PHL
54060000208610

WITHDRAWN

Excavation of the Iron Age, Roman and medieval settlement at Gorhambury, St Albans

THE
PAUL HAMLYN
LIBRARY
DONATED BY
THE PAUL HAMLYN
FOUNDATION
TO THE
BRITISH MUSEUM
opened December 2000

D1348490

English Heritage

Archaeological Report no 14

Excavation of the Iron Age, Roman and medieval settlement at Gorhambury, St Albans

David S Neal, Angela Wardle and Jonathan Hunn

with contributions by Justine Bayley, Sarnia Butcher, P E Curnow, G B Dannell, Brenda Dickinson, Kay Hartley, Martin Henig, Alison Locker, Yvonne Parminter, Andrew Pye, Michelle Ramsay, Valery Rigby and Angus Wainwright

Historic Buildings & Monuments Commission for England

1990

30109 0 10688300

Copyright © Historic Buildings and Monuments Commission for England 1990

First published 1990 by Historic Buildings and Monuments Commission for England
23 Savile Row, London W1X 2HE

Printed by Page Brothers (Norwich) Ltd, Mile Cross Lane, Norwich

British Library Cataloguing in Publication Data
Neal, David S (David Stanley) *1940–*
Excavation of the Iron Age, Roman, and medieval settlement at Gorhambury. – (Historic Buildings and Monuments Commission for England)
1. Hertfordshire. St. Albans houses, Country. Gorhambury antiquities excavation of remains.
I. Title II. Wardle, Angela III. Hunn, Jonathan IV. English Heritage V. Series
936.2585

ISBN 1–85074–250–2

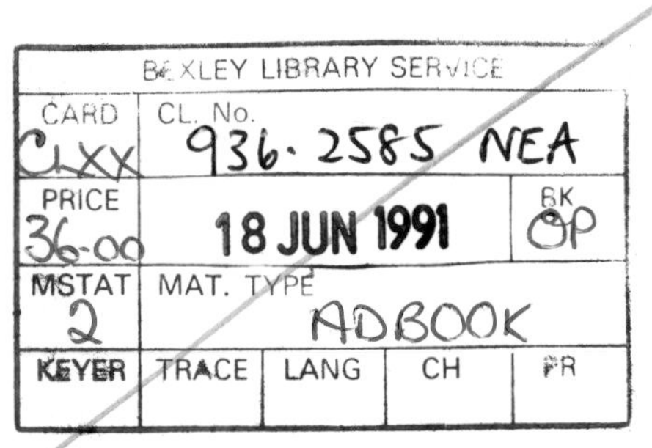

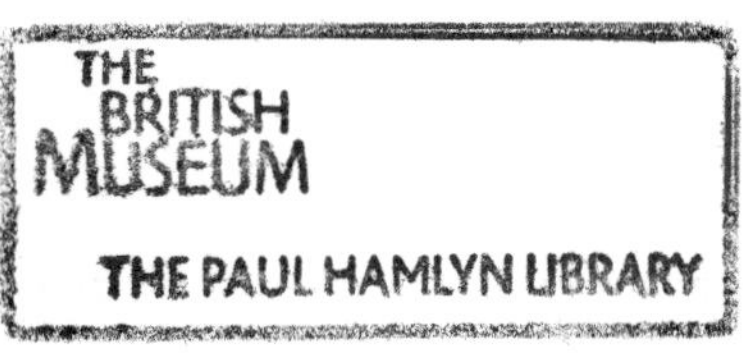

936.2585 NEA

Contents

List of illustrations

Acknowledgements

It is a pleasure to record my debt of gratitude to the numerous people who have assisted in the project, especially the volunteers, some of whom came for the full 12 years. My sincere appreciation also extends to the supervisory staff, particularly those who also saw the project through and have made significant contributions towards the written report. Site supervisors included (in alphabetical order) N Doggett, M Gorman, M Harrison, A Hunn, J Hunn, Miss M A Nation, A Pye, A Wainwright and Dr A Wardle. The arduous task of running the finds shed and dealing with hundredweights of pottery was undertaken by Miss G Cousins, Miss M Hawley, Mrs F Hunn, Miss N Robinson and Miss G Walker. Site photography between 1956 and 1961 was by James Brown of Verulamium Museum, who continued his work into later excavations. As the scale of the project increased and the presence of a full-time photographer was required, this duty was then undertaken by M Gorman and P Ramsay respectively. The committee members are thanked most warmly for their help and encouragement, but the writer would like to single out the work of the Treasurer, H W Mathew ('Dan') who worked unstintingly for twelve years undertaking an ever-increasing burden, paying staff, dealing with accounts and arranging audits. My sincere thanks. Thanks must also be extended to a few individuals, notably Mrs M Cousins and Dr and Mrs D O'Reagan who gave invaluable help in a variety of ways. Also to the late A Stilwell, the Gorhambury Farm Manager. His unfortunate death during the excavations was a tragedy – he will always be remembered for his keen interest and ready assistance. B F Rawlins, who worked on the excavations from 1956–61, has also been a keen supporter of the project and provided every assistance. Specialist contributions to the report have been made by Miss J Bayley (metalworking and analysis), Miss S A Butcher (brooches), P E Curnow (coins), G Dannell (samian), Miss B Dickinson (samian stamps), Mrs K Hartley (mortaria), Dr M Henig (intaglios), J Hunn (the Gorhambury Survey), Mrs A Locker (animal bones), Mrs Y Parminter (coarse pottery), A Pye (flints), Miss V Rigby (potters' stamps), A Wainwright (snails and seed identification and also for taking samples of small mammals, birds and fish) and Dr A Wardle (miscellaneous small finds). Other contributors are recorded in the text. Most of the publication drawings are the work of the writer but the illustrations of D Honour, J Thorn, Ms H Riley and F Gardiner of the Ancient Monuments Drawing Office are acknowledged, as are various staff of the Ancient Monuments Laboratory for conservation and other specialist help. These include Miss G Edwards, Miss J Watson, Miss J Bayley, and N Balaam. The writer is also indebted to Mrs Anna Eborall for typing the manuscript.

Lastly I would like to record my appreciation of the Earls of Verulam, Patrons, for permitting the excavations and allowing camp sites and spoil-heaps to rise so close to Gorhambury House. They always took an active interest in the project – but for them it would never have taken place. Likewise but for the enormous help and encouragement given by J Hunn and Dr A Wardle the excavation and its reporting would have been a more arduous task.

DSN

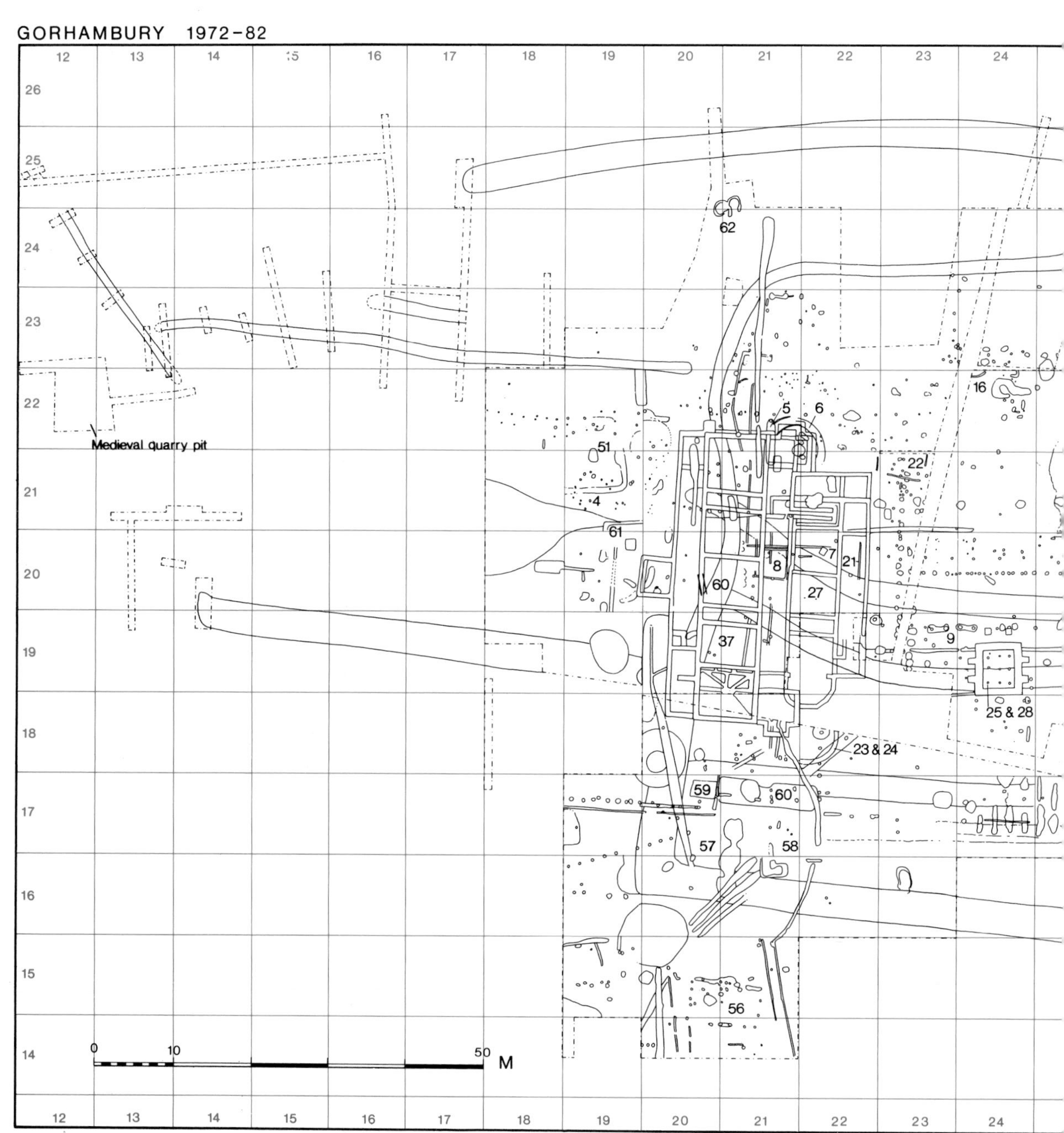

Fig 1 Overall plan of site, all features shown (Scale 1:800)

Introduction (overall plan Fig 1)

From 1963–8 the writer directed excavations on a Roman villa at Gadebridge Park, Hemel Hempstead, a villa located about five miles west of Gorhambury (Neal 1974) (Fig 2). The work included the excavation of courtyards, outbuildings and a bath-house and at the time was a rare example of virtually total excavation of a villa complex. As with many villas in Hertfordshire a timber phase of *c* AD 75 gave way to a masonry building which by the fourth century had developed into a large and luxurious establishment.

From 1969–71 the writer also undertook an excavation of a nearby villa in the grounds of Boxmoor House school, then being enlarged (Neal 1976). Only limited work was possible here although the site produced a most interesting timber villa dated *c* AD 100. Many architectural aspects of the villa were similar to those of Gadebridge; by the Antonine period both had reached a peak of affluence, and were of winged corridor plan, although the wings at Boxmoor were less extended. In the fourth century the courtyards of the two villas appear to have been transferred from the south side to the north, as were their facades. At Gadebridge this transfer was associated with the construction of large tower rooms at both ends of the building. The villas shared more varied fortunes in the fourth century but unusually there was little evidence for occupation at either of them beyond *c* AD 350. Most of the Gadebridge villa was demolished at that time, excepting a small cottage, and the Boxmoor villa had contracted to almost half its original size. The latest masonry phase saw the construction of a row of buttresses propping the building up.

It was unfortunate that the presence of recent buildings prevented the complete examination of the Boxmoor site and, although the timber phase was of more than local interest, we were left with yet another example among hundreds throughout England of a house which has been excavated in isolation from its outbuildings, with little idea of the size or nature of its agricultural buildings or associated estate, other than what could be surmised from the fairly regular distribution of villas 1–1½ miles (1½–2 km) apart along the valley bottoms. Since Gadebridge Park remained alone in having been totally excavated, it was realized that until another neighbouring villa was fully excavated conclusions regarding trends in growth, decline and economy could never be positive;

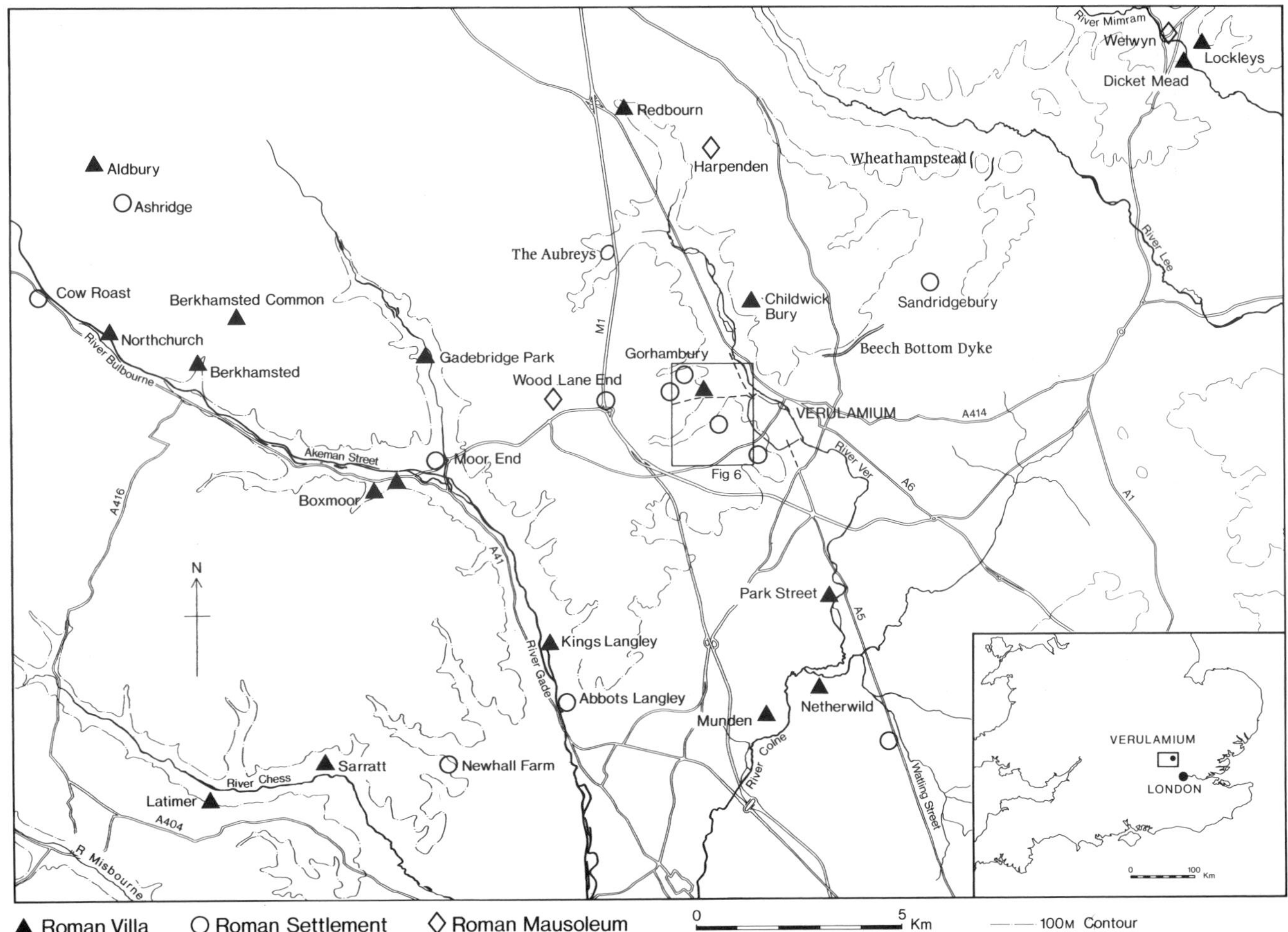

Fig 2 Location map showing site of nearby villas and the river systems. The insets show the location of Verulamium and the extent of the area covered by Fig 4

it was not possible to understand the interrelationships between sites, to study how they compared or contrasted or to test whether the decline of the villas noted near Hemel Hempstead in *c* AD 350 was typical of other villas around Verulamium.

With the aim of fully excavating another villa, a number of sites around Verulamium were studied for their potential but the villa at Gorhambury (Fig 1) was an ideal choice for, like the villas at Barton Farm outside Cirencester and Norfolk Street outside Leicester, for example, it was an unusual case of a villa situated close to a cantonal capital. More especially, the site was unencumbered by development, being situated in open farmland (Fig 3) and with ancient earthworks surviving in woodland areas – every part of the site was available for excavation or survey. Another reason for choosing Gorhambury was that ploughing was damaging the main house which had already been partially excavated by the St Albans and Hertfordshire Architectural and Archaeological Society under the direction of J Lunn and later by Dr Ilid Anthony (Anthony 1961), both previous directors of Verulamium Museum. This work had been initiated in 1956 by the late Earl of Verulam to understand whether crop-marks along the 'Avenue' 350m east of the present house indicated the position of the manor house preceding Sir Nicholas Bacon's, demolished in *c* 1560. The possibility that here lay the site of the early manor built by Abbot Geoffrey de Gorham in about 1130 was recorded in a manuscript by Charlotte

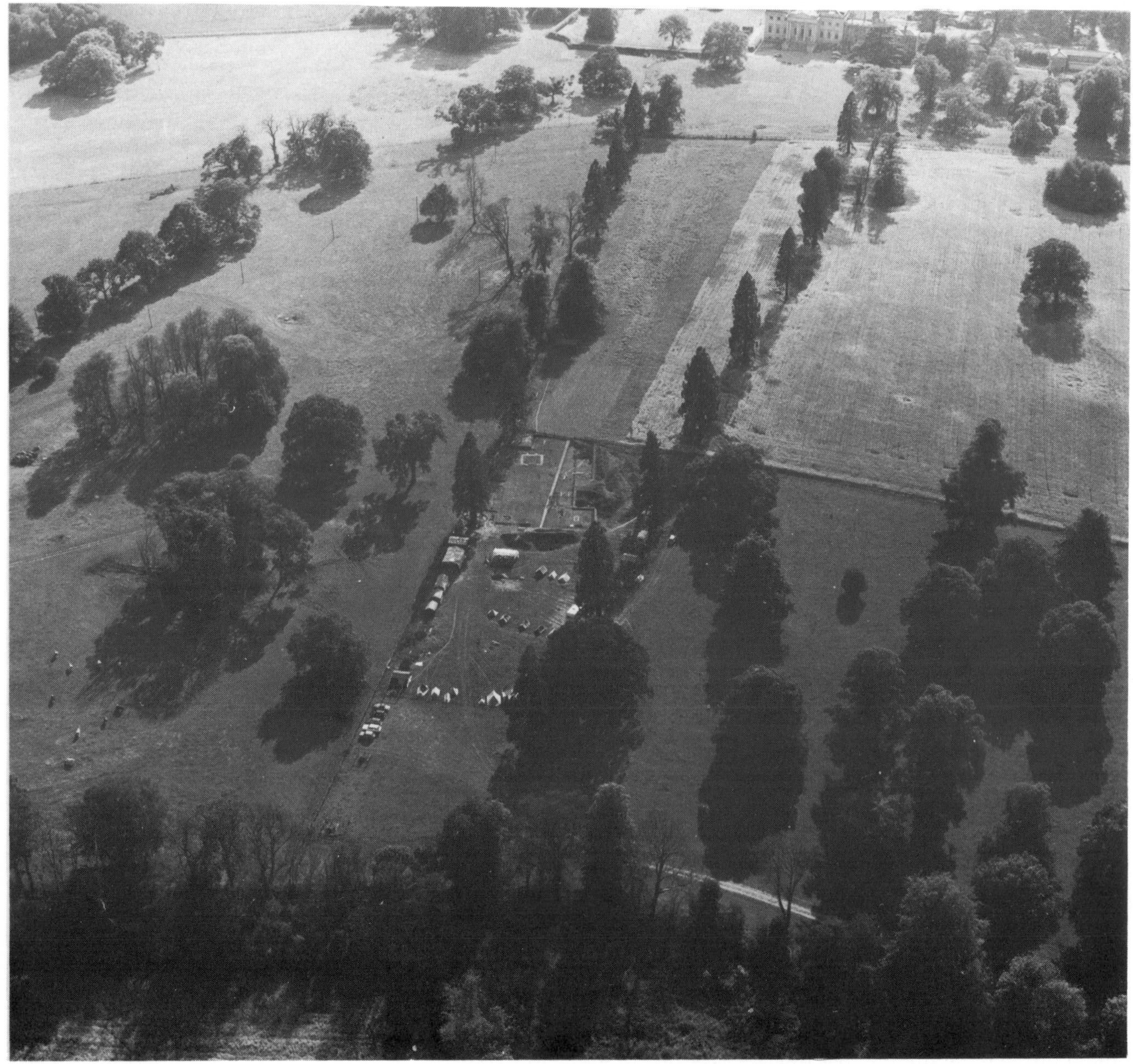

Fig 3 Aerial view of site looking towards the west. Gorhambury House can be seen in the distance

Fig 4 Excavation of the cellar in progress, 1959

Grimston (Grimston 1821) who commented on prominent parch marks being visible during periods of drought. Excavations by the local society revealed not a manor house but a substantial Roman villa with traces of overlying medieval occupation.

Weekend excavations proceeded until 1961 during which period the southern half of two villas, one a reconstruction of the first, was excavated, including a large cellar (Fig 4) with a polygonal apse. Finds in the cellar, especially stucco in the form of human figures (Fig 5) and moulded painted wall-plaster, indicated a building of some pretension. The presence of Flavian occupation also suggested a long history but, although medieval pottery and features were present, the possibility that the site was also that of the medieval manor was not proven.

An outline of the project was discussed with academic colleagues and the proposals submitted to the Right Honourable 6th Earl of Verulam who agreed to the venture, becoming the Committee's Patron. On his sad death in 1973 his son John succeeded as 7th Earl. At its conception the project was expected to take about six seasons – the time spent excavating the Gadebridge Park villa – but in the event the site proved to be more complex and extensive, resulting in the project taking double that time – twelve seasons. The first season's work began on the main villa, re-excavating areas exposed between 1956 and 1961. Although the policy of the project was total excavation, this could not always be realistically achieved; it was considered unnecessary to re-excavate the cellar and neither was it practical to excavate completely stretches of ditches which, in most cases, were between 2 and 3m deep and filled with heavy clay and flint. The presence of parkland trees also prevented total stripping, but fortunately nowhere did they appear to mask significant archaeological deposits. Virtually the total exposure of the villa enclosures was achieved; in addition an attempt was made to survey the surviving earthworks of Gorhambury (Fig 6) in an effort to study any link there might have been between the boundaries of the Roman and medieval estates and to find evidence, if any, for continuity of those boundaries into the present century. It was also necessary to establish how these earthworks related to those in Prae Wood first excavated by Sir Mortimer Wheeler (Wheeler and Wheeler 1936).

Fig 5 Stucco in the form of a human face, hands, feet and a cloak found in the cellar, 1956

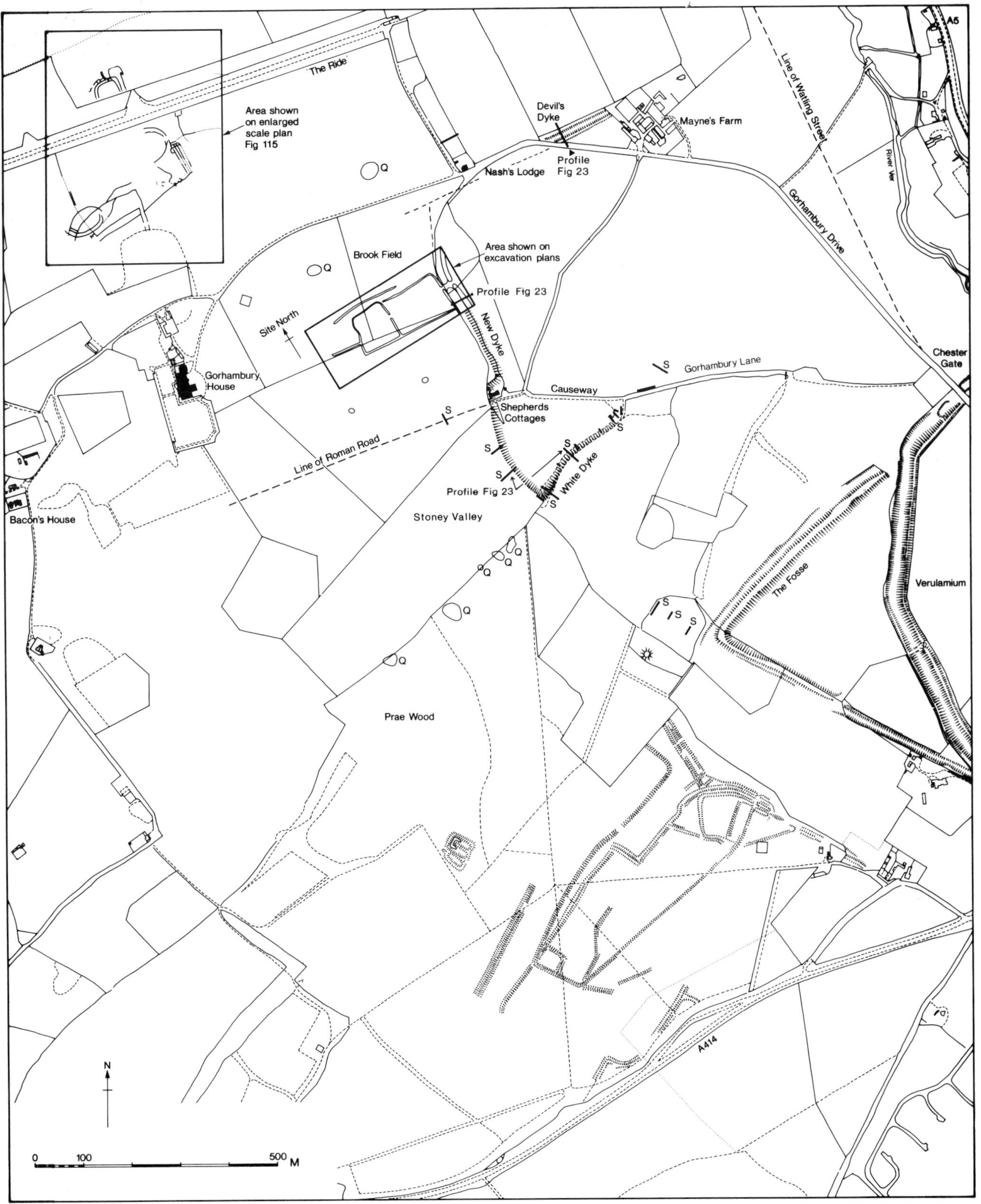

Fig 6 Map showing location of Gorhambury villa in relation to Verulamium and the earthworks in Prae Wood

The topography

Gorhambury villa (National grid ref TL 117079) and the present house of 1777–84 lie about ¾ mile (1 km) north-west of Verulamium, St Albans, in the South Chilterns – a belt of chalk hills stretching from Oxfordshire across Buckinghamshire and Hertfordshire into Cambridgeshire (Fig 7). The north edge is scarped but the southern slopes are more gradual and indented by a series of river valleys with fairly fast-flowing streams which have created regular blocks of land. These rivers, from east to west, include the Mimram, Lee, Ver, Gade, Bulbourne, Chess and Misbourne, and flow mainly south-east or south into the River Colne before reaching the Thames west of London. The exceptions are the Mimram and Lee which take a more direct course. Between the river valleys are plateaux of higher ground above the 350ft (100m) contour frequently capped with clay and flint; glaciation has deposited pockets of gravel and sand. The clay is variable in depth; in some areas, especially west of Gorhambury near Leverstock Green, for example, it is very thick and was dug in earlier centuries for brick and tile production. Elsewhere on the plateau, however, the chalk may be capped by only one or two metres of clay and has fingers of chalk rising close to the surface. Although the plateau has clay, where it is mixed with gravel and flint it is remarkably well drained and provides good arable soil. Generally the valley slopes are covered by a friable chalky clay loam and the valley floors contain fine alluvium on river gravels.

The villa itself overlooks the River Ver to the east and occupies a narrow spur of land running west–east

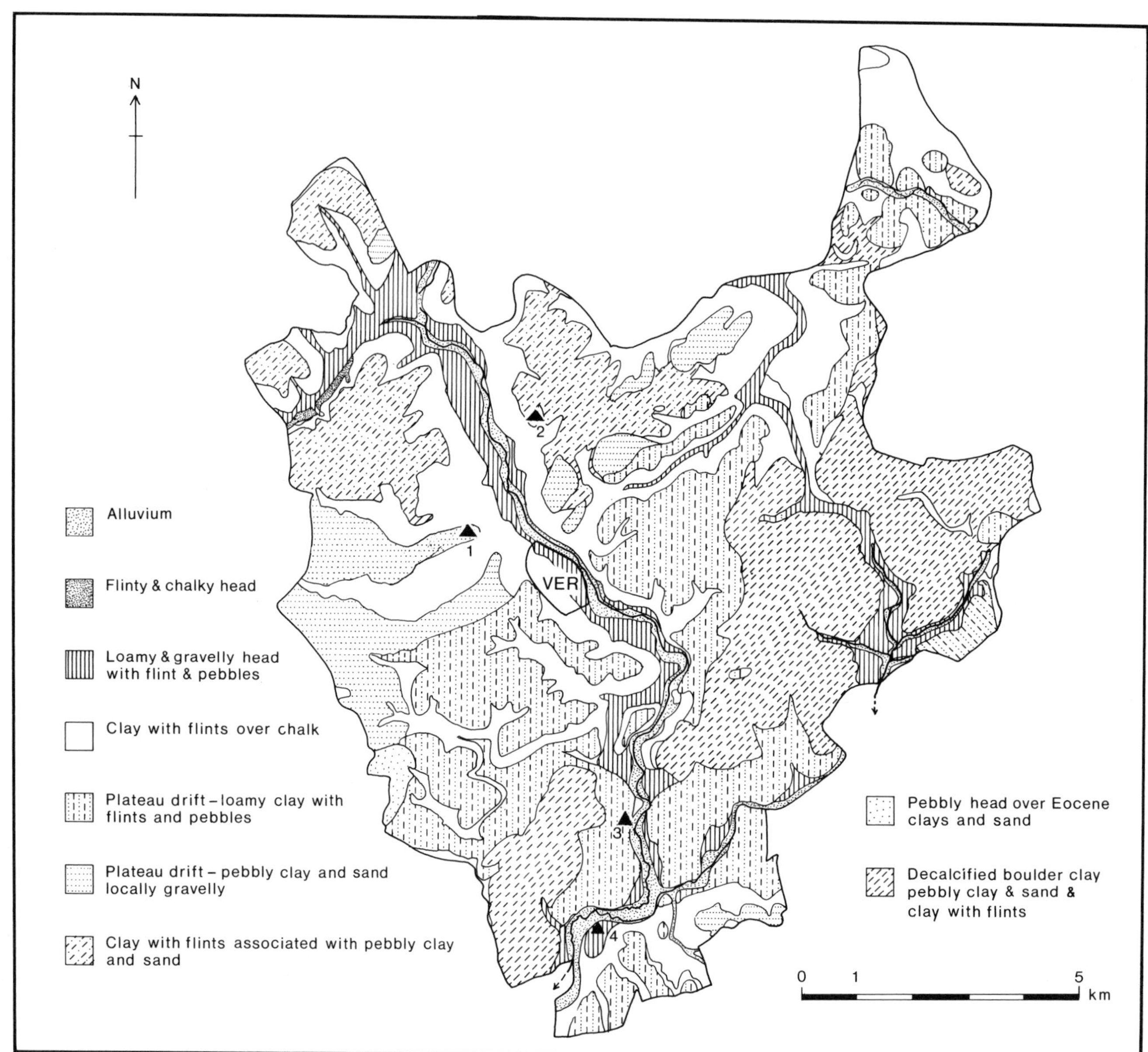

Fig 7 Geological map of the Verulamium region. Villas along the River Ver include 1 Gorhambury, 2 Childwickbury, 3 Park Street and 4 Netherwild

sloping down into the river valley (Fig 6). On either side of the villa, to the north and south, the terrain dips fairly sharply into valleys covered with chalky loam on the slopes and gravelly soil on the bottoms. In Roman times, however, these valleys probably had streams, for in medieval times the northern dip was known as Brook Field and river gravels and aquatic molluscs have been located in cuttings in Stoney Valley to the south (p 216). The southern valley separates the site from the higher plateau occupied by Prae Wood which extends towards the western margins of the Roman city of Verulamium and south to the present-day St Albans–Hemel Hempstead road, the A414, the present modern boundary of the Gorhambury Estate. The valley to the north of the villa is flanked by another ridge now occupied by 'The Ride' – an avenue of trees defining a nineteenth-century racecourse. This ridge extends further towards the river than that occupied by the villa and forms a natural boundary, shared by the present northern limits of the Estate. The eastern limit of the Estate is the river and the western extent the boundary between St Michael's parish and Leverstock Green, close to the M1 motorway. The existing limits of the Gorhambury Estate define, generally, the extent of the survey.

The current land use can be divided into three categories: woodland, parkland and arable. The woodland area is confined to the higher, more sandy, soils of Prae Wood. Until the 1950s the parkland extended all around Gorhambury House as far, south-east, as Prae Wood; now it is limited to small areas east of the house and covers part of the villa complex. The remainder of the estate is under arable cultivation.

The structure and conventions of the report

The excavation covered an area roughly 300 by 100m (3 hectares) and resulted in the discovery of over 60 buildings dating from the Neolithic to the medieval periods, over 3000 small finds, hundredweights of pottery and bone and the accumulation of over 400 site plans. A plan of virtually every structure is provided in this report together with the number of the grid square it occupies: the excavation grid is shown on Fig 1. Appendix 1 (p 222) lists the plans of the grid squares with their archive plan (AP) number. The original archive is preserved in Verulamium Museum with a copy in the National Monuments Record (NMR).

Co-ordinates of small finds are expressed in six figures divided eastings–northings; they are prefixed with the four figure grid-square co-ordinate but to avoid possible confusion with context numbers, grid square or area numbers are prefixed with 'area' or, in the report on the artefacts, shown in bold type.

Every structure described has a sequential building number (different from the context number apportioned on the excavation). When a building has been extended and that extension or phase is integral, it shares the same number, but if the building has been replaced, even if it shares a similar architectural form and location, a new building number is allocated. References to phases refer specifically to phases of an individual building complex and are not applicable across the site. For pottery, when an archive vessel (AV) is recorded in the text it refers to a drawn vessel in the archive. Bracketed numbers accompanying the AV numbers are the context under which the pottery and card indexes are arranged. A list of objects by context appears as Appendix 5; drawings of associated groups of pottery arranged in context order can be inspected in the site archive (Verulamium Museum).

The excavations

Introductory summary of developments (Table 1)

Note: Many of the pre-Roman Iron Age buildings cannot be related with confidence to either period and therefore they have all been described in a separate section following Period 5.

As with the pre-Roman Iron Age it is impossible always to be precise as to the date of the Roman buildings and therefore the era has been divided into six sections (Periods 6–11).

The prehistoric period

Introduction

The main content of this report deals with the occupation of the area from the pre-Roman late Iron Age onwards. However, an analysis of the flintwork indicates the presence of man in early prehistoric times. Three burin spalls are attributed to the Mesolithic period but occupation of the site itself seems to have begun in the Neolithic with the construction of a rectilinear building, Building 1, and the deposit of a considerable scatter of flint including a significant proportion of blades. Although there is little structural evidence for the Bronze Age, apart from palisades, this period is represented by two fine early scrapers and, perhaps more significantly, by the remains of two urns. There then seems to be a gap in activity for, apart from the occasional sherd, there is little material of early Iron Age date.

Table 1

Period	*Period plans*	*Date range*	*Buildings or enclosures constructed in this period*
1	Fig 8	Neolithic	Building 1
2		Bronze Age	Palisades possibly associated with field systems
3	Fig 12	Late Iron Age	Enclosure A. Entrance on west
4	Figs 12, 26	Late Iron Age	Enclosure A remodelled with entrance on east and the creation of another enclosure (B) to the west. Gates, Buildings 2 and 3 constructed
5	Figs 12, 26	Late Iron Age	Construction of massive dyke system east of Enclosure A. Enclosure B sub-divided. Buildings 4–15 erected
6	Fig 45	*c* AD 43–62	Buildings 16–20. Timber buildings including rectilinear and circular huts constructed in Enclosures A and B. Some buildings burnt, possibly the result of the Boudiccan uprising
7	Fig 47	*c* AD 62–100	Buildings 21–26. Principal buildings replaced
8	Fig 56	*c* AD 100–175	Buildings 27–36. Construction of first masonry buildings including the villa, Building 27
9	Fig 73	*c* AD 175–250	Buildings 37–46. Original masonry villa demolished and new villa (Building 37) constructed
10	Fig 96	*c* AD 250–300	Buildings 47–50. Following a period of abandonment, trackways restored and some earlier buildings repaired. New building comprised merely simple huts
11	Fig 101	*c* AD 300–350	Buildings 51–55. Construction of two large timber barns and other simple huts. Villa possibly abandoned
12	Fig 106	11–14th C	Buildings 56–62. Medieval croft associated with palisade enclosure and corn-drying or malting ovens

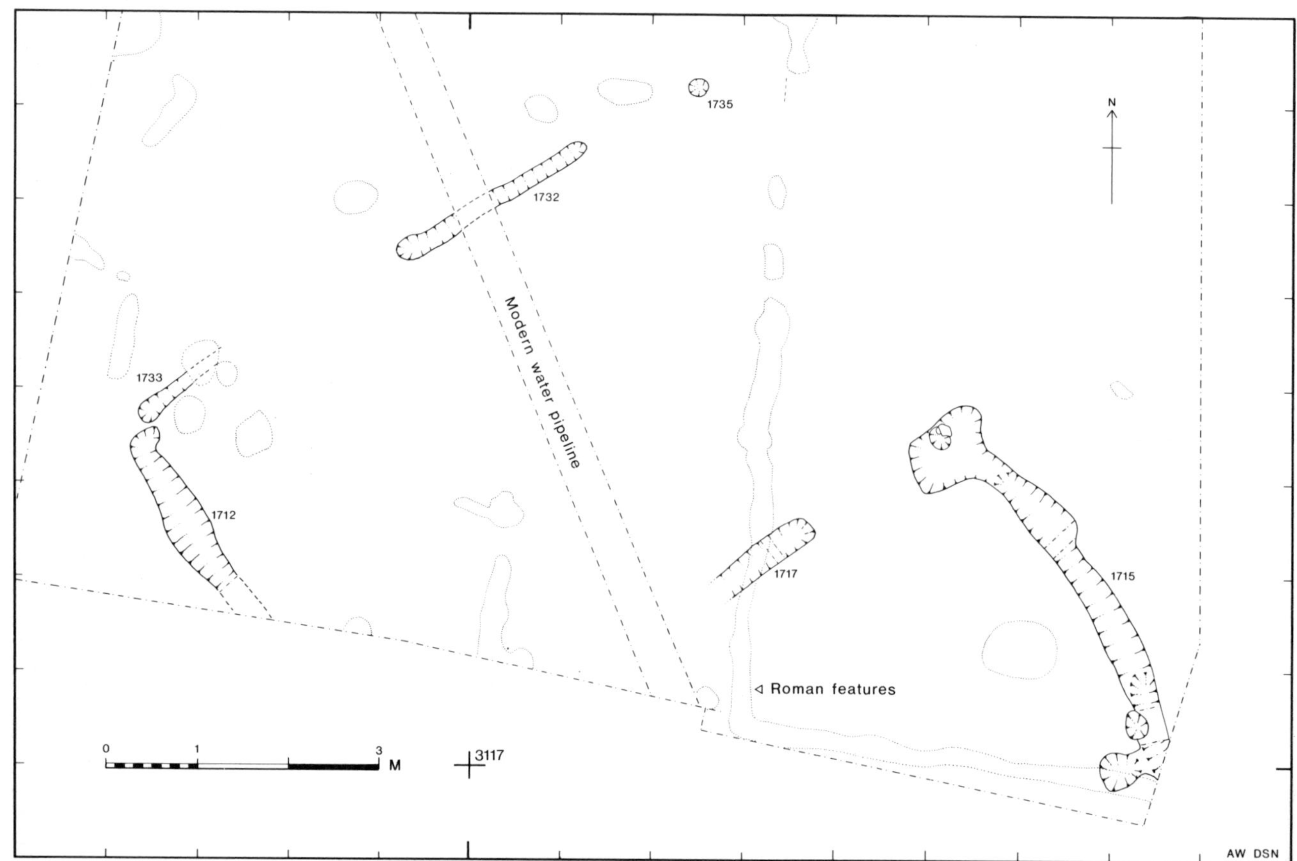

Fig 8 Plan of Building 1, late Neolithic, Period 1 (Scale 1:80)

Period 1, Neolithic

Building 1 (Figs 8 and 9)

The earliest occupation is represented by slots located in area 3116–17, partially truncated on the south by a later east–west enclosure ditch and a modern water pipeline. Lengths of five slots were discovered (1712, 1715, 1717, 1732 and 1733) with U or V-shaped sections between 0.20 and 0.30m wide and between 0.20 and 0.35m deep. They were packed with orange clay and all contained considerable quantities of charcoal which, in the case of 1715, ran along the outer side of the cut, suggesting a wattle wall. The upper fill also contained charcoal but included burnt daub; no associated floor surfaces survived. As the slots were intermittent the overall plan of the building is doubtful, but it would appear to have been about 7m wide overall by at least 9m long and to have been divided into two areas by a cross wall (1717) where an opening 1.20m wide might represent an entrance. Whether the building was a house or had some other function remains uncertain. Sherds of calcined crushed flint-tempered fabric were found in the upper filling of 1715, including four rim sherds (Fig 152, Nos 1–4); charcoal of mature oak from the same feature was submitted to Harwell (HAR 3484) for radiocarbon analysis, giving a result of 4810±80 BP (3513–3389 cal BC, Pearson *et al* 1986) – late Neolithic. Four other sherds, including a rim, of flint-tempered fabric were recovered from a Roman palisade (1716) cutting these features and may have been derived from the same source.

Also included in the slots were four 'typically Neolithic blades' (see p 219); Neolithic flintwork was also found in unstratified levels over much of the site.

Period 2, Bronze Age

The Bronze Age is represented by the remains of two possible urns (contexts 424 and 1020) situated in areas 2022 and 2520 respectively. The first was very shattered, weighed approximately 2500 grammes and was set into a shallow pit; no rim survived. Although no ashes were found in or associated with either of the urns their function is assumed to have been funerary. A small Bronze Age urn with suspension holes around the rim (Fig 152, No 5) was also found in area 3916 to the south-east of the site; it occupied a small pit (2031) shown on Fig 40. Scatters of Bronze Age sherds were located elsewhere, but not in sufficient concentrations to suggest discrete areas of settlement. Structural evidence in the form of possible palisade trenches was also located; one ran east–west beneath

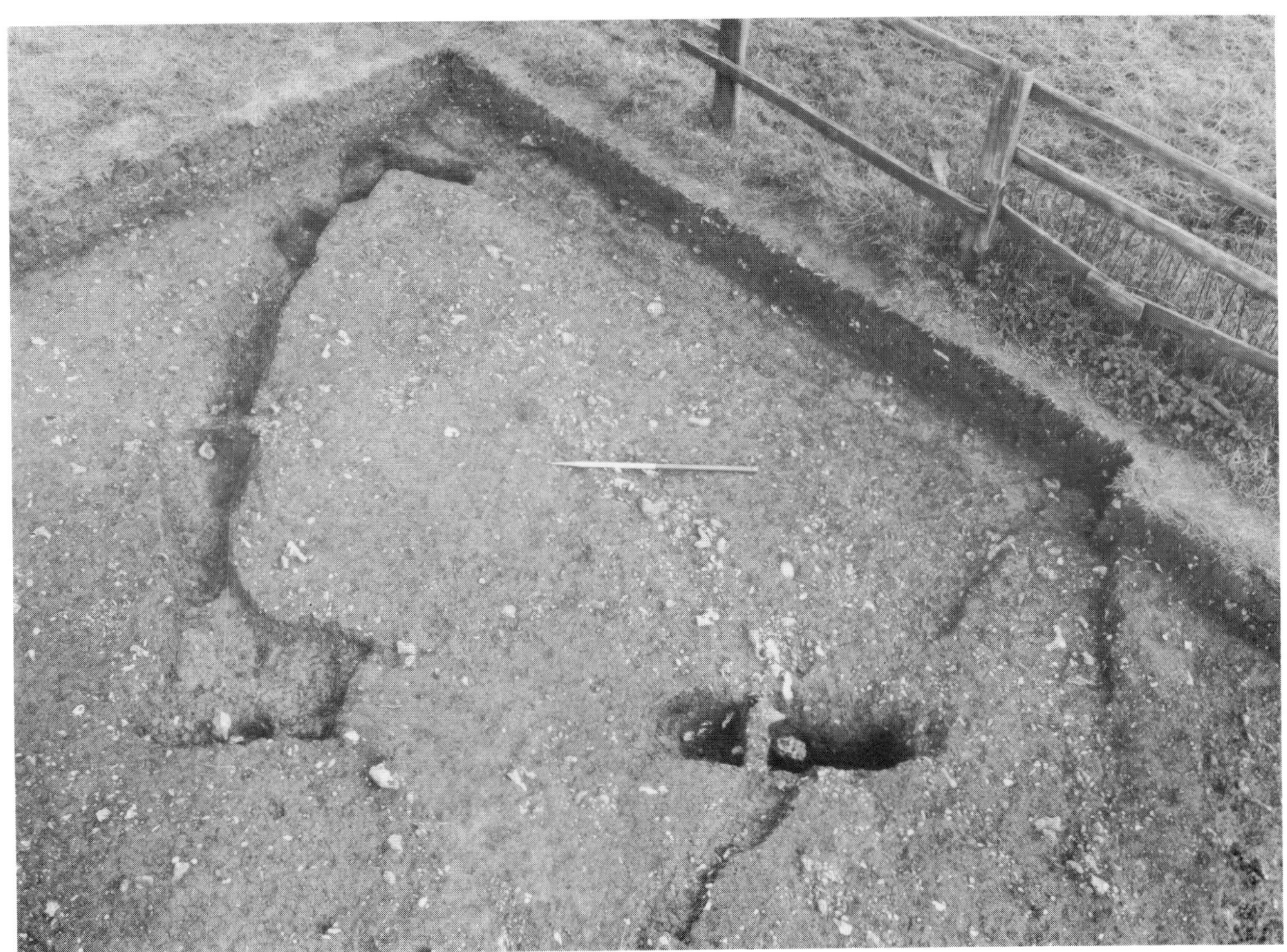

Fig 9 View of Building 1 showing wall slots; late Neolithic; view south-east

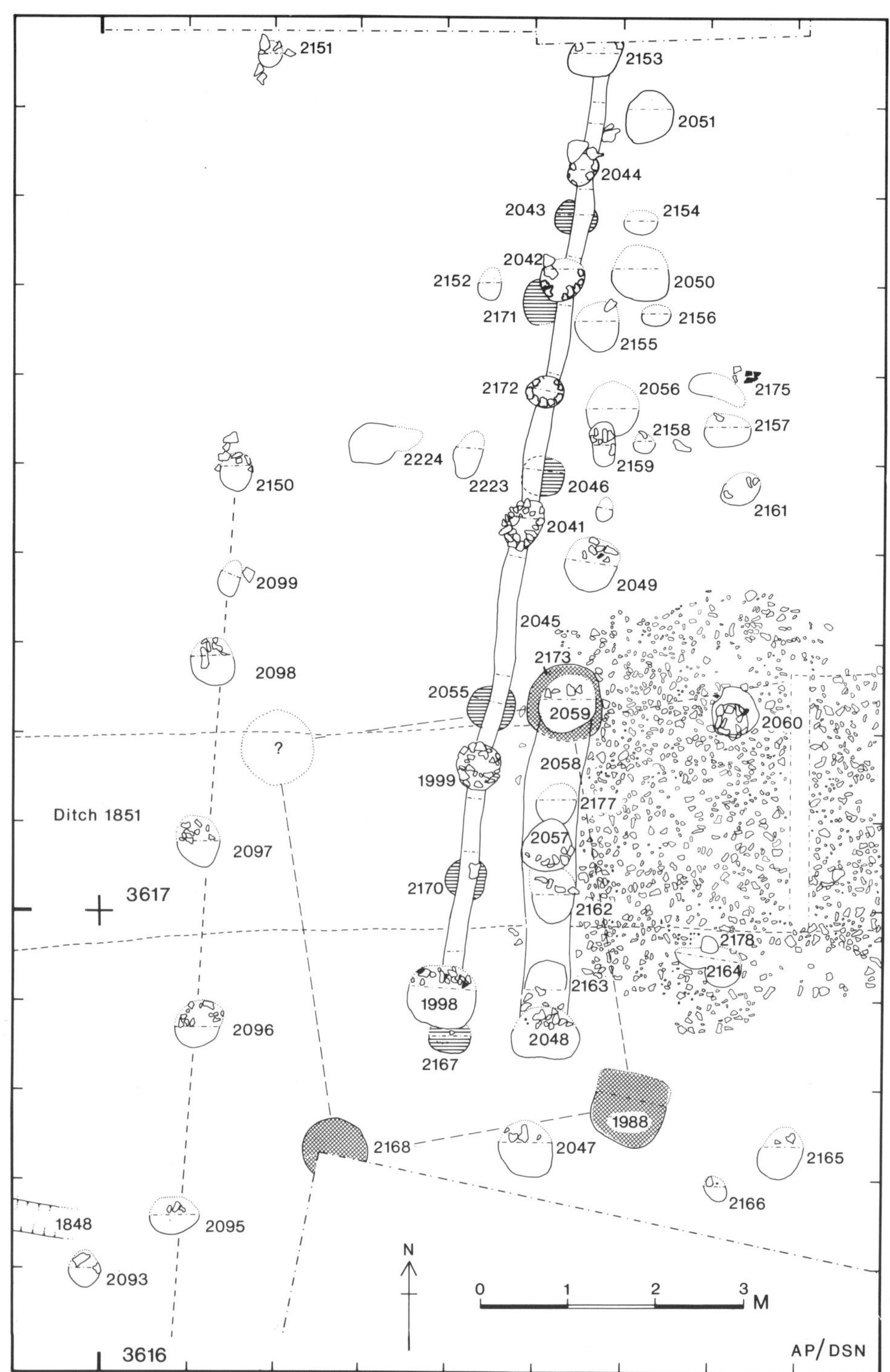

Fig 10 Plan showing postholes 1988, 2059 and 2168 in area 3616–17, which belong perhaps to an Iron Age granary; the later palisades and postholes demonstrate how the same boundary was replaced on at least five occasions (Scale 1:80)

the causeway into a later enclosure, context 2653, area 39–4019 (Fig 13). Its limits were not established but it was U-shaped in profile and about 0.75m wide. A length of another palisade trench (1591, Fig 18), ran north–south across area 2820. It was narrower, 0.25m wide. Only Bronze Age pottery was found in both trenches; although this does not necessarily prove an associated date another distinguishing aspect of these features, compared to those of later periods, is their leached-out soil. The later the period the more organic and less indurated the fills. This period is also represented by a scatter of flint including two fine scrapers (p 219; nos 15 and 16).

There is a slight suggestion from the overall plan that there might be some relationship or continuity between the alignment of these palisades and the later Iron Age earthworks. It is possible that fixed boundaries were influencing the location of later dykes; perhaps the palisades represented field divisions.

Periods 3–5, c AD 20–43, the late Iron Age

Between the Bronze Age and the Belgic period a scatter of Iron Age sherds of flint-tempered fabric is virtually the only trace of occupation. Apart from area 3616 where postholes 1988, 2168 and 2173 (Fig 10) may conceivably be part of a four-post granary, one part of which was destroyed by the cutting of Ditch 1851, there are no associated structures or ditches. It was not until the pre-Roman Iron Age therefore that the site saw more intensive activity in the form of a sequence of rectangular enclosures, aligned east–west following the ridge (Fig 11). These enclosures were associated with the Belgic oppidum of Verulamium, traditionally centred on Prae Wood, and with enclosures elsewhere in the vicinity. The sequence of the enclosures will be described first followed by a description of the buildings, although it must be emphasised again that few of the buildings attributed to the late Iron Age can be related with confidence to specific periods. Just because some buildings happen to be 'within' the enclosures they are not necessarily contemporary.

The enclosures: summary (Fig 12)

The first enclosure, Enclosure A (Period 3), measured about 115 by 60m and had antennae ditches flanking an opening on the west side. Other entrances were situated on its south, north and possibly east sides (p 13). In a later period (Period 4) the south side of the enclosure and the antennae ditches were filled in and the enclosure extended south 21m on its east side and 6m on its west. It had an eastern entrance.

The new southern ditch was also extended west for 140m and along its length had a dog-leg turn. Ninety metres north another east–west ditch was dug. It ran alongside the north ditch of Enclosure A for about 40m to form a parallel droveway; it was not straight but curved slightly towards the south. There is no evidence that these new ditches continued further west or that the extension (Enclosure B) had a west side at this period.

In Period 5 a huge dyke was dug to the east of Enclosure A and within Enclosure B a separate square compound was made by cutting a sinuous ditch

Fig 11 Reconstruction drawing by David S Neal showing Enclosures A and B in relation to the major system of dykes; view north-west

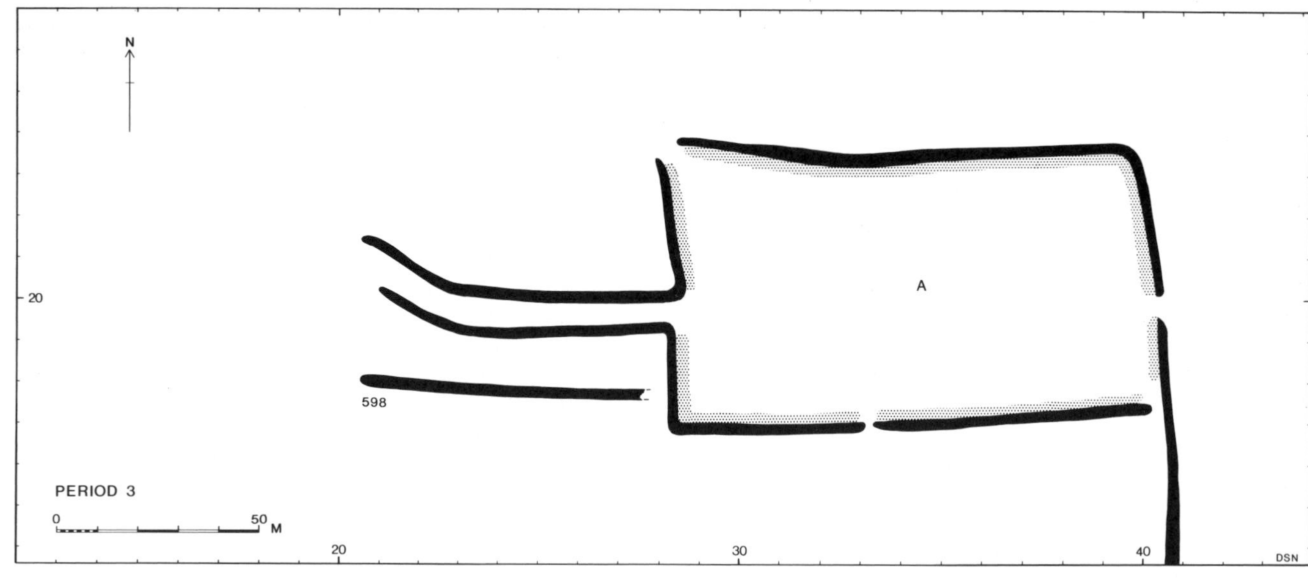

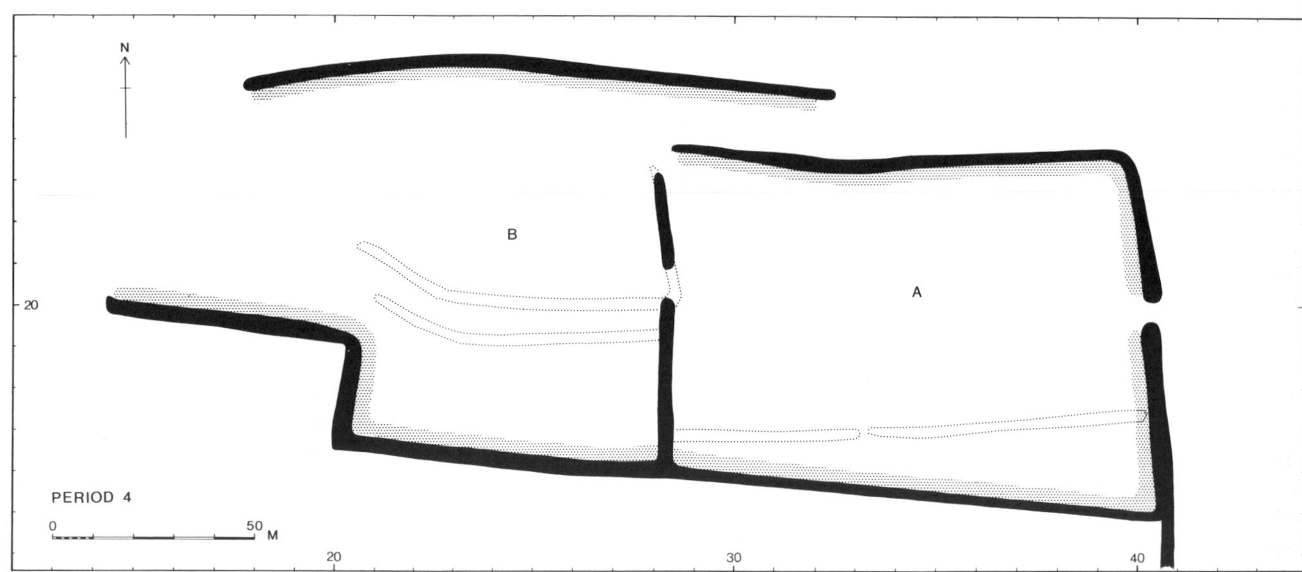

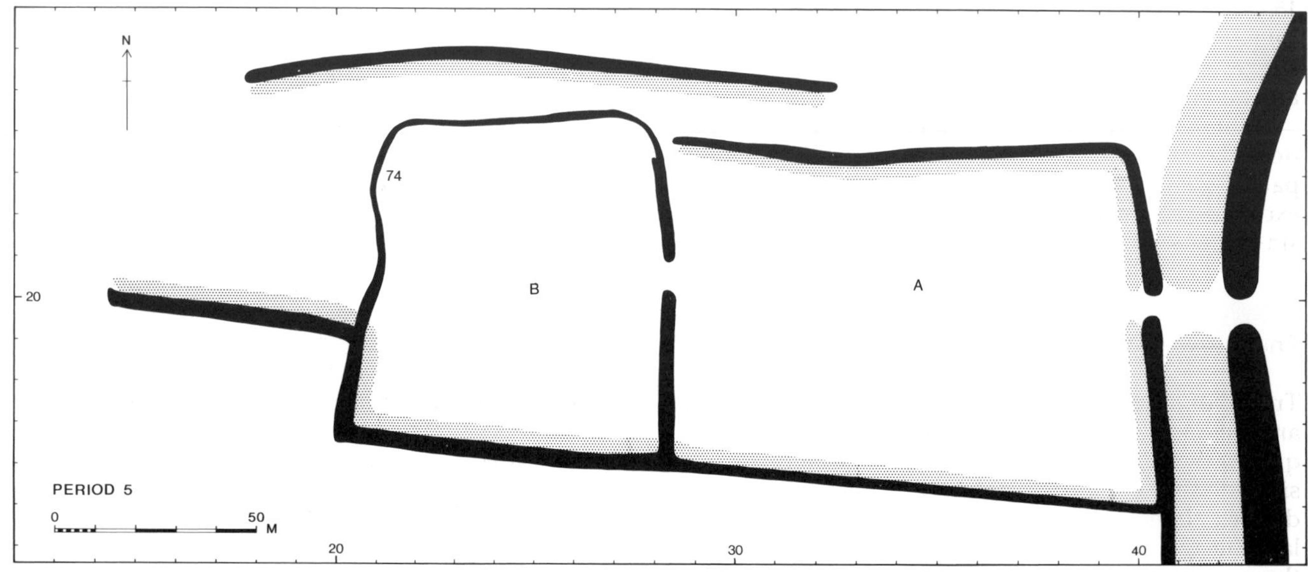

Fig 12 Block plan showing sequence of Enclosures A and B, Periods 3–5

from the dog-leg northwards and then east to join the north-west corner of Enclosure A.

Enclosure A, Period 3

The Enclosure A ditches were V-shaped in profile, 3m wide and about 1.20m deep; later remodelling removed all traces of banks. The antennae and the southern ditch were the only sections to survive for they were later backfilled and remained unaffected by recuts. The presence of causeways in the north-west corner and the south side is not in doubt, but evidence for the east ditch and entrance is more problematical. There is a north–south ditch (2927, Fig 13) beneath the main causeway into the later Iron Age (Period 4) enclosure (area 4019–20) which might represent the original east cutting. However, this need not be related to Enclosure A and it is possible that the causeway and flanking ditches are in fact contemporary with the first enclosure. Ditch 2927 could therefore be related to unexplained earthworks in area 4022 and 4024. In Period 4 the ditch on this side extended south of the enclosure into area 4013 and the same possibly applied in Period 3. Also of uncertain phasing is ditch 598 running east–west from area 2017 to 2517 south of the antennae and with its western terminal roughly on the same line; its eastern side probably stopped at or before the west side of Enclosure A – certainly it never ran further east into the enclosure itself. In its lowest fill (1407) were four body sherds of undiagnostic 'Belgic' pottery.

Dating evidence

The most reliable dating evidence comes from a group of pottery (Fig 153, Nos 8–21) from the lower filling (105) of the southern antenna ditch (area 2219, Fig 1). An associated assemblage (104) was found in the same ditch further east in area 2419 sealed by Building 28. The pottery included burnished cordoned jars and grooved wares of similar type to an assemblage (Fig 153, Nos 22–31) from the ditches flanking the causeways (1804). The completeness of the vessels suggests that they represent a contemporary group and are not residual.

Another small group of pottery was located in the north-west corner of Enclosure A, area 2823, where part of the original terminal of the Phase 1 ditch was excavated. Its primary fill contained fragments of a simple jar similar for example to Fig 153, No 9.

Enclosures A and B, Period 4

Traces of internal banks (571, Fig 14) were found around most of Enclosure A and extension B; the quality of their preservation varied but on the south side in area 22–2316 the tail of the bank showed as a distinct band of clay with occupation deposits lapping against it. The sharpness of this feature raised the possibility of there having been a sleeper beam for a revetment, but if so no indentation for it was found. The ditches varied in size. Generally they were originally about 2m wide and deep but at the terminals flanking the eastern causeway (Figs 13 and 15) they were about 2.50m deep and 4m broad, possibly to raise a bank higher than elsewhere and give the illusion of strength – more than the enclosure truly had. A distinctive feature of the ditches is their steeper, perhaps once almost vertical, inner sides.

The new east entrance and 5m wide causeway (Fig 16) was defended by a gateway (Building 2, Fig 13) represented by three pairs of opposed postholes, those to the west being the earliest (Nos 2359 and 2388). The postholes (Fig 17) flanked an entrance about 2.50m wide; their depth, almost one metre, indicated the emplacement of substantial posts, perhaps intended not merely to support gates but also to revet the bank. The post-pits were oval in plan, presumably to facilitate the tilting of the posts into their sockets, and were packed with clay and flint. In the southern post-pit was a single sherd of 'Belgic' furrowed ware. Another gate (Building 3, Fig 18) was made through the ditch separating Enclosures A and B. This was also represented by two large postholes (Nos 1566 and 1567) about 0.90m deep and set 2.70m apart. In the upper filling of 1566 was a Gallo-Belgic sherd. As the causeway here was built over an earlier ditch (2820) later road metalling (1551) had subsided into it (Fig 19).

Dating evidence

The date of the Period 4 remodelling is based on two groups of pottery, from the ditch terminals flanking both causeways. Ditch 1720 (Fig 15) to the east contained sherds of two native 'Belgic' forms (as Fig 153, No 8) from early levels, specifically layer 2391 (sections C–D, Fig 15) which also contained two coins of Cunobelin (coins B5 and 11), both sealed by clay associated with the construction of the Period 5 dyke. Recovered from the filling of the ditch terminals (1281) flanking the causeway into Enclosure B – especially context 1804 – were 19 kilograms of pottery; a complete range of types appears in Fig 153, Nos 22–31. Apart from the base of a terra nigra platter they are all of native 'Belgic' fabric, some with furrowed bodies duplicating the forms illustrated from context 105 (Nos 8–21). A coin (B1) of Tasciovanus was also found in this context.

Enclosures A and B, Period 5

The planned extension (Enclosure B) against the west side of Enclosure A was subdivided by a separate enclosure with a ditch (74) extending from the north angle of the dog-leg in area 2019 towards the north-west corner of Enclosure A. The width of Ditch 74 is variable: at its south end it was about 3m wide but towards the north it was reduced to only 1m wide. Longitudinal sections here failed to find any evidence for it having been a palisade trench and it was presumably intended as a boundary and gully skirting a complex of buildings yet to be described (p 23).

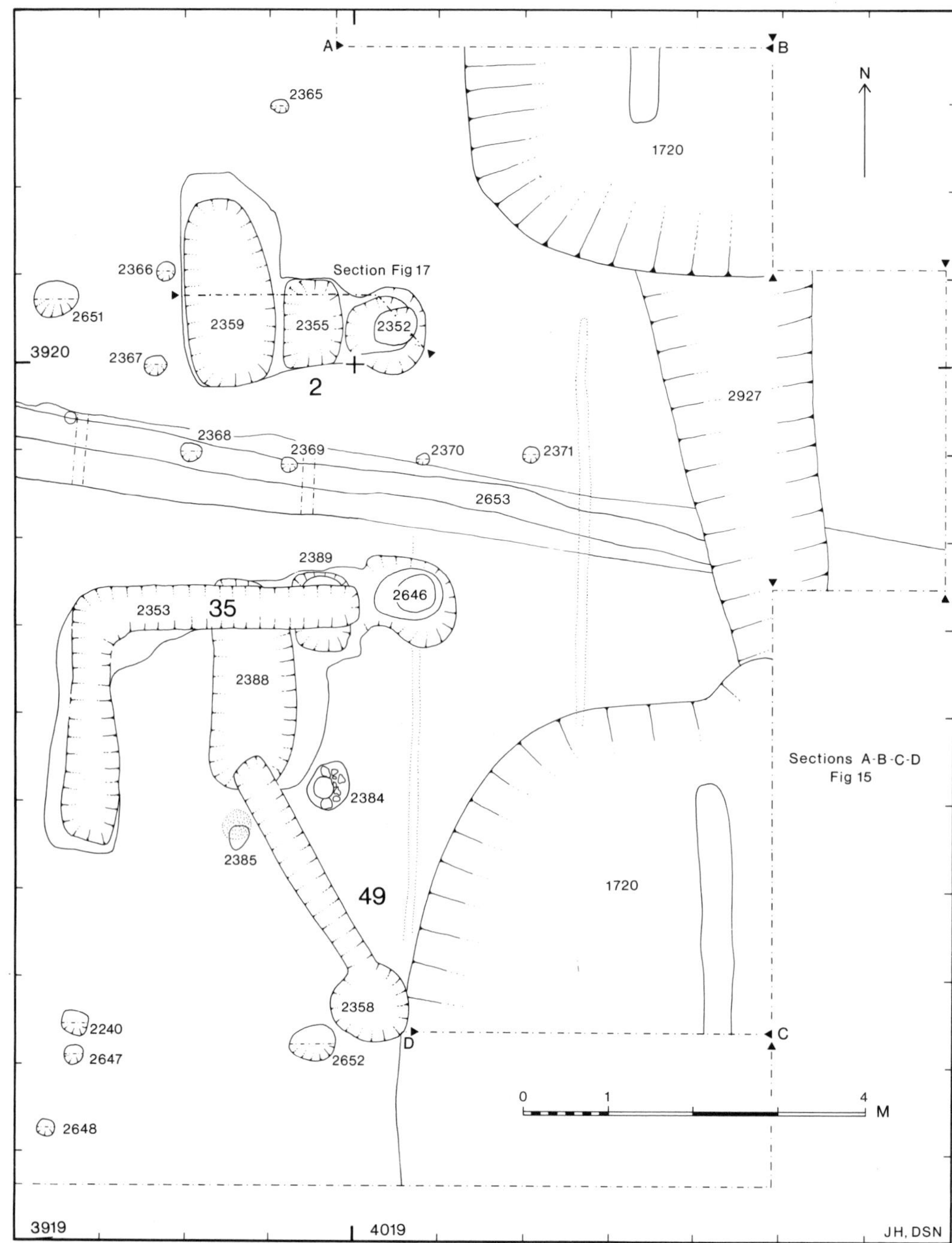

Fig 13 Plan of gate complex (Building 2) on east side of Enclosure A; also shown are Structures 35 and 49 (Scale 1:80)

Dating evidence

An early first-century date is suggested by pottery in the primary filling (269) (Fig 154, Nos 55–62) from area 2121, which included coarse native jars, also duplicating types in context 105, and a butt beaker dated to the first half of the first century AD. At a later date the ditch was recut and only in a few places was the original primary fill undisturbed.

The dyke (for overall plan see Fig 6)

The major feature of this period was the construction of a massive dyke that probably forms part of the system known as Devil's Dyke, passing Mayne's Farm (Fig 20) and surveyed by Wheeler (Wheeler and Wheeler 1936, 15, Pl 11). In his report Wheeler erroneously assumed the ditch to terminate 175m west of Nash's Lodge, but in reality another arm branches sharply south to follow the present field boundary. This runs adjacent to the eastern edge of Enclosure A towards Shepherds Cottages where it then turns sharply west for about 30m before resuming its southern route across Stoney Valley towards a major lynchet defining the valley from Prae Wood and an arable field to the east. Here the ditch stops abruptly. Its route, however, is represented by the line of the lynchet, for the dyke proceeds east for about 190m where it appears to terminate. Conceivably the boundary might be reflected in the line of the

N S
571 4 1 501 29 549 29 1264 1423 3251 424 1425 1026
A Area 2316

S N
3016 3110 3017 3111 3117 3112 3115 3114 3116
B Area 3023
0 1 2 M

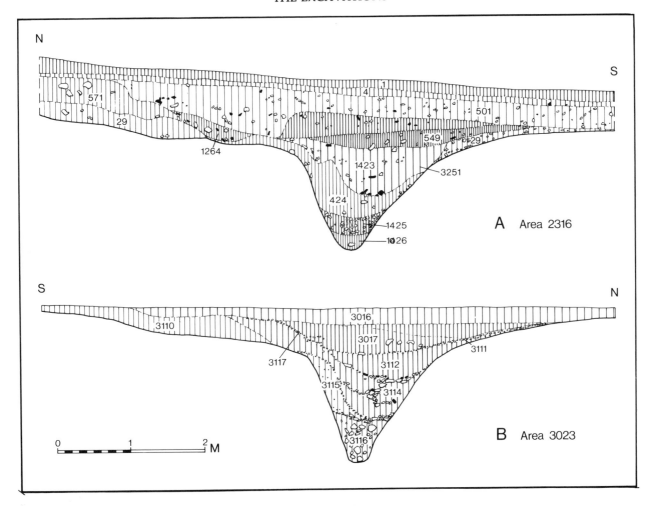

Fig 14 Sections across enclosure ditches: A area 22–2316, B area 3023 (Scale 1:50)

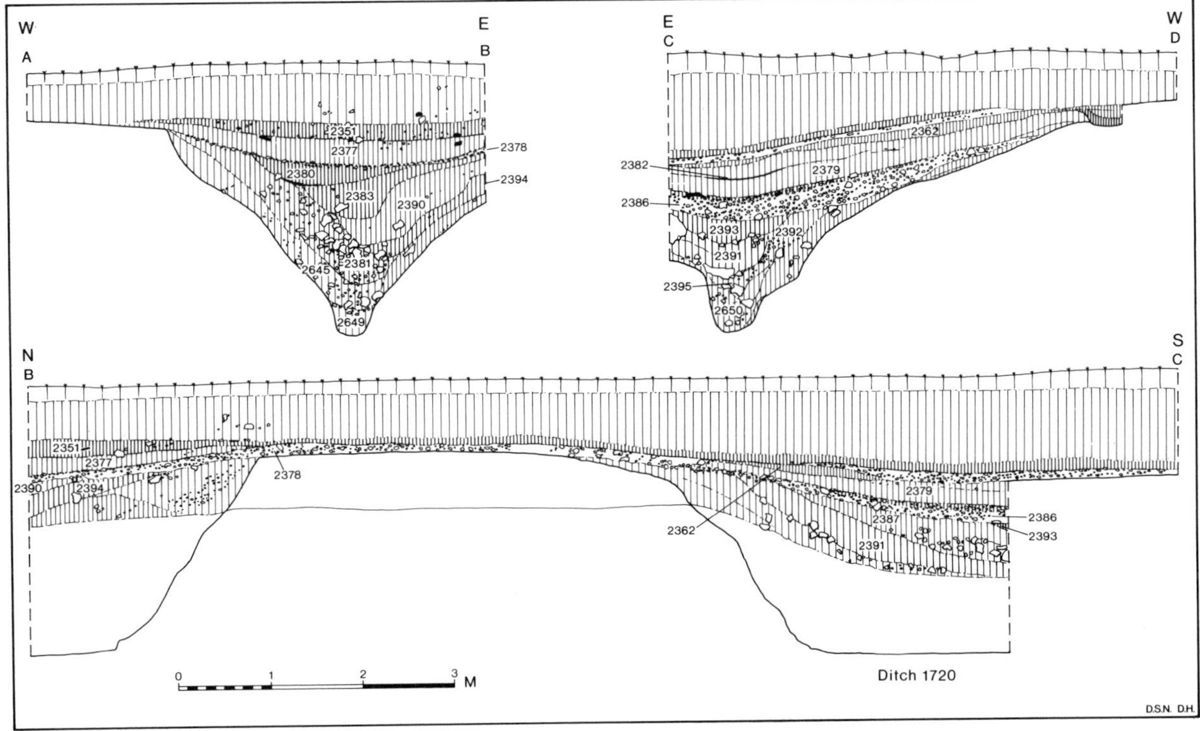

Fig 15 Sections across ditch terminals and causeway on east side of Enclosure A, area 3920 (Scale 1:80)

Fig 16 View east of gate complex (Building 2) and causeway on east side of Enclosure A

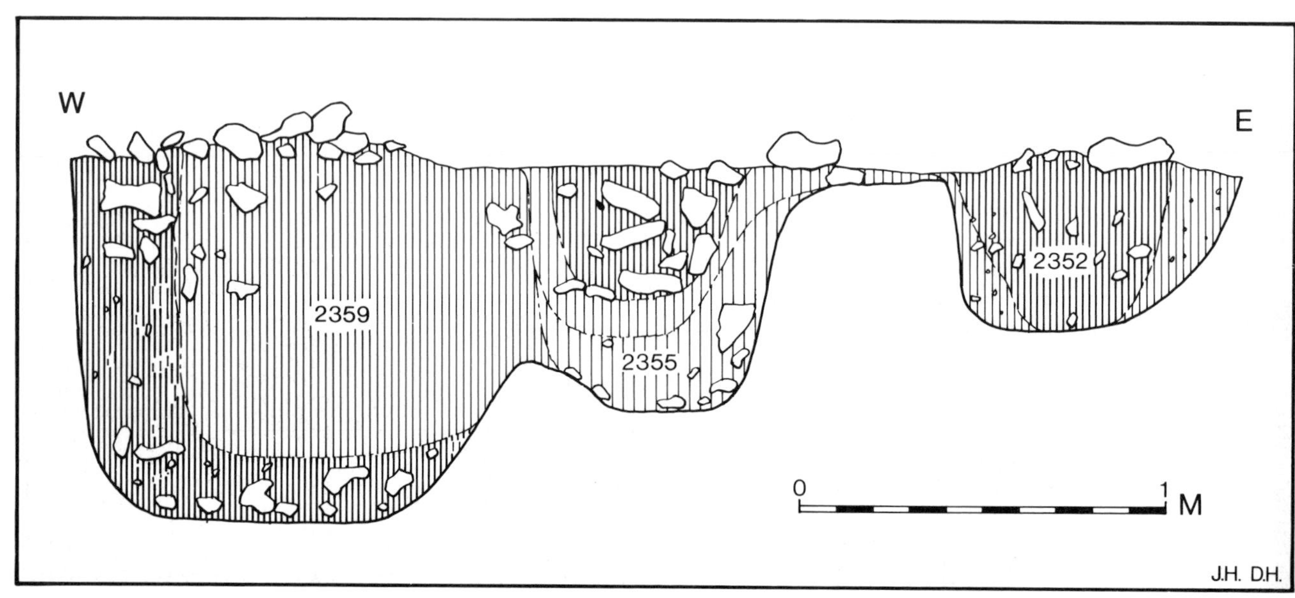

Fig 17 Sections across northern set of gate postholes, Building 2, area 3920 (Scale 1:20)

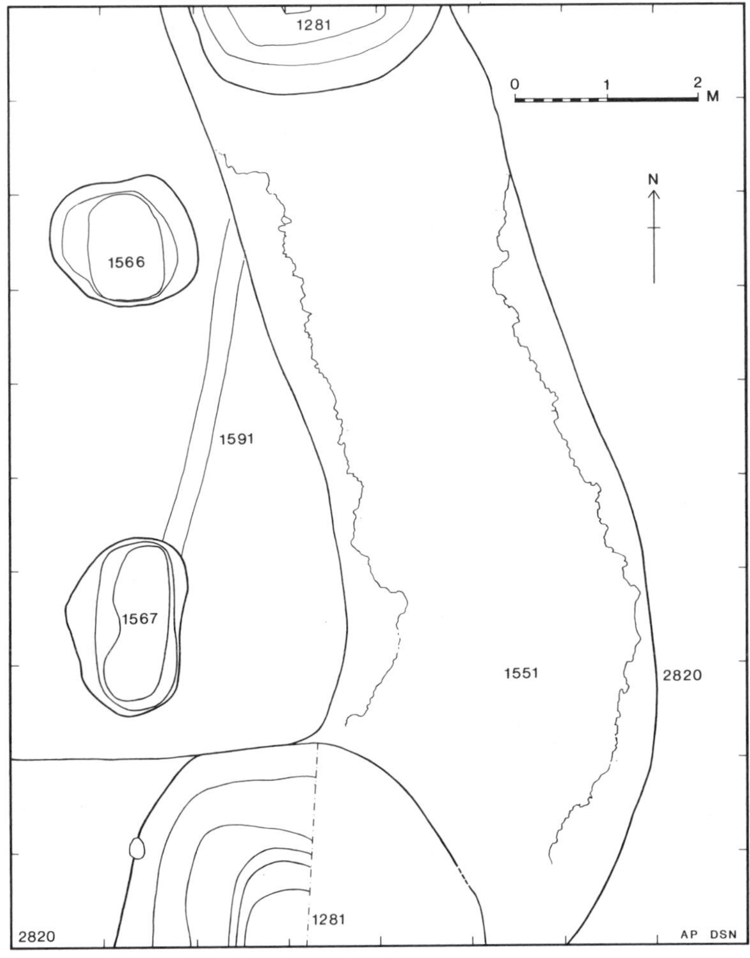

Fig 18 Plan of late Iron Age gateway, Building 3, Enclosure B, area 2820 (Scale 1:80)

Fig 19 View east of late Iron Age gateway, Building 3, Enclosure B, area 2820

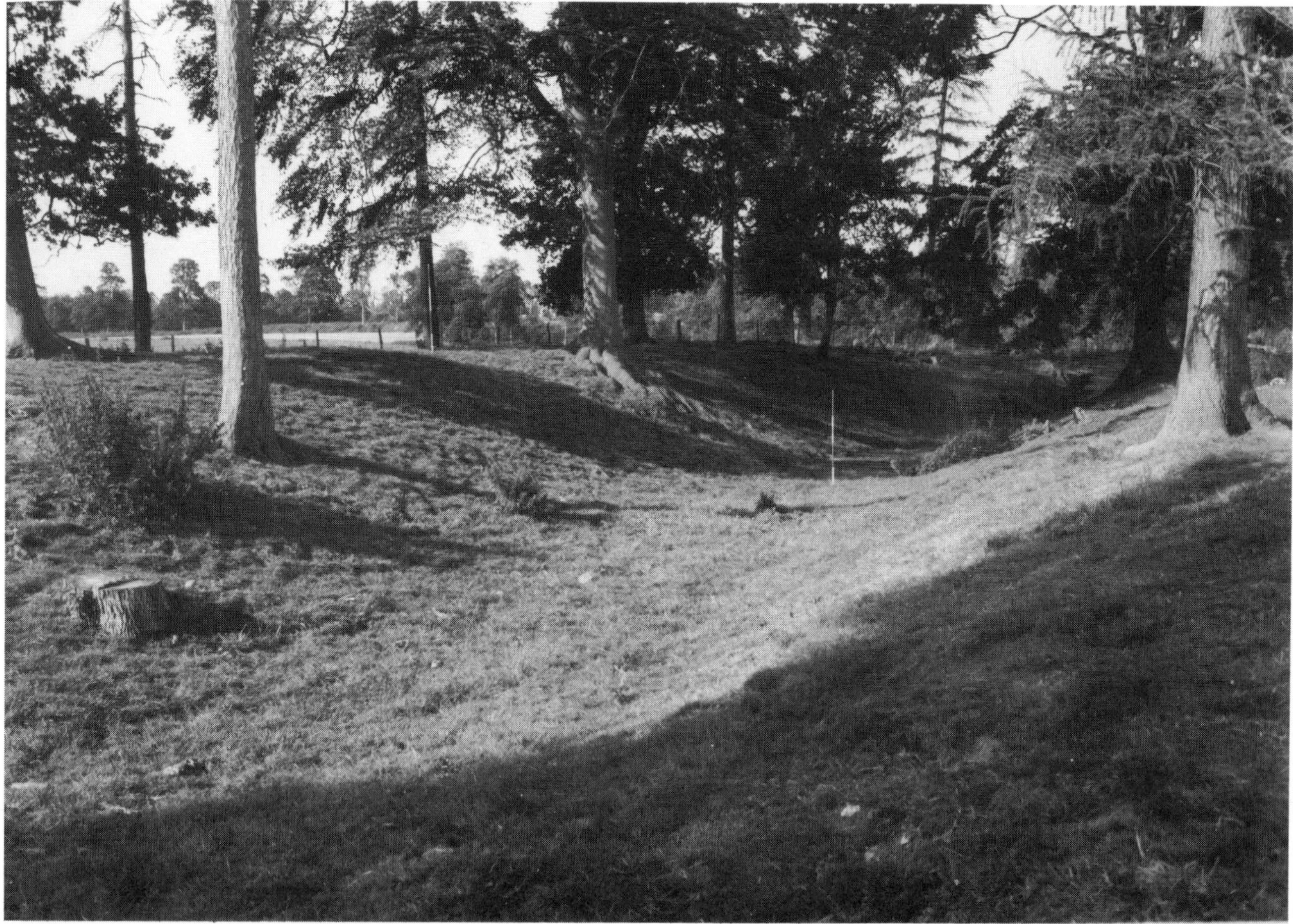

Fig 20 View south-west along Devil's Dyke close to Maynes Farm (Fig 6); the southern return of the dyke is represented by a hedgerow in the far distance

trackway leading westwards from Chester Gate. If so the area of land enclosed was approximately 60 hectares.

Woodland prevented the excavation of the dyke terminals flanking the causeway but a contour survey (AP Nos 304–310) east of the enclosure indicates a broad causeway across the dyke on the line of the enclosure's original entrance. Further south a long section (Fig 21) was obtained across areas 40–4315 where the ditch was V-shaped and originally about 9m wide by 4m deep: its clay external bank still stands 2m high and 14m wide (Fig 22). Allowing for erosion it is estimated that its 45° slope from bank top to dyke bottom was originally 12m. Its primary filling contained sherds of undiagnostic Belgic pottery, but from the presence of abraded late Antonine wares in layers 1708 and 1707 it appears to have been kept cleared out and to have remained a prominent boundary. One of the vessels was a grey ware bowl similar to *Ver* I, 973 (Frere 1972) dated AD 155–60. The eastern ditch of Enclosure A was retained although the internal bank appears to have been removed in places, perhaps to provide extra material to construct the new bank or to provide more room for buildings.

A second section was machine-cut across the dyke where it passes over Stoney Valley (Fig 23) – partly to prove its location (it is largely ploughed out) but also to obtain environmental evidence as here the lower, damper, conditions made preservation possible. Samples for pollen proved negative but mollusca of the species *Planorbis planorbis* and *Pisidium amnicum* suggest that the areas behind the bank and the ditch itself were filled with water for some considerable time. The south terminal and the western end of the east–west dyke (AP Nos 427–9) were found intersecting one another close to the modern field boundary. Further east a profile (Figs 23, comparative profile, and 24) revealed a bank and ditch pre-dating the dyke and with its bank on the opposite, northern side. In its filling (3529), sealed by the later banks were sherds from a cooking pot similar to Fig 153, No 13, dated at Prae Wood AD 5–40/45 (Thompson 1982, form C7–1). The new V-shaped dyke was 6.50m wide by 3m deep, but ploughing on the lower slope had denuded its northern edge, reducing its proportions by at least a metre. The bank survives 1.70m high (Fig 25) and is predominantly of chalk. In the medieval period the boundary was known as Whyt Dyke presumably because of its chalk sides. Machine trenches further east failed to locate the dyke beyond 190m; chalk quarrying may have destroyed it but it was not found in the quarry face further east nor in a field north-west – a direction indicated by its slight north-east shift in alignment. The route of the earlier ditch is also

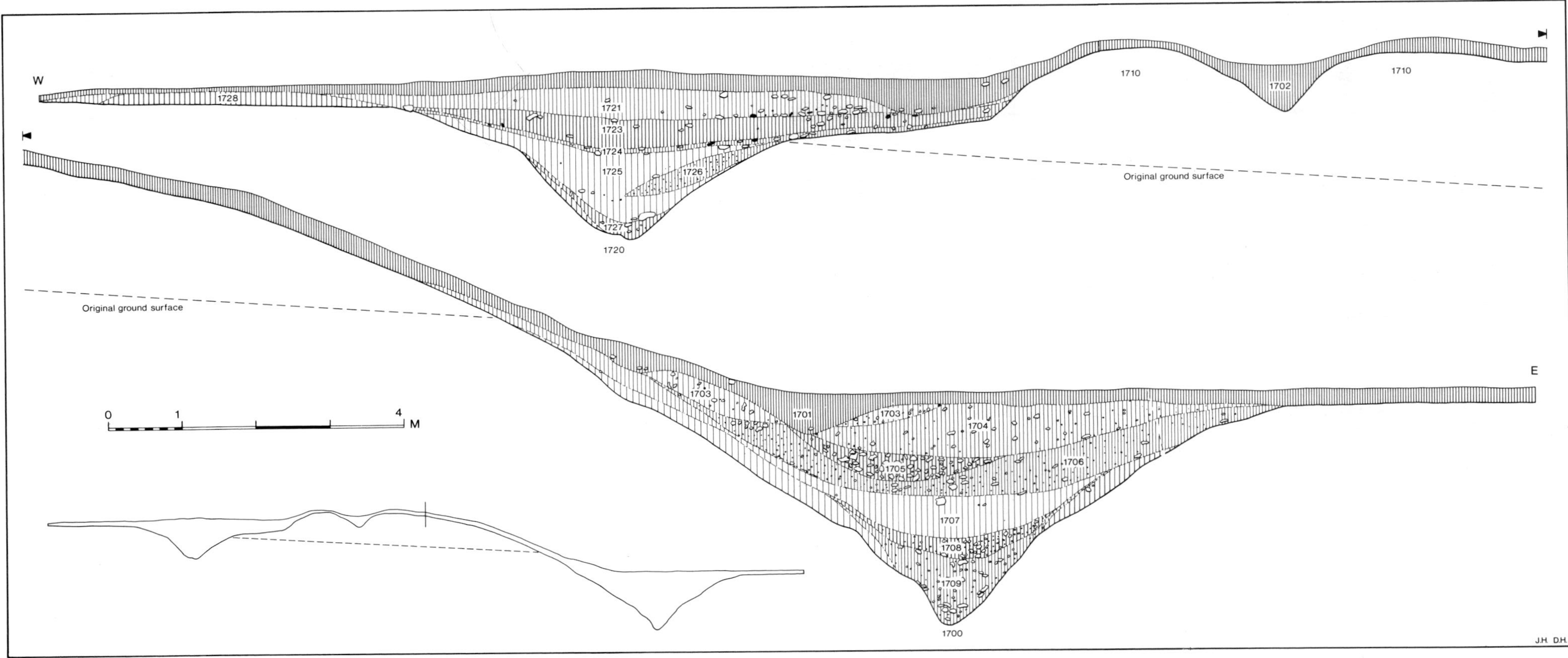

Fig 21 Sections across 'New Dyke' on east side of Enclosure A, area 40–4315, late Iron Age, Period 5 (Scale 1:80)

Fig 22 View west showing ditch and bank of 'New Dyke' situated on east side of Enclosure A, area 4315

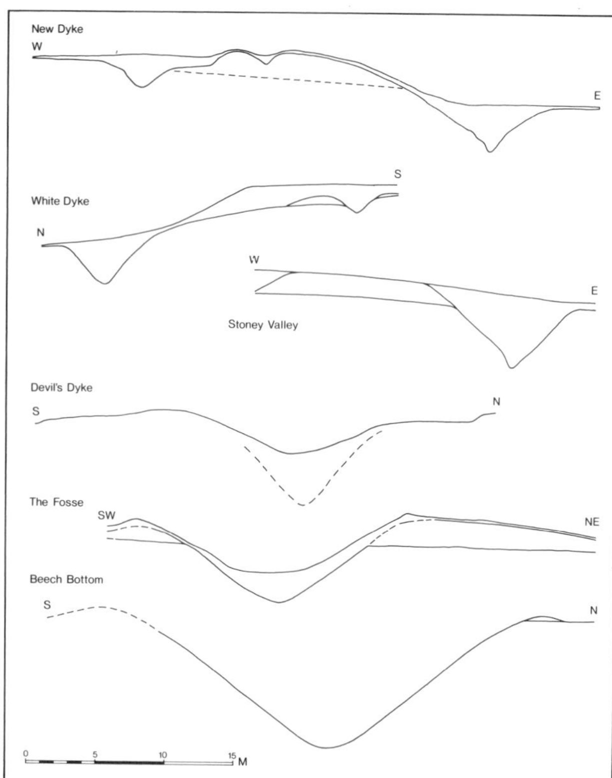

unknown but like the example beneath the causeway into Enclosure A (2927, Fig 13), it may have already defined the boundaries we see today.

Wheeler's description of Devil's Dyke is incorrect. For many years its bank was assumed to have been on the south side (Wheeler and Wheeler 1936, 15), where a shallow 'bank' survives, but the main bank is really on the north and has been utilised as an embankment for Gorhambury Drive close to Nash's Lodge. Confusion has arisen because the bank alongside the earthwork at Mayne's Farm (Fig 20) has been removed to enlarge a field; the shallow bank to the south, therefore, which is probably a negative lynchet, has received unwarranted attention.

It can now be seen that the relationship of bank to ditch throughout its length is consistent – the ditch is always on the downhill side – and follows a similar contour except where it dips towards the river or crosses Stoney Valley. There is no evidence for another dyke linking the two arms but the river, or

Fig 23 Comparative sections showing scale of 'New Dyke', area 40–4315, and 'White Dyke' south-east of the site, in relation to other dyke systems in the Verulamium area (see Fig 6)

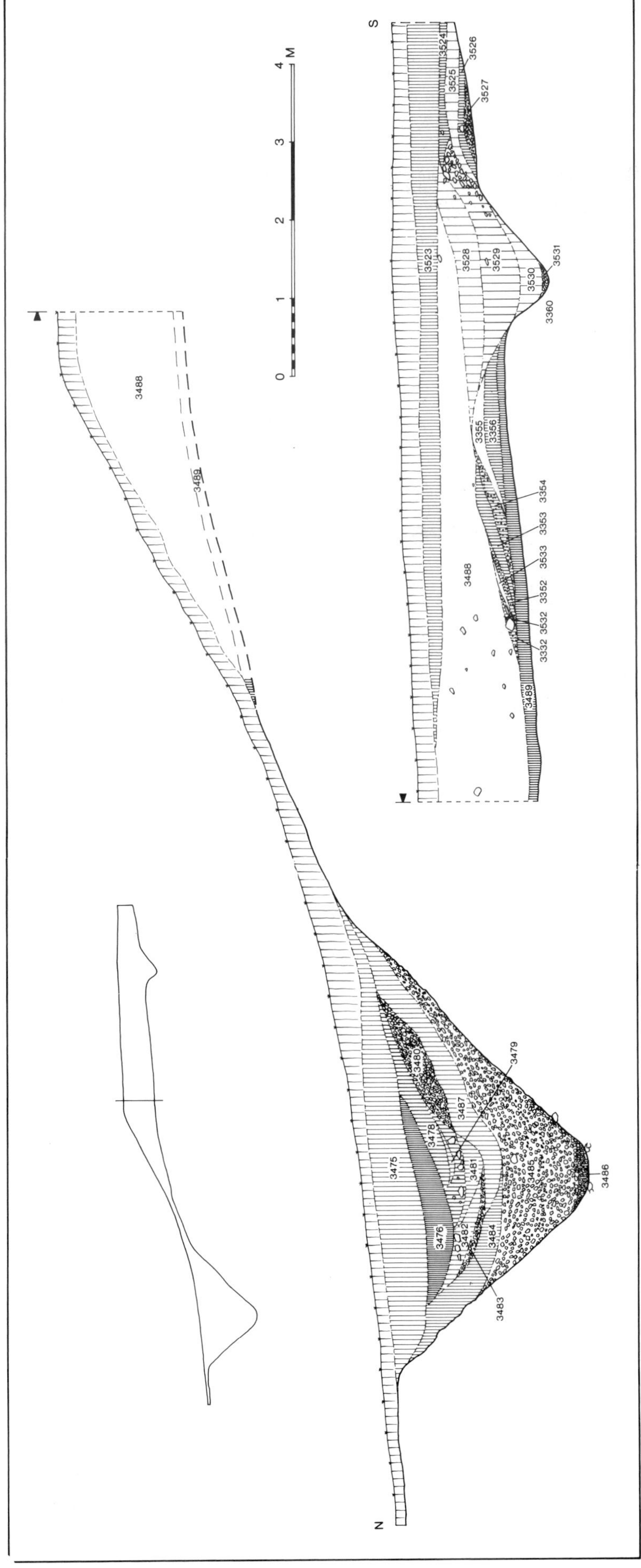

Fig 24 Section across 'White Dyke'; for location see Fig 6 (Scale 1:80)

Fig 25 *View south of 'White Dyke' south of Stoney Valley; for location see Fig 6*

marsh, could perhaps have created an eastern boundary. Nor is there evidence that the dyke ever continued south to link with the Fosse even though both features (and the western defences of Verulamium) are on a similar line and much the same distance from the river. Three machine-cut trenches close to the Fosse (Fig 6) failed to locate evidence for a connecting dyke and confirmed that a linear feature here is a gravel pit.

No molluscs were recovered from Dyke 1700 adjacent to Enclosure A but evidence from the molluscs removed from White Dyke (Fig 24) suggests that the primary ditch fillings (3531 and part of 3530) were dominated by *Vallonia excentrica*, which prefer an open habitat. Open country species, particularly *Pupilla muscorum*, were also dominant in the buried soil both beneath the bank (3356) associated with Ditch 3360 and the later bank (3488) of White Dyke indicating that prior to Period 5 possibly much of the surrounding area was open grassland. Similar evidence for open grassland species was also recovered from the early fills of the later dyke which implies that an open habitat continued. However, as the dyke filled up there was an increase in snails preferring a woodland habitat, which may merely reflect the surrounding environment of the ditch. It is of interest to note that the primary filling (3531) of the earlier ditch also contained species typical of shaded habitats, suggesting the presence of a nearby hedge.

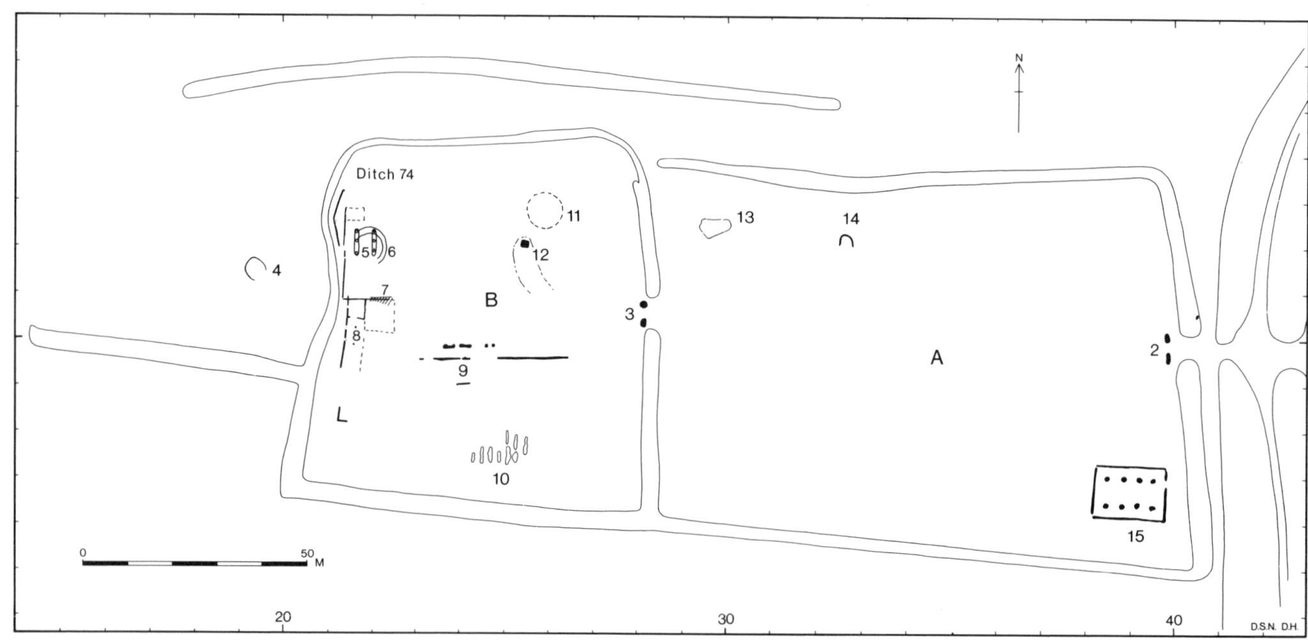

Fig 26 *Block plan showing Iron Age buildings within Enclosures A and B, Periods 3–5*

The buildings, nos 2–15 (Fig 26)

Apart from the gates (Buildings 2 and 3), 12 buildings of the early first century have been identified. They include, working from west to east, a sub-rectangular hut (Building 4, Fig 27), area 1921, a six-post granary (Building 5, Fig 28), which was replaced by a circular house (Building 6, Fig 28), area 2122, replaced again further south by a small hut (Building 7, Fig 32), and yet again by a rectangular house or proto-villa (Building 8, Fig 33). In area 23–2419 there was evidence for a rectangular post-built house (Building 9, Fig 33) while further south in area 24–2517 seven shallow trenches perhaps represent a foundation for a granary erected alongside the south bank of Enclosure B (Building 10, Fig 35). However, there are grounds for arguing that buildings 8 and 9 were constructed in the early–mid first century (p 28). North, in area 25–2623, ephemeral traces of the circular chalk floor of a hut (Building 11, not shown in detail, see Fig 26) on the same stratigraphic horizon and associated with a flint-lined tank (Structure 12, Fig 36) were located and further east, in area 2922 another hut (Building 13, Fig 37), utilising flint, occupied the north-west corner of Enclosure A. Slight traces of a structure (Building 14, Fig 39) were located in area 3221, while situated in the south-east corner, area 38–3916, was a large rectangular aisled barn (Building 15, Figs 40–44).

Certain relationships can be observed. Buildings 5, 6, 7 and 8 are stratigraphically in sequence; Buildings 7 and 8 were constructed over the antennae ditches of Period 3 and because Building 8 respects the alignment of Ditch 74, the primary fill of which contains Belgic material, the structure can be assigned to Period 5. Buildings 9 and 10 were also constructed over horizons in a ditch attributed to Period 3, and the fact that Building 10 was constructed against the enclosure bank confirms its association with Period 4 or 5. There is no stratigraphic link between Building 11 and the enclosure ditches. This is also the case with Building 13, although this seems to have been built against the tail of the bank and, if so, follows the Period 4 remodelling. Stratigraphically Building 14 has no relationship to these features. Building 15 seals the filling of the Period 3 enclosure and belongs to either Period 4 or 5 – the latter is the more likely as the interval between its east wall and the ditch leaves little room for a bank, which was probably levelled after construction of the Period 5 dyke. The discovery of two almost complete native vessels in Pit 2669 (Fig 90) in the north-east corner of the Period 3 enclosure, area 3922, might suggest the presence of a building here, but no structural trace was found and it is possible the pottery was associated with a burial.

Had it been feasible to clear extensive lengths of the Enclosure A ditch, concentrations of pottery from the primary filling might have provided clues to the main areas of occupation. Recutting prevented this, however, and the only reliable groups came from the infilled ditch sealed by the causeway (Fig 18) into the Period 4 'enclosure B' and sealed by the backfill in the antennae, particularly the southern arm (see p 13). The presence here of almost complete vessels (Fig 153,

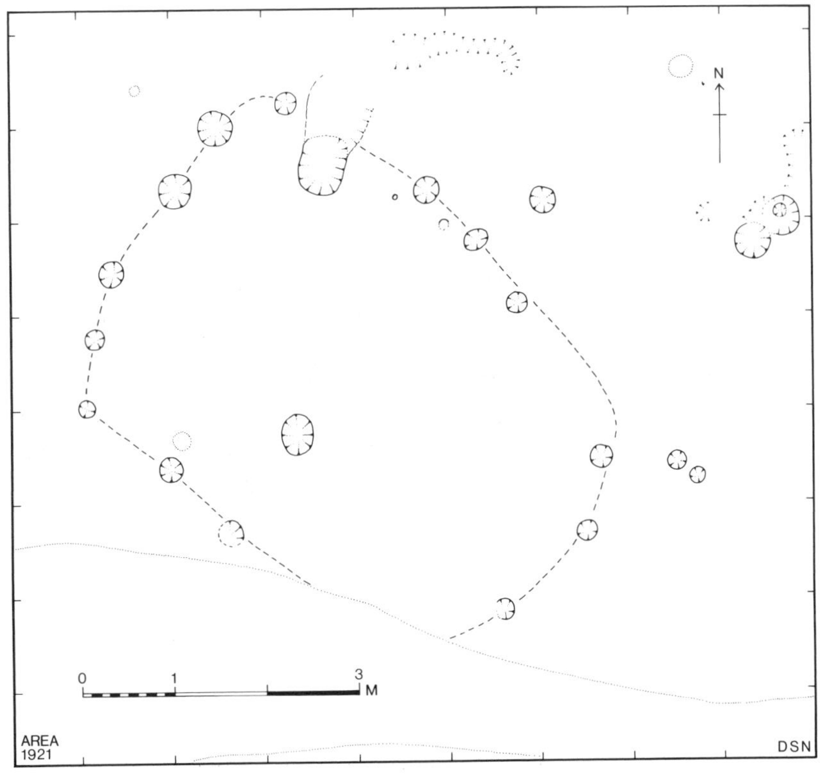

Fig 27 Plan of Building 4, Periods 3–5 (Scale 1:80)

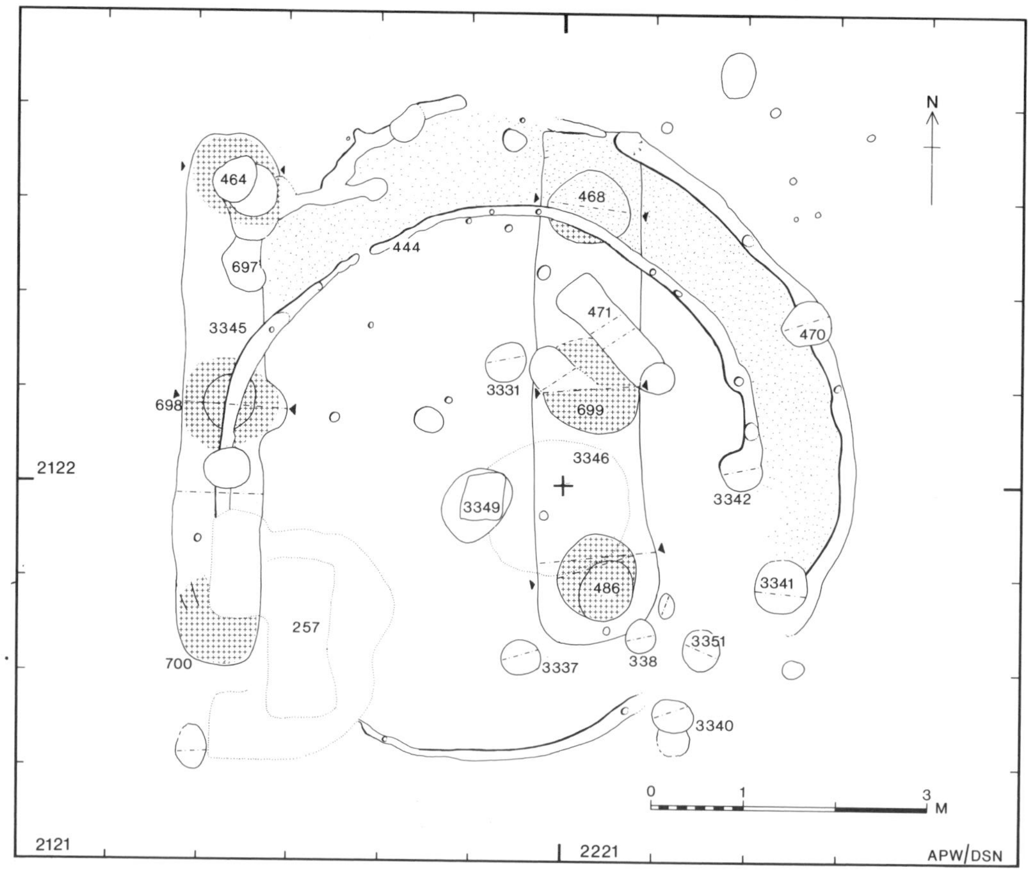

Fig 28 Plan of Buildings 5 and 6, Periods 3–5 (Scale 1:80)

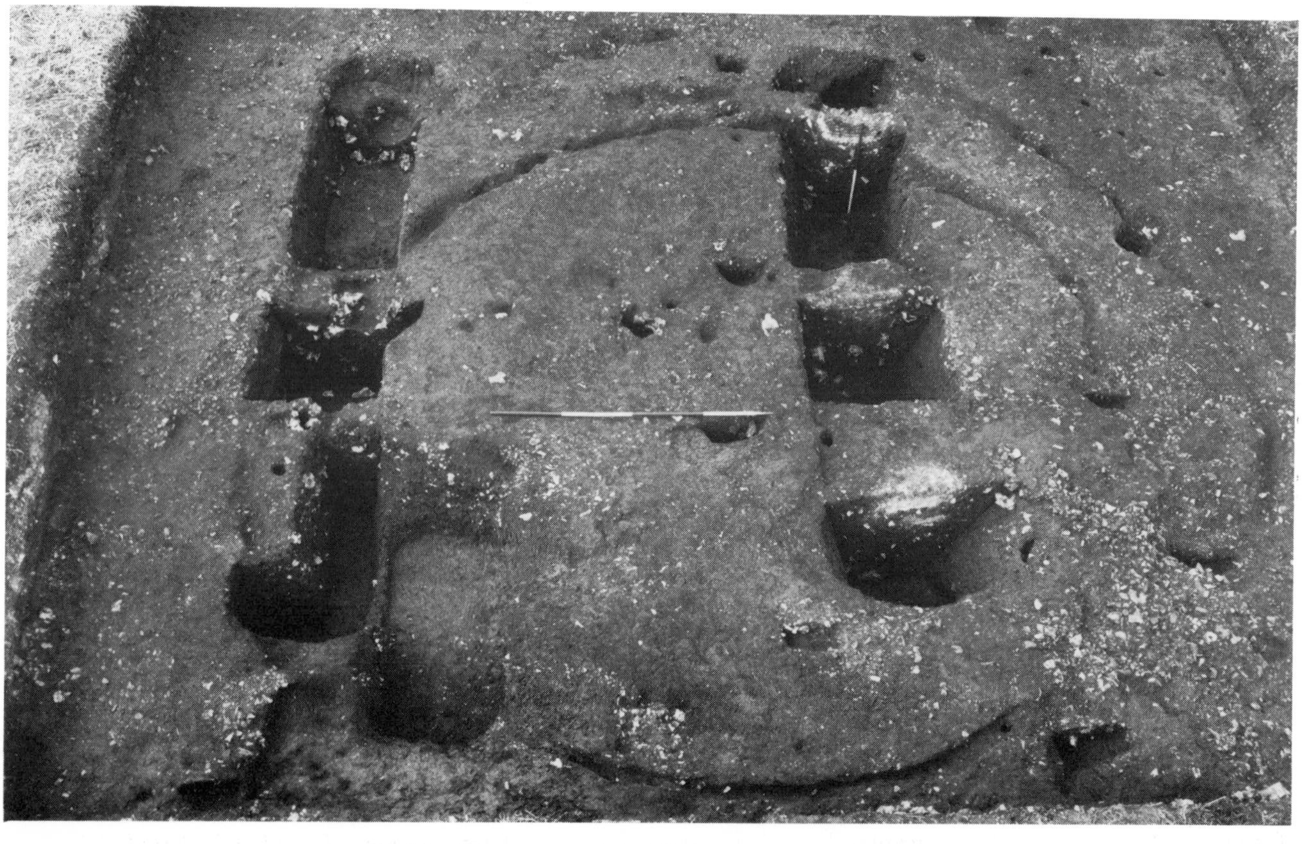

Fig 29 View north of Buildings 5 and 6, Periods 3–5

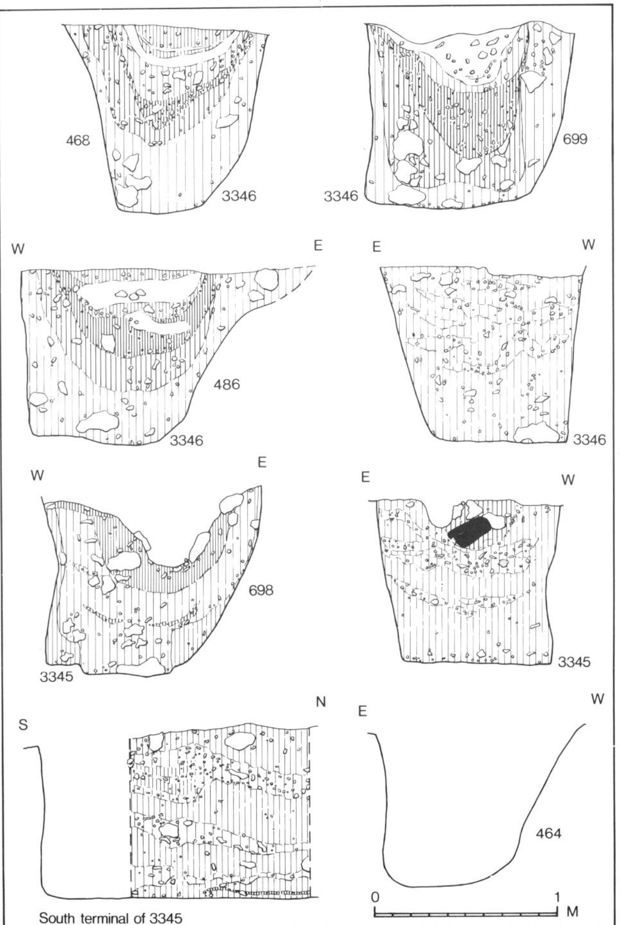

Fig 30 Sections across post-trenches, Building 5, Periods 3–5 (Scale 1:40)

Nos 8–21) is perhaps significant, for it possibly implies occupation very close by; if so, the assemblage could have been associated with Buildings 4, 5, 6 or 11 or some other unrecorded dwelling. The existence of the Period 4 causeway, with its gate (Building 3, Fig 18) on the western – outer – side, emphasises the importance of the new 'enclosure B' in this period. This is perhaps further emphasised by the discovery from around Buildings 5 and 6 of five British coins, a single Republican piece (No 1) and an issue of Augustus (No 4). The native coins included one of Tasciovanus 20 BC–AD 10 (B2), and four of Cunobelin, AD 10–40 (numbers B6, 10, 12 and 13).

Building descriptions

Building 4 (Fig 27)

Building 4, located in area 1921, was a sub-rectangular hut of post construction measuring about 4 by 6m. It was orientated north-west to south-east and had a total of 14 postholes, those on the south having been partially truncated by a ramp into a medieval quarry-pit. There was no obvious evidence for an entrance although a gap 1.70m wide on the north-east side may represent one: if so the entrance could have faced Buildings 5 or 6. Its postholes had also been truncated by a later hut (Building 50); there was little dating evidence although one of the postholes contained a single sherd from a Gallo-Belgic beaker. From the absence of Roman pottery, the form of the building, and the possibility that an entrance faced Buildings 5 or 6, emphasising its link with one of those structures, an early first-century date is likely.

Building 5 (Fig 28)

Located in area 2122 (approx) Building 5 was about 5m square and comprised two parallel trenches 3m apart, each about 5m long by 1m wide and deep (Fig 29). Set at either end and in the middle of each trench, opposite one another, were three pairs of postholes (Fig 30) packed with clay, which was also used to level-up the 'floor'. It had no hearths or other internal features. Six-post structures are usually interpreted as granaries and, although Building 5 is unparalleled in its size and in having post-trenches, its function is believed to have been the same. It is

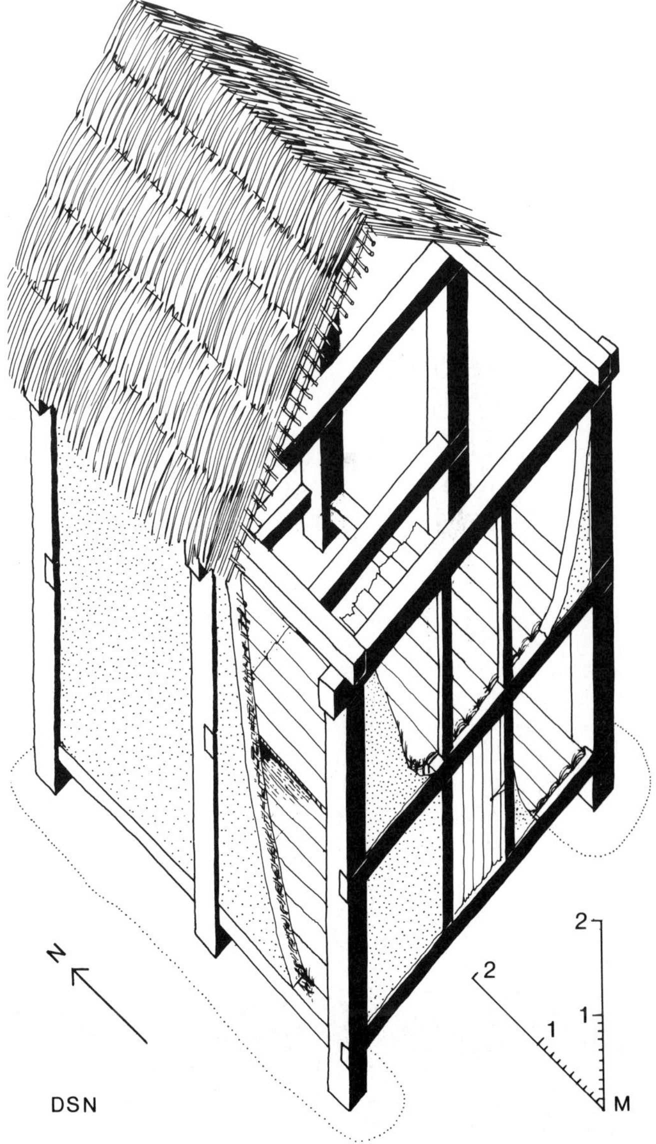

Fig 31 Reconstruction of Building 5, Periods 3–5

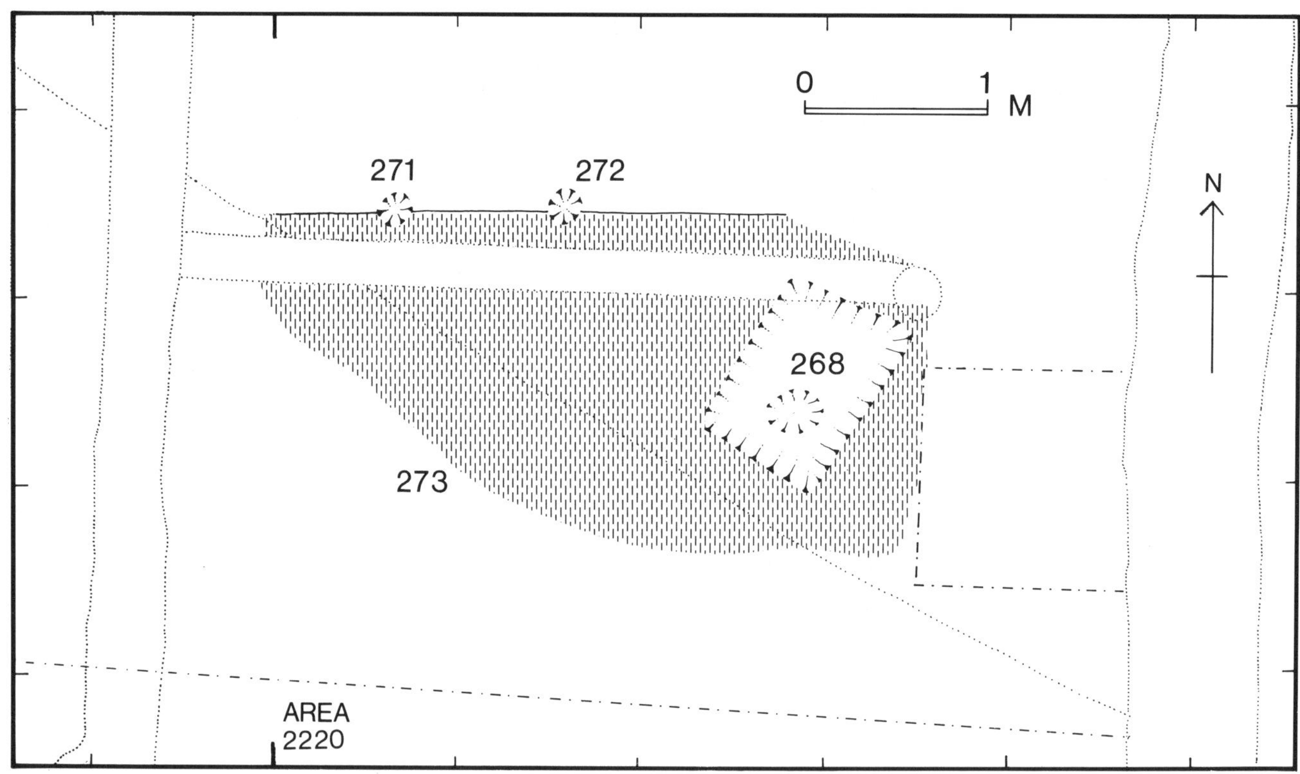

Fig 32 Plan of Building 7, Periods 3–5 (Scale 1:40)

uncertain why construction trenches rather than post-pits were necessary but in many respects digging a continuous trench is easier than digging within the confines of pits, and trenches would have allowed more flexibility, lengthways, to make adjustments in setting the posts. Their depths perhaps indicate that the posts were initially free standing for construction purposes, but the width of the sockets, 0.75m (Fig 30), also implies considerable load-bearing capacity and height, possibly to provide a raised floor clear from vermin and to allow the circulation of air to prevent the grain decaying or overheating. If the clay spread was a floor then the grain might have been stored at first-floor level. Alternatively, if the clay spread was not a floor, the building could have had two raised floors, as shown on the reconstruction (Fig 31), one about a metre off the ground and the second above head height. Such an arrangement would allow seed and food grain to be stored separately (see p 34).

The post-sockets were subsequently filled by chalk and cob associated with Building 6. In posthole 464, this material sealed a large body-sherd of native fabric with oblique striations similar to Pot No 61, Fig 154. Small fragments of grog-tempered fabric were also found in the clay packing of posthole 486.

Building 6 (Fig 28)

The granary was dismantled and its post-sockets sealed by Building 6, a circular house 7.30m wide externally, with walls 1m wide constructed in cob puddled between hurdles bedded into shallow concentric 'U'-shaped trenches (Fig 29). It had a central hearth. On its south-west side the slots were destroyed by later constructions but on the south-east side there was a gap in its wall associated with a series of postholes (Nos 3340, 3341, 3351 and 338) indicating the probable position of an entrance. Other associated features included a shallow pit (3349) cutting the hearth and a rectangular cist (471). There was no evidence to suggest that the wall trenches represented two phases, one an enlargement of the first.

No pottery was found in the house but beneath the floor of the north wing room of the second masonry villa (Building 37), which sealed the structure, was a Republican coin (No 1) which may conceivably have come from its floor. Five British coins, one of Tasciovanus and four of Cunobelin (already referred to, p 25), came from the area surrounding the building.

Building 7 (Fig 32)

This was located in area 2220 and was probably a hut represented merely by an occupation deposit (273) mixed with charcoal, with a straight north edge associated with two postholes (Nos 271 and 272). It sealed the cob spread from Building 6 and was sealed in turn by the floors of Building 8. The size of the structure is not known but, if the extent of the spread is an indicator, was no less than 3.50 by 1.75m. The floor was cut by a sleeper beam associated with Building 8 which also cut a shallow rectangular pit (268) containing charcoal, believed to have been an oven. No pottery was present.

Building 8 (Fig 33)

Building 8 was of sleeper-beam construction supporting wattle-and-daub walls. Its plan is not fully understood; a main 'block' aligned north–south, 4.50m wide by 15m long, had at least three rooms with puddled clay floors (Rooms A–C). Its southern extent is uncertain as it was erased by later buildings, but at the north-east was another room (D) or 'wing' 5.60m square, with a rammed chalk floor, sealing Building 7.

Extending north from the building into areas 2121–22 was another sleeper beam (266), 20m long, which seemed to turn east to define the north edge of a rectangular area of occupation material (465), 4 by 2.50m, with fragments of a native storage jar (AV2), a small jar as No 32, Fig 154, and a copy of a terra nigra platter (AV3) of unusual fabric. It may have been a floor, the long wall forming the west side of an open-sided shed, but no postholes supporting a lean-to were discovered. Sharing the same strati-

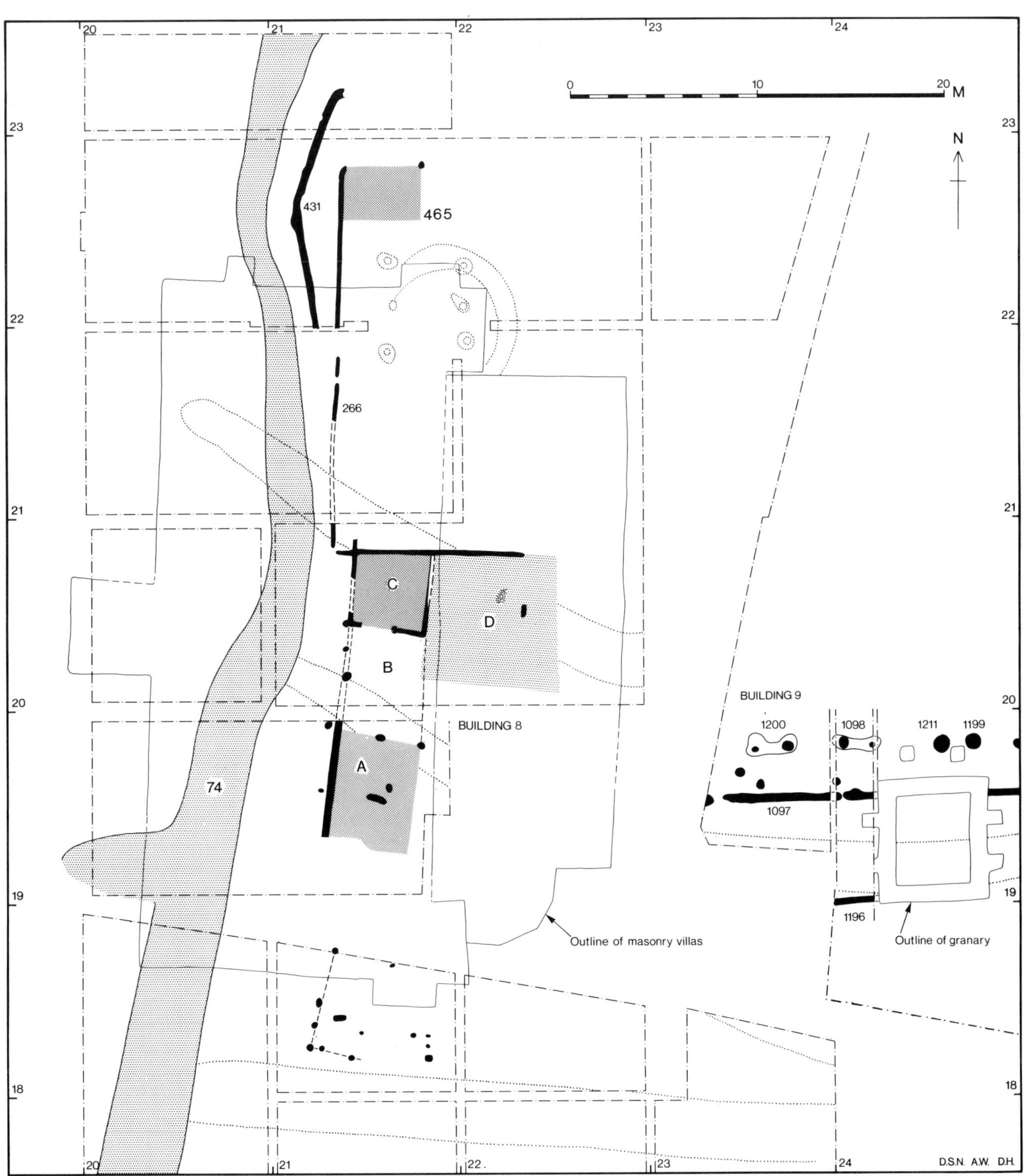

Fig 33 Block plan of Buildings 8 and 9, Period 5

Fig 34 View north showing Ditch 74 and palisades associated with Building 8; they are sealed by Building 37. The eastern palisade is medieval

graphical horizon was a palisade (431) separating the building from the adjacent ditch (74) (Fig 34). Traces of burnt daub along the line of the sleeper beams indicate that the buildings burnt down.

Further south in area 2118 were six posts forming a right-angle; they contained an identical fill to the sleeper beams (clay with small granules of chalk suggesting a cob construction). As they are on a slightly different alignment they probably represent either a separate rectangular hut or, more likely, a fence.

The original plan of the structure cannot be established with certainty. The presence of the north-east 'wing' might suggest a wing-room but there is no evidence for a corridor to the east which such an architectural design might have had, nor any evidence for a corresponding room to the south. A building of this date could have had a peristyle plan similar to some south Gaulish houses, but there is no evidence. The relationship of the structure to Building 9 (Fig 33) is also uncertain. It is stratigraphically possible that they formed part of the same building but, if so, the overall plan is even more difficult to visualise. In the absence of definite evidence, Buildings 8 and 9 must be assumed to be separate and 8 probably comprised little more than L-shaped living quarters with subsidiary outhouses.

Dating evidence

Unfortunately it is impossible reliably to equate levels associated with the building with those in Ditch 74, but the fact that the palisade (431) follows the alignment of the ditch implies that the two were contemporaneous. Only in a few places was the ditch not recut: in area 2121 the lowest fill (269) contained a group of nine Belgic vessels (Fig 154, Nos 55–62) yet elsewhere similar horizons (eg 259) produced early Roman wares including a samian vessel of Tiberian date, and a mortarium of Sheepen Type 14 (Niblett 1985, fig 50), AD 20–60 (No 1, p 194). On the present evidence Building 8 can be assigned to the late Iron Age, although at the very end of the Period 5 sequence (there is a possibility therefore that its construction could have taken place in the early years of the Roman period and be of Period 6).

Sealing the building was a layer of clay (35) which extended south into area 2117 where it was cut by a cesspit (622) containing Claudian-Neronian samian and a bone wrist-guard (Fig 141, No 973). The coarse pottery groups from pit 622 contained mostly 'Belgic' vessels in fabric 20. Fine wares included a Lyons ware roughcast beaker (as *Ver* 30 and 31, AD 49–70, Frere 1972) and two Gallo-Belgic rims of unusual form (AV (648)5 and (649)4). It would seem therefore that the building may have been burnt before the Boudiccan rebellion of AD 61–2. Also in the pit was a coin of Cunobelin (Br 10), and another of Republican date (No 3), and mineralised seeds including coriander, fig, lentils, field pea, sloe, bullace, *ribes* species, blackberry and grape.

Building 9 (Fig 33)

Building 9, area 23–2419, shared the same horizons as Building 8 and its postholes were packed with the same distinctive clay mixed with granules of chalk, and sealed by the same horizon of clay, numbered here 1081. It had three pairs of postholes, two pairs (Nos 1098 and 1200) contained at either end of a figure-of-eight shaped pit. These probably supported the north wall of the building with the opposite side possibly represented by a sleeper beam (1196) 7.50m further south. The relationship of an east–west slot (1097) is uncertain. It is tempting to suggest that it was the main north wall of the building, making the room about 5m deep, and that the three pairs of posts supported a verandah. However, this slot shared the same alignment as a palisade which extended about 40m east into area 2719 (see overall plan, Fig 1) so that its relationship to the structure, if any, remains uncertain. Pottery from the filling of the postholes was exclusively of native fabric, as was pottery from an occupation level adjacent to the slot, including a fragment from the shoulder of an imported amphora.

Building 10 (Fig 35)

This lay in area 24–2517 and was distinguished by a row of seven shallow U-shaped trenches each about 700mm wide by 100mm deep, probably formed to bed split tree-trunks or joists supporting a raised floor. It was built against the tail of the Period 4 bank. No evidence for walls was found but if the limits of the trenches approximate to those of a superstructure an overall dimension of about 13 by 7m can be assumed. The presence of a raised floor suggests that the building was a granary. No pottery was found in the trenches which were sealed by a pebbled surface (1269) containing first-century pottery. An undisturbed level (1403), sharing the same stratigraphic horizon as the U-shaped trenches but over a nearby ditch, contained rim sherds of 16 Belgic ware vessels (AV Nos 1–6) and a single rim sherd from a Claudian samian bowl. In the pebbled surface (1269) was a one-piece brooch dated AD 43–75 (No 4, Fig 121).

Building 11 (detailed plan not published – see Fig 26)

Other features occupying the 'inner enclosure' in this period included a semicircular chalk spread (736, AP 133) partially sealed by Building 29 and located in area 25–2622. It was about 8m in diameter and possibly represented a hut floor. It was associated with a scatter of exclusively late Iron Age sherds but its perimeter was ill-defined and no related slot or postholes were traced.

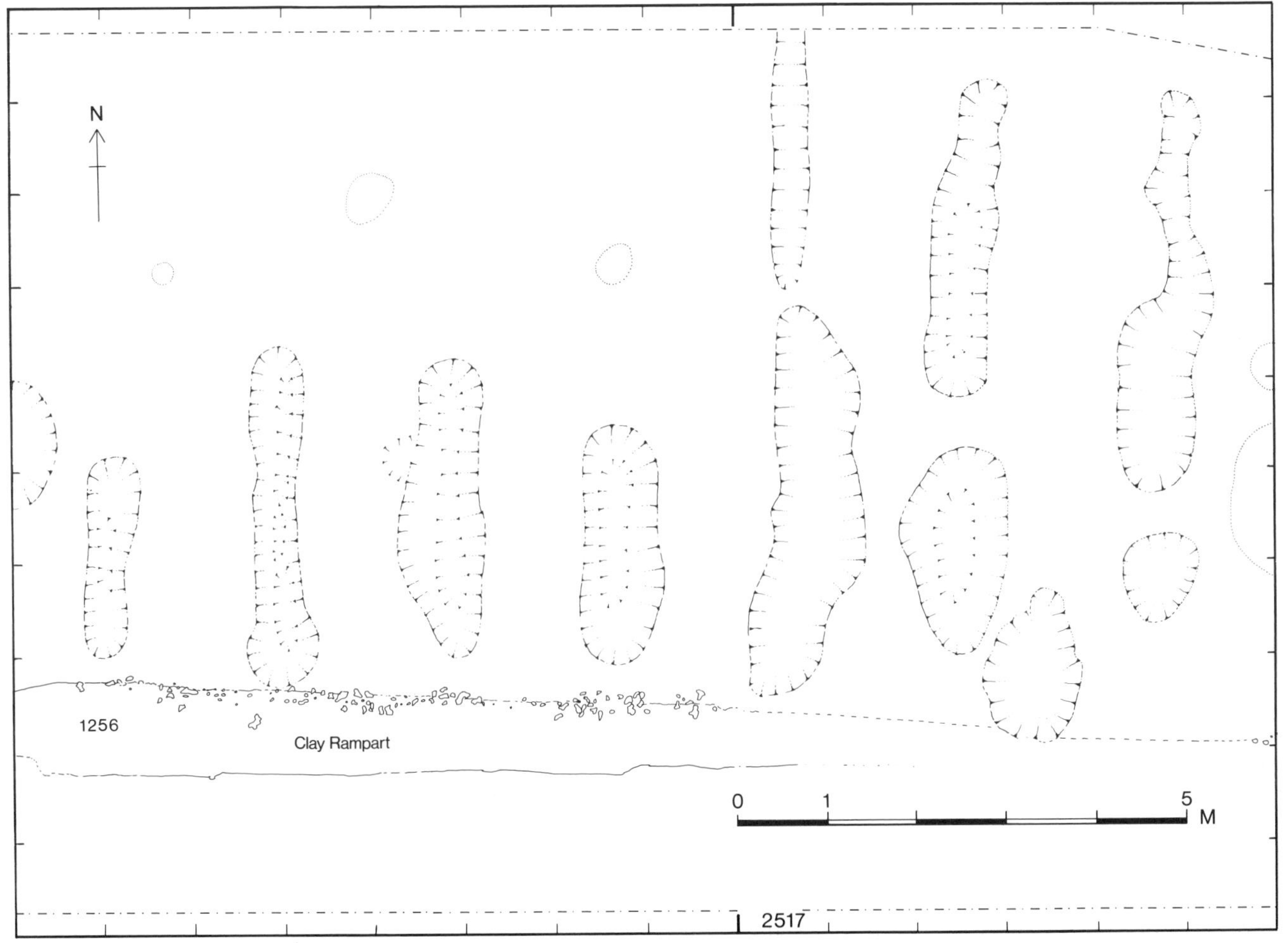

Fig 35 Plan of Building 10, Period 5 (Scale 1:80)

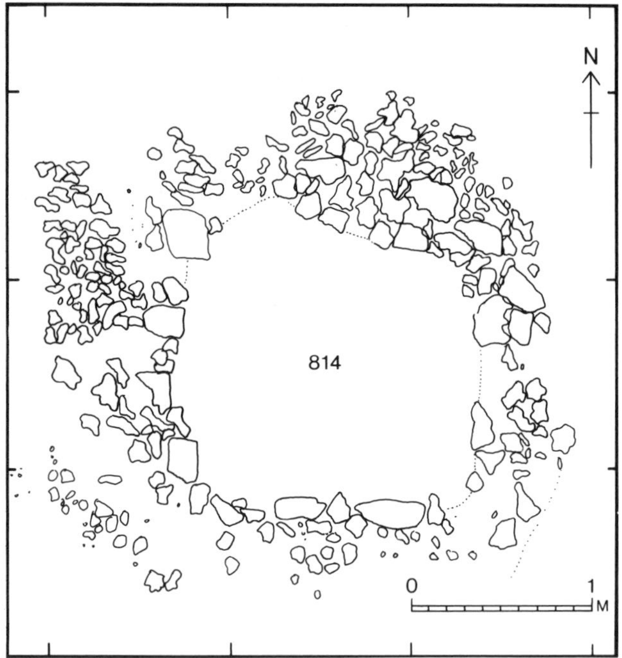

Fig 36 Plan of Structure 12, Period 5 (Scale 1:40)

Structure 12 (Fig 36)

This lay directly south of Building 11 in area 2522 and comprised a pit (814) 1.70m square by 0.54m deep, lined with flints. Curving south-east from it was a spread of flint (713) lining a shallow hollow (Fig 1) and containing a native jar similar to No 36, Fig 154. Sealing both was a layer of clay. Also sealed by the clay were two brooches: No 30 found inside the feature, and No 18 within the hollow. No 18 (Fig 121) is an Aucissa brooch dated no later than AD 43, and No 30 is a Colchester one-piece brooch dated *c* AD 10–60. The pit is believed to have been a water-tank, possibly marking the position of a 'spring' and a potential reason for the importance of the inner enclosure. It is unlikely to have been an abundant supply but its presence would have reduced the need to carry water from the river. It is of interest to note that during the excavation a little water always collected in the feature, even in dry weather.

Building 13 (Fig 37)

This occupied the north-west corner of Enclosure A, area 29–3022, and was a flat-bottomed hollow (1693) 6.60 by 3.60m overall. No sleeper beams or postholes were found, but along the north side (and possibly the east side also) was a row of large flint nodules (1686) suggesting that either the tail of the bank was reveted, or that the foundation was a support for a wall (Fig 38). Pottery from the feature was in two distinct horizons. The primary level (1679) contained a large quantity of native pottery from at least 36 vessels (Nos 32–50, 52 and 54, Fig 154), an imported terra nigra platter, and an imported butt-beaker (Nos 51 and 53 respectively). In a secondary level (1678) was a fine-ware beaker (AV No (1678) 8). The only small objects were a spindle whorl and a sling shot (Nos 1025 (Fig 145) and 1031). Although the function and original plan of the feature is uncertain the floors and pottery scatter suggest a dwelling. The presence of imported vessels in the primary levels and their absence in context 105 (p 000) in the filling of the Period 3 antennae ditch would suggest that the hut belongs to the later occupation, probably Periods 4 or 5.

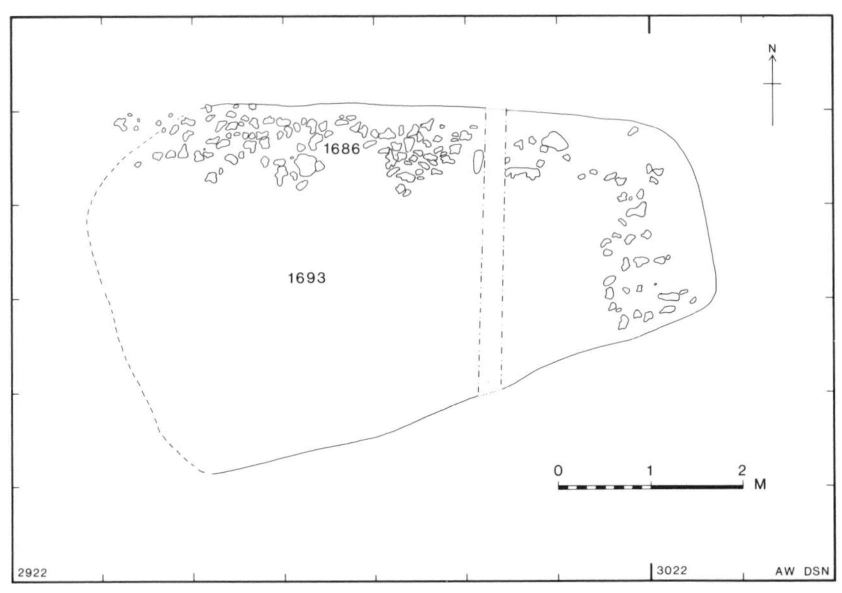

Fig 37 Plan of Building 13, Period 5 (Scale 1:80)

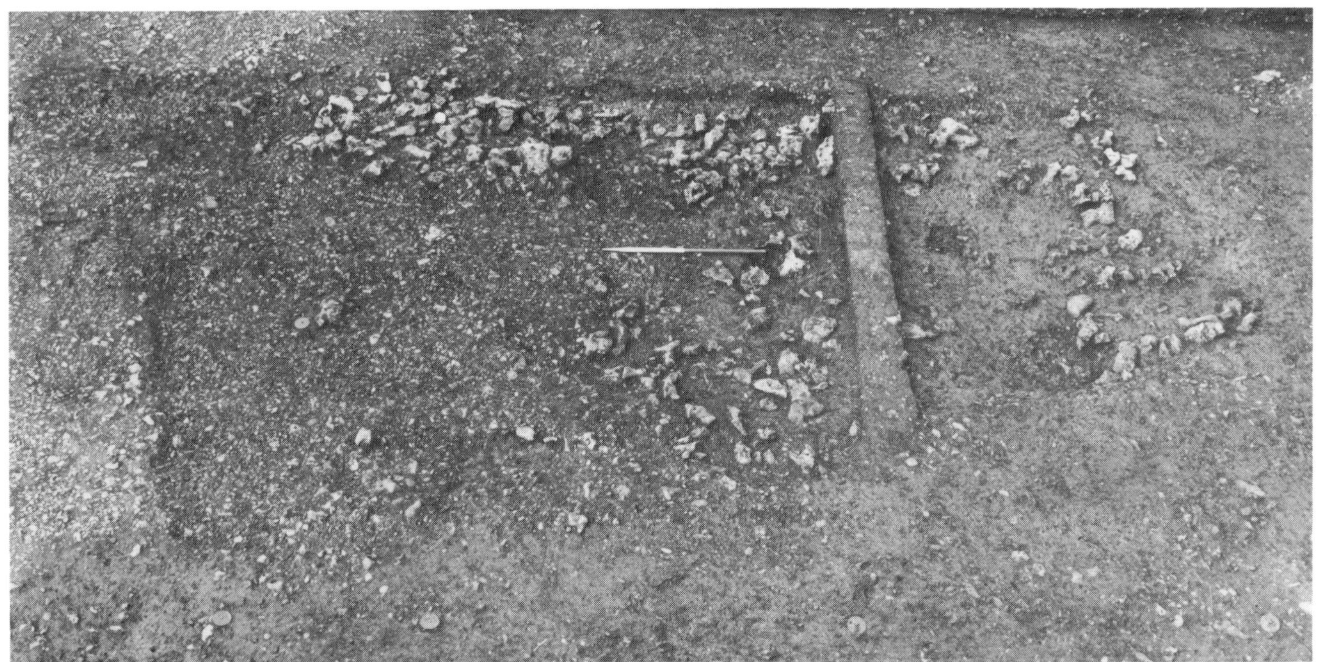

Fig 38 View north of Building 13

Structure 14 (Fig 39)

This was an oval enclosure or pen located in area 3222. It was 3m wide with a U-shaped trench (3184) filled with clay perhaps derived from a wattle wall. On its south side was a spread of cobbles (3185) containing a coin of Tasciovanus (No B3) and two sherds of flint-tempered pottery of Iron Age date; it perhaps marks the position of a south-east facing entrance. The function of a pit (3182) on the north side is not understood but since its sides were fired red and a deposit of charcoal (3181) was found inside, it may have been an oven. The feature contained early first-century sherds and a fragment of daub.

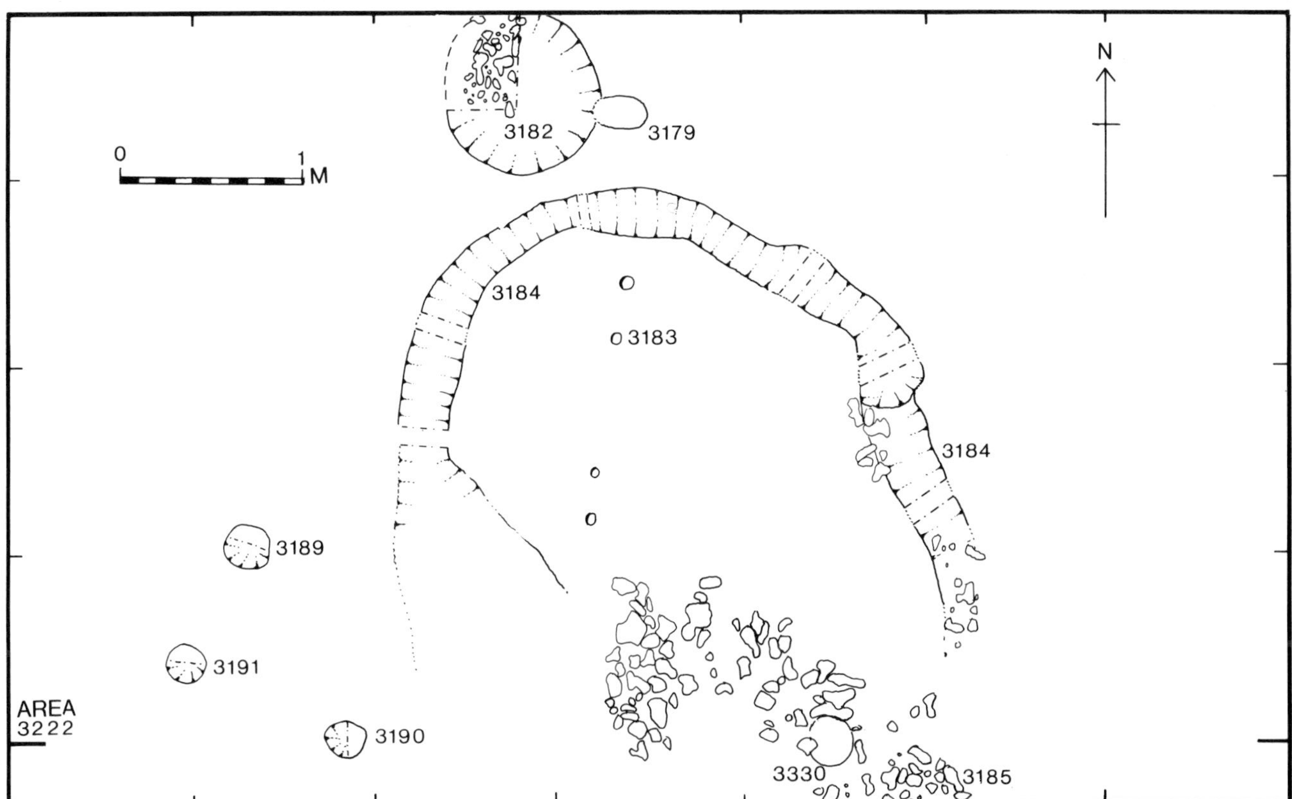

Fig 39 Plan of Building 14, Periods 3–5 (Scale 1:40)

Building 15 (Figs 40–44)

Building 15 was reconstructed on numerous occasions (see overall plan of complex, Fig 40, and sequence of development, Fig 41). Each reconstruction has been given a separate building number and will be described under its appropriate period, but in order to be able to follow subsequent developments the description of Building 15 is followed by a list of successive building numbers together with a list of associated illustrations. Figure 41 also lists the various building numbers.

The structure occupied the south-east corner of Enclosure A and, since it was built over the Period 3 ditch, belongs to either Period 4 or 5. Period 5 is the more likely as there is little space for the bank between the east wall of the structure and the ditch, which strongly suggests the bank was already levelled: levelling also took place following the construction of the dyke elsewhere. Earlier Iron Age occupation in area 3916 is attested by the presence of a cooking pot with suspension holes (Fig 152, No 5) in a shallow pit (context 2031, Fig 40).

The building, of aisled form, measured 16.50 by 11.50m (Fig 42) and had four pairs of post-pits (Nos 2237/2240, 2069/2241, 2236/2006, 2250/2249) forming three bays each about 2.50m wide. The post-pits, about 1.0m wide by 0.5m deep (Fig 43), contained slight evidence for post-pipes between 0.40 and 0.50m wide: flanking the postholes was an aisle 2.25m wide. The outer wall was represented by a U-shaped trench between 0.30 and 0.60m wide, complete for most of its length, except where it was destroyed in the north-west corner and a 1.50m gap in the east wall. This gap might represent an entrance but, if so, its position almost opposite a pier is unusual. More likely, the main entrance was on the north side where entrances and yard surfaces existed in later periods.

As with other buildings of the period, the postholes were packed with light orange clay and some contained in their filling small sherds of native ceramic-tempered pottery with no Roman wares. A rim (AV1) from a native storage-jar was found in the east wall-trench (2191). A pre-Roman date is not proven, but located along the north wall of the building and within it was a layer of occupation material (2198), with native pottery preserved in a hollow caused by subsidence of the floor into the underlying ditch. Pottery represented included forms similar to 12, 17, 18, 22, 49, and 56 (Figs 153 and 154). Included also was a fine-ware butt-beaker, probably imported, of unusual form (AV11).

The absence of postholes along the wall-trenches strongly suggests that the side walls were not load-bearing, and therefore the main posts must have supported virtually the whole weight of the roof, probably of steep but fairly uniform pitch from apex to eaves. Because no load-bearing supports existed in the side walls and their distance from the main posts

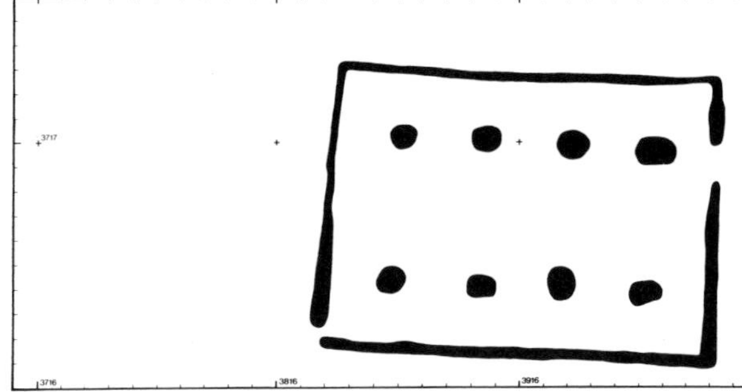

BUILDING 15

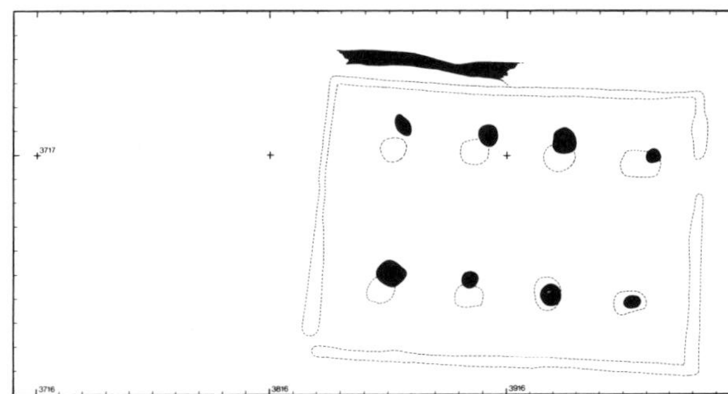

BUILDING 20

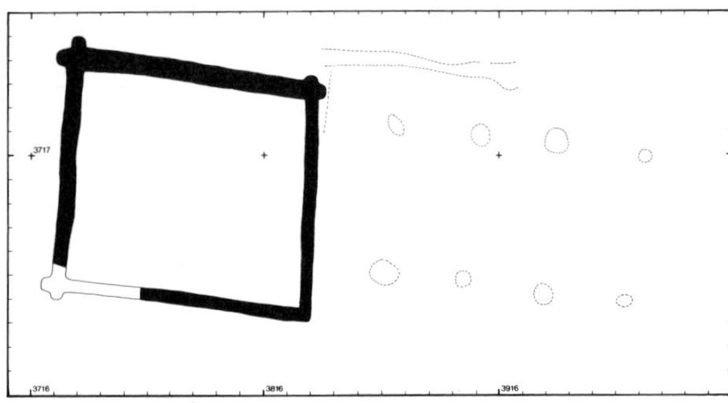

BUILDING 34

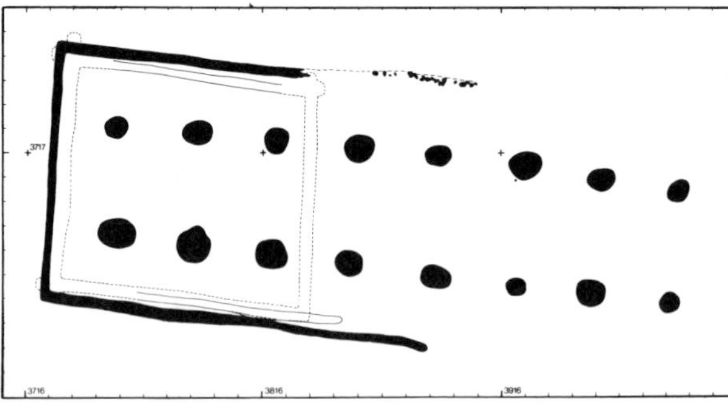

BUILDINGS 39/40

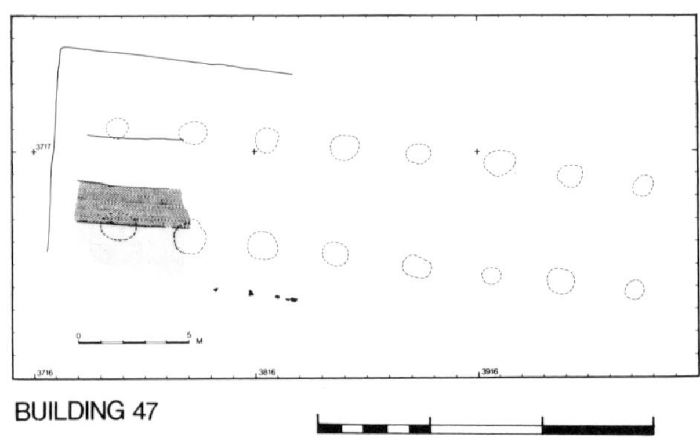

BUILDING 47

0 5 15 M

Fig 41 Sequence of development of complex in south-east corner of Enclosure A

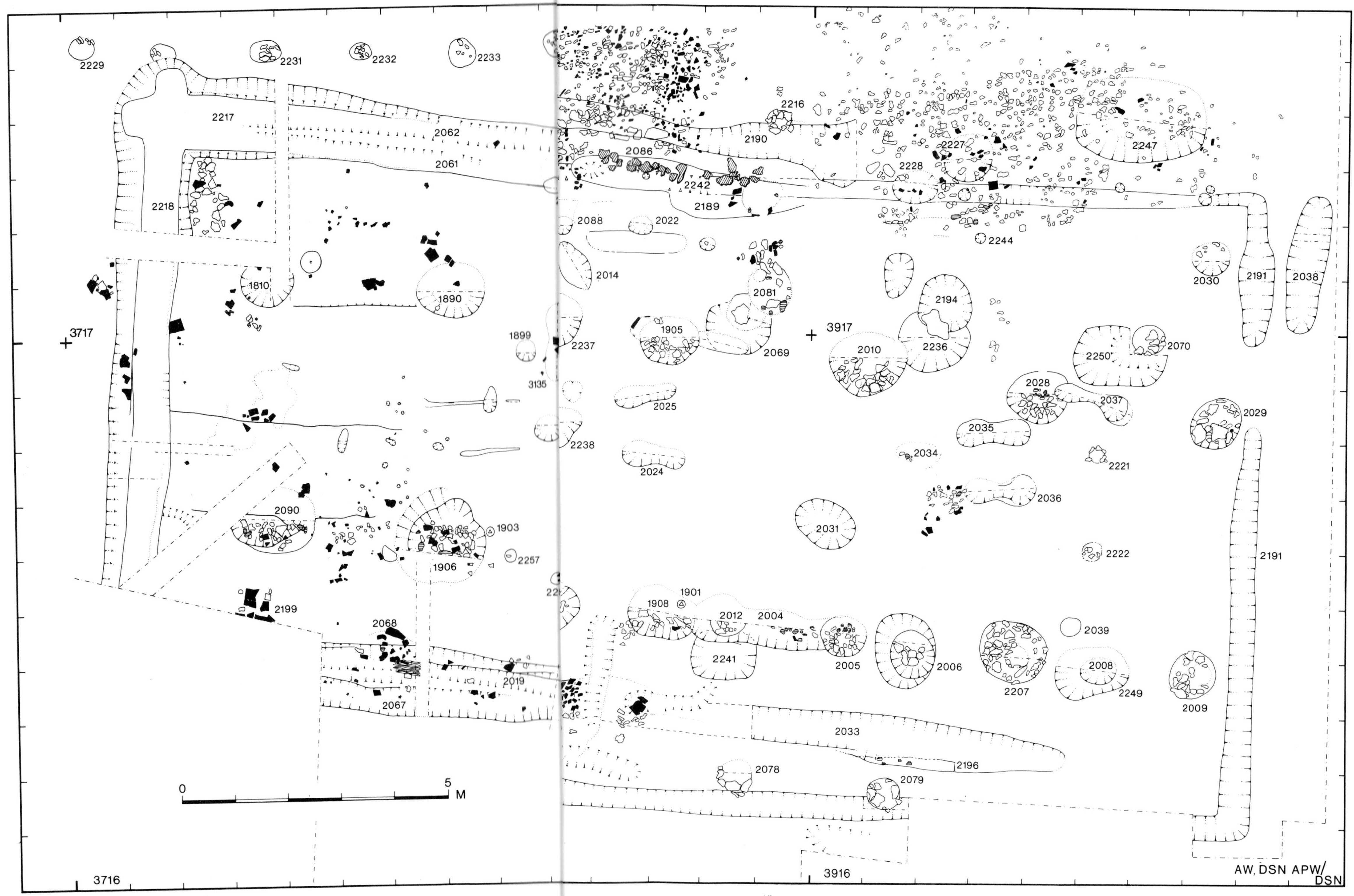

Fig 40 Overall plan of building complex in south-east corner of Enclosure A incorpo[r]
and 47; for sequence of buildings see Fig 41 (Scale 1:80)

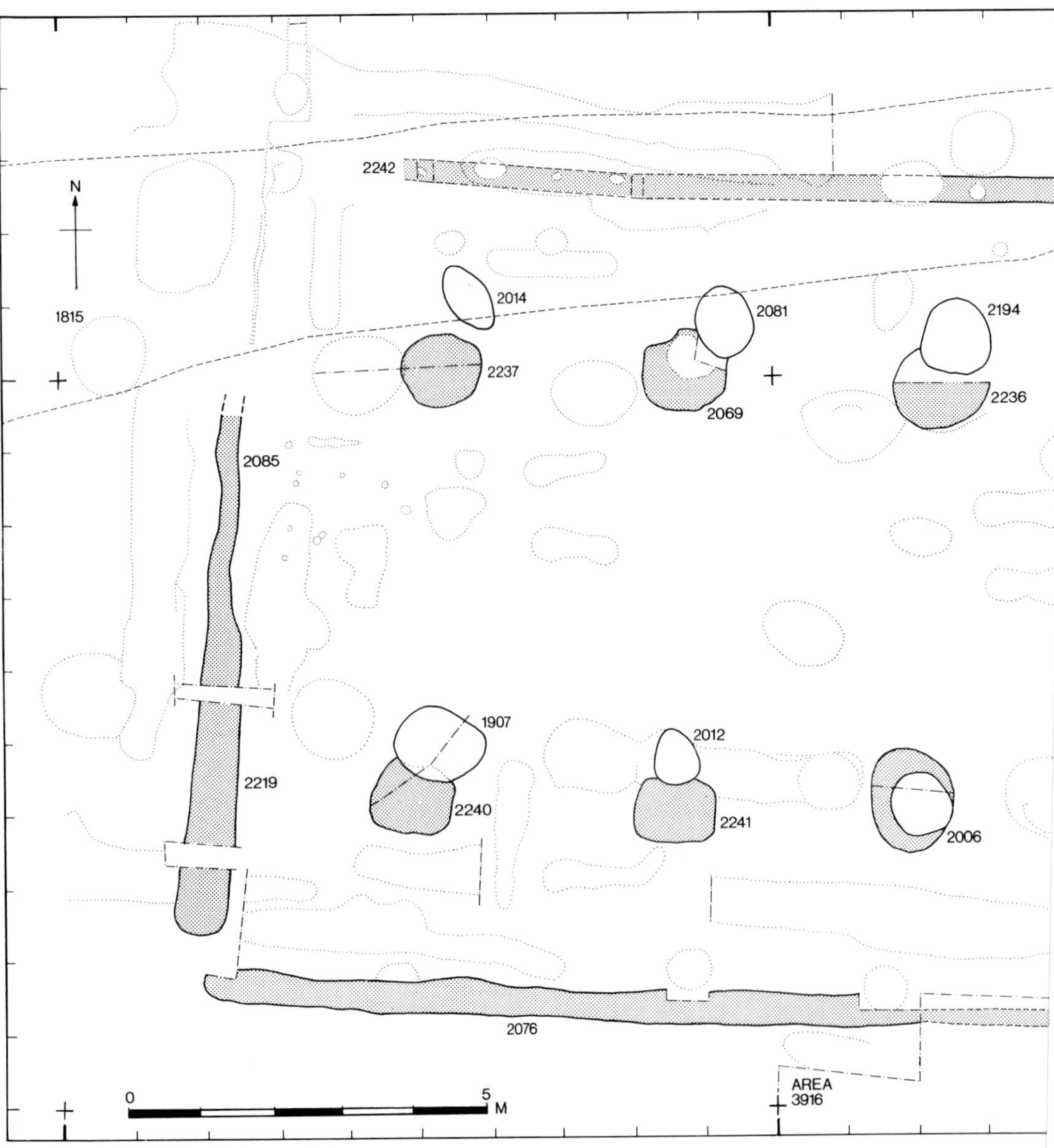

Fig 42 Plan of Buildings 15 and 20, Periods 5 and 6 (Scale 1:100)

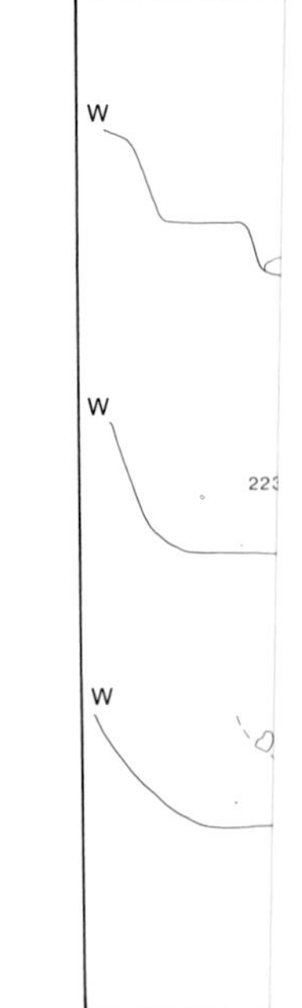

Fig 43 Profiles across postholes, Building 15, Period 5 (Scale 1:40)

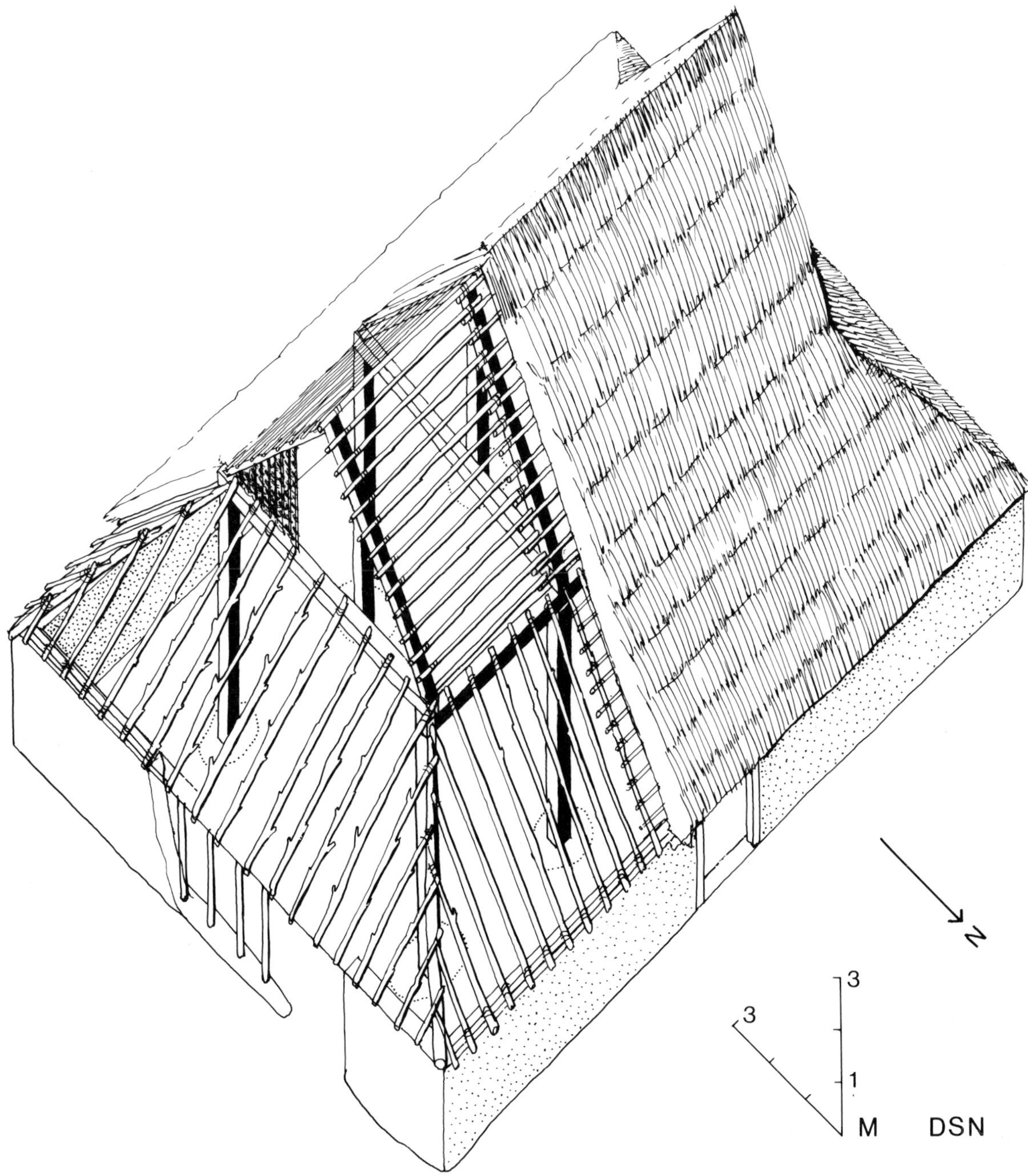

Fig 44 Reconstruction drawing of Building 15, Period 5

was constant all round the building, it is possible that the roof pitch at the east and west ends was the same as that over the aisles on the north and south. If so, assuming that the east and west end posts supported principal rafters, the ends of the building probably had gablets – as shown on the reconstruction (Fig 44). Its walls are assumed to have been wattle-and-daub and its roof thatch. Along the north wall (2242) were patches of charcoal suggesting that the building had burnt down.

Later buildings on the same site include Building 20 (Figs 41 and 42), Building 34 (Figs 41 and 71), Building 39 (Figs 41, 80 and 82), Building 40 (Figs 41, 80 and 82) and Building 47 (Figs 40, 41 and 81).

Discussion

Enclosures A and B

The presence of at least four causeways and a western opening into Enclosure A, Period 3, suggests that the enclosure was not intended for defence; the antennae ditches indicate, perhaps, the movement and separation of stock. The same function might apply in Period 4, since stock could be controlled through the droveway separating the north–west corner of Enclosure A and the east–west ditch a little further north. Why Enclosure B was not given a west side is not understood but perhaps it was never finished. The Period 5 ditch subdividing this area enclosed a series of buildings and was almost certainly designed to keep stock, or intruders, out.

Whether the Period 5 additions to the enclosure and the construction of the huge dyke to the east are contemporary is uncertain, but that the dyke is later than Periods 3 and 4 is demonstrated by the way the tail of the bank partially fills the Period 4 ditch (1726, Fig 21). Although this could be taken to represent slippage and cannot on its own constitute sufficient evidence for phasing, the construction of an enclosure post-dating the dyke would hardly need its own ditch or gateway at this point.

The dyke

It is possible that there is an association between the dyke and the enclosures, not only because a substantial causeway was provided between the two but also because the dyke's course veers west to enable it to run alongside the enclosure, perhaps for extra security. The presence of a second causeway is also indicated near the dog-leg at Shepherds Cottages since a Roman road crosses it at this point, possibly making for a pre-existing gap. It is tempting to suggest therefore that the same proprietor controlled lands on both sides of the dyke. What was the dyke's function? One might assume at first that a monument of such proportions must be defensive but the fact that the arms of the dyke do not extend to the river precludes this. The most likely explanation therefore is that it was a huge stock kraal. It was sufficiently strong to deter rustling and it provided a demonstration of the social status and wealth of the owner of the actual enclosure (for discussion of the function of this area in the Roman period, see p 100).

The buildings

It seems from the concentration of buildings and finds that Enclosure B was, or became, the main living compound. The inhabitants appear to have had some status, as demonstrated by the number of British coins and early brooch types found there. One of the first buildings, Building 5, however, appears not to have been domestic, but a large granary of unusual construction, with its two trenches each originally containing three massive posts. The size of the post-sockets indicates considerable load-bearing capacity. It is interpreted as a two-storey tower granary; the idea of two-storey or tower granaries in a late Iron Age context may seem fanciful but elevated granaries designed for maximum ventilation were a common feature of Roman Republican estates in Italy (Vitruvius, Book VI, 4) and it is not inconceivable that the basic type was known in Britain. Certainly four- and six-post granaries of less substantial construction are common on late Iron Age sites.

When the postulated granary, Building 5, was demolished it is possible that it was replaced by Building 10, which had a raised floor indicative of a granary. The site of Building 5, however, was used for Building 6, which appears to have been domestic, as suggested by the centrally-placed hearth and the artefacts found. The construction of Building 6 is unusual in that its cob walls were faced on each side with wattles. This was the only building found on the site with this method of construction; the possibility that the slots used for bedding the wattles represent two separate phases is discounted (p 26).

That this area of the site became residential is further supported by the nature of later buildings. Building 6 was replaced by Building 7, a rectilinear hut which, although only of simple form, probably represents the adoption of Roman architectural styles. The same applies to Building 8 which followed; it was probably a much larger complex. The wealth of Belgic pottery and domestic occupation material around the building, especially in the adjacent ditch (74), strongly suggests that it was a house and that Enclosure B, throughout Periods 3–5, was the nucleus of the settlement.

Enclosure A perhaps remained a stock-yard although parts of the enclosure were given over to human habitation, demonstrated by the presence of occupation levels in Buildings 13 and 15. The relationship between the buildings occupying the two enclosures therefore is uncertain, but possibly a distinction existed between them and Enclosure A was not just for stock but also for workers – a social and functional difference pertaining in later periods. The aisled building (Building 15) would perhaps have accommodated workers' families, wintered stock, and stored hay and equipment. Although the dating evidence cannot disprove an early Roman date for Building 15 there can be little doubt that it is one of the earliest aisled buildings yet to be discovered in Britain and might be paralleled by a native-style timber-framed building found in insula XVII at Verulamium (Frere 1983, 105). Of particular significance is that when it was rebuilt its architecture remained the same.

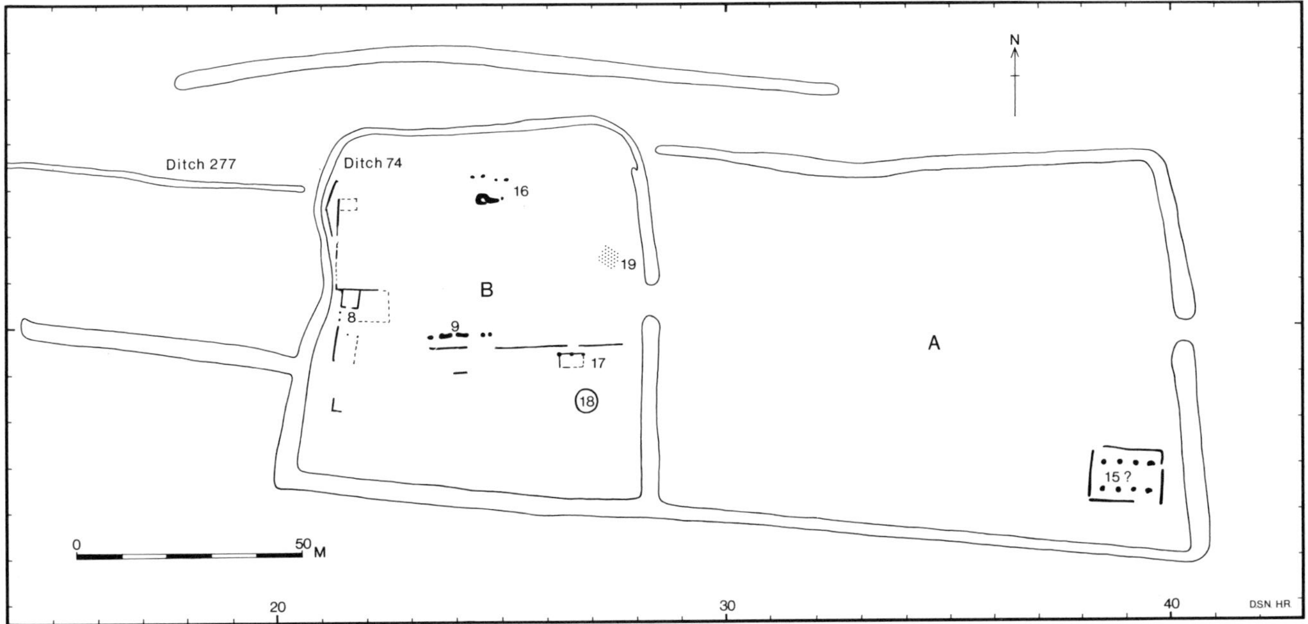

Fig 45 Block plan showing buildings of c *AD 43–62, Period 6*

The Roman period

Period 6, c AD 43–62 (Fig 45)

The enclosures

The Iron Age enclosures of Periods 3–5 remained relatively unchanged although the east side of Enclosure A, which had become redundant owing to the construction of the dyke, was gradually filled. The main gate-posts were replaced slightly further east (Nos 2355 and 2389, Building 2, Fig 13); no new gate was made between the Enclosures A and B and it is assumed to have been abandoned. The banks remained extant.

Enclosure B was further sub-divided by a Ditch, 277, which extended 70m west from the Period 5 ditch (74). As previously, this area of the overall 'enclosure' had no western side. The ditch was about 2m wide by 1m deep with a V-shaped profile – considerably smaller than earlier examples. Pottery from its primary fill (315) included a range of first-century native forms, but the presence of a Central Gaulish samian bowl (Drag 37) of Antonine date indicates that the ditch remained open for some considerable time. Also in the filling were fragments of a large dish in Pompeian red ware (Fabric 179). (For further comment on this ditch see p 70.)

The buildings, nos 8–9, 16–20

Period 6 possibly includes Buildings 8 and 9 (Fig 33) already described (pp 27–9) and perhaps constructed in the years preceding the conquest, Structure 16 (Fig 46), area 2422–23, Structure 17 (Fig 45), area 2619, a circular hut, Building 18 (Fig 45), area 26–2718, and ephemeral traces of another rectangular hut, Building 19 (Fig 45) in area 2721. They all occupied the Period 5 sub-division of Enclosure B, were all of timber construction and had been burnt. Occupation material associated with them suggests a Neronian date. In Enclosure A it is possible that Building 15 extended into this period.

The inner enclosure, Enclosure B

Structure 16 (Fig 46)

This lay on the north side of the enclosure, area 2422–23; its limits are uncertain but a row of postholes including Nos 3273, 3289, 3279, 3274 and 3290 appear to define the north side of a hut. Its west side is equally ill-defined but two concentrations of postholes may be related. There was no evidence for posts along a south side but possibly it was an open-sided shed or screen sheltering a corn-drying oven (744) with a flue in the plan of a question-mark. Its lowest filling (744B) contained small sherds of mid first-century native and Roman pottery; the structural postholes contained no pottery. Although the higher proportion of native to Roman fabrics might suggest a mid first-century date it is possible that the Roman pottery extends into the later first century and therefore the structure should go with Period 7.

Building 17 (detailed plan not published – see Figs 1 and 45)

This putative structure is interpreted as an animal pen and was located in area 2619 close to a gap through an earlier east–west palisade (1152) which continued the

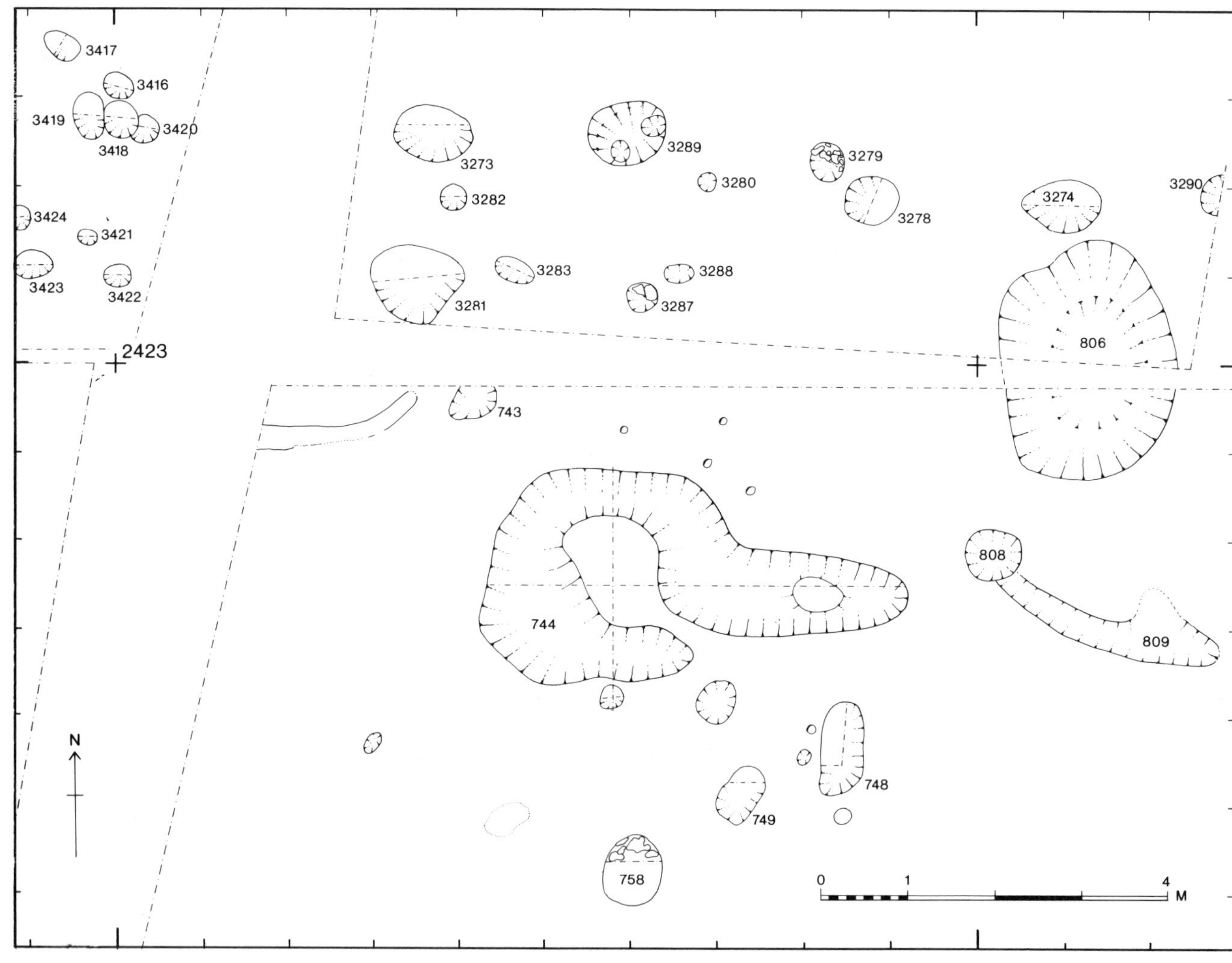

Fig 46 Plan of Building 16, Period 6 (Scale 1:80)

line of the palisade or sleeper beam (1097) contemporary with Building 9 (Fig 33). A rectangular spread of occupation material (1140), including native and mid first-century Roman pottery, had subsided into the filling of the Period 3 antenna ditch and was bounded by a series of postholes. Also in its filling was a coin of Nero (No 16) and a La Tène-derivative brooch (No 1, Fig 121) of first-century date, and brooch No 39 (Fig 122), a Colchester two-piece of *c* AD 50–90. Pottery types (AV 1–23) included, for example, *Ver* 147 (Frere 1972) dated AD 60–100 and a Lyons ware bowl as *Ver* 28 (ibid) dated AD 49–60. The presence of the palisade indicates that the enclosure was probably subdivided and, because the palisade follows the line of an earlier Period 3 ditch, it is possible that an existing boundary, however slight, dictated its course.

Building 18 (detailed plan not published – see Figs 1 and 45)

Building 18 was represented by an earthen floor (1080) approximately 5m in diameter situated in area 26–2718, and had a circular chalk hearth. Two postholes indicated the position of its north wall and on the south a shallow U-shaped feature was possibly a wall-trench or gully. It was sealed by a layer of clay (1079) and truncated on the west side by Building 29. The latest pottery in the clay sealing the floor was a jar similar to *Ver* 175 (Frere 1972) dated AD 60–75.

Building 19 (detailed plan not published – see Figs 1 and 45)

In area 2721 were general spreads (eg 839) of first-century material associated with a scatter of postholes and traces of burning. In places they were disturbed and contaminated but originally were sealed by a layer of clay (768), possibly the levelling of the bank alongside the nearby north–south ditch. The postholes and burning were probably associated with a structure but its plan was not recovered. The pottery included south Gaulish and Les Martres-de-Veyre samian ware (Nos 1947 and 1964 respectively).

The outer enclosure, Enclosure A

Compared to Enclosure B, Enclosure A seems to have been sparsely occupied in this period except in the south-east corner which saw the construction of Building 20, a reconstruction of Building 15.

Building 20 (Figs 41 and 42)

In plan this was virtually identical to Building 15, but its north-west angle was moved about one metre north, putting most of the post-settings slightly north-west of their original location. Only the eastern pair of postholes was in the same place. Its walls were also a little further north; on the north side its position was represented by a trench 7.50m long. No pottery was recovered from the postholes which, therefore, precludes positive attribution of the building to Period 6 – it could belong to Period 7. However it certainly pre-dates Buildings 34, 39 and 40 which are of second-century date.

Summary of Period 6

There were no major changes to the site in this period and it is possible that a number of structures from Period 5 continued in use. Building 20 replaced the earlier aisled building (15) in form and location indicating perhaps that Enclosure A remained a farmyard. The transition of the late Iron Age settlement into the early Roman period was smooth. However, it is inconceivable that the Boudiccan uprising of AD 61–2 had no impact on the site; it is tempting to suggest therefore that the burning of buildings noted in Enclosure B was no accident and that, like Verulamium, the Gorhambury settlement was also sacked.

Period 7, c AD 62–100 (Fig 47)

The enclosures

No distinction can be observed between the earthworks of Periods 6 and 7 except that ditches close to buildings were increasingly being used as rubbish pits and filling up. No attempt was made to level them deliberately. For example, layer 77 in Ditch 74 (Fig 33) was extensive, with very large quantities of Flavian and earlier pottery (AV 1–175) and residual imported fine wares (p 181). The latest samian is dated AD 75–90. Much of the pottery is Belgic in fabric; following the policy of full publication of Belgic forms these types are shown on Fig 155 (Nos 63–86; for list of vessels see Table 14). Small finds from this ditch were also numerous, the more important being a fan-tailed brooch (No 15, Fig 121) dated AD 10–50 and a Colchester two-piece brooch (No 34, Fig 122) dated AD 50–80. Iron objects include a linch pin (No 471, Fig 133); a crucible with traces of gold was also found (No 1034, Fig 145).

A palisade (1848) was built 10m north and parallel to the south ditch of Enclosure A. At its west end, area 3117, it turned north and petered out; at its eastern end (2045) it turned north across area 3616–17 where many phases of fence lines were excavated (Fig 10). It probably extended up to and turned west to run along the south side of a trackway between the two causeways; a stretch of another palisade was located in area 32–3319 (Fig 1). It would appear possible, therefore, that the southern half of the outer enclosure was sub-divided into three units: a central rectangular plot flanked by square paddocks, the eastern paddock having domestic and possibly farm buildings. No trace of structures of the period has been identified in the other paddocks. The northern half of the enclosure was probably also fenced, as traces of a palisade (2778) were found along the north side of the

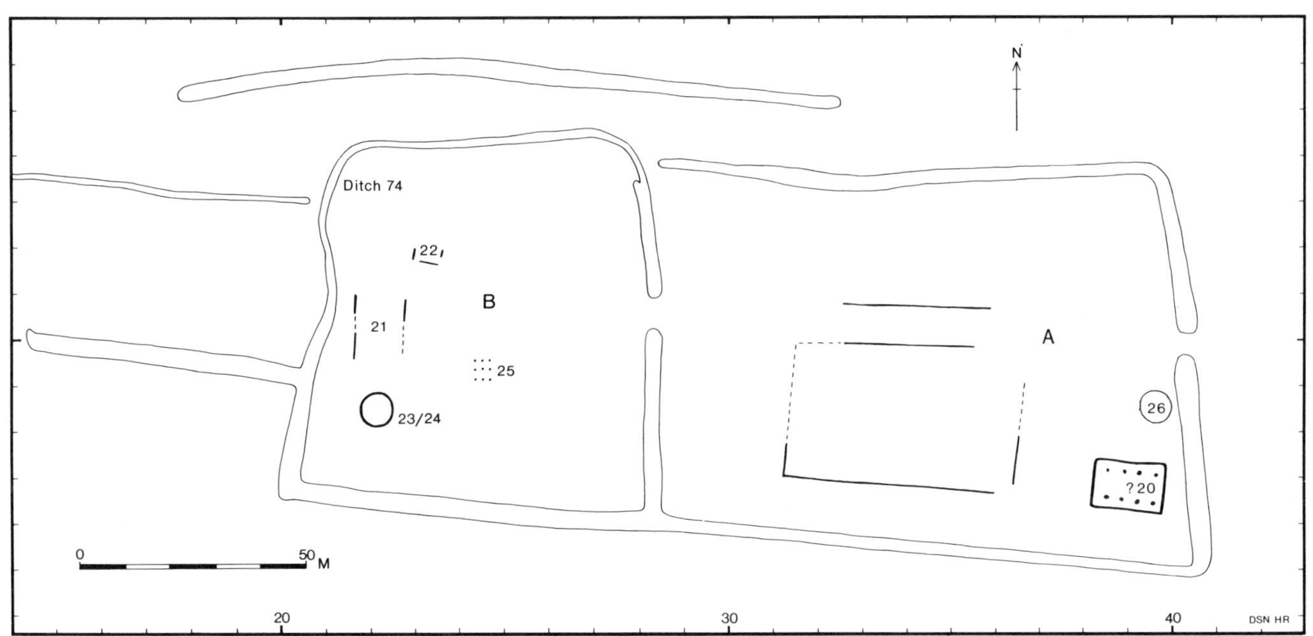

Fig 47 Block plan showing buildings of c *AD 62–100, Period 7*

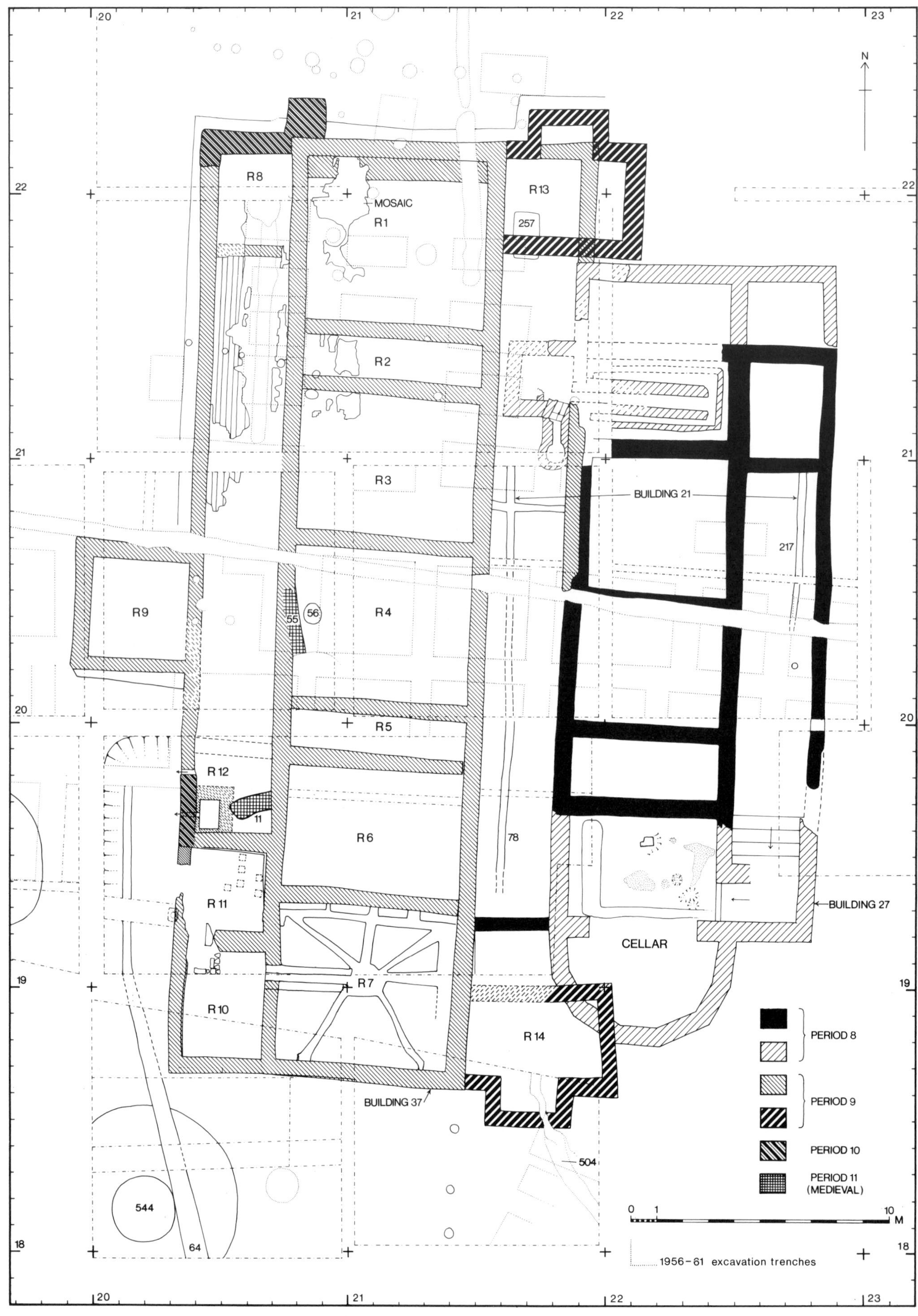

Fig 48 Plan of main villa complex in Enclosure B incorporating Buildings 21, 27, 37 and medieval Structure 60 (Scale 1:200)

road in area 34–3520, but there was no evidence for further sub-division. Unfortunately dating evidence for this palisade was lacking.

The buildings, nos 21–26

There was later first-century reconstruction in Enclosure B and in the south-east corner of Enclosure A. Buildings in the former include Building 21 (Fig 48), area 21–2220, Building 22 (Fig 49), area 2321, two circular huts, Buildings 23 and 24 (Figs 50 and 51), area 21–2218 and a granary, Building 25 (Figs 52 and 53) in area 2419. The outer enclosure had Building 26 (Figs 54 and 55), area 3918 and it is also possible that Building 20 (Figs 41 and 42) was constructed in this period.

Building 21 (Fig 48)

The main house site, previously occupied by Building 8, was replaced by Building 21, which was constructed over and cutting into the clay which sealed and levelled the earlier building; the clay contained mid first-century sherds. Evidence for its overall plan is slight owing to later development but two sleeper beams, features 78 and 217, areas 21–2220, ran north–south beneath the east and west corridors of the later masonry villa (Building 27). Associated with them were floors of trampled clay. A coin of Vespasian (No 20) came from 217. They were not timber verandahs of the subsequent building as the plan might suggest, but are probably the outer corridor walls of an earlier timber house, the main block of which lies directly beneath the stone house. Charcoal in the slots indicates that the building burnt down. The eastern sleeper (217) was underpinned with stones. Unfortunately these levels were disturbed by previous excavation trenches and it was not possible to correlate the stratigraphy remaining in the earlier baulks. Nevertheless the extensive deposit (layer 77) in the nearby north–south ditch (74) is believed to represent occupation material associated with this period (for comments on the pottery from this context see p 181).

Building 22 (Fig 49)

Building 22 to the north-east, in area 2321, was a rectangular hut about 6 by 4.50m, represented by slots for sleeper beams, 3325, 3326 and 3449, forming its west, south and east sides respectively; no north wall survived. It ran almost at right-angles to Building 21 but there was no indication that they ever linked. Dating evidence is slight but sherds from the filling of wall slot 3326 indicate a first-century date. It was sealed by a cobbled surface (140) associated with the first masonry villa (Building 27).

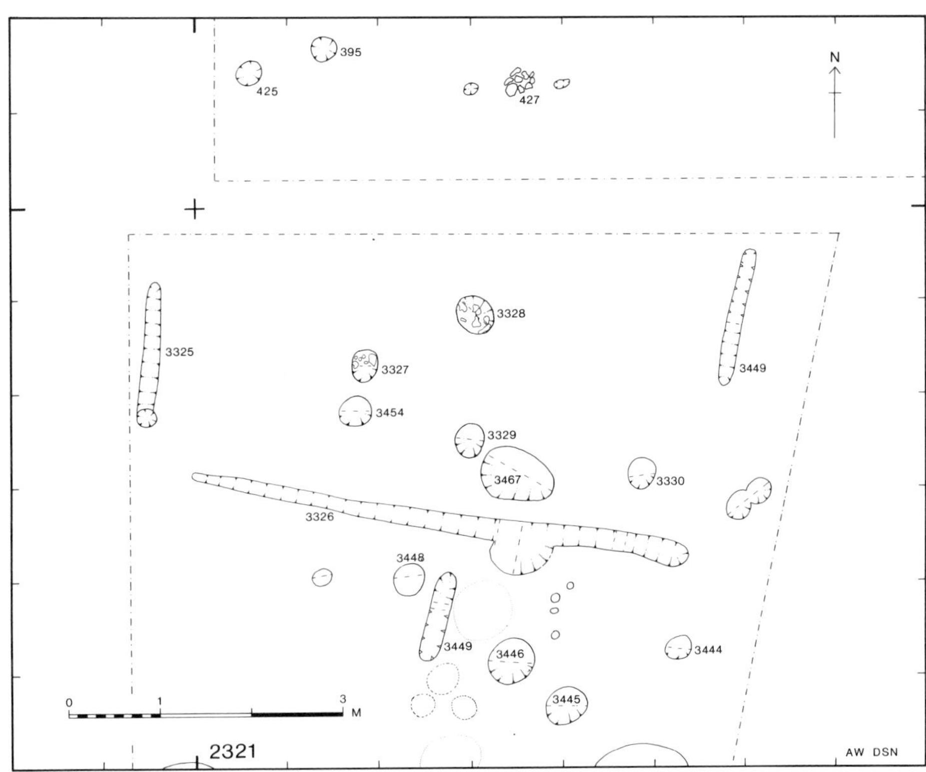

Fig 49 Plan of Building 22, Period 7 (Scale 1:80)

Buildings 23 and 24 (Figs 50 and 51)

Building 23 was a circular hut with a pebbled floor (691) and traces of two hearths, constructed over the levelling clay of the preceding period. On its east side was a rectangular area of chalk (661) possibly representing the floor of a porch facing into the enclosure. A coin of Claudius (No 8, allowing for wear dropped *c* AD 75) was recovered from the floor surface sealed by the floor of Building 24, a reconstruction which maintained the same plan. This reconstruction is dated no earlier than *c* AD 97 since a dupondius of Nerva (Coin No 27) was found in a layer (615) cut by the second-phase drip-trench (628). The later hut (Fig 51) had a chalk floor (638) with a central hearth (692). Between the hearth and a rectangular porch (639), also with a chalk floor, was a shallow circular hollow caused by wear. Possibly this was due to threshing, or some other activity which had scuffed the floor. The wear is unlikely to have been created by foot traffic as neither the porch floor nor the floor of the hut near the threshold had suffered similarly. Around the inside edge of the drip trench were traces of burnt clay, presumably from a wattle-and-daub wall. No stakeholes were observed.

The second building was burnt, but whether this event was contemporary with the destruction of Building 21 is unknown; on the evidence, the second phase could have been contemporary with the earliest phase of the masonry villa. A coin of Claudius (No 7) was recovered from a layer of loam post-dating the huts, which in turn was sealed by a cobbled path (614) associated with later phases of the first masonry house (Building 27).

Building 25 (Fig 52)

The granary in this period was located about 16m south-east of the main house and was represented by nine postholes beneath and filled by the rubble foundation for the floor of Building 28, a later masonry granary (Fig 53). It was rectangular, 3.40 by 2.80m, with its postholes up to 0.45m deep and about 0.30m wide. Many of them were tapered, indicating that sharpened posts had been driven in. Presumably the posts supported a raised floor, typical of many granaries. It could be argued that the postholes represent floor supports to an earlier phase of the masonry building, especially since the alignments of

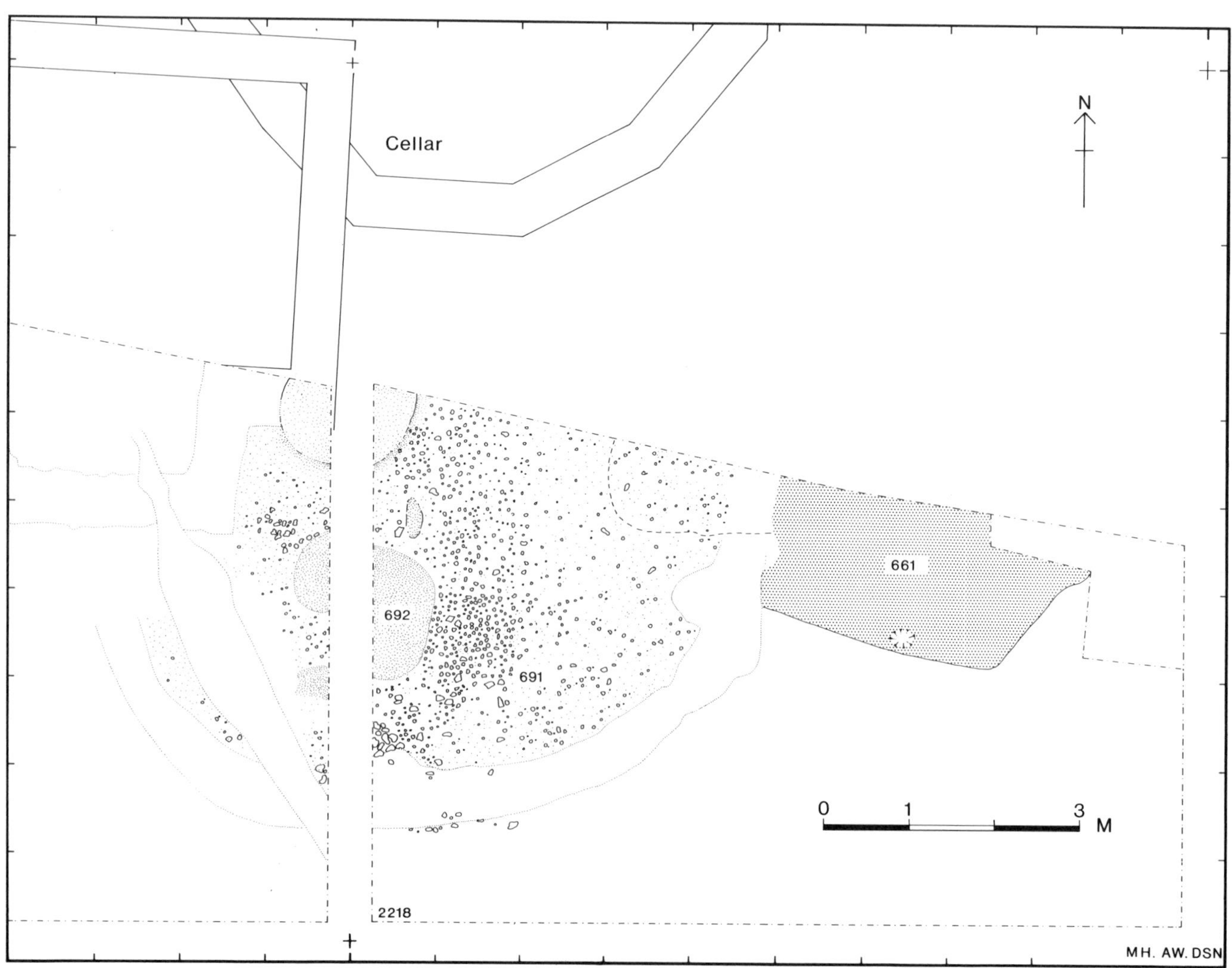

Fig 50 Plan of Building 23, Period 7 (Scale 1:80)

the holes and walls correspond so closely. However, as the internal width of the later structure was only 4m, its raised floor could have been spanned in one, the ends of the joists resting in wall sockets and less susceptible to decay. There was no dating evidence from the postholes, or the floor make-up sealing them (990), which is associated with Building 28. Tile in this material, although conceivably coming from Building 28, is more likely to represent destruction of the first building and therefore would suggest that the granary had a tiled roof, was built towards the close of this structural period, and was demolished some time in the early second century: similar to Building 24.

Building 26 (Fig 54)

Building 26 in the south-east corner of the outer enclosure was a circular hut, 7m in diameter, apparently with 15 posts set approximately 1.40m centre to centre (Fig 55). There was no evidence for intermediate walls or divisions, although a hole for a ridge-post occupied the centre. The postholes varied between 0.20 and 0.30m wide and 0.15 and 0.20m deep and were filled with clay; the south side of the hut was destroyed by a late nineteenth-century trackway. No dating evidence was found but it was sealed by cobbles (2001) associated with a yard with second-century pottery and occupation of the aisled hall, Building 39/40. Although the lack of dating evidence precludes reliable attribution of the building to Period 7 the more organic, darker soil filling the postholes, compared to those of earlier periods, and the presence of slag in posthole 1968 suggest a Roman date.

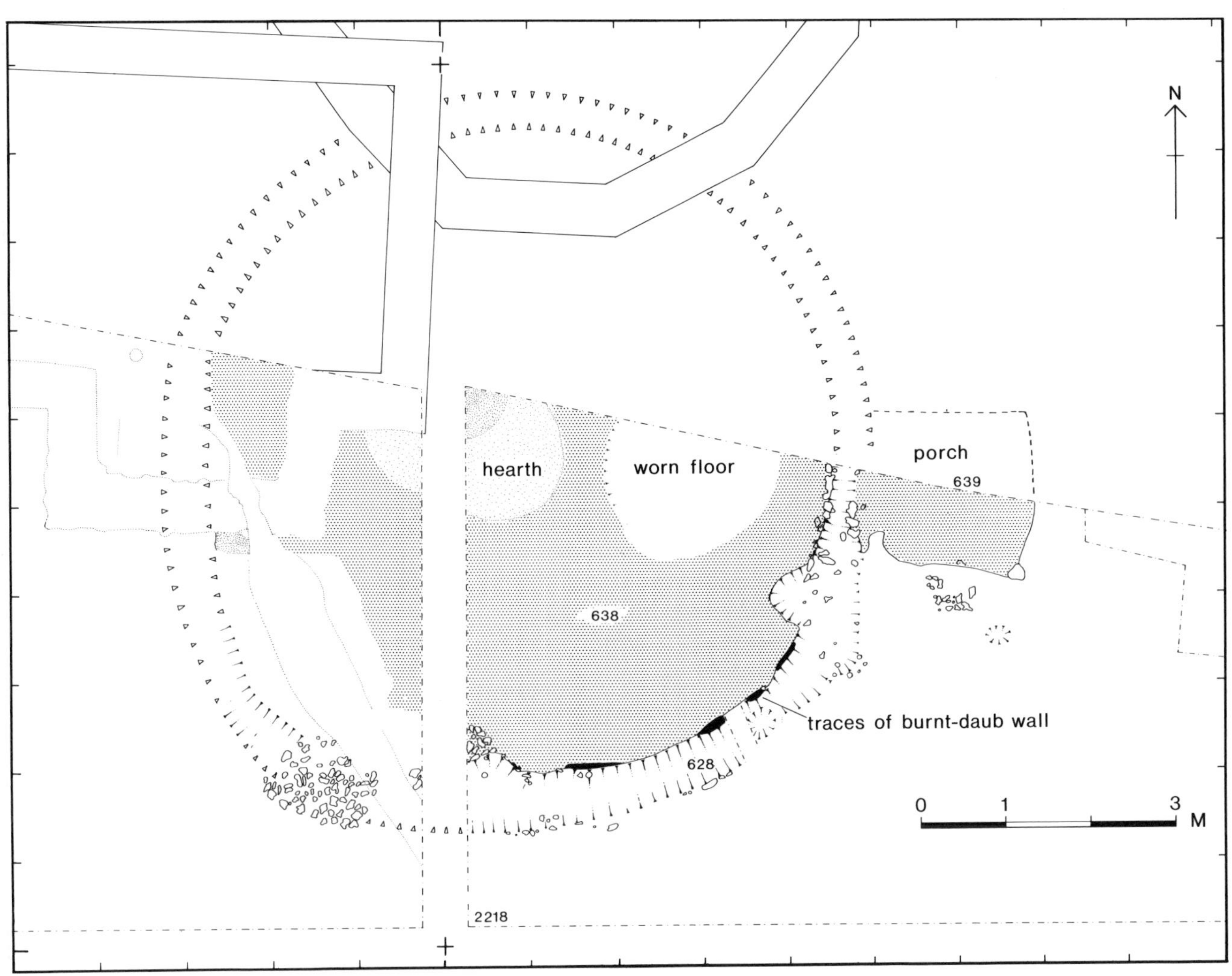

Fig 51 Plan of Building 24, Period 7 (Scale 1:80)

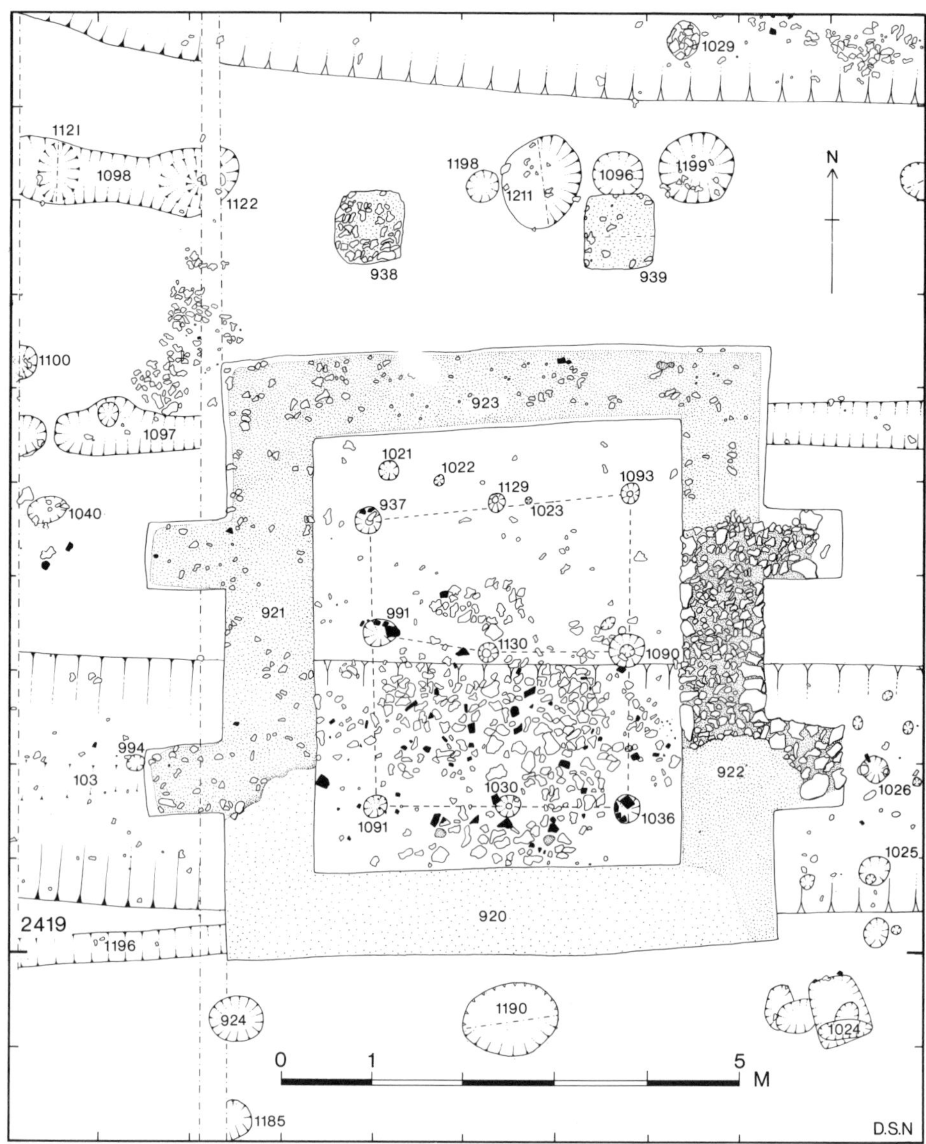

Fig 52 Plan of tower granary, Building 28, Period 8, with postholes of earlier timber granary, Building 25, Period 7, beneath (Scale 1:80)

Fig 53 View north of tower granary, Building 28, Period 8; the postholes belong to an earlier granary, Building 25, Period 7

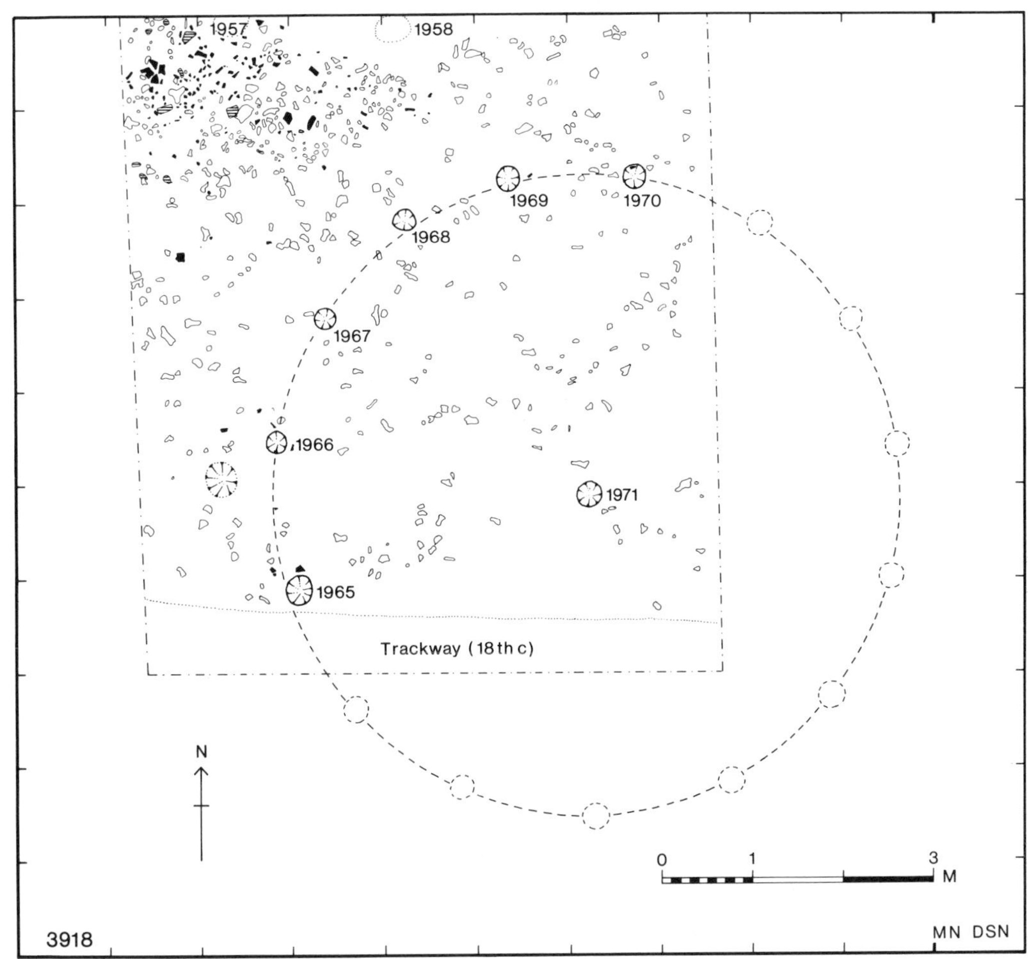

Fig 54 Plan of Building 26, Period 7 (Scale 1:80)

Fig 55 View north of Building 26, Period 7

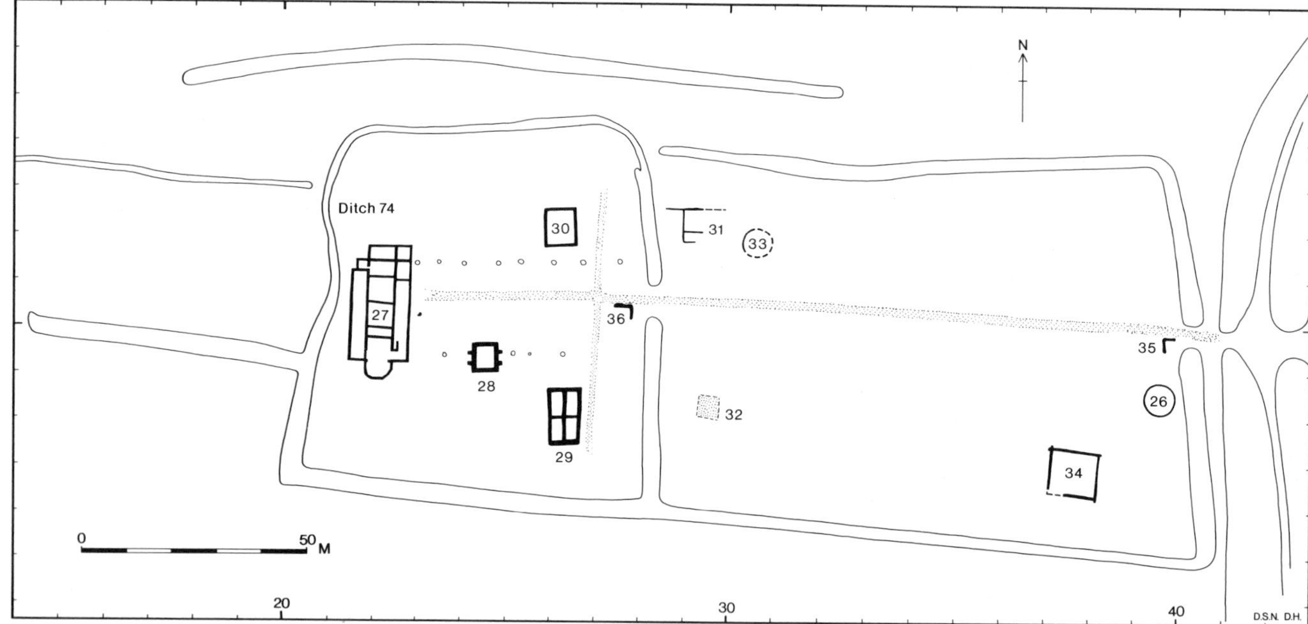

Fig 56 Block plan showing buildings of c *AD 100–175, Period 8*

Period 8, c AD 100–175 (Fig 56)

From *c* AD 100 onwards the site saw major reconstruction in masonry, converting what was perhaps a disparate assortment of huts into a fully Romanised villa of some luxury. However, elements of the overall plan were retained, demonstrating that the basic layout of the site stayed unchanged, including the sub-division of the area into two main enclosures, or inner and outer courtyards.

The enclosures

No additions were made to the earthworks which by now, although remaining prominent as both banks and ditches, were being backfilled piecemeal. The evidence of the snails would also suggest that by this period many of the enclosures were delineated by hedges, since species preferring a woodland habitat were found in many places. Ditch 74 and the north angle of the adjacent dog-leg, were infilled (layer 63, 1972 = layer 76, 1975) as was most of the ditch separating Enclosures A and B. The north and south perimeter ditches saw less infilling although trackways, which will be described in detail under Period 9, began to be made across them. The latest pottery in Ditch 74, sealed by levels associated with the first masonry house, is dated no later than *c* AD 100 with the following *Verulamium* vessel types represented: Frere 1972, 326 AD 85–105, 279 AD 75–85 and 206 AD 60–75; Frere 1984, 2011 AD 70–100 (layer 63 AV 1–12, layer 76 AV 1–11). The latest samian is a bowl (Drag 37) of *c* 65–80.

The paddocks flanking the axial trackway across the outer enclosure were retained but the old palisades were replaced by rows of postholes. Whether two or three paddocks existed on the south is uncertain: possibly only the farmyard and a larger paddock to the west. In the inner enclosure the trackway extended right up to the villa, Building 27, and was also fenced suggesting that the road was being kept clear of stock. The inner enclosure was further enhanced by an avenue, 20m wide, of trees or shrubs set into pits spaced between 4 and 6m apart. The pits were filled with a fine homogeneous loam, almost free of stones, implying that the soil had been sieved. Unfortunately no evidence was found for the species planted. The north row had six pits between areas 23–2721; the south row between areas 23–2719 also had six pits, but they were not set opposite one another. In one of the pits in the northern row was an escutcheon (No 199, Fig 126). There was no evidence elsewhere on the site for garden layout.

The buildings

Buildings constructed during this period include the first masonry villa, Building 27 (Fig 48); it had at least three phases and sealed the site of Building 21. A new granary, Building 28 (Fig 52), replaced Building 25 while to the south-east, area 2617–18, a bath-house, Building 29 (Fig 62), was constructed. Directly north, providing symmetry when facing the villa from the east, was a rectangular house (Building 30, Fig 64).

In the outer enclosure, by contrast, buildings were replaced in timber and include a possible corridor house, Building 31 (Fig 67) located in area 2922, while directly south, area 2918, were traces of another simple hut, Building 32, sealed by Building 38 (Fig 69). Directly south-east of Building 31, area 3021, were traces of another hut (Building 33, Fig 70). On the east side of the outer enclosure Building 34 (Figs 40 and 41) was constructed to the west of Building 20 (which may have been demolished), and it is possible from the concentration of finds of this period to suggest that a hut (not catalogued) was also situated to the north, approximately area 3821–22.

The inner enclosure, Enclosure B

Building 27 (Fig 48, reconstruction drawing Fig 57)

This was the principal house in this period and seems to have had at least three phases of construction. From the evidence of thicker footings on the north-west side compared to elsewhere (Fig 58) the villa may have begun as a rectangular block of about three rooms which were rebuilt and extended in Phase 2 by a more sophisticated structure comprising a range, 6.50m by 22.50m, of five rooms including a cross-passage. It had an east-facing verandah with a wing-room to the north. Another verandah probably existed on the west side – this would explain the need for a cross-passage and also explain the presence of an east–west wall, in area 2119. The western north–south verandah wall was probably sealed by the main east wall of the Period 9 villa. In Phase 3 the villa was extended about 3m further north and the extension, together with the original northern room, was provided with a channelled hypocaust stoked from a furnace on its west side. The south wall of the praefurnium had a separate flue through it leading to an oven (Fig 59). Possibly this was designed to enable the stoker to also attend to the cooking – using coals from the furnace. The earlier wing-room was demolished and another added a little further north.

At the south end of the villa a large masonry cellar (excavated from 1956–9, see p 3) was built; it was approached via a wooden staircase with a landing mid-way, where the stairs turned west. The cellar (Fig 4) measured 8.50 by 5.50m internally and had a seven-sided apse at its south end, possibly reflecting the architecture of the ground floor room above. Separating the apse from the main area of the cellar were two responds which acted as buttresses and which may also have supported similar features upstairs. The walls were originally covered in plain render, which remained *in situ* at the foot of the staircase. In the west wall were two rows of three holes associated with the impressions of wooden beams (Fig 60). The excavators interpreted these as holes for brackets and the impressions as those of shelves, but

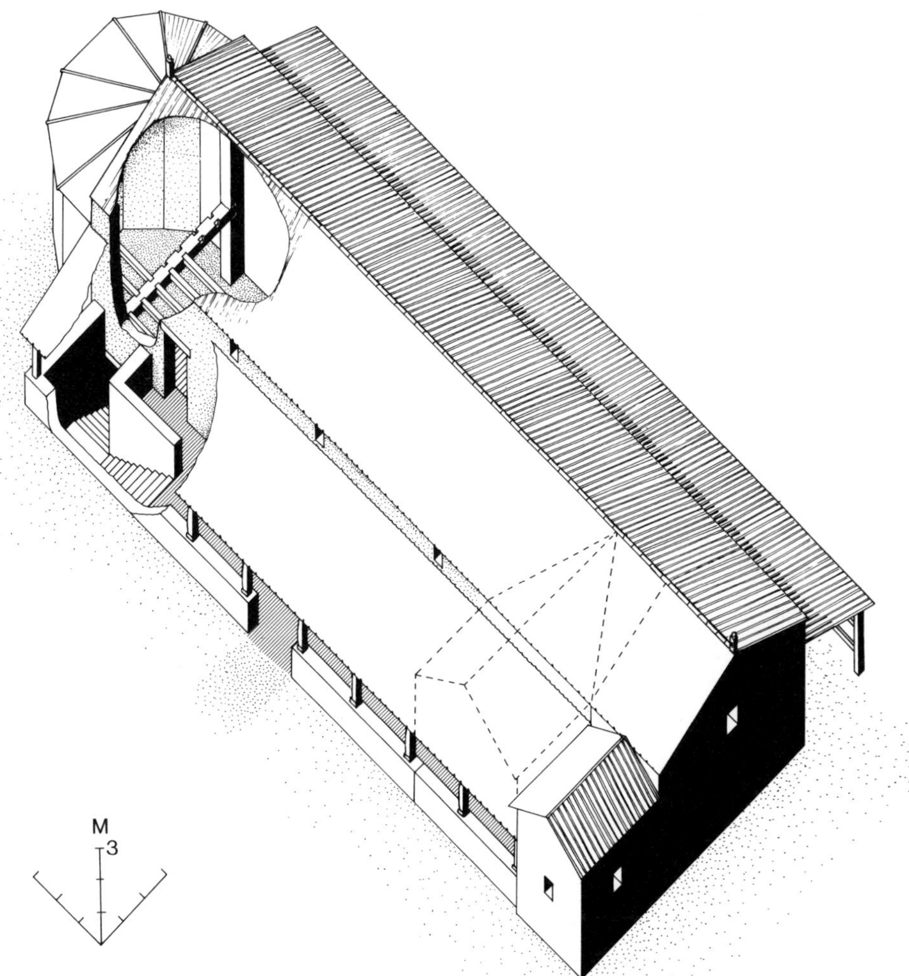

Fig 57 Reconstruction drawing of Building 27 looking south-west. The drawing shows the Period 8, Phase 3, development with its roof 'cut away' to show the staircase descending into the cellar and the northern extensions; the original position of the wing-room is shown by a dotted line

Fig 58 View west towards Gorhambury House showing excavation of the villas, Buildings 27 and 37, in progress, 1974

it is more likely that the holes, since they go through the thickness of the wall, are putlogs and the timber impressions evidence for shuttering. Set into the floor between the responds was either a sleeper beam or more likely a drain, packed or lined with broken roofing tiles. At right-angles, parallel to the west wall, was another, wider, U-shaped feature almost certainly the same drain. In the north area was a large block of oolitic limestone, possibly a pad for a prop supporting the upstairs floor. Also set into the floor (location not known) was a small pot and in a pit opposite the entrance a coin of Hadrian (No 37). The cellar was filled deliberately with flint rubble including large quantities of painted wall-plaster of exceptional quality, with architectural mouldings (Figs 148 and 150: for a report on the plaster see p 169). The debris also included fragments of stucco (Fig 5) in the form of a human torso, hands, feet and a head, possibly that of a child, all in high relief, and suggesting two figures. Folds of drapery painted red were represented. Also in the debris were fragments of mosaic (Fig 151). It is uncertain where the moulded plaster, stucco and mosaic originally came from, but it is tempting to suggest that they ornamented the room upstairs, the stucco figure representing a deity and perhaps occupying the apse. In the upper fill of this rubble was a scored coin of Marcus Aurelius (No 45).

Stucco on Romano-British sites is rare; other than Gorhambury it occurs at Fishbourne (Cunliffe 1971, 50) and Colchester, and together with the architectural reliefs further indicates a lavish dwelling, perhaps superior to most nearby town-houses, although a moulded pilaster from insula XXVII Building 2, Verulamium (Frere 1983, 216 and pl XXI *b*) suggests it was not the only scheme of its type in the area.

Dating evidence

There was no direct dating evidence from beneath the building, but considering the fact that Phase 1 follows the timber house (Building 21), which is related to deposits in Ditch 74 with Flavian pottery, a late first-century date is probable.

In the filling of a latrine (257, area 2121), sealed by Room 13 of the later masonry house, was a fine group of pottery (Fig 156) including many examples from Verulamium, such as *Ver* (Frere 1972) 429, AD 105–40; 435, AD 105–30; 486, AD 110–20; 489, AD 115–30; 610, AD 135–55; 631, AD 120–50; 646, AD 130–50; 671, AD 135–60; 683, AD 135–85; 692, AD 140–50; 931, AD 130–70; 995, AD 150–60; 607, AD 130–40. It also

Fig 59 View west showing flue of oven inserted through the south wall of the praefurnium *on west side of channelled hypocaust, Building 27 (see Fig 48)*

Fig 60 View west showing east wall of Room 14, Building 37, constructed into the cellar of Building 27; the holes in the wall are believed to be for putlogs

contained a riveted samian bowl (No 117). The latrine is believed to be related to Phase 3 of the building, which on the evidence of the pottery probably came to a close *c* AD 175. In the cesspit, and also in the cellar, were fragments of burnt wall plaster, which might indicate that the structure burnt down, although this is far from certain.

Building 28 (Figs 52 and 53)

Situated in area 2419, Building 28 (919) measured 6.40 by 5.80m externally, with footings constructed of alternate layers of rammed flint and chalk, in trenches 0.75m deep. It had pairs of buttresses against its east and west walls (Fig 53), and on its north side, one metre away from the wall, two 0.75m square foundations built in the same materials and of the same depth as the walls. No floor survived but on the south side of the room was a spread of rubble, possibly the make-up for a concrete or *opus signinum* floor. For its relatively small size the depth of footings and the provision of buttresses is unusual. (The buttresses are unlikely to have been provided because of the underlying ditch, which was filled with rammed clay and probably unknown to the builders.)

Fig 61 Reconstruction drawing of tower granary, Building 28, looking south-east, Period 8

The building is perhaps best interpreted as a two-storey tower-granary (Fig 61). The front square foundations are possibly the best indicators of its use. Had they merely supported wooden porch posts they would not have needed such deep footings, and therefore they probably supported masonry piers for an upstairs loading or unloading jetty, serving an upper storey reinforced by the buttresses. The space between the piers, 2m, is sufficiently wide to allow access for a cart. The possibility that an arrangement of nine posts (Building 25) inside the structure might have supported a raised floor has already been discounted (p 40) since they were sealed by the floor make-up; whether the masonry granary had a raised floor is uncertain. No dating evidence was found beneath the building and it is assumed to be associated with the latest phase of the Period 8 villa; however it must be emphasised that the building materials used in each differed.

The proximity of the granary to the villa effectively blocked views across the yards. For this reason it is perhaps not surprising that in the late Antonine period it was demolished when the second masonry villa (Building 37) was constructed. The robber trench of its south wall (920) was used as a rubbish pit; this contained a large group of pottery (AV 1–67) of the period including, for example, Verulamium types (Frere 1972) 459, AD 115–30; 677, AD 135–70; 683, AD 150–160; 687, AD 140–50; 867, AD 150–160; 873, AD 150–180; 1026, AD 120–160 and (Frere 1984) 2315, AD 140–60. The earliest samian was a Drag 37 type bowl of Hadrianic date, and the latest an Antonine form 18/31R. Small finds from this context included a miscellaneous collection of structural ironwork and a drop handle (No 257, Fig 128). Among the skeletal remains were the bones of *rattus rattus* (black rat), one of the earliest examples of this species recorded in Britain (Armitage 1984). Burnt grain was noted, with wheat dominant, and also a snail fauna indicating an overgrown, shaded habitat. Edible molluscs included mussels, whelks and oysters.

Building 29 (Figs 56 and 62)

This is interpreted as a bath-house (1144) measuring about 11.50 by 7m, with a block of four rooms, the two on the west side with sunken floors, 0.30m deep, with their foundations comprising a raft of rammed flint continuous with the wall footings (Fig 63) and containing sherds of first-century native pottery only. Not a single *pilum* or even the impression of one survived, but a dividing wall with three scorched tile-built flues and the presence of *opus signinum* indicated its function. Nor was its furnace located, but this is assumed to have been on the south; in which case the southern room was probably a *caldarium*, the northern a *tepidarium* and a room in the north-east corner, without a sunken floor, a *frigidarium*. The fourth room in the south-east corner perhaps doubled as both vestibule and *apodyterium*. The bath-house may have been demolished in the late Antonine period, perhaps at the same time as the construction of the second masonry villa, Building 37, which had an integral bath suite. The evidence for its date is not

Fig 62 Plan showing destruction rubble sealing the bath-house, Building 29, Enclosure B; superimposed over the rubble are traces of a rectangular hut, Building 52 (Scale 1:80)

good. There was no pottery from the lowest level of destruction rubble (1075) but mixed with this deposit was a distinctive layer of silt representing a period of abandonment dated to the first half of the third century (Period 9). In the fourth century the site of the building was occupied by a sub-rectangular hut (Building 52).

In plan the bath-house recalls the simple *Reihentyp* bath-house at Gadebridge Park dated *c* AD 75 (Neal 1974, fig 8), and more closely the bath-house of *c* AD 100 at Wood Lane End (Neal 1984, fig 7), both less than five miles away.

Parallel to the east side of the bath-house was a metalled pathway (1273) on the same alignment as another path alongside Building 30, area 2721, opposite. They probably joined one another originally. For comments on alignment see entry for Building 30 below.

Fig 63 View south showing foundation of flint rubble for bath-house, Building 29

Building 30 (Fig 56, 64, 65, and 66)

Building 30 (723) spans two periods. In Period 8 its south wall was about 4m north of an imaginary line drawn from the north wall of the second phase villa, Building 27. Likewise, the north wall of Building 29 was the same distance south of a line drawn from the south side of the second phase villa (excluding the apse) demonstrating that both buildings were situated with symmetry in mind, especially from an eastern aspect. It is possible therefore to suggest from the architectural relationships that Building 30 was probably contemporary with Phase 2 of the villa.

The building (Figs 56 and 66) consisted originally merely of a one room structure 7.25 by 8.75m overall, built in flint laid herringbone fashion in yellow mortar on a chalk footing. No floor surfaces or internal features of this phase survived but the entrance was probably on the east side, approached from the path. In a secondary phase, Period 9, the building was extended south and given an *opus signinum* floor (734).

The latest pottery from a levelling layer of clay beneath the building was a south Gaulish samian bowl (Drag 27) of Trajanic date. It also contained a Colchester two-piece brooch of *c* AD 50–80 (No 32, Fig 122). Layer 795, also pre-dating the structure, contained Flavian samian forms Drag 18 and 27, and coarse pottery (AV 1–5). The make-up (847) for the floor of the Period 9 extension had a jar similar to *Ver* 654 (Frere 1972) dated AD 130–50 (AV 1–2).

The function of the structure is uncertain, but its location within the inner courtyard and proximity to the villa suggests that it was of some importance, especially since it was built in flint. The lack of general domestic rubbish immediately around the building precludes it having been domestic and it is suggested that it was the estate office. There is no evidence for it having been a granary as suggested by Black (1981, 165); it must be remembered that the granary, Building 28, was broadly contemporary with its initial phase.

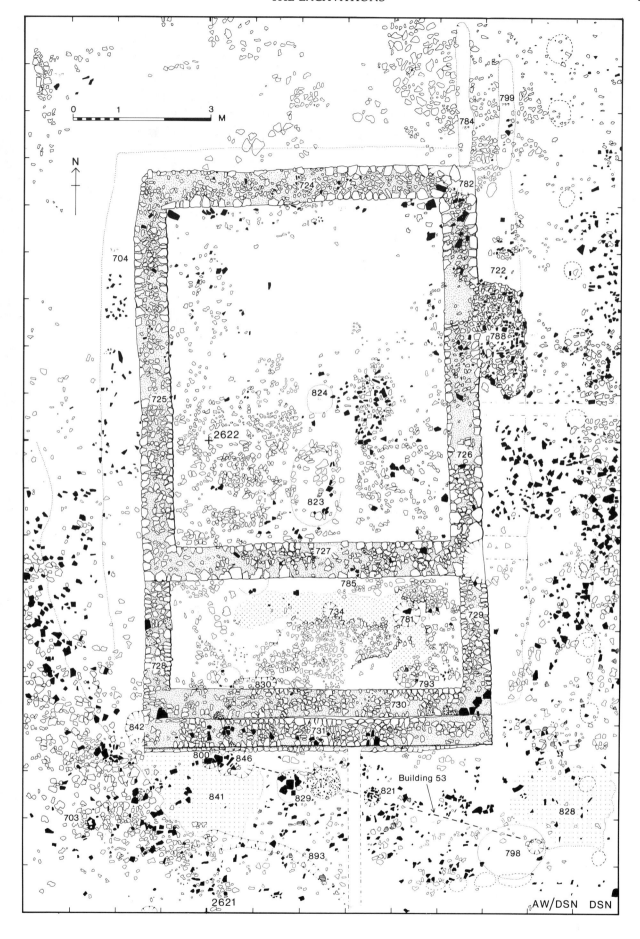

Fig 64 Plan of Building 30, Period 8, with postholes on south side forming a hut, Building 53, Period 11 (Scale 1:80)

Fig 65 View north of Building 30

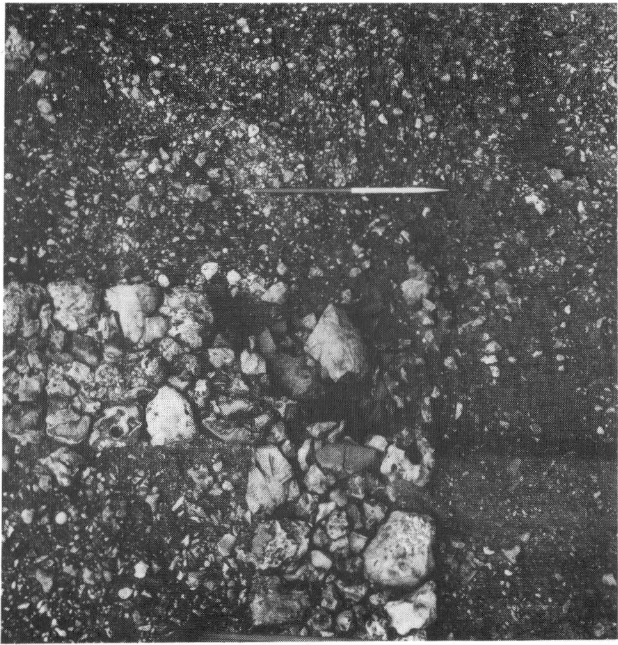

Fig 66 View showing north-east corner of Building 30; the tile quoins were robbed out and subsequently replaced in Period 10 by massive nodules of flint

The outer enclosure, Enclosure A

Building 31 (Figs 67 and 68)

This occupied the north-west corner of the outer enclosure, area 28–2922, and was constructed over the site of an Iron Age hut, Building 13. Owing to ploughing, only about half the building survived but it was of sleeper beam construction and appears to have comprised a rectangular 'room' or 'hall' 10 by 4.50m containing four domestic ovens, 1466, 1469, 1658 and 1672. Oven 1466 contained in its flue a samian dish (Drag 42) of Trajanic date and in the flue of oven 1672 was a reeded-rimmed bowl similar to *Ver* 673 (Frere 1972) dated AD 130–50. The ovens were cut into a clay floor (1461). At the south side was a slot (1467) for a verandah and an area of rubble (1814), perhaps a pathway, leading to it. The western side of the building is not full understood; a west wall (1458) turned west at its north end for at least 2m and may have extended about 6m to meet another north–south slot (1660), built along and respecting the edge of the adjacent ditch (1281), and possibly the west wall to another room. If so, because the room extends south up to the outer verandah wall, it could be termed a wing-room. A problem, however, is the interpretation of two sleeper beams (1654 and 1655) roughly parallel to and 0.70m west of wall 1458. Possibly these represent a narrow passage leading to the back of the building. That the building was of more than a single phase is demonstrated by an east–west post alignment along the south side of the building and the insertion of five post-pads (1624–28) over the north wall, sealing a samian dish (Drag 18/31) of Hadrianic date. In this phase both the original west wall (1660) and the passage wall (1654 and 1655) went out of use, as they were covered by a black occupation layer (1454) which sealed the earlier ditch (1281) and extended up to but not over the north–south wall (1458) to the east. In layer 1454 was a large assemblage of pottery (AV 1–78), mostly in Verulamium fabric and grey wares. Vessels similar to those found in Verulamium include for example *Ver* (Frere 1972) 456, AD 115–40; 499, AD 115–30; 526, AD 105–60; 627, AD 140–50; 650, AD 130–50; 657, AD 145–50; 661, AD 125–45; 663, AD 130–40; 666, AD 130–80; 685, AD 130–40; and 1046, AD 130–75. A mid second-century date is likely for this deposit and the abandonment of the building. Finds from the upper levels of the adjacent ditch included a Colchester one-piece brooch of *c* AD 10–60 (No 27, Fig 121) and a vine-leaf pendant of military type (No 170, Fig 125).

Although of Roman architectural form, the simple timber construction of Building 31 is in contrast to the buildings in the inner enclosure. However, symmetry appears to have been a consideration in its siting since the verandah lined up with the south wall of Building 30, Phase 1, as well as the north wall of the villa. A similar situation possibly prevailed further south where Building 32 (Fig 56), area 2918, possibly lined up with the north wall of the bath-house, Building 29.

Building 32 (Fig 69)

Only the most ephemeral traces of this hut survived, but these comprised a pebbled floor (1631) in area 2918 bounded on the south side by two postholes

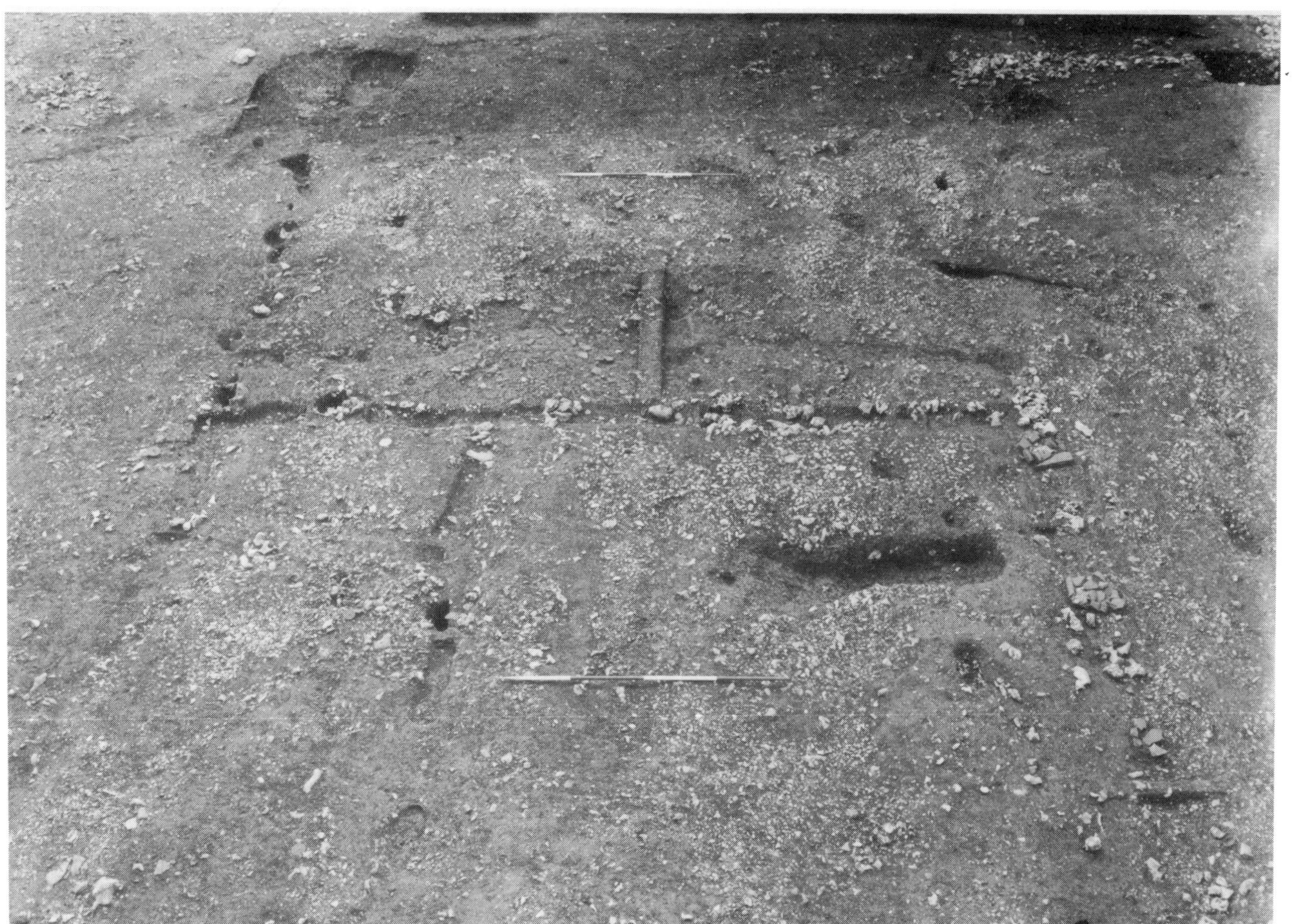

Fig 68 View west of Building 31, Period 8

(1632–3) and a straight edge to the pebbles. The dimensions of the hut are uncertain, nor was there any dating evidence. However it was sealed by Building 38 which, elsewhere, sealed pottery no later than late Antonine. (See also comments on Building 31.)

Building 33 (Fig 70)

Building 33 (3020), area 3021, lies south-east of Building 31 and originally may have been a hut of circular form, represented by a curved gully or wall trench (3208). It was associated with a worn pebbled floor (3205) which had been cut by a pit (3200), possibly a latrine, containing pottery (3226, AV 1–9) of the mid second century, including fragments of a Trajanic samian bowl (Drag 20/27), and two copper alloy rings, Nos 71 and 73 (Fig 122) and a pin (No 101, Fig 123). Sealing the pit was a layer of gravel (3090) which also extended elsewhere throughout the hut and was in turn sealed by a horizon of dark earth (3021) which, on the south-west side, was delineated by a slot (3220) and stakeholes. In layer 3021 (AV 1–40) was pottery of late Antonine date, except for a flanged bowl in black burnished ware; a coin of 323–4 (Coin No 239) was also found. The evidence, however slight, might suggest that in the early fourth century the second-century house site was reused.

Building 34 (Figs 40 and 41)

This was situated in the south-east corner of the outer enclosure, area 37–3816, and measured 10 by 11m, with its floor terraced into the slope of the land so that its west side was about 0.40m deeper than outside. Its walls rested on four massive sleeper beams (Fig 71) between 0.50 and 0.75m wide, set into broad trenches (2217–2220); at the angles the ends of the beam trenches projected beyond the wall line indicating lap joints (Fig 72). No internal features could be identified with this structure except possibly a north–south gully 2226 containing pottery (AV 1–12) including Verulamium forms (Frere 1972) 379, dated AD 100–130, and 405 and 515, dated AD 105–115. It was erected on the west side of Building 20 in such a position as to suggest that conceivably the earlier aisled building was retained. Its architectural form and function are both in doubt. Such massive walls, wider than any other timber building on the site, imply that the structure was of great strength,

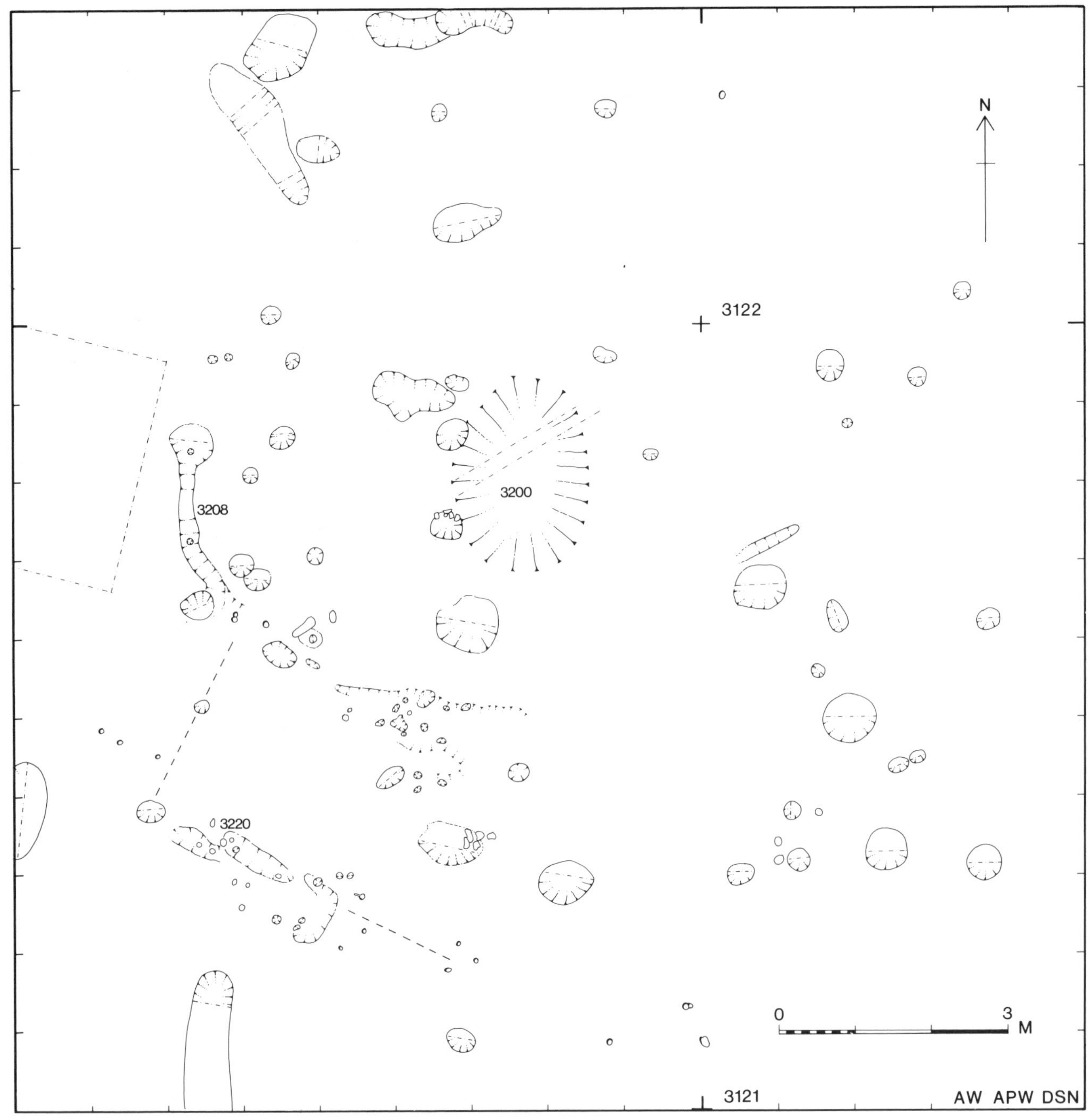

Fig 70 Plan of Building 33, Period 8 (Scale 1:80)

possibly spanned in one, as the lack of internal supports might suggest. Such strength is reminiscent of first-century military architecture and indeed its inspiration may have been derived from that source: it was probably a store-house or barn, possibly on two levels. If it was a store its place in the farm-yard was appropriate. Its north-east corner was cut by a shallow cesspit (2185) containing sherds ranging in date from AD 115–50, including for example Verulamium types (Frere 1972) 440, AD 110–40, and 455, AD 115–30. In the Antonine period the building was demolished (there is no evidence that it burnt down) and replaced by Building 39.

Structures 35 and 36 (Figs 13 and 1)

Space does not allow plans and descriptions of the numerous groups of post-settings or other small structural features, but Structure 35, area 3919, and Structure 36, area 2720, are of potential interest. They were both located alongside the trackway close to the entrances into the inner and outer enclosures respectively and comprised L-shaped foundations of rubble or set masonry. The similarity between their plans and locations may not be merely coincidence; the absence of other walls precludes their being gate-houses. Perhaps they reveted an earthen ramp (vestiges of the earlier banks) designed to facilitate the loading or unloading of vehicles and the mounting of horses.

Fig 71 View west showing terracing for Building 34 (Fig 41) and later aisled buildings, Buildings 39/40

Fig 72 View east showing beam trench at north-east corner of Building 34; a quern associated with Building 40 can be seen top right

Summary of Period 8

Period 8 sees the introduction of masonry buildings, including the construction of a small, luxurious villa with a cellar and high quality interior decoration. In front of the villa were two rows of pits representing an avenue of trees or shrubs and an attempt at garden landscape. The villa replaced a timber building (Building 21) destroyed by fire. Other timber buildings in Enclosure A were also rebuilt in masonry (perhaps to avoid the same mishap recurring), including the granary, Building 25, which is likely to have been double-storeyed, conceivably for the separation of seed corn. Further evidence of luxury included a small bath-house, Building 29, which was sited close to the entrance into Enclosure B and could also have been for the use of estate workers.

In contrast to Enclosure B, the buildings in Enclosure A continued to be of timber, including Building 39 which replaced the aisled building. It was of massive construction, and even though there is no direct evidence for its purpose the strength of its timbers, greater than any other on the site, suggests that it possibly had another storey and was a store; it was not domestic. The presence of timber buildings only in Enclosure A in this period highlights not only the working role of this part of the site but also the lower status of its buildings and inhabitants. However, Building 31 in the north-west corner had a fronting corridor and a wing room, indicating that it was basically similar, architecturally, to the masonry villa. If so, it is possible to speculate that it was occupied by somebody of somewhat higher status than the other occupants of Enclosure A, possibly a foreman and his family. Its proximity to the villa compound may also support this.

Of further interest is the re-use of sites of earlier buildings, indicating that the basic plan of the settlement was established in preceding periods. However, that an attempt was being made to arrange the buildings symmetrically is evident, for example, from the pairing of Buildings 29 and 30.

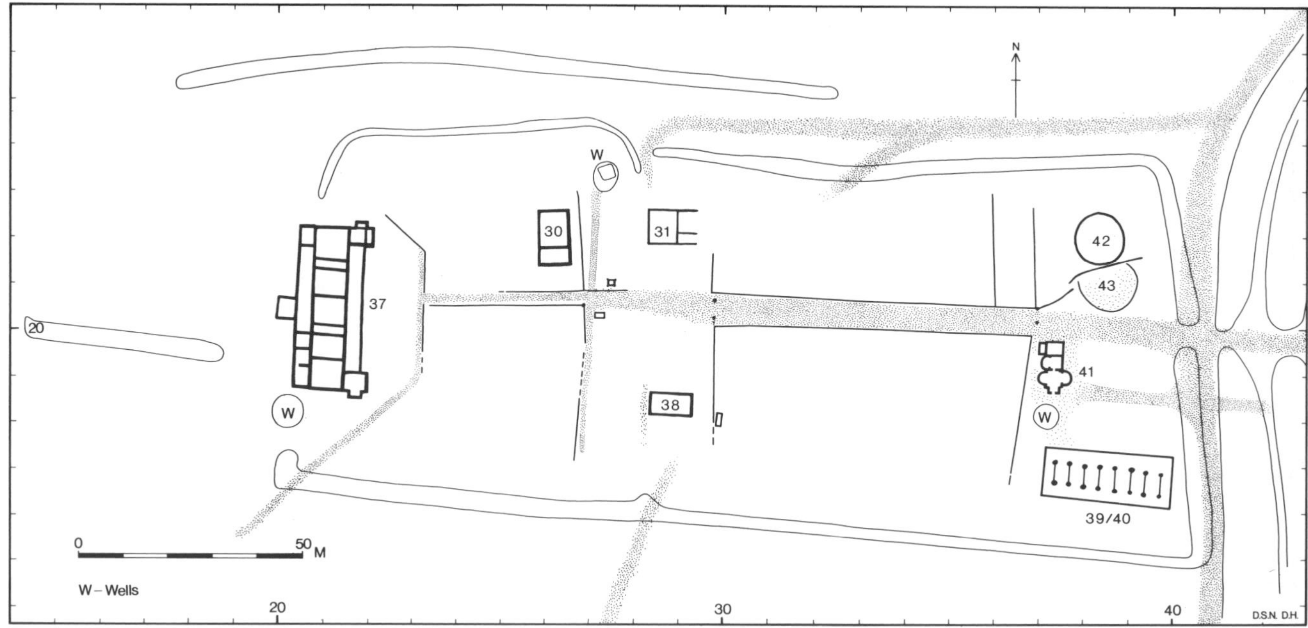

Fig 73 Block plan showing buildings of c *AD 175–250, Period 9*

Period 9, c *AD 175–250* (Fig 73)

The enclosures

The ditch dividing the two enclosures was finally filled up and the boundary replaced by a new fence 14m further east. Where the fence crossed the line of the approach road to the villa, area 2920 (Fig 1), a new gate was provided – it was represented by two large postholes. The inner enclosure (B) was further sub-divided by another fence: it ran north–south on the west side of an existing pathway linking Buildings 30 and 29 (the latter appears to have been demolished in this period). There was a gate through the fence where it met the approach road, area 2620; the gate-post was represented by a larger and deeper posthole (Fig 1, Archive plan 119). Sealed beneath the trackway in area 28–2920 was a Bagendon brooch of AD 10–50 (No 19, Fig 121).

The farmyard in Enclosure A to the east was already fenced-off from the adjacent paddocks, but the fence was probably rebuilt and provided with yet another road-gate in area 3720 (Fig 1, Archive plan 327). This gate was hinged on a pivot utilising a quern of Hertfordshire Puddingstone (Fig 74 and No 1057, Fig 147). The fence continued north of the road and divided this area into two, isolating Building 42 and Structure 43 (Fig 90) from a new paddock to the west. This boundary was probably 'temporary' for it was replaced twice on slightly different alignments. Another fence 9m west of the gate possibly represents the west side of a separate compound. (For an appreciation of the number of times particular fences were replaced on the same alignment see Fig 10, the southern alignment of the fence just described. Here the fence was replaced on at least three occasions.) The consequence of these changes was the creation of at least seven enclosed yards: three, or possibly four, in the area designated Enclosure A, and four in Enclosure B.

The presence of so many gates hints at stock control, and would have meant some inconvenience to those approaching the main villa from the east. It is not surprising therefore that trackways began to cross the enclosure banks: these tracks might represent separate routes into the paddocks. Three trackways were situated along the south side of the enclosures: one close to the angle in area 2016, another at what was the junction of the two enclosures in area 2816 and another on the east side at about 4014. All the tracks on this side probably joined a Roman road 400m south (Fig 6) which was aligned east–west, and ran towards the Chester Gate of Verulamium (see p 96). The causeway by the main entrance was also widened, as was the road across it, which spread into the filled-up

Fig 74 View showing quern of Hertfordshire puddingstone utilised as a gate pivot situated in area 3720

ditches. This road turned sharply to the south suggesting that a new gap was made in area 4017, perhaps to provide direct access to the farmyard, further evidence being an east–west road with cart-ruts located north of the aisled building, Buildings 39 and 40, in area 38–3917 (AP No 286). Further north a trackway ran north-east/south-west along the 'inside' line of the massive bank and, at area 4124 close to the enclosure, forked, one route running south to cross into the enclosure via the causeway and another continuing west to cross the enclosure in area 3223, where another trackway has been located.

The buildings

Buildings and structures of Period 9 include the second masonry villa, Building 37 (Fig 48) and a rectangular barn or workshop, Building 38 (Fig 69), in area 28–2918. The outer enclosure saw the erection of Building 39 (Fig 80) and its replacement, Building 40. Further north, in area 3718–19, a new bath-house, Building 41 (Fig 85), was constructed, while north of the road there was a new circular house and an animal pen, Building 42 and Structure 43 (Fig 90). Other structures were erected and Buildings 30 and 31 enlarged. Buildings 27, 28, 29, 32, 33 and 34 were demolished. Alterations to existing buildings will be described first.

The inner enclosure, Enclosure B

Building 30 (Fig 64)

This was given a southern extension (Fig 65) with an *opus signinum* floor (734) sealing, in its make up (847), a jar similar to *Ver* 654 (Frere 1972) dated AD 130–45. These additional walls differed in construction to those of the earlier work, in that they incorporated considerable quantities of puddingstone, tufa and tile, suggesting the re-use of materials from buildings demolished elsewhere. They also had rammed chalk footings. Shortly after its construction, the extension subsided into the hollow associated with Structure 12, and was reinforced by a retaining wall (731) with a triple-offset foundation. Contemporary with these repairs a new floor was laid. The entrance into the building on the east side was retained; the building, therefore, faced the same direction as the main villa. A timber-lined gutter (704) was added around the building; it was not observed on the south side, possibly because it was sealed by the added retaining wall. It contained hundreds of small flakes of tile probably representing frost fractures from the roof. Unfortunately there was no evidence for the function of the structure in this period; as already suggested (p 50) it could have been an office or a small dwelling for a bailiff or steward. At the close of this period the quoins were robbed-out (Fig 66).

For Periods 10 and 11 alterations to this building see p 71.

Building 37 (Fig 48, reconstruction drawing Fig 75)

Building 37, a new villa, was constructed over the west ditch bordering the previous house, Building 27 (Fig 34). Why a new site should have been chosen is uncertain but Building 27 could have remained occupied while the new house was being erected. It was of three phases: Phases 1 and 2 are assigned to Period 9; Phase 3 was attributed to the late third century and is described under Period 10 (p 71). The Phase 1 house, built in flint bonded in pale-yellow mortar, comprised a rectangular block 35 by 8m, of seven rooms, including two through-passages linking corridors 3m wide on the east and west sides. The facade of the villa now faced west, because the corridor on this side has a wing-room (8) at its north end and at the axis, projecting west, was a 'square' porch (9). At the south end of the corridor and of the same width was a simple three-roomed *Reihentyp* bath-house with the *caldarium* and furnace at the south end (Fig 76). With the provision of an integral bath-suite within the villa, the isolated bath-house, Building 29, was demolished and a new bath-house (Building 41, Fig 85), perhaps for workers and staff, built in the outer courtyard. On the east side the main west wall of the previous house became the foundation for the new eastern verandah wall; the only new footing provided for this wall was a short length projecting from the north-west corner of the original building, area 2121–22.

A western aspect did not long prevail for in Phase 2 the facade reverted back to the east where two new wing-rooms with *exedrae* (Rooms 13 and 14) were constructed, the one on the south side projecting over the loose fill of the earlier cellar, necessitating the sinking of its foundation 2.25m deep to the level of the cellar floor (Fig 4). Around the north side of the house and its verandahs was a timber-lined gutter similar to that around Building 30.

Shortly after, or during, construction it was realised that the north wall of the building might subside into the underlying ditch. Consequently the wall was more than doubled in thickness by a foundation of flint and tile rubble bonded in off-white mortar. It sealed an internal offset of the original wall (Fig 77).

Owing to medieval disturbance and plough damage the nature of the floors in this period is uncertain. However, in all cases their original sub-floors were of rammed chalk, which in Room 1 was paved with a mosaic comprising arrangements of guilloche and scrolls (Fig 78) (see p 174) and in Rooms 2 and 3 with plain coarse tesserae; no floor surfaces survived in other rooms nor was any painted plaster of this period worth noting recovered. The western corridor was paved with a coarse tessellated pavement decorated with alternate rows of red brick and cream limestone tesserae, which ran up to and butted the outer side of the south wall of the wing-room (8). Had the pavement post-dated the wing-room it would have sealed its foundation. Instead, when the wing-room was demolished and transferred to the eastern side (Room 13) the area of the room was paved with a coarse plain red tessellated floor which also sealed the earlier south foundation. No attempt was made to

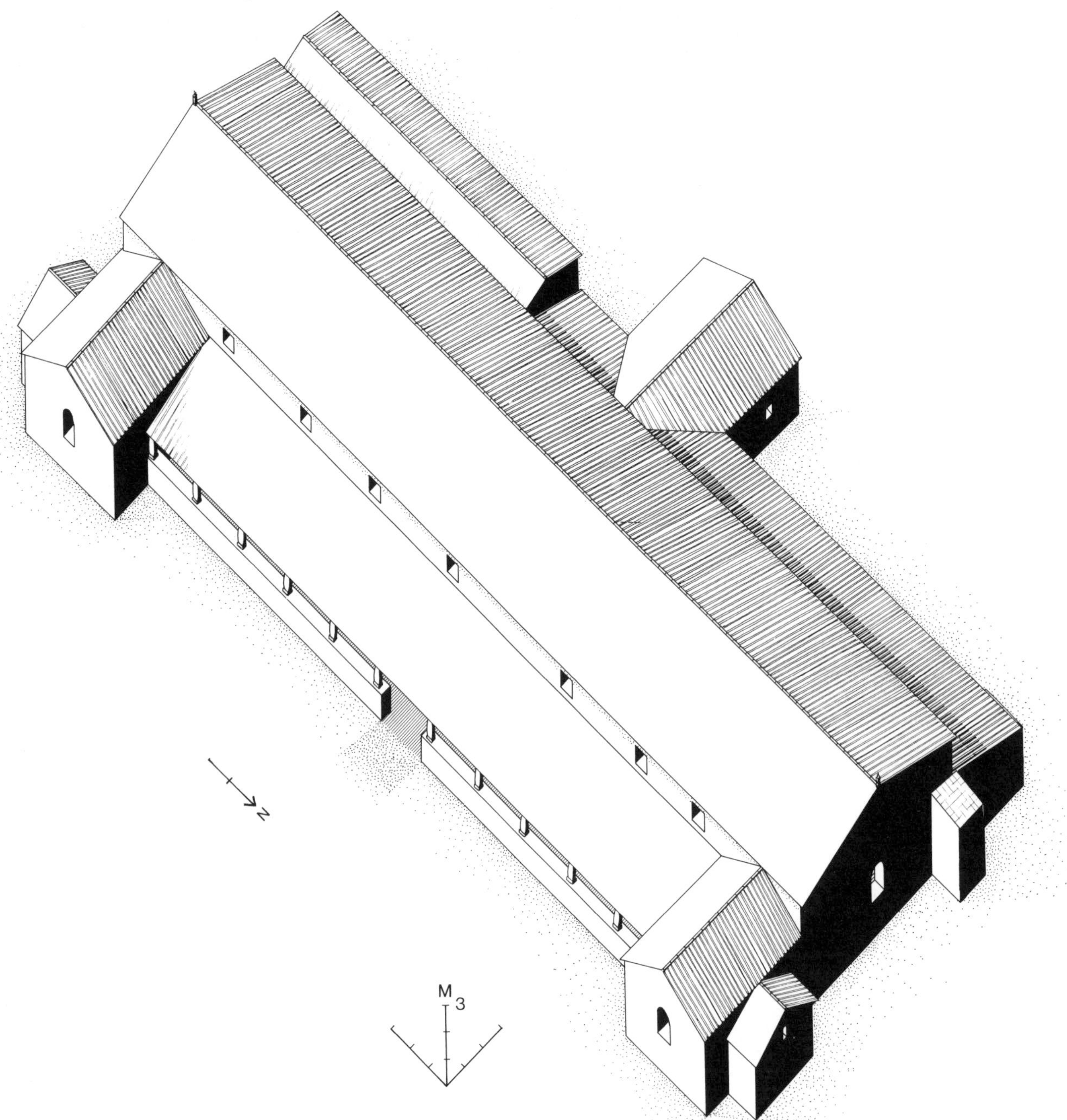

Fig 75 Reconstruction drawing of Building 37 looking south-west and showing the final phase of development with a buttress against the north wall, Period 9

continue the pattern of red and limestone tesserae. There is no evidence for the mosaic and tessellated floors in Rooms 1–3 sealing earlier examples: the rammed chalk was no more than a foundation, and it can be assumed that the mosaic floors are contemporary with the construction of the building.

Dating evidence

Building 37 could not have been constructed earlier than AD 161, the earliest date assignable to a coin (No 45) found in the destruction rubble in the cellar. How long the coin remained in circulation is not known because it had been deeply scored in antiquity, but a date *c* AD 175 is suggested by a group of pottery (Fig 156), analogous to examples from Verulamium, in a cesspit (257) sealed by the eastern corridor and the south wall of Room 13. Antonine pottery was also found in layers of clay and chalk make-up for the floors (layers 42 (AV 1–2), 45 (AV 1–31) and 67 (AV 1–47)). How long Building 37 remained habitable in the period under discussion is doubtful, since most of the pottery pre-dating the building and in occupation levels (275, AV 1–59), associated with and to the north of Room 1, is indistinguishable in type and of the same date. However, later vessels up to *c* AD 200, for

Fig 76 View north showing bath-suite (Rooms 10–12) in Building 37; the chalk-built union jack hypocaust can be seen on the right

Fig 77 View north showing north wall of Building 37 with rubble foundation overlain by mosaic pavement in Room 1

Fig 78 Mosaic pavement found in Room 1, Building 37; photographed in 1960

example Verulamium types *Ver* (Frere 1972) 1077, AD 150–200, and (Frere 1984) 2599, AD 200–250, are also represented. None of these groups contain colour-coated wares such as those represented at Verulamium from *c* AD 200 onwards. Sealing these levels was a layer of humus representing a period of abandonment. Occupation levels north of the villa (275 and 369) also contained domestic and personal items including a large number of bone pins and needles, cosmetic implements, and three styli.

Building 38 (Fig 69)

Building 38, area 28–2918, was constructed in flint and re-used roofing tile bonded in yellow mortar, and measured about 9 by 5m; it sealed Building 32 on the east and was constructed over a layer of heavy rubble (1283) filling north–south ditch 1281. It was poorly preserved, since it had been levelled for the construction of a later barn, Building 55 (Fig 79), although where the west wall had subsided into the underlying ditch several courses of masonry survived. However the superstructure is likely to have been mainly of timber and daub, as against the west wall was a

Fig 79 View north showing masonry building 38 with barn, Building 55, superimposed

deposit of collapsed clay daub (1521) with many iron nails; in the daub was a coin of AD 350–351 (No 283).

The function of the building is not known but the absence of ovens perhaps precludes its having been domestic: it may have been a workshop. Evidence is slight, but there may have been an entrance in the north wall facing Building 31 on the opposite side of the yard. The flint rubble underlying the building, filling the ditch, was mixed with tile and represented the destruction rubble of a major building. It is tempting to suggest that it came from the nearby bath-house, Building 29. Running north–south along the line of the ditch and west of the building was a pathway (1555 and 1477) which crossed the enclosure bank and ditch further south in area 2816. Pottery in the rubble sealed beneath the building included late Antonine forms similar to examples from Verulamium such as *Ver* (Frere 1972) 960 dated AD 145–200; 969, AD 140–90; 970, AD 155–160; (Frere 1984) 2114, AD 140–80 and 2131, AD 170–225. The latest samian ware included a Central Gaulish Antonine dish (Drag 18/31).

The outer enclosure, Enclosure A

Buildings 39 and 40 (Figs 40, 41 and 80)

This was an aisled barn situated in the south-east corner of the enclosure and over Building 34. It measured 29 by 11m and comprised eight pairs of postholes forming seven bays, each 3.40m wide centre to centre (Fig 81). The posts were 0.30m square and set into circular pits 0.80m wide by 0.75m deep and packed with clay and flint (Fig 82). Posthole 1810 contained an axe (No 363, Fig 131). Its floor at the western end utilised the terrace excavated for Building 34 and consequently the widths of the buildings accord. The outer walls, represented by the impressions of sleeper beams, for example 2062 on the north and 2067 on the south (Fig 83), were placed just outside the limits of the previous structure. Unfortunately, the east wall of the building was not exposed and is assumed to lie beneath a deeply-rutted farm track, although it is possible that the east wall (2191) of the earlier barn may approximate to its position. The width of the aisles, about 2.25m, corresponds to the distance between the west end wall and the first pair of posts (Nos 1810 and 2090) suggesting either that the aisle roof was a simple lean-to resting against a gablet over the first pair of posts, or was carried up to meet an apex supported by principal rafters on the second pair of posts, Nos 1890 and 1906.

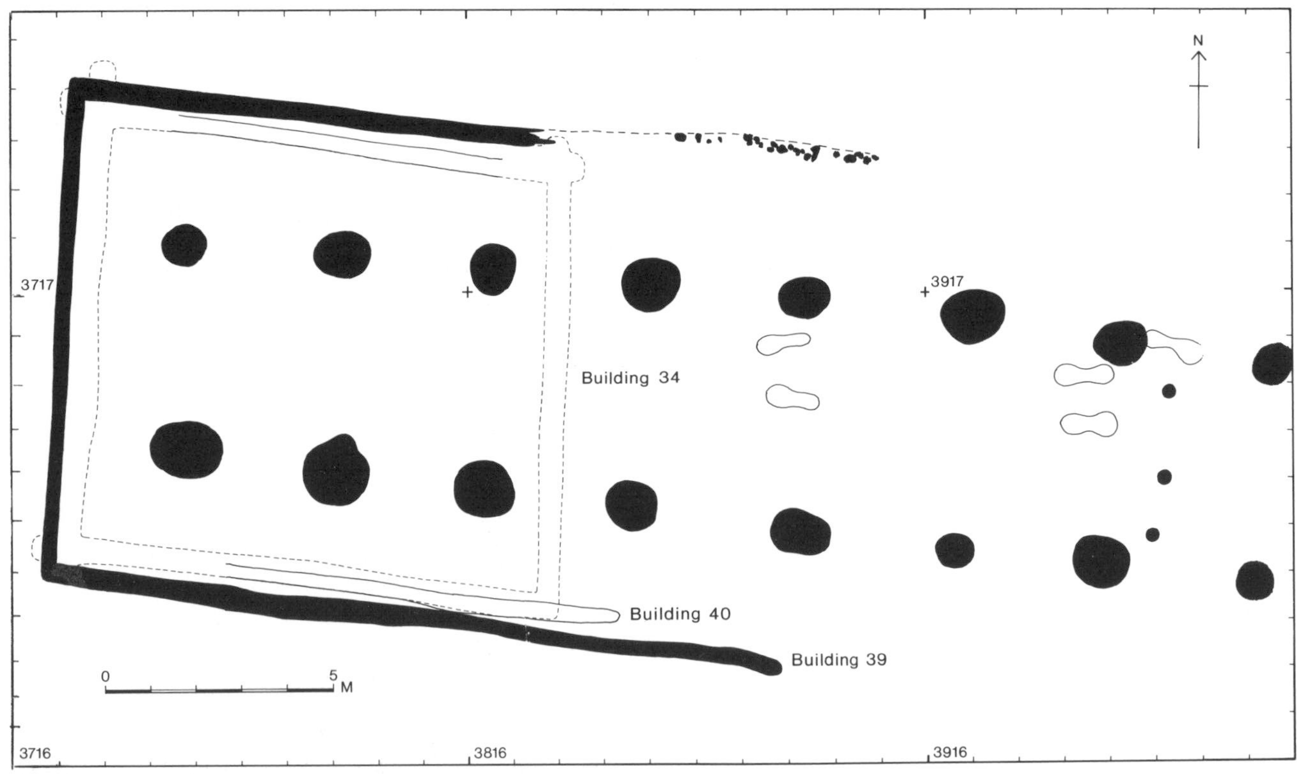

Fig 80 Plan of Building 34 (dotted) with Buildings 39 (in black) and 40 (outline) superimposed, Period 9 (Scale 1:160)

Fig 81 View west showing Building 39/40; the trenches for Building 34 can be seen in the distance

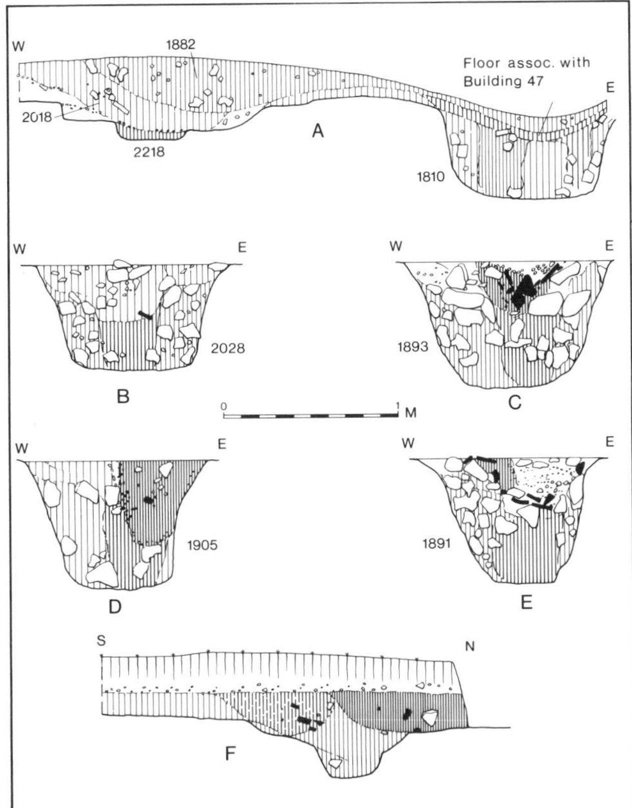

Fig 82 Sections across postholes and slots associated with complex in south-east corner of the outer enclosure, Buildings 34, 39 and 40 (Scale 1:40)

Fig 83 View showing charred beam of south wall of Building 40

No internal features can be confidently assigned to Building 39 for it was completely reconstructed, its replacement being designated Building 40 (Fig 80). The earlier posts were withdrawn (or they may have rotted) and for a short time the holes were left vacant, for they silted-up; the silting was sealed by the new packing material (for example posthole 1891, Fig 82). The plan of the building was the same except that its width was slightly less; its north and south walls (2061 and 2019) were moved slightly inwards making the aisles marginally narrower (1.90m). As with Building 39 the main entrance was on the north side, where there was a row of stones (2242) suggesting that a door cill was underpinned, and north of the structure there were cobbled surfaces and spreads of crushed tile.

Over the floor were numerous features (not necessarily all of the latest phase) including five ovens on the eastern side of the nave. Another oven was found on the west where there was a rotary quern (No 1058, Fig 147) close to the north-west pier (No 1810). Against the south wall was a small hoard of iron objects (Fig 84) including a mount from a cart (No 470, Fig 133); also in the building was a large swivelled cauldron-hook (No 529, Fig 134).

Fig 84 View showing hoard of ironwork against inside edge of south wall, Building 40

The building was probably a barn; it is perhaps significant that it was the fifth on the same site, and apart from Building 34 all these had aisled plans. However, the presence of so many ovens, a quern, and other items of domestic rubbish implies that this building, and perhaps the others also, doubled as habitation.

Unlike many aisled farm-houses in Britain, Building B from Winterton, Lincs, for example (Stead 1976, 26, fig 15), it had few sub-divisions separating stock from occupants. That stock were kept in the building is perhaps indicated by a north–south row of postholes (Nos 2221, 2222 and 2039, Fig 40), a possible attempt to screen off cattle at the east end of the barn, and by a U-shaped trench (2033) along the east side of the south aisle. This was probably a runnel for the collection of dung from animals stalled in three bays separated by postholes 1909, 1908, 2005 and 2207. The width of each bay is sufficient to stall two animals and therefore as many as six could have wintered there. Significantly perhaps, there were no ovens in the southern half of the nave, possibly to allow access for stock. Perhaps the building was occupied by family groups who shared it in the winter with stock and farm equipment. Hay could have been stored in the loft which could have provided additional sleeping quarters. The swivelled cauldron hook is a significant find for it suggests communal cooking, as does a

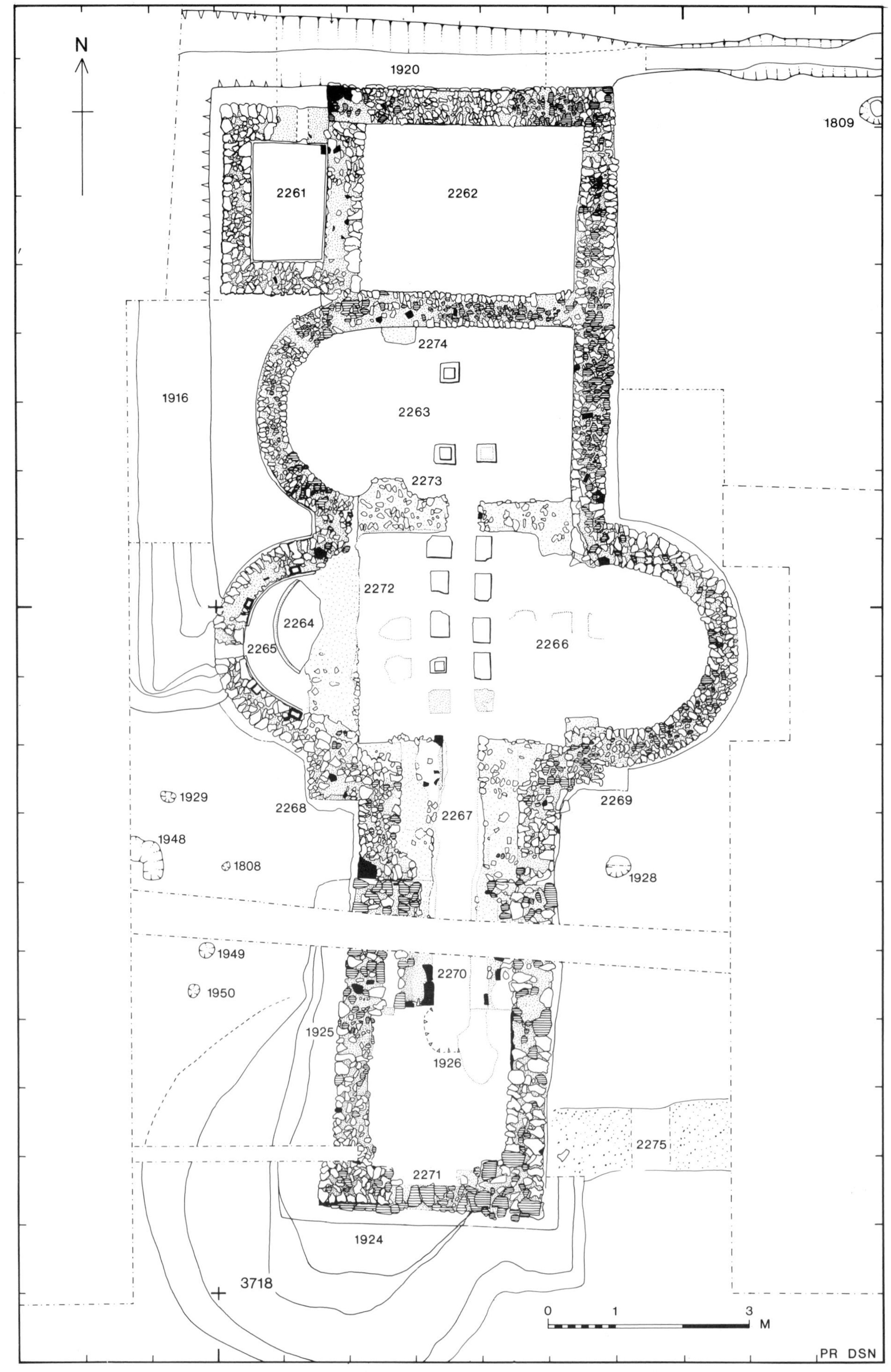

Fig 85 Overall plan of bath-house, Building 41, Periods 9 and 10 (Scale 1:80)

massive mortarium by the potter Verecundus (No 5, p 194) dated AD 160–200. Another interesting find, but out of context, is an emerald, once from a large and showy ring (No 1011, Fig 143). The building burnt down; charred sleeper beams were found on three of its sides (Fig 83). Although a spread of tiles was found north of the building insufficient tiles were found elsewhere to suggest that it had a tiled roof. More likely its roof was of thatch.

Dating evidence

Sealing the north-west corner of the building and extending over posthole 1810 was a layer of clay (1882, Fig 82, A) which also sealed a layer of humic clay (2018) representing a period of abandonment noted elsewhere on the site. Clay 2018 sealed a group of pottery (AV 1–51) lying at the interface and directly over the sleeper beam for the west wall. The range of pottery is similar to types published from Verulamium and dating from the late second to the early third centuries – for example *Ver* (Frere 1972) 867, AD 150–60; 873, AD 150–80; 878, AD 135–80; 879, AD 130–70; 929, AD 140–80; 957, AD 150–75; 974, AD 140–200; 986, AD 155–60; 999, AD 140–60; 1061, AD 200–25; (Frere 1984) 2129, AD 180–210; 2258, AD 150–200; 2462, AD 130–80; 2464, AD 140–80; 2553, AD 150–200; and 2564, AD 230–80. The latest samian forms included a 31R and a Curle 15, both Central Gaulish. A coin of Lucilla, AD 161–80, was also found in this layer (No 47). Two vessels in calcite-gritted ware should be mentioned. In *Verulamium* III (Frere 1984), forms 2192 and 2194 are dated AD 310–70 and AD 350–400 respectively. However, providing the Gorhambury sherds are not intrusions, the writer considers that in view of the total absence of flanged bowls from the deposit, the types should be dated earlier: no later than the early third century. A similar range of pottery (2015, AV 1–8), some from the same vessels, was found north of the barn over a cobbled surface. Here too the deposit was sealed by humic soil (numbered 2015 but equating with 2018). A coin of Faustina II (AD 161–80, No 46) was found in posthole 1890, sealed by Building 47 which was constructed over the west end of Building 39/40, sealing the clay (1882) and pottery just described. The pottery listed would seem to be later than that associated with the villa proper and therefore it is possible that the farm was occupied longer than the villa.

Among the small finds in the occupation level (2065) of Building 40 was a considerable amount of structural ironwork, including, for example, split-spiked loops (No 639, Fig 136), wall spikes (No 662), fragments of hinges (No 400) and rings (No 744, Fig 137). Other finds include a hipposandal (No 488, not illustrated); there were no objects of copper-alloy. The quern (No 1058, Fig 147) came from this layer.

The cobbled area to the north produced a number of iron tools and implements including a plane blade (No 367, Fig 131), a ploughshare tip (No 414, Fig 132), a large cleaver (No 432, Fig 132), a water-pipe collar (No 559, not illustrated) and various staples, timber studs, ferrules and other fittings. Nowhere on the site, however, were water-pipe collars found in lines, indicating the direction of a piped supply.

The probability that this part of the site was a separate entity to the villa is perhaps further supported by the presence within the stockade of a bath-house (Building 41, Fig 85) presumably serving the community living at this end of the farm and perhaps also the farm-hands living elsewhere on the estate. It was built 12m north of the aisled barn, separated from it by a well. The west wall of the bath-house and the west wall of the barn shared the same alignment.

Building 41 (Figs 85 and 86)

The bath-house (1915) was of three phases, the first two probably of the period under discussion and the third of the late third century (Period 10). Phase 1 was built of flint and chalk, Phase 2 of flint only and Phase 3 of very large nodules of chalk and flint. In all phases the mortar was pale yellow.

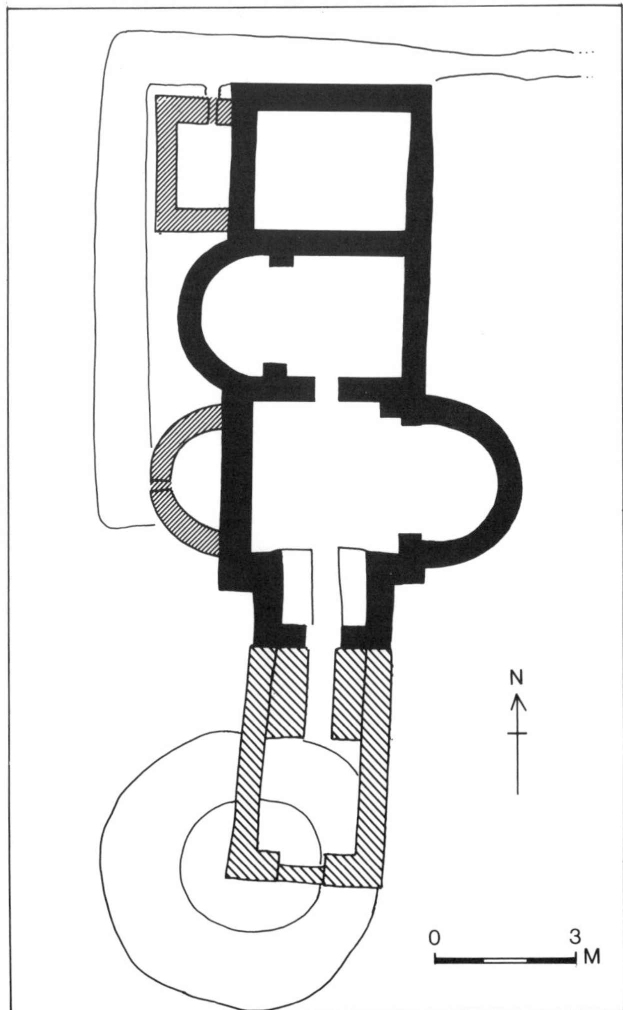

Fig 86A Plan of bath-house, Building 41, showing sequence of phases and reconstruction drawing, Periods 9 and 10

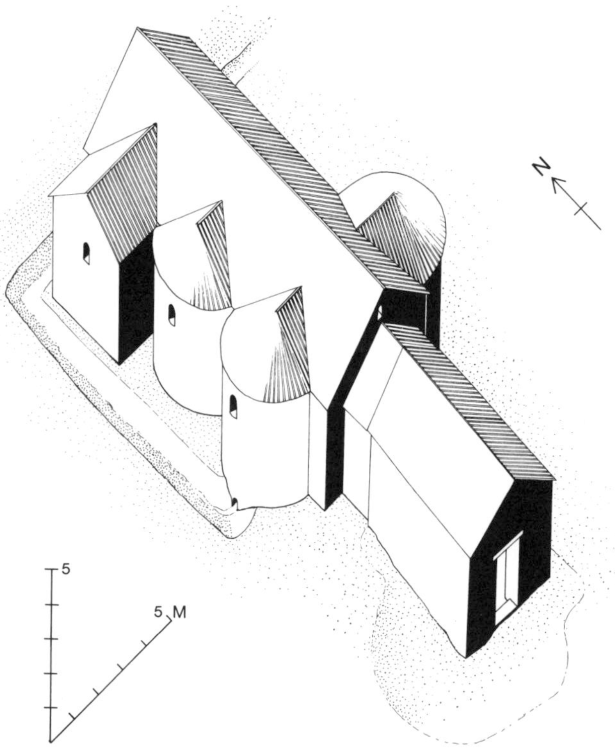

Fig 86B Reconstruction of bath-house, Building 41, Periods 9 and 10

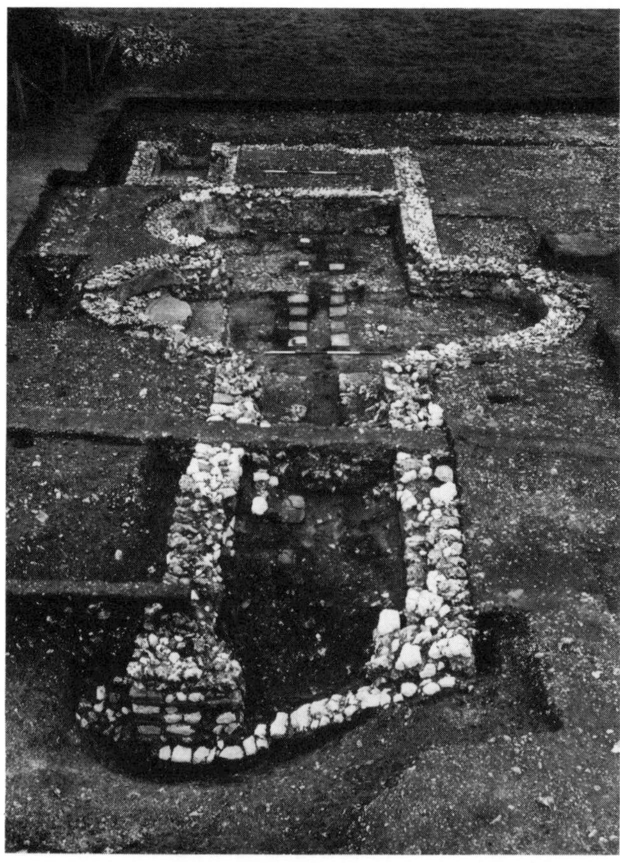

Fig 87 View north of the bath-house, Building 41; in the foreground can be seen the south wall of the praefurnium *sunken into an underlying well*

It began as a simple three-roomed block orientated north–south with a 'square' projection at the south end (Fig 87) enclasping the furnace cheeks for a boiler stand or *testudo*. The southern room (2266) therefore was the *caldarium*, the next (2263) the *tepidarium* and the northernmost (2262) the *frigidarium* (Fig 88). In Phase 1 the *caldarium* had an apse on its eastern side and the *tepidarium* a shallower apse on its western side. Neither contained plunge-baths since they had no drains; presumably they contained basins. However a heated plunge-bath (Fig 89) was provided in Phase 2 when the west wall of the *caldarium* was breached and a bath installed – matching that on the east, but slightly smaller. It had the remains of four vertical flue-tiles with square side vents. The plunge drained into a V-shaped gully (1916), conceivably originally timber-lined, that flowed north, turning east at the north end of the building. The drain also served a rectangular cold plunge-bath added onto the west side of the *frigidarium* and with a drain in its north wall (Fig 88). It originally had a tiled floor bedded in *opus signinum*.

Despite additions to the building in Phase 3 there is no reason to assume that the square pilae surviving in the *caldarium* and *tepidarium* are not original.

Dating evidence

Unfortunately there was little dating evidence for the first two phases; the latest pottery from the lower fill of the drain, prior to it being recut, included two Antonine forms only. The Phase 3 additions to the structure and its decoration will be described under Period 10.

Building 42 (Fig 90)

This lay in the north-east corner of the outer enclosure, area 3821–22, and appears to have been of two phases. It was represented by a curving clay wall (2670) set into a shallow U-shaped trench (Fig 91), which cut a late Iron Age pit (2669), possibly a burial, containing two almost complete vessels including a native jar and an imported terra rubra fine-ware cup. It is probable that the trench was originally a drip-trench around an earlier circular house and had become a refuse tip. At the bottom of the trench were a number of late second-century forms (2670, AV 1–10) such as types published from Verulamium including *Ver* (Frere 1972) 634, AD 140–50; 654, AD 130–65; (Frere 1984) 2308, AD 135–90; and 2455, AD 155–20.

However, perhaps the building in phase 2 was slightly enlarged, for the trench was filled and the pottery sealed with thick clean orange clay probably representing a wall. The south-western half of the building was ploughed out but, assuming it to have been circular, its diameter is likely to have been about 12 metres. Inside the building were 21 ovens, both circular and pear-shaped; from the lack of industrial waste the ovens are assumed to have been domestic. They were mainly concentrated on the east side of the hut, but appear to surround a central area with a posthole (2339) possibly for a roof support. There was a 3m wide clear space between the ovens and the north-east wall; possibly this was a sleeping or living area. Pit 2846 pre-dates the hut.

Oven 2303 had a sherd of samian ware from an Antonine form 33 cup and a flanged bowl as *Ver* (Frere 1984) 2462, AD 130–80. Oven 2565 had a rim from a Verulamium ware jar dated no later than the early third century, and oven 2303 contained a rather fine leather mount (No 168, Fig 125).

Structure 43 (Fig 90)

Outside, to the south-east, was a circular shallow hollow with a concentration of compact cobbling (2665) separated from the hut by a palisade (2841) which was later replaced by a row of postholes – 2842, 2843, 2844, 2840. Another row of postholes extended south-west from posthole 2556 towards the gate leading from the farmyard along the trackway towards the inner enclosure (see block plan, Fig 73). The cobbling thinned towards the palisade and, on the south-west side, was cut by a drainage gully (2345) which curved around the cobbling, respecting the hollow. The nature of the feature in this period is uncertain but since there is clear evidence for it having become a pen in Period 11 (Fig 92, see discussion p 73) perhaps it served the same function. Finds associated with the cobbles included an enamelled copper alloy ring (No 61, Fig 122) of second-century date, and miscellaneous metalwork.

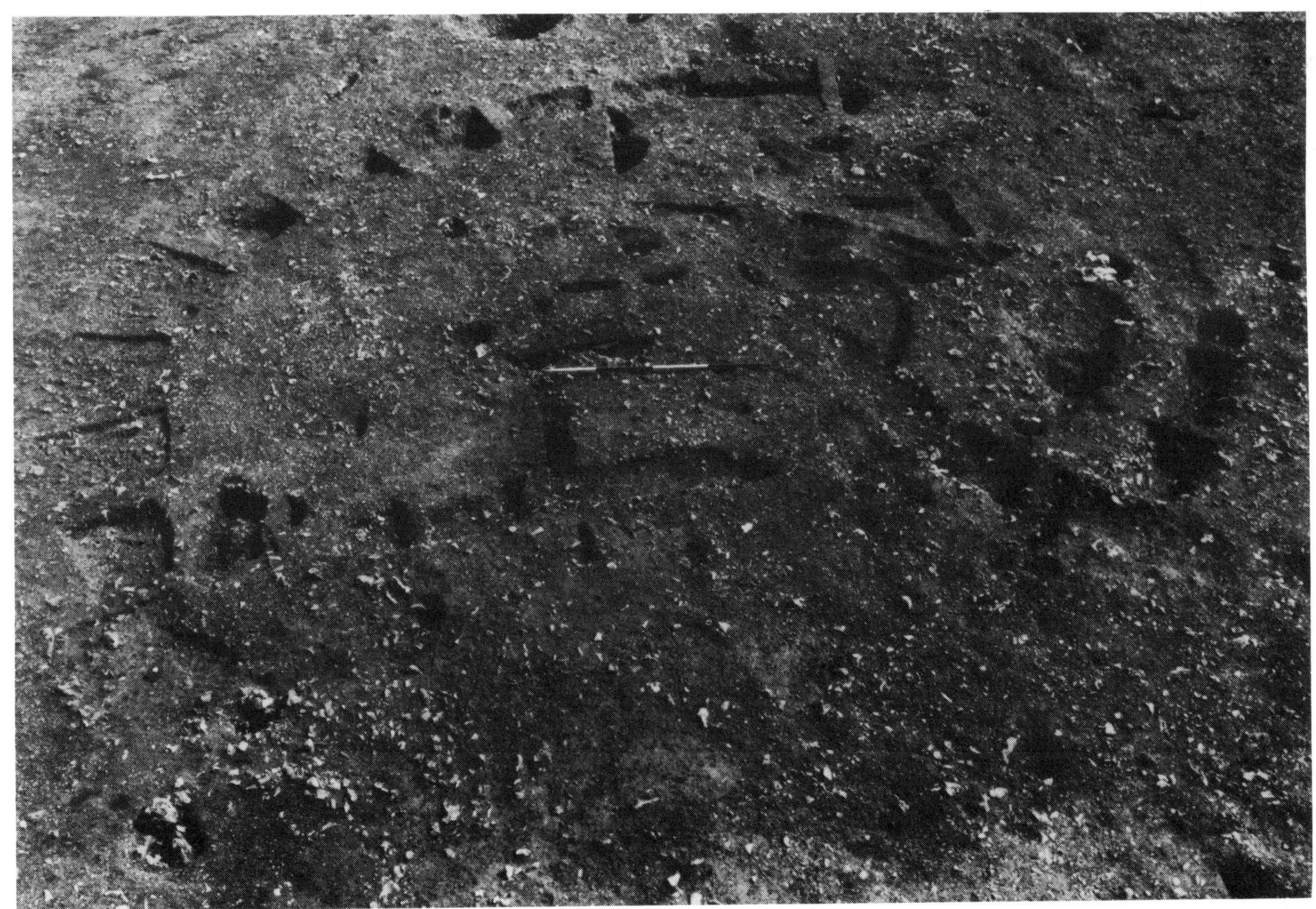

Fig 91 View east of Building 42

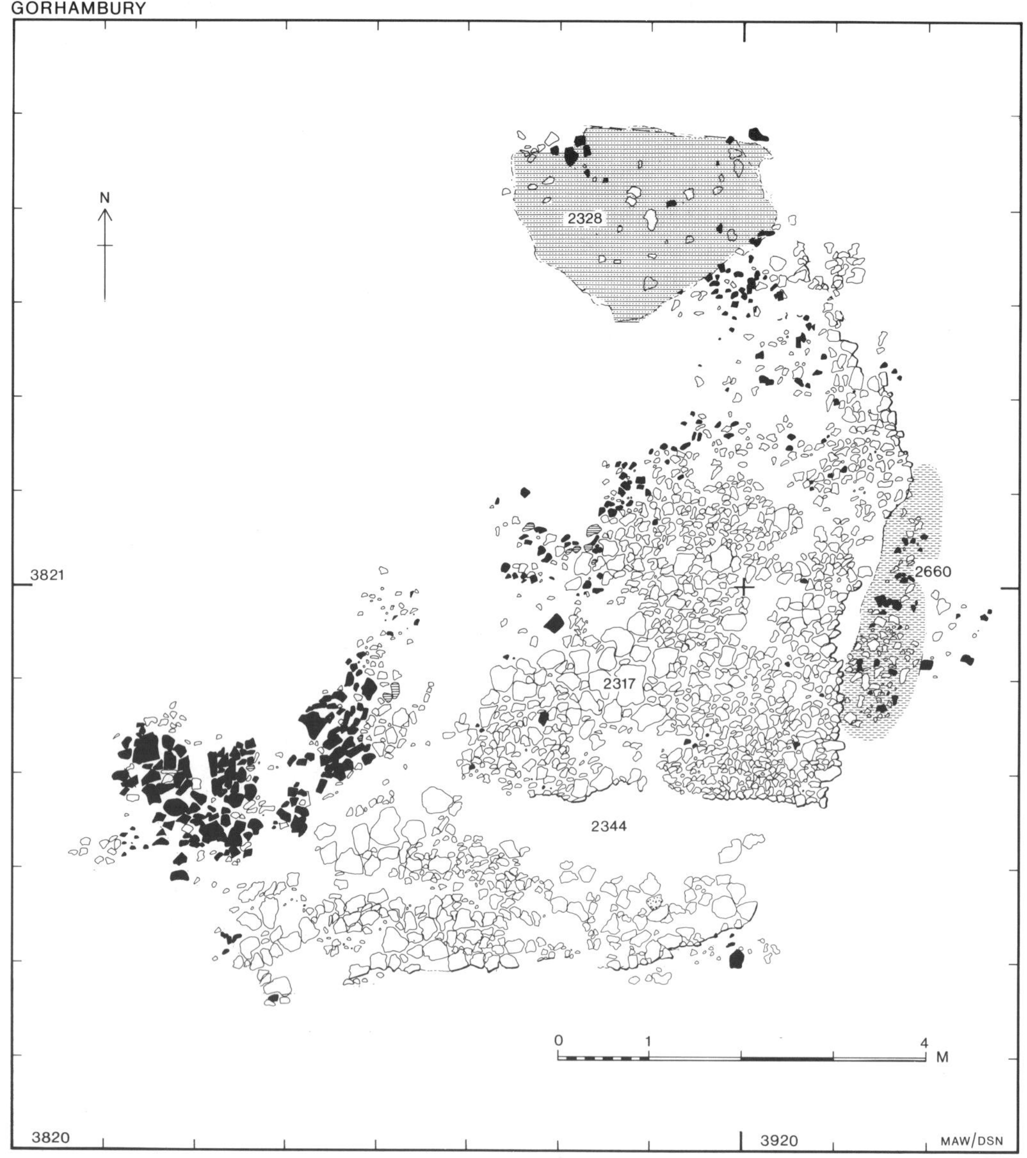

Fig 92 Plan of Structure 43 showing latest levels, Period 10 (Scale 1:80)

Structures 44–6 (Fig 1)

Structures 44–6 were all similar to one another both in plan and construction and therefore only a single example (Structure 44 (1052), area 2720) is illustrated (Fig 93).

They were located in areas 2720, 2721 and 2918 respectively; another (257) (already referred to on pp 46 and 58, but not numbered individually there) was found beneath Room 13 at the north end of the east corridor of the second masonry house, Building 37 (Fig 48), but it was disturbed by later footings. They were similar in construction, each with a rectangular trench, about 2 by 1m by 1m deep; their sides were lined with planks set horizontally (Fig 94). The floors were flat, suggesting that they too were lined, and had postholes at their outer corners. The structures are interpreted as privies, the posts supporting a simple roof and possibly a seat as shown on the reconstruction (Fig 95). Structures 44 and 46 were sufficiently large to seat two or three persons. Structure 45, being only 1.50m long, might only have accommodated one or two persons. All the examples are dated to the late Antonine period and were probably intended to be emptied to supply manure for the fields or alternatively for leatherworking.

In Structure 46 was a copper alloy 'file' or 'rasp' perhaps originally from a toilet set (No 153, Fig 124).

Summary of Period 9

The most significant event of this period was the construction of a new, larger, masonry villa to the west of the earlier house. As at Gadebridge, the facade was moved to the opposite side of the villa, away from the courtyards, although this aspect did not last long, for the facade was moved back to its original position. The new villa incorporated its own bath-suite, at the expense of Building 29 which was demolished. A new bath-house, Building 41, probably for estate workers, was constructed in the farmyard, Enclosure A. The tower granary, Building 28, was also demolished and appears not to have been rebuilt, for there is no

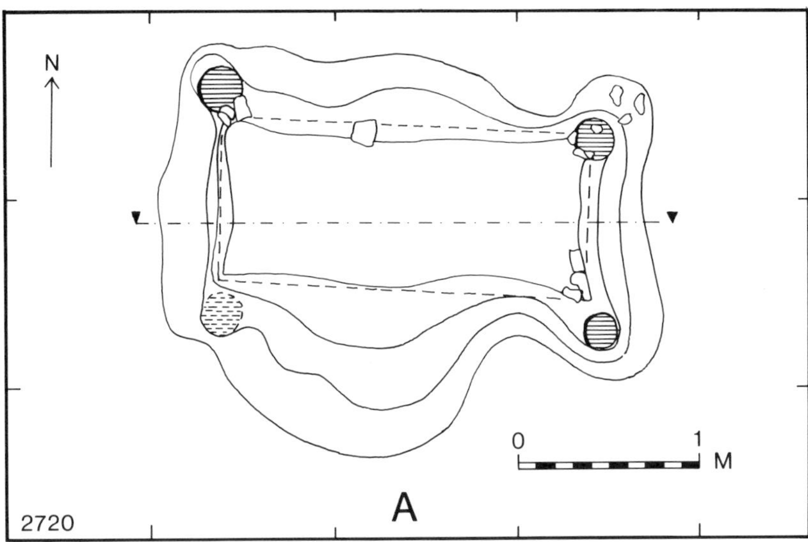

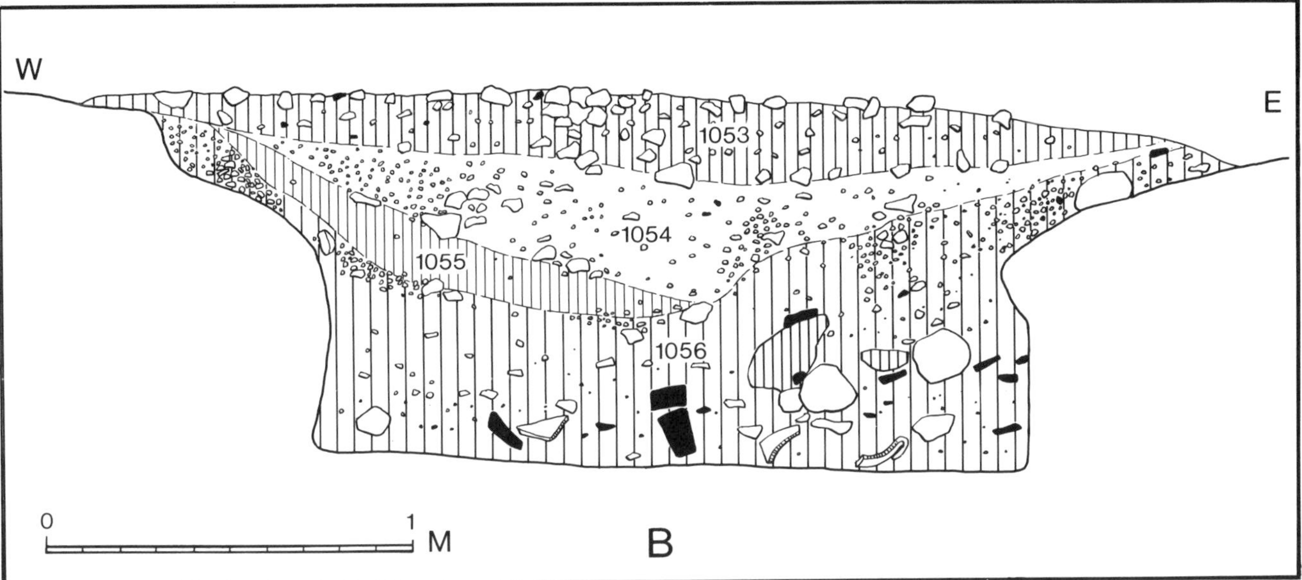

Fig 93 Plan (A) and sections (B) of privy, Structure 44, Period 9; it is of similar form to Structures 45 and 46 (Scales: plan 1:40, section 1:20)

Fig 94 View south of privy, Structure 44, showing plank-lined trench

Fig 95 Reconstruction drawing of privy, Structure 44

obvious candidate among the other buildings for its replacement. Whether this signifies a move away from a primarily arable system of agriculture to stock is not known, although it is perhaps significant that from this period onwards there is a marked increase in the number of stockades about the site.

In Enclosure A, Building 34 was dismantled and replaced by Building 39, another aisled barn used jointly for occupation and housing stock. It is contemporary with the new bath-house, and hints at considerable activity on this part of the site. The bath-house was far too large merely for residents and it is assumed that it was also used by estate workers living outside the enclosures.

Following the reconstruction of the villa and many outbuildings in masonry there would have been little need, perhaps, for substantial repairs and alterations for many years. However, although few additions were made towards the close of the period, this is likely to have been the consequence of a decline in the status or economy of the estate and the possible abandonment of buildings. The reason for suggesting this is that over many of the features there were deposits of brown humic soil, derived naturally. It sealed horizons around Building 30 and also robber pits cutting out the quoins at the angles of the building (Fig 66), but, more significantly, it sealed the trackways, especially where they cross the infilled ditches, for example in areas 2816, 4019 and 3423 (Fig 73). The same humic deposit also sealed much of the eastern farmyard, including the west end of Buildings 39 and 40, its preservation here being probably due to ponding against vestiges of the enclosure banks. At a later date the trackways were restored with fresh metalling, which sealed the humic soil. For evidence of this in area 4019 see sections across ditch terminals, Section B–C, Fig 15, p 15. Here the original road was represented by 2386 and the brown humic soil 2379, which has the subsequent metalling over it. Elsewhere on the site a similar soil has been noted in the upper levels of ditch 74 north of the masonry villas and as layer 278 in the east–west ditch (277) (area 1923). Here the level could be related to waterlogging and the formation of ferromanganiferous pipes, caused by iron in the soil building up around rotted plant roots, perhaps from a hedge. The humic soil was not observed in levels beneath the villa, Building 37.

There is another reason for suggesting the decline or abandonment of buildings. The wells associated with the previous periods, situated in areas 2017–18, close to the south-west corner of the masonry villa, in area 2723 in the north-east corner of the inner enclosure, and another close to the bath-house, area 3718, went out of use and were replaced. Details of the new wells will be described under Period 10 (p 71) but suffice to state here that a decision to sink at least two new wells to depths in the region of 30m (depth estimated from the still-open medieval well at Bacon's House) must have been taken reluctantly and only as a result of the existing wells having become polluted and abandoned. Timber buildings 31, 40 and 43 were gone; only the masonry houses survived and even these were partially dismantled (see Period 10 description for Building 30, p 71). Reasons for the abandonment are considered more fully later (p 94) but it probably took place in the early decades of the third century – an event noted on other sites in the region.

That the abandonment of the site was not total, however, is suggested by the coin series, with five coins of coin Period VI (AD 161–93) (see p 105), three of Period VII (AD 193–333), and four of Period VIII (AD 222–59). Whilst the degree of wear might indicate that some of these coins could easily have been in use, and therefore lost, in the third century, lack of wear of other examples would strongly suggest a date of deposition not too far removed from their date of issue. Considerably more activity at Gorhambury is demonstrated by these coins than for example at Gadebridge, where the coin loss for the same periods is three, one and one respectively: the presence of the coins appears at variance with the evidence for abandonment demonstrated by the humic soil.

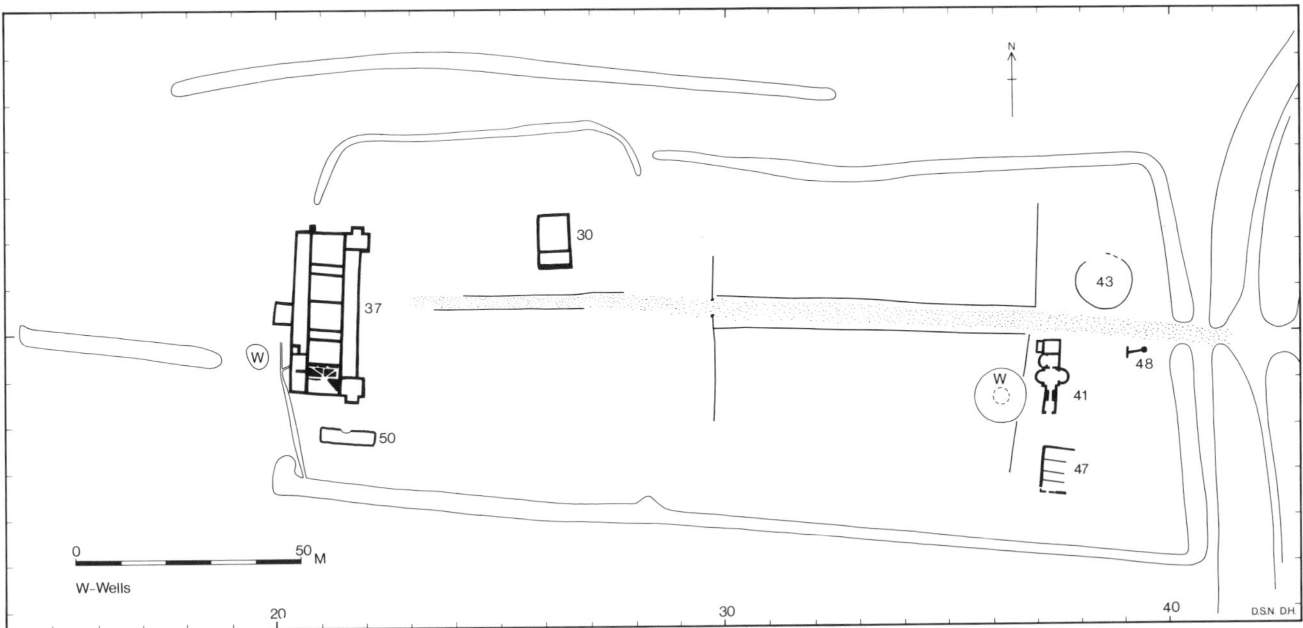

Fig 96 Block plan showing buildings of cAD 250–300, Period 10

Period 10, c AD 250–300 (Fig 96)

There appears to have been renewed occupation from the middle of the third century, when new trackways were put down over the horizons of humic soil. Associated with these levels was a dramatic increase in coin loss. Ratios of later third-century issues to coins of the early third century are frequently high and a similar pattern can be observed at Gadebridge (Neal 1974, fig 52), but when the numbers are compared, 141 to 63, the ratio of loss at Gorhambury is more than double and implies considerably more trading on site. This cannot be explained by the Gorhambury assemblages being a dispersed hoard for they were concentrated in three localities (Fig 1) – south of the villa, Building 37, south of Building 30, and spread about the farmyard in the outer enclosure. This last group can be sub-divided into three: 42 coins in areas 38–3920–21 north of the road, another 33 south of the road east of the bath-house, and a smaller group of 9 coins associated with Building 47, sealing Building 40.

The implication, therefore, is that from the middle of the third century Gorhambury, or at least its farm, was 'reoccupied'. Apart from the restoration of trackways over the humus, this reoccupation also involved the repair of the villa and its bath-suite, and the bath-house. New wells were dug. Building 47, perhaps a stable, was built over Building 40 and a sunken hut, Building 50, constructed south of the villa in area 21–2217; Building 30 was repaired. It is also possible that Buildings 54 and 55 are of this period, but as this is uncertain they have been described under Period 11; Building 38 must have been demolished before Building 55 was constructed.

The enclosures

Apart from restoring trackways across the ditches, no substantial changes were made; slippages of the dyke bank continued to occur and consequently the enclosure ditches continued filling up. The division of the site into two main enclosures was probably retained, since the dividing fence in areas 2918–20 had at least three phases and was utilised as the east wall of Building 54, constructed in either Period 10 or 11.

The buildings

Building 30 (Fig 64)

By the middle of the third century Building 30 was ruinous and its tiled quoins robbed out, the resulting pits becoming filled with brown humic soil which also filled a flint-lined pit (823) cutting the main room. However, the structure was sufficiently sound to merit renovation because the robbing pits, eg 782 and 842, were filled with massive nodules of flint to act as foundations for repairs (Fig 66). In Period 11 the structure had an industrial function and the same possibly applied in Period 10. Two parallel slots (784 and 799) at right-angles to the north wall belong to this phase: they cut a gutter (704) which was now filled up. Their function is not understood but possibly they supported an external staircase rising to a store in the loft space. For further comments relating to features cutting this building see Building 53 (p 79).

Building 37 (Fig 48)

If not ruinous, the villa must have been seriously neglected for, like Building 41 (the bath-house), its well was abandoned and the bath-suite (Rooms

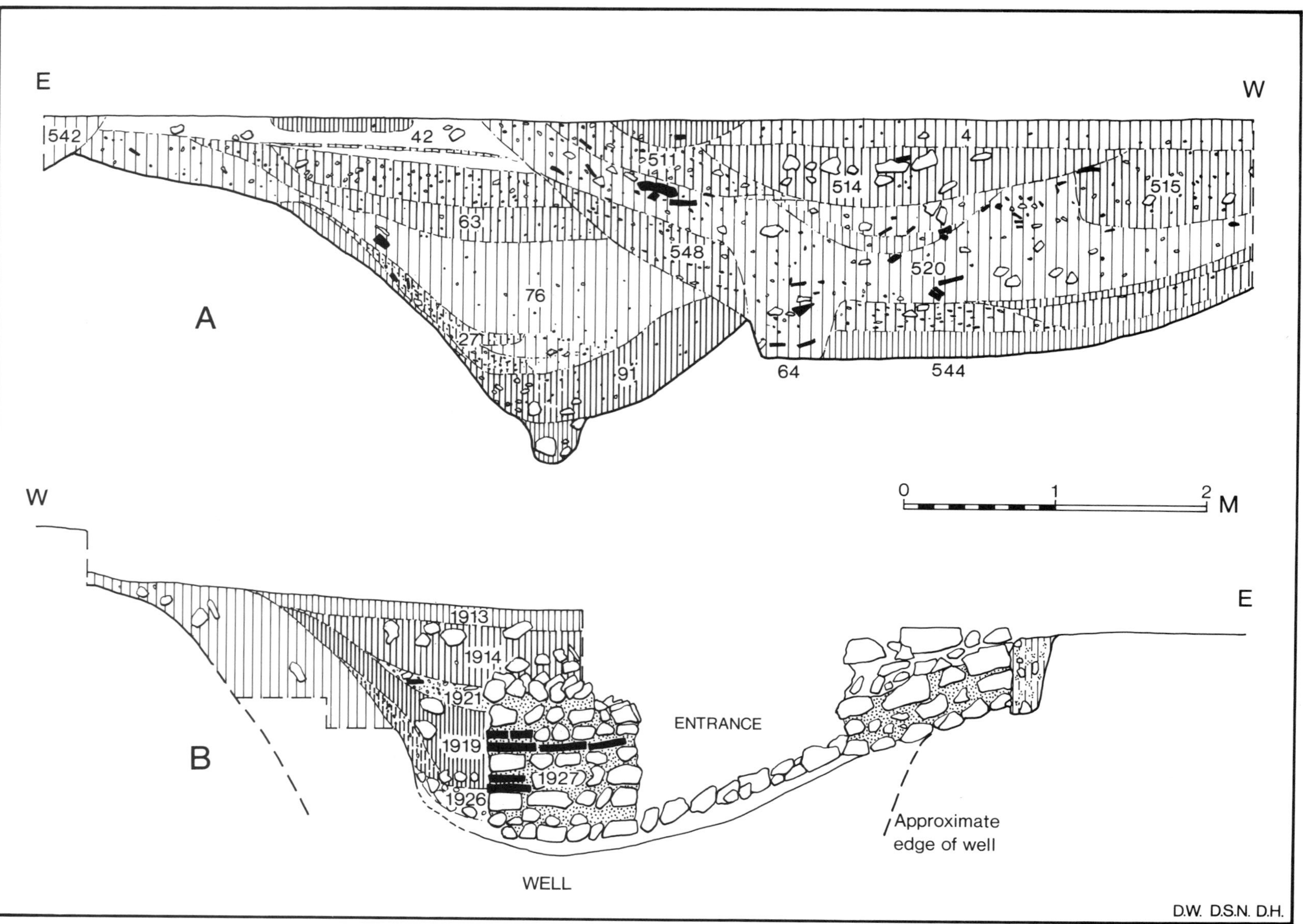

Fig 97 Section A, area 2918, shows the well weathering cone (544) 'cutting' the ditch of the inner enclosure and subsequently cut by drain 64 leading from the bath-suite, Building 37. Section B, area 3718, shows the south praefurnium *wall (1927), Building 41, subsided into the well pit (Scale 1:40)*

10–12) lay in serious disrepair. The bath-suite was rebuilt incorporating considerable quantities of chalk; the earlier *Reihentyp* layout was retained but the *caldarium* (10) was converted to a *praefurnium* and a new stokehole constructed through the dividing wall between the old *caldarium* and the *tepidarium* (Fig 76). On its east side the *praefurnium* also served a stokehole for a new chalk hypocaust (Room 7) with its flues in the plan of a Union Jack: the room is likely to have been primarily a living room but it could have doubled as a *tepidarium*. The *frigidarium* was given a small square plunge-bath with a drain (64) on its west side discharging into a timber-lined gully. This ran south and cut the upper filling of a well (544) situated in area 2018 (section, Fig 97 A). The well contained large numbers of snails including, not surprisingly, species favouring a shaded and overgrown habitat. Of the 978 shells identified from this context 880 were of the species *Discus rotundatus*. However, a small proportion of open habitat species was found, perhaps washed in from surrounding yards. Among the finds was an oyster shell containing haematite and possibly used by a wall painter as a palette. In the bottom of the drain was an unworn coin of Carausius, AD 287–293 (No 210). A new well was dug close by in area 1919 (Fig 1).

The north wall of the villa was reinforced by a substantial buttress to prevent subsidence into the underlying ditch. The buttress sealed the earlier timber-lined gutter. The villa continued to face east.

Building 41, Phase 3 (Figs 85–88)

There is no evidence that the bath-house was also dismantled or robbed for tile in the preceding period. However, the possibility that it was abandoned is suggested by the need to recut its well to the west in area 35–3618 (Figs 1 and 96) and to recut the surrounding drainage gully (1916). The earlier well was deliberately filled-up and its final level of clay cut by a foundation trench for a *praefurnium*, constructed in flint with considerable quantities of chalk. A new furnace was built to the north with a pair of *testudo* supports flanking the flue; later the flue was moved slightly to the east. The earlier *testudo* stand was dismantled, although the *caldarium* was retained. In the south wall of the *praefurnium* (section, Fig 97 B) was an entrance 1.30m wide with the impression and rebate for a wooden cill. The walls flanking the entrance stood one metre high, their preservation being due to their having subsided into the underlying well (Fig 87). The decoration (or lack of it) in the bath-house is of interest mainly because nowhere was there evidence for more than plain red-painted walls and *opus signinum* floors – no mosaic or plain tesserae (although the rectangular plunge-bath (2261) had a tiled pavement). However, of unusual interest were fragments of *opus signinum* from the apsidal plunge-bath floor (2264) of the *caldarium* (Fig 89): it was coated with blue frit – a pleasant relief from an otherwise unimaginative and plain decor, although in harmony with the colour of the windows which had blue glass panes. Fragments of Egyptian blue frit, perhaps used in preparation of pigment, were found in areas 2317, 2318 and 2321.

There was no dating evidence from beneath the structure, since the underlying well remains unexcavated, but in deposits post-dating construction and demolition were coins ranging in date from AD 270–335. In the gully north of the *frigidarium* was a coin of Victorinus (Coin No 107).

Structure 43, Phase 2 (Fig 92)

The cobbled hollow (Structure 43, Phase 1) already described (p 67) was levelled with large flints (2317) and, as with the metalling of the phase 1 feature, the stones again formed an edge on the south-east side indicating that they were set against pre-existing limits. There was little evidence for a boundary, however, except for a spread of clay (2660), which may have been the residue of a retaining wall. Further north a layer of chalk (2328) continued the edge already noted and had a straight south-east side suggesting that it had also been set against an internal division. The function of the structure is uncertain but such heavy metalling would have been an ideal standing for animals. In dark soil over the feature were many coins. Apart from a single issue of Faustina (No 42), 42 of them were of the later third century and 10 of the early fourth century. Their concentration here indicates trading on the spot, with the possibility that stock were kept in the pen and being sold. In support of this is the presence of eight fragments of hipposandals and an ox-goad (No 407, Fig 131). Interpretation of the form of the structure is doubtful: the outer edge of the metalling is not curved but composed of five straight lengths suggesting perhaps that it was polygonal with originally about seven sides. Domestic buildings of similar type have been found at Stanwick, Northamptonshire (Neal, in progress) and Catsgore, Somerset (Leech 1982).

Building 47 (Figs 40 and 41)

Building 47 is located in area 3716–17 and was constructed over the west end of the aisled buildings (Buildings 39 and 40) utilising the existing terrace. Unfortunately the limits of its outer walls are uncertain but its west wall seems to have shared the same position, approximately, as the west end of the earlier barns which had now been removed. Floors associated with the hut sealed two pairs of postholes (Fig 40), Nos 1810, 2090, 1906 and 1890: the last contained a coin of Faustina II, AD 161–80 (No 46). The floors were represented by three distinct regular spreads, the northern one being of chalk and the others clay, each separated by a narrow slot for a partition. The floors did not extend east over the second bay and were laid in the north 'cubicle' over a thick layer of clay (1882), which also sealed the north-west corner of the earlier barn (Section A, Fig 82), including posthole 1810. What function the structure served is doubtful but the size of the 'cubicles', each about 5 by 2m, might suggest it was a stable, 5 by 8m overall, divided into four stalls – assuming the original width of the barn reflects the overall length of the building.

Sealing these horizons was a black occupation deposit (1881) forming a rectangular spread and containing seven radiate coins, none later than issues of Tetricus II. With the absence of early fourth-century issues a later third-century date is likely for the structure. A group of pottery (AV 1–37) would confirm this.

Nevertheless there is evidence for early fourth-century occupation close by since an oven (2024, Fig 40) containing a coin of AD 330–7 (No 270) was found in the general area of the earlier barn and another coin of AD 321 (No 240) was found in a stakehole cutting the filling of feature 2004 further south-east (no other fourth-century issues were found on this part of the site). What these features represent is uncertain; it might be argued that perhaps Building 47 extended further east, incorporating Building 40, and that only the west end of the earlier barn was replaced. However, on the evidence available the oven is unlikely to be related to the buildings under discussion; it is conceivably associated with an unrecorded structure.

Structure 48 (Fig 98)

This lay in area 3919 and was a T-shaped corn-drying oven built in chalk and fragments of oolitic limestone, normally used around Verulamium for decorative mouldings and presumably stripped from Period 8 or Period 9 buildings. Its flue (1951), which cut an earlier lime-slaking pit (1961), was aligned east–west and contained a flanged bowl ((1953) AV 1) and at its extremity the skeletons of a dog and a chicken. A thick deposit of charcoal along the flue was sieved for carbonised grain, which can be divided into the following species: 50.2% *T spelta*, 35.9% *T dicoccum* and 13.7% *T aestivum*.

Structure 49 (Fig 13)

Close to and on the east side of the corn-drying oven just described was another furnace or oven (2358). Its function is not fully understood but it was built into

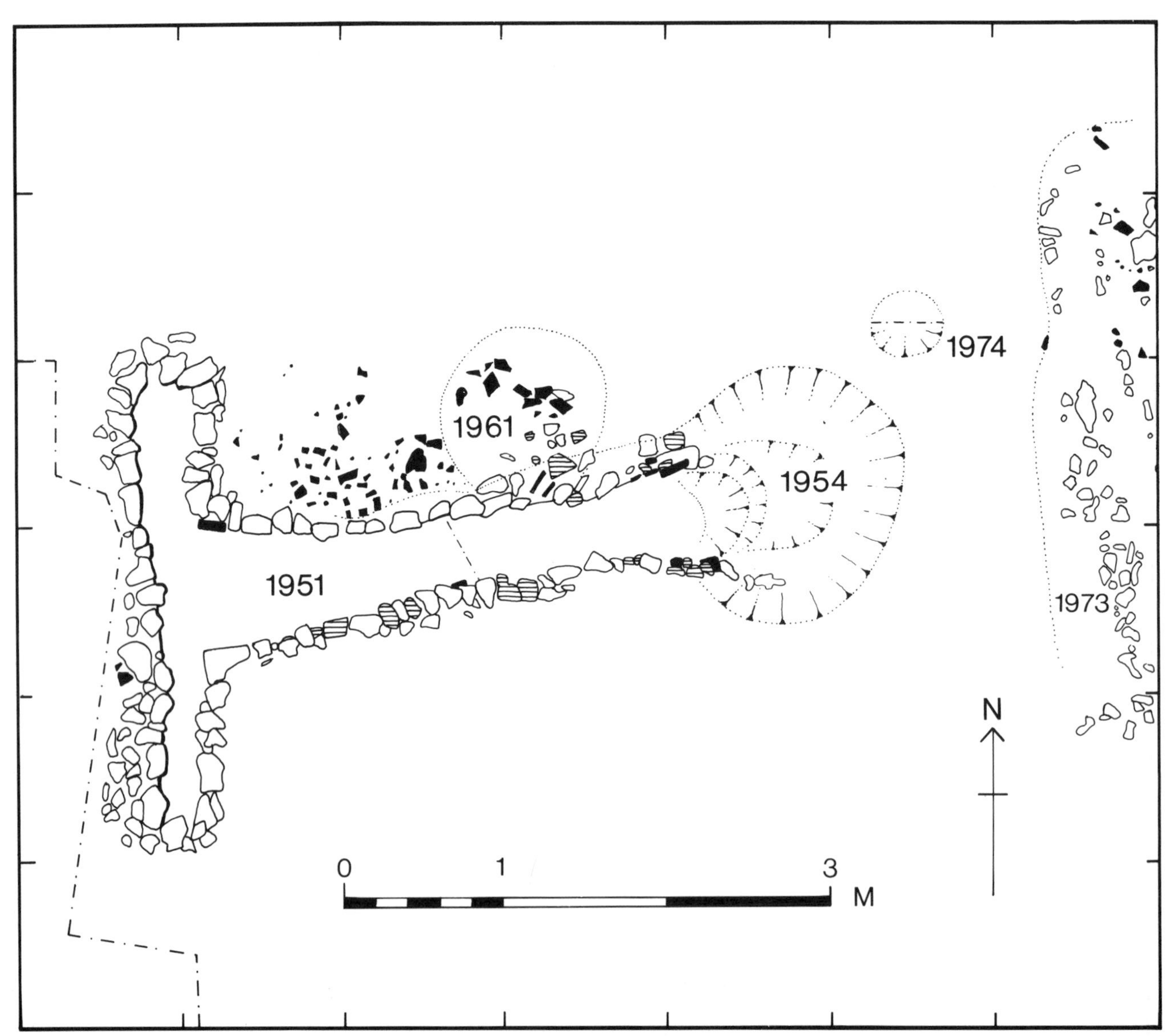

Fig 98 Plan of T-shaped corn drying oven, Structure 48, Period 10 (Scale 1:40)

the vestiges of the bank and the assumed ramp for Structure 35. Its flue was 2.70m long and had a bowl-shaped furnace at the south-east end. It was filled with a chalky 'cob-like' material. This could represent material from the collapsed superstructure but it is possible that it was the remains of lime. If so, the structure may have been a small lime kiln. It contained a body sherd from a small first-century jar; it cut the humic soil extending over much of this part of the site and therefore must belong to either Period 10 or 11.

Building 50 (Fig 99)

This lay south of the main house, area 2117, and comprised a rectangular hollow (492) 12.50 by 3m by 0.35m deep, with a level floor and a short ramp on its north side indicating the position of an entrance (Fig 100). Its south side shared the inner edge of the enclosure bank. No walls were observed but the feature has much in common with a sunken-hut or 'grübenhaus' more commonly associated with the early Saxon period. A possible posthole existed at the east end. In levels (562) on its floor were three irregular radiate coins of *c* AD 270 (Nos 137, 181 and 183) and pottery (AV 1–54) including flanged bowls. Objects comprised an intaglio from a ring (No 1013, Fig 143), a copper alloy hairpin (No 95, Fig 123), an iron saw-blade and a pruning hook (Nos 375, Fig 131 and 418, Fig 132); these suggested that the building was a 'dwelling' rather than merely a byre. Objects of interest from its upper fill included a silver spoon (No 239, Fig 128), a glass pin (No 988, Fig 142) and a spindle whorl (No 1024, Fig 145). It recalls three similar structures dated to the late second century excavated by Dr Stead in 1966 fronting the Silchester Road outside Verulamium (Stead and Rigby 1989). With the lack of associated features interpretation as to its superstructure is speculative, but perhaps it had turf walls which supported a simple thatched, ridged roof. It was abandoned in Period 11 and filled with mixed rubble (495). Sealed beneath the rubble were molluscs indicating a shaded, overgrown habitat. Presumably these entered after the abandonment of the building, but of particular interest are two specimens of *Oxyloma pfeifferi*, a species of permanent wet places, perhaps derived from reeds used for bedding or thatch. At the eastern end of the feature was an area of green cess which produced fly pupae.

Summary of Period 10

Following a period of abandonment, represented by horizons of humic soil, some of the earlier buildings were restored, including the villa (Building 37) and the bath-house (Building 41). Apart from some timber huts and possibly barns no masonry buildings were constructed; it was necessary to sink two new wells. Most of the activity in this period seems to have been centred on the farmyard, where relatively large

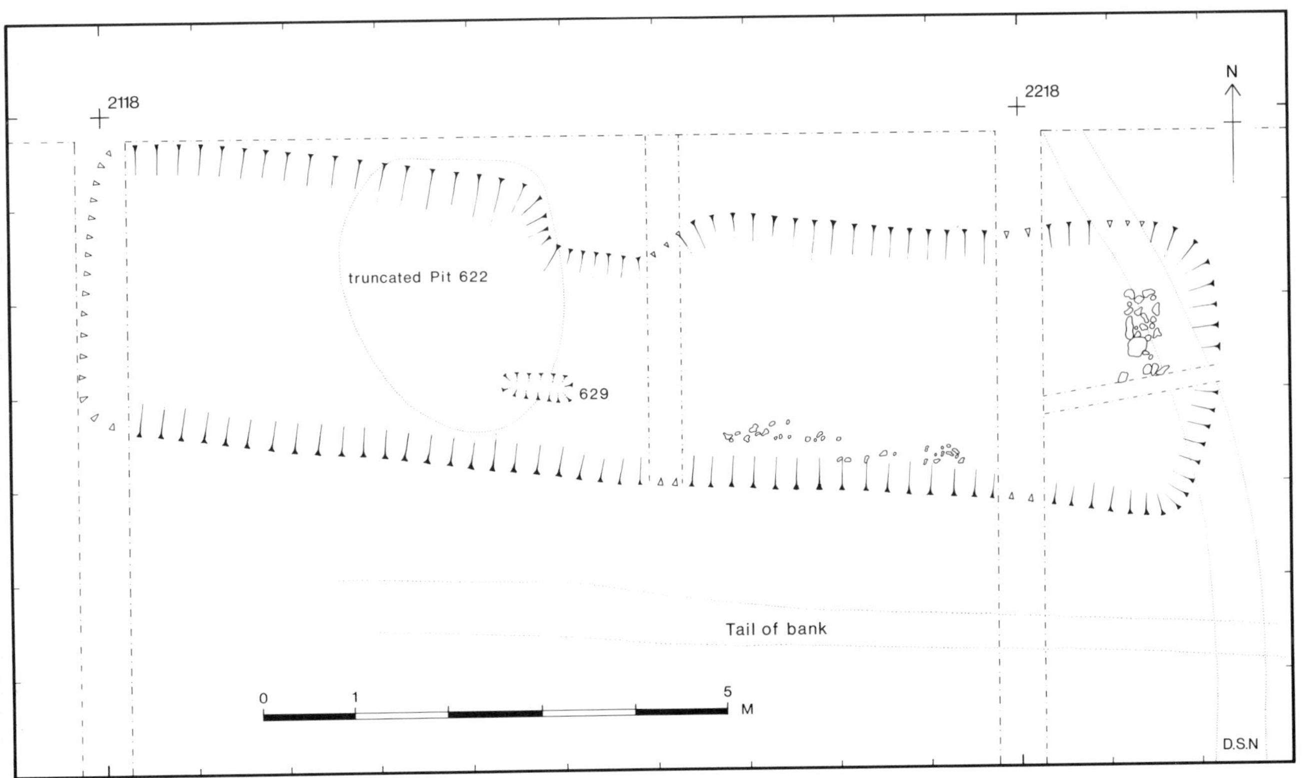

Fig 99 Plan of sunken hut, Building 50, Period 10 (Scale 1:80)

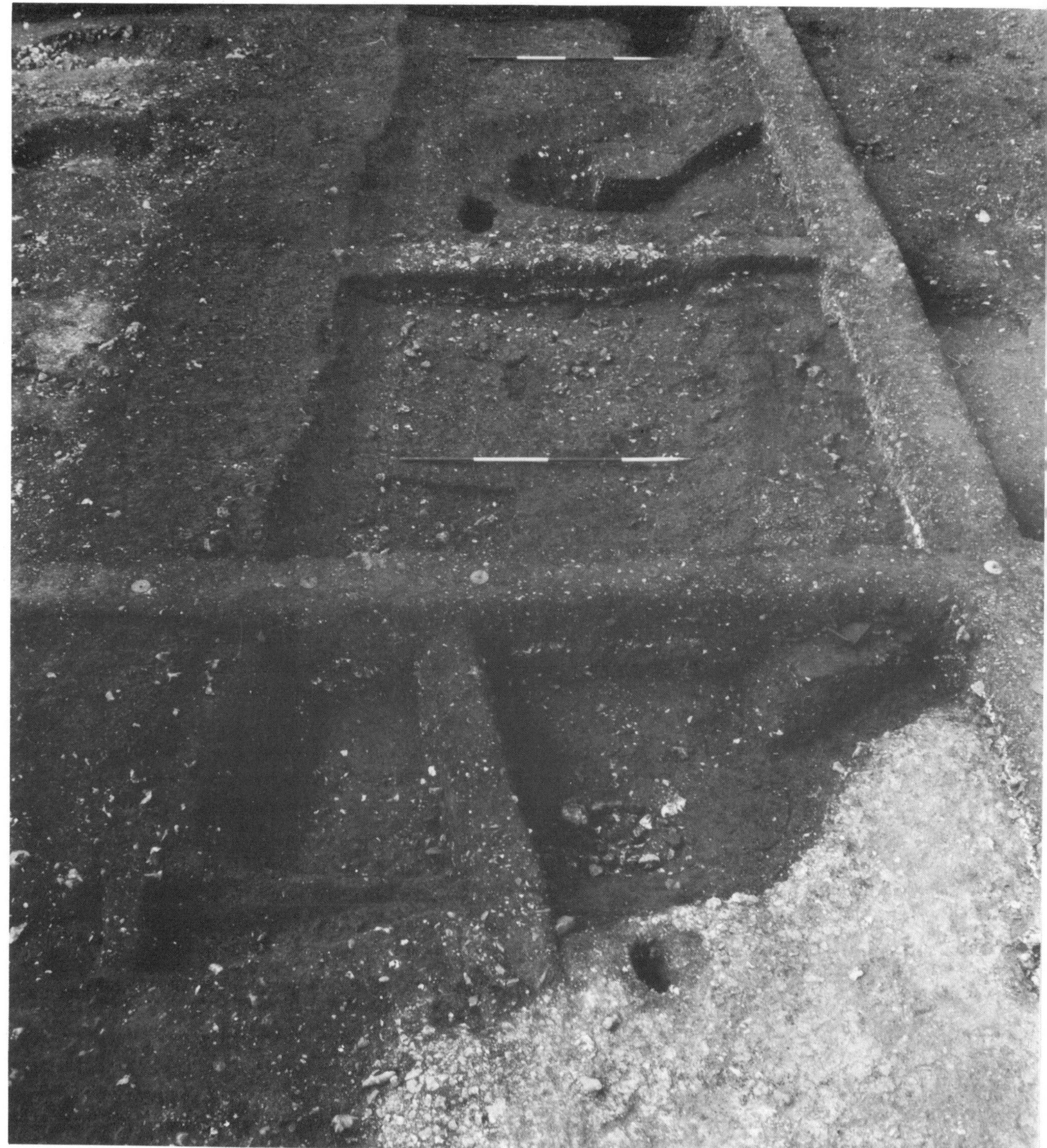

Fig 100 View west of sunken hut, Building 50

numbers of coins were recovered. One group was associated with a small circular (or polygonal) stock pen. The aisled building was removed to make way for a small hut (Building 47) divided into cubicles; it was probably a stable. A structure (Building 50) to the south of the villa had a sunken floor rather like a grübenhaus. Personal items on its floor attest that it was for domestic use although its strange form suggests that it might have been built and occupied by migrant workers.

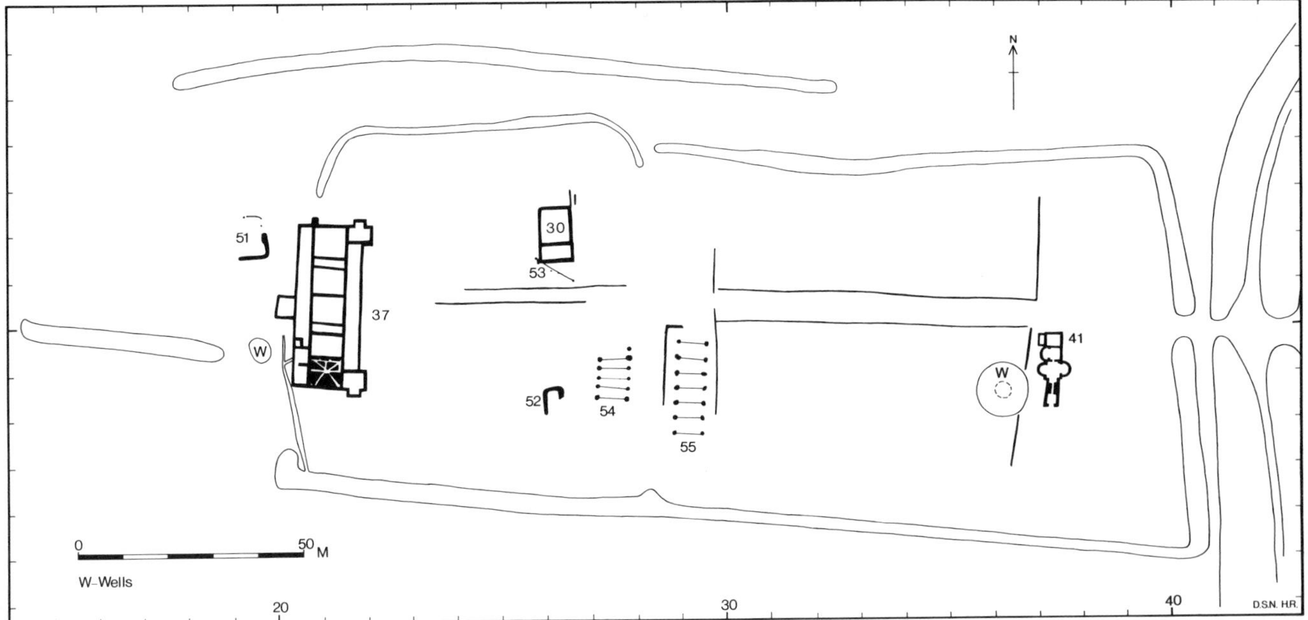

Fig 101 Block plan showing buildings of c *AD 300–350, Period 11*

Period 11, c *AD 300–350* (Fig 101)

On many villa sites these decades, especially the first two, see an enormous increase in activity, with the redevelopment of buildings with mosaics and sometimes, as at Gadebridge Park for example, the provision of grandiose bathing establishments (Neal 1974, 60). However, this revival was not shared by Gorhambury, which saw little reconstruction – indeed from *c* AD 335 there is a real decline. As already stated (p 71) the coin loss for the period, 20.7%, is remarkably small and only 7% more than the combined loss of British and first-century Roman issues. With such a dearth of fourth-century coins their distribution pattern should perhaps be considered with caution, but there is a general scatter over most of the site suggesting that the whole complex was being utilised. It could be argued that the percentage of fourth-century coins recovered to those of earlier periods may not be a true reflection, since not only have the later levels been disturbed by ploughing but the topsoil was removed by machine. Nevertheless the same technique of removing overburden was adopted at Gadebridge, so the figures are likely to be a fairly accurate reflection of loss. The largest concentrations were associated with three new huts, Building 51 (Fig 102), area 1921–22, Building 52 (Fig 62), constructed over the site of the Period 8 bath-house (Building 29) and Building 53 (Fig 64), immediately south of Building 30, area 2621. Two large barns, Building 54 (Fig 103), area 2718, and Building 55 (Fig 69), area 28–2918–19, may also have been constructed in this period, although there is a possibility that they date to the later third century, Period 10. From the evidence of the animal bones, the proportion of cattle increased in the fourth century, and it is possible therefore that ranching rather than mixed farming was being practiced.

The buildings

Building 51 (Fig 102)

Situated in area 1921–22, little of the structure (186) survived the plough except for the very lowest course of mortared chalk and flint footings, set directly onto the clay subsoil without foundation trenches. The footings were lost on the west side but the indications suggested a hut about 9.50m square. Its south-east corner was probably rounded, and perhaps the other corners also. Along its north side were concentrations of tile suggesting ploughed-out post-pads. Associated with it were external mortared floors which stretched towards the villa; they were sealed by destruction rubble (110) containing quantities of fourth-century pottery (AV 1–18) similar to the following forms published from Verulamium: *Ver* (Frere 1972) 1179, AD 310–15; (Frere 1984) 2354, AD 270–400; 2359, AD 270–400; 2472, AD 280–380; 2473, AD 310–400 and 2490, AD 310–50. There was also a coin of Severus Alexander (No 60, AD 222–35); other finds included an intaglio (No 1017, Fig 143) and several bone pins (Nos 936, 938 and 941, Fig 140). On the line of the east wall was a hearth possibly indicating several phases. Huts with rounded corners are unusual in Hertfordshire, but the construction technique has been observed at Stanwick, Northants (Neal, in progress), in the angles of rectangular cottages of fourth-century date. It strengthens the angles of the buildings, and removes the need for quoins.

Building 52 (Fig 62)

The first bath-house (Building 29) was robbed in the Antonine period but its location must have been

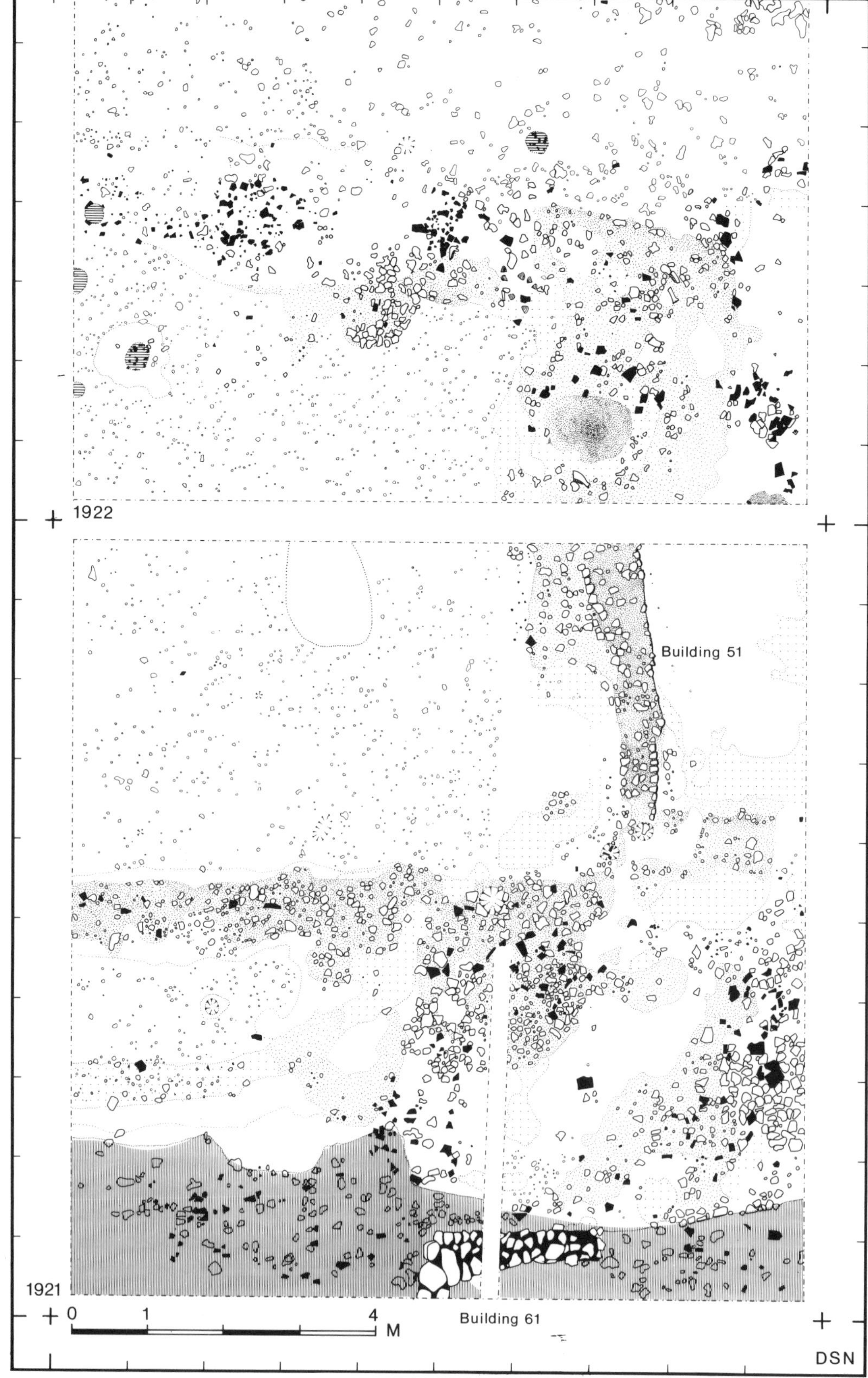

Fig 102 Plan of Building 51 (Period 11) and medieval Structure 61 built over filled-in ramp into medieval quarry pit (Scale 1:80)

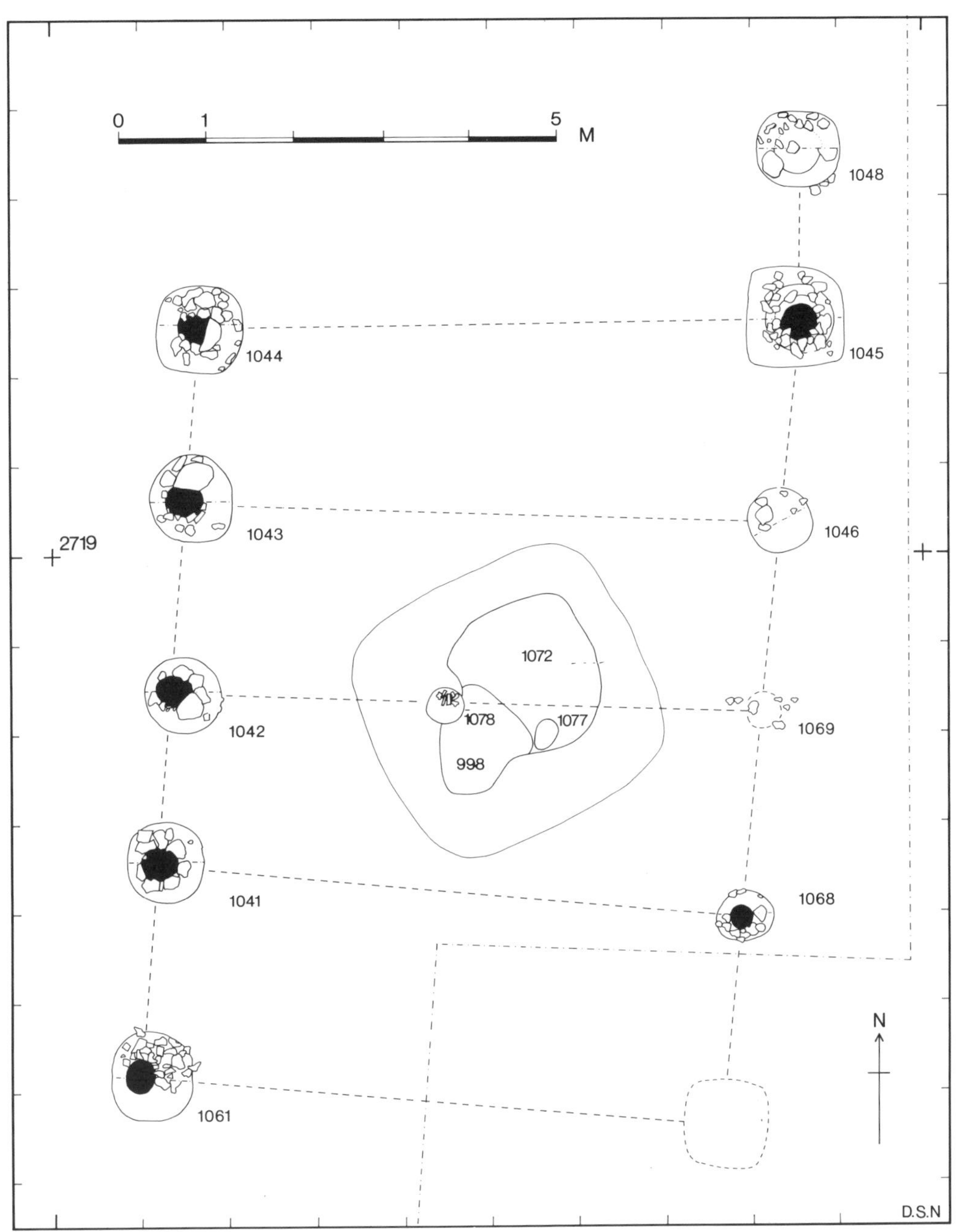

Fig 103 Plan of Building 54, Period 11 (Scale 1:80)

visible as a hollow throughout the third century. Its site was used for a small hut (995), the unmortared flint walls of which (1064, 1065, 1070 and 1276) conform remarkably closely to the sunken area of the earlier *caldarium* and *tepidarium*. It was built upon the rubble filling of the robber trenches and appears to suggest a sub-rectangular structure at least 9m long by about 4m wide. Possibly it was originally of more complex form because sealing the robber trench for the south wall of Building 28 was a layer of chalk (1275) with a kerb of flint on its south side. A spread of smashed tile (1272) to the south possibly indicated the location of a path leading towards the chalk, which may have been a threshold. It sealed a coin of Tetricus (No 131). The stump of another wall (1066), 1.60m long, survived in the north-east corner. Quantities of fourth-century pottery (AV 1–26) were found within a dark occupation level (996) in and around the structure, and included a number of flanged bowls (not common at Gorhambury) such as material published from Verulamium. These include *Ver* (Frere 1984) 2472, AD 280–380; 2475, AD 265–300 and 2486, AD 350–410+. The horizon also contained a coin of AD 341–8 (No 280).

Building 53 (Fig 64)

This was located on the south side of Building 30, area 2520. Little structural evidence for it was found

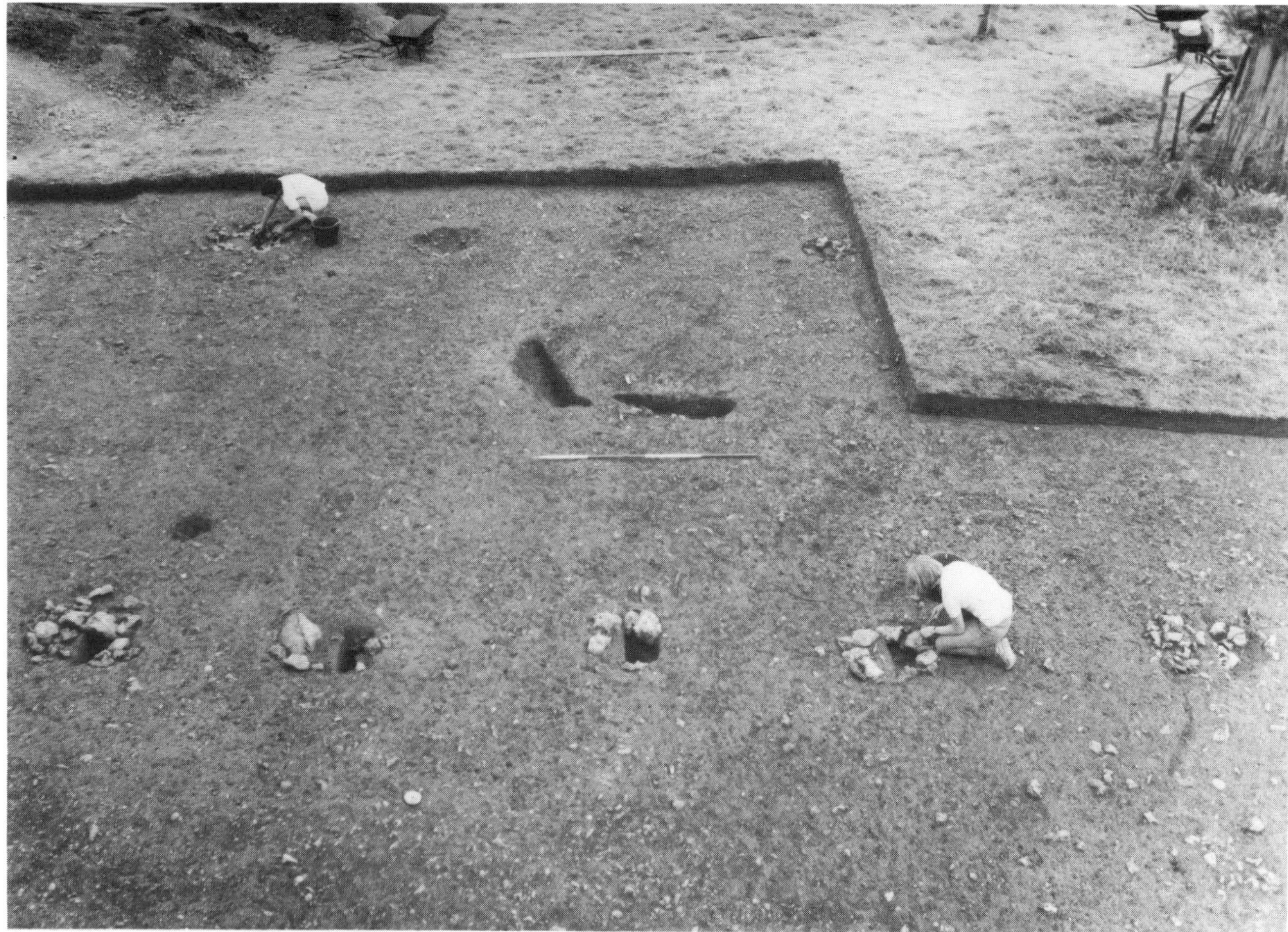

Fig 104 View east of Building 54

except a line of postholes and post-pads including Nos 842 (recut), 800, 846, 821 and 798, diverging from the south-west corner of the earlier building. Another post-pad (822) was found at the east corner of the masonry building; there was no evidence that the masonry building was razed even though other postholes, eg 734, 781 and 793, cut its floors, as did an infant burial (845). However, between the main alignment of postholes and pads and a fence delineating the road a little further south was a spread (721) associated with hundreds of nails and other small fragments of iron and snippets of sheet-bronze, suggesting the presence of a workshop. Of particular interest was the discovery of three weights (Nos 226, 227 and 228, Fig 126), two discs of bronze interpreted as weights (Nos 220, 221, Fig 126), and the arm of an iron balance (No 555, Fig 134). Other discs of identical type (Nos 222 and 223, Fig 126) were also located in Ditch 1281, areas 2822 and 2820. Related to these levels were several hearths, perhaps smithies; two others were also found inside Building 29. Slag was found in a pit cut by posthole 798 and two other fragments from the general spread were residue from the melting-down of bronze. Coins associated with this structure included issues of Gallienus, AD 259–68 (No 74), Maximianus, AD 300–5 (No 223) and a *Providentiae Augg/Caes*, AD 324–330.

Several hundred rim sherds (721, AV 1–218) were also present, many of them from flanged bowls and Nene Valley beakers of early fourth-century date. Of particular interest, but residual, is a quadruple vase or candlestick holder (No 118, Fig 157) in Verulamium region fabric: it is related to the more common form of triple vase eg *Ver* (Frere 1972) 887, dated AD 150–70. From the evidence of coins this occupation may have begun in Period 10 and continued to the middle of the fourth century.

Building 54 (Fig 103)

This occupied the south-east corner of the original inner enclosure, area 2718; it was a barn (1000) 7 by 8.30m overall, represented by five pairs of postholes forming four bays, each about 2m wide centre to centre (Fig 104). Its posts were set into flint-packed postholes but because they were only about 0.30m deep are assumed to have been pads rather than sockets. For this reason the structure is believed to have been pre-fabricated (for reconstruction see Fig 105). No evidence for its cladding was discovered but its very absence indicates that it might have been thatched or perhaps had pegged boarding – no deposits of clay which might have indicated wattle-and-daub infill were found. Inside and pre-dating the barn was a cesspit, and cut into its upper level was a corn-drying oven (998) of oval plan. A 10kg sample of its filling contained 14 grains of wheat and barley (GS

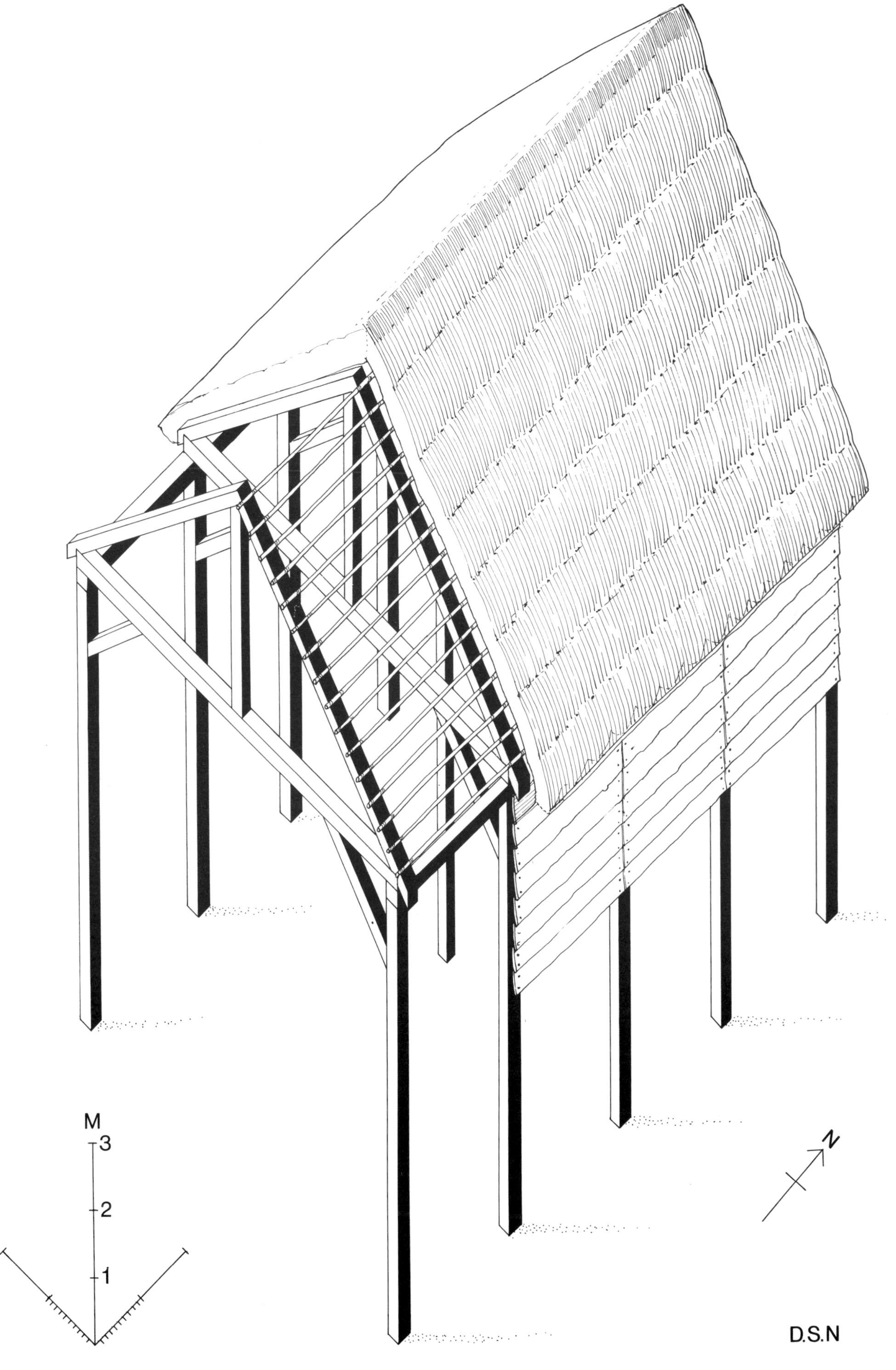

Fig 105 Reconstruction of Building 54

2335). Also in the barn, between posts 1042 and 1069, was a single posthole (1078), possibly to reinforce a tie-beam. Posthole 1042 contained an Irregular Radiate of *c* AD 270 (No 161). Outside the north-east corner was another, single posthole (1048) the purpose of which is doubtful, but possibly it supported an external staircase rising to the loft-space. The possibility that the structure may have formed part of an aisled building prompted the excavators to inspect the area carefully for postholes or other evidence for aisle walls. No evidence for aisles was found nor dating evidence for the period of use of the building.

Building 55 (Fig 69)

This barn was built in the south-west corner of the original outer enclosure, area 28–2918–19, over the site of and with one of its postholes (No 1507) cutting the north wall of Building 38. It was much larger than the barn previously described and had seven pairs of postholes, spaced 3.25m centre to centre. Its overall size is uncertain – on its west side was a slot (1449) for an aisle wall which slightly changed in width and alignment along its length, indicating the emplacement of four horizontal timbers. The slot did not continue along the full length of the building and at the south end stopped adjacent to the penultimate bay. At its north end it turned east for 4m where it stopped, perhaps marking the position of an entrance. It was not found on the other side of the supposed entrance, nor was there a slot on the east side. Instead the 'aisle' here was represented by numerous postholes forming a fence leading south from the road, an alignment repeatedly replaced. Here, too, the fence did not extend the full length of the building but also stopped at the penultimate bay, opposite the end of slot 1449 on the other side of the building.

The aisles were the same width. Why they failed to extend the full length of the barn is uncertain but possibly the barn was of two phases, the first constructed without aisles and later the 'alley' between the barn and the fence roofed over and a corresponding addition placed opposite. If so, perhaps the two southern bays were now abandoned – certainly two phases have been noted elsewhere as postholes 1508 and 1512 were replaced. No internal features were discovered and it is believed to have been a hay barn without provision for accommodation. Like Building 54 the absence of nails and tiles suggests a thatched roof and perhaps pegged or wattle cladding. There was little evidence for dating other than body sherds of Much Hadham oxidised ware in posthole 1514.

Summary of Period 11

Period 11 continues to see a general rundown of the site and unlike many villas there is no early fourth-century revival. The only major rebuilding comprised the construction of two barns (Buildings 54 and 55) both of which occupied the inner enclosure close to the villa. It appears therefore that this part of the site was incorporated into the farm, as is also suggested by the construction of a hut (Building 53) where industrial work was carried out.

Conclusion

Reasons for the complete failure of the villa in the middle of the fourth century, together with other sites in the region, are considered in the Discussion (p 89) and it is sufficient to state here that from the third century we see a steady decline. A drop in activity *c* AD 335 is suggested by the coin evidence and from then on some sort of presence at the site is represented by only a few coins. Groups of pottery of this period are equally sparse and we must assume that the villa as a luxury home was abandoned, although it is likely that the farm estate remained operational but administered from elsewhere, conceivably from within the town. Unfortunately there is no evidence for Saxon occupation and it is not until the medieval period that the site was reöccupied.

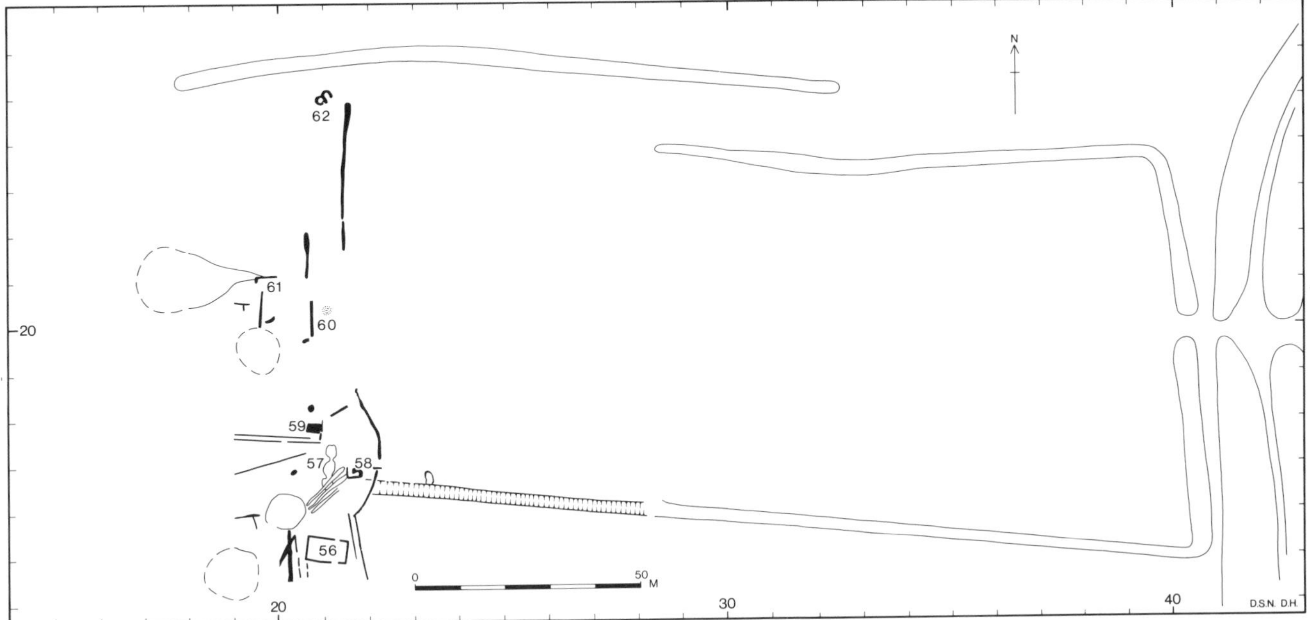

Fig 106 Block plan showing medieval features, Period 12

The medieval period (Fig 106)

Period 12

The medieval occupation is probably associated with a croft and is unlikely to be the early manor of Abbot Geoffrey de Gorham, built about 1130, which perhaps lies just to the north-west of Bacon's House (Fig 6) where a moated enclosure has been observed on aerial photographs (AP 3199 RP CPE/UK/1779, 10/10/46). Why the Roman site should have been utilised is uncertain but two factors are relevant. The original enclosures, now formed into one, were still a prominent feature and could have been a useful ready-made enclosure for stock; it was probably hedged. Secondly, the villa provided a quarry for building materials and it is possible that part of the ruin of Building 37 (Fig 48) was incorporated into the new complex (see p 86).

Occupation was concentrated exclusively to the west side of the site; preservation over the villa itself was poor, but to the south where associated levels were protected by the enclosure bank preservation was good. Horizons over the ditch in area 2016–17 indicated two distinct levels associated with two groups of pottery. In the earliest (549) shelly wares (Nos 119 and 120, Fig 158) of the Bedfordshire area were represented, together with local reduced grey wares (Nos 121–130) while the later levels (eg 501) produced reduced grey wares only. With the presence of two horizons, two periods might possibly be postulated – the first starting in the late eleventh or early twelfth century and the second extending into the early fourteenth. A few locally-made glazed jugs of this period are also present but there is a dearth of products from the Surrey kilns. Had occupation continued into the fifteenth century Surrey wares might be expected. There are no post-medieval ceramics.

However, although the pottery evidence might indicate two periods, the individual buildings and structures cannot be subdivided easily into phases even though, in places, gully cuts gully and walls are built over infilled medieval quarries. Unfortunately our knowledge of what was happening on the site at this period is not sufficiently broad to reconstruct a reliable chronological framework of development as presented for the Roman periods. Consequently developments of this date are presented on a single overall plan; buildings and structures are described briefly as for the earlier periods.

The evidence of mollusca indicates a disturbed open habitat, perhaps with patches of undergrowth, hedgerow and long grasses. Three specimens of *Clausilia bidentata*, which prefer a wooded habitat, were found but these could have arrived in firewood.

The enclosures (Fig 106)

The area of the two enclosures was probably a single field, perhaps delineated by a hedged bank and with the Roman ditches visible as shallow hollows; only on the south side was one of these recut (1264) in areas 21–2716 (Archive plan 200). Medieval occupation is confined to the west side of a palisade trench (234) running north–south, located in areas 2121–24. It divided the enclosure into two with its north end meeting the Roman bank; it cut the northern room of the villa, Building 37, but was not found elsewhere over the main block of the villa, possibly because it had been removed by earlier excavations. However, it

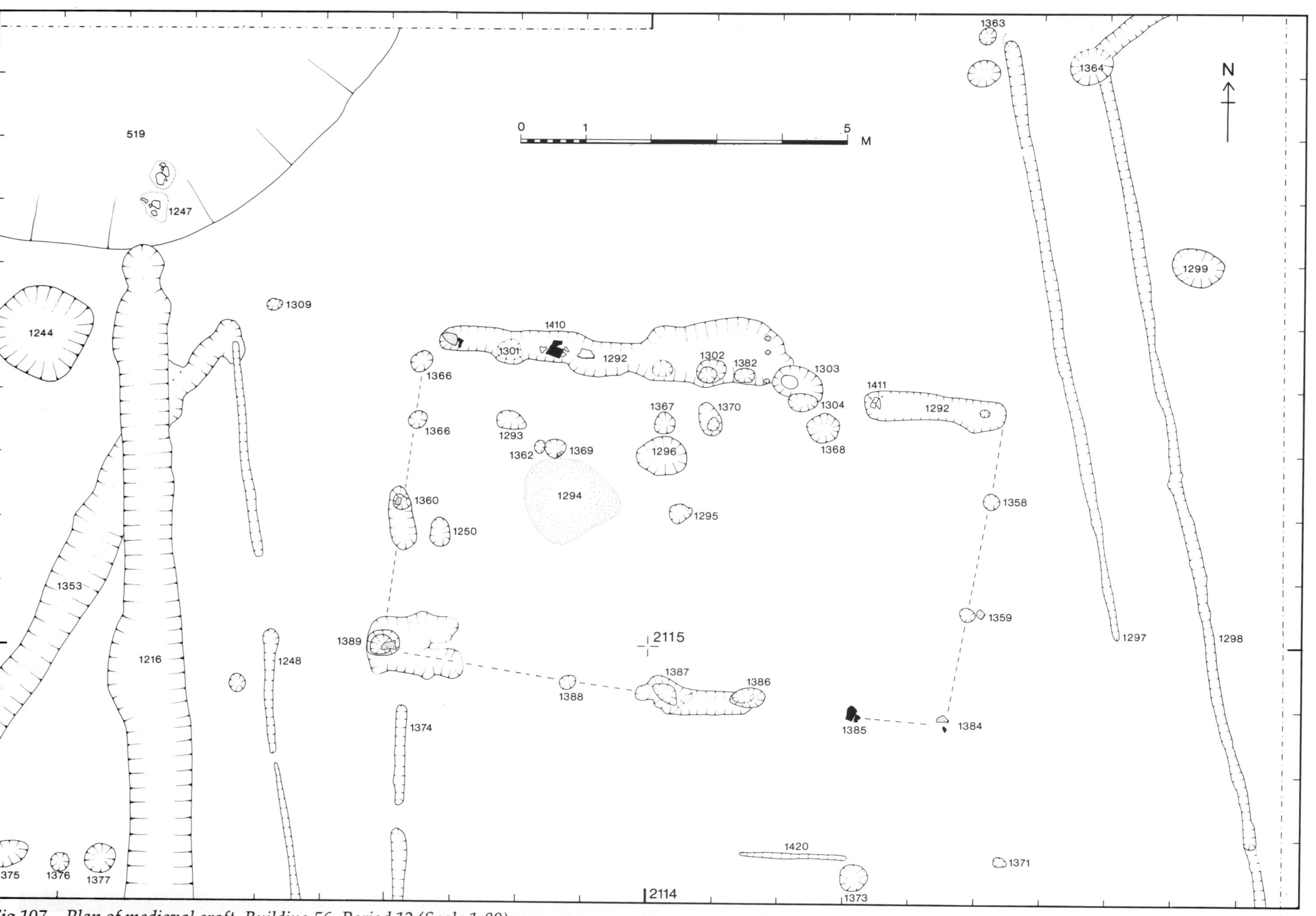

Fig 107 Plan of medieval croft, Building 56, Period 12 (Scale 1:80)

cut the southern wing-room (Room 14, Fig 48), from which point it curved eastwards in a broad semi-circular sweep before re-establishing its earlier alignment (1298) in area 2115. Mid-way along the curve, in area 2217, was a gap indicating the position of an entrance. The location of this palisade, over the ditch, might suggest that the Roman boundaries were abandoned, but the recutting of the ditch and the presence of two fences (573 and 574, Fig 111) in areas 19–2017, following the alignment of the enclosure bank, would refute this. The east boundary of the enclosure was probably the dyke since it remains a prominent boundary today.

The buildings

Building 56 (Fig 107)

This was a small croft (1306) in area 20–2115 (Fig 108) and was of post construction, with the posts on the northern side set in a shallow U-shaped trench interrupted towards the east by an entrance opposite another through the south wall. The two entrances mark the position of a cross-passage separating two rooms, that to the west having a central hearth (1294). To the west was a gully (1216) draining a pond-like hollow (519). In the pond, if such it was, were a number of vessels in local reduced wares (Nos 158–170, Fig 158). It cut another earlier gully (1353) at the north end of which, running south, was a palisade slot (1248) forming an alleyway between it and the building. Another palisade ran south from the south-west corner of the building and terminated at the same line as palisade 1248 opposite. However, this termination was probably the result of plough damage rather than intent. On the east side of the croft the palisade (1298) running south from the villa also terminated; again plough damage was the probable cause. Between it and the building was another palisade which was either a replacement or formed part of a single droveway facilitating the separation of sheep. The palisades are assumed to be contemporary with the croft, although this could not be demonstrated stratigraphically.

Structure 57 (Fig 109)

Located in areas 2116–17, this was a lime-kiln (1340) constructed into the slope of the Roman enclosure bank. It had three connecting chambers probably representing two phases: in the first the central oval chamber was probably the furnace, with the south chamber the stoking-pit. In a later phase a new

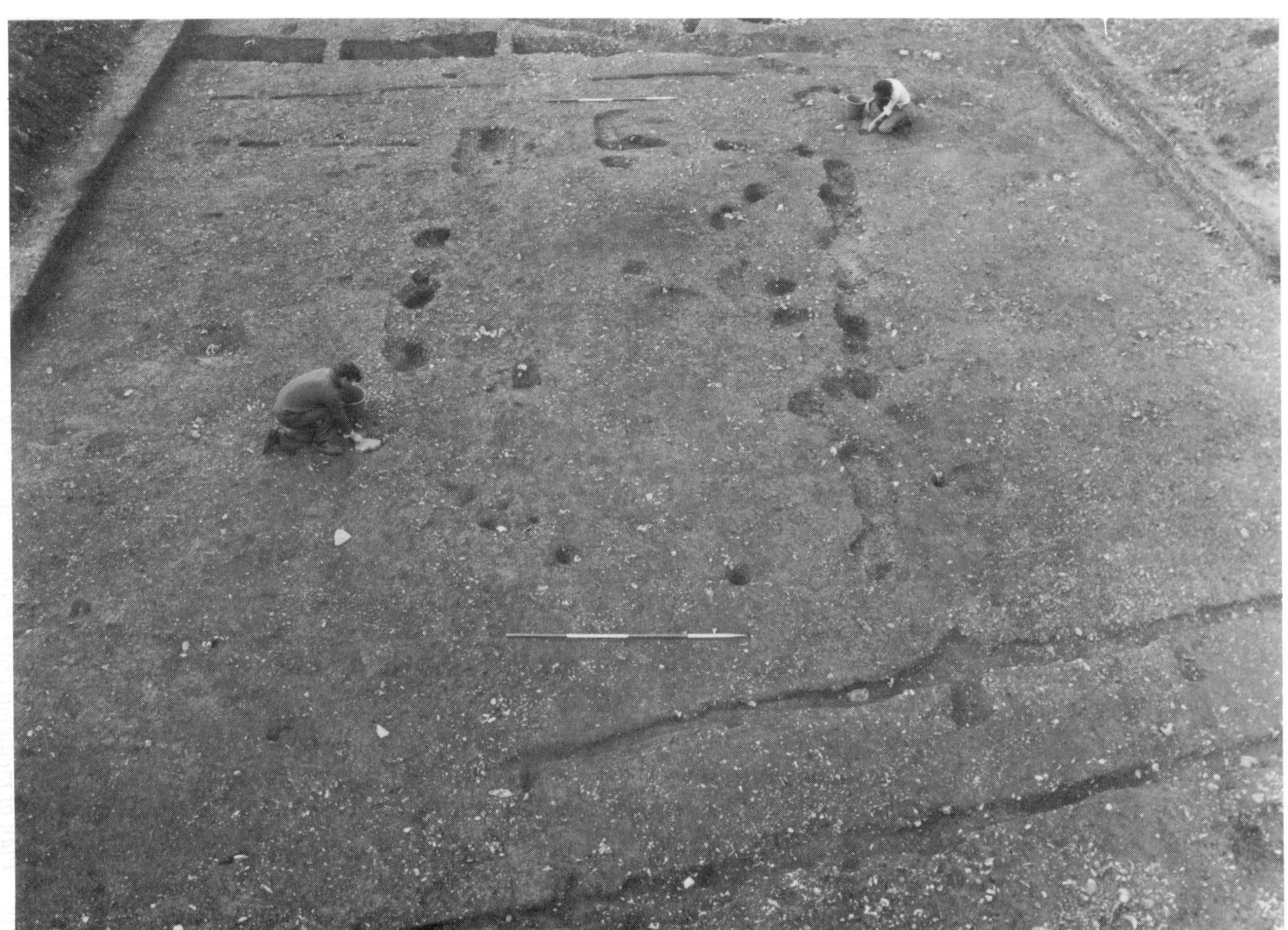

Fig 108 View east showing medieval croft, Building 56, under excavation

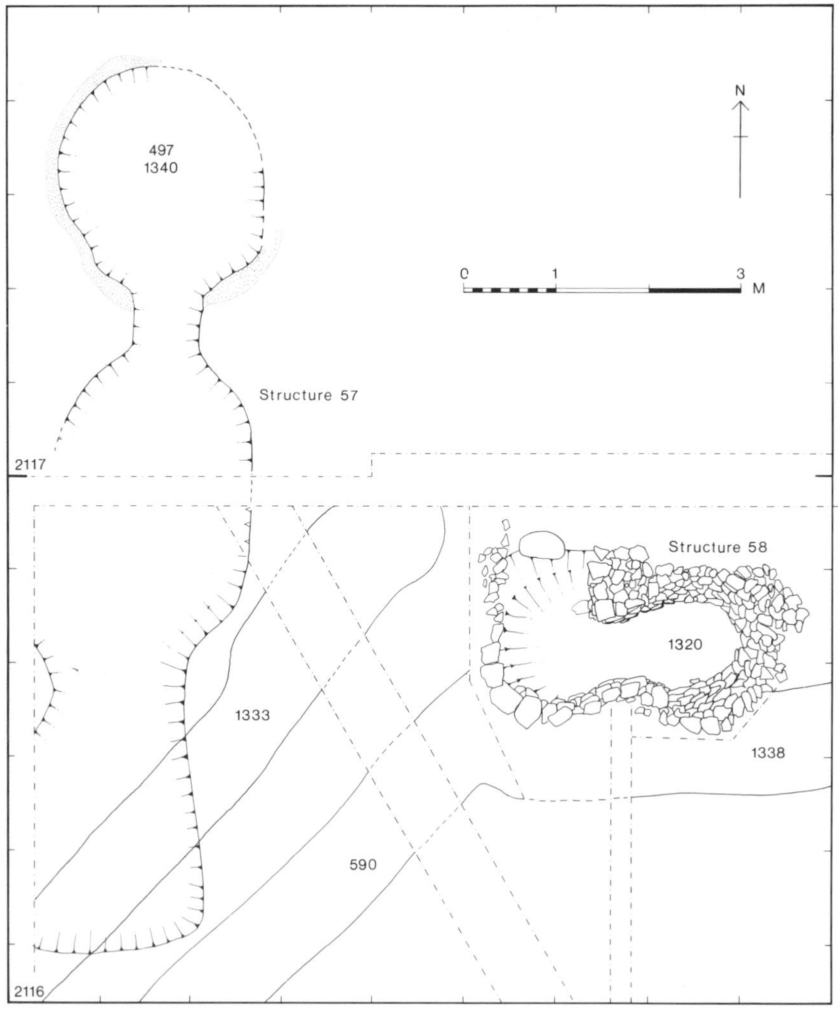

Fig 109 Plan of lime kiln, Structure 57 (497), and malting oven, Structure 58 (1320), Period 2 (Scale 1:80)

furnace was cut to the north and the old furnace utilised as a firing chamber. A thick deposit of lime covered the north chamber, supporting its interpretation as a kiln. Pottery in the filling included sherds of Hertfordshire grey ware.

Structure 58 (Fig 109)

This was situated 3m east of the previous structure and was a malting oven (1320) (Fig 110) constructed in large flints and also built into the slope of the enclosure bank with its walls, 0.80m high, lining the sides of a pit. Its mouth, situated on the north side at the bottom of a steep ramp, was built of flints in orthostatic setting and had been intensely burnt. A 6kg sample of charcoal (1331) in the bottom of the feature produced several hundred grains of barley. Hertfordshire reduced wares were found in its filling (1322) including Nos 144–157, Fig 158.

Structure 59 (Fig 111)

This comprised a rectangular area, 2.20 by 3.30m overall, of rammed cob and flint surrounded by a flint kerb. Along its east side was a narrow slot with numerous stakeholes, and along its south side, 2m away, another two palisades (573 and 574) the northern of which (574) is probably contemporary with the structure. Its south side also perpetuated the alignment of the bank. Built into the feature was a glass linen smoother (No 1006, Fig 142). The function of the structure is uncertain but it was possibly a hard-standing for a hay or wood stack – it is perhaps too wide for a staircase and in any event there was no evidence around it for a house.

Building 60 (Fig 48)

Building 60 was the remains of a wall (55) built upon and slightly diagonal to the west wall of Room 4, Building 37, areas 2019–20. On the floor of the room, to the east, was a hearth (56) associated with Hertfordshire reduced wares. One stump of wall does not make a building, but the impression gained was the possibility that part of the villa wall here remained standing into the medieval period and that it was utilised for the construction of a house or hut – hence the medieval hearth. Another, curved, stump of wall (11) cut the *frigidarium* of the bath-suite (Room 12)

Fig 110 View north showing malting oven, Structure 58

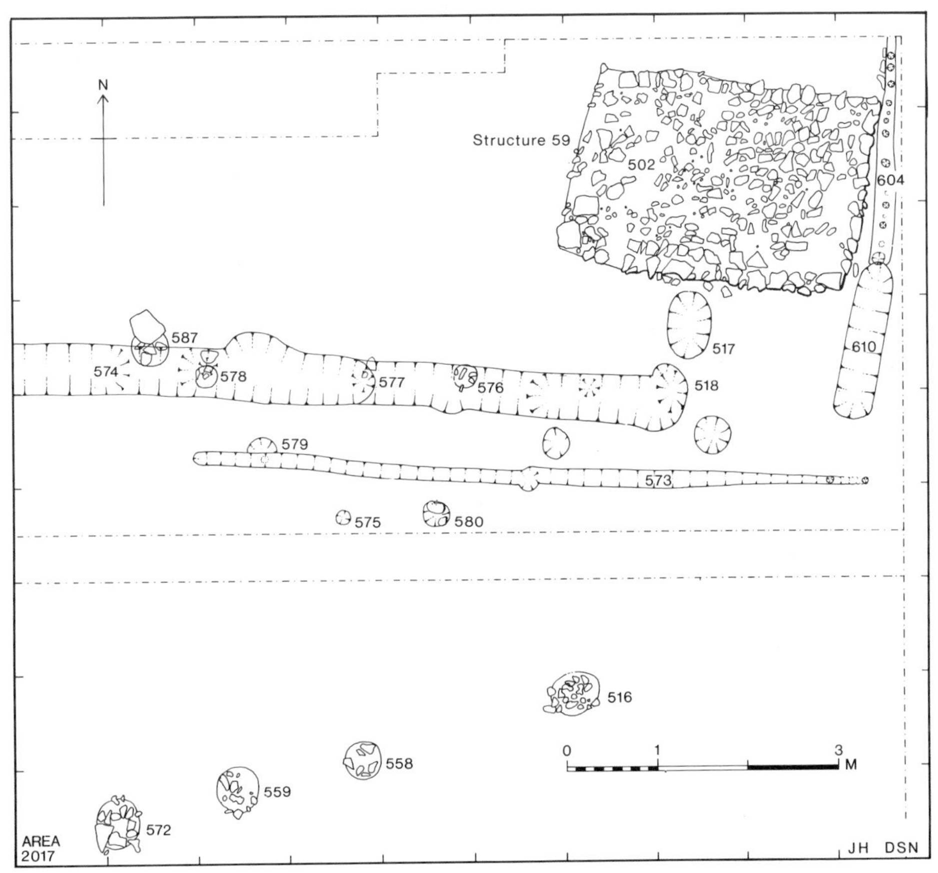

Fig 111 Plan of Structure 59, Period 12 (Scale 1:80)

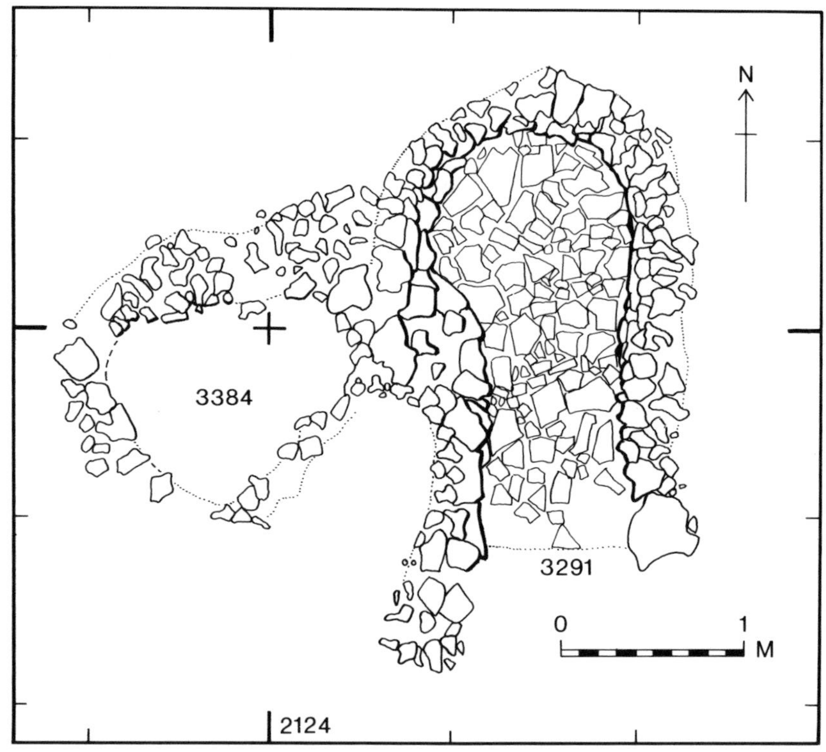

Fig 112 Plan of malting oven, Structure 62, Period 12 (Scale 1:40)

and contained in its rubble fragments of Purbeck Marble veneer, perhaps stripped from the Roman buildings. Postholes with tile packing also cut the outer west corridor wall: they are assumed to be of medieval date.

Building 61 (Figs 102 and 106)

In areas 18–1920–21 was a large quarry pit connected to the surface by a ramp (159) running east–west and containing sherds from three vessels in Hertfordshire grey ware of thirteenth–fourteenth century date. It was levelled in the medieval period and its ramp sealed by an L-shaped wall, probably the north-west angle of a building. To the south were fragments of palisade trenches orientated north–south and east–west, but their relationship to the feature under discussion was not established.

Another large quarry pit was also located to the west of the site in area 12–1322 (Fig 1, Archive section 418). It contained fairly large quantities of medieval pottery, which suggested the presence of further buildings, but ploughing is likely to have destroyed all traces of them.

Structure 62 (Fig 112)

This was a large bread or malting oven of two phases situated in area 2124–23. In the first phase (3384) it was constructed in flint and chalk and orientated east–west with the stokehole on the east side. When it was rebuilt (3291) it was re-orientated north–south with the stokehole at the south end. It measured 1.70 by 3m overall and was also constructed in flint bonded with chalk; it had a tile floor made from re-used Roman material. As with the ovens further south it was built into the south side of the enclosure bank which even here must have been a prominent earthwork in the medieval period. There is no dating evidence for this structure, but a medieval date is likely.

Summary of Period 12

Regrettably, the medieval complex is too nebulous for worthwhile discussion and interpretation. However, it does suggest the presence of a medium-sized farm associated with a croft on the south side, and buildings and a stock enclosure over the site of the villa. Its presence demonstrates a new settlement on the site after some 500 years, since there is no evidence for post-Roman or Saxon occupation. The probability of the late Saxon manor being located close to Nicholas Bacon's house of 1563–8 has already been noted (p 83). The continual change of settlement pattern at Gorhambury, however, is demonstrated by the gradual decline of Bacon's house and the construction of the present Gorhambury House 400m east of Bacon's house and the same distance west of the villa complex, between 1777 and 1784. It was designed by the architect Sir Robert Taylor. Further changes in 1826 saw demolition of the south range, built between 1788 and 1790. Meanwhile the ruins of Bacon's house remain standing, a memorial to the longevity of many great estates (see Rogers 1933).

General discussion

by David S Neal and Jonathan Hunn

Pattern of settlement and communications (Fig 2)

More Roman villas have been examined, though only partially, within the orbit of Verulamium than any other Roman town in Britain. The extent of this work allows us to suggest a general picture of the development of the countryside, and to relate it to the economic fortunes of Verulamium. Other villas excavated include Lockleys (Ward-Perkins 1938) and Dicket Mead (Selkirk 1971) on the River Mimram; Park Street (O'Neil 1945; Saunders 1961), Netherwilde (Neal 1976, fig LXIX) and Munden (*VCH Herts*, **4**, 165; Anthony 1960, 7) on the Rivers Ver and Colne; Gadebridge Park (Neal 1974) and Kings Langley (Wardle 1982) on the River Gade; and Boxmoor (Evans 1853; Neal 1976) and Northchurch (Neal ibid) on the River Bulbourne. Further west in the Chilterns other villas excavated include Latimer (Branigan 1971) and Sarrat (*VCH Herts*, **4**, 163) on the River Chess, and High Wycombe (Hartley 1959) on the River Wye. Numerous other sites (Branigan 1967) have also been explored but only superficially and these will not be included in the discussion; however their locations serve to emphasise the settlement pattern along the river valleys and their regular distribution. For example 1½ miles (2 km) divides Gadebridge Park from Boxmoor, and about the same distance separates Boxmoor from Kings Langley and other sites north-west along the Bulbourne. As Branigan has pointed out (Branigan 1967, 132) the distance between villas further west in the Chilterns is greater, nearer 2–2½ miles (3–3½ km). The nearest villa to Gorhambury is Childwickbury – an unexcavated site on the opposite side of the valley 1½m (2 km) away and the same distance from the town.

East of Verulamium the distribution of villas contrasts markedly; there is a dearth of villas until Lockleys/Dicket Mead on the River Mimram, a distance of 7½ miles (12 km); curiously, none is known along the River Lee. The reason for this could be the presence of slightly more sandy, marginal soil in this area, but it is possible that the area up to the Lee was included in the *territorium* of the Roman city and devoid of private villas, analogous for example to the situation around both London and Canterbury (Wacher, 1974, 193). Elsewhere some cantonal capitals, such as Leicester and Cirencester, have villas close to the town, but Verulamium is unique, so far, in that it has two.

South of Verulamium the Park Street, Netherwilde and Munden villas all lie close to Watling Street although, apart from Childwickbury and Gorhambury, there are no known villas along Watling Street north of Verulamium. Again the reasons are not understood but a temple-site at Friars Wash near Redbourn may have had land holdings stretching south towards Verulamium and the estate boundaries of Gorhambury and Childwickbury. The same situation possibly also applied to the north-west. In this direction the next known site to Gorhambury is the temple-mausoleum complex at Wood Lane End (Neal 1983; 1984), which may also have had land holdings meeting the Gorhambury villa boundary.

Pre-conquest farmsteads

Two villas, Lockleys (Ward Perkins 1938) and Park Street (O'Neil 1945), have long been regarded as type sites where the transition from native farm to villa could be demonstrated. In her classic report Mrs O'Neil described how the Park Street villa began with several simple pre-conquest rectilinear huts which were probably destroyed at the time of the Boudiccan rebellion. By *c* AD 100 the main house was rebuilt in masonry. As with so many rescue excavations the work was hurried, in advance of an approaching gravel quarry, and although the main house and its forerunners were excavated, the overall plan remained enigmatic. The excavation of a bath-house and two other buildings at Park Street between 1954 and 1957 (Saunders 1963) helped to complete the picture, but served further to highlight the size of villas in general and the dispersed character of the Park Street villa in particular. However, there are elements of the overall plan (Fig 113) which might suggest that its layout was established in the pre-conquest period and that its later plan was dictated by the presence of earlier buildings and their function. We have seen at Gorhambury how the same site was repeatedly used for the main house and many of the farm buildings, particularly the aisled building, whereas logically it may seem easier to have rebuilt on a clear site. Possibly tradition was an element in the layout and retention of house sites, but separate areas may have had specific functions and status, and perhaps the radical notion to remodel and place the villa on areas originally occupied by workers' buildings, or vice versa, could have been socially unacceptable.

The relationship of the Gorhambury aisled building to the villa finds parallels in villas and aisled buildings on numerous other sites, as far afield as Winterton, South Humberside (Stead 1976, 82, fig 42) and Sparsholt, Hants (Johnston 1972, 16). The isolation of such aisled buildings from the main houses implies a clear social and functional distinction. Initially they were primarily agricultural buildings with provision for workers, but by the fourth century some had developed an increasingly residential role, incorporating bath-suites and mosaics – Rooms 3 and 5, Building D from Winterton, for example (Stead 1976, fig 22) – while at the same time allowing provision under the same roof for stock or other agricultural activities.

The provision of rooms and bath-suites within aisled buildings reflects a fundamental change in the way of life, and perhaps status, of their occupants. However, at Gorhambury there is no evidence that the lifestyle changed, as is evident from the architectural uniformity of the various rebuilds and the lack of private rooms. Nor was any attempt made to embellish the building by adding a facade with

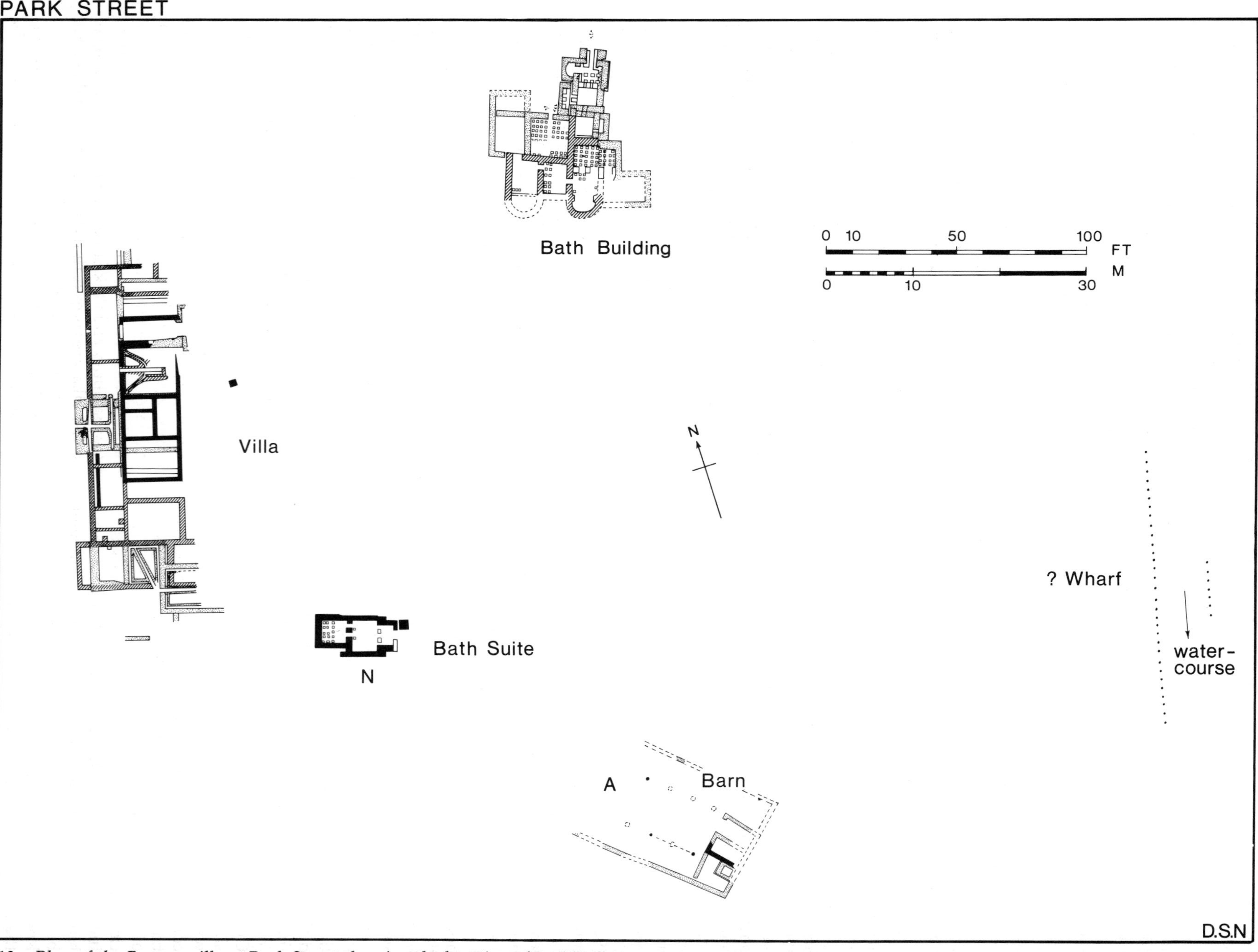

Fig 113 Plan of the Roman villa at Park Street showing the location of Building A

corner projections such as at Stroud, Hants (Smith 1963, 5), and numerous other sites. Had the Gorhambury villa survived as a luxury house into the fourth century, perhaps the situation would have been different.

It had been generally assumed that the introduction of aisled farmhouses took place in the Roman period (Smith 1963, 24) and that their main concentrations are to be found in Hampshire and Lincolnshire. Aisled houses have not previously been recognised in Hertfordshire and therefore to find a particularly early building complex with five periods prior to the early third century was surprising. It is paralleled within Verulamium however by the discovery of an early barn below Insula XVII (Frere 1983, 105). At Gorhambury the excavation was on a scale unprecedented for a villa in the south of England and it would occasion no surprise to the writers if examples were discovered on other sites, perhaps remote from the main house, or beneath aisled buildings previously believed to be of third or fourth century date. (For further discussion on aisled buildings see Hadman 1978.)

There may have been one such building at Park Street. Building A discovered in 1954–7 (Saunders 1967, 112) was of uncertain plan and function. About 3m north of the surviving south wall were two large postholes, with an isolated posthole further north and lying about the same distance south of a stump of masonry possibly marking the line of the north wall of the building. Reinterpretation of its plan (Fig 113) might suggest that the building was a barn or aisled hall 13m wide and that the postholes belonged to three pairs of aisle-posts. The excavator concluded (Saunders 1967, 121) that the structure may have been intended for farm workers and that the later insertion of two small baths at the east end was for their use. At least two phases are indicated by this reconstruction, but the discovery of native pottery and a coin of Tasciovanus in levels beneath the building serves further to emphasise the possible longevity of the house site. The provision of a bath, independent of the main bath-house on the opposite side of the yard, highlights the social division within the complex – a subject we shall return to later.

The Park Street excavation provided more information on buildings of the late Iron Age in Hertfordshire than Wheeler's excavations in Prae Wood, where the difficult clay subsoil obscured structures hinted at by the presence of hearths and domestic ovens. Parallels for the Park Street huts were located at Skeleton Green, Braughing, in 1971 (Partridge 1981) when eight single-roomed huts, one with an annexe, associated with a wealth of pre-conquest finds and linked by cobbled pathways, were discovered. However, essentially it was an 'urban' site and, although the nature of the artefacts indicates wealth, the juxtaposition and closeness of the buildings suggest the houses of individual traders with little or no evidence for social hierarchy. Nor could their architectural development be studied, as the site was abandoned in the early Roman period and later became a cemetery. Nevertheless the apparent cill-beam construction common at Skeleton Green is typical also of Gorhambury, although Building 8 at Gorhambury seems to be larger and architecturally more complex, with at least four rooms and connecting lean-to sheds. We can assume therefore, if building size can be regarded as an indicator, that the occupants of Gorhambury were of a higher social class, as is also hinted at by the quality of the buildings which followed.

Late Iron Age farmsteads in the south-east of Britain often comprised circular or sub-rectangular enclosures, usually with a south-east facing entrance, containing a number of circular huts and four or six-post structures interpreted as granaries. One of the first of these enclosures to be excavated, Little Woodbury, Wilts (Bersu 1940), had at least two huts and a group of granaries close to the western defences. At Wakerley, Northants (Jackson 1978), there is a double-ditched enclosure with traces of eight circular houses. They were not all contemporary, but arranged around the periphery of the enclosure leaving a yard in the centre, between the houses and the main entrance. The largest of the houses, presumably occupied by the chieftain, was situated directly opposite the main entrance, similar to the buildings at Gorhambury, while facing one another on the north and south sides of the yard were two pairs of buildings, the smaller one presumably of lesser status, being near the gate. To what extent this layout is coincidental is uncertain but pairing of buildings and the provision of a yard can be seen at many sites. At Whitton, Gwent, for example (Jarrett and Wrathmell 1981) at least five circular houses were arranged inside a small sub-rectangular enclosure about 65m wide, also with an east-facing entrance. Like Wakerley and Gorhambury one structure was situated directly opposite the main gate and, from its position, can be interpreted as being the principal house. The early layout at Whitton dictated the form of the subsequent villa, for a new Roman-style house was built over the old, still facing the gate across the yard. The circular outbuildings to the south, perhaps intended for staff or retainers, were also rebuilt and incorporated a small bath-suite and perhaps a tower granary. The main house was of the most basic type consisting of a range of rooms with wing-rooms at either end linked by a verandah. Unlike the earlier periods when *all* the buildings were of similar form, the outbuildings now consisted of obviously inferior rectangular sheds. A social order had emerged. This is not to imply that none existed before but that there is no evidence for it in the architecture apart from size.

The native style buildings at Whitton are of Roman date but there is a similar situation at Gorhambury in the pre-conquest period. The two enclosures form inner and outer yards, the inner containing the principal apartments and granary, and the outer, subsidiary buildings and an aisled building possibly housing workers. The social distinction that existed in the late Iron Age was carried through into the Roman period. To what extent we can use the evidence from Gorhambury and Park Street in our understanding of other villa sites is questionable as so many villas have been inadequately excavated, but there are elements in the plans of some villas, especially in the area of the Catuvellauni, which suggest that they too might be based on earlier layouts. Clearly, early artefacts are an indicator of pre-Roman occupation but so too, perhaps, is the architecture.

At Gorhambury the reconstruction of buildings on earlier house platforms created a scattered or rather unplanned look to the overall layout. There are no deep integral wings or long outbuildings flanking courtyards such as the late Antonine arrangement at Gadebridge. The villa at Hambleden, Bucks (Cocks 1921), situated close to the River Thames, also had an assortment of buildings apparently lacking planning. Early occupation however is suggested by a British bronze and a Roman coin series starting with six issues of Claudius, three of Nero, five of Vespasian and five of Domitian. The presence of native coarse pottery is not in itself significant, as native fabrics continue in the Chilterns into the third quarter of the first century, but among the sherds are five stamped terra rubra and terra nigra platters. The coins and pottery indicate an early foundation not apparent in the site description owing to the superficial excavation. Again there are elements about the plan which suggest affinities with Gorhambury and Park Street. The main house was divorced from the outbuildings, which were situated on either side of a yard enclosed by a wall and gate; there was no ditched enclosure. The outbuildings were probably aisled as is implied by the location of corn-drying ovens along the centre of the building, possibly placed in the nave to leave the aisles clear for stock.

Whatever the evidence for halls at Park Street or Hambleden, the examples at Gorhambury and Verulamium serve to demonstrate that this type of building already existed in Britain before the conquest and was not necessarily a Roman innovation. A hall or longhouse provided accommodation for workers, sheltered stock (especially in the winter) and stored farm equipment.

The economic base of the Iron Age enclosure at Gorhambury remains uncertain. Unfortunately the recovery of bones from associated levels was poor owing to fragmentation but they indicate a mixed range of species with cattle, pig and sheep represented, cattle being the dominant type. Wild game included red deer, with roe deer and hare coming from first-century levels. However, it is perhaps the structural evidence which provides the best clue, for the presence of two large Iron Age granaries (Buildings 5 and 10) serves to emphasise the importance of grain as a resource, further symbolised by the wheat-ear on coins of Cunobelin. Cattle or horse ranching is perhaps the explanation for the dykes east of the complex, since much of the land they define is fairly rich meadow bordering the west bank of the river; close to the river it was perhaps too damp for arable cultivation. The erratic nature of the dyke system and the apparent lack of linear earthworks connecting the smaller dykes in Prae Wood rules out their being solely defensive and part of an overall work – more likely they delineate property. This is perhaps reinforced by the discovery at two separate points along the dyke (see p 20) of earlier ditches on the same alignment, which suggests that the boundaries were fixed in preceding periods. The scale of the dyke points to the co-ordinated and collective labour of a tribal group and therefore the relation of the excavated farmstead to the land delineated by the dykes (the provision of a causeway and the axial arrangement) highlights the importance of the site and the status of the family who occupied it.

Early first-century enclosures

Although the Childwickbury villa is unexcavated the aerial photographs suggest a winged corridor villa similar in plan to that of Gorhambury and probably of second-century date. It too appears to have been set in an enclosure on a 125m contour and serves to highlight the importance of both sites, especially since they lie so close to Verulamium. As we have already seen, Gorhambury has a long history, with a late Iron Age farmstead, and the presence of the enclosure at Childwickbury (Fig 114) might suggest that this villa developed in a similar way.

Neither the Gorhambury nor the assumed Childwickbury enclosures are isolated examples around Verulamium; three others lie on the 110–115m contour west of the River Ver. One (257) in Prae Wood was surveyed by Wheeler (Wheeler and Wheeler 1936, pl XI) and later by Hunn (Hunn 1980, fig 4). It was rectangular and had at its south end a linear earthwork with a dog-leg similar to the Period 4 ditch at Gorhambury; there was an entrance in its south-east corner. Further south-east, on the opposite side of the Silchester Road, was another enclosure (259) at right-angles to Wheeler's ditch (Hunn ibid) and with a ditched droveway along its north-west side. The sequence within this enclosure is not understood but it appears to have been divided into three yards, the northern of which had a barn (Freeman MS). The third enclosure lies 1½ miles (2 km) north of Gorhambury at Beaumonts Hall near Redbourn, and shares a similar geographical location and distance from the river. This was also rectangular and appears from the aerial photographs to have had, as at Gorhambury, a more imposing ditch and causeway on its east side facing the river. There is also evidence that the enclosure was sub-divided. We cannot be certain that all these sites contained Iron Age farmsteads but their presence does indicate that the heavy clay with pebbles on the plateaux around Verulamium was being exploited. Gallo-Belgic pottery and imports of wine amphorae suggest that the aristocracy had assimilated aspects of 'Romanisation' before the conquest, as the excavations at Skeleton Green (Partridge 1981) demonstrate. If the other enclosures did contain pre-Roman farmsteads it might also explain why Verulamium became a *municipium* under Claudius (Frere 1983, 28), for perhaps 'Romanisation' was already advanced and the farms were producing large surpluses of grain as the late Iron Age granaries at Gorhambury might suggest. The conquest need not have affected the area adversely and since the residents were peaceful, and perhaps 'won themselves favour by abandoning the cause of Togodubnus and Caratacus' (Frere 1983, 28), they may have been rewarded by self-governing status. This would also partly explain the short military occupation of only one or two years. It may be objected that if the enclosures were farmsteads, why

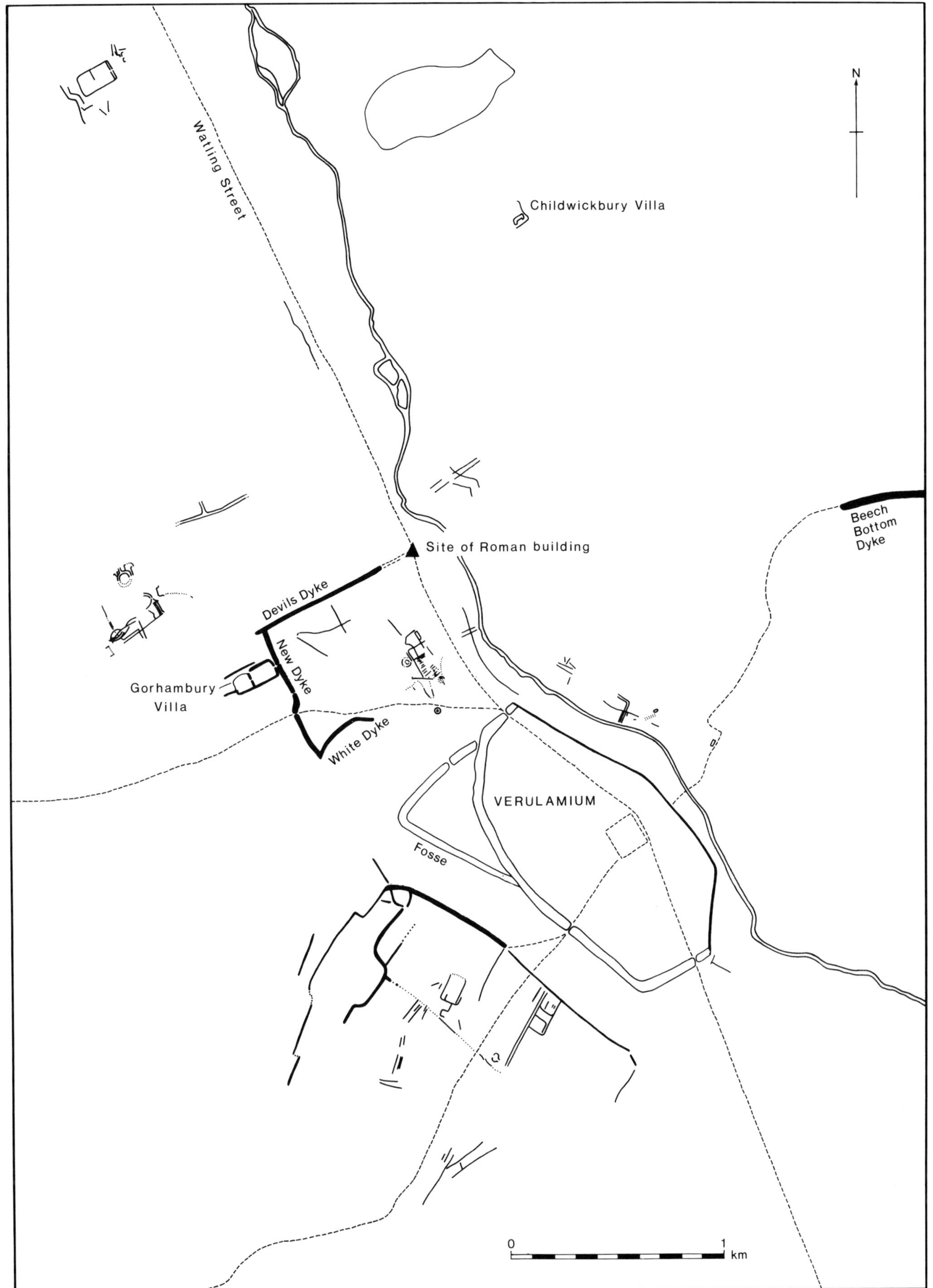

Fig 114 Plan showing earthworks around Verulamium (based on field survey and aerial reconaissance)

did only some develop into villa-estates? The answer may be that under tribal control their boundaries would have been notional and cattle and stock could perhaps be grazed over wide tracts, but as self-supporting private farms they may have been too small and uneconomic to survive the realities of Roman taxation.

The winged corridor villa to the end of the second century

The winged corridor form of the two Gorhambury masonry villas is very similar to others in the locality and typical of many elsewhere in Britain, especially the south-east. It appears with a symmetrical plan as early as *c* AD 100 at Boxmoor, where it was constructed in timber and had one of its rooms decorated with painted wall-plaster (Neal 1976, 58). A timber villa also appears at Gadebridge *c* AD 75 but whether it had a winged corridor plan is not known. By the Antonine period all the villas in the neighbourhood of Verulamium had winged corridor plans, although they varied in size and in the case of Gadebridge and Kings Langley had extended wings enclosing a small court. Gadebridge had a range of rooms 42m long, Park Street 41m, and Boxmoor 39m. At 35m Gorhambury was no longer exceptional.

However, as noted elsewhere (Neal 1978, 47), although the villas may have varied in scale, by the Antonine period the number of rooms in each is very similar and, allowing for accommodation over cellars, was between 9 and 12 rooms. Walthew (1975, 199) has stressed that the provision of masonry footings for many villas in the early second century, combined with interior decoration and domestic comfort, was well in advance of the contemporary situation at Verulamium, where masonry does not appear to have been widely used for private building before the mid second century. However, by this date there is a close relationship between the winged corridor architecture of the countryside and the town, where if anything the buildings became larger, for example Verulamium Building IV 8 with a total length of 61m.

In this period there was considerable prosperity in the town, as manifested by the fine mosaics and wall plaster furnishing many of the houses. The villas in the locality were also embellished at this period: Boxmoor had at least two mosaics, one of which was of exceptional quality (Neal 1981, fig 8); and the first masonry villa at Gorhambury also had at least one mosaic pavement, as did Park Street (O'Neil 1945, 27) and High Wycombe (Hartley 1959, pl IX). Curiously, although the Gadebridge villa was larger than the others it had no mosaics or even tessellated pavements (excepting the bath suite) in the second century. All it had was plain *opus signinum* floors and imitation ashlar rendering on its walls.

Until the late Antonine period it is possible to relate the growth of the town houses and villas. It was a period of stability and the countryside around Verulamium was sufficiently fertile to merit investment in land. Markets for produce were close at hand and either considerable surplus and profits were being produced to pay for the construction of the villas, and perhaps ultimately the town houses, or the land was deemed sufficiently profitable to be accepted as collateral for loans to pay for building work. In such a situation any upset, whether national or local, could alter the economic balance and create insecurity.

It might be expected that the Antonine fire at Verulamium would have done this, but the evidence from Frere's excavations suggests a major programme of reconstruction with no blighted areas. The same applies in the countryside: expansion continued into the late Antonine period, and indeed villas may have prospered as a result of the fire, especially if some of the villa estates were engaged in the supply of building materials such as lime, sand, timber and flint. Hauliers would certainly have prospered.

Nevertheless, by the late second or early third century an event, or sequence of events, took place that was to have a serious effect on the affluence of the villas. It was from this period that most of the villas declined; at Gorhambury this was exemplified by its temporary abandonment.

At Boxmoor the sumptuous house and its mosaics became ruinous at this time, for in the third century it was reconstructed with its walls extending over the borders of the earlier pavements. Unless the villa had been abandoned or had fallen into serious disrepair this reconstruction would have been unnecessary. The rebuilding, in large blocks of flint and of crude construction, also saw the corridor moved from the south side to the north. The building was no longer luxurious and appears to have become a working farm-house.

At Northchurch a mass of tile debris over the corridor sealed pottery of *c* AD 160 and it was suggested that the Period 2 villa was abandoned *c* AD 170, possibly as the result of flooding (Neal 1976, 11), but was reoccupied in the third century. In retrospect, to postulate the abandonment of a villa because of flooding was perhaps unwise; if the flood only damaged buildings there is no reason for it to have halted occupation, other than temporarily. If flooding had occurred, perhaps it was primarily the result of the abandonment of local drainage schemes or river control, affecting the estate more generally.

Closer to Verulamium, a similar decline can be seen at Wood Lane End, a site about 2½ miles (4 km) west of Gorhambury and close to the main east–west road. Here a massive Romano-Celtic temple-mausoleum set within a trapezoidal enclosure went out of use at the end of the second century, together with related buildings, including a bath-house. The temple was demolished and during the third and fourth century the enclosure turned over to stock, since postholes forming paddocks were cut through earlier buildings (Neal 1984). At Park Street the excavator thought it possible the villa had been abandoned, as this would explain the necessity for the wholesale rebuilding and alteration that took place in the early fourth century (O'Neil 1945, 27).

More dramatic perhaps is the abandonment of the massive *thermae* at Branch Road outside the east gate at Verulamium. It was constructed in the mid second century but by *c* AD 225 (Wilson 1975, 258, fig 12) was abandoned and systematically demolished, leaving only the pilae in a matrix of grey silt perhaps derived from a broken aqueduct. These baths lay on the opposite bank of the river to the town and were effectively isolated by the construction of the city defences. Similarly, the King Harry Lane settlement along the Silchester road west of Verulamium may also have been abandoned since, from the evidence of the coins, occupation ceased in the mid third century (Curnow 1974, 56; Stead 1969). The destruction of the baths and construction of the city's earthen defences were probably contemporary events, for the baths would have provided much needed building supplies to construct gatehouses. To what extent other buildings were also razed for supplies is uncertain but if, as in London in a later context, public monuments were stripped to build the defences, it would appear that sometimes civil authorities took exceptional steps to obtain materials. It is feasible therefore that the demise of the Wood Lane End mausoleum coincided with the events at Verulamium and offered substantial building material not readily available from other sources.

Fitting evidence from excavations into historical contexts is fraught with problems, but nevertheless it has been forcefully argued that the provision of earthen defences and the first masonry gates at Verulamium and many other towns was the work of Albinus, in anticipation of the need to secure the province as a consequence of his withdrawal of the army to reinforce his claim to the Imperial throne. In the event he was defeated by Severus who in AD 197 despatched to Britain Sextus Varius Marcellus to ensure that supporters of Albinus were punished; it is likely therefore that some landowners were executed and their estates and villas confiscated. If so, it is most unlikely that the wealthy estates in the south-east remained unscathed. We cannot prove that this happened at Gorhambury but the site from this period onwards saw very few changes, especially to the fabric of the villa proper. Conceivably the lands could now have come under the control of a neighbouring estate and the main house been occupied by a bailiff.

Another hypothesis is that payment for the provision of defences was the responsibility of the landowners. It is unlikely that Albinus was able to secure Imperial funds for these defences and possibly levies were imposed to pay for them. The provision of gates, as well as being defensive, may also have been intended to control commerce and to act as tax collection points in much the same way as city gates in the medieval period.

The provision of defences would have had a dramatic effect upon the countryside if proprietors of villas who were also owners of property in the town were obliged to share the cost. The need for defences may have made dual householders concentrate on their town houses at the expense of their estates. More generally, it is likely to have been a time of hardship, with a tendency to cut down on property maintenance and less reliance on service trades. Any contraction of the money supply would have had a detrimental effect on the prosperity of the country estates. If property owners were required to contribute towards the cost of wall building it could have destabilised the economic balance. Townspeople who had invested in country property may possibly have called in their loans in order to discharge their debts.

Fourth-century development

During the third and fourth centuries the architectural development of the various villas was more diverse. In stark contrast to Gorhambury Gadebridge, for example, grew in size, with the addition of detached wings flanking what was effectively an outer courtyard. The wing on the south-east shared the same juxtaposition as the Gorhambury and Park Street aisled buildings and also appears to have been part residential and part stables. In *c* AD 325 further additions saw the development of a massive and somewhat grandiose bathing pool on the east side of the baths, which by now was no longer an isolated building but integrated into the villa and forming a north-east wing. However, this show of prosperity was not to last long for the villa was razed in the mid fourth century and it has been suggested (Neal 1974, 98) that this event may have been the result of the owner having been a supporter of Magnentius who suffered in the purges carried out by Paulus following Magnentius' rebellion. Nevertheless, although most of the villa was demolished, a cottage to the north-west, flanking a northern yard, remained occupied to the end of the fourth century and the evidence for stockades suggests that the site was given over to stock rearing. However, although the Magnentian troubles of AD 353 may have affected Gadebridge there are reasons to believe that the demise of the villas around Verulamium had already begun and was due to more complex economic problems.

The excavations at Boxmoor were on too small a scale to recover the level of information recorded at Gadebridge or Gorhambury, although we have already observed that throughout the third and in the early fourth centuries the villa was contracting in size to the extent that it was finally reduced to a block of five rooms, with buttresses arranged along its south side. The pattern of coin loss at Boxmoor is closely comparable with that at Gorhambury, showing a substantial falling-off of issues in Period XIIB (soon after AD 330, see Fig 118), although there is coin evidence for the succeeding period (XIII), with a Fel Temp minim and a Victoria Augg being dated later than *c* AD 355. A single coin of Arcadius was recovered from the excavations of 1851 but its findspot is unknown. The excavation report (Neal 1970) suggested that Boxmoor's demise was also ultimately the consequence of the Magnentian revolt, but this is no longer tenable. As we have observed at Gadebridge, although the villa may have been razed it is always possible that outbuildings, none of which have been excavated, remained occupied. The fact that Boxmoor was reduced to such a basic structure by the mid fourth century also raises the possibility that it was subservient to another neighbouring estate – conceivably Gadebridge. The discovery at Boxmoor of an Imperial lead seal is unsufficient evidence for it having been part of an Imperial estate, and even if it had been, there is no reason why it, with other private villas, should also have been demolished.

As already noted, we find a somewhat similar situation at Wood Lane End. Although not a villa, the monumental Romano-Celtic temple-mausoleum was demolished at the end of the second or early third century and a series of timber stockades was constructed within the earlier temenos, cutting the robbed masonry footings of some buildings. In the north-east corner of the temenos was an area of rubble associated with fourth-century occupation suggesting the presence of a hut nearby (outside the excavated area). Conceivably the original temenos was being used to enclose stock, but whether this work was being organised from the presumed hut, or from a fourth-century farm building discovered about a mile to the east at Breakspears during the construction of the M1 motorway in 1958, is far from certain. Its situation close to the east–west Roman road gave it ready access to Verulamium. What similarities in organisation the original Wood Lane End complex had to the villas can only be speculation, but it is feasible that it had its own farm and estates to support the upkeep of the sacred buildings and staff. Working farm buildings have not been identified in the complex, although Building 3, 14 by 10m with buttresses along two sides, could be interpreted as a granary. If so, it is interesting to note that on no other site around Verulamium is there a granary of comparable size, which raises the question as to whether it collected, perhaps as gifts, more grain than its own farm was capable of producing, especially since its land is somewhat heavier and more clayey than the soils worked by the other sites under discussion.

At Gorhambury the provision of stockades over much of the outer yard and the evidence from the bones, which suggests that the proportion of cattle increased in the fourth century, might imply that the site, as with Gadebridge Park and Wood Lane End, was following a local trend. Unlike Gadebridge Park, the fourth-century reconstruction was mainly repair. On this evidence, it could be argued, as with Boxmoor, that by now it had been incorporated into the holdings of another estate, but its proximity to the town makes it perfectly feasible for the villa to have been controlled by town dwellers.

The demise of the Park Street villa was attributed to barbarian raids of *c* AD 367 (O'Neil 1945, 30) but the coin evidence could suggest that occupation terminated earlier since there are no issues later than 348–61, although subsequent issues are in any event scarce. Since some of these coins were issued after Magnentius' uprising perhaps the troubles of AD 353 did not directly touch the villa, but nevertheless, the lack of coins from AD 361 onwards might reinforce the view that Park Street was also abandoned in this period.

Establishing the geographical limits around Verulamium affected by these changes is difficult, because although many sites have been excavated the work has been on a scale too small for significant numbers of coins to be recovered and it could be argued that occupation continued in unexcavated outbuildings, such as occurred in Building E at Gadebridge (Neal 1974). However, the table of coin loss (p 105) from those local villas producing a reasonable sample, including Boxmoor, Dicket Mead and Welwyn, strongly suggests that these sites were abandoned. This is in stark contrast to villas further west and south such as Hambleden, Bucks, and Moor Park, Herts, which have issues associated with principal buildings continuing to the end of the fourth century. Likewise, coin evidence from villas north of the Chilterns, such as Bancroft, Milton Keynes (Williams and Zeepfat forthcoming), and other sites on the Jurassic limestone, also suggests late occupation. On the present evidence it is possible to postulate that a ten-mile zone of countryside around Verulamium was affected by this decline and that villas beyond this distance were unaffected, possibly because their regional centre was not Verulamium. The general picture which emerges is that of once-rich country houses falling into disrepair or being abandoned, but with the associated farms continuing in use, albeit on a run-down scale.

Communications and resources (Figs 1, 6)

Until recently the westerly route from Verulamium, to link with Akeman Street, was believed to have been via the Silchester Gate, but a Roman road discovered about 200m south of the Gorhambury villa (Fig 6) leading towards Wood Lane End may have been the main road westwards out of the city. It would have joined Akeman Street at the river crossing of the Gade at Two Waters and connected the villas along the Bulbourne and Gade valleys. It survives as a shallow *agger* south of the Gorhambury villa as far west as Bacon's House, where it is ploughed-out, but its east end is probably represented by a causeway across Stoney Valley and a metalled track heading directly towards the Chester Gate at Verulamium.

The *Viatores* (1964, 35–6) first suggested that this trackway (Route 159B) was Roman and assumed that it proceeded in a north-west direction, crossing the area of the villa, and heading towards Cupid's Green. However, no evidence for it passing the villa has been found and excavation of the *agger* south of the villa confirmed the presence of an east–west road with a V-shaped ditch on its north side.

On a local level communication with the villa was via a series of minor trackways. The axial route from the east was always the main approach, but in the later history of the site, as the enclosure became less important, this access lost its prominence and we see the emergence of trackways crossing the earlier ditches. On the north side a metalled road with cart-ruts, found in area 4024, appears to have forked in three directions. One route probably led directly west to enter the 'droveway' between the enclosure ditches in area 4024 – a long established entrance – but another led south-west to cross the ditch in area 2815–16 where metalling was found sealing the infilled ditch. The third and more prominent track appears to have led directly south along the original Period 3 enclosure ditch, possibly separated from the enclosure itself by a hedge: it ran to the main entrance. The northerly route of this series of trackways is uncertain but it probably ran north along the existing field boundary alongside the dyke, and at the foot of the slope, where it is damp, possibly breached the dyke and ran along a causeway cutting off the angle between the north–south route of 'New Dyke' and the east–west alignment of Devil's Dyke. Presumably it made its way east towards the meadows and Watling Street – taking this higher route would have avoided the damper meadows within the area defined by the dyke system.

South of the site a similar situation prevailed. Another trackway ran along the ditch bottom located in area 1413 – parallel to the dyke. A gap through the bank 100m south of this point may represent a later traverse taken by the track, but it originally continued perhaps to join the main Roman road through the dyke just south of Shepherds Cottages. Another track was also found crossing the enclosure ditch in area 2815–16 and is assumed to have provided access into the fields and a link south-west to the main road.

Although no archaeological evidence has been found for the methods used in farming the estate or how specific areas were cultivated, the diverse terrain and soil types provide an opportunity to attempt a reconstruction. Gorhambury occupies a spur of plateau drift of pebbly clay and sand, surrounded on three sides by clay with flints over chalk, with chalky loam and alluvium occupying the valley bottom. Alluvium also stretches west of the river into Stoney Valley and has been observed in trenches south of Shepherds Cottages sealing a shallow deposit of gravel probably formed in Pleistocene times by a stream flowing east. Whether the stream survived into the Roman period is doubtful but conditions here are likely to have been moist, as is perhaps confirmed by its medieval name 'Marshlade'. A stream is also likely to have flowed east in the dip to the north of the site, for in the medieval period it was known as Brook Field. The area would have provided ideal pasturage extending up the valley slopes for a distance of 1½ miles (2.4 km). If these valleys were under pasture the acreage of river meadows required for the feeding of stock would have been less and it would have been possible to keep sheep and cattle closer to the farm. As we have seen, the estate is unlikely to have had meadows on the east bank of the Ver, which probably belonged to the Childwickbury villa.

The construction of dykes across the two stream-beds in the late Iron Age and the later construction of causeways for roads and tracks probably blocked the natural drainage of the area and perhaps created ponds. Evidence of one such pond was found west of the earthwork crossing Stoney Valley; here a large quantity of aquatic molluscs were preserved. Stock could have been watered locally without the need to drive them all the way to the river. Another pond is likely to have formed on the south-west side of the road causeway. Spade cultivation – probably virtually impossible or uneconomic on the higher clay and pebble soil closer to the villa – could have been practised in these lighter chalky-loam soils. Market gardens could also have run alongside Watling Street where a number of rectangular enclosures have been observed on aerial photographs. Field-walking on these areas has located Roman pottery, spread by manuring, a common practice and suggested at Gorhambury by the discovery of four rectangular timber-lined latrines (including Structures 44–6) evidently designed to be emptied regularly. However, the regularity of the plots alongside Watling Street and their proximity to the town might indicate that they were worked by townspeople rather than villa workers.

As already stated, the heavier soils immediately around and west of the villa would probably preclude spade cultivation, and little evidence has been found for the division of the area into small fields or plots. Of the 555 iron objects catalogued from the excavation only one is a spade shoe. It could be argued, however, that unrimmed shovels in oak would leave no archaeological trace, but it is difficult even today using a steel spade to penetrate untilthed soil, and wooden spades are unlikely to have been effective. In contrast six plough-shares have been recovered which indicates the importance of arable cultivation, as does the discovery of granaries of both the Iron Age and Roman periods.

The area available for arable cultivation is extensive and it would have been perfectly feasible to cultivate up to the meadows. However, to the south the Roman road was an effective boundary and the fact that a ditch ran along its north side suggests that this area could have been enclosed. To what extent cereal cultivation could have extended south of Stoney Valley, on the north-facing fields south of an east–west line represented by White Dyke, is unknown, but they are partly under arable cultivation today and are likely to have been so in the Roman period, especially since these fields were protected by the dyke system.

The south-facing fields north of the villa and Brook Field were probably also under cultivation, perhaps worked by a small native-type settlement (Fig 115) centred at TL 112083, observed on aerial photographs and highlighted during field-walking by the discovery of Roman pottery of second-century date. Presumably this settlement was associated with the villa and the houses of bondsmen. Roman pottery has also been located near Bacon's House; manuring may be an explanation for its presence, but it is possible that it marks the site of another minor settlement. The bath-house, Building 41, in the outer enclosure was far too big merely for workers or staff living in the villa complex, and hints at a workforce living elsewhere on the estate. The soils between the villa and Bacon's House are consistent in type and, providing labour was plentiful, could all have been cultivated. It is improbable that the mineralized seeds from Pit 22 (p 28), including fig, lentils and grape, represent plants that were being cultivated; they could have been imported as dried produce.

From the evidence of the bones, cattle would seem always to have been the most important stock, a dominance even more pronounced in the third and fourth centuries despite a smaller quantity of material being available for study. A similar situation was noted at Gadebridge Park where stockaded enclosures were built post *c* AD 350 following the

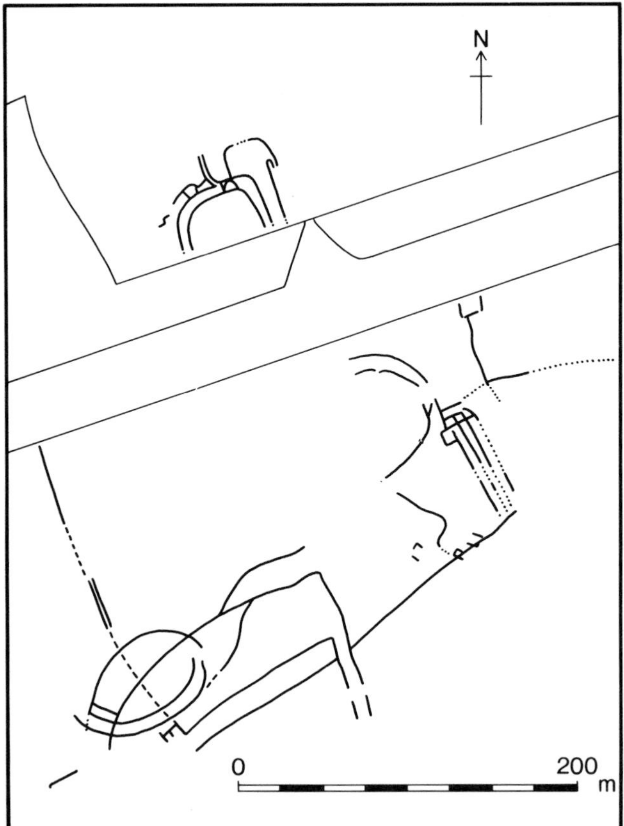

Fig 115 Plan of site revealed by aerial photography north-west of the villa (see Fig 6, inset)

destruction of the main house (Neal 1974, 76). Most slaughtered animals were mature specimens which implies that their primary functions were in breeding, the provision of traction, and giving milk. Culling them for meat and hides was secondary. Conversely there appears to be a greater exploitation of sheep for meat than cattle, and possibly flocks of mature breeding stock were maintained together with a few aged individuals, while some 'fat lambs' and older juveniles were culled. Pigs appear to be better represented in the earlier periods: well over half the pigs were slaughtered within six months, clearly indicating a preference for piglets rather than mature animals.

Just as corn was a vital crop so too was woodland which would have been managed not only to provide timber for the building trades, but coppiced to provide fuel for the estate and the townspeople. West of Bacon's House the plateau rises and the soil conditions become more clayey and it is tempting to suggest that these areas were wooded and provided cover for game such as the red and roe deer identified among the animal bones. Traditionally these areas supported oak which would also have provided winter feed for pigs. From the evidence of molluscs (p 213) it is suggested that woodland may have lain adjacent to or linked with the dykes close to the villa.

Lime was another resource, as at Gadebridge Park. Chalk was readily available especially on the lower slopes; these areas were exploited in the post-medieval period and may have been also in Roman times.

The logistics of gathering flint for building construction need consideration. How was it obtained? It could have been gleaned during field clearance or dyke digging, but this method of retrieval would have been inadequate to supply the demands of masons, who would have required many thousands of tons, especially for the construction of the Verulamium basilica and forum, not to mention the dwarf footing-walls of town-houses and later the city walls. (It has been calculated by J Hunn (forthcoming) that the requirement for flint alone for the city wall (excluding tile and mortar) could have been in the region of 66,000 tons.) In Hertfordshire flint occurs as nodules in the upper clay and dispersed in the chalk, but it is only encountered in tabular form and in density sufficient for its recovery to be economic at considerable depths. Even if chalk for lime or marl for fields was a by-product of these operations, flint must have been an expensive building stone, especially when compared, for example, to limestone which could be quarried along the Jurassic ridge virtually anywhere. No Roman quarries have been positively identified, but a number of large depressions occur in the chalk in various parts of the Gorhambury Estate. Although these are of uncertain date and could be associated with the construction of Bacon's House, their presence does serve to demonstrate possible locations of quarries ('Q' on Fig 6).

The villa estate

In order to reveal the nature of a Romano-British villa it is necessary to attempt to define its territory. The word 'villa' is only an economic term for an estate (Rivet 1969, 175). What is usually referred to as the 'villa' is only the 'caput' of that estate. It is therefore necessary to place the principal dwelling or 'caput' in the context of its associated territory. There have been previous estimates of the sizes of villa estates (Applebaum 1972, 1975; Barker and Webley 1977; Branigan 1977; Finberg 1955; Rodwell and Rodwell 1986). Other efforts have been concerned with tracing the survival of late Roman estates into the early medieval period on a regional scale, eg South Wales (Davies 1979). At Wharram in Yorkshire, it has been suggested that the Roman estate unit formed the basis of the later medieval township (Hayfield 1987, 187). On a smaller scale, individual Romano-British farm units have been investigated at Odell, Beds (Dix 1981), Maddle Farm, Berks (Gaffney and Tingle 1985) and Barton Court Farm, Oxon (Jones 1986).

The majority of previous attempts to define a villa estate have been based on the following methods, either singly or in combination: surviving physical boundaries; the retrospective use of medieval administrative units; estimates based on the capacity of granaries and byres; site-catchment analysis and Thiessen polygons. All these methods have their limitations. However, recent work at Maddle Farm has shown what can be achieved on the micro-regional level by sound fieldwork (Gaffney and Tingle 1985).

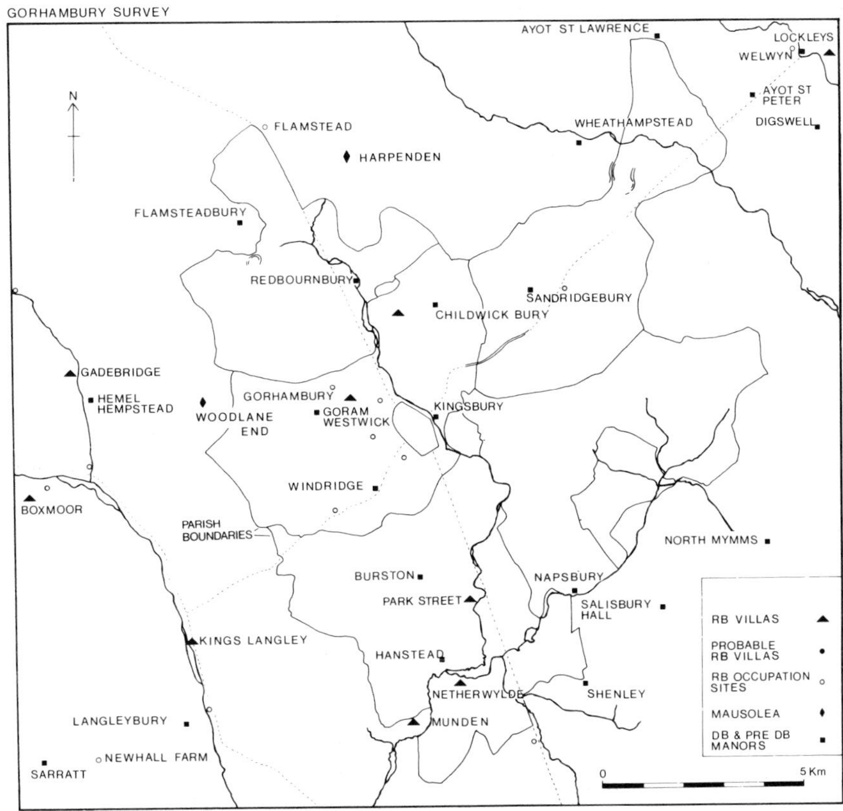

Fig 116 Location of Roman villas and medieval manors in relation to parish boundaries

The following estate sizes have been proposed:

Withington, Glos – 2359 ha (5830 acres) (Finberg 1955, 13)
Ditchley, Oxon – 354 ha (875 acres) (Applebaum 1972, 267)
Bignor, Sussex – 796 ha (1968 acres) (Applebaum 1975, 121)
Gatcombe, Glos – 6070 ha (15000 acres) (Branigan 1977, 195)
Rivenhall, Essex – 1485 ha (3669 acres) (Rodwell and Rodwell 1986, 1)

It can be seen from the above figures that there is a considerable variation in the estimates for estate sizes. In none of the above examples was the centre of the estate completely investigated; at Gorhambury, by contrast, the plan has been fully recovered. Nevertheless, the evidence for its estate is far from complete.

Short of the survival and discovery of clearly defined linear boundaries – perhaps with inscriptions – separating neighbouring estates, the question of how large any individual villa estate was cannot be answered with complete confidence. Nevertheless it is valid to examine whether there is any relationship between Roman estate boundaries and those of the medieval period. At the outset it must be stated that there is not a single direct coincidence of site location between Roman villas and medieval manors, although there is evidence to suggest that some villas and manors may have shared broadly coextensive boundaries. Caution is required in the interpretation of the evidence, particularly in the area south of Verulamium where manors outnumber villas, but it is possible to suggest tentative pairing relationships (Fig 116). For example, Park Street Roman villa and Burston manor, Netherwild villa and Hanstead manor, and Munden villa and Garston manor. North of Verulamium, Gorhambury and Childwickbury exhibit a similar coincidence of villa and manor and, in the case of Gorhambury (whose earlier medieval name was Westwick) the manor probably lay about 800m west of the villa, close to Bacon's House. It is probable that Childwickbury manor lies less than one kilometre east or north-east of the villa.

Although the location of Childwickbury manor is unknown, medieval documentary evidence does allow us to trace the extent of its holdings, together with those of Gorhambury. Here it is relevant to note that both adjoining manors have 'wick' ending names, conceivably based on the Old English loan word 'wic' from the latin 'vicus', meaning dwelling or village. The possibility exists, therefore, that while the names do not contain the *wicham* element more securely related to Roman settlement, its association with estates in which Roman villas are situated may be significant (Gelling 1978, 67–74).

As we have already seen, the known distribution of villas, especially those along the river valleys, suggests a spacing of about 1½ miles (2.4 km). Whether these villas occupied radial locations to the estates and farmed lands on both banks of the rivers is uncertain, but such a location would make cultivation more economic as pasture and arable would be close and not strung out along one side of the valley. In support of this view the evidence so far shows that although villas may occupy different banks of a river, there is not a single instance in Hertfordshire or elsewhere in Britain of villas facing one another from opposite river banks.

There are at least 12 villas and two temple complexes in the topographical area of the rivers Bulbourne, Gade and Ver. If one uses polygons as a model, while assuming both that these are the only sites which existed and that territorial divisions lay midway between estate centres, the following territories can be estimated:

Boxmoor	2967.7 ha (7333.2 acres)
Childwickbury	1519.8 ha (3755.5 acres)
Frithsden	1845.2 ha (4559.5 acres)
Gadebridge	1799.2 ha (4445.9 acres)
Gorhambury	1308.1 ha (3232.4 acres)
Kings Langley	2811.8 ha (6948.1 acres)
Munden	1494.7 ha (3693.5 acres)
Park Street	1736.0 ha (4289.8 acres)
Wood Lane End	2125.4 ha (5251.8 acres)

These figures give an average territory of 1956.4 ha (4834.4 acres), but there is a broad variation in size, perhaps explained by the distances across the plateaux between villas. The postulated territory for the Gorhambury estate is the smallest, possibly owing to its close proximity to Verulamium and the presence of the dyke system north of the city demarking territory which, for the purposes of this hypothesis, is assumed to be related to, and therefore combined with, the city itself although, as we have seen, in the late Iron Age it was probably related to the actual settlement. This change is suggested by the presence of a Roman building (Hunn and Blagg 1984) at the point where Watling Street crosses the line of Devil's Dyke (Fig 6). Perhaps this was an official tax point and the area defined by Devil's Dyke continued its earlier role as a stock kraal, but for public rather than private use in the Roman period. Civic authorities were unlikely to have allowed herds of cattle within the city defences.

Although polygons can provide notional estate areas, this method of calculation fails to consider natural or historic boundaries, such as rivers and dykes. For example, it is possible that the Iron Age earthworks, Devil's Dyke, New Dyke, 'White Dyke' and one in Prae Wood, were also major territorial boundaries in the Roman period, and perhaps they coincide with the medieval township boundary of Westwick. We will therefore examine this boundary in more detail and consider the sizes of local medieval manor estates, beginning with an attempt to outline the boundaries of the major of Gorhambury (Westwick).

Gorhambury villa estate boundaries

(Fig 117; for more detailed map see Fig 6)

Based on sixteenth-century figures the likely acreage of the Gorhambury estate (the Westwick manorial area) was 2451 acres (992 hectares). The eastern limits of the estate were represented by New Dyke and by Devil's Dyke which flanked a strip of land about 250m wide which probably extended to the river. The meadows east of New Dyke and south of Devil's Dyke, perhaps as far south as Kingsbury, were not wholly part of Westwick but were parcelled out between the manors of Kingsbury, Childwickbury, St Mary de Pre and a tiny portion to Windridge. How this unusual subdivision developed is uncertain and it is not until the mid sixteenth century that discrete blocks of land within that area can be discerned. However, to judge from the medieval documentary evidence, the arable land (as opposed to meadow land) to the east of the Iron Age 'New Dyke' belonged mainly to the manor of Kingsbury and St Mary de Pre and formed one common field up to the fringes of Watling Street. The description of the lands of Robert Pleistowe in 1327 in the manor of Kingsbury states that he held half an acre in Morsladefeld between the land of 'St Mary de Pratis' and John de Veer (of Gorhambury) (HRO Gorhambury Deeds XDO). It is uncertain whether the manor of Westwick had arable strips in this field (it is sometimes difficult to draw precise boundaries between estates in the medieval period because common arable fields were often shared by different manors). However, what does seem certain is that the lands bordering the north side of Devil's Dyke were wholly part of the manorial holding of Westwick. There is no evidence to suggest that Westwick held land on the east side of the river.

Further south, the medieval boundary of the estate was defined by the line of the east–west Roman road (Gorhambury Lane), and formed a narrow wedge of land, pointing east, extending to where the road converged with the Iron Age bank, 'White Dyke', which also represented the south side of the estate.

Opposite Shepherds Cottages, the sixteenth-century boundary ran south-west on a zig-zag route following the boundary between lands of Westwick and St Mary de Pre. However, in Roman times, the boundary may possibly have been the same as the township boundary between Westwick and Kingsbury, which coincides with Iron Age earthworks in Prae Wood. Both boundaries converge in the vicinity of the A414 road, from which point the sixteenth-century boundary coincides with the boundary between the lands of Windridge and Westwick. Further south-east it coincides with the parish boundary of St Michael's, Kingsbury, along now extinct lanes except for Bedmond Road, but excludes land held by the nunnery of Markyate south of the A414. Thereafter, it again coincides with the parish and township boundary of St Michael's and Westwick respectively, along Hemel Hempstead Lane. The north-west corner of the estate is delineated by sixteenth-century Plattens Lane (it is no longer extant but originally ran to Watling Street) which also coincides with the parish boundary of St Michael's with Redbourn and the township boundary of Westwick.

The estate areas of the seven medieval manors known in the general vicinity of St Albans are set out in Table 2. With the exception of Westwick they are based on tithe apportionment areas. The demesne areas are based on medieval documentation. These figures give an average size of 2586 ha (6390 acres) for

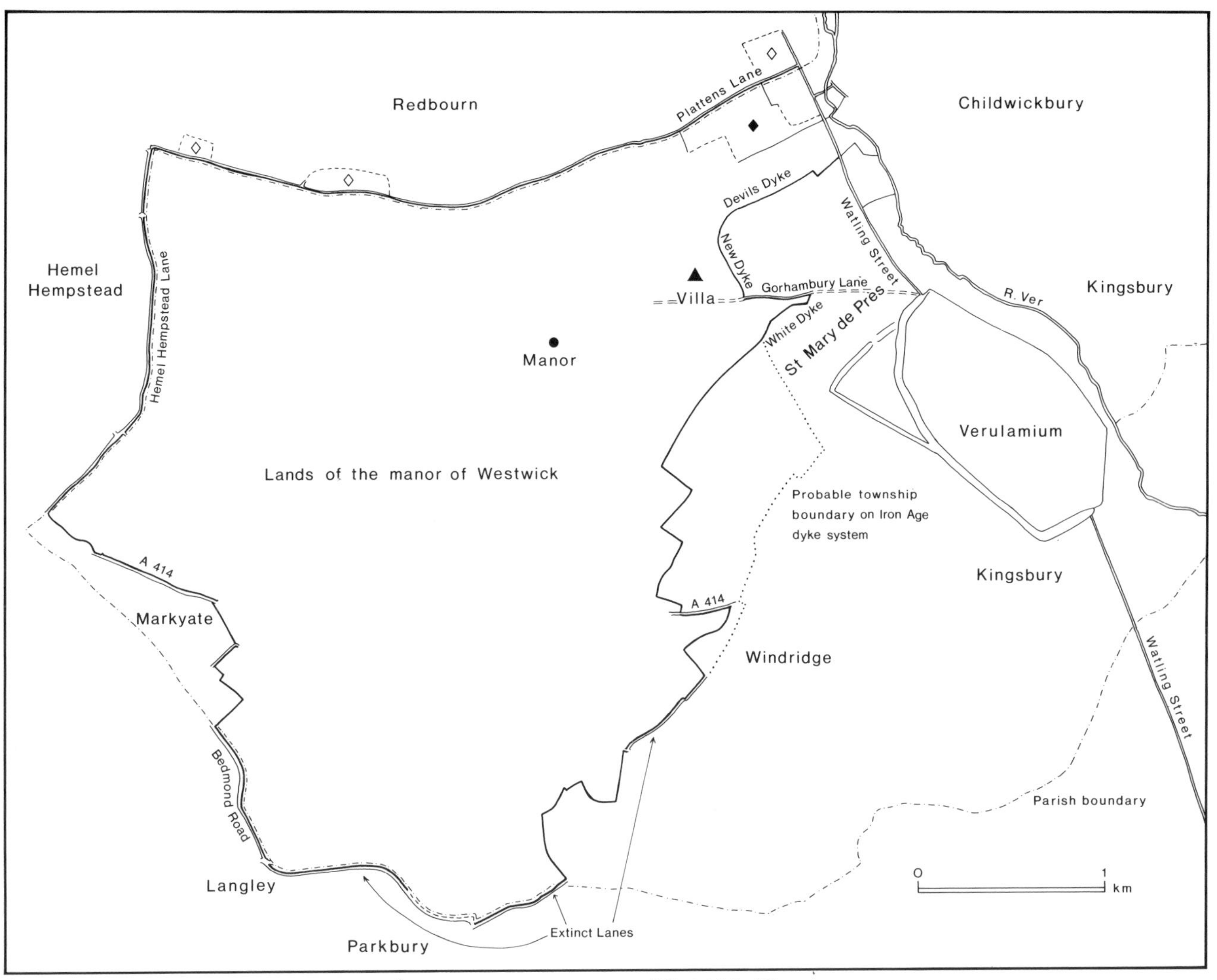

Fig 117 Map showing the lands of the manor of Westwick in relation to the township and parish boundaries

the actual estate and 227.4 ha (562 acres) for the possible demesne area, but whether this reflects the 'demesne' area in the Roman period is impossible to say. However, an independent assessment as to the estate area in the Roman period may be obtained from calculations based on the granary (Building 28). Mrs M Ramsay, using data shown in Appendix 2, has estimated the cubic capacity of the structure and the weight of cereals it might have held. Such an exercise is fraught with uncertainty – what percentage of the capacity of the granary was used for storage, was the storage area divided between seed and food grain and what was the dominant grain type? None of these questions can be answered positively, but by assuming 50% as the storage capacity for either food or seed grain, the estimated quantity of wheat (the

Table 2

	Manorial area (estate)	*Arable demesne area*
Aldenham	2441.5 ha, 6033 acres (19th century)	173.2 ha (428 acres)[1]
Berkhamsted	2222.1 ha, 5491 acres (19th century)	172.8 ha (427 acres)[2]
Flamstead	4492.1 ha, 11100 acres (estimated)	333.4 ha (824 acres)[3]
Park	2333.4 ha, 5766 acres (18th century)	311.2 ha (769 acres)[4]
Tyttenhanger	1462.9 ha, 3615 acres (19th century)	208 ha (514 acres)[5]
Wheathampstead	4159.8 ha, 10279 acres (19th century)	259.8 ha (642 acres)[6]
Westwick	992 ha, 2451 acres (1569)	134 ha (331 acres)[7]

Sources: 1 Cambridge Library K.5.29 AD1314/15 2 PRO C.133.31.3 AD 1264 3 HRO 7593 AD 1331 4 Brit Lib Harley Ms 602 fol 37v 5 Brit Lib Mss 36327 6 Cambridge Library K.5.29 AD 1314/15 7 PRO C.135.10.12

most common cereal on site) that could be stored was about 88,000 lbs. This is calculated as being the yield from about 750 acres (304 hectares) of medium land, more than double the estimated demesne area of Westwick in the medieval period.

The manor of Westwick (Fig 117)

(The later history of the former Roman territory)

The earliest reference to Westwick was in the late tenth century when it was granted by Aethelgifu to St Albans abbey along with Gaddesden, Longford and Munden (*Chron Maj* VI P 13). In AD 996 Aethelred also granted 8 'jugera' of land at Westwick along with Verulamium, Burston and Winchfield. There is no mention of Westwick in Domesday Book, and like Kingsbury, Childwickbury and Burston it was probably included in the entry for St Albans. The reason for this omission was because Westwick was farmed directly by the Abbey's Refectory (*VCH Herts*, **2**, 393). The manor was granted at the request of Archbishop Lanfranc by Abbot Paul (1077–93) to Humbold, a kinsman of Abbot Richard de Albini, successor to Paul as abbot for life (*Gesta Abbatum*, Rolls series **1**, 64), and Abbot Geoffrey de Gorham built a hall at Westwick about 1130 for the use of one of his friends and kinsmen, a benefactor of the church (ibid, 80). The relative was Hugh, the son of Humbold, and Geoffrey appears to have granted it without the consent of the convent to Hugh on his marriage with Abbot Geoffrey's sister (ibid, 95). Thereafter, Hugh took the name of de Gorham (ibid, 65). The nephew of Abbot Geoffrey (Abbot Robert de Gorham), confirmed this grant (1151–66) in the mid twelfth century (ibid, 183; **3**, 400). In 1166 Geoffrey de Gorham held the manor of the Abbot of St Albans for two-thirds of a knight's fee and suit at the Hundred court of Cashio every three weeks (B Lib *Cott Ms Tib* VI fol 260, 236b). In 1212, Geoffrey was succeeded by Henry de Gorham who held 4½ hides for two-thirds of a knight's fee. William de Gorham succeeded Henry, who died about 1230, and lived until about 1278; on his death half the manor was seized as both his sons (William and John) were minors (*VCH Herts*, **2**, 393). In 1292 Hugh de Gressingham conveyed the manor of Gorham and one other moiety to John de Gorham and Isabella his wife (*Feet of Fines Herts East* 20 Edw I 1 no 275), who in 1307 settled the manor on themselves for life with the remainder to Alphonsus de Vere and heirs, and upon failure of such heirs to Hawisia de Vere for life, with remainder to Hugh de Vere for life, and to Thomas de Vere and his heirs forever (*VCH Herts*, **2**, 393; *Feet of Fines Herts East* 35 Edw I no 433).

It is not until the beginning of the fourteenth century that we learn anything about the actual manor. In 1306 a survey was carried out which described Westwick as comprising 'a hall with chambers; a chapel with a certain chamber; a storied edifice beyond the gate with a chamber. A kitchen, a bakehouse, a dairy, a larder with a certain chamber, a granary with a chamber for the bailiff, a dwelling for the servants of the manor, two cow houses, two sheep houses, a pig-sty and gardens'(B Lib *Cott Ms Tib* E VI fol 236 v). There was a second messuage called Newbury which had a dovecote, which was valued almost the same (ie 33s 4d). It is tempting to see in this 'Newbury' the precursor of Gorhambury, for Newbury may have meant the 'new house' or 'newbiggine' (Ekwall 1959, 339). The place of the Gorhams may then have acquired the name 'Gorhambury' at a subsequent date. The earliest record of the name 'Gorhambury' does not occur until 1540 (EPNS, Herts 91). There is evidence of a pre-Dissolution building underlying the foundations of Tudor Gorhambury (G Parnell, pers comm) and so, taken with the topographical evidence, the site of the medieval manor of Gorhambury is reasonably certain.

The main problem of the manorial history of Westwick is understanding its relationship to Gorhambury, which superseded it in name and possibly even in location. The situation is not helped by the conflicting evidence of the fourteenth century. It is extremely difficult to reconcile the evidence of the 1306 survey, when John de Gorham possessed Westwick, with the evidence of the Inquisition Post Mortem of 1327–8 taken after the death of Alphonsus de Vere (PRO C 1 35 10/12). In the 1306 survey Westwick is given the following valuation: Manor 40s; Newbery messuage 33s 4d; rents and customary dues £27 6s 7d; pleas and perquisites 40s; fishing rights 2s; 13 acres of meadow at 52s; 35 acres of wood 8s 9d and 54 acres of pasture 54s. As for the acreage of arable, the record has been damaged but the total area is about 822 acres and valued at £24 12s. The sum total is at least £63.

In the 1327–8 Inquisition Westwick was held in fee of the Abbot and Convent of St Albans by the service of 2 parts of a knight's fee and suit at the Hundred court of the Abbot every three weeks. The capital messuage was worth 6s 8d per annum; rents and customary dues £8 11s 4d; pleas and perquisites of the court 2s per annum; 4 acres of poor and dry meadow 3s per annum; 22 acres of wood of which the underwood is valued at 2s per annum and 305 acres of arable worth 50s 10d per annum. In addition, the service of 6 'customers' each holding a half virgate worth 26s 8d pa, at Christmas 20 hens worth 2s 6d; 10 cocks worth 10d, at Easter 100 eggs worth 4d, at the feast of St Michael's a quarter of oats worth 16d and one clove – total value £13 8s 10d.

There is no mention in the Inquisition Post Mortem of any fishing rights or of pasture; the meadowland is described as being only 4 acres 'dry and poor'; there is less woodland (22 acres as against 36 acres in 1306) and less than half the arable acreage. The valuation seems to be on a different basis, possibly because the 1306 figures express the total value as opposed to the annual value in the 1327–8 figures (Table 3).

Such items as pleas and perquisites, rents and customary dues can only be given as an annual figure. When one examines the value or rent of the two messuages in 1306 (40s and 33/4), and compares them with the 6/8 of the Capital messuage in the 1327–8 figures, there is clearly something wrong. The total value was over £63 in 1306 as against £13 8s 10d in 1327–8. Such is the difficulty in equating the two sets of figures that one is forced to conclude that the

Table 3

	1306			1327–8		
	Acreage	*Value/rent*	*per acre*	*Acreage*	*Value/rent*	*per acre*
Arable	822	£24 11s 11d	8½d	305	50s 10d	2d
Meadow	13	52s	4s	4	3s	9d
Pasture	54	54s	12d	–	–	–
Wood	35	8s 9d	3d	22	2s	1.09d

holding of John de Gorham in 1306 was not the same as that settled in 1307. If part of the manor of Westwick did revert to St Albans Abbey there is no record of it having done so.

Alphonsus de Vere was succeeded by his son John, who became the 7th Earl of Oxford on the death of his uncle Robert in 1331. He was granted free warren in his manor of Westwick in 1329–30 (*VCH Herts*, **2**, 394; Chart R 3 Edw III rot 30). His son the 8th Earl died in 1371, having settled the manor on his wife Maud. On the death of Maud the manor of Westwick was to revert to the crown, but the abbot of St Albans bought the reversion in 1395 from the Countess for 800 marks. This sum bought the manor of Westwick with one toft, 80 acres of land and 6 acres of wood (*Gesta Abbatum* Rolls series, **3**, 376, 400, 455). The figures are impossible to reconcile with the early fourteenth-century evidence. The manor of Westwick remained in the possession of St Albans Abbey until the Dissolution in 1539.

Because of the different sources of medieval evidence it is difficult to give a precise date for a reconstructed map of field systems within the manor of Westwick; however, what material there is can be described as 'medieval' and dates from the early thirteenth to the late fifteenth century with occasional references to the mid sixteenth-century survey. By plotting the evidence for St Michael's parish it is possible to ascertain some aspects of the spatial relationship, though in an incomplete and shadowy way. The impression that emerges is one of an irregular landscape which may, of course, be accentuated by the incomplete nature of the evidence. To the north of St Michael's, the parish of Redbourn shows a regular brick-work pattern of fields in the sixteenth century and a suspicion – for it is no more than that – that the landscape may have been regularly divided in the Roman or earlier periods. To the south of Redbourn the apparent irregular field pattern is a common characteristic of the Chiltern region which has been fully discussed by Roden (Roden 1973). 'The distinctiveness of Chiltern arrangements, as of the country to the south and east, was linked with a history of gradual and piecemeal settlement, in turn reflecting very varied conditions of soil and slope' (ibid, 374).

The principal characteristic of the landscape of the medieval parish of Kingsbury (St Michael's) is the existence of large common arable fields (200, 170, 180, 140 acres) interspersed with smaller field units often held in severalty. The predominant land-holding pattern was one of intermixed arable strips within the larger fields. The existence of woodland and names derived from woodland clearance suggests that the field pattern was certainly influenced by a piecemeal division of the landscape over several centuries. The indication for this is mainly derived from field name evidence, though there is a mention of an assart beside the 'villa de Westwyca' in the late twelfth or early thirteenth century (Chatsworth, St Albans cartulary 517/2).

There is no direct documentary evidence for the form of medieval settlement that overlay the Roman villa. What evidence there is would suggest that the medieval site consisted of an isolated toft surrounded by large common arable fields. It seems probable, to judge by the evidence of the holding of Robert Pleistowe (HRO Gorhambury Deeds XDO, 75) that in the fourteenth century the area to the west of the New Dyke (F 1700) was held almost entirely by John de Vere and if this was so it is just possible that the toft is the one mentioned in the purchase of the reversion by the abbot (*Gesta Abbatum* Rolls series, **3**, 376) in 1395, although the absence of pottery of this date perhaps precludes this.

The post-medieval landscape

The changes brought about by the division of the Abbey's estates after the Dissolution are uncertain; this is partly due to the paucity of information and a suggestion from the evidence that between the late fifteenth and mid sixteenth century there was no dramatic change in the arrangement of field systems. There is, it is true, a reference to the Park of Gorhambury (PRO SC 2 178/83) in 1551, though in the survey of 1569, where the extent of the Park pale was described, the interior was still sub-divided and in a state of cultivation.

The nature of the survey of 1569 has enabled a reconstruction of the landscape to be made with a good degree of confidence. The survey (HRO Gorhambury Deeds XI2) gives the name of each field, its size and its position in relation to surrounding fields and features; it gives the name of the tenant and state of cultivation, although the section on 'Goram and Westwyck' states specifically only if the land was not arable. In addition there is information concerning hedgerows and the occasional mention of topographic features within or adjacent to the field described. The 1569 survey illustrates principally the state of advanced transition from sub-divided open field systems to one where all the field units were cultivated independently of those around them by individual tenants.

With the creation of the first map of the area in 1634 by Benjamin Hare the cartographic era arrived and the landscape evidence assumed a more precise form. Neither the written survey of 1569 nor the map of 1634 gives any hint as to the existence of the Roman site. The more accurate and larger scale plan of the estate in 1766 by Andrew and Davies shows the state of the landscape before the abandonment of Tudor Gorhambury and the construction of the present Gorhambury house (1777–84). The building of the late eighteenth-century house close to the western side of the original park boundary necessitated the expansion of the park eastwards to the Belgic 'New Dyke' and what had been the intended sixteenth-century park pale boundary (HRO GOR Deeds X12). Thereafter the site of the Roman villa lay in the parkland until the early 1960s, when the principal masonry building once again became threatened with cultivation.

Summary

Unfortunately, the post-Roman history of the estate is devoid of reliable archaeological and historical landscape evidence and direct comparisons between the extents of the Roman and medieval periods cannot, therefore, be made. Nevertheless, it is important to explore the historical perspective so that the limitations and potential of the evidence are at least demonstrated. By this means, questions may be raised which, though they cannot be satisfactorily answered now, may in the course of future studies be more fully investigated.

Population

The Roman city of Verulamium was the third largest in Britain; at one time its area was second only to London being 91 ha (225 acres) in the late Antonine period and 80.93 ha (200 acres) in the third and fourth century. About 20 acres has been excavated so far and most of that contains public buildings. It is difficult, at present, to make a realistic estimate of population density within the town. Aerial photographic evidence and pottery scatter suggest that the north-west part of the town was probably never occupied. Frere, using Tacitus, quotes the mortality figure of 70,000 after the sack of London, Verulamium and Colchester (Frere 1967, 261). He estimates a population of about 15,000 at AD 60 and believes the population for Cirencester, Verulamium and Colchester could have approached 20,000 each (Frere 1967, 262). This figure does not include the rural population of the locality.

Comparison with historical sources does at least help to put the problem in perspective. Historically the 127 square kilometres area around Verulamium supported a fairly low population. The first census returns of 1801 covering 126 square kilometres produces a population of 7,679. At the time of the Tithe Apportionment maps around 1841 the figure stood at 13,318. Even at the time of the First Series 6″ Ordnance Survey maps of 1883 the 1881 census shows a population of 17,993. This is the nearest approach to Frere's estimate of 20,000 for urban Verulamium alone.

The question of population in the Roman period will always be contentious. However, on a completely excavated habitation site such as Gorhambury some estimate of population may be made by examining the range and number of buildings present. This at least permits some calculation as to the number of people required to operate such a villa and its associated estate. By using a list of servants made in the mid fourteenth century for St Mary de Pre, a small estate of *c* 360 acres close to Gorhambury, the number and range of inhabitants may be arrived at (see Table 4).

Table 4 Hypothetical population of the Gorhambury villa

Proprietor's family	6–10
Domestic servants	2
Cook(s)	1–2
Maids	2–3
Gardeners	2
Stoker of bath/hypocaust etc	1
Water carrier/drawer of water	1
Head groom/servant	1–2
Tanners	1–22
Driver/drover	1
Carter	1
Shepherd	1
Cowherd	2
Swineherd	1
Woodmen	1–2
Ploughmen	4–6
Bailiff/Steward	1
Smith/Farrier	1
Fisherman/Waterman	1
Total	31–43

This figure does not include workers' dependants or children, but serves to demonstrate that the villa might have required between 30 and 45 inhabitants in order to be a self-contained unit. It is probable that only half that number may have actually lived on the villa site though there is little prospect of ever demonstrating the amount of living space required for the average Romano-British inhabitant. These figures are based on the minimum numbers required to operate a demesne on a more or less self-sufficient level. The question as to the number of tenant cultivators depends, of course, on the size of the estate which on present evidence can only be speculative.

The coins

by P E Curnow

The publication of the results of the excavation of the villa at Gorhambury represents the completion of a major phase in the examination of the villa and analogous sites in this part of the Chilterns. Most of the work has been carried out in the post-war period and much of it, including the two most important and comprehensive excavations, by or under the aegis of the author of the main Gorhambury report. In this the opportunity has been taken to draw together the evidence from the various sites to see if any general conclusions can be suggested. The evidence of coin loss from a number of roughly comparable sites is therefore presented here (Table 5) with comments on the Gorhambury coin list itself. The comments are derived mainly from the evidence of coin loss as provided by the coin lists and as far as possible supporting or contradictory evidence from other sources has been left to be discussed by the excavator. The comparative evidence from both Gorhambury and the neighbouring sites has been presented in as simple a form as possible, by bar charts (pseudo-histograms) (Figs 118–120) together with graphs giving percentages for direct comparison (Fig 120). The period divisions are those used previously by the present writer and are in general agreement with those used by Richard Reece (eg 1972), although the latter uses more subdivisions and divides the Julio-Claudian into two major periods to AD 69 rather than our single period to AD 64, Nero's reform of the coinage (Curnow 1974). However, there should be no difficulty in correlating the two systems, bearing in mind that in British site finds coinage of Nero, prior to the Aes issues commencing in AD 64, is rare.

The coin list for Gorhambury (Table 6) exhibits no intrinsic numismatic surprises but of interest are a semis of Nero and two quadrans of Domitian; also a fine silvered follis of Galerius (No 223) while a single sestertius of M Aurelius has been very heavily scored in antiquity, a treatment occasionally found on Roman coins from Anglo-Saxon sites such as West Stow, Suffolk (Curnow 1985, 77). Whatever the date of its final deposition the last use of this piece is unlikely to have been as a coin. It has, however, been suggested by J Casey that it may have been defaced mistakenly, the portrait being assumed to represent Commodus, whose memory was damned.

Table 5 Coin loss from 13 selected sites (pp 109–110) by period, number and percentages

Coin periods AD	*I* 64	*II* 96	*III* 117	*IV* 138	*V* 161	*VI* 193	*VII* 222	*VIII* 259	*IX* 275	*X* 296	*XI* 317	*XIIA*	*XIIB* 348	*XIII* 364	*XIV* 388	*XV* 402
Gorhambury	26*	13	9	6	4	5	3	4	141	18	7	31	21	3	4	–
285(324)	9.1	4.6	3.15	2.1	1.4	1.75	1.05	1.4	49.5	6.3	2.4	10.9	7.4	1.05	1.4	
Gadebridge	–	5	3	6	3	3	1	1	62	10	7	32	126	17	16	8
300 (309)		1.6	1.0	2.0	1.0	1.0	0.3	0.3	20.6	3.3	2.3	10.6	42.0	5.6	5.3	2.6
Boxmoor	–	–	–	–	1	–	1	–	62	8	8	9	10	5	–	1
105 (106)					0.95		0.95		59.0	7.6	7.6	8.6	9.5	4.7	0.95	
Northchurch	–	–	1	–	1	1	1	1	13	1	–	2	3	1	–	
25			4.0		4.0	4.0	4.0	4.0	52.0	4.0	8.0	12.0	4.0			
Cow Roast (Orchard)	13*	12	6	6	7	3	2	2	64	7	3	11	50	32	58	29
305	4.3	3.9	1.9	1.9	2.3	1.0	0.65	0.65	21.0	2.3	1.0	3.6	16.4	10.5	19.1	9.5
Park St	3	1	–	–	–	1	–	–	11	3	–	1	11	36	–	–
67(75)	4.5	1.5				1.5			16.4	4.5		1.5	16.4	53.7		
Lockleys	2	–	–	1	–	–	–	–	2	1	–	1	4	2	2	
15	13.3			6.6					13.3	6.6		6.6	26.6	13.3	13.3	
Dicket Mead	1	2	–	–	3	10	7	8	130	8	3	6	40	11	1	–
230 (-)	0.4	0.8	–	–	1.3	4.3	3.0	3.5	56.5	3.5	1.3	2.6	17.4	4.8	0.4	–
Welwyn St Marys	–	1	–	2	1	3	–	–	19	–	1.0	1.0	26	7	11	–
72		1.4		2.8	1.4	4.2			26.4		1.4	1.4	36.4	9.8	15.2	
													91			
Hambleden	7	13	10	11	9	6	3	–	98	19	2	*16*	*58*	*17*	29	16
314(519)	2.2	4.1	3.2	3.5	2.9	1.9	0.95		31.2	6.0	0.6	*5.1*	*18.5*	*5.4*	9.2	5.1
													29			
Latimer	–	1	1	–	1	–	3	1	25	2	–	2	–	–	–	1
37 (39)		2.7	2.7		2.7		8.1	2.7	67.5	5.4		5.4				2.7
Verulamium (Frere)	80	130	40	30	30	25	20	30	368	261	13	42	256	148	96	36
1,603	5.1	8.2	2.5	1.9	1.9	1.5	1.2	1.9	23.0	16.0	0.8	2.6	16.0	9.0	6.0	2.2
Verulamium (Wheeler)	52	84	30	25	35	28	25	22	611	331	12	15	71	67	67	27
1,503	3.4	5.6	2.0	1.7	2.3	1.9	1.7	1.5	41.0	22.0	0.8	1.0	4.7	4.4	4.6	1.8
Verulamium (Theatre)	7	19	27	27	38	15	13	23	784	310	42	149	952	836	225	45
3,512	0.2	0.6	0.7	0.7	1.1	0.5	0.4	0.7	21.0	8.8	1.2	4.2	27.0	24.0	6.3	1.3
Verulamium (Lord Verulam)	30	67	30	37	37	43	33	26	505	473	26	69	574	223	160	48
2,368	1.2	2.6	1.2	1.4	1.4	1.7	1.4	1.0	20.0	19.0	1.0	2.7	22.0	9.0	6.1	1.9
Fishbourne	76	52	5	4	–	5	2	1	41	31	3	–	2	1	1	–
224	33.6	22.6	2.2	1.8	–	2.2	0.8	0.4	18.0	14.0	1.4	–	0.8	0.4	0.4	–

* Including the British coins

On turning to the distribution of coins, the pattern of coin loss for the first 300 years of Roman occupation shows no great divergence from the norm set forth by Richard Reece (1972) but does clearly indicate periods of activity at variance with some other villa sites in the neighbourhood – notably Gadebridge (Neal 1974) – although closely comparable to the pre-Constantinian series at Hambleden (Cocks 1921), and incidentally with those from the Frere excavations at Verulamium (Fig 120; Reece 1972). On coin-loss evidence alone it is possible to postulate considerable activity at Gorhambury in both the immediately pre-Roman and early Roman periods with 14 Belgic coins, mainly of Cunobelin, and 12 pre-Neronian pieces, including 4 pre-Claudian denarii. The succeeding Flavian period, with 13 coins, and period III, Trajanic, are also well represented. The remainder of the second century shows consistent but reduced coin loss – as is usual. A

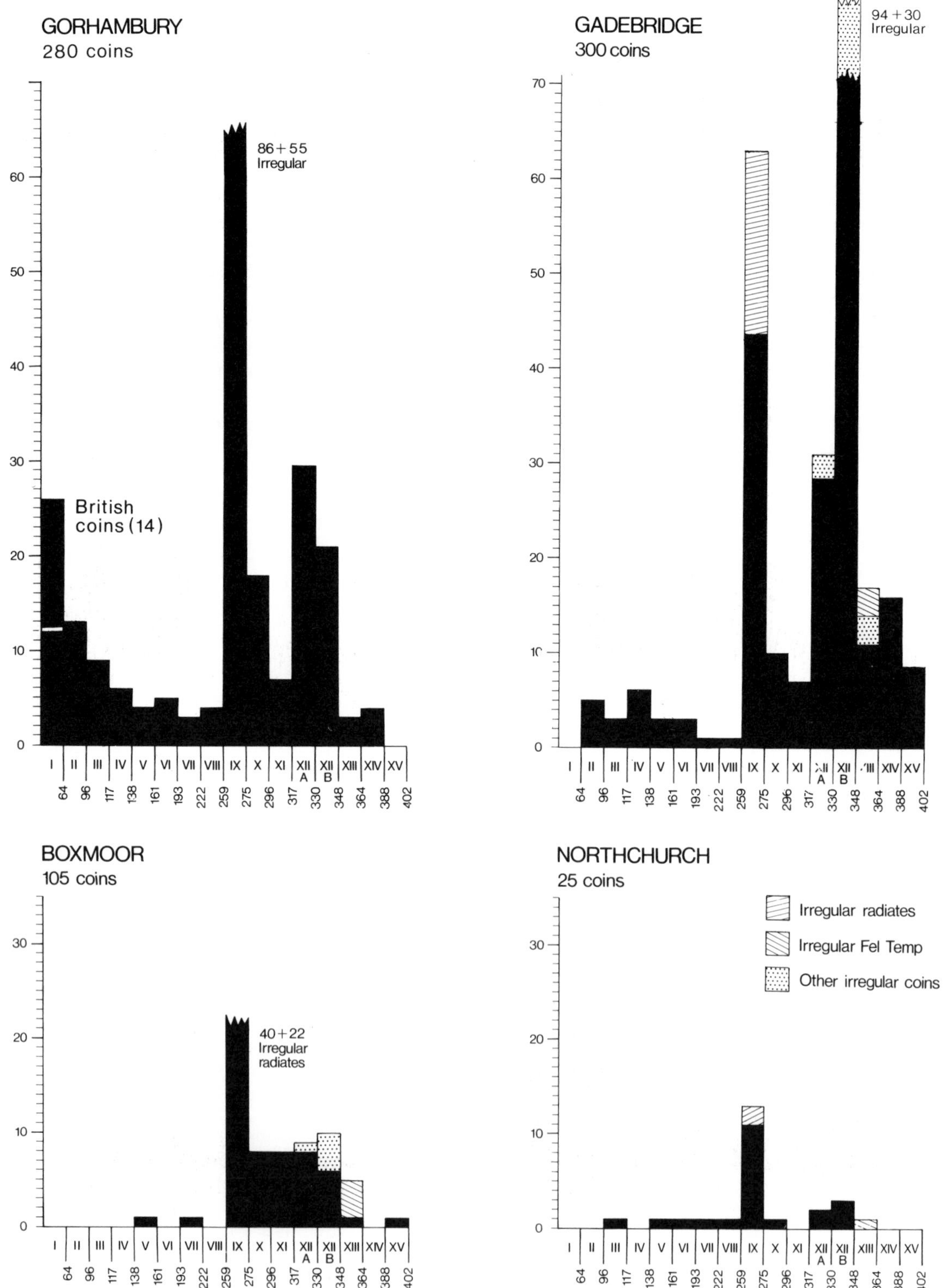

Fig 118 Comparative histograms of coins from the villas at Gorhambury, Gadebridge, Boxmoor and Northchurch

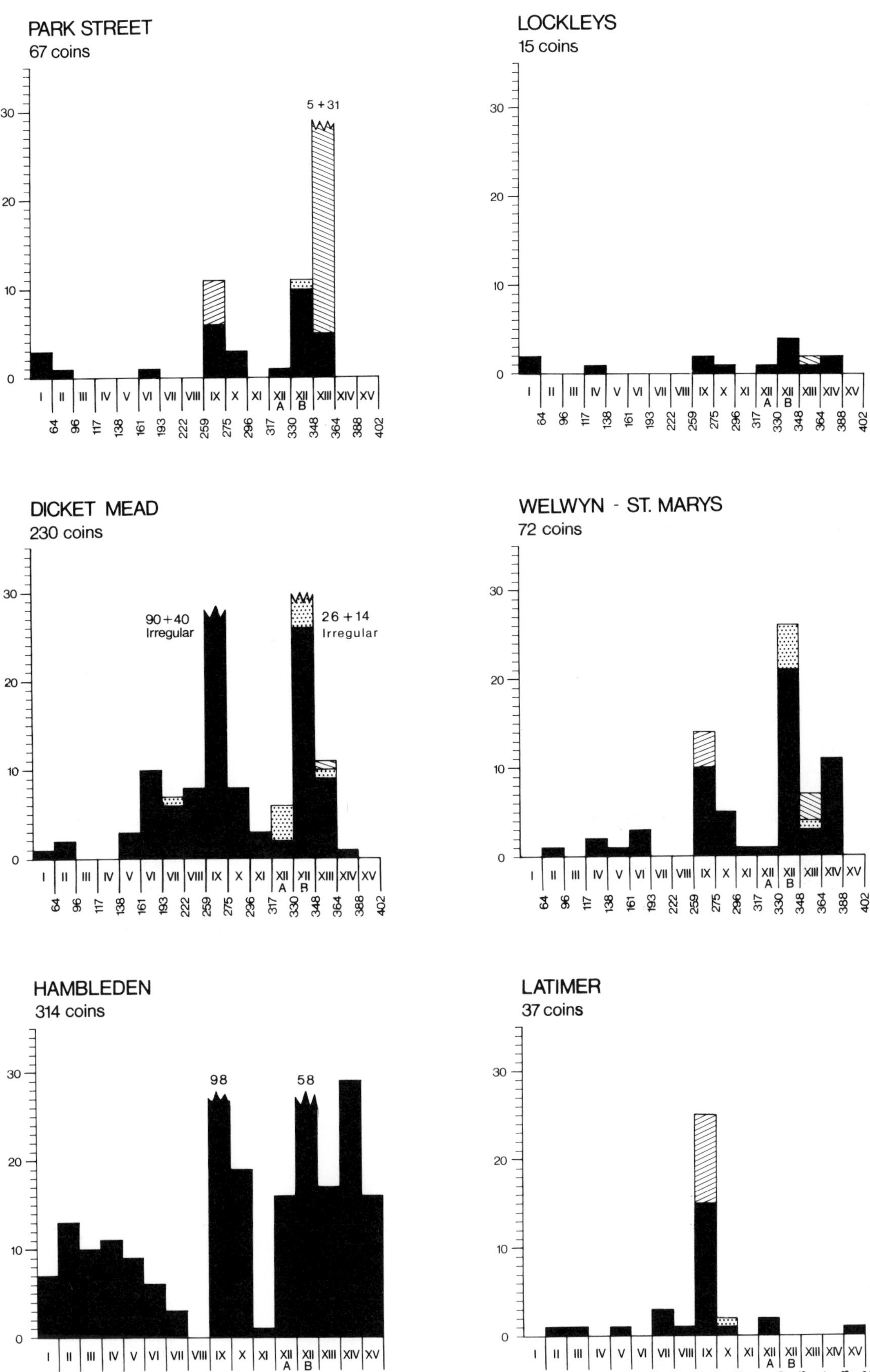

Fig 119 Comparative histograms of coins from the villas and settlements at Park Street, Lockleys, Dicket Mead, Welwyn St Mary, Hambleden and Latimer

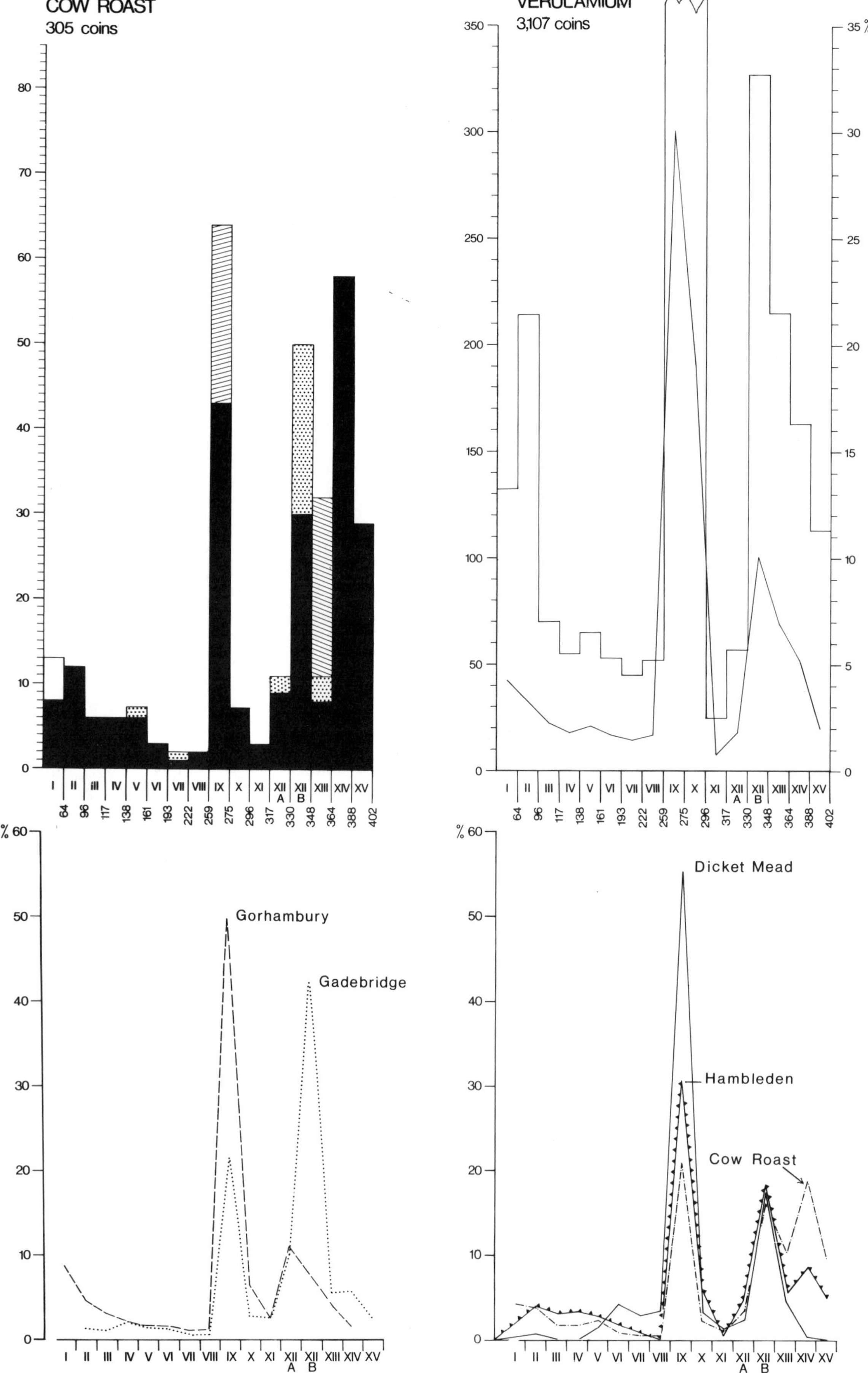

Fig 120 Histogram of coins from the settlement at the Cow Roast, Herts, and graphs showing percentage of coin loss for the villas at Gorhambury, Hambleden, Cow Roast, Gadebridge, Dicket Mead and Verulamium

further seven coins are of the first or second century but cannot be apportioned. The percentage of first- and second-century coin loss is consistently higher than at Gadebridge, notably in periods I and III, but is paralleled closely at Hambleden except for period I where Gorhambury has 9.1% to Hambleden's 2.2%. The Flavian and later Aes coinage from Gorhambury varies considerably in condition and while some, mainly sestertii, are worn enough to have continued in use well into the third century, by no means all are excessively worn and, of the remainder, a number are in very good condition. Much of the evidence therefore represents genuine coin loss not too far removed from the date of issue.

The radiates from Gorhambury represent 49.5% of the total coin loss (Period IX). This is substantially greater than that from Gadebridge (20.5%) as it is for the following period, but it is the lower figure which is the more abnormal since the Gorhambury figure, although high, is not exceptional. In this context it should be noted that in the Verulamium lists analysed by Richard Reece (1972), the radiate copies of the late Gallic Emperors are placed in the post AD 275 period. To get a valid comparison it is therefore necessary to combine periods IX and X in Fig 120. At Hambleden the list omits a very high proportion of unidentified coins, many of which almost certainly should be allocated to this period if a comparison is to be made.

Taking these considerations into account it may be concluded that the late third-century coin loss figures for Gorhambury represent considerable contemporary activity, but by themselves cannot be used to demonstrate a high peak. These figures are in marked contrast with Gadebridge where the total coin list is closely comparable in numbers, ie 285:300 (fully identified coins) derived similarly from a more or less complete area excavation. The Gadebridge figures should probably be seen in the context of a considerably lower level of coin loss for the preceding periods, but there coin loss appears to be growing at this period to peak in the first half of the third century. The contrast in the patterns of fourth-century coin loss at the two sites is striking. Whereas in the period AD 317–30 (XIIA) the figures are almost identical (10.9:10.4%), and also considerably above average for the neighbouring sites, the succeeding period, AD 330–48 (XIIB), shows a sharp divergence. At Gadebridge no less than 42% of the coin loss (126 coins) falls in this period, a uniquely high proportion; however, after *c* AD 350 coin loss falls rapidly from this high point and, while succeeding percentage figures are not incompatible with those, for example, from Verulamium, archaeological evidence, including the location of the late fourth-century coins, indicates that the villa's economy had changed substantially in the later fourth century with the demolition of the main buildings and occupation of a cottage in the northern courtyard.

At Gorhambury, following the somewhat higher than average figure for coin loss in AD 317–30, the succeeding period shows a drastic and highly unusual drop (to 7.4%). Indeed if the series from Latimer, Bucks (Branigan 1971), is dismissed as being too small (only 37 coins in all) to extrapolate from, then it represents a unique trend. The other sites tabulated (Table 5) show that the increase of period XIIB over XIIA varies from near parity at Boxmoor to a sixfold one at Verulamium (Reece 1972) with the average nearer the latter.

Clearly this enormous reduction in what might be expected from the coin evidence for the period AD 330–48 must be a reflection of changed circumstances in the economy of the villa – in either its degree of prosperity or its economic management. That this change was not a short-lived phenomenon is confirmed by the succeeding periods XIII–XV with 3, 4 and no coins respectively, representing only 1% and 1.4%, very much lower than any of the other sites quoted, excepting the very special case of Fishbourne and those with too few coins to provide valid comparisons.

Allowing for the dangers and difficulties attending interpretation of coin evidence when viewed in isolation from other archaeological evidence, the total coin list does nevertheless show significant variations in the pattern of loss which require explanation. The comparison of Gorhambury with Gadebridge seems to the writer to provide a clear example of a considerable change in economic activity taking place in each villa, but at a significantly although not widely different date. At Gadebridge coin loss peaks *c* 320–50 and falls away subsequently while Gorhambury sees a high level of coin loss during the last quarter of the third century and extending to the 330s, after which it drops strikingly. Hambleden with a comparable number of identified coins does not exhibit a similar peak and trough, but is slightly unusual in that it maintains a high level of coin loss to the end of the Roman period.

Smaller coin lists may also have features which depart from the norm in such a way as to illuminate some phase in the history of the site. Amongst the villas in the Verulamium area Park Street is exceptional in its overwhelming proportion of *fel temp reparatio* coinage – mainly copies of AD 353+. Less immediately obvious is the relatively high proportion of the normally rare *folles* coinage of period XI from Boxmoor, where there is a markedly high level of coin loss in the periods IX to XIIA, giving figures more closely comparable to Gorhambury than to Gadebridge.

Table 5 provides coin loss figures for 13 sites, 11 close to Verulamium; the Verulamium lists (Reece 1972) have been subdivided to show coins from the Wheeler and Frere excavations and those in a collection from Verulamium owned by Lord Verulam and are provided for comparative purposes. The Fishbourne coins are included to show a site with a uniquely early coin distribution. The sites more or less local to Verulamium comprise nine which are recognisable as villas and two, Welwyn St Mary's and Cow Roast, which appear to be settlements (although perhaps based on villas).

Of the villa sites three, Latimer, Northchurch and Lockleys, produce series too small for valid conclusions to be drawn but are included for completeness and to illustrate their general 'normality'. Park Street, already noted, is abnormal in the preponderance of *fel temp reparatio* – Fallen Horseman issues, regular and irregular.

Of the villa sites with more substantial coin lists, Dicket Mead falls within the general pattern of the Verulamium lists and of Gorhambury, but coin loss there appears to develop later and fall off earlier. Comments on the Boxmoor list have been given above. Hambleden is not a recent excavation and without a detailed re-examination of the coins it is not possible to allocate some 200 coins to their proper date brackets; even the Constantinian issues are only identified collectively – covering periods XIIA and B and XIII.* Only limited comments are therefore possible. Nevertheless the earlier periods are well represented, and allowing for the unallocated coins – many of which are likely to belong to Periods X (radiate), XII and probably XIII – the periods up to *c* AD 200 would provide very similar percentages to those from Gorhambury and from Verulamium (Wheeler). It is in Periods XIV and XV, however, that Hambleden reveals a considerably higher coin loss rate than on the other villa sites tabulated; this would remain valid even if many of the 200 unidentified coins could be dated, thereby reducing the overall percentage figures.

Of the two settlement sites listed, Welwyn St Mary's, admittedly with only 72 coins, and the Cow Roast (Orchard site) with 305 do show a comparatively high rate of fourth-century coin loss. Reece in his comments on the former, however, points out that the site 'behaves as a remarkably normal rural site of Lowland Britain' (Reece 1986, 144–5). It is nonetheless worth noting that within the local sites discussed here the radiate total is somewhat low.

The Cow Roast site, situated on Akeman Street between Berkhamsted and Tring, has a pattern of coin loss which seems to differentiate it markedly from all the other sites mentioned with the exception of Hambleden. The high rate of late fourth-century coin loss is striking and seems to indicate a period of monetary activity not paralleled elsewhere, especially in the periods from AD 364 to the end of the fourth century (XIV and XV). Even at Hambleden, which is exceptional amongst the villa sites, these late periods are not so marked as at the Cow Roast (Orchard site) where the coin loss represents 19% and 9.5% respectively for these two periods. This atypical pattern can be associated with the interpretation of the Cow Roast site as an important roadside settlement and thus subject to different economic factors from those affecting the villas, especially those around Verulamium. However, the late economic activity at the Hambleden villa should engender a note of caution on interpretation based on coin evidence alone.

The Cow Roast site apart, the villa sites producing a substantial coin series, whilst generally conforming to a pattern within the parameters suggested as normal for lowland Britain, do show significant period variations as indicated above. Finally, the sites and coin lists described here are considered primarily in a local – ie Chiltern and more specifically Hertfordshire – context although even here no attempt has been made to provide an exhaustive list: thus only one of the two major Cow Roast sites is listed (for the other, Marina site, see Reece 1982, 63). Any discursive treatment on a nationwide basis has been eschewed and while most of the sites fall within the major classes Reece has propounded for British rural sites, it is the variations within the overall patterns which seem well worth emphasising.

* Hambleden. In the coin report by Mill Stephenson (Cocks 1921, 189) the periods from AD 317 to 364 (XIIA, XIIB and XIII) could not be distinguished. The 91 coins from these three periods have therefore been allocated in Fig 120 proportionally to the average percentage of total coin finds from seven sites (Gorhambury, Gadebridge, Boxmoor, Dicket Mead, Welwyn St Mary, Verulamium (Frere's excavations) and Verulamium (Wheeler's excavations; the figures for the last two sites are based on Reece 1972).

Table 6 Catalogue of coins

For site context see Appendix 3

British coins

1–3	Tasciovanus	*c*20BC–AD10	AE	Mack 167, 170, 190	79,73,82
4	?Addedomarus/ Dubnovellaunus	*c*15BC–AD10	AE	cf Mack 278/281	75
5–13	Cunobelin	*c*AD10–40	AE	cf Mack 244[26, 248, 249[3], 250[2], 251	81, 73, 73, 77, 76, 75, 81, 74, 74
14	Uncertain Belgic	*c*20BC–AD40	AE	–	82

Roman

* = Coins 'lost' following initial identification

1	Republican		Ar Den*	
2	Republican		Ar Den*	
3	Republican		Ar Den*	
4	Augustus	29BC–AD14	Ar Den (2BC–AD14)	350 (Var IVENVT)
5–12	Claudius I	41–54	Dup, Asses[7]	66[5] Copies of various grades II–IV, 67 Grade I–II copy, 66 or 68/9 Grade I copy, + 1
13–16	Nero	54–68	Dup, Asses[2], Semis	304, 389, +2 (Asses-Victory type)
17–21	Vespasian	69–79	Sest, Dup, Asses[2]	cf 405, cf 478, 497, 500 + 1
			Dup or As	–
22–25	Domitian	81–96	Asses[2], Quadrans[2]	335, cf 333, 434 [2]

26–27	Nerva	96–98	Sest, Dup		64, 84
28–34	Trajan	98–117	Ar Den, Sest[2], Dup[2], Asses[2]		318, 385, 392, 396, 516, 673 + 1
35–40	Hadrian	117–138	Sest, Dup, Dup or As[2], Asses[2]		577b, 716, 750 (but 2e) + 3 (Dup, Dup, or As, As)
41–44	Faustina I (Ant Pius)	138–161	Sest[2], Dup, As.		1074 (but R/ as 328) 1146b, 1162, 1172
45	M Aurelius	161–180	Sest		– (Scored deeply in antiquity)
46	Faustina II (M Aurel.)	" "	Sest		–
47	Lucilla (M Aurel.)	" "	Sest		1763
48–49	Crispina (Commodus)	180–193	Dup or As[2]		680, ?675
50–54	1st or 2nd century	–	Dup, Dup or As[4]		–[5] (Dup ?Trajan)
55–56	2nd century	–	Sest, Dup		–[2] (Sest ?Hadrian)
57–58	Sept Severus	196–211	Ar Den[2]		196, 379
59	Caracalla (Sept Sev)	196–211	Ar Den		166 (Irregular – plated)
60	Severus Alexander	222–235	Ar Den		9
61	Julia Mamaea (Sev Alex)	222–235	Ar Den		343
62	Volusian	251–253	Ant		239a
63	Gallienus (Joint Reign)	253–259	Ant		134
64–74	Gallienus (Sole Reign)	259–268	Ant[11]		157 ΓI, cf 177, 180, 182, 193 I€, 193, ?226, 227–8, 249 ZI, 283, I/N, 287 I€
75	Salonina (Gallienus)	259–268	Ant		68
76–92	Claudius II	268–270	Ant[17]		16 IN, 34, 34/5, 38 I€, 47 IZ, 49, 55 IN 62/3 (but R/ 279), 66/7 IH, 85/6, cf 85, 90–96, 103, cf 103, 107, 187 IT, + 1
93–101	Posth Claudius II	270	Ant[9]		261[3], 266[6]
102–103	Irregular posth Claudius II	*c*270	– [2]		cf 261, 266
104	Claudius II or Quintillus	270	Ant		–
105	Postumus	259–268	Ant		74
106–110	Victorinus	268–270	Ant[5]		57, 71, 78, 114, 118 I*
111–122	Tetricus I	270–273	–[12]		78/80, cf 86, 87/90, 88, 100[3], 122/3, 130–6[2] + 2
123–127	Irregular Tetricus I	*c*270–273	Ant[5]		cf 100, 126, + 3
128–136	Tetricus II	270–273	Ant[9]		255, 270, 270/2 [5], 272 [2]
137–138	Irregular Tetricus II	270–273	–[2]		cf 254, 255
139–158	Uncertain Radiates	*c*270	Ant[20]		– [20] (Types of Postumus [1], Victorinus [2], Victorinus or Tetricus I [2], Tetricus I [2], Tetricus II [2], Tetricus I or II [2] + 9)
159–204	Irregular Radiates	*c*270	–[46] (AE3[21] AE4[19] Minims [6])		
205	Tacitus	275–276	Ant		65
206–220	Carausius	287–293	Ant [15]		98 S | P / MLXXI, cf 121 etc, 165 B | E / MLXXI, cf 243, 475 [S] | P, 878/80, 880, 881, 920, 923 + 4 + 1?
221–2	Allectus	293–296	Ant, Quin		cf 36 (Doublestruck), 55 | / QL
223	GENIO POPVLI ROMANI	300–305	London	Galerius	RIC VI, London 15 (VF Silvered)
224	PRINCIPI IVVENTVTIS	310–312	London	CI	RIC VI, London 229
225	GENIO POP ROM	316	Trier	Licinius I	RIC VII, Trier 120
226–9	SOLI INVICTO COMITI	313–315 317 316 316–317	?London London Trier Trier	CI CI CI CI	RIC VII, London cf 6 RIC VII, London 110 RIC VII, Trier 102(A) RIC VII, Trier 105/35
230–1	VICTORIAE LAETAE PRINC PERP	319–320	London	CI Cr.	RIC VII, London 154, 174
232	Irregular Victoriae Laetae Princ Perp	*c*319	cf Trier	CI	cf RIC VII, Trier cf 213
233	Irregular Virtus Exercit	*c*320	cf Trier	CI	cf RIC VII, Trier cf 292 (but no letters in field)
234	DN CONSTANTINI AVG	320–321	Aquileia	CI	RIC VII, Aquileia 64

235–8	CAESARVM NOSTRORVM	321 320–321 323–324 323–324	Rome Aquileia Lyons Trier	CII CII CII Cr	RIC VII, Rome 236 RIC VII, Aquileia 79 RIC VII, Lyons 211/217 RIC VII, Trier 431
239	Irregular Dn Constantini Max Aug	c323–324	cf Trier	CII	cf RIC VII, Trier 434/9 Hybrid
240–53	BEATA TRANQVILLITAS	320–324	Lyons	CI, CII, Cr	RIC VII, Lyons 133, 148/188, 153
		320–324	Trier	CI[8] Cr	RIC VII Trier 303[2], 305, 341, 347, 368[3], 390
			–	CI, –	– [2]
254	Irregular Beata Tranqvillitas	320–324	–	CI, –	cf RIC VII –[2] cf Trier 303
255–7	BEAT TRANQLITAS	323–324	London	Cr[3]	RIC VII, London 275[3]
258	SARMATIA DEVICTA	323–324	London	CI	RIC VII, London 290
259	PROVIDENTIAE AVGG/CAESS	324–330	trier	–	cf 12
260	SECVRITAS REIPVBLICE	324–330	Trier	Helena	41
261–6	GLORIA EXERCITVS(2 Stds)	330–335	Trier	CI,CII[2]	cf 49, 61, 81
		330–337	Lyons	CII	181
		330–337	–	H of CI[2]	– [2]
267	Irregular Gloria Exercitvs(2 Stds)	c330–337	cf Trier	CI	cf 48
268–272	Wolf and Twins	330–335	Trier	UR	51, 65
		330–337	–	UR	[3]
273	Irregular Wolf and Twins	c330–337	–	UR	– (AE4)
274–277	Victory on Prow	330–335	Trier	C'opolis	59, 66
		330–337	Lyons	C'opolis	cf 185
		330–337	–	C'opolis	–
278	Irregular Victory on Prow	c330–337	cf Trier	C'opolis	cf 59
279	GLORIA EXERCITVS (1 std)	337–341	Arles	CsII or Cn	441–3
280–281	VICTORIAE DD AVGG Q NN	341–348	Lyons/Arles	Cn	274
		341–348	–	CsII or Cn	137/8
282	FEL TEMP REPARATIO (Phoenix)	348–350	–	CsII or C	cf 34/5
283	GLORIA ROMANORVM	350–351	Arles	Mg	421 (Traces of Silvering)
284	VICTORIAE DD NN AVG ET CAE	351–353	Amiens	Mg or Dec	13/14
285	GLORIA ROMANORVM	364–367	Aquileia	Vn	985
286–7	SECVRITAS REIPVBLICAE	364–378	Lyons/Arles	H of VI	cf 280 etc
		364–378	–	H of VI	–
288	Irregular Secvritas Reipvblicae	c364–378	–	H oF VI	– (type of Lyons/Arles)
289–310	Uncertain				[22] (?1st–2nd cent, ?Plated Coin, ?3rd or 4th cent AE3, AE4[5], frags etc [12], ?Roman[2])

Medieval

	Long Cross Penny				Brooke

Modern

	Charles I Maltravers 1/4d	1635–49			
	George III ½d	1775			

Trade token

	John Weidingers	18th cent			

References for the Roman coins

Unless otherwise indicated references to coins are as follows: to AD 324 *RIC*, I–VII; from AD 324 *LRBC*, I, II

Abbreviations for fourth-century Emperors are as follows:

C I = Constantine I		Vn = Valens	
C II = Constantine II		G = Gratian	
Cr = Crispus		V II = Valentinian II	
Cs II = Constantius II		T I = Theodosius I	
Cn = Constans		Ar = Arcadius	
Mg = Magnentius, Dec — Decentius		Hon = Honorius	
V I = Valentinian I			

The artefacts
other than coins, pottery and glass vessels

by Angela Wardle

(Incorporating reports on the brooches by Sarnia Butcher (p 115) and intaglios by Martin Henig (p 160) and including analytical results by Justine Bayley of the Ancient Monuments Laboratory (p 136); the evidence for metalworking by Justine Bayley follows the Finds Catalogue (p 164). For terminology used in the analyses see p 121.)

Discussion

The catalogue illustrates a large number of the small finds from the site, in the hope that presentation of this assemblage will be of value for comparison with finds from other villas. However, a number of uninformative fragments are only described in the site archive. Certain comparisons can be made with the objects from the neighbouring villa at Gadebridge Park (Neal 1974), which are also published in full, and with the general range from sites such as Shakenoak, Oxfordshire (Brodribb *et al* 1968–73).

Considered as a group, the wide variety of small finds from Gorhambury reflects the life of a flourishing villa estate, although individually the objects are not generally of outstanding quality. They range from the personal possessions of the inhabitants, their tools and implements, items which also provide information about the economic activity of the estate, to the structural fittings, decorative features and contents of the buildings themselves. The distribution of particular classes of object is of significance in an assessment of the activity in various parts of the estate and of the function of specific buildings.

Certain items are of especial interest, notably the bronze wing, probably from an eagle statuette (No 194, Fig 126) found in the cellar during the 1956 excavations, which is of particularly fine workmanship, with marked similarities to the Silchester eagle (Boon 1957, 99, pl 15), while the hand with grapes (No 195, Fig 126), came from a figurine. A few objects may have military associations, as for example the vine leaf harness pendant (No 170, Fig 125), which has many parallels in Britain and Germany, a mount with Celtic trumpet design (No 168, Fig 125), and a scabbard runner (No 179, Fig 125) which is of military type.

Among the personalia the site produced 46 complete brooches and various fragments. Sarnia Butcher observes (p 115) that they are almost entirely first century in date, several made no later than AD 43; the majority are types which are common from other Hertfordshire sites including Verulamium. They were distributed widely over the site; several came from levels associated with early buildings (ie Buildings 17 and 21) and many from ditch fills, particularly the north–south ditch between the inner and outer enclosures (Ditch 1281). This ditch produced numerous finds of all descriptions deposited during the second-century occupation of Buildings 27 and 37.

Other items of personal adornment included finger rings, several with intaglios (Nos 1012–1018, Fig 143), two of early first-century date, or gem stones, notably the large and ostentatious emerald found in Building 40 (No 1011, Fig 143). The distribution of these and the more modest rings is random. The eleven bracelets, mostly fragmentary, all from third- and fourth-century levels, represented various common types, and there is a wide variety of hairpins in copper alloy (Nos 86–107, Fig 123), bone (Nos 924–949, Fig 140) and glass (Nos 987, 988, Fig 142). Many bone objects, particularly hairpins and needles, were concentrated in second-century levels in Ditch 74 to the north of the villa (Building 37). There are only a few beads from necklaces (Nos 989–1005) in silver, glass, amber and jet, all widely scattered.

The number of such personal items is broadly comparable with those from Gadebridge Park, with more brooches and hairpins from the larger site of Gorhambury. The greater number of bracelets from Gadebridge, 27 as opposed to 11, is chiefly explained by their presence in a votive deposit.

Among the objects intended for personal use at Gorhambury were numerous cosmetic implements, chiefly tweezers and nail cleaners; one complete set including tweezers, nail cleaner, and scoop (Nos 110–112, Fig 124) came from Ditch 1281. More unusual is a folding implement, probably a knife (No 151, Fig 124), from the same area, and a file (No 153, Fig 124) from the second-century fill of a latrine. Again there are more toilet implements from Gorhambury, which is surprising considering the size of the fourth-century bathing establishment at Gadebridge.

Gorhambury is slightly richer in the quality and variety of small decorative objects and mounts. Three of the four seal boxes, all of recognised types dating from the second century with local parallels, are enamelled. In contrast the iron styli are generally simple. Only four have moulded decoration on the stem and none is inlaid. Apart from the seal boxes, one brooch, a ring, four studs, and a button and loop fastener are enamelled (No 45, 61, Fig 122; Nos 207–212, Fig 126); one stud has niello inlay (No 217, Fig 126).

Items of domestic use include vessels of copper alloy (Nos 229, 230, Fig 126), spoons of tinned copper alloy (Nos 239–244, Fig 128) and bone (Nos 964, 965, Fig 140), bucket handles and fittings of iron and copper alloy (Nos 542, 543, 545–546, Fig 134), a large cauldron hook (No 529, Fig 134) and querns (Nos 1057–58, Fig 147), made of both local and imported materials. There are numerous keys and lock bolts of copper alloy and iron (Figs 128 and 135), all the usual Roman types being represented. Among the objects of copper alloy are various studs and fittings which may be from furniture or small articles such as boxes and chests, while the iron objects include many structural fittings, hinges, clamps, split spiked loops and assorted bindings. The wall plaster, stucco, mosaics and architectural fragments demonstrate the luxury of the villa itself.

Among the iron objects are tools and implements

which are informative about the economic life of the estate. It is notable that many such items are concentrated in the area of the aisled hall in its various phases, and the finds reinforce the interpretation of these succeeding buildings as accommodation for estate workers. The quantity of iron tools is limited but the range covers woodworking tools, including an axe, adze, saw, file and possible plane blades (Fig 131), all from this building complex. A drill bit and mortise chisel came from Structure 43 further north, and a carpenter's gouge from a second-century level over Building 10 (No 372, Fig 131). Several fragmentary chisels came from the area of Building 53. Certain types of chisels and punches were used in metalworking, but apart from the wedges or sets (Nos 389, 390, Fig 131) there are few obvious metalworking tools despite the evidence, from crucibles found in first-century levels, of fine metalworking (including gold) and, from the presence of considerable quantities of slag and scrap iron, for smithing in the fourth century. The evidence for iron and metalworking, which would have been on a limited scale to serve the estate, is discussed by Justine Bayley (p 164).

As one would expect from a farming community there is a group of items broadly associated with agricultural activity and animal husbandry. In the latter category belong ox goads (Nos 406–408, Fig 131), a farrier's butteris (No 404, Fig 131) and a large collection of hipposandal fragments (see below), while a wool comb (No 410, Fig 132, used for the carding of fleece before spinning), shears (No 424, Fig 132), spindle whorls and loom weights (No 1032, Fig 145) show that wool was produced, spun and woven. A bone bobbin (No 971, Fig 141) and many rather coarse sewing needles of copper alloy and bone were also found.

Several agricultural tools were identified, including ploughshare tips (Nos 411–416, Fig 132), a spade sheath and a rake tooth (Nos 405 and 393, Fig 131). For general pruning and harvesting there were knives (Nos 419–423, Fig 132), scythes and sickles (Nos 420–422, Fig 132), the latter in extremely fragmentary condition.

Again, the aisled hall complex produced several of these objects; in the yard to the north was a large cleaver (No 432, Fig 132) and fittings including a water-pipe junction-collar (No 559). Many of the personal and domestic items detailed above, including the emerald, a seal box, a cauldron hook (No 529, Fig 134), querns, keys and numerous fittings suggest that the building provided living accommodation and was not simply a workshop or storage barn. A hoard found in Building 40, the latest phase of the complex in its aisled form, is of interest as it contained, among miscellaneous ironwork, a hooked mount, possibly a cart fitting (No 470, Fig 133), a pruning knife (No 423, Fig 132), a key (No 563, Fig 135), a steelyard (No 556, Fig 134) and two lead weights (Nos 920, 921, Fig 139). From elsewhere on the site, other weights of copper alloy (Nos 220–225, Fig 126) include six flat discs of a type and weight also found at Verulamium (Frere 1972, 160) and Colchester (Crummy 1983, fig 195); five came from the area of Building 53 (Fig 64). Much scrap iron, fragments of bindings, straps and other offcuts, including snippets of bronze, came from around this building; together with the finding there of three-quarters of the smithing slag from the site, this suggests that it was a forge.

While much of the ironwork was scattered over the entire site, the third area of concentration, after the aisled hall complex and Building 53, was Structure 43. This was of two phases, the later of which also produced 52 third- and fourth-century coins. Various tool fragments included a drill bit (No 371, Fig 131), a knife (No 433, Fig 132), an ox goad (No 406, Fig 131), a key (No 564, Fig 135), a stylus (No 613, Fig 136) and numerous miscellaneous scraps. The area also yielded eight fragmentary hipposandals, used as temporary shoes for horses. The whole site produced 25 fragments of hipposandals; apart from Structure 43 these were also concentrated around Building 30 (but possibly associated with Building 53) (five examples), and in the aisled hall complex (seven examples). The remaining five were scattered. The number of fragments is relatively high when contrasted, for example, to the three from Gadebridge Park, but this may simply reflect the more extensive excavations at Gorhambury. There is however an exceptionally large number of complete and fragmentary hipposandals from Verulamium (Manning 1984a, 87), which may reflect its importance as a market centre (Manning points out that horses were normally unshod in the country). The plan and construction of Structure 43 suggests that it may have been a stock pen and the presence of a relatively large number of hipposandals and the many coins supports the theory that horses and perhaps other animals were traded there.

Although the horseshoe was known in Roman Britain (Manning 1976, 31) the horseshoes found at Gorhambury are all from unstratified contexts and likely to be of post-Roman date. Certain other items of Roman date are associated with transport; for example the linch pin (No 471), a swivel ring (No 473), a terret (No 474) and the hooked mount (No 470), all Fig 133. The function of the latter object, found in the hoard described above, is obscure – it may be a binding from a cart. Other examples are known (see catalogue) but the Gorhambury mount is better preserved than most.

Evidence for the leisure activities of the villa's occupants is confined to a few bone and glass gaming pieces and bone dice.

General comparison with the finds from Gadebridge is of interest. The Gorhambury assemblage is larger, as might be expected from the more extensive area excavated, but with certain notable exceptions the relative proportions of the types of objects are broadly similar. Jewellery and personal and domestic items are comparable, with slightly greater numbers from Gorhambury, but the most obvious differences occur in the quantity and type of ironwork. Gorhambury (with 555 published items) has produced nearly twice as many objects and fragments, numbers which reflect the extent and position of the excavated areas. Most of the ironwork, notably the hipposandals, was found in areas well away from the main villa buildings, and the excavation of many buildings and structures with agricultural function is reflected in the greater concentration of agricultural implements and related tools. Both sites produced a similar range of structural fittings.

Other Hertfordshire villas were excavated on a more limited scale, investigation being confined in many cases to the main building. The number of finds is consequently smaller but similar types recur. At Shakenoak, Oxfordshire, about 400 out of approximately 1600 iron objects were illustrated, with 254 objects of copper alloy out of 'several hundred' from Sites A, B, C and H, which contained a villa and outbuildings. A range of personal and domestic items and tools was revealed, with some interesting late Roman material which demonstrates the prosperity of the fourth-century settlement on parts of the site, in contrast to Gorhambury.

Analysis of the numbers and types of stratified finds from Gorhambury reflects the general prosperity and activity at different periods. There is a gradual increase during the first century, rising to a peak in Period 9, late second to third centuries, which is largely due to the numbers of objects lost in the deposits filling the ditches dividing the two enclosures and to the large quantity of ironwork in Building 40. The large number of finds in Periods 10 and 11 is due to the presence of much ironwork in late third- and fourth-century contexts; there are very few stratified objects of intrinsic value or quality. It is likely that the relatively small amount of ironwork surviving in earlier contexts indicates that it was reworked, but with the end of occupation in the fourth century iron objects and scrap were abandoned on the site.

Catalogue

Note: All recognisable objects have been given catalogue numbers and a representative selection has been illustrated. Descriptions and drawings of the unillustrated material can be found in the site archive.

The catalogue has been arranged by material, but objects of similar function in different materials have been cross-referenced in the discussions that prefix each group of catalogue entries. The coding following each entry gives the small find (SF) number, the Ancient Monuments Laboratory (AML) number, the site grid square number (in **bold** type), the coordinates related to that grid square, and the context number (bracketed). The find is then related to a building (if possible) and its archive plan (AP) and archive section (AS). In all cases measurements give the maximum surviving length unless stated otherwise.

Objects of copper alloy (Figs 121–130)

The brooches

by Sarnia Butcher

The alloy identifications are by Justine Bayley; see her discussion of the results on p 121 below.

In view of the long period of occupation of the site it is remarkable that the brooches are almost entirely first-century types. A number are types which occur on exclusively pre-conquest sites and were almost certainly not made later than AD 43: the Langton Down, Rosette, Aucissa, Bagendon and Hod Hill types. The common types of the middle years of the first century are present: the Nauheim derivative and two-piece Colchesters, but there are very few of the later Colchester derivatives or others which are common in the later first century and the early second century, such as the Polden Hill and headstud types. There is one brooch (no 43) which is dated to the Hadrianic–Antonine period on the continent and another (no 44) which is unlikely to be earlier than the second half of the second century.

Nearly all are types which are common in the area, with parallels from St Albans, Colchester, Chelmsford, Baldock and Braughing. The best parallels come from the King Harry Lane cemetery at St Albans (Stead and Rigby 1989). Some, such as the Colchester brooches (both one-piece and two-piece types), were almost certainly made in the area, but the other types have parallels from wider afield, including the continent. The two later brooches cited above were almost certainly continental products.

Fig 121

One-piece brooches: incomplete

1 Highly arched upper bow and first turn of a one-piece spring; the foot, which has broken off, almost at right angles to the upper bow. Catchplate missing. Bronze. Length 58mm. SF 2338 AML 820266 **2619** 4.32 0.97 (1140). Spread associated with Building 17, Figs 2 and 45. AS 164/1

2 Similar profile to no 1 above, with the first turn of a one-piece spring. A group of grooves imitates a binding near the centre of the bow. The foot is missing. Bronze. Length 35mm. SF 26 AML 820031 **1919** 7.00 4.00 (5). Well. AS 22/3

These two brooches might be seen as La Tène brooches of the first century BC but it is more likely that they belong to the following group; they are too fragmentary for parallels to be cited.

Plain brooches with one-piece spring and no crossbar

3 Complete brooch of the type called 'Nauheim-derivative' by M R Hull but which Stead (1986, 109) prefers to follow Wheeler in naming the 'poor man's brooch'. The spring of four turns, with inferior chord, is made from the same strip of metal as the square-sectioned bow which tapers to a very narrow foot bearing a large unperforated catchplate. Bronze. Length 45mm. SF 2931 AML 811385 **2819** 2.30 9.70 (1587). South terminal Ditch 1281, between inner and outer enclosures. First-century level. AS 251/1

4 Similar to No 3 but smaller; broken foot. Bronze. Length 38mm. SF 2514 AML 820284 **2417** 2.70 3.90 (1269). Pebble surface postdating granary, Building 10, Fig 35. AP 184 AS 201/1

5 Generally similar to Nos 3 and 4. The upper bow is broader with three punched circles near the centre. Bronze. Length 38mm. SF 1546 AML 820227 **2622** 8.95 6.25 (786). Gully east of Building 47. AP 123 AS 134/6

6 Similar brooch but with bow of rounded wire (a crease at the back suggests that it was wrought); it has rough grooves scratched across the middle and lower bow and a plain triangular catchplate. Bronze. Length 40mm. SF 3011 AML 811389 **2821** 4.00 2.00 (1594). North terminal Ditch 1281. AS 253/3

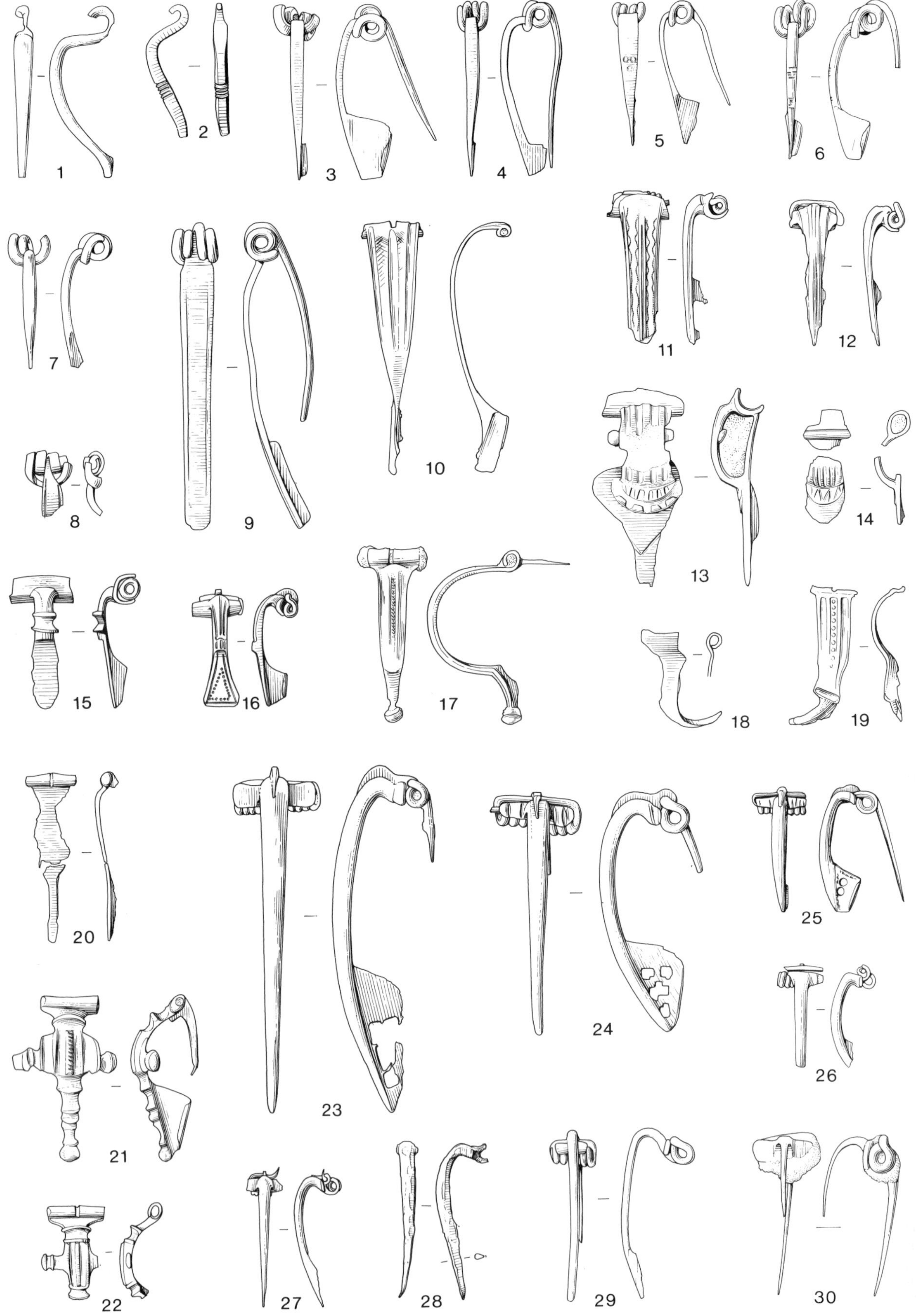

Fig 121 Brooches of copper alloy (Scale 2:3)

7 The upper part of a similar brooch, badly corroded. Bronze. Length 34mm. SF 2967 AML 820334 **2820** 4.00 9.00 (1594). South terminal Ditch 1281. AS 253/3

8 Upper part of a brooch with broad flat bow with marginal grooves; corroded. Bronze. Length 17mm. SF 3295 AML 820348 **3719** 0.50 5.80 (4). Ploughpan

At Camulodunum this type appears in contexts dated to Claudius–Nero (Hawkes and Hull 1947, type VII, 312), while Fishbourne provides related examples in the period AD 43–75 (Hull in Cunliffe 1971, 100).

Strip-bow brooch with one-piece spring

9 The bow is a broad strip, almost flat in profile, ending in a one-piece spring of four turns with inferior chord. Recessed knurled lines run down each side of the bow; broken central catchplate. Bronze. Length 80mm. SF 924 AML 811365 **2018** 2.00 1.00 (544A). Well

A very similar, though smaller, brooch was found at Camulodunum (Hawkes and Hull 1947, pl XCIV no 85, 318) where it was regarded as the forerunner of the Langton Down series; brooches with similar bows, but with a hook holding the chord, have been described as variants of the Colchester brooch (Stead and Rigby 1986, 112, no 52) or 'Simple Gaulish' (Olivier forthcoming). A date within the first century AD is indicated by the one-piece spring.

Early hinged

10 The bow is a thin strip, very wide at the head where it is turned under to hold an axial rod for the hinged pin, but tapering to a very narrow foot, almost at right angles to the arched main bow. The broken catchplate is almost rectangular. The bow has three longitudinal grooves and bands of fine cross-hatched decoration between them. Bronze. Length 67mm. SF 2149 AML 820259 **2620** 0.70 4.80 (721) Building 53, Fig 64. AP 108 AS 133/1

Although somewhat unusual in its details this brooch clearly belongs with the Maiden Castle type which has the same head construction and thin strip bow. Some also have the three grooves and a similar-shaped catchplate: cp Wheeler 1943, fig 84 nos 26 and 27, 261–2, both from a 'Belgic' layer.

Langton Down brooches

11 The upper part of a broad finely-moulded bow with central and marginal ribs and wavy-line decoration of punched dots. The broken head was cylindrical and still contains a spring of seven or more turns. The back of the bow is flat and shows the stump of a central catchplate with large cut-out. Brass/gunmetal. Length 40mm. SF 2070 AML 811383 **2418** 4.50 6.50 (741). Ploughpan

12 Fragmentary brooch of the same general type as no 11. The bow shows a series of grooved mouldings and a slight crest at the top. The spring of seven turns retains only a fragment of its covering cylinder. There is a stump of a central openwork catchplate. Brass/gunmetal. Length 38mm. SF 2085 AML 820252 **2418** 6.50 6.00 (741). Ploughpan

Parallels for these two brooches can be seen in *Camulodunum* (Hawkes and Hull 1947, pl XCIV) including a fragment with the same decoration as no 11. Most Camulodunum examples occurred in deposits of AD 44–61, although some were pre-conquest. In the pre-conquest cemetery of King Harry Lane, St Albans (in use *c* AD 10–43, Stead and Rigby 1989) there were numerous examples, including another parallel for no 11 (seen by courtesy of Dr I M Stead). Skeleton Green (Partridge 1981, fig 71, no 45) has one of the same general type as these two (ie with reeded bow rounded at the head) but it was from a late deposit and Mackreth (ibid, 134 and 141) suggests that these may be later than the straight-headed type. However, the evidence from King Harry Lane shows that they can be pre-conquest.

Rosette brooches

13 Fragmentary. Remains of a cylindrical spring cover are joined by an arched upper bow decorated with longitudinal ribs which appears to be cast in one with the flat main plate. This has a band of chevron decoration at the base of the upper bow and shows remains of a plain zone and a reeded foot. It is probable that an extra repoussé plate was attached over the plain zone as in many of these brooches. Two pellets under the upper bow may be the remains of decorative bolts but the space is obscured by concretion, making it impossible to tell whether the main flat plate is actually cast in one with the head or not: appearances suggest that it only touches. There is the stump of a central openwork catchplate. Brass/gunmetal. Length 53mm. SF 534 AML 820084 **2023** 9.60 2.50 (348). Level over Ditch 74. AS 55

14 Two fragments of a brooch which was probably similar in form and decoration to no 13. Bronze/gunmetal? SF 625 AML 820106 **2023** 6.70 2.00 (409). Posthole. AP 53

Several complete brooches which appear to be similar and which have an attached repoussé plate occur in the King Harry Lane cemetery, St Albans, in use from *c* AD 10–43 (Stead and Rigby 1989). Another from a pit dated Claudius–Nero at Chichester apparently did not have an attached plate and the main plate appears to be cast in one with the head (Down and Rule 1971, 131, fig 6.4). None of the rosette or thistle brooches from Camulodunum is very close to ours; the nearest is no 78, from a period I deposit (Hawkes and Hull 1947, 316, pl XCIII).

Fantail brooches

15 Head with a large plain cylindrical spring cover, now partly broken open; spring missing. The short arched upper bow terminates in two flanged mouldings, below which there is a damaged flat triangular foot. Plain catchplate. Brass. Length 35mm. SF 678 AML 820113 **2123** 1.00 2.00 (77). Ditch 74. Level associatted with occupation of Building 21, Fig 48

Similar brooches have been found in Britain: Hod Hill (Brailsford 1962, 8, C43, quoting another from Woodcuts); Camulodunum (Hawkes and Hull 1947, pl XCV 15, 320– very fragmentary) and Bagendon (Clifford 1961, 176 no 42). Hull (op cit, 320) considered it to be mainly a Rhineland type and quotes several from the area; however it also occurs in France. Dated examples are all from contexts in the first half of the first century AD.

16 In general shape similar to no 15 but the head construction differs. The spring, of about eight turns, is open and attached by means of a rod threaded through a lug behind the centre of the plain almost flat crossbar; the chord is also threaded through a crest forming the upper part of this lug. The arched upper bow is narrow and longitudinally ribbed, with a slight moulding at the waist. The triangular foot has a border of punched dots. The upper surface is tinned or silvered. There is a stout plain catchplate and a slight rib above it which may be a casting flash, as seen on the Lullingstone brooch quoted below. Leaded bronze. Length 31mm. SF 619 AML 820104 **2022** 9.80 6.20 (369). Ditch 74. Associated with occupation of Building 37, Fig 48. AP 51 AS 68/3

An almost identical brooch was found in a first century context at Lullingstone (Meates 1987, 63 no 56). Other generally similar brooches are hinged: eg Rudston (Stead 1980, 94, fig 61 no 15; this is also enamelled and has a cast headloop) and Chew Park (Rahtz and Greenfield 1977, 292, fig 114 no 9).

A wide range of brooches have fantail feet as described by M R Hull and others; within this range there are variations amongst those with the general shape of the two Gorhambury brooches. Until better evidence is forthcoming it seems safest to regard the shape as probably fairly widespread and long-lasting.

Aucissa and related brooches

17 The head is obscured by concretion and it is not possible to say whether it was inscribed with the maker's name, but it is very typical of the Aucissa-type brooches found in Britain. It has the usual features: the highly-arched centrally-ribbed upper bow, the flat head rolled back to form a narrow tube holding the axial rod for the hinge and the short foot ending in a knob which is a separate casting. It seems also to have separate knobs at the ends of the hinge-axis. Brass. Length 46mm. SF 3871 AML 820365 **4019** 5.95 4.37 (2387). First-century level. AP 346 AS 363/3

The type is common throughout the Roman provinces and occurs on both pre- and post-conquest sites in Britain (eg Hod Hill, Camulodunum and Richborough) but is much rarer here in Flavian and later contexts.

18 Fragment of a brooch probably similar to no 17, showing half of the head with hinge-tube and knobbed end, and part of an arched upper bow with central rib. Brass. Length 31mm. SF 1717 AML 820234 **2521** 7.00 8.00 (713). Structure 12, Fig 36. AP 110 AS 132/1

19 This distorted brooch belongs to the 'Bagendon' type, which has the form of the Aucissa except that the upper bow is less arched and is broader, usually either divided or having multiple ribs. The head shows the typical flattening and cross-mouldings but the hinge-tube is missing; the broad upper bow is undivided but has two longitudinal ribs with a row of pellets between; the foot is very narrow. Brass. Length 38mm. SF 2907 AML 820326 **2820** 4.70 4.20 (1551). Trackway over ditch 165. AP 219 AS 253/4

Fairly similar brooches occur in sub-class D of the eponymous type at Bagendon: (Hull in Clifford 1961, 179, fig 32 no 11, fig 33 nos 7 and 8). From both context and morphology they are probably to be dated to the first half of the first century AD.

20 Two badly corroded fragments of a brooch of very thin metal, the head turned back to form a narrow tube for the axial rod of the hinged pin, flat profile, spreading upper bow and very narrow foot. Brass. Length 43mm. SF 987 AML 820129 **2018** 5.50 6.80 (91). Ditch 74. First century level. AS 99/1

This may have been similar to some brooches from Hod Hill illustrated as nos C 89–92 in Brailsford 1962, fig 10; even if not, the head construction suggests that the date must be in the first half of the first century AD.

Hod Hill brooches

21 Badly corroded but complete brooch with rectangular ribbed panel on the upper bow and multiple mouldings down the narrower foot. A collared lug projects from each side of the panel. The pin is hinged in a narrow tube formed by folding back the top of the head. Brass. Length 44mm. SF 1090 AML 811371 **2218** 4.00 3.00 (615). Humus sealing first-century levels. AP 90 AS 103/1

22 The upper half of a brooch similar to no 21 except that the ribbed panel is not much wider than the bow. Brass/gunmetal. Length 24mm. SF 675 AML 820112 **2122** 5.00 2.00 (266). Timber slot. AP 21 AS 68/3

These brooches belong to a well-known sub-type; it occurs at Hod Hill (Brailsford 1962, fig 9, C76), at Colchester (Sheepen, Niblett 1985, fig 75, no 33, context AD 54–57) and on the continent (eg Augst, Riha 1979, nos 911 and 912, taf 33, 131; one found with Claudian pottery). Hull's dating to Claudius–Nero for the general type still seems valid (Hawkes and Hull 1947, 324).

One-piece Colchester brooches

23 Stout tapering rounded bow and plain crossbar. The one-piece spring of nine turns is held by a hook turned back onto the top of the bow. The broken catchplate shows the remains of rectangular piercings. Brass. Length 90mm. SF 1921 AML 811382 **2722** 4.80 6.10 (769). Chalk spread associated with path 770. AP 122 AS 134/5

24 Similar to no 23 although shorter. The spring is of seven turns and the catchplate with its rectangular piercing is complete. Brass. Length 65mm. SF 1197 AML 811374 **2117** 9.00 9.50 (660). First-century level south of Building 23. AP 88 AS 103/3

25 Typical example of the small Colchester brooch. It has a short, flat, slightly ribbed crossbar covering a spring of eight turns formed from the same piece of metal as the bow. The chord is held by a second projection from the head turned back to form a crest on the top of the bow. The bow itself is a plain rounded rod, tapering slightly towards the unmarked foot. The catchplate has two round perforations. Bronze. Length 35mm. SF 2293 AML 820264 **2620** 3.95 9.57 (721). Building 53, Fig 64. AP 108, AS 133/1

26 Similar to no 25 except that only four turns of the spring remain; the foot is missing. Brass/gunmetal. Length 27mm. SF 4030 AML 826326 **3021** 3.00 4.00 (3021). Level over Building 33, Fig 70. AP 400

27 Similar to no 25; spring and foot broken. Brass. Length 35mm. SF 2675 AML 820300 **2822** 4.00 0.05 (1454). Occupation level west of Building 31, Fig 67. AP 255

28 Bow only surviving with the stumps of the two rods forming the spring and its hook. Brass. Length 42mm. SF 1519 AML 820225 **2620** 1.00 6.00 (721). Building 53, Fig 64. AP 108 AS 133/1

29 Very narrow and distorted bow; foot broken. A spring of five turns remains but the hook is missing. Brass. Length 45mm. SF 927 AML 820125 **2217** 2.50 7.80 (530). Posthole, fence line.. AP 86

30 Fragment with spring and crossbar. The bow is so narrow that it looks as if it may have been filed down to form a pin. Bronze. Length 43mm. SF 1917 AML 811381 **2522** 4.00 1.00 (817). Structure 12, Fig 36. AP 117

Nos 23–30 belong to the type first discussed by M R Hull as the 'Colchester' brooch (Hawkes and Hull 1947, 308–310). In general it belongs to the first half of the first century AD; the rectangular fretted catchplate (as nos 23 and 24) is very common amongst the many Colchester brooches in the pre-Conquest cemetery of King Harry Lane, St Albans, (Stead and Rigby 1989) which has no examples of the smaller brooches with plain or perforated catchplate such as nos 25 and 26 above. These occur commonly elsewhere and may be somewhat later in the series.

Fig 122

Two-piece Colchester brooches

31 A stout casting with the typical head construction: the separate spring of eight turns is held both by an axial rod passing through a lug behind the head and by the chord which passes through an upper hole in the same lug. The lug continues as a crest on the upper bow which is otherwise plain except for flanges at the sides. These are distorted near the centre, possibly by heat. The stout catchplate has two irregular perforations. Leaded bronze. Length 60mm. SF 474 AML 820073 **2122** 1.40 3.99 (287). Cobbles. First-century level. AP 55

32 Similar to no 31 but smaller and with fine zigzag decoration down the central rib of the bow. Leaded bronze. Length 41mm. SF 1851 AML 811379 **2621** 5.00 5.80 (849). Clay levelling for second phase Building 30, Fig 64. AS 133/1

33 Spring of eight turns attached as no 31 above; flattish bow with marginal grooves; small foot-knob (rather unusual in this type of brooch). Catchplate with two round perforations. (Leaded) bronze. Length 43mm. SF 1196 AML 811373 **2016** 0.70 7.10 (91). Lower fill Ditch 74. AS 97/2

34 Spring of about six turns, attached as no 31 above; very short crest; groove down centre of upper bow, cross-hatched; cross grooves at foot; catchplate with one round and one triangular perforation. (Leaded) bronze. Length 48mm. SF 139 AML 820037 **2019** 6.50 8.00 (77). Ditch 74. Level associated with occupation of Building 21, Fig 48. AS 23/1

35 Head construction as no 31 above, spring missing; bow has finely moulded ribs and flutes down whole length. The catchplate has one round and one triangular indentation not perforated. Leaded bronze. Length 45mm. SF 25 AML 820030 **1919** 7.00 6.00 (5). Fill of well

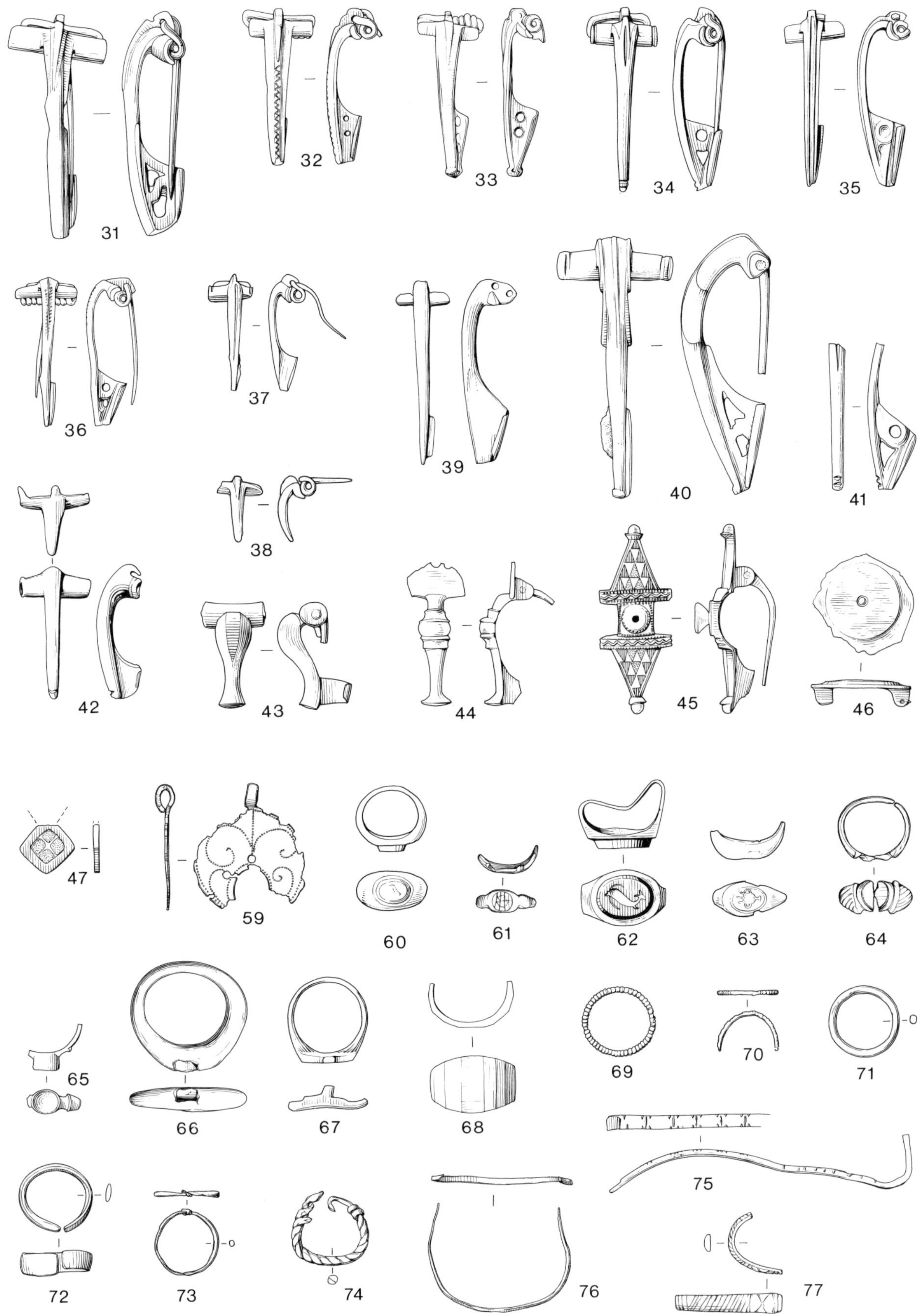

Fig 122 Brooches of copper alloy and other items of personal adornment including pendants, rings and bracelets (Scale 2:3)

36 Spring of eight turns attached as no 31 above; central groove down upper bow, cross-hatched; catchplate has two round perforations. Leaded bronze. Length 39mm. SF 2875 AML 811384 **2022** 3.00 2.00 (1665). Ditch 1281 between inner and outer enclosures. AS 253/1

37 Very small but constructed as the preceding brooches; spring of six turns; plain groove down centre of bow; catchplate plain. Leaded bronze. Length 30mm. SF 2718 AML 820305 **2819** 3.58 9.35 (1521). Ditch 1281. AP 212 AS 251/2

38 The head only of a small brooch of similar construction to no 31 above; no decoration visible. Leaded bronze. Length 17mm. SF 3973 AML 820368 **3420** 4.00 5.60 (2619))

39 The spring is missing but the rest of the brooch survives in good condition and shows the lug behind the head with two holes, as in all the preceding examples. The bow is unusually narrow and lacks any feature; the catchplate is plain. (Leaded) bronze. Length 46mm. SF 2361 AML 820270 **2619** 1.00 2.00 (741). Ploughpan east of granary, Building 28

Nos 31–39 (Fig 122) belong to the type first distinguished as Camulodunum Type IV (Hawkes and Hull 1947, 311) and dated there to the period *c* AD 50–65. Subsequent work has confirmed the dating; the type is absent from the pre-conquest cemetery at King Harry Lane, St Albans, and from Hod Hill. The variety represented by Gorhambury brooch no 32 seems to be particularly common in the area immediately north of London: several have been found at St Albans, Chelmsford and Colchester, and individual specimens at Magiovinium, Wakerley, Wickford and Baldock. The small grooved brooches such as no 36 are also common in this area.

Colchester derivative

40 The pin is hinged in a cast tube and the long arched bow is plain except for a rib at the upper end and two flanges beside the head. The harp-shaped catchplate has two irregular perforations. Leaded bronze. Length 68mm. SF 965 AML 811369 **2018** 1.00 1.50 (544B). Well. AS 99/3

This brooch has no exact parallels but seems to belong to the varied T-shaped developments from the preceding group (two-piece Colchesters) which are most common in south-west Britain. Other hinged brooches with flanged heads of generally similar appearance have been found at Tollard Royal (Wainwright 1968, fig 25 no 206, 135), Charterhouse on Mendip (Bristol Museum, F 1883) and Piercebridge (Butcher in Scott forthcoming). They are probably related to the sprung 'Polden Hill' brooches of otherwise similar appearance and could thus be dated to the later part of the first century AD: cp Camerton nos 9 and 10 (Wedlake 1958, 219, fig 50; one in a context of AD 65–85) and Verulamium (Frere 1972, 114, fig 29 no 9; context AD 85–105).

41 The foot only of a brooch probably belonging to the two-piece Colchester type or one of its derivatives. The pierced catchplate and plain tapering bow with an upper groove are typical of these. Leaded bronze. Length 39mm. SF 2921 AML 811393 **2819** 2.00 9.60 (1586). South terminal Ditch 1281

42 A development of the two-piece Colchester brooch in which the axial rod for the spring was held by loops at the ends of the crossbar and the chord was held by a rearward facing hook on the head. The spring and rod are missing. The rounded bow is plain except for a groove at the foot; plain triangular catchplate. Leaded bronze. Length 34mm. SF 2086 AML 820253 **2519** 1.00 2.00 (741). Ploughpan

This is virtually a 'Polden Hill' brooch except that the crossbar ends of those are more solid. It may belong to an early stage of their development and probably dates to the second half of the first century AD.

Knee brooch

43 The spring is held on a rod between the discoid ends of a semi-cylindrical crossbar, open at the back. The bow is humped at the top, narrows and then flares at the foot. It is plain except for slight faceting and there is a deep cylindrical hollow behind the hump. The catchplate is very narrow but projects a long way. Bronze. Length 28mm. SF 491 AML 820076 **2122** 0.40 5.00 (318). Posthole. AP 55

Several similar brooches were found at Camelon (Butcher in Maxfield forthcoming) where some of them were in Antonine deposits. This would accord with the continental dating for generally similar brooches, although it appears that this sub-type may be a British product (Böhme 1972, 22). Although they have strong military associations several have been found in civil contexts.

Pseudo-bow brooch

44 A 'Pseudo-bow' broocch in which the pin is hinged between two lugs behind a flat semi-circular headplate which has the remains of a broken loop at the top. The bow is reminiscent of some Knee brooches (cp no 43 above), but is much narrower at the top and swells to a tripartite moulding in the centre. The foot is narrow and plain, with a sharply out-turned terminal moulding. The catchplate is small and triangular, unlike those of Knee brooches. There is a cylindrical hollow behind the central moulding. Leaded bronze. Length 36mm. SF 3310 AML 820349 **3716** 6.00 3.80 (2067). Building 40, slot, Fig 40

Similar brooches from Augst are illustrated by Riha (1979, 179, taf 57, nos 1498–1500), who also groups them with plate rather than bow brooches and regards them as a product of the Rhineland and northern Gaul in the Hadrianic–Antonine period. They are very scarce in Britain but one from Colchester (Crummy 1983, 14, fig 11, no 68) has exactly the same headplate and central moulding; its foot is missing but seems to be flared and may have been enamelled, as in a similar brooch from Hofstade (de Laet 1952).

Symmetrical plate-brooch

45 Two triangular plates are joined by an arched central plate which bears a raised stud. The pin is hinged between two lugs behind one of the triangular plates; the other bears the plain triangular catchplate. Each plate has an all-over decoration of triangular enamelled cells alternating with triangles of reserved metal; the three central cells are orange and the others appear greenish. The central stud has a dark blue enamel spot surrounded by an outer ring of enamel which now appears greenish. On either side of the central plate are long bars with moulded wavy line decoration between two lines of beading; the two finials are collared lugs. All the decoration is fine and accurately moulded or cut, and the brooch is in a good state of preservation. Brass/gunmetal. Length 49mm. SF 2997 AML 811388 **2823** 0.70 1.60 (1540). Level over ditches 1483, 1281. AP 227 AS 249/3

Very similar brooches were found at Berzée (Musée de Namur) and at Lenzburg (Ettlinger 1973, 118, taf 14 no 4) which has the same enamel colours and is also described as being of exceptionally good workmanship. There is no dating evidence for these brooches but from the enamel technique they probably date to the later first century (Spitaels forthcoming).

Disc brooch

46 Plate with damaged edges which may have been polygonal rather than round. The centre is slightly raised and has a central ring, or possibly a rivet which once held a stud. The pin was hinged between two lugs and a very small catchplate.

This brooch probably had an applied decorative plate; lacking this it is impossible to identify closely. Brass/gunmetal. Surviving diameter 27mm. SF 2626 AML 820294 **2819** 9.50 2.35. Unstratified from area of Building 55, Fig 69

Fragment

47 Lozenge-shaped plate recessed for enamel: traces of dark ?blue remain. The back is flat and there is nothing to show whether this was part of a brooch or other object. Leaded gunmetal. Length 14mm. SF 38 AML 820042, **2120** 3.00 8.00 (109). Destruction level. AS 4315

48–58 Brooch fragments. Not illustrated. For drawings see AS No 442.

Analytical results for the brooches

by Justine Bayley

Altogether 46 brooches and 9 fragments were analysed qualitatively by energy dispersive X-ray fluorescence (XRF). Small metal samples for quantitative analysis by atomic absorption spectroscopy (AAS) were drilled from 20 of the objects which were sufficiently massive and uncorroded. In most cases the analyses detected zinc, tin and lead in addition to copper, but in widely differing proportions. The detailed results are given in Appendix 4 and the alloys are described on p 136.

As expected, the results show strong correlation between alloy composition and brooch type. Individual types are discussed in turn below, the results for the Gorhambury brooches being compared with those previously obtained for brooches from some 80 sites from all over Britain.

La Tène brooches are normally made of bronze so it is not surprising that the related La Tène derivatives (Nos 1 and 2) are also bronzes. The seven one-piece brooches and the fragment (No 51) are also bronze. Overall about 60% of these types are bronze so the results here are not unexpected although it is a little unusual for all the one-piece brooches from a site to have similar compositions. One early hinged brooch with the head rolled under rather than forwards (No 10) is a variant of the one-piece brooches and is also bronze. This example is not related to the Aucissa (see below).

Langton Down and Rosette brooches are normally brasses with a few percent of tin. The results from the Gorhambury brooches mostly conform to this pattern (too much reliance should not be put on the result given for No 14). The fantail brooch (No 15) has the same cylindrical head as the Rosette brooches and is also brass. The other fantail brooch (No 16) has a head like a two-piece Colchester brooch and its composition is comparable with that of the two-piece Colchester brooches (see below).

Aucissa brooches are normally rather purer brass than the Rosettes etc and the examples here, and the related Bagendon and early hinged brooches, are all brasses. Hod Hill brooches are also related types but compositionally they are rather more varied with only 70% of them being brass, and the rest divided fairly equally between bronzes and gunmetals. The two examples from Gorhambury conform to this pattern.

Colchester brooches are either of one-piece construction or the pin/spring assembly is made separately and then attached. The two types have completely different compositions, the former being brasses (in over 90% of cases) while the latter are leaded bronzes (80%) or more rarely leaded gunmetals or unleaded bronzes. The change of composition is clearly related to the change in method of manufacture, though which came first is impossible to say (Bayley 1985a). It is interesting that two of the eight one-piece brooches here are bronzes though it has been noticed before that these atypical compositions seem to concentrate at relatively few sites.

Colchester derivative types are most often also leaded bronzes (in over 60% of cases) but a whole range of compositions has been noted. The examples here are all leaded bronzes.

The symmetrical plate brooch (No 45) is a brass containing minor amounts of tin and lead. Two comparable, though not identical, brooches from Magiovinium (Butcher in Neal 1989, no 20) and Nor'nour (Hull in Dudley 1968, no 150) are also both brasses as are two brooches from Velzeke in Belgium which have the same sort of enamel decoration as the Gorhambury brooch but are triangular rather than double-ended in shape).

The brooches not discussed above are of types where insufficient analytical data exist to allow comparisons to be made.

Items of personal adornment

Apart from brooches, items of personal adornment included finger rings, bracelets and hairpins. Three of the fourteen rings retain intaglios, discussed by M Henig (p 115), and several have decorative bezels. Their distribution is random, although some came from levels directly associated with the occupation of specific buildings. Nos 53, 67 and 69, from levels in Ditch 1281, were deposited during the second century occupation of the villa, as were Nos 66 and 68 from Ditch 74. The single earring, also from a second century deposit, is of a common type. Earrings as a class of object are more often recognised as a result of recent work by L Allason-Jones, whose typology is used here. The bracelets found at Gorhambury belong to standard types, mostly from third- or fourth-century contexts although No 81 is from a second-century ditch fill. Pins were found in copper alloy, Nos 86–109, bone, Nos 924–954 (Fig 140) and glass, Nos 987, 988 (Fig 142), from contexts dating from the first to the fourth centuries. It is not possible to date specific types from the limited selection of copper alloy pins, although it is likely that those with grooves below a flattened spherical head were produced in the second century (Nos 86–89). Other types can be dated by analogy (see descriptions).

There is no reason to doubt the use of pins in a variety of materials as hairpins, although some could have had a dual purpose as fasteners. They were necessary to support elaborate hairstyles and have been found in sufficient quantity on cemetery sites such as Butt Road, Colchester (Crummy 1983, 19) and Lankhills, Winchester (Clarke 1979, 315), in positions near the head to indicate this function.

Fig 122

59 Crescentic pendant. Both surfaces are tinned and the face has punched decoration, with a small circular hole at the mid-point. Its size suggests that it may have been used for personal adornment, although similar lunate pendants were often horse-trappings used to decorate harness, shown by many examples such as those from Newstead (Curle 1911, pl LXIII 1–4, pl LXIV 4) and Wroxeter (Bushe-Fox 1916, 30, no 32, pl XVIII). An almost identical pendant, not tinned, came from Smith's Wharf, London (British Museum – PRB DR-1-6), dated to the first century AD. A smaller silver lunula of different form found in a grave at Colchester was suspended from an armlet (Crummy 1983, 51, fig 54, 1806). Gunmetal, tinned. Length 33mm. SF 2982 AML 811394 **2820** 2.30 1.00 (1599) South terminal of enclosure ditch 1281. AS 251/1

Rings

60 Ring with intaglio, discussed by M Henig, No 1016, p 161. Diameter 18mm. SF 2645 **2723** 1.95 1.81 (1490). Upper fill of well. AP 207 AS 249/1

61 Oval bezel with circular design in orange enamel. Leaded bronze. Length 16mm. SF 3974 AML 820369 **3921** 2.00 3.00 (2665). Structure 43, Phase 2. Fig 92. Period 10, third century

62 Ring with intaglio = No 1017, p 162. Base silver. Diameter *c* 23mm. SF 56 **1921** 9.50 6.00 (110). Destruction material over Building 51, Fig 102. Period 11

63 Ring with intaglio = No 1018 p 162. Diameter *c* 19mm. SF 2814 **2819** 2.30 8.60 (1569). Upper fill, south terminal of Ditch 1281. Second century

64 Circular bezel, stone missing, and with incised diagonal grooves on the shoulders. Diameter 20mm. SF 2458 AML 811391 **2517** 0.75 7.50 (1263). Level over Building 10, Fig 35. AP 182, 187

65 Oval bezel, the stone missing, with a decorative rib on shoulder. Diameter *c* 21mm. Surviving length 18mm. SF 1597 AML 820229 **2721** 2.05 0.80 (786). Fourth-century spread east of Building 53, Fig 64. AS 134/6

66 Ring with corroded bezel which may have carried a key. For a well preserved ring key, see No 252, Fig 128. Diameter 20mm. SF 618 AML 820103 **2122** 0.20 1.00 (369). Upper fill Ditch 74, associated with occupation of Building 37, Fig 48. Second century. AS 68/3

67 Heavy ring, thickened on one side with a rectangular setting for a stone. Diameter 31mm. SF 2802 AML 820311 **2821** 1.50 9.60 (1552). Level over Ditch 1281 between inner and outer enclosures. Second century. AS 253/3

68 Multi-faceted ring. Diameter 23mm. SF 421 AML 820067 **2022** 8.65 6.40 (275). Ditch 74, fill associated with occupation of Building 37, Fig 48. AS 66/1

69 Ring with continuous beaded decoration. Bronze. Diameter 20mm. SF 2862 AML 820318 **2822** 2.00 2.00 (1662) Ditch 1281 between inner and outer enclosures. Second-century fill. AS 253/1

70 Ring with grooved decoration giving the effect of beading. Diameter 17mm. SF 2122 **2618** 0.10 0.25 (741). Ploughpan in area of Building 29. AS 160/1

71 Plain ring. Diameter 19mm. SF 4089 AML 826334 **3021** 7.30 7.10 (3091). Fill of pit 3200 in Building 33, Fig 70. Second century

72 Penannular ring with oval section. Bronze. Diameter 20mm. SF 3523 AML 820358 **3820** 3.50 3.40 (2301). Fourth-century level over Structure 43, Phase 2, Fig 92. AP 336

73 Ring made from fine circular-sectioned wire. Diameter 17mm. SF 4088 AML 826333 **3021** 7.20 7.40 (3091). Fill of pit 3200, Building 33, Fig 70. Second century

74 Earring made from three strand cable with hooked terminal. (Allason-Jones, Type 6, pers comm). Diameter 20mm. SF 2720 AML 820306 **2818** 3.30 8.00 (1521). Level over Ditch 1281. AS 251/2

Bracelets

The Gorhambury assemblage contains bracelets of the types commonly represented on Roman sites; most come from third or fourth century contexts. For general comparison see the type series from Lankhills cemetery, Winchester (Clarke 1979, 300ff), the collection from Lydney Park (Wheeler 1932, fig 17) and Colchester (Crummy 1983, 37–45).

75 Bracelet decorated with incised vertical lines flanked by V-shaped notches on each edge. Brass. Length 83mm. SF 427 AML 820068 **2122** 2.65 7.50. Topsoil north of villa

76 Single strand bracelet, possibly for a child. Lankhills Type B. Length 38mm. SF 2646 AML 822155 **2819** 8.00 0.50 (1450). Building 55, Fig 44. Period 11. AP 212

77 Fragment with incised line decoration. Bronze/gunmetal (leaded). SF 3394a AML 820352 **3816** 3.00 5.50 (1898). Third-century level over Building 40, Fig 40. AP 282

78 Not illustrated. Fragment similar to No 77, probably from the same bracelet. Bronze (leaded). Length 22mm. SF 3394b AML 820353 **3816** (1898). AS No 77. Fig 123

Fig 123

79 Bracelet decorated with groups of slanting incised lines. Lankhills Type D. Bronze (leaded). Length 74mm. SF 2648 AML 820299 **2819** 7.00 1.50 (1450) Building 55, Fig 69. Fourth-century level. AP 212

80 Four strand cable bracelet. Lankhills Type A3. Gunmetal. Diameter *c* 69mm. SF 3458 AML 820354 **3820** 4.25 9.70 (2301). Fourth-century level over Structure 43, Fig 92. AP 336

81 Bracelet with running dot and circle motif, separated at the terminals by groups of vertical lines with V-shaped chip carving on the outer edges. Present width 82mm. Bronze. Diameter *c* 65mm. Lankhills Type B. Also found at Gadebridge Park (Neal 1974, fig 60, no 155). SF 4209 AML 826341 **2817** 5.10 3.20 (1283). Ditch 1281 between inner and outer enclosures. Second century fill. AS 205/3

82 Crenellated bracelet. Fourth-century type. Length 58mm. SF 3514 AML 820356 **3819** 3.00 1.30. Unstratified

83 Bracelet with incised vertical lines at the terminals. Brass. Diameter 55mm. AML 820020. 1956–61 excavations

84–5 Bracelets. Not illustrated. For drawings see AS No 442.

Pins

For additional pins of bone and glass see Nos 924–963, Fig 140 and 987, 988, Fig 142.

In some cases the full length of the pin has not been illustrated; the text states its surviving length.

86 Pin with three grooves and cordons below a spherical head. Bronze/gunmetal. Complete. Length 99mm. SF 2900 AML 820323 **2821** 3.00 9.80 (1669). Second-century fill of enclosure Ditch 1281 . AS 253/1

87 Pin with spherical head above groove and cordon. Bronze. Complete. Length 92mm. SF 3630 AML 820296 **2823** 0.80 1.50. Unstratified

88 Pin with groove below flattened spherical head. Bronze. Complete. Length 40mm. SF 2429 AML 820280 **2115** Unstratified

89 Pin with groove and cordon below a flattened spherical head. (Leaded) bronze. Complete. Length 102mm. SF 212 AML 820056 **1921** (199). Fourth-century level associated with Building 51, Fig 102 AP 26

90 Pin with oblique incised lines on a spherical head and five grooves on the shaft. (Leaded) bronze/gunmetal. Incomplete. Length 104mm. SF 968 AML 820128 **2117** 5.50 8.00 (566). Level over Building 50, Fig 99, Period 10

91 Pin with spherical head above a flattened shoulder with incised lines on the faces and notched edges. Bronze. Complete. Length 96mm. AML 820008. 1956–1961 excavations

92 Pin with grooved decoration below a domed head. (Leaded) bronze. Complete. Length 112mm. SF 1191 AML 820152 **2217** 6.00 5.50 (615). Humic layer sealing first-century levels. AS 103/3

93 Pin with biconical head and groove and cordon decoration. Bronze. Complete. Length 89mm. SF 2632 AML 820297 **2823** 2.05 0.50. Unstratified

94 Pin with biconical head, the upper surface decorated with incised triangles. (Leaded) gunmetal. Complete. Length 47mm. SF 2373 AML 820271 **2618** 0.25 5.50 (1142). Redeposited clay in Building 29, Fig 62. Period 8, second century. AP 150

95 Pin with biconical head and incised line decoration. Bronze. Incomplete. Length 83mm. Similar examples come from Skeleton Green (Partridge 1981, 107, no 18, fig 55) and Chichester (Down 1981, 169, no 47, fig 8.32). SF 1112 AML 820134 **2117** 4.00 9.50 (562). Building 50, Fig 99, Period 10. AS 101/2

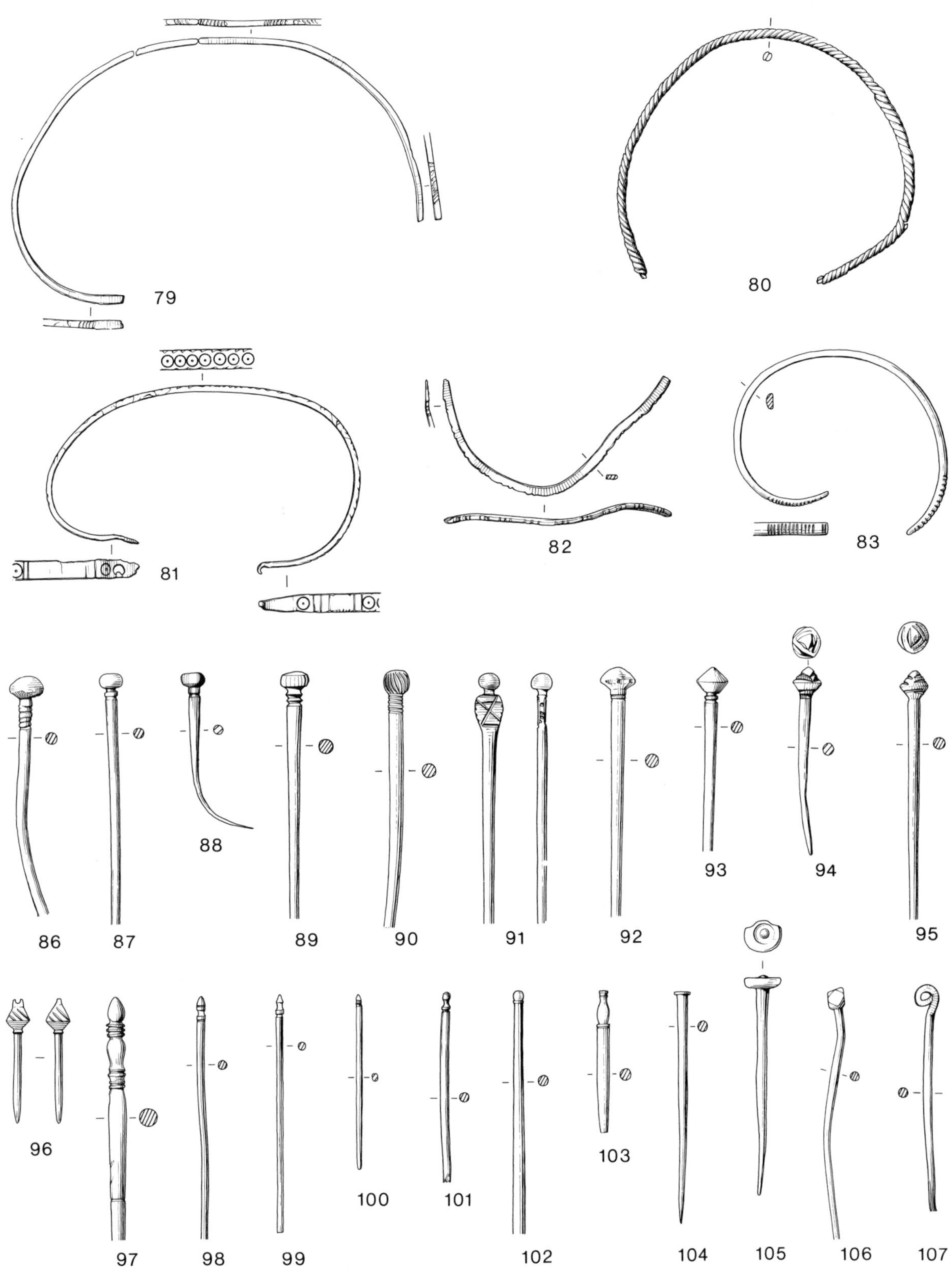

Fig 123 Bracelets and pins in copper alloy (Scale 2:3)

96 Small pin with biconical head, its upper surface decorated with oblique incised lines and surmounted by traces of a small ring. Gunmetal. Complete. Length 31mm. SF 573 AML 820091 **2123** 1.00 4.00 (384). Level over Ditch 74, north of villa. AS 66/1

97 Pin with ovoid head, above elaborate baluster and cordon moulding. Brass/gunmetal. Complete. Length 110mm. SF 3066 AML 811396 **3716** 6.50 9.60 (1881). Third-century occupation deposit over Building 47, Fig 41. Period 10. AP 276

98 Pin with conical head over horizontal grooves and moulding. Bronze. Complete. Length 114mm. SF 632 AML 820108 **2023** 0.15 1.00 (410). Ditch 74, north of villa. AS 67/2

99 Pin with conical head and cordon. Bronze. Incomplete. Length 60mm. SF 483 AML 820074 **2022** 9.00 6.55 (275). Ditch 74, level associated with occupation of Building 37, Fig 48. Second century. AS 66/1

100 Slender pin with two grooves below conical head. Bronze. Incomplete. Length 46mm. Latrine, Strucure 44, Fig 93. AS 161/1

101 Slender pin with spherical head and grooved decoration. Bronze. Complete. Length 103mm. SF 4085 AML 826330 **3021** 7.90 7.00 (3091). Pit 3200, Building 33, Fig 70. Second centtury

102 Pin with small spherical head and single cordon. (Leaded) gunmetal. Incomplete. Length 107mm. SF 385 AML 820064 **2121** 7.50 3.00 (258). Cesspit associated with Building 27, Fig 48. Phase 3, mid second century

Items of personal use

Cosmetic implements

The collection includes a large number of tweezers, nail cleaners and ear scoops which are commonly found on domestic sites, frequently in sets, as Nos 110–112. Eighteen tweezers were found, of which seven came from contexts associated with the first- and second-century villas (Buildings 21 and 37), and three from the aisled hall (Building 39/40). The nail cleaners have been divided into two types: A with a leaf-shaped body which is sometimes decorated, and B with a straight shaft. Type B, dated at Colchester to the mid to late first century (Crummy 1983, 57, Type Ia), may be earlier than Type A, but is found at Gorhambury in a second-century context (No 135). The majority of nail cleaners were again found in association with the first and second century villas; perhaps belonging to the same sets as the tweezers. Ear scoops are less common finds but two of the three came from levels in ditches associated with Buildings 21 and 27.

103 Pin with moulded head and grooved decoration. (Leaded) bronze/gunmetal. Incomplete. Length 36mm. SF 1131 AML 820140 **2017** 5.00 6.00 (545). Clay fill of gully cutting well, third/fourth century. AS 99/4

104 Pin with flat round head. (Leaded) bronze. Complete. Length 58mm. SF 415 AML 820114 **2022** 8.70 6.95 (275). Ditch 74, second century level associated with occupation of Building 37, Fig 48. AS 66/1

105 Pin with flat round head with concentric mouldings. Brass. Complete. Length 55mm. SF 130 AML 820036 **2119** 4.00 6.00 (36). First-century level. AS 23/6

106 Pin with faceted cuboid head. At Colchester this type was found in post-AD 250 contexts (Crummy 1983, 29). Gunmetal. Complete. Length 76mm. AML 820013. 1961 excavations

107 Pin with rolled loop terminal, possibly a buckle pin. Length 65mm. SF 1489 AML 820224 **2520** 7.05 9.50 (721). Level associated with Building 53, Fig 64, fourth century. AS 135/1

108–9 Pins. Not illustrated. For drawings see AS No 442.

Also represented are ligulae or spatulas used as scoops for unguents, cosmetics and medicines. The nine found show a similar distribution to the cosmetic sets. More unusual items include a folding knife, a file and a razor (Nos 151–153).

Fig 124

110-12 Toilet set comprising tweezers (bronze), nail cleaner (bronze) and ear scoop (leaded gunmetal). Lengths 48mm; 45mm; 51mm. SF 2905 AML 820325 **2822** 2.50 0.05 (1669). Ditch 1281, between inner and outer enclosures. AS 253/1

113 Tweezers with incised linear decoration along the edges. Length 40mm. SF 2808 AML 820250 **2418** 8.50 6.50 (741). Ploughpan, south of Building 28

114 Tweezers with incised linear decoration. Length 44mm. SF 535 AML 820085 **2022** 8.00 5.90 (275). Ditch 74, second-century level associated with occupation of Building 37, Fig 48. AS 66/1

115 Tweezers with linear decoration. Length 47mm. SF 1177 AML 820144 **2118** 5.00 1.00 (652). First-century level. AS 101/1

116 Tweezers with linear decoration. Length 50mm. SF 1113 AML 820135 **2118** 1.00 1.50 (628). Building 24, Fig 51, Period 6

117 Tweezers, undecorated. Gunmetal. Length 55mm. SF 3347 AML 820350 **3716** 1.50 8.00 (2018). Occupation level, Building 39/40, Fig 40, 53. Period 9. AS 302/8

118 Large undecorated tweezers with steeply angled arms. Length 59mm. SF 2682 AML 820303 **2723** 2.50 3.85 (1490). Upper fill of well. AS 249/1

119 Tweezers with stamped decoration on the arms. Gunmetal. Length 50mm. SF 3329 AML 811401 **3716** 3.10 6.90 (2090). Posthole, Building 39, Fig 40. AS 301/1

120 One arm of tweezers, bent for re-use. (Leaded) bronze. SF 2966 AML 826478 **2821** 2.00 9.20 (1657). Ditch 1281 between inner and outer enclosures, second century. AS 253/1

121–29 Tweezers. Not illustrated. For drawings see AS No 442. Nos 121–26 are decorated, Nos 127–29 are plain.

130 Nail cleaner. Type A, with linear decoration on the stem. Length 46mm. SF 537 AML 820086 **2022** 7.00 8.90 (369). Second-century fill, Ditch 74, north of Building 37. AS 68/3

131 Nail cleaner. Type A, with linear decoration. Length 50mm. SF 2237 AML 820262 **2419** 0.25 2.80 (1040). Posthole. AP 141

132 Nail cleaner. Type A, with incised decoration on the edges and handle. Length 45mm. SF 605 AML 820098 **2122** 0.50 8.60 (45). Ditch 74, second-century level. AS 43/5

133 Nail cleaner. Type A, with zigzag decoration on the shaft. (Leaded) bronze. Length 49mm. SF 1128 AML 820139 **2016** 2.00 9.50 (91). Ditch 74, first-century level. AS 97/2

134 Nail cleaner. Type A, with notched decoration on the edges of the handle. Length 46mm. SF 1176 AML 820143 **2118** 4.50 2.50 (653). First-century level

135 Nail cleaner. Type B, with straight undecorated body. Length 51mm. SF 602 AML 820097 **2022** 9.00 8.00 (369). Ditch 74, second-century fill north of Building 37, Fig 48. AS 68/3

136 Nail cleaner. Type B, with rolled loop handle. Length 55mm. SF 2623 AML 820292 **2820** 5.10 2.50. Unstratified

137–38 Nail cleaners. Type A. Not iillustrated. For drawings see AS No 443

139 Ear scoop with D-sectioned shaft. Leaded bronze. Length 48mm. SF 2863 AML 820319 **2822** 1.50 5.00 (1651). Over Ditch 1281 between inner and outer enclosures. AS 253/1

140 Ear scoop with fractured ring handle. Bronze. Length 50mm. SF 988 AML 820130 **2018** 5.50 6.05 (91). Ditch 74, first-century level. AS 99/1

141 Not illustrated. As 140. Length 43mm. SF 1209 AML 820148 **2118** 7.00 2.50 (652). First-century level. AS 101/1

142 Ligula with cupped scoop and grooved decoration on the handle. Length 107mm. SF 630 AML 820107 **2023** 9.95 1.00 (410). Ditch 74, north of Building 37. AS 67/2

143 Ligula with flat circular angled scoop. Length 148mm. SF 4211 AML 826343 **3021** 5.00 9.00 (3227). Building 33, Fig 70

144 Ligula with flat circular straight scoop. Length 90mm. SF 634 AML 820109 **2123** 0.50 1.00 (410). Ditch 74, north of Building 37. AS 67/2

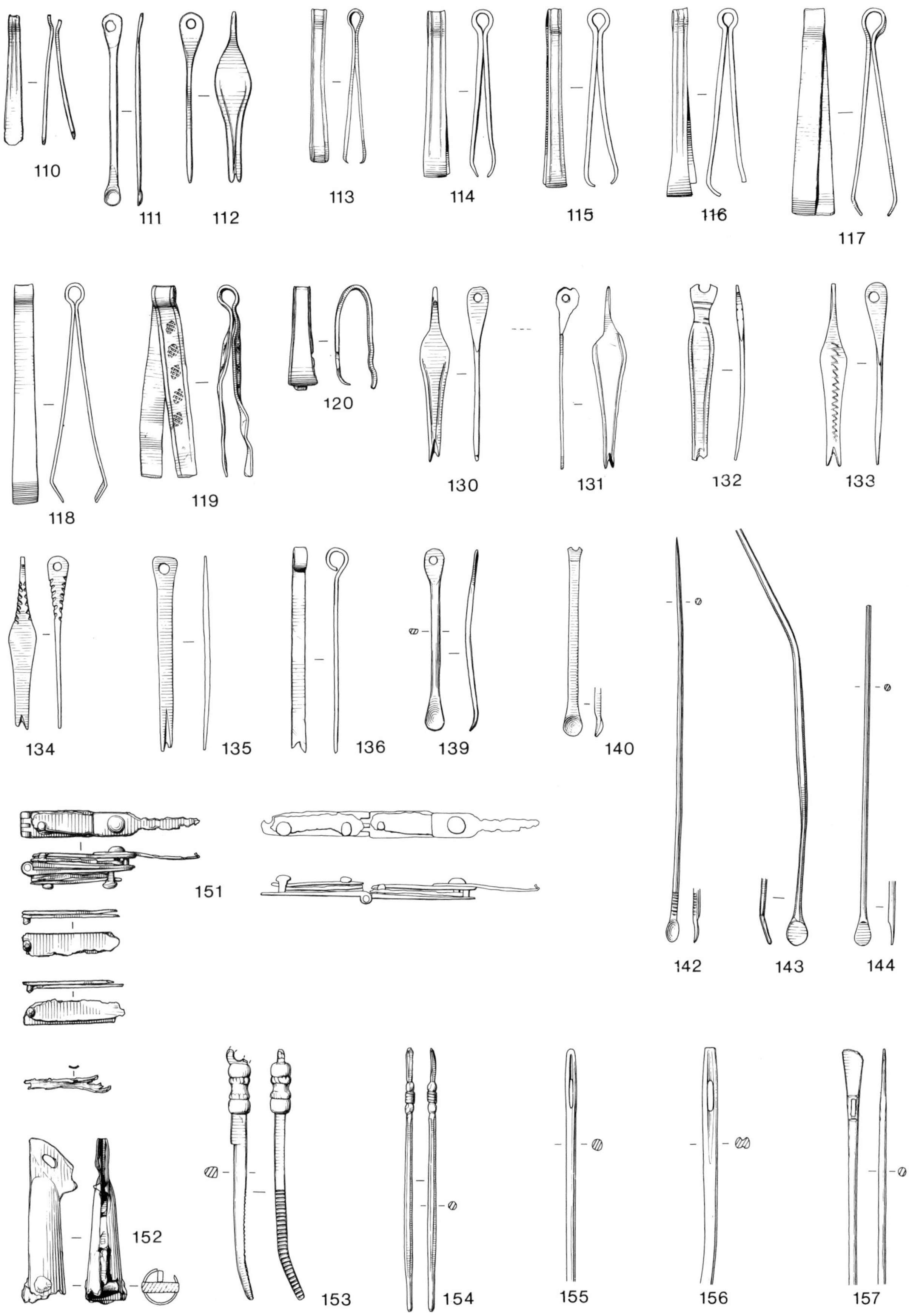

Fig 124 Cosmetic implements and needles in copper alloy (Scale 2:3)

145–50 Ligulae. Not illustrated. For drawings see AS No 443

151 Folding knife. The object is very fragmentary with a central hinge and trace of one blade remaining. Brass. Length 50mm. SF 2976 AML 820338 **2821** 3.00 2.00 (1596). Ditch 1281, between inner and outer enclosures. Second-century fill. AS 253/3

152 Razor. Ferrule from a razor handle with traces of an iron blade. Brass. Length 43mm. SF 3142 AML 811400 **3716** 3.00 8.50 (2002). Third-century occupation material over Building 47, Fig 41. AS 300/9

153 File. The blade is D-shaped in section with serrations on the flat side. The head has baluster and cordon decoration below a fractured suspension loop. Bronze. Length 66mm. A similar implement with coarser serrations comes from a toilet set at Colchester (Crummy 1983, 61, no 1941). SF 3034 AML 820340 **2918** 8.50 1.00 (1642). Latrine, Structure 46. AP 229

154 Spatula. Slender round-sectioned shaft with a pointed end. It is fractured below groove and cordon decoration at the other end, but appears to have had a spatulate blade. It may have been a surgical instrument. Gunmetal. Length 70mm. SF 2978 AML 820335 **2827** 4.00 1.50 (1594). North terminal Ditch 1281 between inner and outer enclosures. Second-century level. AS 253/3

Needles

Of the thirteen copper alloy needles eight are from ditch fills associated with the occupation of the second century villas, Buildings 27 and 37. This distribution is paralleled by the bone needles where seven of the twelve examples are from Ditch 74, to the north of Building 37.

Other items associated with textile production in general include an iron wool comb (No 410, Fig 132), a bone bobbin (No 971, Fig 141), spindle whorls and loom weights of fired clay (Fig 145).

155 Needle with groove above the long eye. This type is relatively slender, resembling modern examples. Such needles are common on Roman sites, as Colchester (Crummy 1983, 67, no 1993). Complete. Length 121mm. SF 594 AML 820094 **2023** 9.50 1.00 (396). Ditch 74, north of Building 37, Fig 48. AS 66/1. A second example, no 158, came from this context

156 Needle with vertical groove above and below an elongated eye which was punched out of a groove made in the flattened head. The top of the head is squared. Complete. Length 139mm. Comparable examples come from Gadebridge Park (Neal and Butcher 1974, 145, no 230, fig 64) and Verulamium (Goodburn 1984, 41, no 123, fig 16). SF 718 AML 820116 **2217** 4.50 8.00 (488). Ploughpan

157 Needle with a flat spatulate head, with incised horizontal grooves above and below the rectangular eye. The type is also found in bone and there are identical examples from Colchester (Crummy 1983, 65, no 1976, fig 66) and Gadebridge Park (Neal and Butcher 1974, 145, no 228, fig 64). The width of the head might imply that these needles were used for sewing coarse material such as hessian. Complete. Brass/gunmetal. Length 134mm. SF 2810 AML 820314 **2819** 1.70 2.10 (1569). South terminal of Ditch 1281 between inner and outer enclosures. Second century. AS 251/1

158–67 Needles. Not illustrated. For drawings see AS No 443. None is complete.

Decorative fittings

Several items with possible military associations are of interest, in particular the mounts, Nos 168–172, and a scabbard runner, No 179.

Outstanding among the miscellaneous decorative items is the eagle's wing, No 194, Fig 126, from the filling of the cellar, while other objects such as a figurine and an escutcheon (Nos 195 and 199, Fig 126) are of good quality. Other items which indicate a degree of luxury include the various enamels, chiefly seal boxes and studs. The distribution of these objects is random.

Fig 125

168 Mount, probably a harness fitting. The object has an asymmetrical pelta with a 'trumpet' motif reminiscent of Celtic design, and may have had a second arm, now lost, to balance the pattern. The mount is cast with a slightly hollow back, but there is no sign of the method of attachment. Similar motifs are seen on mounts from Germany; compare an example from Zugmantel (Oldenstein 1976, taf 69, 908). Brass. Length 56mm. SF 3547 AML 820360 **3821** 1.50 3.00 (2303). From oven in Building 42, Fig 90. Second century. AP 343

169 Decorative mount. Flat, shaped plate with incised decoration on the curved edge possibly from a pelta-shaped mount as one from Zugmantel (Oldenstein 1976, taf 54, 645). Brass/gunmetal. Length 56mm. SF 2347 AML 820268 **2720** 4.50 9.50 (1057). Latrine 44, Fig 93. AS 161/1

170 Harness mount in the form of a stylised vine leaf with bunches of grapes, three studs for attachment on the reverse. The upper edge, which has notched decoration, is fractured and does not appear to have had a suspension loop. The design is similar to that found on first-century 'trifid' harness pendants found in Britain and Germany (Bishop 1988, 96 and 142–144); note especially examples from Colchester (Webster 1958, nos 58, 59, fig 4) and Wiesbaden (ORL no 31, taf X, no 20). Brass/gunmetal. Length 52mm. SF 2759 AML 811392 **2822** 8.90 2.50 (1454). Over Ditch 1281 west of Building 31, Fig 67. Second century. AP 225

171 Pelta-shaped cast mount with hollow back, probably a military fitting. There is a similar object from Richborough (Cunliffe 1968, 105, pl XLVIII, no 223). Leaded bronze/gunmetal. Length 41mm. SF 2341 AML 820267 **2720** 2.20 7.50 (721). Level associated with Building 53, Fig 64. Fourth century. AS 134/3

172 Pelta-shaped mount. A military type often found in Germany as at Holzhausen (Oldenstein 1976, taf 53, no 629); see also Richborough (Cunliffe 1968, pl XXXVII, no 129). (Leaded) gunmetal. Length 35mm. SF 853 AML 811366 **2018** 2.50 3.30 (547). Well. AP 79, AS 99/4

173 Shaped sheet, probably the terminal of a pelta-shaped mount. Length 18mm. SF 902 AML **2218** 6.70 4.00 (506). Second-century level. AS 103/1

174 Thin sheet, semi-circular on one side with a lobe on the other. Length 60mm. AML 820019. 1959 excavations G5 (2)

175 Mount. Rectangular plate with three broad ribs. Leaded gunmetal. Length 32mm. SF3730 AML 820361 **3821** 5.00 1.50 (2302). Building 43, Phase 2, Fig 92. Fourth century. AP 540

176 Decorative boss, probably a harness mount. A central boss is surrounded by four semi-circular mouldings, giving a cruciform appearance. The depth of each semi-circle is 5mm and the metal curves underneath to form a backing plate, making a hole through which a strap could pass. (Leaded) gunmetal. Length 40mm. SF 3141 AML 811399 **3816** 3.40 5.30 (1902). Level over Building 40, Fig 40, 53. AP 282

177 Decorative strip or binding. Sheet with five ribs running lengthwise, folded at each end. Length 70mm. SF 64 AML 820046 **2021** 8.00 5.00 (8). West wall of main range of Building 37, Fig 48

178 Mount. Rectangular strip with a rivet at the squared end. It terminates at the other end in a disc of which half remains (tinned), with trace of central hole. Brass/gunmetal. Length 45mm. SF 2536 AML 820287 **2017** 7.10 6.60 (1413). Ditch 74, second-century level. AS 198/2

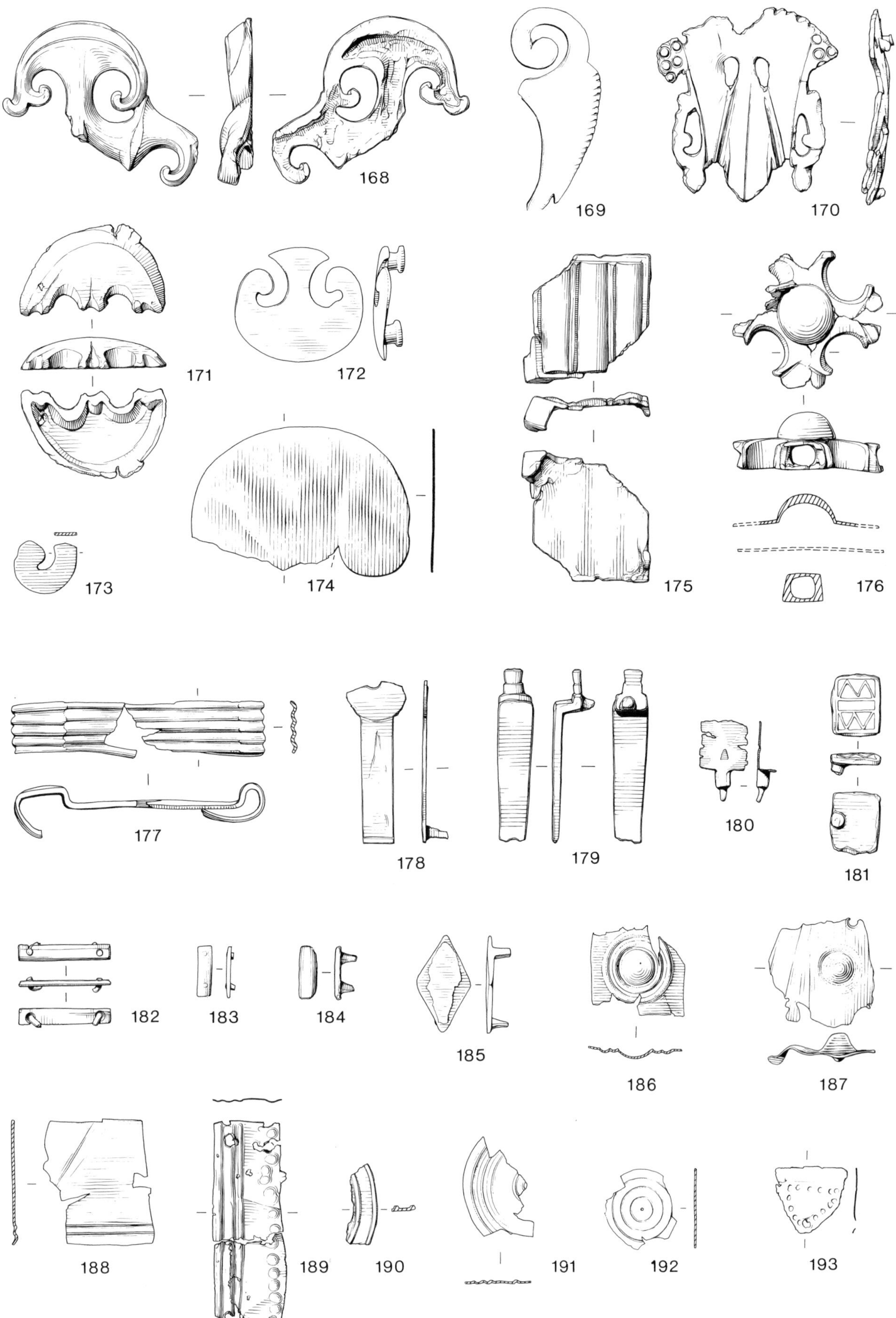

Fig 125 Decorative fittings in copper alloy (Scale 2:3)

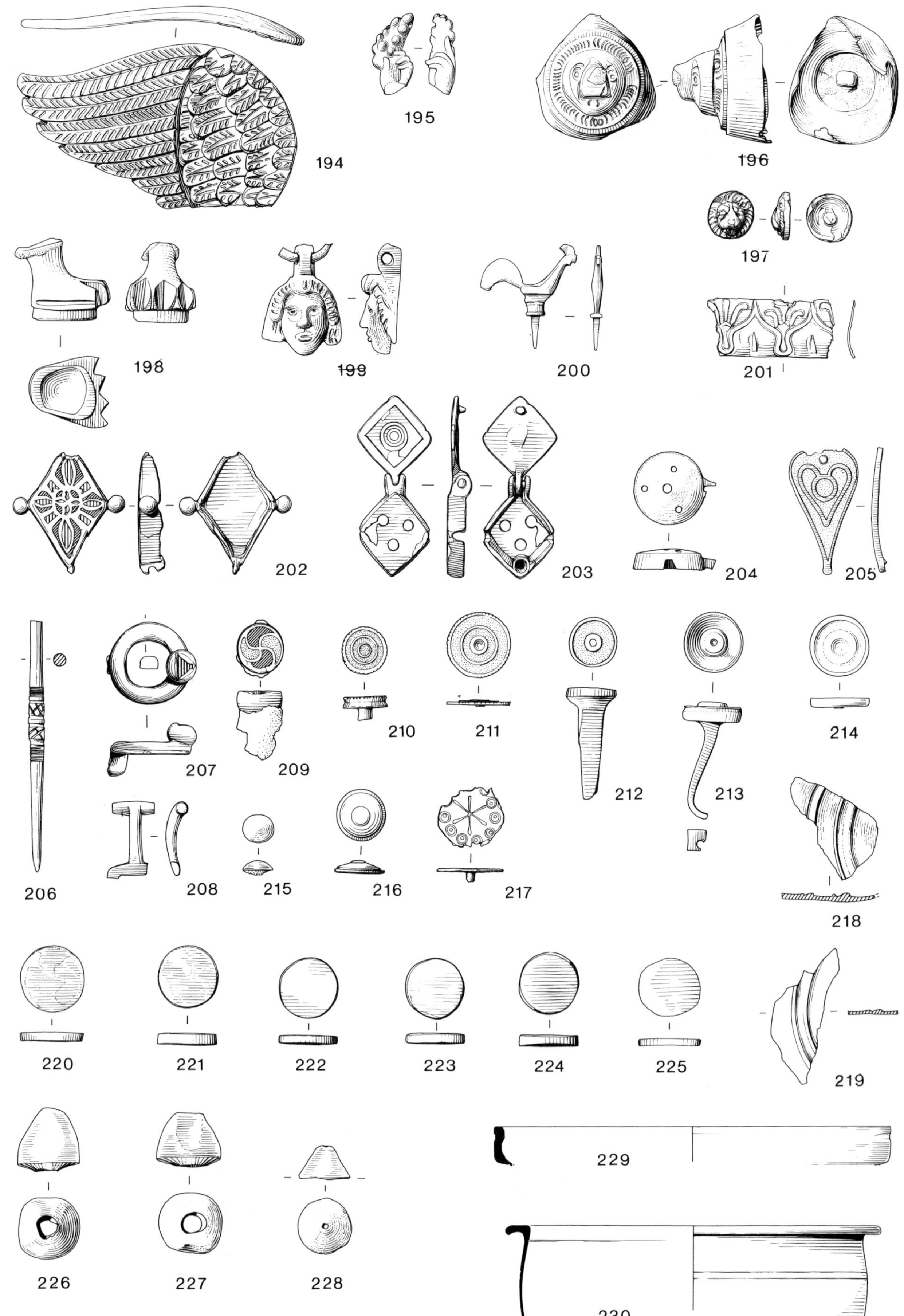

Fig 126 Objects of copper alloy (Scale 2:3)

179 Scabbard runner, incomplete at the lower end. (Leaded) gunmetal. Length 47mm. Comparable examples from South Shields (Allason-Jones and Miket 1984, nos 645, 647), Colchester (Webster 1958, fig 4, no 61), Cirencester, (Webster 1958, fig 3, no 34) and Germany, eg Zugmantel (ORL 8, taf xi, no 28, 26). SF 1850 AML 820241 **2621** 3.00 3.50 (848). Building 30 Period 8, Fig 64. AS 133/1

180 Mount. Rectangular sheet, fractured along its upper edge, the lower bent at right angles, riveted. length 22mm. SF 2420 AML 820278 **2115** 7.65 4.80 (1298). Fill of slot. AP 173

181 Enamelled stud. The central band is enamelled in red and the triangular fields on either side now appear greenish (outer) and buff (inner). The greenish fields may originally have been red. (Leaded) brass. Length 17mm. SF 3434 AML 811402 **3917** 5.50 4.50 (2247). Latrine over ditch 1851. AP 293

182 Mount with two rivets. Length 26mm. SF 4273 AML 826347 **11/1322** (3258). Medieval pit. AS 418/1

183 Mount with two rivets. Length 14mm. SF 781 **2017** 2.85 7.00 (4). Ploughpan

184 Rectangular mount. Length 14mm. SF 4029 AML 820325 **3021** 3.80 5.70 (3021). Fourth-century level sealing Building 33, Fig 70. AP 400

185 Lozenge-shaped mount, with sheet silver on brass. Length 26mm. SF 1208 AML 811375 **2117** 7.50 7.00 (35). Clay levelling, second century

186 Mount. Square sheet with domed centre and concentric mouldings. Length 26mm. SF 1731 AML 820235 **2622** 9.50 5.50 (797). Gully east of Building 30, Fig 64. AS 134/6

187 Mount. Sheet with central boss and iron rivet. Length 30mm. AML 820011. 1956–61 excavations

188 Sheet with two half-round mouldings along the edge. Length 34mm. SF 22 AML 820029 **1919** 5.00 5.00 (6). Upper fill of well

189 Decorative sheeting with mouldings along one edge and a line of repoussé dots on the other. Traces of rivet holes for attachment. SF 2631 **2823**. Unstratified, over Ditch 1281

190 Fragment with traces of enamelling between raised mouldings, probably the rim of a large stud with a band of enamel around one or more fields. (Leaded) bronze. Length 22mm. SF 3067 AML 820342 **3717** 7.50 2.10 (1881). Occupation deposit over Building 47, Fig 41. AP 279

191 Disc with concentric mouldings. Bronze. Diameter 28mm. SF 662 AML 820111 **2123** 0.50 0.50 (77). Ditch 74, associated with Building 21. AS 67/2

192 Disc with concentric circle decoration. Diameter 22mm. SF 719 AML 820117 **2217** 7.00 7.85 (491). Mortar floor. AP 86, AS 103/4

193 Thin sheet with repoussé dots in a triangular pattern. Length 20mm. SF 2407 AML 820275 **2015** 9.10 8.10 (519). Medieval pond. AS 197/1

Fig 126

194 Wing, probably from an eagle, cast in (leaded) bronze, the lower part broken (Figs 126 and 127). The treatment of the feathers shows similarities with the Silchester eagle, cast by the *cire perdue* method and dated to the second century AD (Boon 1957, 99, pl 15; Toynbee 1964, 129, pl XXXVb). The reverse is undecorated. Several wings from bird figurines are known from Roman Britain, the eagle having associations with Jupiter (Green 1976, 19 and pls VIII and IX). One from Colchester, of inferior workmanship, was designed to be inserted into the body of a bird (Crummy 1983, 143, fig 171, no 4271). Like the Gorhambury wing the tips of the primary feathers are raised. A smaller finely worked wing from Uley, Gloucestershire, with a different feather arrangement is interpreted as coming from a Cupid or Victory (Henig 1979, 369, pl LXXIIIb) but the style is very close to the Gorhambury example. (Leaded) bronze. Length 81mm. AML 811364. From upper filling of cellar, 1959 excavations

195 Fragment of a figurine with a hand holding a bunch of grapes, possibly a satyr associated with the god Bacchus, or the god himself. (Leaded) bronze/gunmetal. Length 24mm. SF 1041 AML 811370 **2117** 6.50 6.00 (563). Gravel on side of Ditch 598. Second-century level. AP 80, AS 101/2

196 Lion-headed stud with an iron shank. Length 35mm. Such studs were often used to decorate lock plates particularly on burial caskets, as at Skeleton Green (Partridge 1981, 341ff). AML 820006. 1956–61 excavations

197 Lion-headed stud similar to those used on lock plates. The head is moulded in lower relief than the larger examples. (Leaded) brass/gunmetal. Diameter 13mm. SF 3779 AML 820363 **3821** 9.80 2.00 (2302). Building 43, Phase 2, Fig 93. AP 340

198 Decorative foot in the form of a stylized bird's claw. At the top of the leg are traces of iron suggesting that it may have been affixed to an iron vessel. Gunmetal. Length 22mm. SF 1213 AML 811376 **2217** 7.20 9.00 (694), Building 23. Fourth-century level. Fig 50. AS 103/3

199 Escutcheon from a vessel in the form of a ?female head with a loop on the crown; a fragment of ring remains in the loop. The head has rounded features with full lips and a broad nose; the hair is rolled back from the face. There is no sign that the escutcheon continued below the chin. Like the Medusa mask from Gadebridge Park (Toynbee in Neal 1974, 151ff, pl XXVIIb and fig 55, 42) it was probably one of a pair of handle escutcheons soldered to a vessel such as a small bucket with a swing handle which was inserted into the two rings. Leaded bronze. Length 30mm. SF 1510 AML 811378 **2421** 8.00 3.50 (745). Tree bedding-pit in avenue leading to villa. AP 105

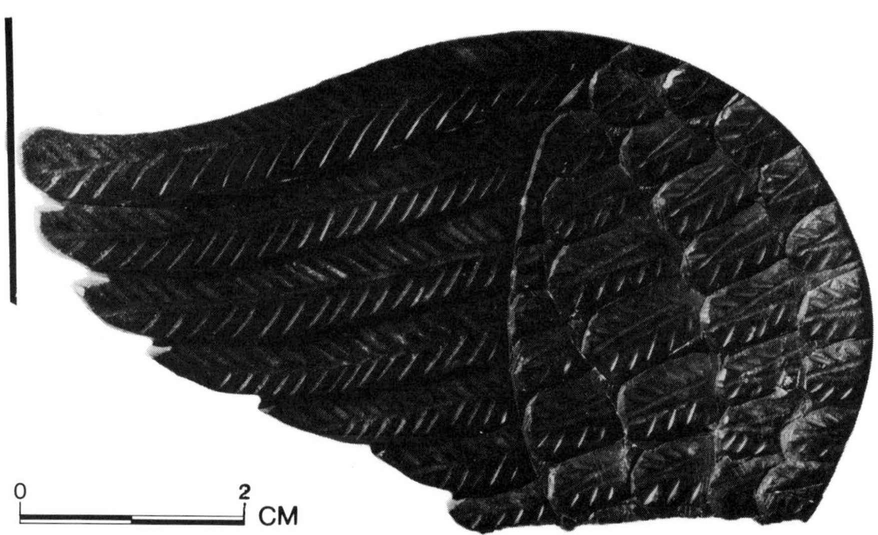

Fig 127 Photograph of the eagle's wing; for description see the catalogue entry for No 194

200 Decorative fitting in the form of a stylized cockerel set on a short square-sectioned shank for insertion into wood or bone. Leaded bronze, tinned. The cockerel was an attribute of the god Mercury (Green 1976, 31). Length 30mm. SF 2233 AML 820261 **2319** 0.30 5.00 (1082). Second-century level. AS 159/1

201 Strip with moulded acanthus-like design. Bronze. Length 86mm. SF 3140 AML 811 398 **3816** 5.30 6.20 (1909). Posthole, Building 40, Fig 40. AS 330/3

Seal boxes (Nos 202–205)

Seal boxes were used to protect the wax seal affixed to a writing tablet or other document. They are often highly decorated, frequently enamelled, and are found in a variety of shapes. The identification of the enamels is by J Bayley and S Wilthew (1986).

The Gorhambury seal boxes are all of recognised types dating from the second or third centuries. They appear to be randomly distributed but are found in levels associated with Buildings 37, 47 and 53.

202 Lozenge-shaped seal box lid with knobbed projections on either side and trace of a hinge at one end. The design, in the form of a stylized flower, is enamelled and made up of many small fields each containing a single colour. Two colours survive: one appears as mid green but was originally red, the other pale green, original colour uncertain. The red fills the background fields and the other colour the petals. Probably second century. (Leaded) bronze. Length 32mm. SF 4207 AML 826340 **2816** 3.00 8.50 (1283). Rubble over Ditch 1281, between inner and outer enclosures. AS 205/3

203 Diamond-shaped seal box enamelled with a design of concentric circles on the lid. The outer zone contains yellow enamel and the central ring, blue. The colour of the central spot is uncertain. The base has three circular holes through which the cords passed. (Leaded) bronze/gunmetal. Length 29mm. SF 3112 AML 811397 **3716** 8.00 6.70 (1903). Building 47, Fig 41. AP 276

204 Base of circular seal box with four holes, with a square notch on the side at right angles to the hinge, as on an example from Verulamium (Goodburn 1984, 36, fig 13, 99). (Leaded) bronze/gunmetal. Diameter 19mm. SF 494 AML 812589 **2122** 4.60 6.00 (234). Timber slot. AP 55

205 Leaf-shaped lid decorated with enamel separated by raised mouldings in a leaf or heart-shaped design. The reserved metal was tinned as was the metal spot. The outer field was red, the heart-shaped field turquoise and the central circular field, now appearing green, may originally have been red. Seal boxes of identical type come from Verulamium (Goodburn 1984, 39 fig 13, 101) and Colchester (Crummy 1983, 103, fig 106, 2525). Second or third century. Leaded bronze. Length 35mm. SF 1456 AML 81137 **2620** 5.70 7.25 (721), Building 53, Fig 64. AP 108, AS 133/1

206 Stylus, or pin shaft, decorated with horizontal grooves and two bands of incised lattice pattern. Leaded bronze. Length 70mm. SF 856 **2018** 1.00 1.50 (520). Well. AS 99/2

207 Button and loop fastener. Ring-headed fastener (Wild Class 2) with blue enamel in the triangular field on the knob. The shank is fractured. Such objects, discussed by J P Wild (1970b, 137), were originally thought to have been fasteners for dress or textiles but are more likely to have been harness fittings. Bronze. Diameter 24mm. SF 2979 AML 820336 **2819** 2.15 1.70 (1597). South terminal of Ditch 1281 between inner and outer enclosures. Second-century fill. AS 251/1

208 Clasp or fastener. T-shaped terminal with a circular cross-section. The fractured lower end is flat. It may be a variant of Wild Class 9 (1970b, 142, fig 2). SF 1250 AML 820151 **2016** 4.00 6.50 (667). Level over Ditch 666. AS 97/2

Studs (Nos 209–217)

209 Enamelled stud. The fields on the head are alternately red and turquoise. (Leaded) gunmetal. Diameter 14mm. SF 1770 AML 820236 **2621** 9.00 6.00 (796). Gully east of Building 53. AS 134/5

210 Stud with two concentric bands of enamel and a central spot separated by reserved metal. The centre and outer zones contained red enamel, the latter containing other colours also, perhaps in a pattern of juxtaposed blocks of different colours. The enamel in the inner ring was too badly decayed for identification. (Leaded) bronze. Length 13mm. SF 1976 AML 811380 **2521** 2.50 9.00 (815). Structure 12, upper fill, Fig 36. Second century. AP 116

211 Stud. The two concentric fields separated by reserved metal have slight traces of enamel which suggest that the design was one of juxtaposed blocks of alternating colours. There was no trace of enamel in the central spot. Bronze. Diameter 18mm. SF 531 AML 820082 **2022** 9.00 7.00 (275). Second-century fill of Ditch 74, associated with occupation of Building 37, Fig 48. AP 50, AS 66/1

212 Stud or mount (?lock pin) with fractured shank. The head has concentric mouldings with inlay in the central spot. The outer zone contains white material rich in calcium but this does not appear to be true enamel. Bronze. Length 30mm. SF 11 AML 820006 **2020** 1.75 8.00 (3). Levelling clay. AS 24/2

213 Lock pin. Flat rectangular shank, now slightly curved, pierced near the end with a circular hole. The circular head has decorative moulding. Compare one from Skeleton Green (Partridge 1981, 109, no 34). Bronze/gunmetal. SF 532 AML 820083 **2122** 0.20 1.00 (275). Second-century fill Ditch 74. Associated with occupation of Building 37, Fig 48. AS 68/2

214 Stud with concentric moulding, shank fractured. Diameter 26mm. SF 252 AML 820089 **2022** 9.80 5.05 (275), Ditch 74, as 213. AP 50, AS 66/1

215 Oval stud. Width 9mm. SF 1520 AML 820226 **2620** 5.40 9.80 (721). Building 53, Fig 64. AP 108, AS 133/1

216 Stud with domed head and central boss. Post-medieval. Diameter 14mm. SF 1380 **2622** 8.00 9.50 (701). Ploughpan

217 Stud with tinning and niello inlay in the form of a dot and circle motif surrounding three crossed lines forming a central star. Tinned brass. Diameter 19mm. SF 2887 AML 820320 **2820** 3.00 9.40 (1575). North terminal Ditch 1281. AS 253/3

218 Fragment with concentric moulding, probably from a mirror. Length 29mm. SF 237 AML 820060 **1921** 9.25 1.50 (199). Fourth-century level associated with Building 51, Fig 102. AP 26

219 Fragment of mirror. Length 38mm. SF 436 AML 820069 **1822** 6.35 2.76 (276). AP 46

Weights

Disc-shaped weights in copper alloy have been found on other sites, eg Colchester (Crummy 1983, 101, nos 2511, 2512, fig 105) and Verulamium (Frere 1972, 160, no 85, fig 36). Gorhambury has produced six weights which were probably used on scale pans. Their present weights range from 3.46 gm to 4.86 gm, which was the weight of the Verulamium example. According to Frere (1972, 160) this may be approximately 1/64 of a Celtic pound of about 309 gm, which was lighter than the Roman pound (of about 325 gm). Alternatively they weigh from three to four scruples (*scripula*), No 225 at 3.46 gm being very close to the weight of one Colchester example of approximately three scruples. There were 24 scruples to the Roman ounce (*uncia*) and 12 *unciae* to the *libra* or pound.

The six flat circular weights were widely spread over the site, with two from second-century levels of Ditch 1281 and two from the area of Building 30/53, while the three conical weights came from Building 53, in a layer that contained much scrap metal.

220 Flat circular weight. 4.81 gm. Leaded bronze. Diameter 18mm. SF 1773 AML 820234 **2721** 2.00 8.00 (773). East of Building 53, Fig 64. Fourth century AS 134/5

221 Weight. 4.86 gm. (Leaded) bronze. Diameter 17mm. SF 1928 AML 820244 **2721** 1.40 2.10 (768). Levelling clay east of Building 30. AS 134/3

222 Weight. 3.92 gm. Leaded bronze. Diameter 17mm. SF 2922 AML 820327 **2822** 2.50 2.10 (1665). Ditch 1281, second-century fill. AS 153/1

223 Weight. 4.79 gm. (Leaded) bronze. Diameter 17mm. SF 2794 AML 822161 **2819** 2.40 7.90 (1569). South terminal Ditch 1281, second-century fill. AS 251/1

224 Weight. 4.33 gm. Leaded bronze. Diameter 17mm. SF 184 AML 820055 **2120** 0.50 8.50 (67). AS 43/5

225 Weight, 3.46 gm. Leaded bronze. Diameter 17mm. SF 2295 AML 820265 **2720** 1.60 4.10 (1052). Latrine 44, Fig 93. AP 155

226 Conical weight, possibly from a steelyard. 1.76 gm. Diameter 17mm. SF 1435 AML 820223 **2621** 1.50 0.50 (721). Building 53, Fig 64, fourth century. AS 133/1

227 Weight as 226. 15.63 gm. Diameter 18mm. SF 1423 AML 820222 **2620** 9.50 8.30 (721). Provenance as 226 AP 108. AS 133/1

228 Weight as 226, fragmentary, 202 gm. Diameter 15mm. SF 1415 AML 820221 **2620** 5.50 9.22 (721). Provenance as 226. AP 108, AS 133/1

Domestic items

Objects of general domestic use included two copper alloy vessels, Nos 229–230, spoons, Nos 239–244, miscellaneous handles, Nos 253–259, and keys, Nos 245–252.

A wide range of metal vessels and cooking pots was used in Roman Britain but with the notable exception of hoards, such vessels, being both more expensive and less durable than pottery, are not found in large quantities on villa sites – the Gorhambury survivals are typical. The spoons are discussed below.

The handles are mostly from furniture. Such fittings were used on many items such as chests, boxes, drawers and cupboards. No 258, however, belonged to a large vessel, perhaps a bucket. Tumbler-lock slide keys as No 245 are found in both iron and copper alloy. Copper alloy examples tend to be smaller and were used for cupboards and boxes while larger iron keys were used for doors. The copper alloy lock bolts were used in tumbler locks. Many iron keys were also found: see Nos 560–604 (Fig 135), where the principal types are described.

Vessels (Fig 126)

229 Rim of wide vessel. Length 82mm. SF 2073 AML 826349 **2419** 5.00 1.50 (741). Ploughpan

230 Rim of vessel with incised line decoration, tinned on the inside. Length 58mm. SF 3899 AML 820366 **3821** 9.95 0.05 (2344). Clay levelling below Structure 43, Phase 2, Fig 92. AP 337

Fig 128

Buckles

231 Buckle with grooved decoration. Length 30mm. SF 2740 AML 820282 **2316** 5.15 4.60 (501). Upper fill Ditch 666. AS 199/2

232 Buckle, tongue missing. Length 26mm. SF 1847 AML 820239 **2520** 9.50 8.00 (859). Posthole. AP 119

233 Circular buckle. Diameter 14mm. SF 2440 AML 920281 **2316** 5.15 4.60 (501). Upper fill Ditch 666. AS 199/2

234 Buckle tongue. Length 25mm. SF 773 **2218** 1.10 1.40 (494). Building 50, Fig 99. AS 103/2

235 Buckle tongue. Length 25mm. SF 36 AML 820041 **1920** 8.00 3.00 (24). Post-medieval trackway

236 Buckle fragment with iron pin piercing a flattened terminal. Gunmetal. Length 24mm. SF 364 AML 820062 **2121** 1.00 1.50 (77). Ditch 74, first-century fill associated with occupation of Building 21, Fig 48. AS 42/7

237 Belt plate with scored decoration, central hole and four prongs. Length 23mm. SF 377 AML 820063 **2120** 1.00 9.00 (77). Ditch 74, aas No 236. AS 43/5

238 Buckle plate with two rivet holes. Length 29mm. SF 622 AML 820105 **2122** 0.50 9.75 (369). Ditch 74, seecond-century level associated with occupation of Building 37. AS 68/3

Spoons

Five of the six spoons are round bowled *cochlearia*, a type common in the first and second centuries. Justine Bayley reports that the single example in which the handle springs from the rim of the bowl, No 243, is wrought and is made of brass, while those with the handle continuing as a rib across the back of the bowl (Nos 240, 241, 242, 244) are cast and mainly made of leaded alloys. This illustrates the use of appropriate materials for different methods of manufacture (Bayley 1986a). An analysis of the spoons from Richborough shows a similar use of brass and leaded bronze for wrought and cast spoons respectively (Bayley 1984). Miss Bayley also observes that it is likely that all the Gorhambury spoons made from copper alloys were originally tinned.

239 Spoon bowl of mandoline form made from base silver. This shape was produced throughout the Roman period with many parallels from Roman Britain including those from Colchester (Crummy 1983, 70, fig 73, 2018, 2019). Length 39mm. SF 961 AML 811368 **2217** 1.00 6.75 (494). Building 50, Fig 99, Period 10, third century. AS 101/2

240 *Cochleare* bowl, tinned bronze. Length 32mm. The type, in which the handle continues as a 'rat tail', is common, as at Verulamium (Goodburn 1984, 40, fig 15, 120) and is also found in bone, Nos 964, 965, Fig 140. SF 859 AML 811367 **2317** 7.20 6.50. Unstratified

241 *Cochleare* with round bowl and thin straight handle. Leaded bronze/gunmetal. Length 87mm. SF 2417 AML 811390 **2727** 0.50 6.50 (1271). Charcoal spread east of Building 29. AP 194, AS 205/2

242 *Cochleare* with fractured handle. (Leaded) bronze. Length 63mm. SF 1644 AML 820052 **2120** 2.00 9.00 (45). Over Ditch 74. AS 43/5

243 *Cochleare*, the handle springing from the rim of the bowl. Tinned brass. Length 51mm. SF 2980 AML 811386 **2819** 2.90 9.00 (1588). South terminal Ditch 1281 between inner and outer enclosures; second-century fill. AS 251/1

244 *Cochleare* with 'rat tail' on the underside of the bowl. Leaded gunmetal, tinned. Length 50mm. SF 2911 AML 811387 **2819** 2.40 2.20 (1584). South terminal Ditch 1281. AS 251/1

Keys and locks

245 Tumbler-lock slide key with rows of teeth arranged on a straight bit, a type commonly found in iron (Manning 1985 92), see also Nos 569, 571 Fig 135. The key has a heavy handle with decorative ribs. Brass. Length 64mm. SF 2983 AML 820339 **2820** 2.60 0.50 (1599). South terminal Ditch 1281. Second century. AS 251/1

246 Lock bolt, used in a tumbler lock. Length 88mm. SF 2628 AML 820295 **2818** 5.00 2.00 (1446). Building 55, Fig 69. AP 212

247 Lock bolt with square and triangular perforations which correspond to the teeth on the bit of a key. Leaded gunmetal. Length 70mm. SF 2888 AML 820231 **2819** 3.10 2.20 (1581). South terminal Ditch 1281. AS 251/1

248 Lock bolt, incomplete. Leaded gunmetal. Length 73mm. SF 388 AML 820065 **2121** 7.50 2.50 (263). Cesspit 257 in Building 27, Fig 48. Second century. AP 35, AS 42/2

249 Lock bolt with triangular perforations forming two 'X's'. Length 61mm. SF 2401 AML 820274 **2417** 2.20 6.50 (741). Ploughpan over Building 10. AS 157/1

250 Lock bolt with one rectangular and two triangular perforations. Length 58mm. SF 2541 AML 820288 **2717** 0.50 0.60 (1271). Charcoal spread east of Building 29. AP 194, AS 205/2

251 Fragment of lock bolt. Length 43mm. SF 165 AML 820053 **2221** 5.00 9.00 (171). Area of Building 27, Fig 48. AP 39, AS 45/1

252 Ring key. Ring with simple lever lock key, the rectangular bit with notches suggesting wards. Such keys generally belonged to small boxes or chests; one was found *in situ* at Colchester (Crummy 1983, 86, fig 90, 2195). Leaded gunmetal. Diameter 18mm. Length of key 17mm. SF 3186 AML 829345 **3716** 5.00 5.00 (2020). Building 47, Fig 41, fourth century. AP 27, AS 301/3

Handles

253 Drop handle with plain flattened terminal. Length 45mm. SF 1662 **2621** 0.10 2.00 (714). South of Building 30, Fig 64

254 Drop handle. Square-sectioned strip with looped terminals. Bronze. Length 50mm. SF 2947 AML 820331 **2821** 3.00 0.00 (1594). North terminal Ditch 1281. AS 253/3

255 Drop handle with knobbed terminals. Brass. Length 51mm. SF 2930 AML 820330 **2821** 4.00 2.00 (1594). North terminal Ditch 1281. AS 253/3

256 Drop handle with looped terminals, one straightened, and central mouldings. Length 100mm. SF 517 AML 820079 **2022** 8.20 6.70 (275). Second century. Fill of Ditch 74, associated with occupation of Building 37, Fig 48. AP 50, AS 66/1

257 Ring handle. Flat circular plate with pierced terminals set at right angles. Length 42mm. SF 2081 AML 820251 **2419** 3.00 0.50 (920). Building 28, Fig 52, robber trench. AP 141

258 Handle of vessel. Round-sectioned iron bar covered with copper alloy which has sprung open. There are traces of lead solder along the join. Length 175mm. SF 3417 AML 801716 **3716** 1.00 6.80 (2192). Slot Building 40, Fig 40. AS 302/8

259 Ring handle from unknown object. Length 15mm. SF 57 AML 820044 **2220** 2.00 8.00 (29). Old land surface. AS 43/3

Structural fittings

The site produced a large number of structural fittings: many of the bindings were used for boxes, chests and items of furniture, as were various rivets, nails and dome-headed studs, a selection of which is published here. Lozenge-shaped pieces of sheeting, as No 269, may have been used as rivets for leather. Nails and studs were found over the entire site but there were distinct concentrations in levels associated with the occupation of the first- and second-century villas. Also represented are split-spiked loops, which are more commonly found in iron, cleats, miscellaneous ferrules and bindings and rings of various sizes which can have a multitude of uses as fittings. Some, as No 306, show signs of uneven wear.

Fig 129

Bindings

260 Angle binding. Heavy riveted plate for strengthening the corner of a chest. Length 61mm. SF 2677 AML 820301 **2723** 2.50 4.00 (1492). Well. AS 249/1

261 Binding. Riveted strap. Bronze. Length 45mm. SF 2884 AML 826469 **2821** 3.00 2.00 (1572). Ditch 1281. AP 220

262 Binding with two iron rivets. Length 45mm. SF 2633 2822 0.60 9.20. Unstratified

263 Rectangular plate with rivet-holes. Bronze. Length 37mm. SF 3012 AML 811395 **2918** 9.00 1.50 (1643). Latrine, Structure 46

264 Binding with iron rivet. Length 30mm. SF 2619 **2819** 2.00 8.85. Unstratified, over Ditch 1281

265 Riveted sheet. Length 30mm. SF 1335 **2621** 8.50 4.00 (721). Building 53, Fig 64. AS 133/1

266 Tapering strip with rivet-hole at the narrower end. Length 26mm. AML 820021. 1956 excavations, unstratified

267 Folded perforated disc. Length 42mm. SF 7 AML 820012. 1956 excavations

268 Perforated disc. Diameter 17mm. SF 2713 AML 820304 **2820** 4.00 8.00 (1551). Trackway over Ditch 165. AS 253/4

Lozenge-shaped rivets, nails and studs

269 Lozenge-shaped sheet, folded to make a rivet. See three examples from Gadebridge Park (Neal 1974, nos 104–6, fig 59). Length 20mm. SF 1598 **2721** 2.00 1.00 (786). Rubble east of Building 53, Fig 64. AS 134/6

270 Binding. Sheet folded over the edge of a second sheet forming a collar. Bronze. Length 16mm. SF 152 AML 820051 **2019** 6.50 8.25 (77). Ditch 74, level associated with occupation of Building 21. AS 23/1

271 Rivet with flat rolled head. Length 22mm. SF 1683 AML 820232 **2421** 7.00 9.95 (721). Building 53, Fig 64. AS 133/1

272 Nail with flat round head and square-sectioned shank. Length 13mm. SF 576 AML 820092 **2022** 9.90 8.00 (369). Upper fill Ditch 74, associated with occupation of Building 37, Fig 48. AS 68/3

273 Nail. Length 17mm. SF 94 AML 820034 **2019** 8.00 5.00 (77) Ditch 74, associated with Building 21. AS 23/1

274 Nail. Length 12mm. SF 769 **2017** 8.10 6.00 (4). Ploughpan, over Ditch 74

275 Nail with square-sectioned shank pinched below the head. Length 17mm. SF 1814 AML 820238 **2621** 1.50 4.00 (787). Building 53, Fig 64. AS 133/1

276 Nail. Length 37mm. SF 484 AML 820075 **2122** 1.80 3.90 (320). Over Ditch 74. AP 55

Dome-headed nails and studs

277 Length 22mm. SF 882 AML 820124 **2117** 4.00 8.00 (539). Redeposited clay, Building 50, Fig 99. AP 80

278 Length 28mm. Five similar nails also came from this context. SF 579 AML 820093 **2022** 9.80 7.50 (369). Second-century fill Ditch 74, associated with Building 37, Fig 48. AS 68/3

279 Length 20mm. Diameter of head 16mm. SF 2666 AML 822157 **2723** 8.80 2.20 (741). Ploughpan

280 Stud with flat head. Diameter 22mm. SF 2804 AML 820313 **2822** 1.60 8.50 (1552). Over Ditch 1281. AS 253/3

281 Length 6mm. Diameter 12mm. SFF 584 **2022** 8.00 7.50 (369). Upper fill Ditch 74. AS 68/3

282 Conical head. Diameter 14mm. Length 8mm. SF 4385 AML 826348 **2319** 2.00 5.00 (1028). Humus overlying first-century levels. AS 159/1

283 Circular head and concave centre. Diameter 14mm. SF 2054 AML 820249 **2319** 5.50 6.00 (741). Ploughpan

284 Diameter 24mm. SF 2678 AML 820302 **2820** 4.10 7.95 (1552). Over Ditch 1281. AS 253/4

285 Stud with lead infilling. Diameter 5mm. SF 637 **2123** 0.50 1.00 (410). Ditch 74. AS 67/2

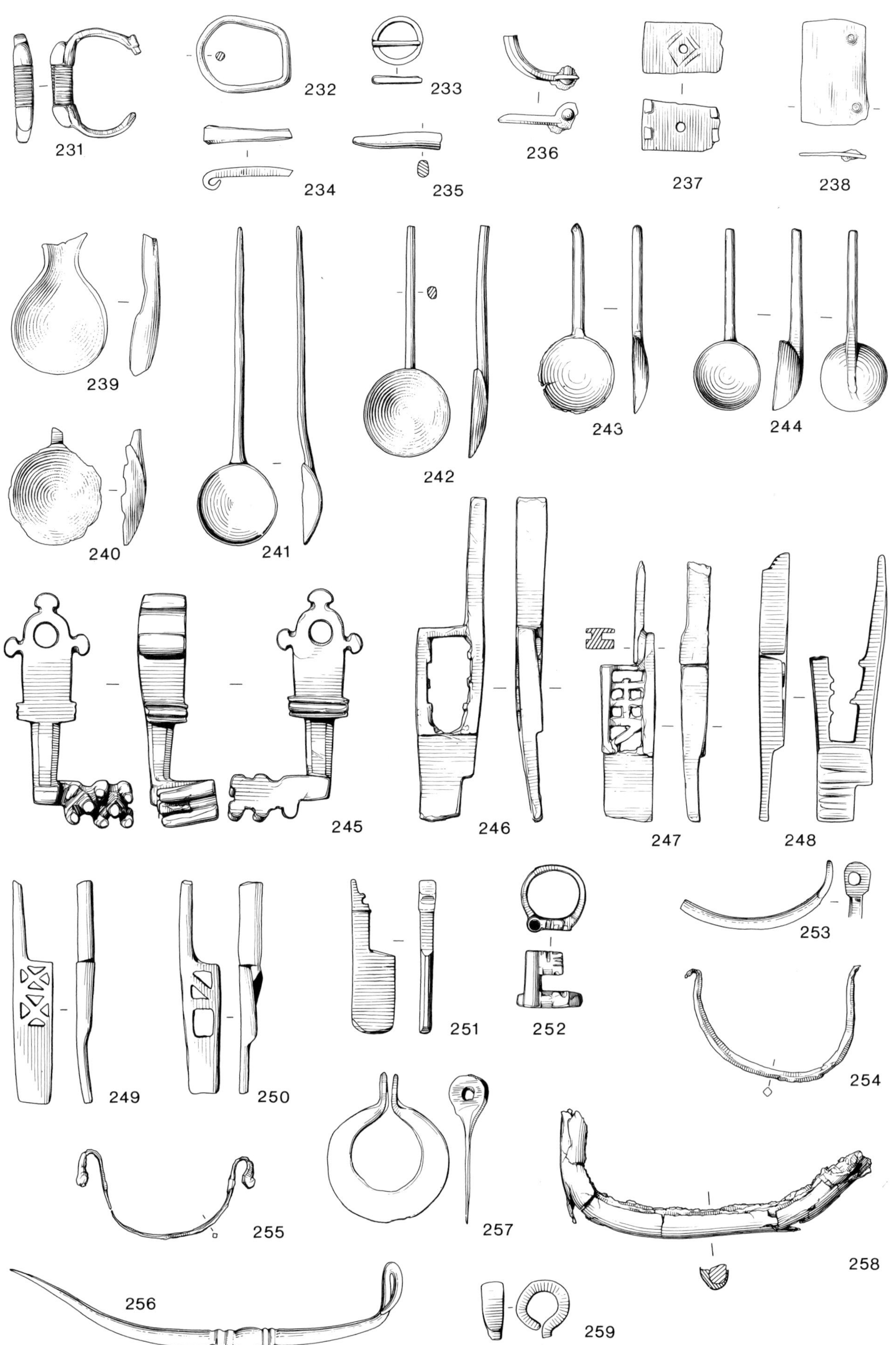

Fig 128 Objects of copper alloy (Scale 2:3)

286 Length 7mm. SF 635 **2123** 0.50 1.00 (410). Ditch 74. AS 67/2

287–91 Dome-headed rivets. Not illustrated. For drawings see AS No 444

292 Split-spiked loop with twisted shank. Length 49mm. SF 711 AML 820115 **2218** 0.50 1.50 (488). Ploughpan, south of Building 24, Fig 51. AS 103/2

293 Split-spiked loop. Length 38mm. SF 967 AML 820127 **2117** 7.00 8.50 (562). Building 50, Fig 99, Period 10, third century. AS 101/2

294 Cleat. Oval plate with an arm at each end. Length 36mm. SF 1149 AML 811372 **2017** 4.00 5.25 (596). Clay loam, second century

295 Hinge fragment. Riveted strap with pierced terminal. Length 52mm. SF 1979 AML 820246 **2721** 3.80 2.00 (768). Levelling clay. AS 134/3

296 Ferrule. Length 39mm. Diameter 8mm. SF 2105 AML 820256 **2518** (741) AS 162/3

297 Ferrule. Strip folded lengthwise to form a tube. Length 33mm. SF 1216 **2217** 8.50 2.00 (641). Levelling clay, first century. AS 103/3

298 Ferrule. Length 48mm. SF 872 AML 820123 **2017** 2.00 9.80 (4). Ploughpan over Ditch 74

299 Ferrule made from a sheet with a decorative cordon at each end. Length 12mm. Diameter 9mm. SF 2822 AML 820315 **2822** 7.80 2.00 (1630). Building 31, Period 8, Fig 67. AP 225

300 Collar ferrule. Diameter 11mm. SF 2803 AML 820312 **2821** 1.80 8.20 (1552). Over Ditch 1281. AS 253/3

301 Spiral ferrule, made from wire. Diameter 15mm. SF 3070 AML 826481 **3416** 4.00 8.00 (1857). Second-century level. AS 299/2

302–05 Bindings. Not illustrated. For drawings see AS No 444.

Rings

306 Heavy ring, worn on one side. Diameter 25mm. SF 1714 AML 820233 **2721** 4.00 2.60 (769). East of Building 53, Fig 64. AP 122, AS 134/5

307 Ring with polygonal section. Leaded bronze. Diameter 26mm. SF 2720 AML 820310 **2833** 1.30 0.30 (1540). Over Ditches 1483, 1281. AS 249/3

308 Ring with asymmetrical section. Diameter 23mm. AML 820013. 1961 excavations below tessellated floor, Building 37

309 Ring. Diameter 21.5mm. SF 3795 AML 820364 **3820** 8.00 6.20 (2344). Structure 43, Phase 2, Period 10, Fig 92. AP 337

310 Heavy ring. Diameter 40mm. AML 820009. 1956–61 excavations, from cellar ramp

311 Large ring with faceted outer edge. Diameter 40mm. SF 2732 AML 820307 **2723** 2.80 3.80 (1535). Well. AS 249/1

312–20 Rings. Not illustrated. For drawings see AS No 444.

Chains

321 Fragments of decorative chain, square sectioned. Brass. Lengths 17mm, 11mm. SF 2901 AML 820324 **2822** 2.00 2.50 (1662). Ditch 1281. AS 253/1

322 Three strand plait. Length 16mm. SF 2563 AML 820289 **2316** 3.50 8.00 (1398). Lime pit. AS 200/2

323 Twisted loop made from fine wire. Length 11mm. SF 2419 AML 820277 **2015** 6.20 3.95 (4). Ploughpan

324 Three figure-of-eight links are joined, one opened out to form a hook. Length 36mm. SF 469 AML 820072 **2022** 0.50 4.00 (317). Pit. AP 50

325 Three links. Brass. Length 60mm. SF 1124 AML 820138 **2017** 4.20 0.25 (91). Ditch 74, first century. AS 97/2

Fig 130

Miscellaneous

326 Mount or inlay, possibly a stylised bird. Length 25mm. SF 2587 AML 820290 **2116** 3.40 5.75 (590). Medieval gully. AP 174, AS 199/3

327 Lid, possibly for flask. On each side of the object is a rivet holding a circular 'washer' with a narrow extension which slots into a hole piercing the side. On the underside is a lead concretion, possibly filling a dome-headed cap. Diameter 14mm. SF 451 AML 820071 **2022** 9.90 6.00 (275). Ditch 74. Associated with the occupation of Building 37. AS 66/1

328 Bracket. Narrow curved strip with a rivet-hole at the flattened end and trace of another at the fracture. SF 2190 AML 820260 **2618** 1.00 6.00 (996). Building 52, Fig 62. AS 160/1

329 Flat curved strip with rounded terminals. Length 39mm. SF 4205 AML 826338 **2816** 3.70 8.90 (3246). Ditch 1281

330 Curved strip. Bronze. Length 86mm. SF 2962 AML 826447 **2822** 2.50 1.00 (1669). Ditch 1281. AS 253/1

331 Strip fractured at one end, with a circular hole. Possibly part of a lock pin. Length 33mm. SF 757 AML 820118 **2016** 5.00 4.00 (501). Ditch 666, upper fill. AS 97/2

332 Fragment of ferrule. Length 23mm. SF 229 AML 820059 **2121** 5.00 1.50 (208). Gully cutting Ditch 74. AS 42/8

333 Crudely-worked ring with flattened surfaces. Length 16mm. AML 820024. 1956–61 excavations

334 Fragment of cast copper alloy. Length 54mm. SF 3520 AML 820357 **3819** 8.00 0.10. Unstratified

3335 Wire. Length 25mm. SF 4210 AML 826342 **2524** 5.00 8.00 (3270)

336 Strip. Length 23mm. SF 725 **2317** 2.00 5.25 (488). Ploughpan. AS 104/1

337 Cast fragment, one edge fractured. Length 14mm. SF 2706 **2819** 8.80 4.40 (741). Ploughpan

338 Cast fragment. Length 38mm. SF 172 AML 820054 **2120** 1.50 9.00 (42). Floor make-up for Building 37, Fig 48. AP 32, AS 43/5

339 Cast fragment. Length 61mm. SF 76 AML 820033 **2119** 9.25 8.80 (71). Building 21, Fig 48

340 Fragment of casting. Bronze. Length 60mm. SF 101 AML 820035 **2019** 8.00 5.00 (63). Ditch 74, first-century level. AS 23/6

Miscellaneous objects of medieval date

341 Miniature barrel padlock with incised wave-and-dash decoration on the polygonal case. The spring mechanism is lost. A projecting chain arm is pierced by a circular hole. (Leaded) bronze. Length 29mm. SF 444 AML 820070 **1923** 9.00 1.50. Topsoil

342 Girth buckle. Large rectangular buckle, the pin and hinge missing. SF 40 1956 excavations. Mixed debris

343 Buckle with moulded decoration on the outer edge; the tongue is lost. Length 29mm. SF 2140 AML 820273 **2720** 6.20 1.80 (741). Ploughpan

344 Buckle pin. Length 34mm. SF 7 AML 820025 **2020**. Topsoil

345 D-shaped buckle. Length 24mm. SF 61 **2021**. Topsoil

346 Hinge. Length 27mm. SF 15 AML 820039 **1921** (4). Ploughpan

347 Pin. Length 29mm. SF 40 **1920** 7.00 4.00 (24). Post-medieval trackway

348 Thimble. Length 22mm. SF 2090 AML 820254 **2520** 4.10 5.60 (741). Ploughpan

349 Blade with thickened back, terminating in a rolled loop, possibly a razor. Length 49mm. SF 2620 AML 820291 **2921** 2.50 4.20. Topsoil

350 Harness bell with central rib, below which is arcaded decoration. It contains an iron pea. This is a common type, see Gadebridge Park (Neal and Butcher 1974, 135, no 82). Diameter 31mm. SF 411 AML 820066 **2122** 4.30 8.30. Topsoil

351 Bell, as 350 but undecorated. Diameter 30mm. SF 4092 AML 826337 **2917**. Unstratified

352 Bell, as 351. Diameter 30mm. SF 1366 **2522** (701). Ploughpan

353 Conical stud with foot on the shank. Length 16mm. SF 3535 AML 820359 **3821** 1.00 4.90 (4). Ploughpan

354 Stud as 353. Length 16mm. SF 3494 AML 820355 **3821** 3.40 8.40 (4)

355 Leather mount. Length 14mm. SF 2123 AML 820257 **2620** 5.00 4.15 (741). Ploughpan

356 Leather fitting. A triangular loop, fractured, terminating in an oval plate, with a shank on the reverse. Length 19mm. SF 2093 AML 820255 **2520** 9.00 1.20 (741)

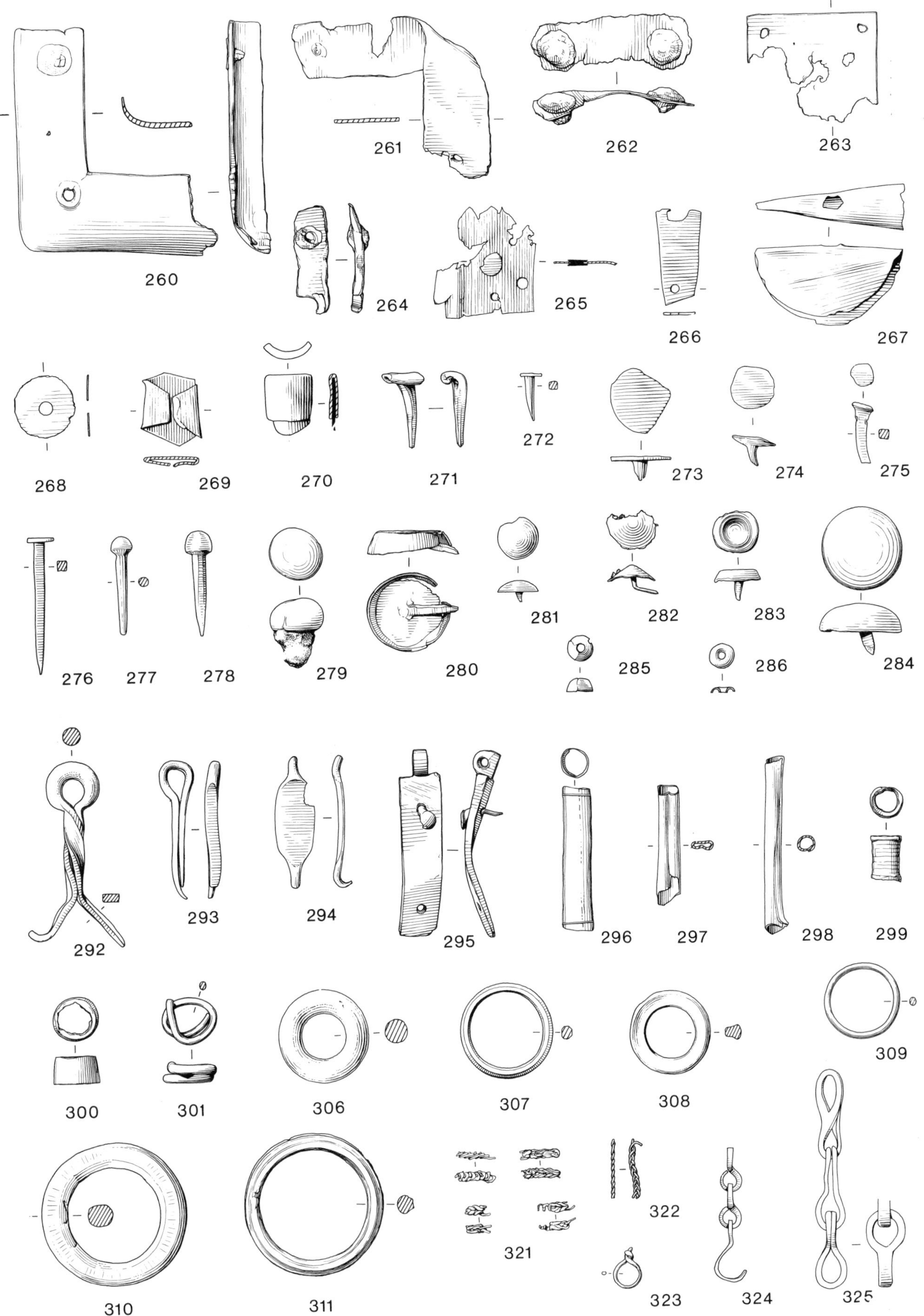

Fig 129 Objects of copper alloy (Scale 2:3)

357 Strap end. Length 20mm. SF 959 AML 820126 **2117** 5.00 8.50 (493)
358 Stud. Diameter 35mm. SF 31 (4)
359 Stud with head in the form of a fleur-de-lis. Length 10mm. SF 3289 AML 820347 **3817** 9.00 1.00 (4)
360 Hinge. Length 30mm. SF 1311 AML 810021 **2721** 2.00 6.50 (701)
361 Stud with flat decorated head. Diameter of head 19mm. SF 44 AML 820032 **2119** 7.00 9.00 (43)
362 Dome-headed stud. Length 24mm. SF 2051 AML 820248 **2419** 4.50 2.50 (741)

Qualitative analyses of copper alloy objects

by Justine Bayley

The list of objects analysed, with results, will be found in Appendix 4.

Introduction

The results of the analysis of the brooches are discussed above (p 121). A total of 125 of the other copper alloy finds from the site were selected for analysis by Angela Wardle. They were chosen to provide groups from dated contexts and also a number of comparable objects of different dates. This was an attempt to see if the date or type of object was reflected in its composition. A number of unique, intrinsically interesting pieces were also analysed.

The analyses, which were the work of Susan Wilthew, were carried out using energy dispersive X-ray fluorescence (XRF). This technique analyses the surface of the objects which were all patinated (corroded) and so does not give quantitative results, as the composition of the corroded surface is not the same as that of the metal of which the object was originally made. However, the presence or absence of individual elements can be detected and a very rough estimate made of the amounts present. In almost all cases tin, zinc and lead were detectable in addition to copper. Their relative proportions varied widely, indicating the use of different alloys.

A whole range of copper alloys was used in Roman Britain, the choice sometimes being a functional one but sometimes apparently dictated by fashion or the availability of supplies. Brasses are mainly copper and zinc while gunmetals contain both tin and zinc in significant amounts. As alloys containing any proportions of the various elements can be made, there are naturally some objects of intermediate compositions which cannot readily be categorised and, furthermore, the analytical method used has produced further results which cannot be interpreted precisely; in the tables of results both groups are described as eg 'bronze/gunmetal' which implies some degree of uncertainty. This emphasises the point that composition is a continuum and there are no hard and fast divisions between the different alloys. Sometimes other uncertainties exist; in these cases the alloy name is followed by a question mark. Those objects described as '(leaded)' contain a few percent of lead while 'leaded' alloys contain more than this amount.

Use of alloys

The analytical results are summarised in Table 7 to show the breakdown of the alloys used at different periods. It is assumed that all metalwork is contemporary with the contexts in which it was found though this may not be so.

The varying frequencies reflect the different sample sizes rather than any significant differences in alloy usage with time although there are a few specific points that emerge.

The proportion of objects where lead is a major constituent of the alloy is far lower than on many other Roman sites though this may be due in part to the selection of specific types of object for analysis, many of which are wrought rather than cast and hence have to be made of low lead or lead-free alloys. If all the objects where lead is present in more than trace amounts are counted, the 'leaded' proportion rises to 42% which is comparable with results obtained for groups of objects from other sites with occupation throughout the Roman period.

Relatively few objects are brass or zinc-rich gunmetal (brass/gunmetal); none of these contain more than a few percent of lead and most of them far

Table 7 Summary of XRF results (objects other than brooches)

Alloy	*'leadfree'*					*(leaded)*					*leaded*					
	1	*2*	*3*	*4*	*?*	*1*	*2*	*3*	*4*	*?*	*1*	*2*	*3*	*4*	*?*	*Total*
brass	2	7	2		4					1						16
brass/gunmetal		2	1		3				1							7
gunmetal	1	4	2	1	3		1	1		5		3	1	1		23
bronze/gunmetal	1	2	1		2			4		2			1		3	16
bronze	5	18	2	1	8	1	5	2	1	9		4	1		5	62
Totals	9	33	8	2	20	1	6	7	2	17	0	7	3	1	8	
	72=58%					33=27%					19=15%					124

Key: 1 first century; 2 second century; 3 third/fourth century; 4 fourth century; ? undated context

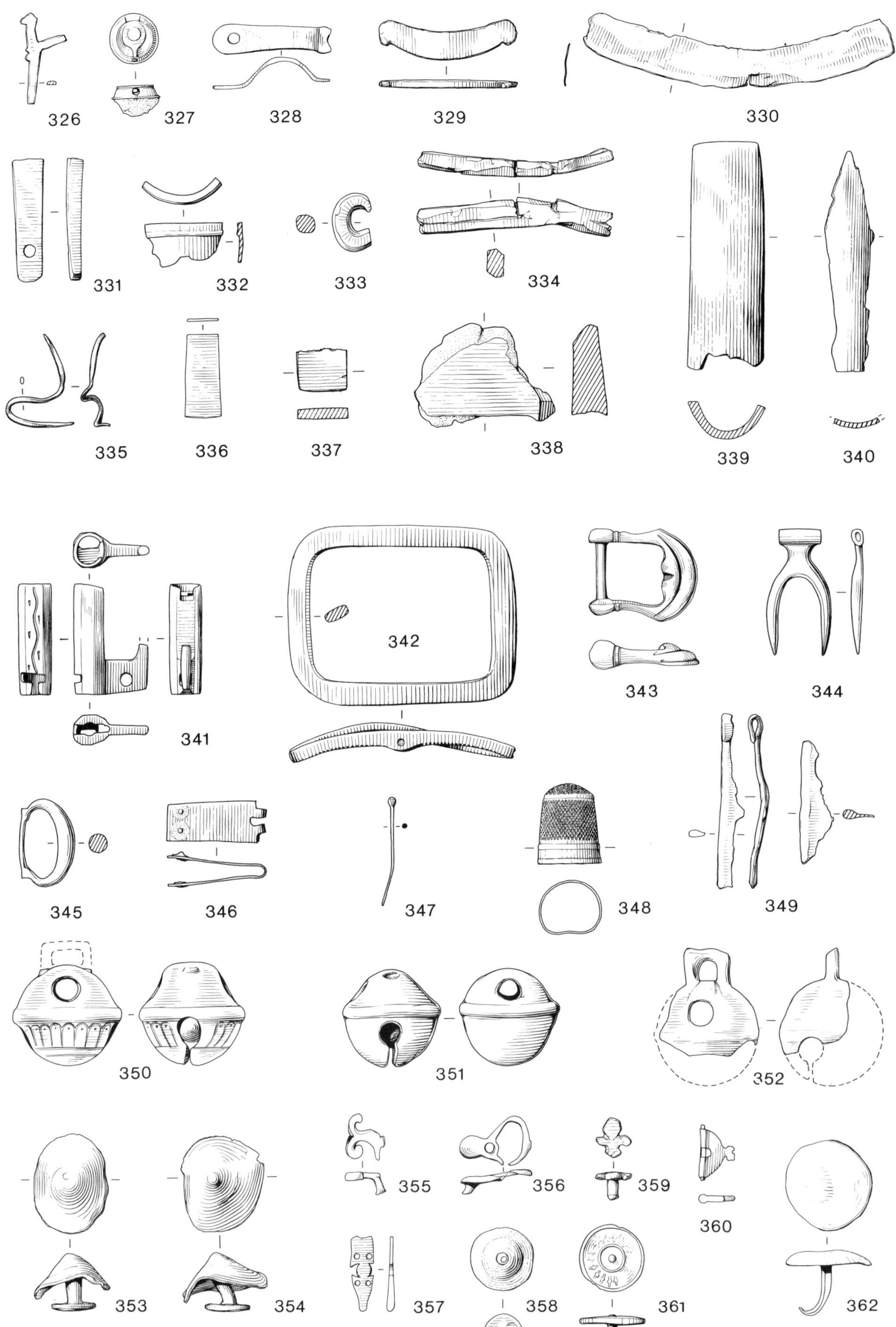

Fig 130 Objects of copper alloy (Scale 2:3)

less. This is normal in Roman metalwork where it is only the bronzes and, to a lesser extent, gunmetals which are normally leaded. What is absent here, but might have been expected, is a high proportion of brass among the first-century finds. On the Sheepen site at Colchester where most of the finds are dated to between the conquest and AD 61 nearly 40% of those analysed (excluding brooches) were brass. It was suggested that the high proportion of brasses might reflect the early date of the site and/or the types of objects, many of which were military fittings (Bayley 1985b). The lack of brass among the early Gorhambury finds suggests that date is not the overriding factor and lends support to the thesis that the widespread use of brass (apart from in coinage and brooches) is associated with the military.

If individual object types are considered, there is no significant difference between the alloys used to make eg pins and the overall alloy distribution. This suggests that the craftsmen used whatever metal came readily to hand, provided its properties were suitable for the intended method of manufacture.

Any lead-free or low-lead bronze, gunmetal or brass can be hammered to shape and then filed and polished. The most noticeable difference would be in the colour of the metal; bronzes are pinkish-brown while brasses are golden yellow and alloys of intermediate composition will have intermediate hues.

If an object was to be cast then lead was often added to the alloy as it makes the melt more fluid and makes it easier to produce a sound casting. This could not be done if the finished object was going to be subjected to stresses. This is why leaded alloys cannot be used for wrought work as the hammering produces cracks in the metal. The more heavily leaded objects from Gorhambury all appear to be cast.

The spoons are mainly of the type that has a small circular bowl on a thin straight handle. These can be subdivided into those where the handle springs from the rim of the bowl, which are wrought (No 243, fig 128), and those where a continuation of the handle runs as a rib part way across the back of the bowl, which are cast (Nos 240–2, 244, fig 128). The wrought spoon is brass while three of the four cast spoons are leaded alloys, which neatly illustrates the use of appropriate metals for different methods of manufacture. Traces of tinning survive on three of the five copper alloy spoons; it is likely that they were all originally tinned. Similar spoons from Richborough have also been analysed; there four out of five wrought spoons were brass and four out of five cast spoons leaded bronze (Bayley 1984).

Objects of iron (Figs 131–138)

The site produced approximately 600 iron objects, excluding nails, of which 250 are illustrated and described in detail. Drawings and descriptions of 302 other objects can be seen in the site archive. It was felt that publication of a large proportion of the assemblage would be of value both for the interpretation of the present site and for future quantitative comparison with other villa sites. All the iron was radiographed by the AM Laboratory prior to drawing.

Tools

The examples are chiefly carpenter's tools, found in the villa outbuildings, notably the aisled hall, Building 39/40, which produced a typical axe (No 363), adze and plane blades and a file (Nos 364–368), also fragmentary chisels, Nos 386 and 388 (not illustrated). The drill bit and a mortise chisel came from Structure 43 (Nos 371, 376) but other tools, such as the saw, chisels and gouges, were widespread; significantly however, none came from the villa area. Despite the evidence for metalworking there are few obvious tools. Exceptions are the wedges or sets (Nos 389–390) and possible smith's punches (Nos 394 and 395), from Buildings 40 and 42.

Fig 131

363 Axe, with a lugged oval eye set below a heavy notched poll. The blade is triangular in longitudinal section. Its front face runs slightly outward, the rear face more so, as Manning Type 3 (Manning 1985, 14). Length 140mm. SF 3418 AML 811358 **3717** 3.70 1.50 (1810). From posthole in Building 39/40. Fig 40. AP 278, AS 302/8

364 Adze blade. Triangular blade with triangular cross section. Length 80mm. SF 3389 AML 811357 **3917** 5.00 9.98 (2001). Yard north of Building 39/40, Period 9, Fig 40. AP 285

365 Blade, from plane? Flat plate, now bent with an edge at one end, possibly from a plane but perhaps a reinforcement or binding. Length 95mm. SF 3145 AML 811244 **3817** 1.00 6.50 (1904). Over cobbled yard north of Building 39/40, Period 9, Fig 40. AP 285

366 Plane blade? Heavy rectangular plate with plano-convex section, fractured at both ends, becoming markedly thinner towards one end with an oval nail hole. Length 95mm. SF 3272 AML 811301 **3716** 7.80 4.80 (2020). Third-century occupation material associated with Building 47, Fig 41. AP 277, AS 301/2

367 Plane blade? Heavy rectangular plate, with one convex face and square rivet hole. Planes are known from Verulamium, Silchester and Caerwent (Manning 1972, 166, no 14). The carpenter's plane had a wooden body or stock with iron fittings and reinforcements and an iron cutting blade, missing on the Verulamium example. It is possible that this object which has a marked edge at one end is such an 'iron'. Length 180mm. Width 40mm. SF 3256 AML 811288 **3817** 8.00 4.80 (2001). Yard north of Building 39/40, Fig 40. Late-second or early-third century level. AP 285

368 File. Rectangular file with 6 teeth to 10 mm on one face. Length 100mm. SF 3297 AML 811313 **3917** 4.50 3.50 (2016). Upper fill of Ditch 1851. AP 292

369 File? Heavy rectangular-sectioned bar with tang, possibly a metalworker's file, although no teeth are visible on the radiograph. Length 108mm. AML 791324. 1956–61 excavations. Topsoil

370 The object has a square-sectioned body which tapers to a blunt edge, with a shoulder between the distorted tang and body. It lacks the striations of a file and is now thought to be a rake prong: see No 417 below. Length 125mm. SF 3178 AML 811257 **3716** 7.50 4.30 (2020). Third-century occupation material associated with Building 47, Fig 41. AP 277, AS 301/3

371 Drill bit. Pyramidal head of drill bit of characteristic form (Manning 1985, 25). Length 113mm. SF 3548 AML 814762 **3820** 5.50 3.50 (4). Ploughpan over Structure 43, Fig 92

372 Gouge (carpenter's). Fragment of stem and blade. Length 88mm. SF 2503 AML 810523 **2517** 4.50 7.00 (1263). Level over Building 10. AP 182

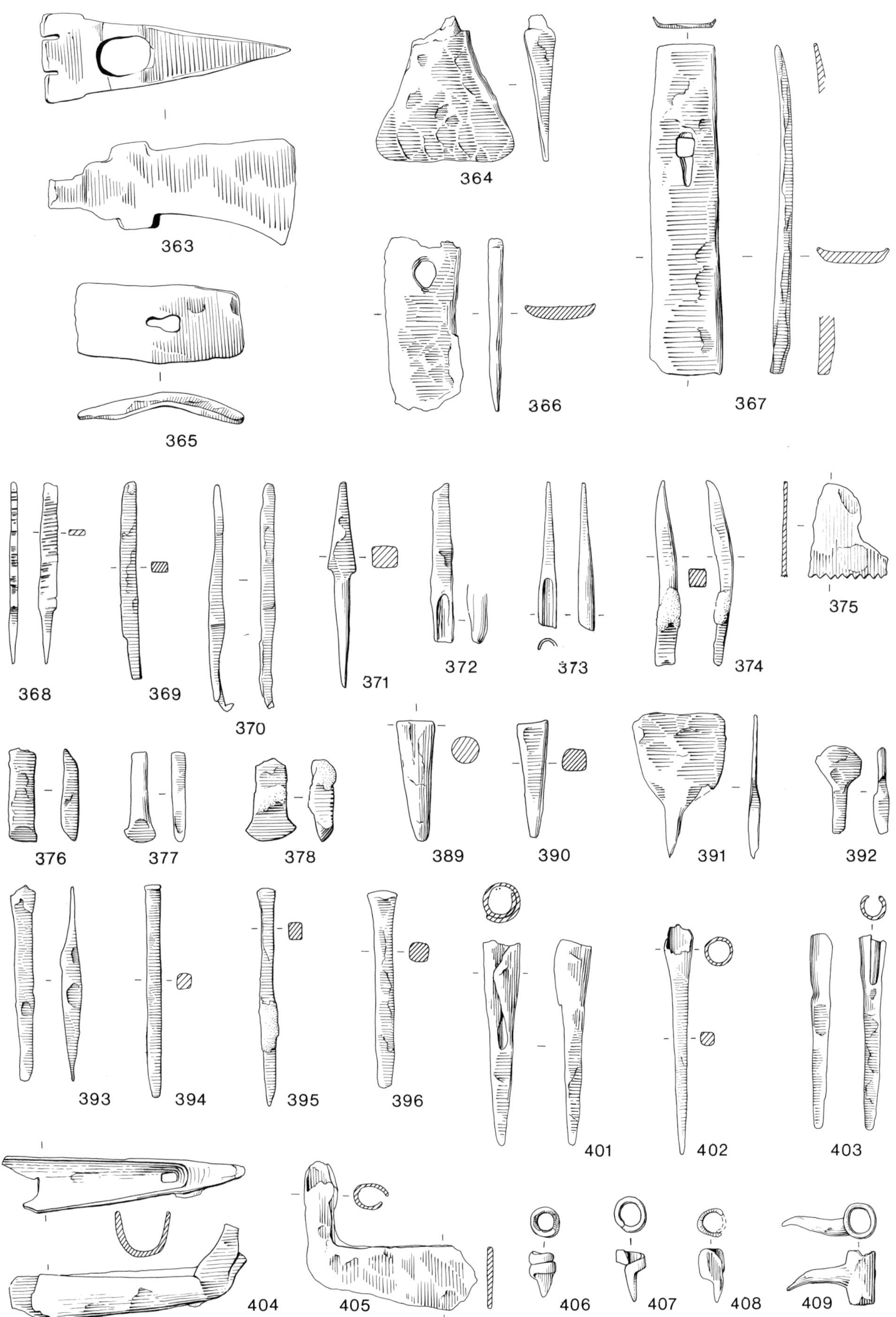

Fig 131 Objects of iron (Scale 1:3)

373 Gouge with a tang and a U-shaped blade. Length 83mm. SF 4296 AML 823960 **12/1322** (3258). Medieval pit. AS 418/1

374 Chisel. Fragment with tang and chisel edge. Length 100mm. SF 601 AML 791699 **2022** 9.00 5.00 (45). Ditch 74, second century. AS 42/7

375 Saw blade with six teeth to the inch (25mm). The teeth are not raked and the fragment may be from a bow saw, in which the blade is held under tension, but the piece is too small for certainty. Similar fragments came from Gadebridge Park (Manning 1974, 163, 356–60). Length 45mm. SF 1043 AML 802857 **2117** 9.00 8.00 (562). Building 50, Period 10, Fig 99. AS 101/2

376 Chisel. Bar with flattened chisel edge, bevelled on one side, fractured at the upper end; probably a mortise chisel. Length 50mm. SF 3493 AML 814747 **3821** 2.75 3.10 (2301). Fourth-century level over Structure 43, Phase 2, Fig 92. AP 340

377 Chisel. Mortise chisel with splayed blade, bevelled on one edge. The square-sectioned stem is fractured. Length 50mm. SF 3281 AML 811307 **3716** (2002). Building 47, Fig 41. AS 300/9

378 Chisel blade. Length 45mm. AML 791319, 1956–61 excavations, from cellar ramp

379–88 Gouge and chisels. Not illustrated. For drawings see AS No 445.

389 Wedge or set. Round-sectioned bar tapering to a blunt point. Length 68mm. SF 2581 AML 810533 **2817** 1.50 2.00 (1286). Ditch 1281, between inner and outer enclosures. AS 205/3

390 Wedge or set. Square-sectioned tapering bar. Length 65mm. SF 2606 AML 810538 **2116** 2,20 6.80 (1334). Medieval gully 1333. AS 199/3

391 Tanged tool with wide flat blade, fractured. Length 90mm. SF 3229 AML 811279 **3716** 5.00 7.50 (2032). Building 47, Fig 41, Period 10, floor. AS 301/1

392 Fragment of triangular blade with tang. Length 50mm. SF 3944 AML 814906 **3822** 1.50 1.00 (2691). Slot in Building 42, Fig 90. AP 343

393 Chisel? The object has a broad chisel edge at one end but is incomplete. Length 109mm. SF 1582 AML 810120 **2622** 4.50 2.50 (744). Corn dryer. AP 106, AS 132/2

394 Punch or chisel. Square-sectioned stem with tapering chisel edge and battered head. Length 119mm. SF 3674 AML 814789 **3822** 2.00 10.00 (2330). Slot within Building 42, Period 9, Fig 90. AP 343

395 Punch. Square-sectioned stem with chisel edge. Length 119mm. AML 791303 1960 excavations. Ditch fill

396 Punch. Rectangular-sectioned bar with tapering chisel edge and battered head. Length 109mm. SF 3324 AML 811327 **3717** 4.00 1.00 (2065). Second or third century, Building 40, Figs 40 and 80. AP 277 AS 302/8

397–400 Chisels. Not illustrated. For drawings see AS No 445.

401 Socketed point. Square-sectioned tapering bar with ferrule. Length 114mm. SF 3302 AML 811318 **3816** 1.00 1.00 (2018). Building 39/40, Period 9, Figs 40 and 80. AS 302/8

402 Point with ferrule. Length 124mm. SF 1454 AML 810078 **2321** 8.90 1.30 (741). Ploughpan

403 Socketed tool. The blade is lost but it could have been a punch or chisel. Length 108mm. SF 3891 AML 814886 **3820** 5.00 8.00 (2301). Fourth century level over Structure 43, Phase 2, Fig 92. AP 336

Agricultural implements

The site produced a varied group of items associated with agriculture and animal husbandry. The well-preserved farrier's butteris came from levels pre-dating the second-century villa while the ox goads (Nos 406–408) are from structures in the outer enclosure. Goads in the form of either a spiral socket or a simple ferrule with a projecting spur are commonly found on Romano-British sites, especially in the south (Types I and II, Rees 1979, 75, H). Simple spiked ferrules may have been used for the same purpose (ibid, Type III).

The wool comb (No 410) from the third-century Building 47 is unusual in having been altered from a double to a single-ended type.

The surviving plough shares are all of the short socketed type, placed on the tip of a wooden bar-share to protect it. The form was introduced in the late Iron Age and continued into the Roman period, although there was a general tendency for shares to become larger as more of the wood was replaced by metal, culminating in all-metal bar-shares. The different types are discussed by Rees (1979, 49). The plough share tips appear to have a completely random distribution and many are very worn, from use, not from subsequent corrosion. Several agricultural tools have been identified, including a spade sheath (No 405) from Building 39/40, and a rake prong (No 417). Nos 370 and 899 may also be rake prongs. Various blades came from scythes, sickles and pruning hooks (Nos 418 and 419) or were used for general purposes. The distribution of these items is scattered but most came from Enclosure A, several from the area of the aisled building (Building 40).

404 Farrier's butteris with a U-shaped blade used for paring horses' hooves. The handle is missing. There is a parallel from Gadebridge Park villa (Manning 1974, 159, fig 69, 345). Length 135mm. SF 93 AML 791339 **2020** 8.20 6.30 (86). Clay levelling over ditch 74, pre-dating Building 37. Second century

405 Spade sheath for use with a wooden blade. The mouth is straight and the surviving arm deeply grooved for the attachment of the blade, Type 2A (Manning 1985, 44, fig 10). Length 110mm. SF 3338 AML 811336 **3716** 1.10 8.90 (2073). Building 39/40, Period 9, Fig 40. AP 277, AS 300/9

Ox goads (Nos 406–408)

406 Length 26mm. SF 3457 AML 814741 **3820** 3.80 5.20 (2301). Level over Structure 43, Phase 2, Fig 92. AP 336

407 Length 28mm. SF 4050 AML 823856 **3021** 5.00 4.50 (3021). Fourth-century level over Building 33, Fig 70. AP 400

408 Length 34mm. SF 3216 AML 811275 **3617** 5.00 5.00 (4). Ploughpan, area of Building 40, Fig 40

409 Simple ferrule with a spur projecting at right angles. Width 50mm. AML 791309, 1956 excavations, 'mixed debris'. It is possible that this object may be a hinge: see No 627

Fig 132

410 Wool comb. Length 196mm. The comb has teeth at one end, which are welded into slots in the rectangular plate, and a tang or handle set into a slot at the other end. Radiographic examination shows that the comb was originally double-ended and the handle is a later addition. Such combs were used for carding a fleece before spinning and examples have been found on the continent where they are usually double-ended, as at Pompeii, Aquileia (Gaitzsch 1980, ii, taf 11, no 47, taf 42, nos 195, 196), and Lyon (Rue des Farges, Musée de Gaule Romaine, Lyon). British examples include double-ended combs from Worth, Kent, Great Chesterford, Essex, (Manning 1985, 34, pl 14, D1–D3) and Baydon, Wilts (Wild 1970a, 153 fig 9, pl Ib), but combs with teeth at one end only have been found on several East Anglian sites and may have been a local type (Manning 1985, 34). A wall-painting from the workshop of Verecundus at Pompeii, shows carding combs in use. They are set vertically in posts and the wool is pulled through the teeth (Wild 1970a, 25, and pl II). The Gorhambury comb is unusual in having a broad tang and may have been adapted when one set of teeth became damaged. SF 3184 AML 811263 **3716** 8.00 4.40 (2020) Building 47, third-century occupation layer, Fig 41. AP 277, AS 301/3

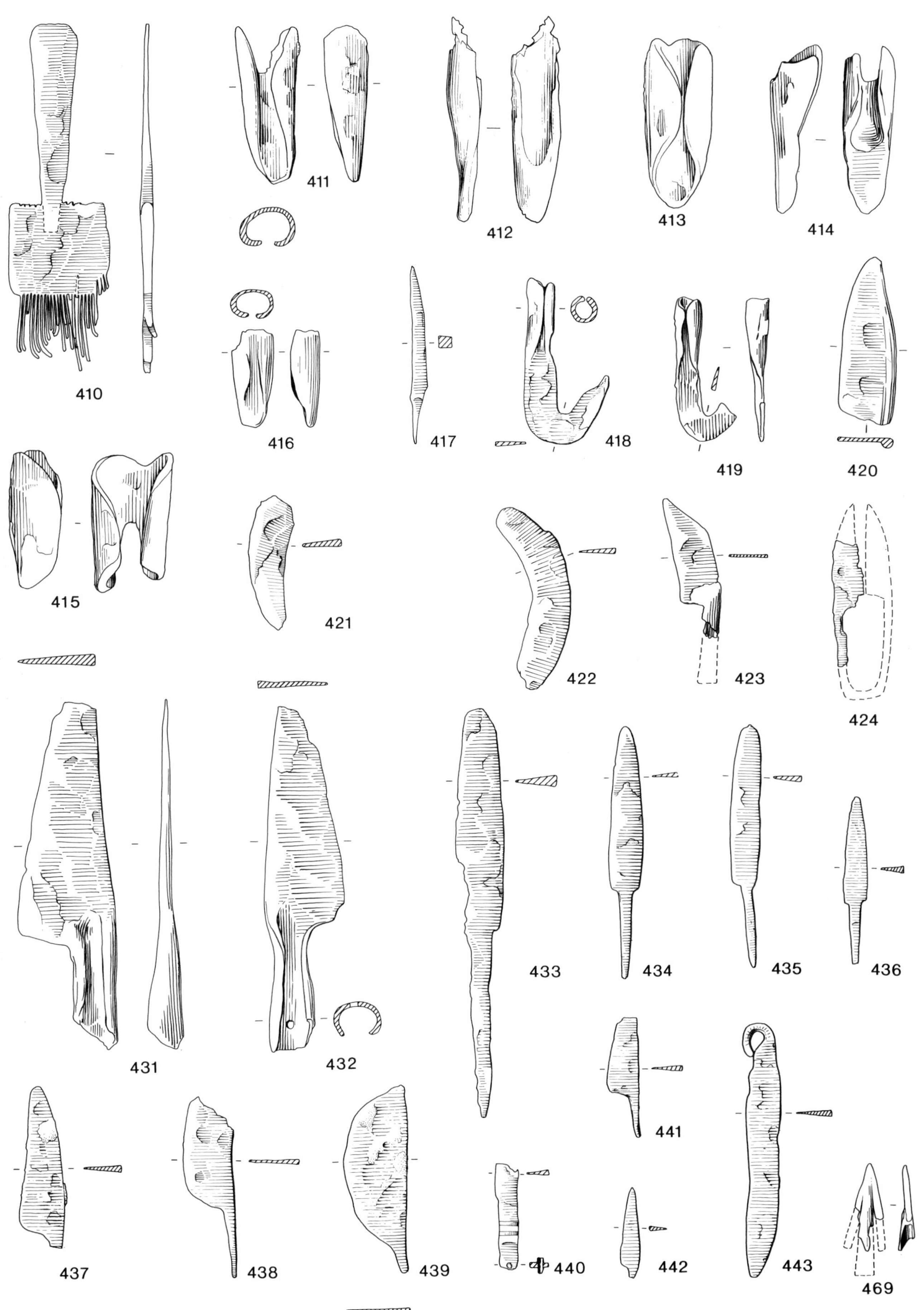

Fig 132 Objects of iron (Scale 1:3)

Ploughshares (Nos 411–416)

411 Short blade tapering to a blunt end. The open socket has round flanges and a slightly flattened back similar to an example from Slonk Hill, Sussex (Rees 1979, fig 51). Length 90mm. SF 219 AML 791358 **221** (179). Cobbled surface, first-century level. AP 39

412 Length 115mm. SF 4223 AML 823942 **2424** 5.00 9.00 (3285). First-century level in Ditch 3130. AS 425/6

413 Length 96mm. SF 1588 AML 810144 **2422** 8.40 5.25 (748). Posthole. AP 106

414 Length 96mm. SF 3200 AML 811271 **3817** 8.20 4.80 (2001). Cobbled yard north of Building 40, Period 9, Fig 40. AP 285

415 The blunt point completely worn away. Length 80mm. SF 1505 AML 810108 **2622** 0.50 6.10 (736). Building 11, Fig 26

416 Length 57mm. SF 2641 AML 810551. Unstratified

417 Rake prong. Square-sectioned tapering tooth with fractured tang. Such prongs were set in a wooden beam or clog; similar examples from many sites include Great Chesterford and Borough Hill, Daventry (Manning 1985, 59, pl 25, F66, F63), London (Rees 1979, 738) and Stanwick, Northants (excavations in progress). A well-preserved rake from Newstead shows the method of construction (Curle 1911, 283, pl LXI, 7). Length 99mm. SF 1392 AML 810050 **2621** 5.00 9.00 (701). Ploughpan. (For another possible rake prong see No 370, fig 131)

418 Pruning hook with sharply curved blade and short open socket. Manning Type 2, with comparable examples from Icklingham, Suffolk, and Bayford, Kent (Manning 1985, 57, pl 24, F46, F48). Length 90mm. SF 1028 AML 802853 **2117** 8.00 8.50 (562). Building 50, Period 10, Fig 99. AS 101/2

419 Pruning hook, with hooked blade of similar type to 418 (see also Rees 1979, 684, fig 199d). SF 3196 AML 811268 **3816** 3.50 4.00 (2019). Fill of slot in Building 40, Fig 40. Third century. AS 301/3

420 Fragment of blade with thickened back, possibly from a sickle or scythe. Length 99mm. SF 2828 AML 810579 **2917** 9.00 0.50 (1642). Latrine, Structure 46

421 Curved blade, possibly from a sickle. Length 75mm. SF 2855 AML 810589 **2823** 0.90 5.60 (1495). Layer in Ditch 1483, outer enclosure. AS 249/3

422 Curved blade possibly from a sickle. Length 105mm. SF 3143 AML 811243 **3816** 2.00 4.50 (1898). Fourth century; over Building 47, Fig 41, AP 282

423 Blade with angled handle, possibly a type of pruning knife. Length 90mm. SF 3269 AML 811298 **3716** 5.25 4.50 (2066). From hoard of ironwork within Building 40, Fig 40. AP 277

424 Shears. Fragment of blade and handle which would have continued into a U-shaped spring, similar to example from Tarrant Hinton, Dorset (Manning 1985, 34, pl 14, D4). SF 1304 AML 810019 **2626** 7.00 4.00 (701). Ploughpan

425–30 Shears. Not illustrated. For drawings see AS No 445.

Cleavers and knives

The site produced two large cleavers, both from Building 40, and 36 identifiable knives and blades. Where condition permits, the classification used is that of Manning (1985, 109, fig 28). The wide distribution of the knives does not permit analysis but there are several from Buildings 21 and 37. They include a wide range of general purpose implements.

Cleavers

431 Socketed handle. The back of the blade is slightly concave and the worn edge, broken at the tip, was straight. Length 196mm. SF 3271 AML 811300 **3717** 0.80 0.90 (2018). Second or third century occupation material, Building 39/40, Fig 40. AS 302/8

432 Type 2 (Manning 1985, 122). The socket has a single nailhole. The straight back continues the line of the socket and the edge is convex. There are parallels from London (Manning 1985, 122, pl 57 Q99) and Verulamium (Manning 1972, 174, fig 65, 40). Length 198mm. SF 3334 AML 811333 **3817** 5.00 7.00 (2001). Yard to north of Building 40, Period 9, Fig 40. Late-second or early-third century. AP 285

Knives

433 Centrally-placed tang. The triangular-sectioned blade has a straight edge and back. Length 230mm. SF 3452 AML 814738 **3820** 8.20 7.70 (2301). Level over Structure 43, Phase 2, Fig 92. AP 340

434 Tang set on the mid line of the blade, which has an almost straight edge. Length 142mm. SF 3723 AML 814812 **3821** 5.70 1.20 (2302). Level over Structure 43, Phase 2, Fig 92. AP 340

435 Straight-edged blade and tang set below the mid line of the back. Length 138mm. SF 1046 AML 802859 **2117** 9.00 8.50 (494). Building 50, Fig 99

436 Central tang. Type 16 (Manning 1985, 109, fig 28). Length 93mm. SF 4348 AML 823975 (3400). Fill of medieval pit. AS 418/1

437 Example with arched back, continuing the line of the tang. Type 13 (Manning 1985, fig 28). There are parallels from Gadebridge Park villa (Manning 1974, 167, fig 72, 407, 409, 410). Length 92mm. SF 337 AML 791369 **2121** 1.00 2.00 (77). Ditch 74, associated with occupation of Building 21, Fig 48. Period 7

438 The tang continues the line of the back and the wide blade has a convex cutting edge. Length 100mm. SF 740 AML 802804 **2218** 1.50 0.45 (488). Ploughpan

439 Wide blade with convex edge. Length 105mm. SF 50 AML 791311. 1955–61 excavations

440 Fragment with non-ferrous metal inlay on handle. Length 61mm. SF 1696 AML 810207 **2620** 4.10 9.60 (721). Associated with Building 53, Fig 64. AS 133/1

441 Straight back which continues the line of the tang and a straight-edged blade. Type 2a. Length 67mm. AML 791310. 1961 excavations

442 Type similar to 437. Length 50mm. SF 271 AML 791362 **2121** 0.50 3.00 (45). Over ditch 74, mid second century. AS 42/7

443 Example with looped terminal and parallel-sided blade. The terminal may be a distorted tang but it appears to have been bent deliberately to form a suspension loop. Length 142mm. SF 125 AML 791350 **1921** 9.00 6.00 (110). Third or fourth century destruction material west of Building 37. AP 26. AS 40/2

444–68 Knives. Not illustrated. For drawings see AS No 446.

469 Arrowhead. This is extremely fragmentary but appears to be socketed and barbed. Length 50mm. Roman examples are known from Gadebridge Park (Manning 1974, 172, fig 73, no 474) and Whitton, Gwent (Jarret and Wrathmell 1981, 190, fig 75, no 3). A tanged arrowhead from Fishbourne may be medieval (Cunliffe 1971, 134, fig 60, no 50) although the Gorhambury example seems from the context to be of Roman date. SF 1793 AML 810272 **2622** 9.50 5.00 (797). Fill of gully east of Building 30, Fig 64. Second century. AS 134/6

Transport

The unusual mount, No 470, from a hoard in Building 40, may be a cart fitting; the terret is from the same building. A linch pin found in levels associated with Building 21 is of a standard type.

Hipposandals were temporary horseshoes for use on metalled roads. The usual classification is that of Aubert (1929) but the Gorhambury examples are too fragmentary for identification of the specific types which are illustrated by Manning (1985, 64, fig 16).

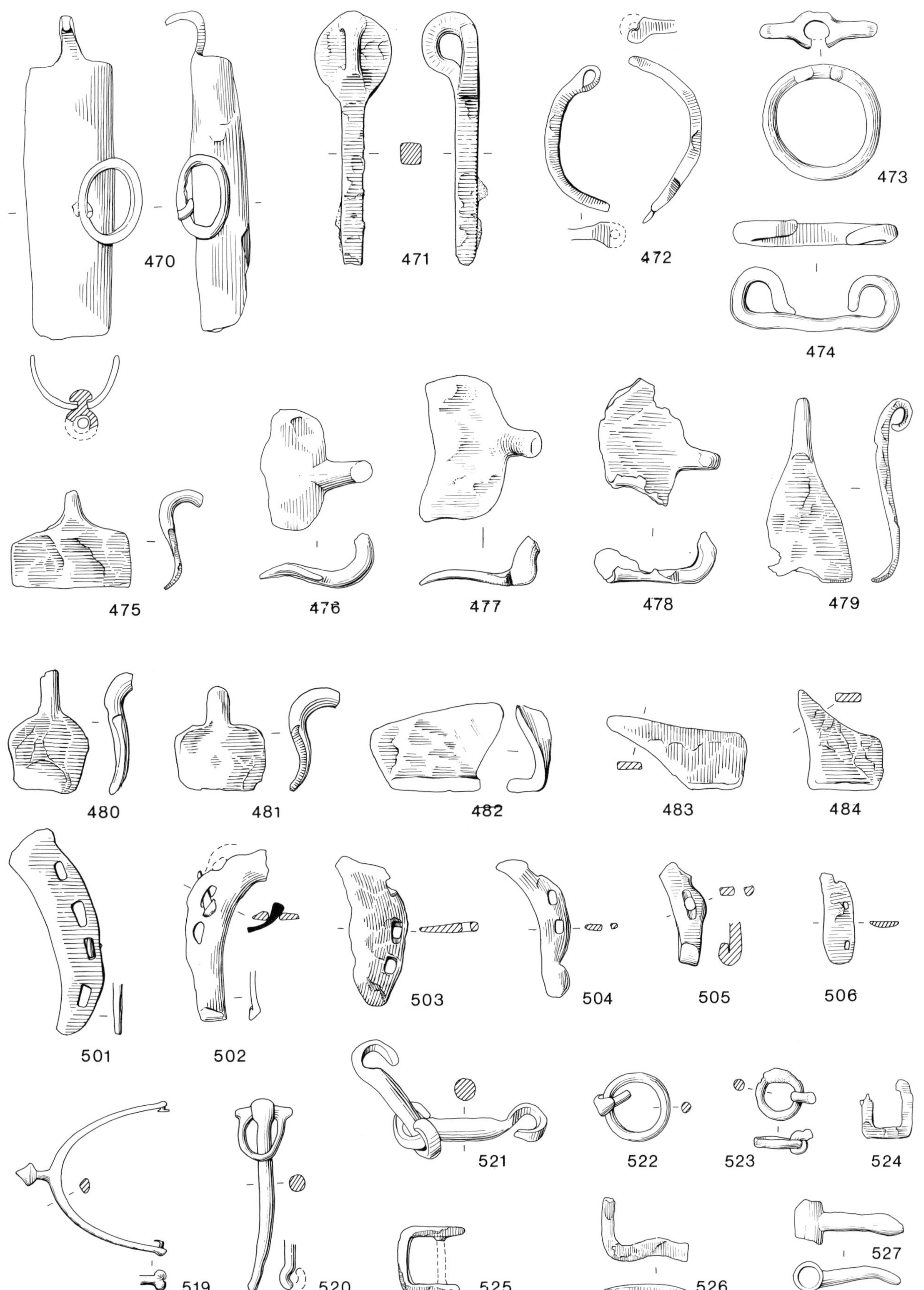

Fig 133 Objects of iron (Scale 1:3)

The distribution of the 25 fragments is of significance, with concentrations within the area of the aisled hall (Building 39/40), Structure 43, which may have been a stock pen, and Building 53. Horseshoes are known to have existed in Roman times but are rarely found in stratified contexts. The examples from Gorhambury, all fragmentary, are no exception and all could date from the medieval period: they are from post-Roman levels. A few items included here are of medieval date.

Fig 133

Cart fittings

470 Hooked mount. A semi-cylindrical mount with an upturned hook at one end and a ring riveted in a central position on the convex side. Several identical but less complete examples are known, from Benwell, Newcastle on Tyne (Manning 1976, 34, no 101), Silchester (Reading Museum), London (Museum of London) and Dorchester on Thames (Manning 1984b, 149, no 45), while objects that are similar are known from Germany (ibid, 149). Professor Manning has suggested they were a type of cart fitting, but their exact function remains uncertain. The Gorhambury example appears to be complete as it retains both hook and ring. Length 179mm. SF 8270 AML 811299 **3716** 5.25 4.50 (2066). From hoard of metalwork within Building 40, Fig 40. AP 277

471 Linch pin with spatulate head and loop. This is the most common type found in Roman Britain, as at Verulamium (Manning 1972, 174, fig 64, 33–35). Length 138mm. SF 347 AML 791373 **2121** 0.50 5.00 (77). Ditch 74, fill associated with occupation of Building 21, AD 43–62. AS 42/7

472 Shackle. Two curved bars, one complete with a single eye at each end, (one fractured). One eye survives on the second bar. Length 93mm; 80mm. These appear to be two bars of a shackle as Manning 1985 (81, fig 22, 3); they would have been fastened to the end of a chain, the outer ends riveted. Shackles used on humans and animals are fairly common finds from Roman Britain and are discussed in detail by Manning (ibid, 82). SF 3362 AML 811346 **3917** 2.00 2.80 (2016). Layer over ditch 1851, north of Building 40. AP 292

473 Swivel ring. Diameter 66mm. SF 3676 AML 814791 **3821** 4.00 2.00 (2302). Fourth-century level over Structure 43, Phase 2, Fig 92. AP 340

474 Terret, a double loop used as a rein guide. Length 95mm. SF 3134 AML 811240 **3816** 5.00 5.50 (1898). Third or fourth century level over aisled building complex, Building 40, Fig 40. AP 282

Hipposandals

475 Heel. Length 57mm. SF 3896 AML 814891 **3820** 6.00 9.00 (2344). Building 43, Phase 2, Fig 92. AP 337

476 Heel with base of the rear hook. Length 68mm. SF 1360 AML 810040 **2721** 2.00 0.70 (721). Fourth century; associated with Building 53, Fig 64. AS 134/3

477 Fragment of sole and rear hook. Length 82mm. SF 4074 AML 823872 **3021**. 7.00 8.00 (3091). Fill of pit 3200, Building 33, Fig 70

478 Part of sole, wings and rear hook. Length 72mm. SF 2600 AML 810536 **2116** 9.00 5.00 (549). Upper fill of Ditch 666, southern ditch inner enclosure. AP 69 AS 199/2

479 Sole and rear hook. Length 96mm. SF 3433 AML 811361 **3917** 5.50 4.50 (2247). Upper fill of latrine north of Building 39/40, Fig 40. AP 293

480 Fragment of sole and rear hook. Length 67mm. SF 3490 AML 814746 **3821** 2.50 9.00 (4). Ploughpan over Building 43, Fig 92

481 Heel. Fragment of sole and rear hook. Length 65mm. SF 3535 AML 814757 **3820** 8.50 3.00 (4). Ploughpan over Building 43, Fig 92

482 Wing and fragment of sole. Length 80mm. SF 2452 AML 810511 **2517** 5.00 5.00 (1258). Levelling clay over Building 10. AP 186

483 Wing of hipposandal. Length 85mm. SF 3534 AML 814756 **3821** 5.00 1.50 (2302). Building 43, Phase 2, Fig 92

484 Wing of hipposandal. Length 70mm. SF 3722 AML 814811 **3820** 5.00 9.00 (2302). Building 43, Phase 2, Fig 92. AP 336

485–500 Hipposandals. Not illustrated. For drawings see AS No 447.

Horseshoes

501 Branch with four rectangular nailholes, one nail remaining. Length 110mm. SF 2476 AML 810517 **2316** 7.00 6.80 (1264). Medieval level over Ditch 666. AS 200/1

502 Branch with lobate edge and two nailholes; small calkin on heel. Length 101mm. SF 2459 AML 810514 **2316** 4.50 4.75 (501). Medieval level over Ditch 666. AS 200/1

503 Branch with two rectangular nailholes. Length 86mm. SF 2629 AML 814922 **2723** 2.00 4.00 (741). Ploughpan

504 Fragment of branch with rectangular nailholes. Medieval. Length 83mm. SF 2406 AML 810501 **1916** 8.05 2.10 (519). Medieval pond. AP 69, AS 97/1

505 Heel with calkin, fragment of wavy-edged arm and nailhole. Length 55mm. SF 1093 AML 802871 **2016** 9.00 5.50 (549). Upper fill ditch 666. AS 97/3

506 Fragment with two nailholes. Length 50mm. SF 565 AML 791695 **2123** 6.00 1.00 (234). Medieval. AS 67/1

507–518 Horseshoes. Not illustrated. For drawings see AS No 448.

519 Spur. The arms terminate in simple rivets. The pyramidal prick is set on a short neck. It has traces of white metal plating which XRF analysis shows to be silvering with traces of gilding (J Bayley). Medieval. Length 90mm. SF 786 AML 802812 **2116** 1.70 9.60 (499). Fill of oven 497

520 Snaffle bit. Cheek piece and one link. Length 106mm. AML 791326. Unstratified, from 1960 excavations. Medieval or post medieval

521 Two link snaffle bit. Length 120mm. SF 3327 AML 811330 **3918** (24). Post-medieval trackway

Buckles

522 Circular. Diameter 39mm. SF 2175 AML 810462 **2419** 5.60 0.50 (920). Fill of robber trench, Building 28, Fig 52. Second century. AP 141

523 Circular. Diameter 28mm. Probably modern. AML 791300 1956–61 excavations

524 Square, fragment. Width 32mm. SF 2076 AML 810436 **2419** 7.00 1.00 (920). Provenance as 522

525 Rectangular. Length 40mm. SF 3456 AML 814740 **3921** 2.70 3.00 (2301). Level over Building 43, Phase 2

526 Length 46mm. SF 917 AML 802845 **2217** 1.50 6.00 (562). Primary fill of Building 50, Fig 99. AS 101/2

527 Tongue, possibly from a girth strap. Length 63mm. SF 1446 AML 810074 **2721** 3.20 1.00 (721). Associated with Building 53, Fig 64. AS 134/3

528 Not illustrated. Length 64mm. SF 1402 AML 810054 **2721** 0.50 1.50 (721) Building 53, AS 134/3

Items of domestic use

The cauldron hanger, No 529, is of note, particularly for its location within Building 40, highlighting its domestic use. The site produced miscellaneous handles, some of which may have belonged to utensils: No 533 shows the decorative twisting characteristic of many items, such as ladles or flesh-hooks. Most finds are from specific buildings. A bucket handle, No 542, came from a second-century ditch fill and there are also bucket side mounts used to bind and strengthen wooden buckets. Miscellaneous items include two steelyards; No 556 was found in the

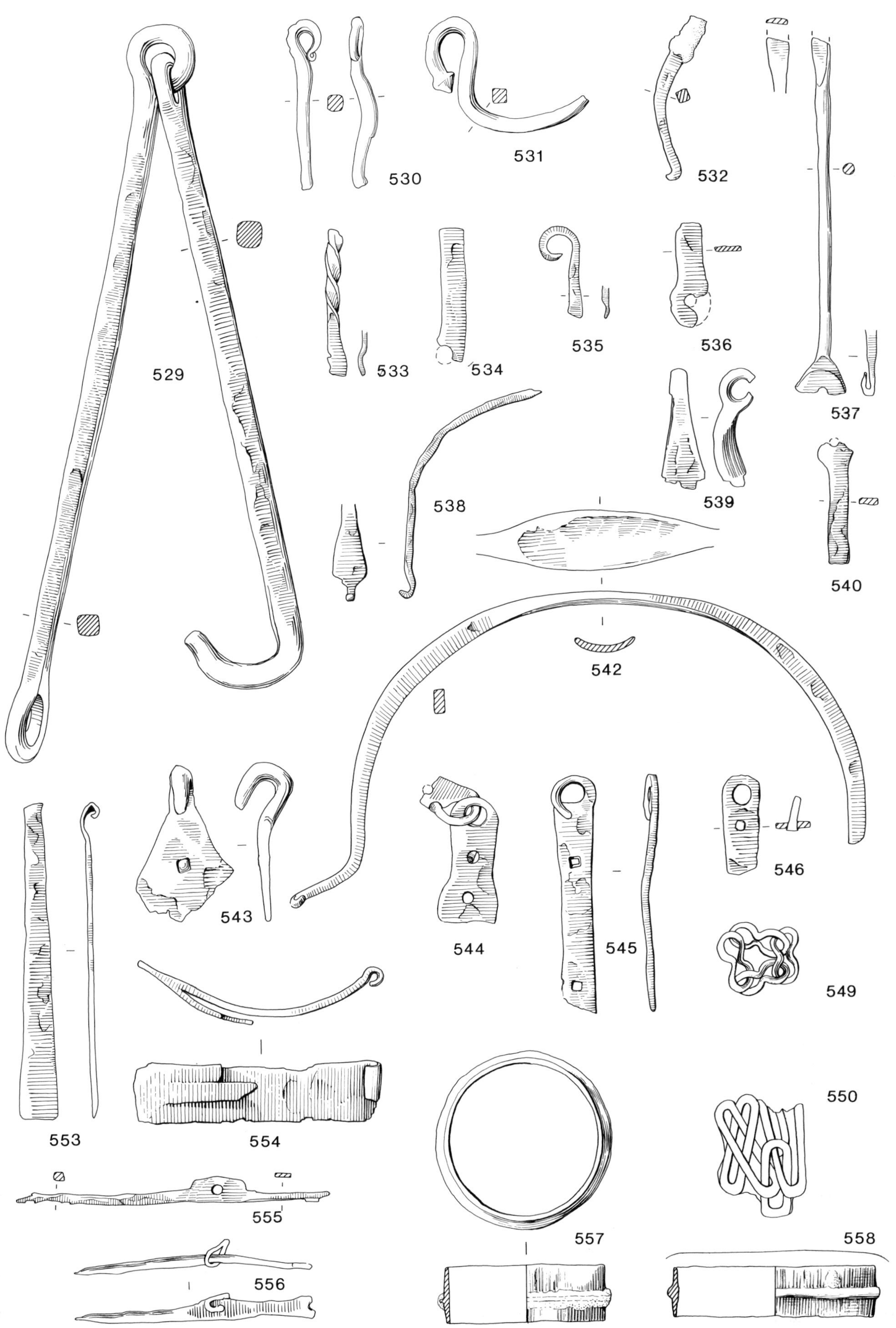

Fig 134 Objects of iron (Scale 1:3)

hoard within Building 40, with two lead weights, Nos 920 and 921.

Water-pipe junction-collars have been included here. Several were found but none *in situ*.

Fig 134

529 Cauldron hanger. Two square-sectioned rods are linked. One terminates in a loop at each end, the other has one loop and a stout hook. The arms lack the decorative twisting seen on Iron Age and early Roman types (Manning 1985, 100). Length of arms 430 and 530mm. SF 3419 AML 811359 **3816** 9.50 3.20 (2033). Gully within Building 40, Fig 40. AP 282

Handles (Nos 530–543)

530 Bar with decorative looped terminal, possibly a handle. Length 94mm. SF 1379 AML 810047 **2622** 1.50 8.00 (735). Clay north of Building 30. First century. AS 133/1

531 Drop handle. Rectangular-sectioned bar with one loop remaining, terminating in a knob. Length 100mm. SF 3194 AML 811266 **3917** 2.50 4.00 (2016). Upper fill of Ditch 1281, second century. AP 292

532 Handle with hooked terminal, possibly from a bucket. Length 94mm. SF 633 AML 791704 **2123** 0.50 1.00 (410). Ditch 74, second century. AS 67/2

533 Fragment of handle with twisted stem. Length 91mm. SF 1466 AML 810086 **2620** 2.20 7.80 (721). Associated with Building 53, Fig 64. AP 108 AS 133/1

534 Flat strap with trace of a ring at the terminal, possibly a handle. Length 77mm. SF 3319 AML 811325 **3816** 2.00 5.50 (2017). Level associated with Building 47, Fig 41. AS 301/4

535 Handle fragment. A strip is curved into a looped terminal. Length 50mm. SF 1712 AML 810236 **2621** 2.50 1.50 (787). Fourth century, Building 53, Fig 64. AP 120 AS 133/1

536 Flat strap handle with trace of ring terminal. Length 58mm. SF 3316 AML 811323 **3917** 5.00 4.00 (2016). Upper fill Ditch 1851, second century. AP 92

537 Handle. Round-sectioned rod with flattened circular terminal, folded and pierced with a central hole. The lower end is also flattened but fractured. Length 202mm. SF 3176 AML 811255 **3716** 8.00 6.00 (2020). Third century, Building 47, Fig 41. AP 277, AS 301/3

538 Handle. Flat bar which widens at the hooked terminal. Length 140mm. SF 780 AML 802811 **2018** 0.75 5.50 (4). Ploughpan, south of villa

539 Handle. Heavy curved bar which widens at one end and terminates in a ring at the other. Length 70mm. SF 3336 AML 811335 **3817** 6.00 7.00 (2001). Cobbled yard north of Building 40, Fig 40. AP 285

540 Strap handle with ring terminal. Length 70mm. SF 3999 AML 814918 **3921** 1.00 1.00 (2665). Cobbles in Structure 43, Phase 1, Fig 90, second century. AP 341

541 Not illustrated. Handle made from rod of circular section. Length 108mm. SF 3856 AML 814877 **3820** 2.20 7.00. Gully, Structure 43, Fig 90. AP 336, 338

542 Bucket handle. Rectangular-sectioned bar, widened at the mid-point to form a shallow U-shaped grip, with one hooked terminal remaining; this would have fitted into a side mount. Length 310mm. Comparable examples come from Borough Hill, Daventry and London, Moorgate Street (Manning 1985, 103, P16, P17, P47). SF 2937 AML 810604 **2822** 2.50 2.00 (1663). Over Ditch 1281, second century. AS 253/1

543 Handle mount. Triangular plate with nail hole and hooked terminal. Length 86mm. A similar mount comes from Dorchester on Thames (Manning 1984b, 145, fig 33, no 32) SF 2221 AML 810480 **2618** 1.25 6.00 (1063). AS 162/2

544 Loop hinge. Strap with two nail holes and round eye, through which passes the loop of a second riveted strap. Such hinges were commonly used on lids. Other types of hinges are represented at Gorhambury, see Nos 622–629. SF 3121 AML 811238 **3716** 5.80 9.90 (1880). Humus over Ditch 1851. AP 274

545 Bucket side mount, as example from Northchurch (Neal 1976, 23, fig XIII, 25). Length 130mm. SF 884 AML 802826 **2117** 9.70 8.50 (538). Posthole

546 Strap with rounded terminal and large eye below which is a rivet-hole, probably a bucket side mount. Length 55mm. SF 3197 AML 811269 **3816** 1.75 4.50 (2017). Level associated with Building 47, Fig 41. AS 301/4

547–48 Bucket mounts. Not illustrated. For drawings see AS No 448.

549 Chain made from four figure-of-eight links of a common type. Length of link 45mm. SF 3335 AML 811334 **3817** 5.00 7.00 (2001). Cobbled yard north of Building 39/40, Fig 40. AP 285

550 Fragment of chain with at least four oval links. Length of link 60mm. SF 2835 AML 810584 2823 9.00 9.00 (1495). Upper level Ditch 1482. AP 227, AS 249/3

551–52 Links. Not illustrated. For drawings see AS No 448.

553 Tweezers. Flat strip, rolled at the upper end, which is fractured and appears to be part of a spring. The lower end appears to be complete. The object resembles a large padlock key but the metal seems to be too thin for this purpose. Length 182mm. SF 3326 AML 811329 **3717** 4.00 2.00 (2065). Building 40, occupation level, Period 9, Fig 40. AP 277, AS 302/8

554 ?Padlock bolt. Strap with rolled loop terminal and fragments of three springs. Length 142mm. There is a similar example from Baldock (Manning and Scott 1986, 157, fig 66, 557). SF 16 AML 791315. 1956 excavations. For further keys and lock bolts, see Fig 135

555 Steelyard. Rectangular-sectioned bar, widening into a flat plate with a lug at the junction, both ends fractured. Length 185mm. There are comparable examples from Icklingham, Suffolk (Manning 1985, 107, pl 52, P42, P44). Steelyards are also found in copper alloy as at Gadebridge Park (Neal and Butcher 1974, 129, fig 56, 47). SF 1602 AML 810186 **2621** 9.00 7.00 (786). Rubble spread east of Building 30, Fig 64. Fourth-century level. AS 134/6

556 Steelyard, with corroded round-sectioned arm, suspension hole and flat plate with trace of another pierced lug at the fractured end. Length 137mm. SF 3267 AML 811297 **3716** 5.25 4.50 (2066). Hoard in Building 40, Fig 40. The hoard also contained two lead steelyard weights Nos 920 and 921, Fig 139. AP 271

557 Water-pipe junction-collar. The stop ridge which separated two sections of wooden pipe can be seen clearly on the outer surface. Both faces retain wood impressions, identified as oak by J Watson, AM Laboratory. Diameter 102mm. Pipe collars come from many sites: eg Verulamium (Manning 1984a, 99, nos 112–115, fig 43), Gadebridge Park villa (Manning 1974, 165, 374–7, fig 70) and Fishbourne (Cunliffe 1971, II, 28, fig 55, 4). SF 201 AML 791335 **2220** 5.00 1.50 (201). Early second-century level. A second collar of identical diameter came from this context. AP 51

558 Water-pipe junction-collar. Diameter 110mm. AML 791323. 1956–61 excavations, unstratified

559 Not illustrated. Water-pipe junction-collar as 557. Diameter *c* 110mm. SF 3355 AML 811342 **3817** 2.00 5.10 (2001). Cobbled yard north of Building 40, Fig 40. AP 285

Fig 135

Keys

The collection from Gorhambury illustrates the range of keys used in the Roman period, from the simplest latch lifter, Nos 600–604, to tumbler-lock lift and slide keys, padlock keys and rotary lock keys. There are no complete locks, but several fragments of barb-spring padlocks, Nos 594–599. Tumbler-lock lift keys lifted the tumblers to free the bolt which was then pulled manually. They were either T-shaped or more commonly L-shaped. L-shaped lift keys are found throughout the Roman period. They have from two to four teeth on the bit. The handle, which is frequently thicker than the stem, usually terminates in a loop or eye.

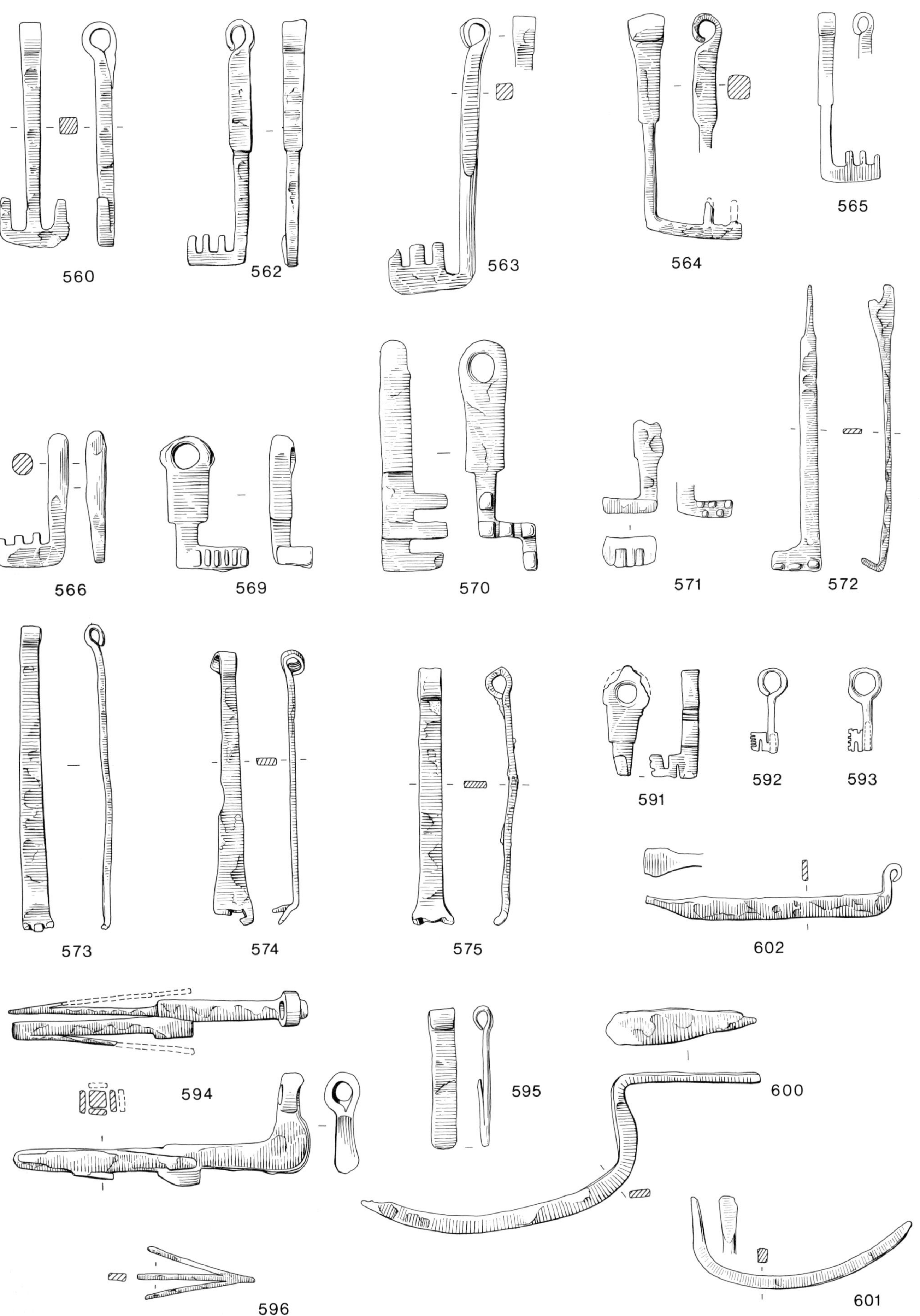

Fig 135 Objects of iron (Scale 1:3)

Tumbler-lock slide keys lifted the tumblers which then moved the bolt to allow it to be withdrawn. They take two forms (Manning 1985, 92, fig 25, 4 and 7) with the teeth either arranged in a single row on an L-shaped, Z-shaped or curved bit, or arranged in more complex patterns on a straight bit. This type is also commonly found in copper alloy (see No 245 and bolts Nos 246–250).

Barb-spring padlocks are frequently found on Roman sites. The Gorhambury collection includes two bolts and numerous keys which are L-shaped with a long flat stem and a rectangular bit, pierced with at least one hole. In operation the key compressed the springs, as can be seen on bolt No 594, allowing the bolt to be withdrawn.

Lever locks, which are more complex than tumbler locks, were used in the Roman period, although they are less common and the keys, three of which were found at Gorhambury, have a more modern appearance. All the Gorhambury examples have a hollow stem, which fitted over a pivot in the lock, with a rectangular bit set to one side. This was pierced with slits corresponding to the wards in the lock.

Of the various types found at Gorhambury, barb-spring padlock keys are the most numerous (nine examples) followed by L-shaped lift keys (seven), although there are fragments of handles which could belong to either type. Slide and T-shaped lift keys are less common. There is no particular pattern of distribution, although many were found within buildings rather than in general spreads, with several from the aisled hall and from Buildings 30 and 51.

560 T-shaped. A common type with one tooth on each side of a rectangular stem which terminates in a looped handle. There are many parallels, for example from the Gadebridge Park villa (Manning 1974, 179, fig 75). Length 128mm. SF 546 AML 791690 **2022** 8.05 7.00 (369). Upper fill Ditch 74, level associated with occupation of Building 37, Fig 48. AP 51, AS 68/3

561 Not illustrated. AS 560. One tooth is missing and the shank is fractured. Length 122mm. SF 472 AML 791679 **1922** 5.50 3.95 (314). Turf level. AS 65/3

L-shaped lift keys

562 Three teeth and a square-sectioned stem with looped terminal. Length 140mm. SF 2064 AML 810433 **2319** 6.00 4.00 (741). Ploughpan

563 Three teeth on a wide bit. Length 160mm. SF 3265 AML 811296 **3716** 5.25 4.50 (2066). Hoard in Building 40, Fig 40. AP 277

564 Two teeth on a long bit and with a rolled loop handle. Length 130mm. SF 4000 AML 814919 **3821** 9.50 4.50 (2844). Posthole associated with Structure 43, Phase 1, Fig 90. AP 342

565 Three teeth and rolled loop handle. Length 96mm. SF 3304 AML 811320 **3816** 1.20 4.20 (2017). Associated with Building 47, Fig 41. AS 301/4

566 Three teeth. The stem is circular in cross section and appears to be complete, without the usual loop. Length 76mm. SF 3119 AML 811237 **3716** 9.50 6.50 (1910). Posthole, Building 40, Fig 40. AS 300/2

567–68 L-shaped lift keys. Not illustrated. For drawings see AS No 449.

Slide-keys

569 Six rectangular teeth on a straight bit. The handle is flat and broad with a large eye. Length 81mm. SF 2722 AML 810565 **2918** 8.00 5.00 (741). Ploughpan, area of Barn 55, Fig 69

570 Z-shaped bit with five rectangular teeth; heavy handle with circular eye. Length 130mm. SF 1706 AML 810253 **2521** 9.00 1.00 (812). Cobbles south of Building 30. AS 133/1

571 Straight bit, with five circular teeth in two rows. Handle fractured below the eye. Length 55mm. SF 1429 AML 810067 **2421** 5.00 5.00 (741). Ploughpan

572 Straight bit with three rectangular teeth. The handle is unusually long for this type. Length 162mm. SF 1328 AML 810030 **2721** 1.30 1.80 (701). Ploughpan

Barb-spring padlock keys (Nos 573–575)

573 Bit incomplete. Length 174mm. SF 440 AML 791674 **1922** 9.00 0.50 (110). Fourth-century destruction material over Building 51, Fig 102. AS 65/2

574 There is a rectangular hole in the bit. Length 156mm. AML 791313. 1959 excavations

575 Trace of a rectangular hole on the incomplete bit. Length 147mm. SF 52 AML 791347 **1921** 9.00 9.00 (110). Fourth-century destruction material over Building 51, Fig 102. AP 26, AS 40/2

576–590 Padlock keys and handle fragments. Not illustrated. For drawings see AS No 449

591 Lever lock key. The bit has deep slits in the top and bottom and two notches in the outer edge. The handle is heavy with a circular eye. Length 62mm. SF 1192 AML 802880 **2217** 8.50 7.80 (615). Humus sealed by second-century levels. AS 103/3

592 Lever lock key with hollow shank, one slit on the underside of the bit and four on the outside edge. Ring handle. Length 49mm. SF 3136 AML 811241 **3816** 0.10 6.00 (1910). Posthole, Building 40, Fig 40. AS 300/2

593 Lever lock key of same type as 592. Length 48mm. SF 1558 AML 810132 **2521** 8.60 1.80 (702). Rubble west of Building 30. Fourth century. AS 132/1

594 Bolt from a barb-spring padlock, Type 1 (Manning 1985, 91, fig 25, 10), with two spines and four springs. The square-sectioned haft terminates in an upturned ring. Length 173mm. SF 3521 AML 814751 **3820** 8.00 5.20 (2301). Fourth-century level over Structure 43, Phase 2, Fig 92. AP 336

595 Spring, possibly from a simple lock. Length 81mm. SF 2799 AML 810576 **2819** 2.30 9.60 (1569). South terminal of Ditch 1281. Second century. AS 251/1

596 Fragmentary spring, possibly from a padlock. Length 68mm. SF 958 AML 802840 **2117** 4.00 8.00 (562). Building 50, Fig 99. AS 101/2

597–599 Lock springs. Not illustrated. For drawings see AS No 449

Latch lifters

600 Flat handle and curved stem, broken at the upturned tip. Length 246mm. SF 2830 AML 810580 **2917** 9.00 9.50 (1642). Latrine 46

601 Short flattened handle, fractured blade. Length 135mm. SF 4201 AML 823936 **2816** 4.35 9.00 (1283). Ditch 1281. AS 205/3

602 Fractured flat handle, the blade terminating in a rolled loop. Length 152mm. SF 3877 AML 814880 **4017** 10.00 9.65 (2372). Upper fill Ditch 1720, Outer enclosure. AS 363/4

603–604 Latch lifters. Not illustrated. For drawings see AS No 450

Fig 136

Styli

These were often made of iron and there are 17 examples from Gorhambury, contrasting with two from Gadebridge and the exceptional number of 74 from Hambleden, Bucks (Cocks 1921, 198).

The classification is Manning's (1985, 85, fig 24), summarised here, the variation between types lying

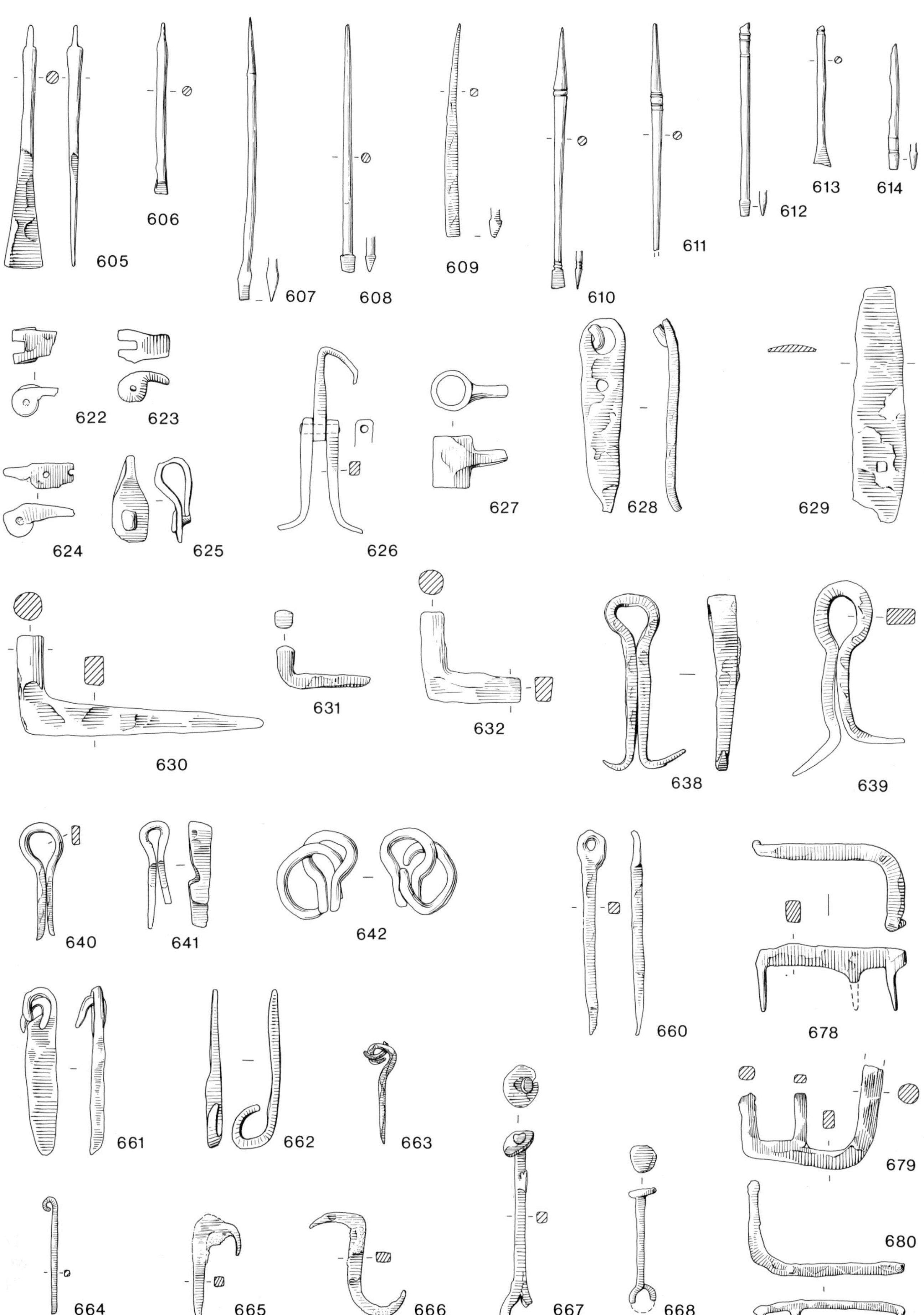

Fig 136 Objects of iron (Scale 1:3)

chiefly in the method of separating the point from the stem and in the shape of the eraser. In Type 1 the slender stem tapers to a point at one end and is flattened to form an eraser at the other. Type 2 has a distinct point with a shoulder between it and the stem and a similar simple eraser. In Type 3 the point and eraser are clearly separated from the stem which can be shaped and Type 4 has moulded or inlaid decoration. At Gorhambury Types 1, 3 and 4 are represented, generally from widely scattered areas, although there are three examples from Ditch 74 in levels associated with occupation of Building 37.

605 Type 2A. The eraser is wide and blade-like and the point is separated from the stem by a marked shoulder. Comparable examples come from London (Manning 1985, 86, N19, N20, pl 35). They are apparently rare outside London, although one was found at Baldock (Manning and Scott 1986, 153, fig 66, 520). It may be a first to early second century type. Length 139mm. SF 2876 AML 810596 **2821** 4.50 8.50 (1622). Posthole associated with Building 31, Fig 67. AP 223

606 Type 2. Slight shoulder between stem and point. Eraser broken. Length 98mm. SF 3279 AML 811305 **3716** 8.50 5.50 (2020). Third-century level, Building 47, Fig 41. AP 277, AS 301/3

607 Type 1. The stem tapers into the point, which is raking without a shoulder. Length 159mm. SF 2391 AML 810501 **2718** 5.00 9.00 (1149). Cesspit 1082, early second-century level. AS 162/3

608 Type 1. Plain stem tapering to a point, and flattened eraser with a slight shoulder. Length 145mm. SF 411- AML 823884 **3023** 5.00 8.00 (3107). Ditch 1481, north of outer enclosure. Second century. AS 99/3

609 Type 1. Tapering stem with simple flattened eraser. Length 122mm. SF 901 AML 802829 **2018** 3.10 2.75 (550). Well. Early fourth-century level. AS 99/3

610 Type 4, with two concentric mouldings at the junction of the stem and point and also above the eraser. Length 146mm. SF 482 AML 810323 **2022** 9.00 6.55 (275). Second-century fill of Ditch 74, associated with occupation of Building 37, Fig 48. AS 66/1

611 Type 4. As 610 with concentric mouldings on stem, eraser missing. Length 90mm. SF 580 AML 810325 **2022** 9.90 5.50 (369). Ditch 74, second-century level, associated with occupation of Building 37, Fig 48. AS 68/3

612 Type 4, with concentric mouldings on stem. Point missing. Length 109mm. SF 591 AML 810328 **2022** 5.00 9.00 (369). Provenance as 611. AS 68/3

613 Type 4, with moulding on stem. Point and eraser fractured. Length 82mm. SF 3816 AML 814056 **3820** 4.50 9.00 (2344). Clay levelling below Structure 43, Phase 2, Fig 92. AP 337

614 Eraser with moulding above, as Type 4. Length 73mm. SF 583 AML 810327 **2122** 7.00 7.00 (389). Second-century level

615–621 Styli. Not illustrated. For drawings see AS No 450

Structural fittings

The site produced a wide range of structural fittings. Three types of hinges are represented, with several strap hinges, including one example (No 626) of a type rarely found in Britain, one fragment of loop hinge (No 628), and L-shaped hinge staples (Nos 630–637), which were used with drop hinges. The longer tapering arm, square or rectangular in section, was driven into the door jamb while the short arm of circular section carried the U-shaped hinge. Distribution of the hinges is very random but some can be ascribed to particular building levels. There are 22 well preserved split or double-spiked loops of various sizes, also ring- or loop-headed pins which had the same function. The many clamps and joiner's dogs, used for clamping pieces of wood, include some three pronged examples (Nos 678–680), but only one T-staple (No 711) used for securing box flue tiles. There were nails from all areas (as Nos 724–741) and rings which could have had many functions, for example as attachments to split spiked loops, linking sections of chain or in horse tack. Four of the fifteen complete examples come from Building 40. Much of the structural ironwork was from the buildings themselves and is widely distributed but with concentrations in the aisled building (39/40) and its successor Building 47, also in Structure 43 and Building 53, inevitably chiefly in late levels.

Hinges

622 Strap hinge. One arm only, fractured, with two plates pierced for a central pivot. Length 26mm. The type is common, with complete examples from London (Manning 1985, 127, R14, pl 59), Fishbourne (Cunliffe 1971, II, 128, fig 56, 12–16) and Verulamium (Manning 1984a, 98, fig 42, 102–105). SF 695 AML 791714 **2222** 5.00 5.00 (29). Old land surface

623 Strap hinge. Fragment as 622, with two plates and fractured arm. Length 29mm. SF 550 AML 791691 **2122** 7.00 8.00 (337). Rubble, area of Building 37, Fig 48. Second century. AP 55

624 Strap hinge. One tapering arm with single nailhole and one plate, pierced for pivot. Length 41mm. SF 498 AML 791683 **2122** 0.20 5.00 (319). Fourth century. AP 55

625 Fragment of small drop hinge. Length 46mm. SF 2245 AML 810486 **2419** 5.80 0.50 (920). Building 28, Fig 52, robber trench. AP 141

626 Strap hinge with three tapering spikes arranged one and two on each side of a central pivot. It is a rare type in Britain, although more common in Germany. It is found at Baldock (Manning and Scott 1986, 157, no 563, fig 68) with four spikes, and Great Chesterford (Manning, 1985, 127, R17, pl 59) with six spikes. The spikes were driven into the wooden door and jamb. Length 110mm. SF 2177 AML 810460 **2419** 5.80 0.50 (920). Provenance as 625

627 Cylindrical ferrule with projecting spur of circular section, possibly part of a hinge, similar to those found in bone. Length 42mm. SF 1542 AML 810125 **2521** 4.60 6.00 (703). West of Building 30. Fourth-century level. AS 132/1. For another possible example see No 409

628 Strap from loop hinge, with fragment of the looped terminal of the second strap through the eye. Length 108mm. SF 891 AML 802827 **2018** 5.00 4.00 ((63). Ditch 74. First-century level. AS 301/4

629 Strap from hinge with one nail hole. Length 134mm. SF 3342 AML 811388 6.00 2.10 (2017). Building 47, Fig 41. AS 301/4

630 L-shaped hinge staple. Complete. Length 147mm. SF 3248 AML 811286 **3817** 5.00 4.80 (2001). Yard to north of Building 40, Fig 40. AP 285

631 Small hinge staple. Length 55mm. SF 217 AML 791356 **2021** 4.00 5.00 (162). Timber-lined drain cutting Building 37. AP 29, AS 41/5

632 L-shaped hinge staple; the rectangular arm is incomplete. Length 55mm. SF 3115 AML 811234 **3716** 3.50 6.50 (1881). Third-century occupation level, Building 47, Fig 41. AP 276

633–637 L-shaped hinge staples. Not illustrated. For drawings see AS No 450

Split spiked loops

638 Complete, with bent arms where they have been hammered back. Length 100mm. SF 218 AML 791357 **2221** 3.00 5.50 (179). Building 37, Period 9. AP 39

639 Complete. Heavy example. Length 115mm. SF 3340 AML 811337 **3717** 3.80 2.40 (2065). Occupation layer, Building 39/40, Period 9, Fig 40. AP 277, AS 302/8

640 Complete. Length 67mm. SF 899 AML 802828 **2018** 3.30 2.90 (550). Well. AP 79, AS 99/3

641 Considerable wear on one side. Length 60mm. SF 407 AML 791667 **2022** 2.50 9.00. Topsoil

642 Ring through head. Length 54mm. SF 31180 AML 811259 **3716** 7.40 4.40 (2020). Third-century level, Building 47, Fig 41. AP 277, AS 301/3

643–659 Split spiked loops. Not illustrated. For drawings see AS No 450

Ring-headed pins, loop-headed spikes and wall hooks

660 Length 115mm. SF 949 AML 802838 **2318** 5.00 2.00 (591). Overlying Ditch 104. AP 95, AS 104/2

661 Length 95mm. SF 3387 AML 811355 **3717** 4.00 1.30 (2065). Occupation level Building 40, Period 9, Fig 40. AP 277, AS 302/8

662 Length 90mm. SF 47 AML 791346 **1921** 9.00 3.00 (110). Fourth-century destruction material over Building 51, Fig 102. AP 26, AS 40/2

663 Length 57mm. SF 3851 AML 814875 **3821** 4.00 2.00 (2346). Structure 43, Phase 2, clay levelling, Fig 92. AP 337

664 Length 66mm. SF 1752 AML 810257 **2621** 2.00 0.50 (787). East of Building 53, Fig 64. AP 120, AS 133/1

665 Wall hook. Length 54mm. SF 4302 AML 823965 **2319** 8.00 7.20 (3312). Drain along east wall Building 27, Fig 48. AP 377

666 S-shaped wall hook. Length 67mm. SF 503 AML 791684 **2222** 0.50 2.50 (339). Drain north of Building 37, Period 9, Fig 48. AP 61

667 Loop-headed spike with washer. The shaft may have been driven through wood and secured with the washer in order to give sufficient strength for suspension. Length 111mm. SF 3260 AML 811292 **3716** 1.00 9.00 (2018). Over Building 39/40, Period 9, Fig 40. AS 302/8

668 Loop-headed spike with washer, as 667. Length 70mm. SF 3994 AML 814916 **3821** 9.50 4.50 (2844). Posthole in Structure 43, Phase 1, Fig 90. AP 342

669–677 Loop-headed spikes and hooks. Not illustrated. For drawings see AS No 451

Clamps and joiner's dogs

678 L-shaped clamp with three arms, a variety of joiner's dog. Length 88mm. SF 16 AML 791325. 1956–61 excavations

679 L-shaped clamp with three arms. Length 85mm. SF 2961 AML 810606 **2822** 2.50 1.00 (1669). Ditch 1281. Second century. AS 253/1

680 L-shaped clamp with three arms. Length 133mm. SF 804 AML 802817 **2018** 1.00 1.50 (520). Upper fill of well. AS 99/2

Fig 137

Joiner's dogs

681 Length 90mm. SF 4001 AML 814920 **4013** (1723). Over Ditch 1720, AS 254/1

682 Length 78mm. SF 25 AML 791345 **2121**. Topsoil

683 Length 72mm. SF 2155 AML 810457 **2720** (741). Ploughpan

684 Length 82mm. SF 3908 AML 814896 **3821** 9.00 1.50 (2344). Stucture 43, Phase 2, Fig 80. AP 337

685–700 Joiner's dogs. Not illustrated. For drawings see AS No 451

Cleats

701 Length 45mm. There is a comparable example from the Gadebridge Park villa (Manning 1974, 179, no 568, fig 75). SF 3724 AML 814813 **3821** 4.10 0.50 (2302). Structure 43. Phase 2, Fig 92. AP 340

702 Length 53mm. SF 3246 AML 811284 **3716** 3.00 9.00 (2002). Building 47, Period 10, Fig 41. AS 300/9

703 A large example with wide oval plate and short arms. Length 87mm. SF 1069 AML 802865 **2018** 1.00 1.75 (544). Well. AS 99/3

704–707 Cleats. Not illustrated. For drawings see AS No 451

Staples and clamps

708 Staple. Length 70mm. SF 3819 AML 814859 **3820** 7.00 9.00 (2346). Levelling clay below Structure 43, Phase 2, Fig 92. AP 337

709 Large staple or joiner's dog. Length 67mm. SF 3190 AML 811265 **3917** 6.00 3.00 (2015). Humus over Ditch 1851, north of Building 40. AP 291

710 Clamp. Length 92mm. SF 1878 AML 810298 **2721** 3.80 5.10 (769). Chalk spread east of Building 30, Fig 64. AS 134/5

711 T-staple, used for securing box flue tiles. Length 95mm. SF 3646 AML 814781 **3821** 5.00 3.00 (2301). Silt over Structure 43, Phase 2, Fig 92. AP 340

712–723 Clamps and staples. Not illustrated. For drawings see AS No 451

Nails

The site produced a large quantity of nails, of which only a few representative types are listed here. The classification used is that given by Manning (1985, 184). Type 1 was by far the commonest comprising 95% of the total; the remainder were of Type 2, with a few less common examples.

724 Type 1 with flat round head and square-sectioned shank. Length 136mm. SF 3543 AML 814758 **3820** 8.50 8.00 (2302). Structure 43, Phase 2, Fig 92. AG 340

725 Type 1. Length 132mm. SF 113 AML 791341 **2019** 8.00 5.50 (77). Ditch 74. First-century fill, associated with Building 21, Period 7, Fig 48. AS 23/1

726 Type 1, complete. Length 126mm. SF 3775 AML 814844 **3818** 4.20 0.50 (2457). Loam. AP 333

727 Type 1, complete. Length 96mm. SF 3166 AML 811249 **3718** (1919). Furnace of Bath-house, Building 41, Fig 85. AS 303/1

728 Type 1. Length 60mm. SF 238 AML 791359 **2021** 5.00 1.00 (120). Pit cutting mosaic pavement, Building 37, Fig 48. AP 29

729 Type 2, with triangular head of the same width as the rectangular-sectioned shank. Length 74mm. This type is less common than Type 1, but is found on many sites including the Gadebridge Park villa (Manning 1974, 173, fig 74, 500). SF 3117 AML 811236 **3716** 6.50 5.50 (1906). Posthole, Building 39/40, Fig 40. AP 277, AS 300/1

730 Type 2, almost complete. Length 101mm. SF 190 AML 791354 **2021** (163). AP 50, AS 41/5

731 Nail with flat round head. Length 53mm. SF 100 AML 791348 **2021** 8.50 5.00 (130)

732 Nail with rectangular-sectioned shank flattened to form a round head. Length 53mm. SF 336 AML 791499 **2121** 0.50 4.00 (77). Ditch 74. First-century level associated with Building 21, Period 7, Fig 48. AS 23/1

733 Horseshoe nail. Length 28mm. SF 802 AML 802815 **2016** 1.50 2.00 (4). Ploughpan

734 Nail with domed head and rectangular shank. Length 136mm. SF 2890 AML 810600 **2918** 9.00 0.50 (1448). Latrine, Structure 46, Fig 2

735 Nail with flat square head and rectangular shank. The shape is similar to Manning's Type 3, although the head is less stout. Length 76mm. SF 1923 AML 810309 **2723** (701). Ploughpan

736 Type 7, with wide flat circular head and short tapering square-sectioned shank. Length 60mm. SF 1654 AML 810210 **2721** 2.00 0.50 (786). Rubble east of Building 30, Fig 64. AS 134/6

737 Type 7, with wide flat head and short stem. Length 46mm. SF 3257 AML 811289 **3817** 8.50 4.50 (2001). Yard north of Building 40, Fig 40. AP 285

738 Horseshoe nail. Length 24mm. SF 849 AML 802823 **2018** 2.50 2.50 (4). Ploughpan

739 Hobnail. Type 10. Length 14mm. SF 1511 AML 810109 **2521** 8.00 2.00 (702). Rubble west of Building 30, Fig 64. AS 132/1

740 Tack with domed head. Length 13mm. SF 739 AML 802803 **2218** (488). Ploughpan

741 Type 8. Head of a dome-headed nail. Diameter 78mm. AML 791322. Destruction material from 1956 excavations

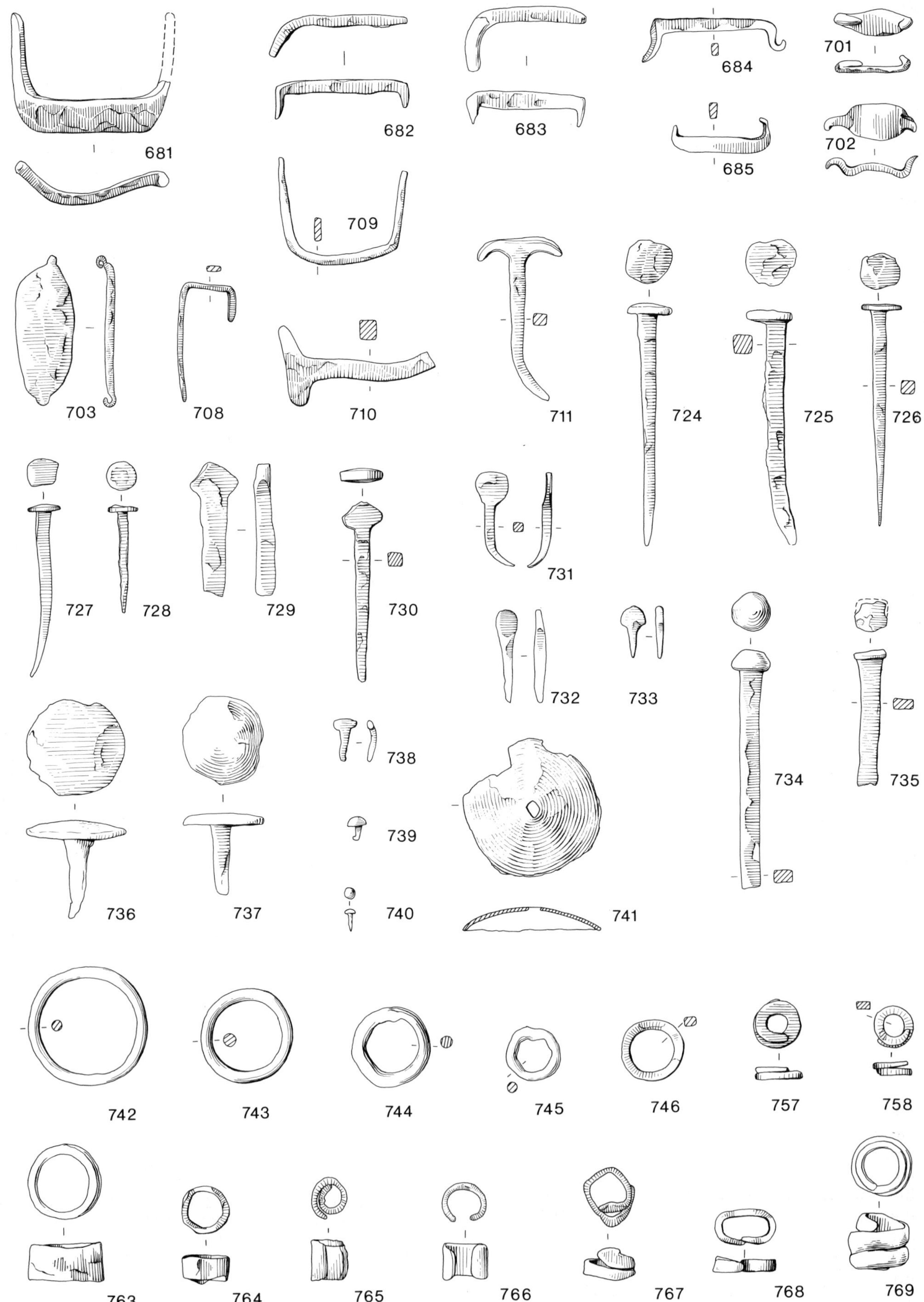

Fig 137 Objects of iron (Scale 1:3)

Rings

742 Diameter 70mm. SF 1875 AML 810279 **2621** 7.00 4.20 (848). Eavesdrip south of Building 30, Fig 64. AS 133/1
743 Diameter 55mm. SF 1777 AML 810265 **2621** 9.00 6.20 (796). Gully east of Building 53, Fig 64. AS 134/5
744 Wear on one side. Diameter 49mm. SF 3325 AML 811328 **3717** 3.00 2.50 (2065). Occupation material, Building 40, Period 9, Fig 40. AP 277, AS 302/8
745 Diameter 32mm. SF 1211 AML 802882 **2117** 4.00 9.00 (659). Cesspit 622, Fig 99. AP 80, AS 100/3
746 Ring with rectangular cross-section. Diameter 37mm. SF 3152 AML 811246 **3817** 6.30 5.50 (2001). Yard north of Building 40, Fig 40. AP 285
747–56 Rings. Not illustrated. For drawings see AS No 452

Split rings

757 Split ring. The overlapping terminals are complete and the object appears to have the function of a split ring rather than a spiral ferrule. Diameter 28mm. SF 38 AML 791337 **2119** 2.00 6.00 (20). Clay floor make-up from Building 27, Period 8, Fig 48. AS 23/6
758 Split ring. Diameter 23mm. SF 335 AML 791368 **2121** 0.50 3.50 (77). Ditch 74, first-century level, associated with Building 21, Period 7, Fig 48. AS 42/3
759–762 Split rings. Not illustrated. For drawings see AS No 452

Ferrules

763 Diameter 40mm. SF 3245 AML 811283 **3717** 7.00 3.00 (2061). Building 40, slot, Fig 40. AS 301/5
764 Diameter 36mm. SF 3225 AML 811277 **3917** 6.00 5.00 (2001). Yard north of Building 40, Period 9, Fig 40
765 Made from a wound strip. Diameter 23mm. SF 831 AML 802821 **2317** 8.15 4.20 (556). Gully fill. AP 93, AS 104/1
766 The ends are not joined. Diameter 26mm. SF 3086 AML 811231 **3717** 4.00 0.05 (1888). Building 47, Period 10, Fig 41. AS 301/1
767 Spiral type, both ends fractured. Diameter 30mm. SF 1323 AML 810027 **2721** 7.50 4.20 (701). Ploughpan
768 Length 35mm. SF 2072 AML 810434 **2419** 9.00 1.50 (741). Ploughpan
769 Spiral type. Diameter 30mm. SF 2130 AML 810451 **2419** 2.90 2.00 (920). Building 28, Fig 52. Robber trench. AP 141
770–788 Bindings. Not illustrated. For drawing see AS No 452

Straps, bindings and miscellaneous fragments

The site produced large numbers of fragmentary straps, bindings and miscellaneous fragments. A selection is illustrated, with many fragments from Buildings 53 and Structure 43. This distribution pattern is repeated for the unillustrated material where much comes from layer 721 to the south of Building 53. Most is scrap iron and it is thought that the area was used for smithing. The other major concentration is in Structure 43.

The miscellaneous material includes chiefly bars of uncertain purpose but there are also possible tools and implements as No 899, which may be a rake prong. The unillustrated fragments are bars and rods, with random distribution.

Fig 138

Riveted straps

789 Two nailholes, one nail remaining. Length 120mm. SF 2848 AML 810588 **2918** 9.50 0.50 (1641). From latrine 46, Fig 2
790 Strap with dome-headed nail. Length 50mm. SF 649 AML 791707 **2123** 0.50 0.75 (410). Ditch 74. AS 67/2
791 Strap with nail *in situ*. Length 50mm. SF 3526 AML 814753 **3821** 7.15 0.30 (2302). Building 43, Phase 2, Fig 92. AP 340
792 Three circular nailholes, possibly from a hinge. Length 130mm. SF 3768 AML 814837 **3821** 5.40 1.80 (2302). AS 791. AP 340
793 Two nailholes. Length 79mm. SF 2744 AML 810569 **2922** 2.00 5.70 (1451). Building 31, Fig 67. AP 234
794 Strap with nailhole at point of fracture. It expands at one end, possibly for a hinge. Length 105mm. SF 3228 AML 811278 **3716** 1.50 9.00 (2003). Building 47, Period 10, Fig 41, floor surface. AP 277, AS 301/1
795 Two circular rivet-holes. Length 94mm. SF 3199 AML 811270 **3816** 2.00 4.50 (2017). Building 47, Fig 41. AS 301/4
796 Curved strap with rivet-hole. Length 52mm. SF 3381 AML 811352 **3716** (2002). Building 47, Fig 41. AS 300/9
797 Rounded terminal and two nailholes. Length 85mm. SF 1427 AML 810065 **2520** 9.00 9.50 (721). Fourth-century level, Building 53, Fig 64. AP 108, AS 133/1
798 Right-angled strap with nailhole at point of fracture. Length 74mm. SF 3677 AML 814792 **3816** 5.00 1.00 (2462)
799 Length 80mm. SF 1488 AML 810103 **2520** 8.20 9.90 (721). Fourth-century level, Building 53, Fig 64, layer containing much scrap iron. AP 108, AS 133/1
800 Length 70mm. SF 2457 AML 810513 **2617** 5.00 3.00 (996). Humus sealing bath house Building 29, Fig 62. AS 160/1
801 Length 64mm. SF 1486 AML 810101 **2520** 9.50 9.95 (721). AS 799
802 Folded strap, scrap metal. Length 30mm. SF 1416 AML 810056 **2520** 9.60 9.99 (721). AS 799
803 Fragment of scrap iron. Length 38mm. SF 1426 AML 810064 **2520** 9.65 9.95 (721). As 799
804 Folded strap, scrap. Length 33mm. SF 1417 AML 810057 **2620** 8.00 9.80 (721). As 799
805 Thin triangular plate with curved edge. Purpose uncertain. Length 121mm. SF 2059 AML 810431 **2419** 3.00 1.50 (741). Ploughpan
806 Plate or strap, waisted at the centre, but fractured at both ends. Length 60mm. SF 2864 AML 810590 **2918** 9.20 0.20 (1641). Fill of Latrine 46, Fig 2
807 Fragment of ?bladed tool. A triangular plate, fractured, with projecting ?tang. Length 65mm. SF 403 AML 821587 **2220** 4.00 3.00 (29). Old land surface. AS 43/3
808 Square-sectioned shank terminating in an L-shaped triangular head. Length 90mm. SF 3773 AML 814842 **3821** 4.00 3.50 (2302). Structure 43, Phase 2, Fig 92. AP 340
809 Strap with a nailhole at the point of fracture. The other end is curved to form a socket or ferrule. Length 90mm. SF 3932 AML 814901 **3820** 5.00 9.50 (2344). Levelling below Structure 43, Phase 2, Fig 92. AP 337
810 Strap curved along its width, possibly a fragment of handle. Length 62mm. SF 3893 AML 814808 **3820** 7.00 8.50 (2344). As 809
811–895 Straps. Not illustrated. For drawings see AS Nos 453, 454, 455

Miscellaneous rods and bars

896 Curved fragment with square section and a thickened terminal. Length 60mm. SF 319 AML 791367 **2221** 7.00 2.00 (233)
897 Square-sectioned curved bar, possibly a fragment of shackle. Length 105mm. SF 2831 AML 810581 **2822** 1.50 6.00 (1456). Clay over Ditch 1281. AP 225
898 Rod, circular in section, terminating in a point. Length 215mm. SF 2960 AML 810605 **2922** 7.20 3.50 (1678). Clay over Building 13, Fig 37 AS 252/3
899 Rod with pointed terminal and a distorted tang, possibly a rake prong. Length 140mm. SF 2808 AML 810577 **2818** (741). Ploughpan

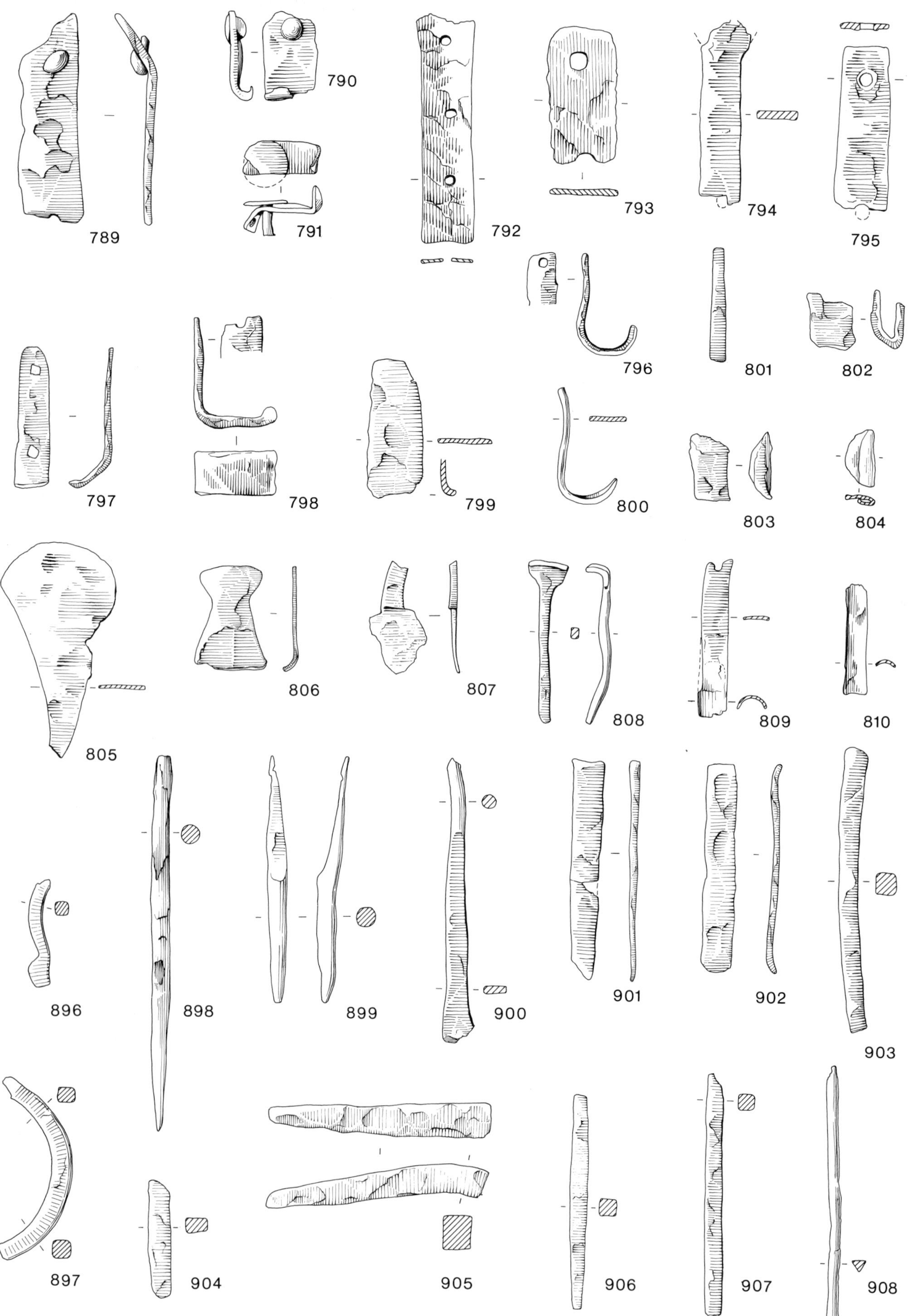

Fig 138 Objects of iron (Scale 1:3)

900 Flat strap or blade tapering into a round-sectioned tang. It is fractured at both ends but may be a chisel. Length 162mm. SF 3146 AML 811245 **3816** 1.00 6.50 (1910). Posthole, Building 40, Fig 40. AP 283, AS 300/2

901 Bar with rectangular section. Length 54mm. SF 3947 AML 814909 **3822** 6.50 4.50 (2670). Slot, Building 42, Fig 90. AP 343

902 Strap. Length 117mm. SF 1536 AML 810122 **2421** 2.00 0.80 (741). AS 141/1

903 Heavy square-sectioned bar. Length 160mm. SF 4002 AML 814921 **4013** (1724). Cobbles over Ditch 1720. AP 343

904 Bar. Length 67mm. SF 1522 AML 810116 **2620** 5.20 9.35 (721). Fourth-century level, Building 53, Fig 64. AS 133/1

905 Heavy tapering square-sectioned bar, possibly fragment of hinge staple. Length 135mm. SF 1329 AML 810031 **2721** 4.20 6.40 (701). Ploughpan

906 Bar, square in section, tapering at one end. Possibly a punch. Length 120mm. SF 1669 AML 810118 **2621** 9.00 8.50 (787). Fourth-century level, Building 53, Fig 64. AP 120, AS 133/1

907 Bar, square-sectioned, one end tapering but fractured. Length 135mm. SF 118 AML 791425 **2019** 5.00 4.50 (77). Ditch 74, first century. AS 23/1

908 Bar with triangular section. Length 145mm. SF 581 AML 810326 **2022** 9.80 9.00 (369). Ditch 74, north of villa, second-century level. AS 68/3

909–918 Miscellaneous fragments. Not illustrated. For drawings see AS No 455

Objects of lead

Twenty-six fragments or objects of lead were found. Apart from the items described below these included one fragmentary weight from Structure 43, Fig 92, and two plugs, unstratified, used to repair pottery. The remaining pieces were fragmentary, without recognisable form or function, and their contexts ranged from first-century to post-medieval levels.

Fig 139

Weights (Nos 919–921)

For weights of copper alloy see Nos 220–228, Fig 126.

919 No suspension loop, presumably used with a pan balance. Diameter 35mm. Weight 164.5 gm. 1959 excavations, from cellar ramp

920 With traces of an iron suspension loop. Diameter 40mm. Weight 218.30 gm. SF 3266 **3716** 5.25 4.50 (2066). With No 921, below, this came from the hoard of metalwork within Building 40, Period 9, AD 175–250, Fig 40. The hoard also included an iron steelyard, No 556, Fig 134. AP 271

921 With iron suspension loop. Length 45mm. Diameter 23mm. Weight 49.95 gm. SF 3268 **3716** 5.25 4.50 (2066). From hoard, as No 920

922 Lead plug used to repair the base of a ceramic vessel, a fragment of which survives. Length 82mm. SF 1035 **2218** 9.00 0.50 (506). Second century. AP 89, AS 103/1

923 Waste fragment, folded strip. Length 88mm. SF 557 **2022** 9.90 3.00 (275). Second-century fill of Ditch 74, associated with occupation of Building 37, Fig 48. AS 66/1

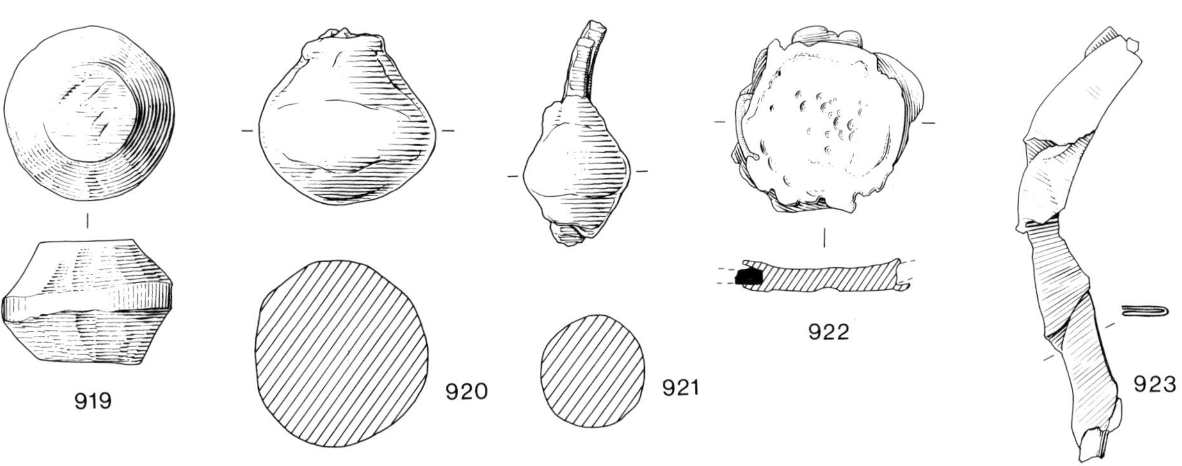

Fig 139 Objects of lead (Scale 2:3)

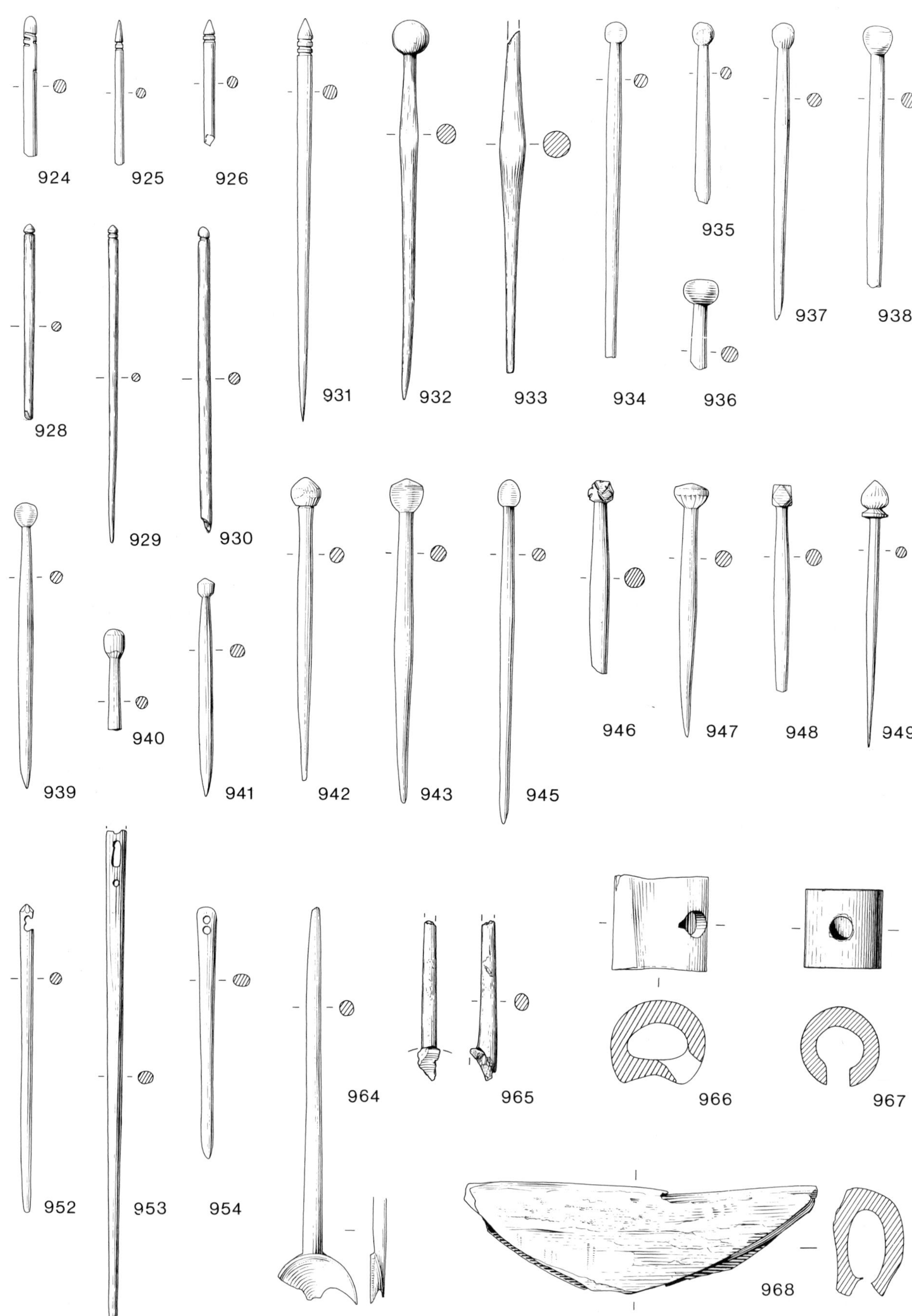

Fig 140 Objects of bone (Scale 2:3)

Objects of bone

The bone includes such items of personal adornment and domestic use as hairpins, needles and spoons, objects which are also found in copper alloy. Miscellaneous fittings and tools comprise bone hinges (Nos 966–967), a handle grip (No 968), several awls (Fig 141) and a bobbin (No 971), while dice and gaming pieces shed light on leisure activities. The typology used for pins is that proposed by Nina Crummy (1979, 157–63); the dates of the Gorhambury contexts agree with the date ranges of the pins from Colchester (Crummy 1983, 19–25). It is notable that there was a concentration of bone pins and needles in levels associated with the second-century villa, Building 37, and in the terminals of Ditch 1281 at the entrance to the inner enclosure, which was filled during the second century.

Fig 140

Pins

924 Grooved decoration below a conical head. Incomplete. Type 2, date range AD 50–200. Length 37mm. SF 545 **2022** 8.00 6.80 (275). Ditch 74. Level associated with the occupation of Building 37, Fig 48. AP 50, AS 66/1

925 Grooved decoration below a conical head. Incomplete. Type 2. Length 38mm. SF 702 **2022** 8.00 6.80 (275). As 924

926 Two grooves below a conical head. Incomplete. Type 2. Length 33mm. SF 586 **2022** 9.00 9.50 (369). Ditch 74, associated with Building 37, Fig 48. AP 51, AS 68/3

927 Not illustrated. As 926. Incomplete. Length 54.5mm. SF 578 **2122** 0.10 9.00 (369). As 926

928 One groove below a conical head. Incomplete. Type 2. Length 51mm. SF 2898 **2822** 2.00 0.50 (1668). Ditch 1281. AS 253/1

929 Two grooves below conical head. Length 84mm. SF 2877 **2822** 2.30 3.75 (1657). Ditch 1281. AS 253/1

930 One groove below a conical head. Type 2. Length 80mm. SF 2158 **2419** 3.00 1.50 (920). Building 28, Fig 52, robber trench. AP 141. A second fragment also came from this layer

931 Three grooves below a conical head. Type 2. Length 106mm. SF 559 **2022** 9.00 8.00 (369). Ditch 74, as 926. AP 51, AS 68/3

932 Spherical head, Type 3. According to Crummy (1983, 22) this type was made from *c* AD 200 until the end of the Roman period. Length 100 mm. SF 3058 **3716** 4.00 7.00 (1881). Occupation material, Building 47, Fig 41. AP 276

933 Pin with a swelling shaft, characteristic of Type 3. Head missing. Length 58mm. SF 3167 **3719** 4.00 8.00 (1920). Gully north of Building 41, Fig 85. AS 303/7

934 Spherical head, Type 3. Incomplete. Length 88mm. SF 1783 **2621** 9.00 4.00 (796). Gully east of Building 53, Fig 64. AS 134/5

935 Spherical head, Type 3. Length 47mm. SF 1600 **2621** 9.50 9.50 (786). East of Building 30, Fig 64. AS 134/6

936 Flattened spherical head. Incomplete. Length 24mm. SF 50 **2021** (110). Destruction material over Building 51, Fig 102. AP 26, AS 41/3

937 Spherical head, Type 3. Length 78mm. SF 920 **2018** 1.75 1.05 (584). Well. AS 99/3

938 Flattened spherical head. Incomplete. Length 69mm. SF 115 **2021** 1.20 2.80 (110). Destruction material over Building 51, Fig 102. AP 26, AS 41/3

939 Spherical head, Type 3. The point has been re-worked. Length 75mm. SF 867 **2218** 5.50 4.00 (509)

940 Elongated spherical head with flattened sides. Length 26mm. SF 162 **1920** 1.00 5.80 (151). Gully. AP 25

941 Spherical head with flattened sides and pointed top, a variant of Type 3. Length 57mm. SF 48 **2021** 1.00 3.00 (110). Destruction material over Building 51, Fig 102. AP 26, AS 41/3

942 Spherical head with conical top. Type 3, head B. Length 80mm. SF 1085 **2018** 1.00 0.45 (595). Well. AS 99/4

943 Spherical head with conical top. Type 3, head B. Length 85mm. SF 727 **2018** (2). Backfill of earlier excavation trenches

944 Not illustrated. As 940. Incomplete. Length 88mm. SF 1318 **2721** (701). Ploughpan

945 Oval head, variant of Type 3. Length 90mm. SF 926 **2218** 3.20 1.20 (506). Destruction level, second century. AP 89, AS 103/1

946 Spherical head with incised decoration. Length 50mm. SF 4, 1956 excavations

947 Lenticular head, the underside with grooved ribbed decoration. Type 3, variant of head C. Length 66mm. SF 892 **2018** 3.90 2.95 (550). Well. AS 99/3

948 Faceted square head, Type 4. Length 54mm. SF 14 **1919** (4)

949 With reel below a conical head. Length 70mm. SF 464 **2022** 7.00 0.90 (26). Gully cutting corridor, Building 37, Fig 48. AS 41/5

950–51 Pins. Not illustrated. For drawings see AS No 456

Needles (Nos 952–963)

Needles were also found in copper alloy, Nos 155–167, Fig 124.

952 Eye formed by drilling two circular holes. Length 81mm. SF 1117 **2218** 3.90 2.00 (615). Humus sealed by second-century levels. AP 90, AS 103/1

953 Unusual type with central elongated eye with small circular eyes on either side. Length 130mm. SF 173 **2120** 3.00 8.00 (20). Floor make-up for Building 27, Period 8. First or early second century. Fig 48. AS 23/6

954 With two circular eyes. The tip is broken but appears to have been reworked. Length 66mm. SF 246 **2121** 3.00j 1.00 (109). Destruction material associated with Building 27. AS 43/5

955–963 Needles. Not illustrated. For drawings see AS No 456

964 Spoon with circular bowl, the handle continuing as a 'rat tail' on the underside (see also Nos 240–246 for examples in copper alloy). Length 104mm. SF 1214 **2217** 9.00 1.00 (660). Destruction material. AP 88

965 Spoon. Section of handle with fragment of bowl. Length 42mm. SF 4405 **2022** 9.90 6.00 (369). Upper fill of Ditch 74, associated with Building 37, Fig 48. AP 51, AS 68/3

966 Hinge. Section of bone hinge with one circular hole. Length 25mm. The function of these hinges, which are frequently found, is discussed with examples from Verulamium by Waugh and Goodburn (1972, 149). SF 1642 **2521** 7.00 6.00 (711). Levelling clay below Building 30, Fig 64. AP 118 AS 133/1. For possible iron hinges of this type see Nos 409 and 627

967 Hinge fragment with one circular hole. The piece is well finished. Length 21mm. SF 2970 **2723** 2.50 3.00 (917). Well, upper fill. AP 132

968 Handle. Worked bone, possibly used as a grip for a rope handle. Length 94mm. SF 280 **2121** 0.50 0.50 (77). Ditch 74, associated with Building 21, Fig 48, AD 62–100. AS 42/3

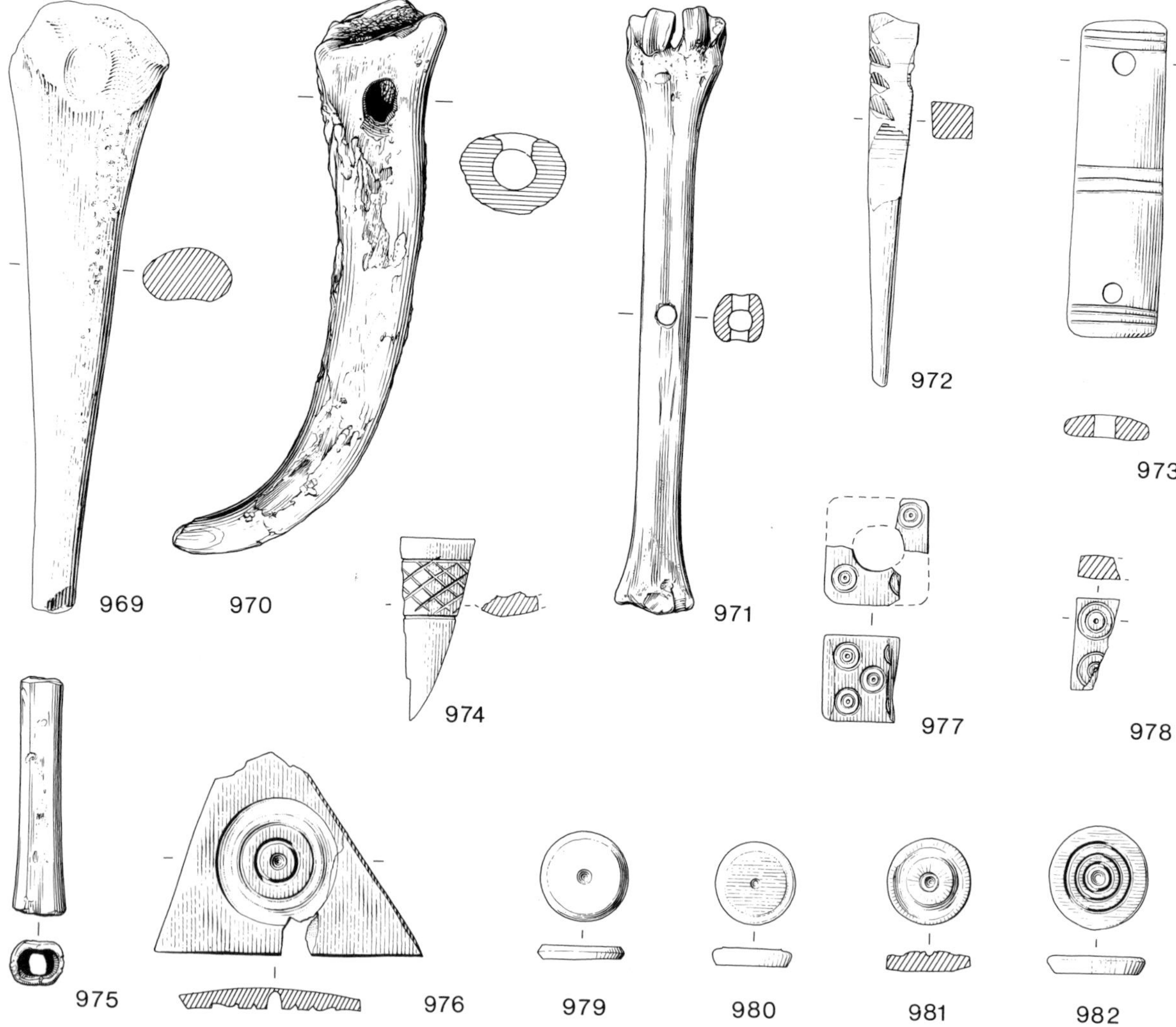

Fig 141 Objects of bone (Scale 2:3)

Fig 141

969 Awl with fractured point. Length 210mm. SF 15, 1956 excavations

970 Red deer antler, worked, with pierced circular hole at the wider end. Length 210mm. SF 4407 **2217** 3.40 9.50 (615). Humus sealing first-century levels. AP 90, AS 103/3

971 Bobbin. Long bone pierced transversely in the centre of the shaft. Such implements found elsewhere in Iron Age and Roman Britain have been interpreted as bobbins (Wild 1970a, 34), for example at South Shields (Allason-Jones and Miket, 1984, 56, 2.144) and Winterton (Stead 1976, fig 122, no 205). Length 122mm. SF 4404 **2821** 2.50 0.50 (1804). Ditch 1281. AS 253/3

972 Awl with broken tip and roughly worked shank. Length 75mm. SF 1567 **2621** 7.50 5.00 (787). Fourth-century level associated with Building 53, Fig 64. AP 120, AS 133/1

973 Archer's wrist guard with incised linear decoration. Length 63mm. SF 1207 **2117** 4.00 9.00 (648). Cesspit 622, late-first century. AS 100/1

974 Fragment of knife handle with incised lattice decoration. Length 37mm. SF 1652 **2621** 4.00 1.40 (787). As 972. AP 120, AS 133/1

975 Handle. Length 47mm. SF 4406 **2123** 0.50 1.00 (410). Ditch 74, second century. AS 67/2

976 Inlay. Triangular fragment with decoration of concentric circles. Length 56mm. 1956 excavations

Dice and gaming pieces

Gambling was a popular pastime and the dice have a modern appearance. The counters, which are lathe-turned, were used in board games as were glass counters (Nos 1007–1010) which are occasionally found in sets, as at Lullingstone (Cool and Price 1987, 139, fig 57) where the 30 pieces may have been used for a form of backgammon known as *ludus duodecim scriptorum* or *tabula*. Other games, such as *ludus latruncularum*, may have required a different number of counters. The Gorhambury counters of bone and glass are all stray finds and do not form a set.

977 Die. Fragments of die with a central hole. The values are marked by a double ring-and-dot motif. Length 17mm. SF 180 **1921** 9.90 9.00 (194). Humus. Second century. AS 41/5

978 Fragment of die or counter. Length 18mm. SF 1421 **2620** 1.00 9.05 (721), Building 53, Fig 64. AP 108, AS 133/1

979 Gaming piece with flat surfaces and central lathe indentation. Dameter 17mm. SF 544 **2022** 9.00 7.00 (275). Ditch 74, associated with occupation of Building 37, Fig 48. AP 50, AS 66/1

980 Gaming piece with flat surfaces and a central lathe indentation on one face. Diameter 17mm. SF 1044 **2117** 9.50 6.00 (563). Ditch 598, second century. AS 101/2

981 Gaming piece with concentric grooves on the obverse. Found with No 986. Diameter 17mm. SF 414 **2221**. Topsoil

982 Gaming piece with three concentric grooves on the obverse and bevelled edge. Diameter 17mm. SF 900 **2018** 6.00 5.00 (63). Ditch 74, first-century level. AS 99/2

983–986 Gaming pieces. Not illustrated. For drawings see AS No 456

Objects of glass

The objects of glass are chiefly personal ornaments. Although it has been suggested that glass pins may have been used as stoppers for unguent bottles rather than hair pins at South Shields (Allason-Jones and Miket 1984, 275), examples have been found in sufficient quantity close to skulls in cemetery sites such as Colchester (Crummy 1983, 28, nos 461–465) and Lankhills (Clarke 1979, fig 73) to indicate that they were in most instances hair pins. The Gorhambury pins are more slender than the South Shields examples.

There are only a few beads. Five of the six gadrooned melon beads are made from the usual turquoise frit; one (No 989) is of blue glass. Four come from first- or second-century contexts. The other beads are of various forms; four are from levels in the aisled building but are unlikely to have been from the same necklace. The glass gaming pieces, all of standard plano-convex form, are discussed with the bone counters above (p 158) and a linen smoother of medieval date is illustrated here.

Fig 142

Pins

987 Blue glass pin with an oval head and twisted shaft, similar in form to one from Colchester (Crummy 1983, 28, no 462, fig 25). Length 53mm. SF 712 **2018** 7.45 9.50 (9). Rubble over chalk hypocaust

988 Translucent green glass pin with slender shaft twisted below a spherical head. Incomplete. Length 28mm. SF 956 **2117** 4.00 8.00 (494). Building 50, Period 10, Fig 99. AS 103/2

Beads (Nos 989–1005)

989 Melon bead of dark blue glass, as example from Colchester (Crummy 1983, 30, no 524 fig 32). Diameter 32mm. SF 533 **2022** 9.50 8.50 (275). Fill of Ditch 74 associated with occupation of Building 37, Period 9, Fig 48. AS 66/1

990 Melon bead, turquoise frit. Height 15mm. SF 1130 **2017** 4.15 0.25 (91). Ditch 74, first-century level. AS 97/2

991 Melon bead, turquoise frit. Diameter 17mm. SF 3192 **3817** 1.50 2.10 (4). Ploughpan, area north of Building 40

992 As 991. Diameter 16mm. SF 2891 **2820** 3.50 9.00 (1551). Second-century trackway over Ditch 165. AP 219, AS 253/4

993 Not illustrated. Melon bead as 991. Height 16mm. SF 2282 **2319** 8.06 3.50 (1028). Second-century level. AS 159/1

994 Not illustrated. Melon bead as 991. Height 16mm. SF 2091 **2420** 1.00 1.00 (741). Ploughpan

995 Annular bead. Dark blue glass with white paste band and marvered purple trails. First-century type. Surviving length 17mm. SF 135 **2220** 6.50 8.50 (135). Humus pre-dating Building 21, first century. AS 45/1

996 Annular bead in blue glass. Diameter 20mm. SF 1980 **2721** 4.40 3.00 (768). Levelling clay, first century. AS 134/3

997 Annular bead in translucent pale green glass. Diameter 17mm. SF 492 **2122** 1.10 5.30 (287). Cobbles. AP 55

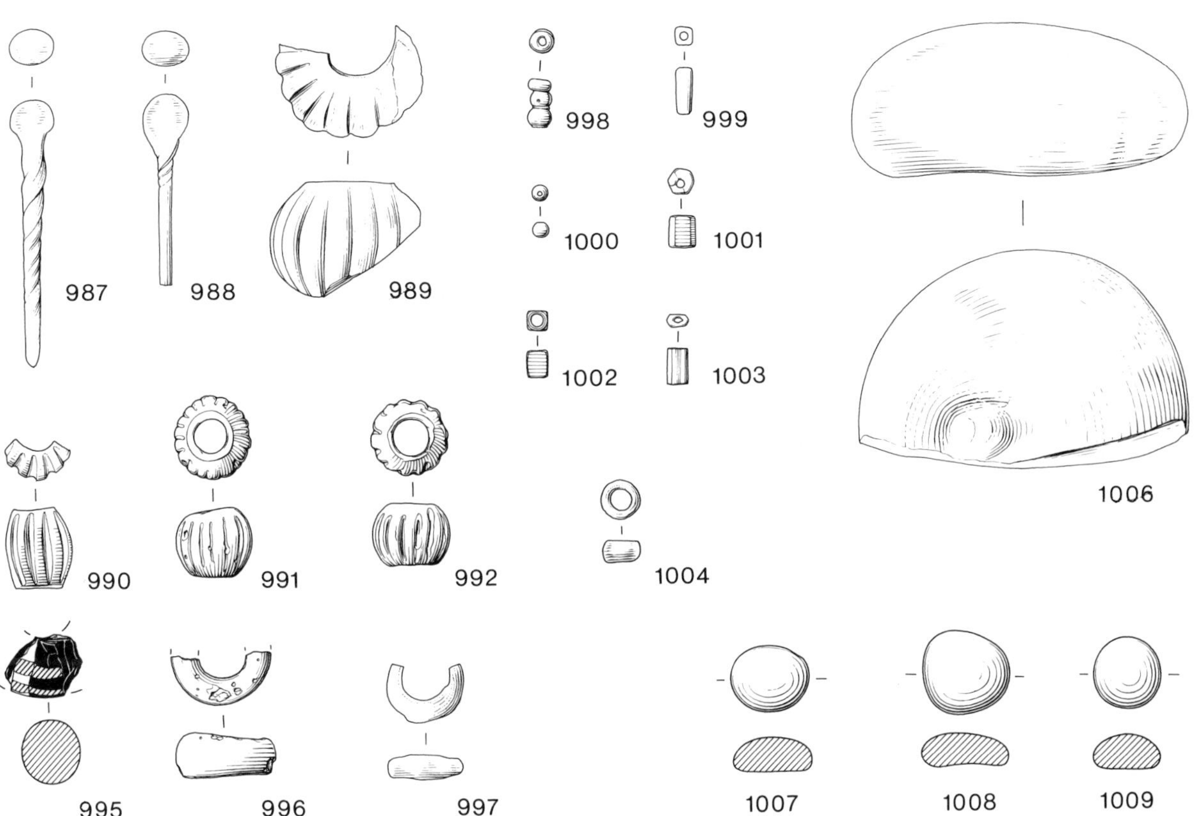

Fig 142 Objects of glass (Scale 2:3)

998 Triple-segmented long bead in green glass. Length 10mm. SF 3431 **3917** 1.00 8.40 (2001). Yard north of Building 39/40, Period 9, Fig 40. AP 285

999 Rectangular green glass bead. Length 10mm. SF 782 **2016** 2.00 1.80 (4) Ploughpan

1000 Spherical green glass bead. Diameter 3mm. SF 3120 **3716** 6.50 5.50 (1906). Posthole, Building 40, Fig 40. AP 277, AS 300/1

1001 Hexagonal bead in green glass. Length 4mm. SF 3139 **3816** 5.50 5.50 (1898). Fourth-century level over Building 40, Fig 40. AP 282

1002 Rectangular bead in green glass. Length 5mm. SF 4208 **3021** 2.00 8.00 (3021). Level over Building 33, Fig 70. AP 400

1003 Hexagonal long bead in green glass. Length 7mm. SF 3118 **3716** 6.50 6.50 (1883). Occupation level over Building 47, Period 10, Fig 41. AP 276 AS 301/2

1004 Annular bead in silver. Diameter 8mm. SF 41 AML 821588. 1956 excavations

1005 Not illustrated. Amber bead, fragment. Length 8mm. SF 2736 **2821** (701). Ploughpan

1006 Linen smoother in opaque greyish green glass. From the context this is of medieval date. The flattened glass ball was used to polish linen to a smooth finish and such implements have been found on sites dating from the Roman period onwards (Wild 1970a, 84). Length 68mm. SF 1132 **2017** 8.80 8.30 (502). Structure 59, Fig 111. Medieval

Gaming pieces

1007 Translucent greenish-white glass. Maximum diameter 17mm. SF 2812 **2819** 2.30 8.50 (1569). South terminal Ditch 1281 between inner and outer enclosures. Second century. AS 251/1

1008 Opaque blue glass. Diameter 19mm. SF 334 **2121** 0.20 9.00 (77). First-century fill of Ditch 74, associated with occupation of Building 21, Period 7, Fig 48. A second example in black glass came from this level

1009 Opaque green glass. Diameter 14mm. SF 3144 **3716** 5.00 4.00 (2003). Floor surface, Building 47, Period 10, Fig 41. AP 277, AS 301/1

1010 Not illustrated. Black glass. Diameter 15mm. SF 2925 **2819** 3.00 9.90 (1686). South terminal Ditch 1281. AS 251/1

Fig 143

Gemstone

1011 Emerald. The opaque stone is triangular in section with one fractured corner. Fine hair-line fractures cover the surfaces. It was identified as an emerald by Mrs M E Hutchinson who has provided the following note (AM Lab Report No 3627): 'The stone has been cut as a three-sided prism with the long axis parallel to the long axis of the original crystal. The two top facets meet at approximately 72°. All the surfaces have been cut and polished and the facets have not been produced by cleavage nor are they the original crystal faces. In a damaged area on the top of the stone are rod- or tube-shaped inclusions on each end. From its physical characteristics the stone can be identified as a beryl-variety emerald. The physical constants are: weight 8.9576g (44.78 carats); refractive index: 1.585, 1.591 DR 0.006; spectrum: faint chromium spectrum; cut: triangular prism.' The stone was examined by J Ogden who identified it as of Egyptian provenance, from a large ring originally with a gold setting (Neal 1982, 365).
27.5 × 17.5mm. SF 3191 AML 814713 3816 0.00 4.10 (2004). Building 40, Period 9. Late second to third century. Fig 40

The intaglios

by Martin Henig

Figs 143 and 144

In the account which follows, the devices are described as they appear in impression. Left and right are, of course, reversed on the actual gem. Ring types and shapes of intaglios are listed after Henig 1978, 35, fig 1.

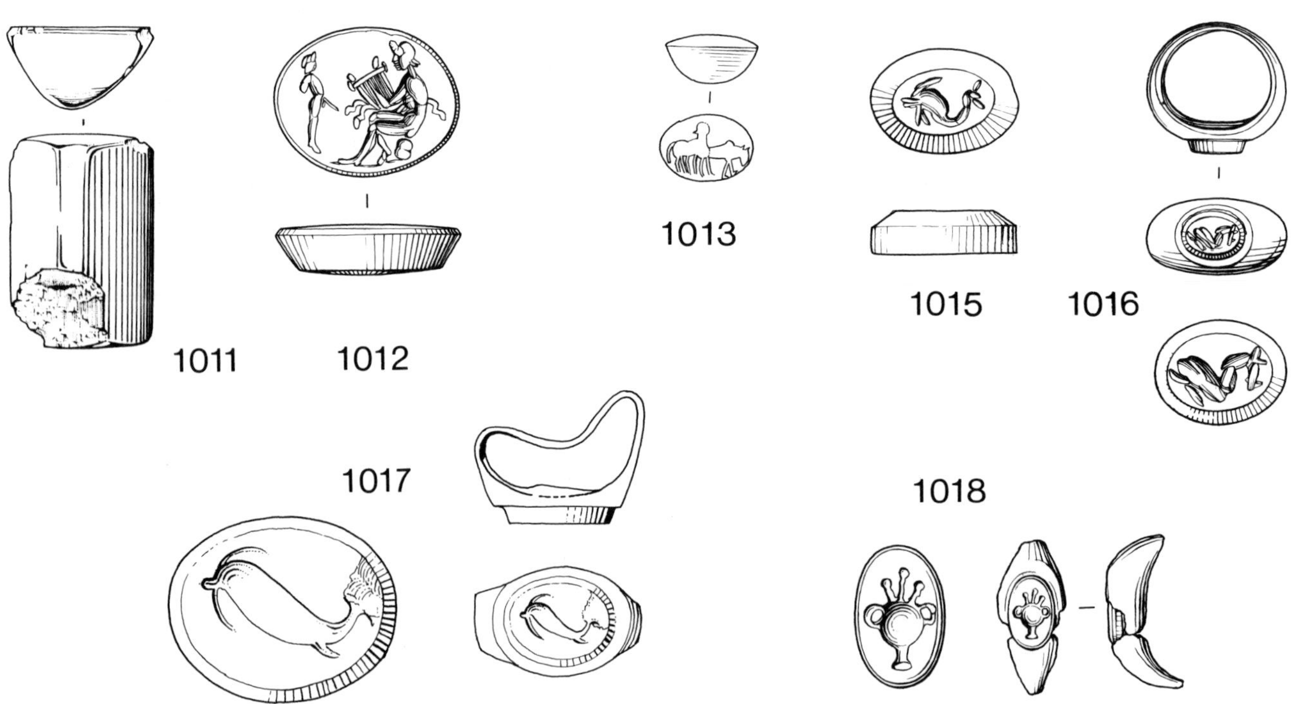

Fig 143 Gemstone of emerald (No 1011) and intaglios (Scales: gemstone 1:1, intaglios 2:1)

1012 Cornelian. Shape A5. 12 x 10 x 2.5mm Youthful satyr, nude with prominent tail placed, however, somewhat too high on his back sits upon a rock in profile to the right. He plucks at the strings of a lyre. Before him stands an image of Priapus. There is a groundline. For other gems depicting lyre-playing satyrs see Maaskant-Kleibrink 1978, no 342 (with a sacred column in front of him, rather than Priapus); Krug 1980, no 322. Intaglios portraying Silenus as a lyre-player are fairly common. An aedicula containing an image of Priapus is generally shown on these stones, eg ibid, no 394; Richter 1971, no 188; Henig 1986, no 182. Also note gems which show seated satyrs pouring out wine in front of images of Priapus upon columns, ibid, no 188. Zazoff 1975, no 872; Zwierlein-Diehl 1979, nos 1065, 1066 and a seated satyr playing with a baby in front of a Priapus column, Henig 1978, no 156 (Ruxox Farm, Bedfordshire). The controlled classicism of the design and the crispness of execution places the gem into Maaskant-Kleibrink's 'Wheel Style' group (1978, 154) and assigns it to the Augustan period. For style we may compare it with all the gems cited above – except perhaps the last which is nevertheless earlier than stated – and also with a plasma from Chichester portraying the satyr Marsyas, likewise seated upon a rock (Henig 1978, no App 108 = Henig in Down 1981, 174–6). The theme evokes harmony and fecundity in the countryside, a *leitmotif* of Augustan state propaganda.
SF 1622 **2422** 0.02 6.10 (751). Clay spread, in area of Building 16, Period 6, Fig 46

1013 Leek green plasma. Shape B2. 5.5 x 4 x 3mm. The intaglio is of diminutive size, evidently intended for insertion in a ring of slight dimensions (see Henig in Cunliffe 1971, **2**, 88–9, and pl xviii no 2 for a small gold ring containing such a gem). Two quadrupeds stand, overlapping one another, in profile to the right, the animal in front lowers its head to browse. There is a groundline. Close inspection suggests that the beasts, which have cloven hoofs, are cattle: indeed on the front one, two horns can clearly be seen. Compare Fossing 1929, no 1366 for two cattle, and for groups Henig 1978, no 599 from Bath and Maaskant-Kleibrink 1978, no 558. The subject is the theme of three poems in the Palatine Anthology (ix, 746, 747, 750), two of them apparently written in the first century BC. The idea of cattle being penned in on a tiny gemstone seems to have fascinated the poets. Incidentally, horses are sometimes depicted in pairs, one beast with head raised and the other lowered (eg Furtwängler 1896, no 2499; Henig 1978, no 588, also from Bath). Material, style of cutting and miniature scale suggest a date perhaps as early as Augustan times and certainly no later than the middle of the first century AD (see Maaskant-Kleibrink 1978, 196).
SF 1029 **2117** 8.00 8.50 (562). Primary fill, Building 50, Fig 99. AS 101/2

1014 Fig 144. Intaglio in private possession, said to be from 'excavations at Gorhambury', submitted to Mr D T-D Clarke of Colchester Castle Museum who provided details. Nicolo. Shape F4. 12 x 10mm. Bonus Eventus stands to front and faces left. He holds a patera in his outstretched right hand, and a corn-ear in his left hand. Groundline. The type is a common one and amongst gems from Britain alone we may note twenty published examples (Henig 1978, nos 203–219; App 21; App 22; App 65; and App 115). It is suggested (ibid, 77) that the type derives from a statue by Praxiteles. The gem probably dates to the second century AD

1015 Nicolo. Shape F4. 9.5 x 7 x 2.75mm. A dolphin swims towards the right. Compare Henig 1978, no 646; Sena Chiesa 1966, no 1404 for material and style. The intaglio may be dated to the early or middle second century AD.
SF 2588 **2116** 8.10 6.40. Unstratified

1016 Red cornelian. Shape ? A6 set in a silver ring, type 5. Gem: upper face 7 x 5mm, the sides bevelling outwards to 8 x 6mm; it stands 2mm clear of the bezel of the ring. External diameter, 18mm (internal 15mm); width across bezel 9.5mm. The small size of the ring indicates that it was designed for a woman. A dolphin swims towards the right; cf Henig 1981. The schematic style of cutting (Maaskant-Kleibrink 1978, 326, Incoherent Grooves Style) and the form of the ring date this to the second half of the second century AD.
SF 2645 **2723** 1.95 1.81 (1490). Well

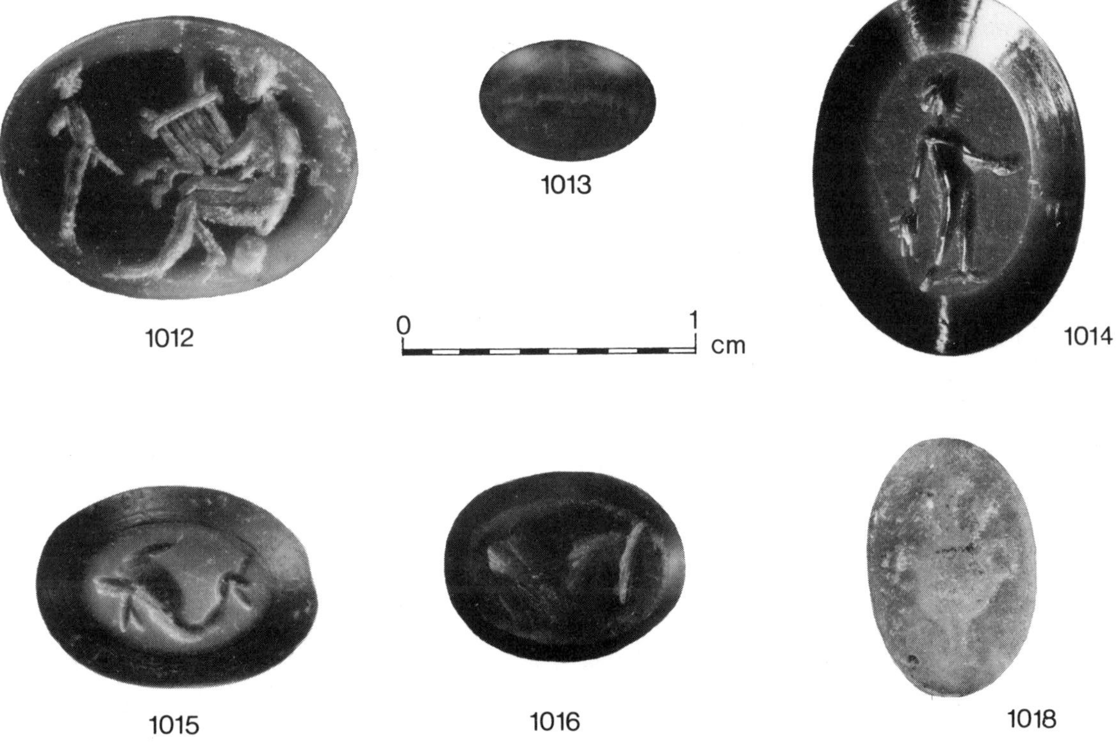

Fig 144 Photographs of the intaglios

1017 Glass with upper blue surface on dark ground, moulded in imitation of nicolo. Shape F2/F4, set in a ring of base silver, type 11. Gem: 14 × 10mm. The ring is bent but has a diameter of c 23 mm. A dolphin swims towards the right; cf Henig 1978, no 647. It is probable that this ring dates to the third century; rings of this form are normally of bronze.
SF 56 **1921** 9.50 2.00 (110). Fourth-century destruction material over Building 51, Fig 102. AP 26, AS 40/2

1018 Moulded, white glass. Shape F set in the remains of a bronze ring, type 3. Gem: 8.5 x 5.5 x 1.5mm. The lower part of the hoop of the ring is lost but it evidently had a diameter of some 19mm; width across bezel 9mm. A cup with two handles contains three plant-sprays. Intaglio and ring identical to Henig 1978, no App 199 (Wroxeter); also note no App 198. The ring is certainly no later than the second century AD, but it may be earlier. The last intaglio cited was found in a 'Belgic hut' at Canterbury.
SF 2814 **2819** 2.30 8.60 (1569). South terminal of Ditch 1281. Second-century fill

The early dating of No 1012 and probably also of No 1013 (conceivably also of No 1018) matches those proposed for two gems and two glass intaglios from the Verulamium excavations (Henig in Frere 1984, 141–2 nos 1–4). This may be accounted for by the fact that signet gems were treasured from generation to generation and by the presence at Verulamium of Roman soldiers and merchants. However the evidence of certain Catuvellaunian coin devices suggests that some signet rings may have reached Britain before AD 43 (Henig 1972).

The three dolphin intaglios are later in date. They allude to the realm of Neptune: after death, souls were thought to traverse the sea to the Blessed Isles. In the first century obsession with death attained such a pitch that Petronius felt impelled to satirise it in the *Cena Trimalchionis*. It is unlikely that many of the inhabitants of Roman Britain were quite as morbid as Trimalchio, but other-worldly imagery is certainly widespread (Henig 1977). In a purely local context it is of some interest that dolphins and a fountain (Neal 1981, 100–101 mosaic 73) and other marine devices (Neptune himself and a bivalve shell) occur on mosaic pavements from the city.

Objects of fired clay

The objects range from fragments of pipeclay figurines which have religious associations to utilitarian spindle whorls and loom weights (Nos 1023–1032). The crucibles provide evidence for metalworking which is discussed in detail by Justine Bayley (p 164).

Fig 145

1019 Fragment of pipeclay ?figurine. Head with elaborate hair style or head-dress above a crudely modelled face. Length 67mm. SF 9. 1956–61 excavations

1020 Fragment of pipeclay figurine, probably of the Venus-type, in the fine pinkish-white fabric of the Allier district of France. Part of the lower legs and a piece of drapery, roughly scored to represent folds remain. It is very similar to a fragment from Gadebridge Park (Neal 1974, 197, no 719, fig 87). Such figures were manufactured in central Gaul and Cologne in the first and second centuries (Green 1976, 20). Height 40mm. SF 458 **2222** 0.20 3.20 (139). Robber trench, Building 37

1021 Fragment of pipeclay figurine, part of the base and drapery surviving. Height 63mm. SF 2920 **2821** (1651). Layer over Ditch 1281, second century. AS 253/1

1022 Pottery counter in Oxfordshire ware. A large number of pottery roundels identified as counters was found at Colchester (Crummy 1983, 93). Width 17mm. SF 2125 **2518** 8.00 3.50 (741). Ploughpan

Spindle whorls (Nos 1023–1030)

1023 Spindle whorl made from a body sherd in coarse grey fabric. Diameter 27mm. SF 1647 **2620** 4.25 9.65 (721). Fourth-century level, Building 53, Fig 64. AS 133/1

1024 Spindle whorl made from body sherd. Diameter 29mm. SF 766 **2117** 8.00 9.50 (494). Building 50, Period 10, Fig 99. AS 100

1025 Spindle whorl in coarse grey fabric. Diameter 33mm. SF 3035 **2922** 7.00 6.00 (1679). Building 13, Period 5, Fig 37. AS 252/3

1026 Spindle whorl, in coarse cream fabric. This is the maximum size practicable for a pottery spindle whorl. Diameter 52mm. SF 4152 **2424/25** (3142)B. Fill of Ditch 74

1027 Spindle whorl made from pot base. Diameter 39mm. SF 1852 **2621** 2.10 0.40 (848). Eavesdrip fill, south of Building 30, Phase 2, Fig 64. AS 133/1

1028 Spindle whorl, in grey fabric. Diameter 44mm. SF 1204 **2118** 8.00 2.00 (652). Humus, first-century level. AS 101/1

1029 Spindle whorl of red-brown fabric. Diameter 34mm. SF 110 **1920** (158)

1030 Spindle whorl made from ceramic-tempered sherd. Diameter 60mm. SF 525 **2222** 2.60 3.80 (367). AP 61, AS 66

1031 Not illustrated. Oval sling shot in red-brown fabric, grooved at one end. Length 33mm. SF 4409 **2922** 8.00 7.50 (1679). Building 13, Period 5, Fig 37. AS 252/3

1032 Loom weight. Triangular, of late Iron Age form, c 0–AD 50. Reconstructed height 18mm, width 176mm. SF 1870 **2522** (809). AP 115, AS 132

Crucibles

Five crucible fragments were found, three of which are illustrated here. They were examined by Justine Bayley who has reported on the evidence for metalworking.

1033 Fragment of circular crucible in fine soft grey fabric. Miss Bayley reports that it contained gold droplets, with traces of copper and zinc. External diameter c 68mm, thickness of wall 9mm. SF 391 **2220** 6.50 8.00 (135). Level pre-dating Building 21, first century. AS 45/1

1034 Hemispherical thumb pot in a fine fabric containing organic matter and little mineral temper. It contained droplets of gold and there was evidence that scrap gold had been melted and then removed. There were also traces of copper and zinc. External diameter 33mm; internal depth 11mm; thickness of wall up to 10mm. SF 138 **2020** 9.50 1.50 (77). Fill of Ditch 74 associated with occupation of Building 21, Fig 48. A
A fragmentary unillustrated crucible also came from a first century fill of Ditch 74. It had been used to melt copper alloys and contains traces of copper, tin, lead and zinc. Surviving length 36mm, thickness of wall c 9mm. SF 103 **2019** 7.00 7.00 (76). Ditch 74

1035 Small crucible in fine soft fabric with quartz inclusions. It contained silver with traces of copper, zinc and lead. External diameter c 40mm. Height 32mm. Thickness of walls 7mm. SF 1734 **2620** 8.80 7.50 (756). Second-century level. AS 133/1

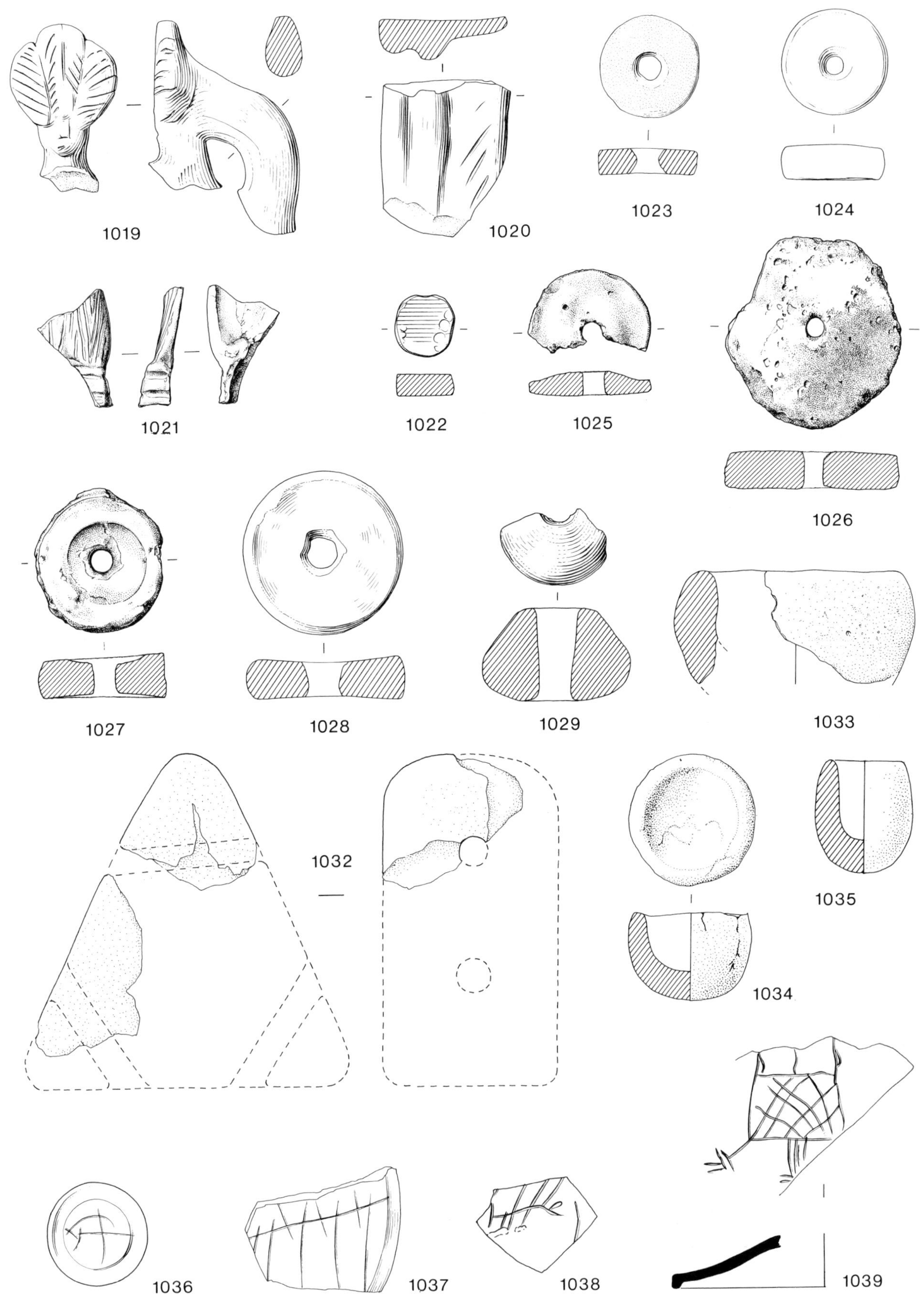

Fig 145 Objects of fired clay (Scale 2:3)

Evidence for metalworking

by Justine Bayley

(AML Report No 28/86)

Summary

A total of 16 kg of slag was examined; most was smithing slag. Parts of five crucibles used to melt gold, silver and copper alloy were also found in first- and second-century contexts.

Ironworking

The total weight of slag from the site was just over 16 kg and three-quarters of this came from area 2621, directly south of Building 30 and assigned to Building 53; it also produced quantities of offcuts or scrap iron. The majority of the slag was iron smithing slag which would have formed in a blacksmith's forge. Some of the pieces were plano-convex 'cakes' of slag which collected at the bottom of the hearth while others were just irregularly shaped lumps. Small quantities of smithing slag are normally found on any settlement site of Iron Age or later date so this material is not unexpected here.

In addition to the smithing slag there was also a small quantity of fuel ash slag which forms when silicate materials such as clay are heated strongly in contact with the ash in a fire. This fluxes them, producing a lightweight, glassy, vesicular slag. On its own, fuel ash slag is only an indicator of high temperatures but in association with smithing slag, as here, it is probably an additional residue of the blacksmith's work.

Non-ferrous metalworking

The major evidence is five crucible fragments. In addition, the site produced about ten small dribbles or blobs of copper alloy. These could have been metal spilt from crucibles but could also have formed if metal objects accidentally fell into a fire or were inside a building that burnt down. They should only be considered as evidence for metalworking if their contexts associate them with finds such as the crucibles.

The crucible fragments were examined and the deposits on them analysed qualitatively by energy dispersive X-ray fluorescence (XRF). Four were hand-made and of not very refractory fabrics, and a fifth was wheel-thrown.

SF 103 (not illustrated and not listed in the catalogue) had obviously been used to melt copper alloys as droplets of corroded metal were trapped in the crucible slag near the rim. XRF detected major amounts of copper, tin, lead and zinc so the metal being melted was a leaded gunmetal containing significant amounts of all these elements. The fabric was fairly fine and soft but contained a few quartz grains. It had been affected by heat, showing slight vitrification and a vesicular structure, especially near the rim. The wall was about 9mm thick.

No 1034 (Fig 145) was a fairly complete hemispherical thumb pot. Tiny droplets of gold were trapped in the vitrified surface layer inside the crucible and a 'tide mark' near the bottom indicates that a prill of gold had solidified in the crucible and had then been removed from it. This suggests that scrap gold, perhaps manufacturing waste such as filings, or a gold object, had been melted to give a piece of metal that could then be worked into a new object.

A rim fragment (No 1033, Fig 145) also contained gold droplets. In both No 1034 and 1033 XRF detected traces of copper and zinc in addition to gold.

In crucible No 1035 (Fig 145) XRF detected silver together with minor amounts of copper, zinc and lead.

The fifth crucible (not listed in the catalogue) is in a Verulamium region, wheel thrown fabric. Its height is 72mm and its width 55mm. XRF detected copper and zinc.

The soft fabrics and handmade forms of most crucibles suggest a native rather than a Roman metalworking tradition. The typical late Iron Age crucible is triangular in plan but only SF 103 could possibly have been of this type. The other four vessels are definitely circular. Circular handmade crucibles are a well known first-century type on sites as widely spaced as Sheepen, Colchester (Bayley 1985) and St Sepulchre Gate, Doncaster (Bayley 1986b).

The contexts producing the crucibles range in date from first century (for No 103 and No 1034) through late first (for No 1033) to second century (for No 1035). This could be interpreted as showing intermittent working of a range of metals over more than a century or, alternatively, all the evidence can be thought of as originating in the first century when the metalworking took place, the later finds being redeposited. The general similarity (though with specific differences) of the crucible fabrics can be used to argue either for or against a single period of metalworking. What can be said is that it was only a very small-scale operation at any time. This being so, it is interesting that the analyses show that not only copper alloys but also gold and silver were being melted and presumably worked at Gorhambury.

Graffiti (Fig 145)

1036 Base with graffito. Diameter 27mm. SF 549 **2022** (275). Second-century fill of Ditch 74 associated with occupation of Building 37, Period 9, Fig 48

1037 Base with graffito on underside consisting of one horizontal line crossed by eight vertical lines. Fabric 12. Length 43mm. SF 784 **2118** (494). Building 50, Fig 99. AS 103/2

1038 Sherd with graffito. Fabric 114. Length 33mm. SF Pot 2 **2133** (318). Posthole. AP 55

1039 Lid with graffito representing a human figure on the inside. The figure wears a tunic, the skirt decorated with a lattice or chequered pattern. The upper part has a single vertical line while two curving lines might represent breasts or arms. The legs and feet are indicated below. Fabric 57. Height of figure 80mm. SF 497 **2022** (275). Pot No (275) 63. Second-century fill of Ditch 74 associated with occupation of Building 37. AS 66/1

For additional graffiti on tile see Nos 1061 and 1062 (Fig 147) and on sherd p 184.

Objects of stone

For worked flint see Fig 168, p 218.

Shale bracelets are frequently found on Roman sites and these examples (Nos 1042–1044) are of standard type. Shale was also used for utilitarian items such as spindle whorls and vessels (Nos 1048–1050). The marble palette (No 1051) is of interest as an imported item. A large number of hones were found; only a small selection is illustrated here.

Fig 146

Jet and shale

1040 Jet bead of irregular trapezoidal shape with a faceted upper surface, pierced with two holes. Length 15mm. SF 3113 **3716** 8.00 6.60 (1881). Occupation level, Building 47, Fig 41. AP 276

1041 Shale bracelet with notched decoration on the outer face. Original diameter 69mm. SF 46 **2019** 2.00 8.50 (37)

1042 Shale bracelet with notched decoration on both sides. Original diameter 69mm. SF 1590 **2621** 6.00 1.60 (787). Building 53, Fig 64. Fourth century. AP 120, AS 133/1

1043 Shale bracelet with notched decoration on both sides. Original diameter 76mm. SF 858 **2018** 0.25 0.80 (546). Well

1044 Shale bracelet. Original diameter 55mm. 1956 excavations. Mixed debris

1045–47 Shale bracelets. Not illustrated. For drawings see AS No 459

1048 Shale spindle whorl. Diameter 29mm. SF 2738 **2818**. Unstratified

1049 Vessel. Base of shale vessel with three concentric grooves. Diameter 38mm. SF 1589 (2721) 2.00 1.00 (786). Rubble east of Building 30, Fig 64. AS 134/6

1050 Fragment from the wall of a shale vessel. Length 42mm. Original diameter 137mm. SF 3174 **3717** 1.50 7.80 (2018). Building 39/40, Period 9, Fig 40. AS 302/8

1051 Marble palette with bevelled edges. Such palettes were used for the mixing of medicines and cosmetics. Surviving length 34mm. SF 2813 **2819** 2.00 9.40 (1569). Upper fill south terminal Ditch 1281. AS 251/1

Hones

Large numbers of hones of various dates were recovered from the site, of which a small selection is published here.

1052 Sandstone hone with worn angled surfaces. Length 43mm. SF 2394 **2319** 4.00 4.00 (1195). AP 136

1053 Fine grained stone, deeply grooved by use on the upper surface. Length 62mm. SF 3407 **3716** 9.90 1.00 (2032). Gully Building 39/40, Period 9, Fig 40. AP 282

1054 Rectangular hone. Length 52mm. SF 2194 **2419** (920). Robber trench, Building 28, Fig 52. AP 141

1055 Rectangular hone. Length 58mm. SF 3173 **3717** 4.00 4.00 (2018). Building 39/40, Period 9, Fig 40. AS 302/8

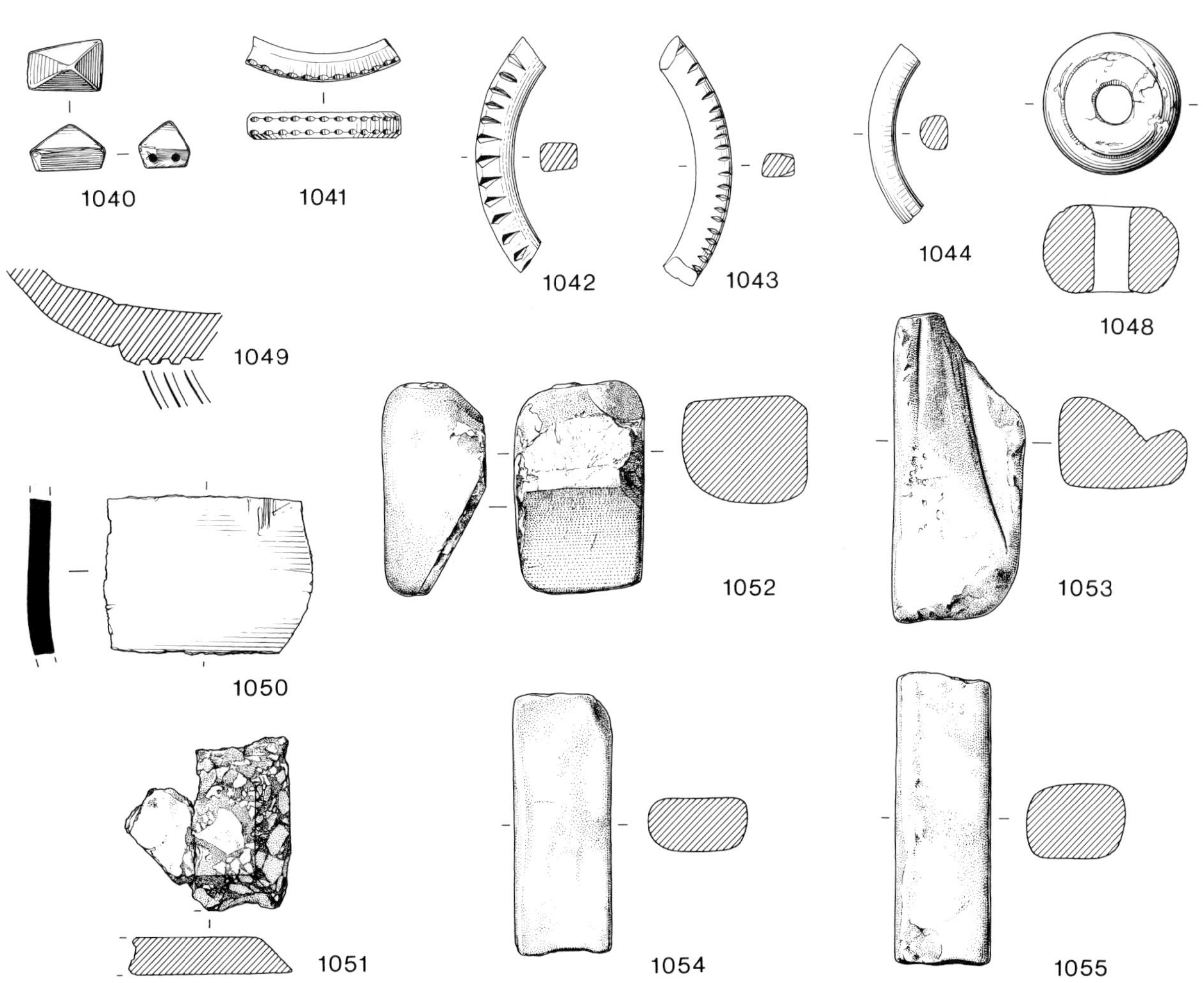

Fig 146 Objects of stone including jet and shale (Scale 2:3)

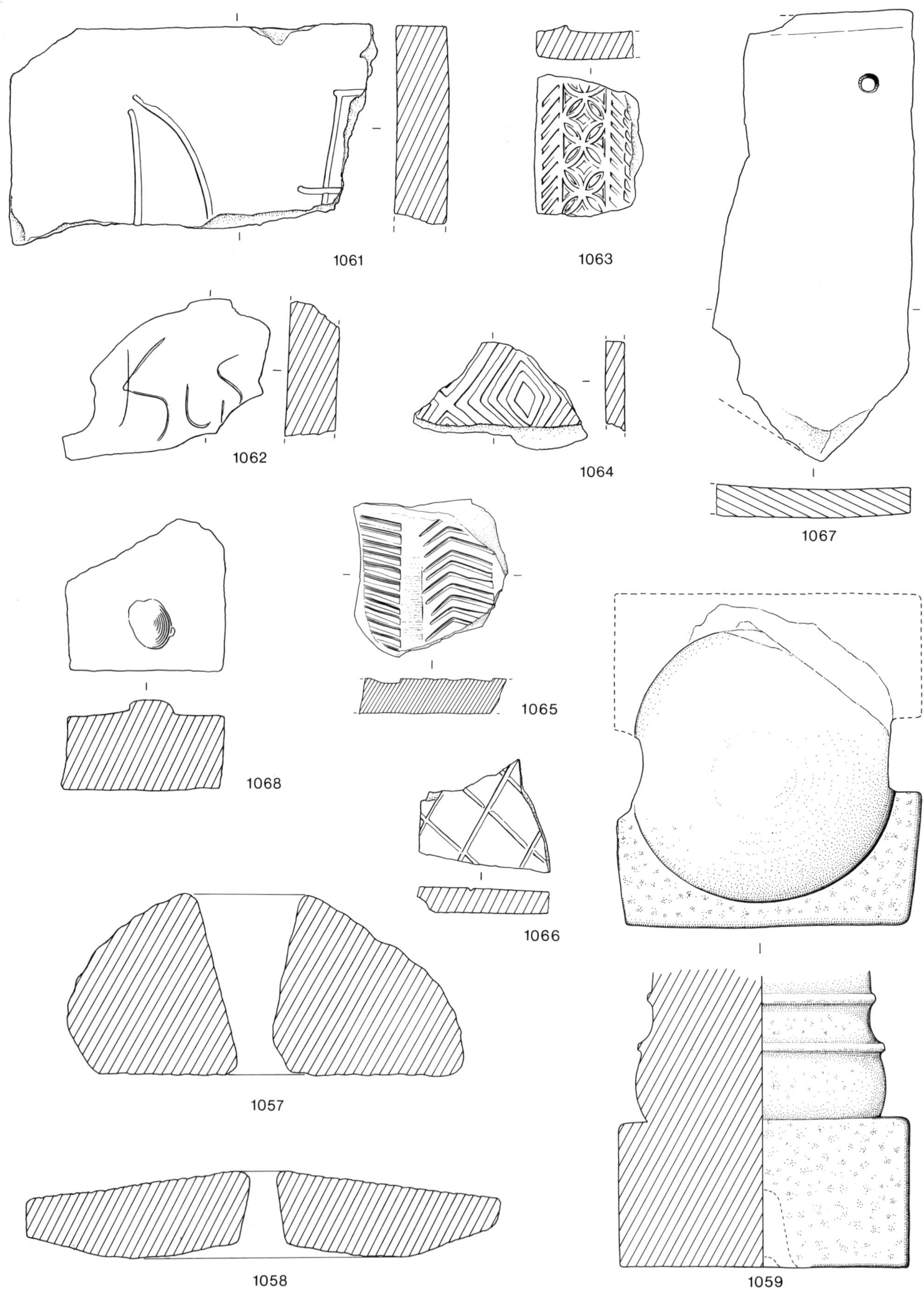

Fig 147 Querns, architectural fragments and tile (Scale 1:4)

Fig 147

Querns

Querns from the site were of three basic types. The earliest are saddle querns, one example being found re-used as a timber support in the Phase 2 aisled hall, Building 20 area 3817 (No 1056, not illustrated). Another came from area 2720. A Roman type of the first century AD is the beehive rotary quern in Hertfordshire puddingstone found re-used as a door pivot along the trackway in the outer enclosure, area 3720 (No 1057). Only fragments were found elsewhere but the type is well represented locally, for example at Gadebridge (Neal 1974, 193, fig 84, nos 697, 698). The most common quern is the flat type found at Gorhambury in millstone grit (as No 1058) and Neidermendig lava. No complete examples were recovered in either material and it is of interest to note the considerable wear on many fragments, reducing one to as little as 10mm in thickness. Many of the fragments were found in the terminals of ditch 1281 between the inner and outer enclosures, area 2820, levels associated with the occupation of Buildings 27 and 37.

1056 Not illustrated. Saddle quern. Length 435mm. SF 3421 **3817** 7.00 4.00 (2086). Building 39/40, Period 9, Fig 40, re-used as door pivot

1057 Beehive quern in Hertfordshire puddingstone. Diameter 310mm. SF 4016 **3720** 1.90 4.40 (2606). From trackway in outer enclosure, used as a gate pivot

1058 Rotary quern in Millstone grit. Diameter 360mm. SF 3333 **3717** 3.50 1.20 (2065). Occupation level, Building 39/40, Period 9, Fig 40. AS 302/8

Building materials (Fig 147)

Architectural fragments

Few architectural fragments were found; all are of oolitic limestone. A fragment of dwarf column with lathe-turned moulding (1060), heavily abraded and burnt, was found in second-century levels in area 2817. It seems to be of the same type as No 1059 which is reputed to have been found at Gorhambury in 1956. The latter is not recorded however and it is possible that it was found elsewhere on the estate; it has been reworked with rebates on either side. Also of interest was a fragment (not illustrated) with a notch and two 'square' projections suggesting a dentilled frieze although this is far from certain. A rectangular block of oolitic limestone was recovered from the floor of the cellar in 1959 but it lacked mouldings and was presumably a quoin.

Scattered over the site were fragments of Purbeck marble veneer. Some were found in medieval contexts but it is unlikely that such elegant material would have graced a manor house, although it is known to have embellished Bacon's house. It is possible that the veneer was stripped from the Roman villa or from buildings in Verulamium.

1059 Column drum. Oolitic limestone with lathe turned mouldings. Rebates later cut in opposite sides. Diameter 218mm. From 'Gorhambury', 1956

1060 Not illustrated. Column drum as 1059. SF 2578 **2817** 1.00 2.80 (1282). Second-century level in Ditch 1281

Tile

A large quantity of tile was recovered from the site, mainly fragments of tegula and imbrex associated with the masonry buildings (unlike Gadebridge there is no evidence for stone slates). As usual, many had the imprint of dog and cat paws and one had imprints of sheep or goat; another had the nail impressions from a boot. They were almost entirely in a hard red fabric but a small fragment of tegula was in an unusual white-cream fabric.

One roof tile (No 1065) is of interest in that although it appears to have been a tegula it lacked flanges and one side was deliberately angled by knife trimming. The underside of the tile was also knife trimmed. Such a tile could have been used for cladding rather than on a roof.

The next group were flue tiles, the majority coming from the destruction rubble filling the bath-house, Building 41. Unlike the roofing tiles these were almost entirely in shelly ware with combed decoration, in contrast to the pilae and hypocaust floor tiles which were in red fabric. Among the collection were fragments of voussoirs indicating a barrel vault.

Fragments of flue tiles with roller-stamped decoration, kindly examined by E Black, were dispersed widely over the site and probably originated from the robbing of the earlier bath-house, Building 29. Compass (No 1063), chevron and lozenge patterns (No 1064), from Lowther's Dies 11, 16 and 36 respectively (Lowther 1948), were represented. Examples with roller-stamped decoration were always in a hard red fabric. Other flue tiles of the same material had lattice and comb scored decoration, while two hypocaust floor tiles were inscribed (Nos 1061, 1062, Fig 147).

Another group was represented by thick flat tiles with circular bosses, as No 1066. The earliest appearance of this type is in a Flavian context from a ditch pre-dating the masonry buildings; they are believed to be spacers for firing.

1061 Floor tile with graffito. Surviving length 270mm. Thickness 40mm. SF 4836 **2026** 9.40 5.90 (3122) g. Medieval oven

1062 Floor tile with graffito. Surviving length 180mm. Thickness 37mm. SF 3890 **3820** 5.00 6.00. Structure 43, Phase 2, Fig 92. AP 336
Mark Hassall comments: The graffito reads . . .]K S[. . . Almost certainly for: numeral]KA!(endas) S[EPT(EMBRES), '(so many days before)the Kalends of September', ie a date in the latter part of August.

Relief-patterned flue tiles

Ernest Black has kindly commented on Nos 1063, 1064 and 1065

1063 Lowther Die 11. The fabric is light orange with occasional minute red and black inclusions and frequent larger white inclusions, producing the same effect as Die 2 tiles from Verulamium (Lowther 1948). The surface colour is white. Length 102mm. Thickness 20mm. SF 2495 **2017**. Unstratified

Fig 148 Examples of painted plaster; no 14 is part of a coved frieze supported by pilasters in relief (see Fig 149); for key to colour conventions see Fig 151 (Scale 1:4)

1064 Similar to Dies 18 and 84. The diamond and lattice design matches the pieces published by Frere (1984, 113, no 16), identified there as Die 18, but it is clear from the larger Gorhambury example that they are neither Die 18 nor Die 84, although close to the latter. There are several dies of the same pattern that are broadly contemporary and copy some prototype: Nos 18, 46, 51, 84, 85, 89, 101, the Gorhambury die being the eighth example. It is interesting to note that Die 36 was also found at Gorhambury (No 1065) and that Dies 36 and 84 were found together at 11 Ironmonger Lane, London in a late first century (?) context. Length 130mm. Thickness 15mm. SF 2952 **2822** (1657). Ditch 1281, Antonine fill. AS 253/1

1065 Die 36. The tile is 24mm thick and there is part of an oval or circular vent in the side *c* 38mm from the junction with the face. Length 102mm. SF 707 **2022** 9.50 5.00 (369). Antonine deposit in upper fill of Ditch 74

1066 Tile with scored lattice design. Length 90mm. Thickness 18mm. **2817** 2.00 3.00 (1286). Ditch 1281, Antonine deposit. AS 205/3

1067 Tegula. The tile appears to be a tegula but lacks the flanges. One side has been angled by knife trimming and it may have been used for cladding rather than on a roof. Length 330mm. Thickness 211mm. **2718** (1062). Posthole

1068 Tile with circular boss on the upper surface. This type also appears in a late first-century context in a level associated with Building 21, and may have been used as a spacer for firing. Length 120mm. Thickness 55mm. **2718** 5.00 8.50 (1149). Cesspit 1072. AS 162/3

Interior decoration

by David S Neal

The painted wall plaster and stucco

(Figs 148–150)

Introduction

The excavations of 1972–82 recovered no painted wall plaster of note, mainly because the two villas had been excavated in earlier years. This dearth of material, however, is more than compensated by the finds of 1956–60, mainly from the cellar, which amount to 62 boxes of wall plaster and 4 boxes of stucco preserved in Verulamium Museum. Every piece of this material has been examined, but it should be emphasised that no attempt has been made to reconstruct the fragments. Given many months of constant work this might prove worthwhile but whether significantly more information would be forthcoming is doubtful. To facilitate further research, the box numbers of the material are given.

Painted plaster has been recovered from the following areas: A in the filling of the cellar (Building 27, Fig 48); B filling the foundation trenches associated with the construction of the second masonry villa (Building 37); C in a gully alongside the bath-suite (Rooms 10–12) associated with Building 37; and D in the destruction rubble of the bath-house occupying the outer enclosure (Building 41, Fig 85). In the upper fill of the well in area 2018 was an oyster shell containing haematite and probably used as a wall-painter's palette.

Fig 149 Fragment of painted moulded coving found in the cellar in 1956

Building 27: the cellar

A Most of the wall plaster from the cellar was excavated between 1956 and 1958. It was found strewn over much of the cellar floor and in the first 300mm of its fill, suggesting that it was thrown in from above rather than having fallen from the cellar walls, which had no painted plaster *in situ*. Apart from a large angled piece with coving found in 1956 (Fig 148, 14), nowhere was it found in slabs sufficiently large to merit lifting with scrim and plaster of Paris.

Building 37

B Decorated fragments were recovered from the filling of the foundation trenches alongside the east–west walls dividing Rooms 4–6 (Fig 48). It was not possible to establish its decoration, but it almost certainly pre-dates the building and came from Building 27. It is associated therefore with material found in the cellar.

C The excavations of 1972 recovered small fragments of painted plaster from a gully alongside the bath-suite (Rooms 10–12) which would seem to be related to material found in the same feature in 1959. This has *opus signinum* backing and is likely therefore to have come from the actual bath-suite or some other room requiring waterproofing. Material in this group includes fragments in boxes 142, 158 and 173. The first has white backgrounds with red and yellow bands suggesting the outlines to a series of panels. Box 158 has a fragment with obtuse right-angled, black, yellow and white lines, also with areas of red and green, but its place in any scheme of decoration is not known. Its surface has been keyed for subsequent rendering, but it is doubtful whether this was ever applied as no trace of mortar adheres. A fragment in Box 173 has a white background and what appear to be three concentric bands, yellow, green and red (Fig 148, 1). Such an arrangement might have decorated a ceiling: these frequently had white backgrounds (Davey and Ling 1981, 40).

Building 41

D Fragments of plain red plaster painted on *opus signinum* were found in the rubble fill of the hypocaust and blue frit was painted on the floor of the plunge-bath (2264) occupying the western apse. This was perhaps a deliberate attempt to harmonise with the light from the windows which appear to have had blue glass panes. Three fragments of Egyptian blue frit were found towards the villa and may have been the material used to paint the floors.

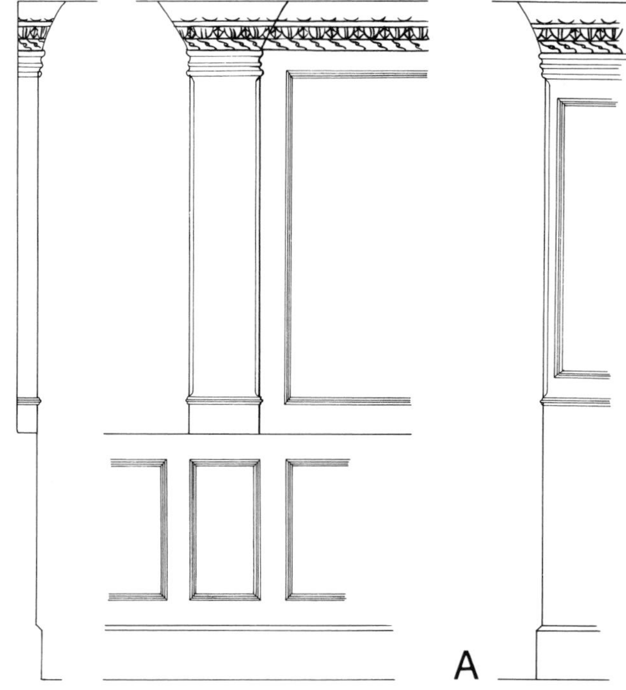

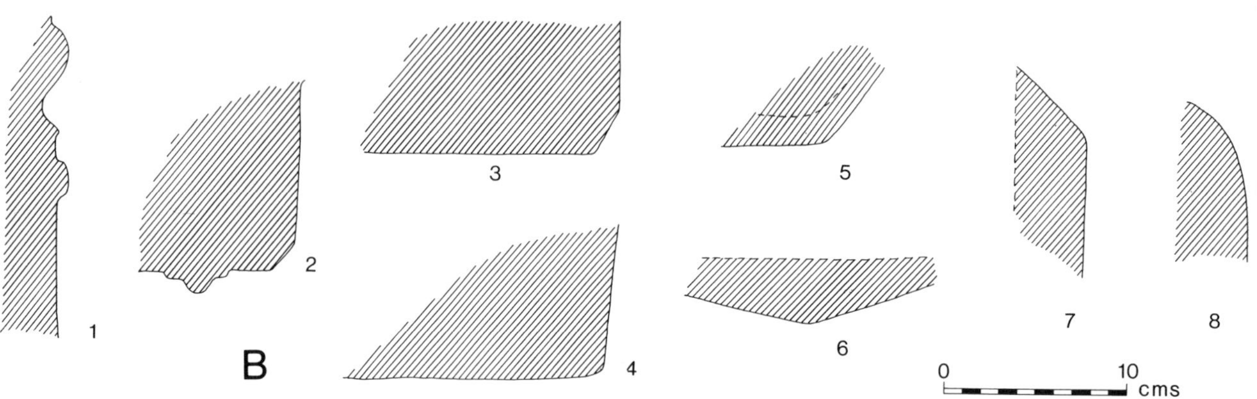

Fig 150 (a) Hypothetical reconstruction of wall plaster in relief found in the cellar; (b) sections of mouldings in relief (Scale 1:4)

The painted ornament

The painted ornament from Building 27 can be divided into seven groups:

Group 1 Panels

		Box numbers	Fig no
1.1	Red panels outlined black	130, 133–136	148,2
1.2	Red panels outlined green	?149	
1.3	Black panels outlined red	131, 138	
1.4	Black panels outlined green	132	
1.5	Green panels outlined black	1 9, 167, 177	148,4
1.6	Panels with door/window reveal	131, 177	148,5

Group 2 Floral or vegetal motifs

2.1	Leaves	131	148,6
2.2	Flowers	169, 177, ?179	148,11
2.3	Indeterminate free style ?vegetation	138, 143, 154, 160, 167–170	
2.4	?Tree trunk	143	148,9

Group 3 Geometric designs

3.1	Zig-zag	159	
3.2	?Octagons	173, 222	148,7
3.3	Circles	?167, 177	
3.4	?Lozenges	222	148,8

Group 4 Repeating motifs

4.1	Guilloche	165, 175, A, Z, 221	148,14
4.2	Ovolos	173, 175, 222	148,12
4.3	Ladder pattern	164	–
4.4	Egg and dart	173	148,14

Group 5 Marbling

5.1	Olive green flecked pale green	144, 146, 150, 161–166, 168, 171, 172, 174–176, 221, A	
5.2	Pink flecked black	174	
5.3	Mottled green on black	148	
5.4	'Worm' type. Green on green	142, 143	148,10
5.5	'Worm' type. Black on pink	147	
5.6	'Worm' type. Red on red	158	
5.7	Conglomerate	153	
5.8	'Fried-egg' type	173	148,13

Group 6 Architectural ornament in relief

6.1	Pilasters	141, ?150, 162, 166, A	150,1
6.2	Architraves	153, 156, 165, 171, 174, 221	150, 1
6.3	Simple mouldings	161, 162, 164–166, 168, 171, 172, 176	150,2
6.4	Reveals*	135, 138, 139, 144, 151, 161, 168, 172	150,3–8
6.5	Coving	175	148,14

Group 7 Stucco (Fig 5)

7.1 Human head
7.2 Hands
7.3 Feet
7.4 ?Parts of a torso
7.5 Red painted drapery

* It is uncertain whether the reveals came from doorways, windows or recesses, or changes in the vertical faces of the walls reflecting changes in construction, such as studded clay walls on masonry footings; cp the example from Insula XXI, Building 2 at Verulamium (Davey and Ling, 1982, no 41E).

Although the plaster was found in the cellar, there is no evidence that it decorated its walls, which lacked plaster *in situ*. More likely it, together with fragments of mosaic, was thrown into the cellar from the room above which may have been a reception room or *triclinium*. The polygonal foundation in the south wall of the cellar is assumed to have supported an apse upstairs. A further problem is whether all the material decorated the same room; its diverse character might suggest two schemes from separate rooms.

The bulk of the material, Group 1, comprises fragments of red panels outlined black, and red plaster with a narrow fillet of black outlined white (boxes 130, 135–7, 139, 141, 146, 157, 159 and 168). It is assumed that these occupied the main wall above dado level and were divided by vertical spaces similar, for example, to a number of paintings at Verulamium including Nos 41B and 42 (Davey and Ling 1981, figs 42 and 45) dated *c* AD 180. It must be emphasised, however, that there is no evidence for the dimensions or colour sequence of the panels, which appear to have been broken sometimes by door or window splays (Fig 148, 5).

To what extent these panels were further ornamented is also uncertain but the leaf (2.1, Fig 148, 6) might indicate a border of repeating leaves. Some panels might have had floral or vegetal motifs such as small red flowers with green leaves (2.2, Fig 148, 11); perhaps these originally formed swags. The free-style vegetation of 2.3 possibly came from a dado but whether a supposed tree-trunk (2.4, Fig 148, 12) also came from this or the main zone is not known.

How the geometric designs of Group 3 linked with this arrangement is difficult to visualise. The zig-zag pattern of 3.1 is represented by a single fragment and impossible to place in any scheme, but it is suggested that the octagons and circles of 3.2 (Fig 148, 7) and 3.3 may have decorated a ceiling. However, caution must be expressed here considering that on a third- or fourth-century wall at Collingham, Yorks, circles have been found decorating a frieze (Davey and Ling 1982, pls XXXVII and XXXVIII). The ?lozenge fragment represented by 3.4 (Fig 148, 8) is also a single piece and it is perhaps unlikely that it forms part of the general scheme being described.

The repeating motifs of Group 4, which include ovolos (Fig 148, 12) and egg and dart, could come from a painted frieze above the panels; they are painted red on a cream background and differ in colour and type to similar ornament painted on the coving associated with the plaster of Group 6.

Much of the marbling of Group 5 is assumed to have decorated a dado, especially 5.3–8 which imitate wall veneers. However the olive green marbling of 5.3 is associated with architectural reliefs now to be discussed.

The material of Group 6 is the second largest class of material and is represented by architectural mouldings in relief and not *trompe l'oeil*. They are painted olive green with white, pale green and, occasionally, black flecks. There is not a single example of Group 1 plaster with similar treatment nor of reliefs of Group 6 having coloured bands or evidence for painted panels. It would seem therefore that the groups decorated different rooms or walls.

Apart from a moulded pilaster from Insula XXVII, Building 2 in Verulamium (Frere 1983, 216 and pl XXIb) the material is without parallel in Roman Britain and therefore difficult to interpret. However, although the plaster is now in fairly small fragments a letter and a sketch addressed to Joan Liversidge from Sheila Cregeen dated 5 November 1956 would suggest that a large corner piece complete with a 'blue and white and black area of decoration' was found and attempts made to lift it. Presumably the fragments in Verulamium Museum with plaster of Paris backing form part of this piece. A reconstruction (Fig 148, 14 and Fig 150A) based on the sketch and the actual fragments shows a right-angle turn or dog-leg in a wall with a broad entablature supporting a pale green-blue coved frieze painted, in ascending order, with bands of guilloche, egg-and-dart, and a fragmentary band with a series of curved lines, such as might have come from a wave pattern or scroll. These motifs are in black with white highlights. The sketch also suggests that on either side of the angle are right-angled fillets forming panels; these fillets, or others of similar type, occur in boxes 171 and 176.

However, a problem in the overall interpretation is that altogether there are five fragments of architraves with returns and none indicate a return deeper than 100mm. Some of these angles have fillets in relief, as represented on the sketch, but others do not. Although part of the room may have had a deep recess, perhaps a door reveal or conceivably the angle formed by the apse, the other fragments of architrave suggest a more complex arrangement with less depth.

Guessing what this arrangement might be is fraught with difficulty, especially since the material is so unusual, but a clue is perhaps provided by examples of *trompe l'oeil* painted decoration from elsewhere. On a wall from Insula XXVIII, Building 3 at

Verulamium (Davey and Ling 1982, No 44, pl XCII), the panels forming the main zone are divided by narrow vertical panels painted with columns standing on top of a dado which acts as a podium. Only a modest attempt has been made to simulate perspective and there is little architectural detail, so that the podium or dado appears to be an integral part of the overall scheme. It is dated between *c* 150 and *c* 155–60. At the 'Painted House' at Dover (ibid, No 14, fig 23) the intervals between panels are painted with illusionistic pilasters and semi-columns on plinths resting on a podium supported by the dado. This example is dated to the second half of the second century and also serves to demonstrate the popularity of dividing panels along the main fields with illusionistic columns.

Clearly these examples are based on a class of interior architectural decoration in true relief. Although no examples of the latter have hitherto been found in Britain it is quite possible that the Gorhambury reliefs came from such a scheme. The architraves could have rested on pilasters, projecting 100mm from the wall face and standing on a podium 'supported' by the dado. The quantity of plaster showing architraves is small, however, so this moulding appears not to have run between the columns – a detail confirmed by the fragments of a painted coved frieze (Fig 148, 14) which lacks an architrave separating it from the panels below.

Two fragments of marbled olive-green plaster with white painted flutes are curved and may have come from door reveals or, more likely, columns framing a doorway such as was found at Boxmoor (Davey and Ling 1981, no 3, 84).

The stucco (Fig 5)

Considerable time has been spent trying to establish the composition of the stucco of Group 7, but without success. However, the human head is possibly that of a child at half life-size as it is small in relation to a hand and feet which probably came from an adult. The head would also seem to be small in comparison to fragments possibly from the upper torso of a figure and also red-painted folds of a cloak. The presence of red pigment on the cloak might indicate that the whole relief was painted. There is no evidence for the gender of the adult figure but it is assumed to be female and this is substantiated in part by the fragments of torso which are gently contoured. Whether the scene represents a deity with a child can only be speculation and there is no evidence for attributes.

Unlike the plaster of Groups 1–6 the stucco was applied on a wall studded with iron nails which acted as supports. Perhaps string or hair linked the nails – a technique used until recent times – although there is no evidence for this. What room or wall it originally decorated is also speculative, but conceivably it occupied a recess, perhaps represented by the architectural fragments in plaster shown on Fig 150, or an apse in the room above the cellar.

Stucco from Roman Britain is rare, the only pieces known to the writer coming from Fishbourne (Cunliffe 1971, 50) and Colchester. These, however, formed part of repeating, moulded, patterns and therefore the Gorhambury example is, to date, the only 'free-style' composition known. The plaster and stucco is assumed to have decorated the phase 3 masonry villa which was demolished *c* AD 175 (Building 27, Period 8).

The mosaics

Evidence for three mosaics was found. These include Mosaic 1, represented by fragments from the rubble filling of the cellar in Building 27, and Mosaics 2 and 3, paving Room 1 and the west corridor respectively of Building 37.

Mosaic 1 (Fig 151)

Five boxes of fragments and individual tesserae were recovered from the excavation of the cellar between 1956 and 1959. They were associated with the wall plaster and stucco (pp 169–72). In assessing the mosaic every fragment with ornament was drawn, but unfortunately they are insufficient to enable a reconstruction of the overall scheme to be made. However, it is possible to classify them into five groups and establish some of the motifs and patterns employed. These are described below.

Group 1

Fragments of Group 1 are the most numerous and are mainly of plain white tesserae; one fragment (Fig 151, 1) has five rows of tesserae (75mm wide) adjoining two courses of red tesserae; the white tesserae almost certainly come from an outer white band surrounding the actual mosaic, the red tesserae being part of a coarse broad border.

Group 2

The second most common group of fragments (Fig 151, 2–5) are certainly from a band of simple guilloche worked in white, yellow and red with dark grey outlines. No 4, the edge of a band of guilloche, has six rows of white tesserae which are probably part of the surrounding band (Group 1). If so, it is possible to suggest that the guilloche also bordered the mosaic but whether on all four sides is impossible to say. The band of guilloche would have been 170mm wide, somewhat wider than usual and a further indicator that it bordered the pavement where coarser workmanship is often found.

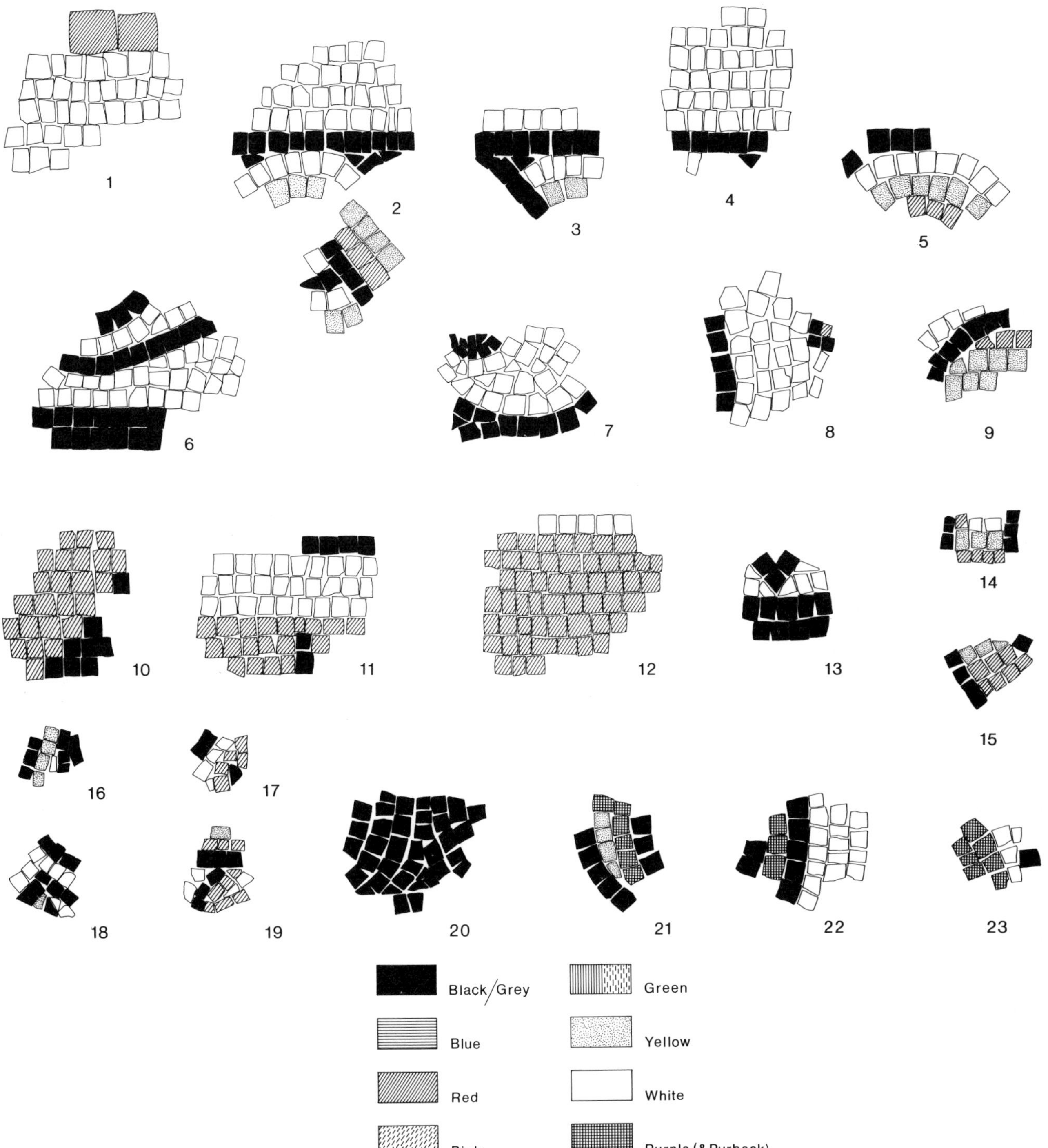

Fig 151 Examples of mosaic fragments found in the filling of the cellar and colour conventions (Scale 1:4)

Group 3

The identification of the third most common group of fragments (Fig 151, 6–10) is doubtful but it possibly formed part of a scroll similar perhaps to that represented on Mosaic 2 (Fig 78). No 9 may be part of a heart-shaped bud in white, red and yellow and outlined in dark grey; such ornament commonly embellished scrolls although it is also a standard petal motif.

Group 4

These are represented by a high proportion of red tesserae; two fragments, one of which is illustrated (Fig 151, 10), have areas of red and black tesserae separated by a staggered line. Such a design may represent part of a series of stepped triangles, although this motif is rare in polychrome. More commonly stepped triangles, of whatever colour, would have a white background. Alternatively, the design may have come from a small square quartered across the angles and forming triangles, each triangle alternating red and black. Another fragment of red (No 11) has traces of two dark grey lines at right angles (but not joining) one another. Its place in any motif or scheme is uncertain.

Group 5

The fifth group is a miscellaneous collection of fragments probably coming from the ornament within the central area of the floor rather than repeating patterns forming borders. Fragments 17–20 could be part of a complex flower motif with red-tipped petals. No 21 is of interest as the dark grey tesserae throughout are arranged in 'concentric' formations. This technique of laying tesserae would never be found in Britain on plain rectilinear areas of colour and therefore the fragment could have come from a bold alternating black and white composition of concave-sided squares, or from the interspaces between interlaced circles. Fragments 22–3 could have come from the bowl of a cantharus; they have dark grey 'outlines' bordering yellow and light grey tesserae, the latter being of Purbeck marble. Only one other fragment has Purbeck marble (No 4); the infrequency of this stone compared to the materials of the other tesserae might suggest that it was being used only sparingly and for special ornament.

Dating

As we have seen (p 46), Building 27 was constructed *c* AD 100 and demolished *c* AD 175 to make way for Building 37 which partially sealed the destruction rubble filling the cellar. What date within this period the mosaic was built is uncertain but it is more likely to be associated with the latest phase (Phase 3) of the building: *c* AD 150.

Mosaic 2

This mosaic paved Room 1, Building 37, and originally measured approximately 4.30 by 4.90m; the room was 6.35 by 7m. It was found in 1961 but by the time it was re-excavated in 1973 and 1974 it had suffered from ploughing. The drawing (rear cover) shows the condition of the pavement in 1961; it has been prepared from oblique photographs (Fig 78) taken at the time of its discovery and surveys made during the writer's excavations.

Unfortunately too little remains for a reliable reconstruction of its scheme, which could have been square or rectangular. The former is the more likely and will be assumed for the purposes of this description. From inside outwards its decoration consists of two concentric bands of simple guilloche in dark grey, red, yellow and white (the same colours are employed throughout). This is bordered in turn by a broad band of four-strand guilloche and voluted scrolls terminating in red, yellow and white heart-shaped leaves set within a linear frame. Along one side of the main scheme is a 'make-up' panel of three-strand guilloche converting what was probably a square scheme into a rectangle. A similar strip of guilloche probably existed on the opposite side of the pavement. It has a broad border of coarse grey limestone tesserae.

It is of technical interest that the mosaicist made an error terminating the three-strand guilloche at the end of the 'make-up' panel and that the pavement has a high quantity of fired clay tesserae: both the red and yellow tesserae come from smashed roofing tile.

In the first report on this pavement (Neal 1981a, Mosaic 60) the scheme was assumed to be of concentric type where bands of various ornament surround a square central panel. Later the writer revised his opinion on the likely overall scheme (Neal 1981b) and now believes it could have come from a scheme of overall meander worked in simple guilloche and developing squares in a quincunx arrangement, such as a mosaic from Toft Green, York, found in 1853 (RCHM *Eburacum* pl 24).

A tessera of opaque green glass was found overlying the mosaic during the excavations of 1961, but it is improbable that it ever came from the pavement under discussion. Such finds occur individually on a large number of sites; if they occurred in larger numbers a case could perhaps be made for their coming from ceiling or wall mosaics but this is improbable here.

Dating

Although the pavement sealed a secondary reinforcement wall against the north wall of the villa there is no reason to assume that it is not contemporary with the initial construction of the villa, which was no earlier than *c* AD 175 and was abandoned temporarily *c* AD 250 (Period 9, p 70).

Mosaic 3

This was originally 8m long by 2.90m wide and paved the western corridor of the villa. It was of the simplest type being composed originally of 13 alternating bands of red and buff tesserae, each band being about 200mm wide (possibly with a wider central stripe). Corridors with similar decoration are to be found within the town-houses of Verulamium and Silchester.

Dating

See Mosaic 2.

The pottery

The coarse pottery

by Yvonne Parminter

Introduction

This report describes all classes of pottery from prehistoric to medieval. Fabric descriptions are to be found on p 188.

No form series for the Roman pottery has been compiled since it was considered that it would duplicate Miss M G Wilson's extensive pottery catalogue published in the reports on the Verulamium excavations (Frere 1972 (Pot Nos 1–1293); 1983 (Pot Nos 1294–1896); 1984 (Pot Nos 1897–2697)). This catalogue has been used to parallel much of the Gorhambury pottery; parallels quoted from the Verulamium catalogue are assigned the Verulamium publication number only (expressed as *Ver* 1234, for example).

Although this policy has been adopted for most of the Roman pottery the large stratified groups of late Iron Age pottery have, in a few cases, been published as groups. Drawings of some of these vessels are already published in simplified form in Thomson 1982. The same form numbers and categories are used to indicate which of the various zone types are present; the information given in the list of Belgic forms (p 177) is based on these.

Although forms are referred to the sources quoted, the assemblage has been fully examined by fabric, and percentages of local and traded wares are presented (Table 8). The lack of statistical work within the Verulamium volumes is therefore partly redressed as it is likely that the percentages of local and traded wares, at least for the first and second centuries, reflect the trading pattern within the town itself. However, it is less likely to reflect the pattern of pottery fabrics in the third and fourth centuries since in this period the Gorhambury villa was in decline and perhaps only a limited range of late pottery arrived there.

Method

To facilitate the dating of individual contexts and the preparation of an archive, every rim from separate vessels, context by context, was sketched onto a card. This archive accompanies the pottery in Verulamium Museum. When an archive vessel (AV) is recorded in the text it refers to a drawn vessel. Bracketed numbers accompanying the AV numbers are the contexts under which the pottery and card indexes are arranged.

The total assemblage was examined using a x20 binocular microscope; rims and sherds were then placed in a numerical fabric series, and each individual vessel rim given a form category. In the fabric description list (p 188), fabric numbers are not consecutive, having been amalgamated as work progressed. A Munsell soil colour chart was used for final colour identification. Rims and sherds were recorded on coding sheets indicating fabric, form, weight, vessel diameter, decoration, base form and dimensions. This information was finally programmed into a computer, the results providing the data for the detailed constituents of this report.

The total weight of body sherds recovered from the excavation was about 1337 kilograms. This can be divided into the following groups:

1	Early prehistoric	4.498
2	Late Iron Age and Roman	1290.000
3	Medieval	42.463

Early prehistoric

Fabric Nos include 50, 66, 124, 140, 154, 157, 160, 187, 188, 192, 213.

Early prehistoric pottery was found scattered over a wide area of the site but fairly thin-walled, flint-tempered pottery (Fabric 66) (Fig 152, Nos 1–4) was found associated with Building 1 (area 3116–17, p 9, and included four rim sherds. Charcoal found with the sherds was submitted to Harwell for C14 tests (Harwell report No 3484) which gave a result of 4810±80 BP (3513–3389 cal BC (Pearson *et al* 1986)), 2860 bc, late Neolithic.

Pottery descriptions

Forms represented by Nos 1, 2 and 4 appear to come from fairly large, wide-mouthed jars. No 1 has a simple rim while No 4, identical in fabric (and conceivably therefore from the same vessel), has a slight bead. No 2, a much thicker-walled vessel in a finer grey fabric, probably came from a larger form; No 3 appears to be a bowl. Other body sherds in Fabric 66 were also recovered; these could not be joined with the rims illustrated but suggest gently rounded profiles and perhaps originally came from Nos 1 and 4.

A second group of prehistoric pottery is identified as Bronze Age and was also widely scattered about the site. However, a rimless urn, very fragmented, with sherds weighing approximately 2500 grammes, was found in area 2022 (context 424) and a heavy concentration of sherds, almost certainly forming another vessel, was found in area 2520 (context 1020). These are believed to have been funerary. Unfortunately both vessels were too fragmentary for worthwhile illustration but the former was large, with a body diameter of about 400mm.

A third vessel attributed to the Bronze Age by C Saunders of Verulamium Museum is represented by No 5, Fig 152, a fairly straight-sided urn in Fabric 192. It has holes, perhaps for suspension or a covering, around its rim. Its original soot-blackened surface survives in places (elsewhere the flint tempering is revealed) and it is soot-blackened internally.

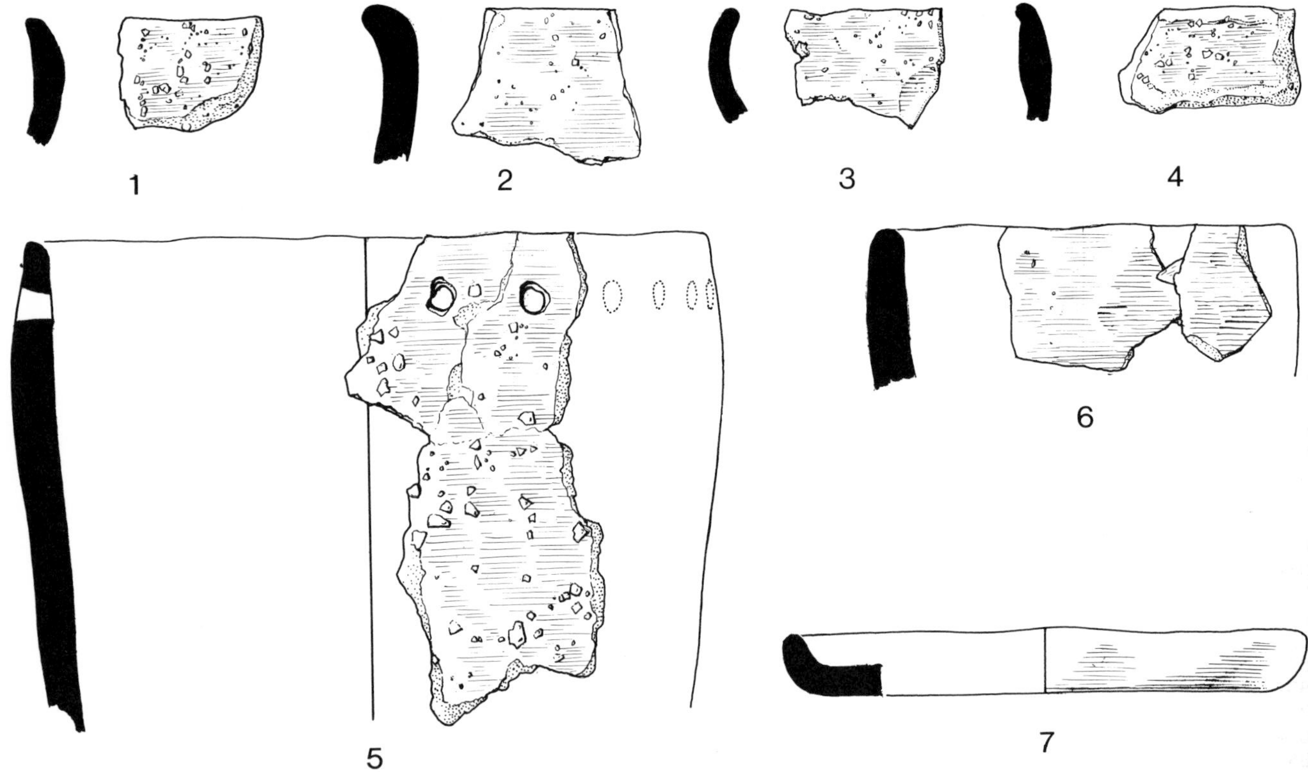

Fig 152 The prehistoric pottery, Nos 1–7 (Scale 1:2)

The Belgic and Roman pottery

Table 8 Summary of wares*

Fabric group and numbers (Fabric descriptions pp 188ff)		*Numbered vessel rims*	*%Total*	*Weight*	*%Total*
Verulamium area cream ware	1, 23, 161	1855	15%	252.88k	19.60%
Verulamium reduced ware	17, 22, 36	353	2.85%	27.18k	2.10%
Belgic ware	20	1108	8.96%	254k	19.68%
Later Belgic ware	37, 49, 71, 76, 80, 86, 88, 92, 96	142	1.14%	32.36k	2.50%
Belgic shelly ware	52, 97, 1111, 193	6	.04%	.60k	.04%
E Herts/W Essex grey ware	16, 27, 175	1138	9.21%	81.46k	6.31%
Imported fine ware	9, 73, 78, 106, 122, 143–4, 145. 153, 162, 173–4, 179, 201	90	.72%	6.91k	.53%
Local fine ware	167, 170, 177	147	1.18%	13.12k	1.01%
Misc grey ware	7, 53, 56, 72, 110, 112, 149, 185, 206	162	1.31%	13.26k	1.02%
Mortaria	1, 14, 35, 47, 65, 77, 79, 220	119	.96%	16.52k	1.28%
Imported mortaria	68, 168, 205	14	.10%	5.42k	.42%
BB1 ware	5	252	2.03%	9.24k	.71%
BB2 ware	12, 95	134	1.08%	3.82k	.29%
Local BB ware	119, 137	116	.93%	16.28k	1.26%
Hadham ware	11, 18, 164	189	1.52%	21.84k	1.69%
Nene Valley ware	13, 189	133	1.07%	17.27k	1.33%
Shelly ware	6	76	.61%	16.64k	1.29%
Oxford ware	2, 44, 48,	83	.67%	5.81k	.45%
Micaceous grey ware	90, 159	21	.16%	2.28k	.17%
Micaceous oxidised ware	21, 38, 94	70	.56%	4.30k	.33%
Amphorae	4, 181, 200, 202	22	.17%	43.10k	3.34%
Pink grogged ware	127	16	.12%	12.20k	.94%

* Table 8 is a summary of information from the computer catalogues. The first column gives the fabric numbers, later amalgamated, of the more common fabrics, the second the number of drawn rims from separate vessels and the third, their percentage of the total weight. The last two columns indicate the weight of each fabric by body sherds only and their percentage of the overall total.

Table 9 Belgic forms in Fabric 20 (Fabric described p 188)

Thompson form nos	*Context nos*	*AV nos*	*Published pot nos*
Pedestal urn base			
A1	1679	5	54
Finer ware jars			
B1–1	1679	11 & 16	34 & 40
B1–2*	1804	37 & 40	–
B1–3	77	105	63
B1–4*	1679	8 & 23	33 & 35
B1–5	105	6	15
B2–1	1679	15	42
B2–2	1679	13	39
B3–1	1804	8	23
B3–3	1669	74	–
B3–4	77	111	–
B3–5*	77	72	65
B33–6	1804	17	22
B3–8	105	9	17
B3–10	1679	20	37
B5–2	1595	4	–
B5–4	131	11	–
B5–5	1804	46	28
Coarser ware jars			
C1–2	77	54	68
C1–3	1804	45	30
C1–4	77	48	69
C5–1*	1804	44	29
C5–3	77A	4	85
C6–1	1804	18	27
C7–1*	105	10	13
C7–2*	105	3	14
Bowls			
D1–1	77	91	71
D1–2	105	14	8
D1–4	105	12 & 4	9 & 10
D2–1	77	45	73
D2–3	269	5	55
D2–4	1804	30	–
D2–5	77	88	74
D3–1	1651	2	–
D3–2+	77	66	75
D3–4	3141	13	–
Cups			
E1–1	1679	22	47
E1–2	105	13	16
E1–4	1804	42	25
E2–1	1679	39	44
E2–3	1588	6	–
E3–1	77	76	76
E3–3	77	115	–
E3–5	105	15	18
Platter copies and shallow bowls			
G1–1*	1587	2	–
G1–2	1679	41	50
G1–3*	1679	9	49
G1–4	1804	2	31
G1–5	91	65	–
G1–6	77	3	77
G1–9	1679	40	45
G1–10	77	57	79
G1–11	77	9	80
G2–2	77	47	81
G2–3	77	26	82
G2–4	885	8	–
G2–5	2334	2	–
G2–6	77	28	83
Girth beakers			
G4+	1679	25	48
Butt-beakers			
G5–1	1804	6	24
G5–2	1679	2	52
G5–3	77	116	84
G5–5	269	1	62
Grog-tempered jugs			
G6	1804	20	26
Lids			
L1	269	4	57
L2	77	83	–
L6	77	64	86
L7	1590	10	–
L8	105	7	19
L9	3141	9	–
Tripod vessel			
S1	1792	1	–
S2	1073	6 ('Legs' only)	

The Late Iron Age ('Belgic') pottery

As can be seen from Table 8, 'Belgic' ware (grog-tempered fabric, Fabric 20) is the second most common fabric from the villa with 1256 numbered vessel rims represented, including the 'later Belgic ware'. The fabric comprises 22.20% of the total weight of body sherds examined.

Belgic pottery was found throughout the site but, not unexpectedly, the greatest number of vessels came from the ditches of Periods 3–5, *c* AD 20–43 (pottery groups from contexts 105, 1804 and 269, Figs 153 and 154), but much continued into post-conquest levels, especially in context 77 (Fig 155), the fill of Ditch 74. Here it has been noted that the fabric of the later pottery gradually became sandier and the vessels more 'Romanised', having lost the finer variations of the traditional forms. Grog is still present but more finely crushed.

Table 9 defines the form group and number, based on the Belgic grog-tempered form series published by Thompson (Thompson 1982) together with the context and archive vessel number from the Gorhambury card index record; the vessels are in Fabric 20 only. The table indicates also the local Hertfordshire area forms as defined by Thompson, and forms particularly comparable with pottery groups from Prae Wood. Forms marked with an asterisk are found in the Zone 7 area (Hertfordshire and the Chilterns) and those with a + symbol are found particularly at Prae Wood. All the Thompson forms are fairly common in the 'Belgic' pottery from Gorhambury with the exception of form S2 (tripod vessels). Forms B3–8, D1–1, D3–4, G1–11, G2–4 and G4 are present together with others in the later 'Belgic' fabrics.

Pottery groups in Fabric 20

Context 105 (Period 3; Fig 153, nos 8–21)

The potttery from context 105 (Period 3) (Table 10, Fig 153, nos 8–21) is represented by semi-complete vessels and probably includes little residual material. It has been fully illustrated therefore and is used as the main 'type series' of native wares, further supplemented by pottery from contexts 1804, 1679, 269 and 77 (A–C) which broadens the range. The types represented are related to Thompson's form numbers and the archive vessel number is given. All the forms fit into the Prae Wood date range of AD 4–40/45.

Table 10 Pottery from context 105, illustrated examples

Nos	*Vessel type*	*Thompson form no*	*AV no*
8	Fine bowl	D1–2	14
9	Fine bowl	D1–4	12
10	Bowl	D1–4	4
11	Coarse jar	C7–1	5
12	Coarse jar	C7–1	11
13	Coarse jar	C7–1	10
14	Coarse jar	C7–2	3
15	Fine jar	B1–5	6
16	Bowl	E1–2	13
17	Fine jar	B3–8	9
18	Cup	E3–5	15
19	Lid	L1	7
20	Base	(none given)	8
21	Coarse jar	C6–1	16

Context 1804 (Period 4; Fig 153, Nos 22–31)

This group of pottery (Table 11), from the ditch terminals flanking the causeway linking Enclosure A and B, is all Belgic in fabric and form, and comparable to the pottery from Prae Wood (Thompson 1982), the exception being a terra nigra platter base (AV 23), very micaceous and paralleled at Skeleton Green in a group dated to *c* AD 20 (Partridge 1981). Common vessels in the group are storage jars (form C6–1 (No 27)) and simple jars with everted rims and neck cordons. Furrowed jars such as No 12 are numerous. Less common are the E1–4 plain carinated cups (No 25) and the jug form G6 (No 20), a Camulodunum 165 copy (Hawkes and Hull 1947, pl LXIII). The latter has a direct parallel in the Prae Wood pottery, there dated *c* AD 30–50; two similar jugs are among the Gorhambury assemblage. Additional forms in this group are represented by examples from other contexts: these include Nos 8, 9, 12, 17, 21, 32, 34, 35 and 37 on Figs 153 and 154.

Table 11 Pottery from context 1804, illustrated examples

Nos	*Vessel type*	*Thompson form no*	*AV no*
22	Fine jar	B3–6	17
23	Fine jar	B3–1	8
24	Barrel butt-beaker	G5–1	6
25	Cup	E1–4	42
26	Jug	G6	20
27	Storage jar	C6–1	18
28	Coarse jar	B5–5	46
29	Coarse jar	C5–1	44
30	Coarse jar	C1–3	45
31	Platter	G1–4	2

Context 1679 (Period 4 or 5; Fig 154, Nos 32–54)

This context (Table 12) represents a primary layer of occupation material within Building 13 situated in the north-west corner of Enclosure A, area 29–3022. The whole group is in Fabric 20, except for a number of early prehistoric vessels, one imported terra nigra platter (No 51) and a fine ware imported butt-beaker (No 53).

Table 12 Pottery from context 1679, illustrated examples

Nos	*Vessel type*	*Thompson form no*	*AV no*
32	Bowl	D1–2	14
33	Fine jar	B1–4	8
34	Fine jar	B1–1	11
35	Fine jar	B1–4	23
36	Fine jar	B3–1	1
37	Fine jar	B3–10	20
38	Coarse jar	C7–1	6
39	Fine jar	B2–2	13
40	Fine jar	B1–1	16
41	Bowl	D1–4	17
42	Fine jar	B2–1	15
43	Fine jar	B3–10	26
44	Cup	E2–1	39
45	Platter	G1–9	40
46	Fine jar	B3–10	33
47	Carinated cup/bowl	E1–1	22
48	Girth beaker	G4	25
49	Platter	G1–3	9
50	Platter	G1–2	41
51	Terra nigra platter	–	38
52	Barrel butt-beaker	G5–2	2
53	Gallo-Belgic butt-beaker	–	36
54	Pedestal base	A1	5

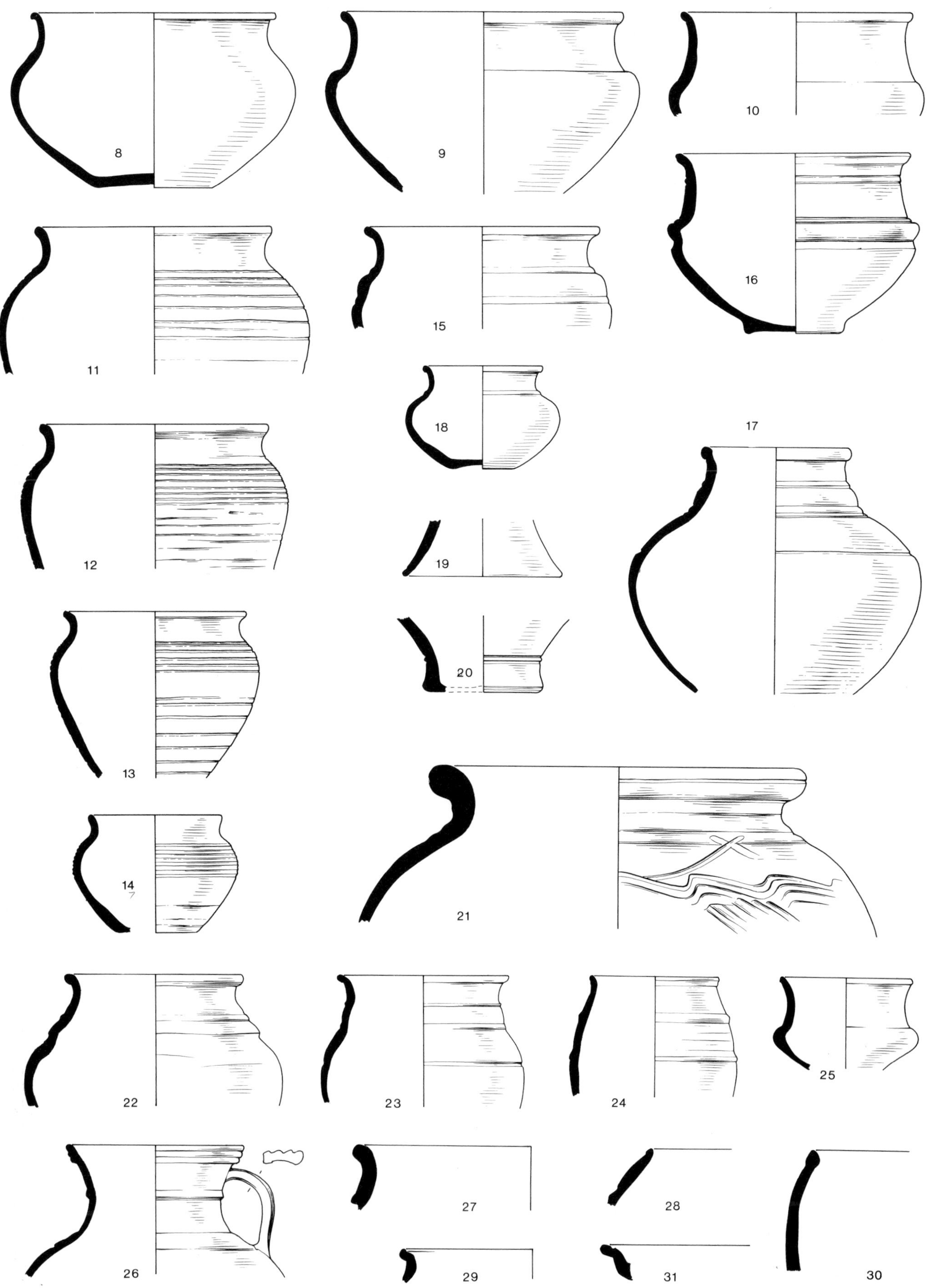

Fig 153 Late Iron Age pottery, Nos 8–31 (Scale 1:4)

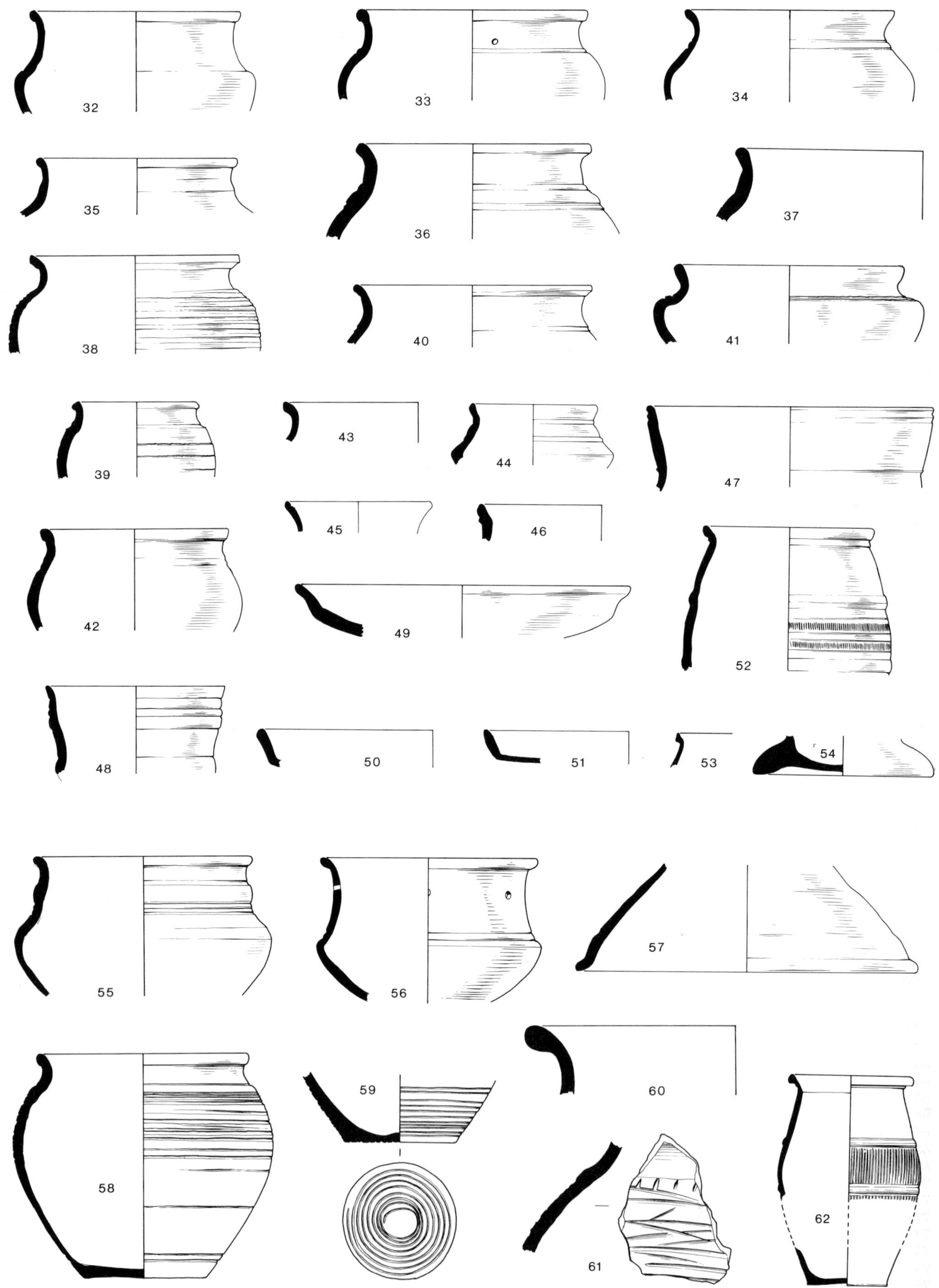

Fig 154 Late Iron Age pottery, Nos 32–62 (Scale 1:4)

Context 269 (Fig 154)

Context 269 (Table 13) represents the primary fill of Ditch 74, attributed to Period 5. All vessels but one are in native fabric 20, grog-tempered, black or dark grey. The exception is No 55, a copy of a Camulodunum 113 butt-beaker (Hawkes and Hull 1947, pl LVII) in a Belgic fabric without grog but tempered with fine shell. Of interest is a base from a coarse jar (No 59) with spiral decoration. There is a parallel at Skeleton Green (Partridge 1981, Fig 31.82) with a group dated *c* AD37. Another base (not illustrated, AV 11) has a wide central hole drilled out, possibly reused as a spindle-whorl.

Table 13 Pottery from context 269, illustrated examples

Nos	*Vessel type*	*Thompson form no*	*AV no*
55	Bowl	D2–3	5
56	Bowl	D1–2	6
57	Lid	L1	4
58	Coarse jar	C7–1	7
59	Coarse jar (base)	?C7–1	3
60	Storage jar	C6–1	2
61	Striated sherd from storage jar	C6–1	8
62	Butt-beaker	G5–5	1

Context 77 (including 77 a–c; Fig 155)

This was a layer of occupation material, possibly derived from Building 21, in the filling of Ditch 74. Apart from a wide variety of Roman coarseware forms (Table 15) and first-century imported fine wares, there was a range of Roman pottery in Fabric 20, probably the work of native potters. These are illustrated and listed, again with the Thompson form numbers (Table 14). On the evidence of published examples from Verulamium the deposit is dated no later than *c* AD 75.

Table 14 Pottery from context 77, illustrated examples

Nos	*Vessel type*	*Thompson form no*	*AV no*
63	Jar	B1–3	105
64	Jar	B1–5	98
65	Jar	B3–5	72
66	Jar	B3–8	145
67	Jar	B3–10	2
68	Jar	C1–2	54
69	Jar	C1–4	48
70	Jar	C7–1	15
71	Bowl	D1–1	91
72	Bowl	D1–4	86
73	Bowl	D2–1	45
74	Bowl	D2–5	88
75	Bowl	D3–2	66
76	Cup	E3–1	76
77	Platter	G1–6	3
78	Platter	G1–9	22
79	Shallow bowl	G1–10	57
80	Platter	G1–11	9
81	Bowl	G2–2	47
82	Bowl	G2–3	26
83	Bowl	G2–6	28
84	Butt-beaker	G5–2	116
85	Butt-beaker	G5–5	4
86	Lid	L–6	64

The Roman pottery

As stated in the introduction, the Roman wares could, almost without exception, be paralleled by pottery published in *Verulamium* (Frere 1972; 1983; 1984) and therefore little is illustrated; most of the deposits were from the upper filling of earlier ditches and contained much residual material. However two contexts were of significance: context 77 in Ditch 74, which contained the assemblage of native types previously noted (Fig 155) and context 258, the filling of a timber-lined latrine (257) sealed beneath Building 37 (area 2121, Fig 48) and believed to be related to the occupation of Building 27 (Table 16 and Fig 156). The latest date of the pottery from context 77 is *c* AD 75 and from context 258 *c* AD 175.

Context 77

Some coarse wares from this deposit are listed below; the deposit also contained stamped first-century fine wares described by Valery Rigby (p 195).

The general assemblage included:
Terra nigra butt-beaker (Fab 78) AV1.
Terra rubra butt-beaker (Fab 201) AV4 (77c).
Gallo-Belgic butt-beaker (Fab 9) as *Camulodunum* 113, AV5.
Lyons ware cup and beakers (Fab 144) AV1, AV4, AV56, AV118, AV151.
Mica-dusted beakers (Fab 162) AV40, AV108, AV365.
North Gaul eggshell-ware cups (Fab 173 and 174) AV 147, AV4 (77B stamped Silvanus *c* AD 60–85).
'Pompeian' red ware dishes (Fab 179) AV41, AV52.

Apart from Fabric 20, the most common fabrics in this deposit were Fabrics 1 and 16. Forms in these fabrics are set out in Table 15 and the same fabrics are listed in Table 17, which shows the range and number of vessel types over the whole site.

Table 15

Fabric 1	*Fabric 16*
AV13, *Ver* 206, AD 60–75	AV5, *Ver* 133, AD 60–75
AV18, *Ver* 212, AD 60–75	AV6, *Ver* 148, AD 60–75
AV23, *Ver* 173, AD 60–75	AV27, *Ver* 27, AD 60–75
AV61, *Ver* 334, AD 85–105	AV45, *Ver* 150, AD 60–75
AV73, *Ver* 211, AD 60–75	
AV112, *Ver* 245, AD 85–105	

Fig 155 Late Iron Age pottery from context 77, Nos 63–86 (Scale 1:4)

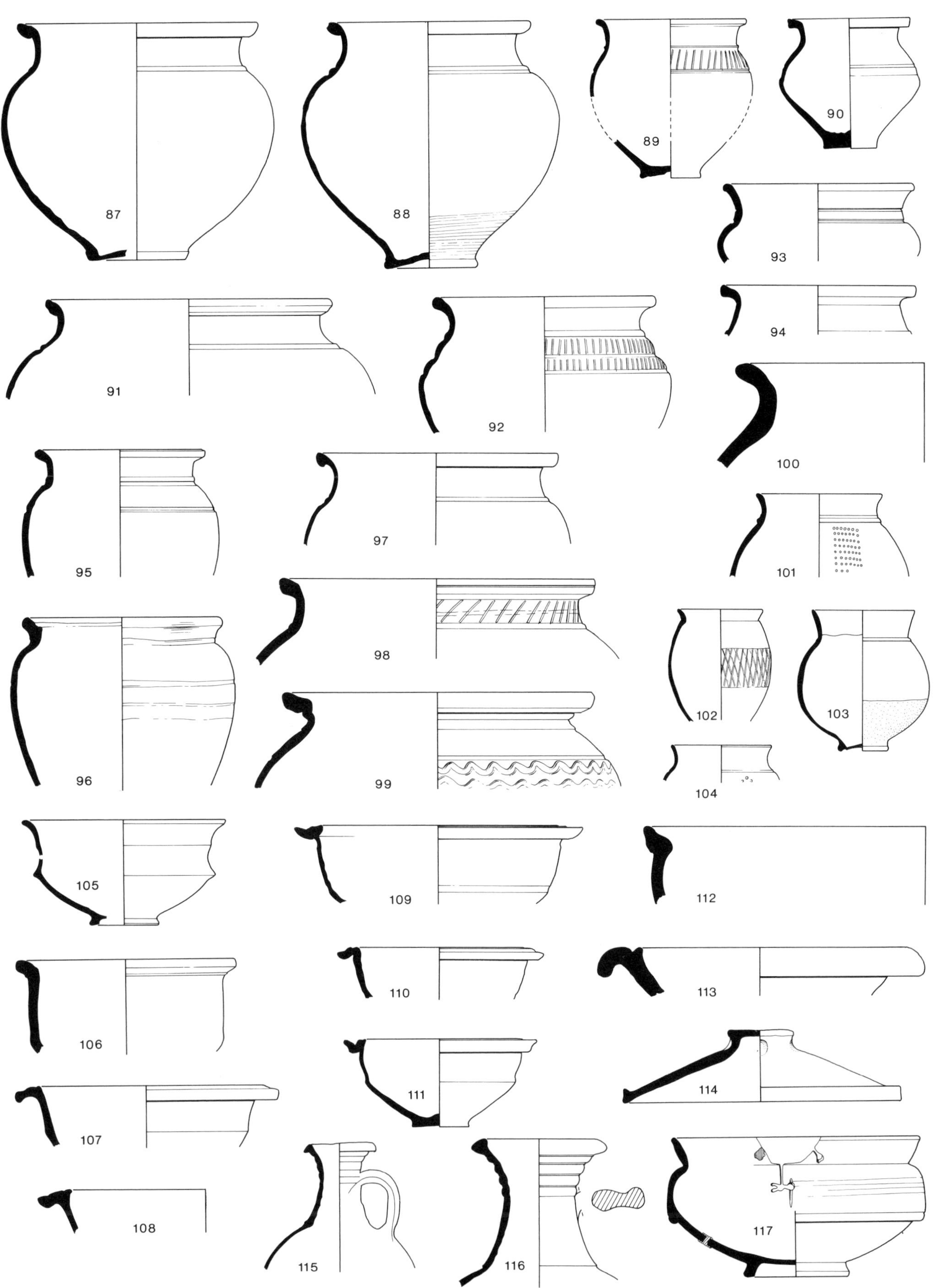

Fig 156 Roman pottery from the filling of a latrine, Nos 87–117 (Scale 1:4)

Table 16 Pottery from context 258, Fig 156

Nos	*Vessel type*	*Ver no*	*Date*	*AV no*
87	Jar	881	135–80	2
88	Jar	281	90–105	12
89	Jar	–	–	45
90	Beaker	646	130–50	1
91	Jar	647	130–50	14
92	Jar	610	135–55	15
93	Jar	–	–	39
94	Jar	486	105–15	34
95	Jar	435	105–30	30
96	Jar	666	130–80	26
97	Jar	873	150–80	27
98	Storage jar	–	–	42
99	Storage jar	–	–	23
100	Storage jar	–	–	41
101	Beaker	428	110–60	10
102	Beaker	429	105–40	24
103	Beaker	–	–	36
104	Beaker	604	110–60	19
105	Bowl	–	–	40
106	Bowl	489	115–30	17
107	Bowl	692	140–50	25
108	Reeded-rim bowl	2432	120–45	6
109	Reeded-rim bowl	671	135–60	33
110	Reeded-rim bowl	931	130–70	5
111	Reeded-rim bowl	683	135–85	4
112	Bowl	2419	130–60	28
113	Mortarium (stamped)	760	110–50	7
114	Lid	–	–	44
115	Flagon	808	150–155/60	9
116	Flagon	809	150–155/60	8
117	Samian form Drag 44	–	Antonine	13

Several sherds had graffiti. These included a lid with a human figure wearing a baggy tunic (No 1039, Fig 145) and a grey ware base inscribed around the circumference . . .]LAỊONVS IΛΛ[. . ., Ian[varius(?) Be]latonus (Hassall and Tomlin 1982, 413).

Miscellaneous forms (Fig 157)

Vessel 118, Fabric 1, AV 24, from context 721, to the south of Building 30, is a 'quadruple vase' or perhaps a candle holder (Young 1977, 91). More commonly this class of vessel has a triple arrangement of cups on a base ring but from the distribution of holes on the ring, leaving space for another two, it would seem there were originally four cups. Since the Verulamium potteries largely died out towards the end of the second century, this piece is probably Antonine.

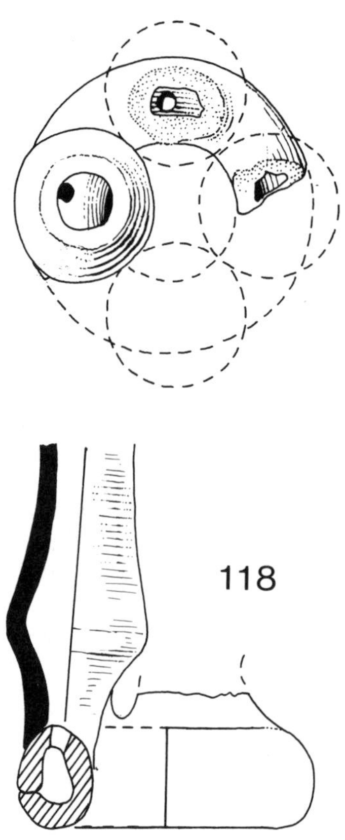

Fig 157 Quadruple vase or candle holder in Verulamium region fabric, No 118 (Scale 1:2)

Table 17 Ratio of vessel types in Fabrics 20, 1 and 16

	Fab 20	*%*	*Fab 1*	*%*	*Fab 16*	*%*
Jars	862	79.3	924	55.3	661	68.0
Beaker jars	14	1.3	12	0.7	71	7.3
Storage jars	88	8.1	18	1.1	–	–
Bowls	54	4.9	430	25.7	106	10.9
Shallow bowls/platters	58	5.3	50	3.0	85	8.7
Beakers	2	0.18	6	0.4	33	3.4
Flagons/jugs	2	0.18	120	7.2	6	0.6
Lids	7	0.64	110	6.6	10	1.0
Total count of vessel forms %		*Fab 20*		*Fab 1*		*Fab 16*
Jars		35.22		37.76		27.01
Beaker jars		14.43		12.37		53.57
Storage jars		91.66		16.98		–
Bowls		9.15		72.88		17.96
Shallow bowls/platters		30.05		25.90		44.04
Beakers		4.87		14.63		80.48
Flagons/jugs		1.56		93.75		4.68
Lids		5.51		86.61		7.87

Discussion

Fabric 1, the cream gritty fabric produced in the Verulamium region, including Brockley Hill, was one of the most common Roman fabrics and formed 19.60% of the total. The same figure applies to reduced wares (Fabric 22) which have a similar fabric description to Fabric 1 and which are also likely to be products of the Verulamium region. From Period 6, *c* AD 43–62, until Period 10, *c* AD 250–300, by which time the variation of forms had declined, this ware provided the bulk of the basic heavier household vessels including jars of all sizes, bowls, flagons and mortaria. Less common forms included face jugs, local copies of amphorae, tazzae, and the quadruple vessel. Together with grey ware Fabric 16, which provided the finer table wares, Fabric 1 continued to dominate the villa pottery. By Period 11, *c* AD 300–350, traded wares from the later industries had superseded 1, 16 and black burnished wares (although these may have been copied and produced locally: cp Fabric 119); Oxford and Nene Valley colour-coated products as well as Much Hadham oxidised vessels replaced the grey wares. Shell-tempered fabrics provided large jars and bowls, and pink grogged fabric, 127, perhaps the late continuation of Fabric 20, provided some storage jars. However there are relatively few late products such as shelly wares from Harrold (Beds), Oxford or the Nene Valley (as can be seen in Table 8) when compared with other villas outside the region. For example, at Bancroft, Bucks, large groups of fourth-century pottery indicate a flourishing occupation to the end of the fourth century. At Gorhambury all indications are that the villa was in decline, or perhaps that there had been a change of status in the estate. As the Fabric 1 industry diminished, perhaps due to economic depression in the area, it became a local supplier only and the range of forms was limited to simple jars with 'wedge'-shaped rims and both flanged and large bowls.

Apart from the Verulamium industry itself it would appear that most pottery, until the fourth century, when Oxford and Nene Valley wares were traded, came from the south or east of Verulamium: the London area, east Hertfordshire and west Essex. If first-century fine ware imports arrived via traditional trade routes from Colchester to Verulamium, it is possible that this pattern continued and that the products of nearby mid first-century kilns (perhaps those at Hadham) producing fine table wares became part of the traded merchandise. Many of the fine grey ware vessels in Fabric 16, while not identical with true Hadham reduced fabric, 18, are essentially similar and it is suggested that the Hadham area kilns could have produced them. Paler buff-grey 'London' wares and soft, underfired, micaceous grey wares also bear a great resemblance to the same fabric.

It can be seen from Table 17, which compares the frequency of vessel types in Fabrics 20, 1 and 16, that jars were the dominant product. Next to jars, storage jars were the most common in Fabric 20 but a much reduced percentage (1.1% compared to 8.1%) of this class of pottery was produced in the Verulamium region kilns, while none are represented in Fabric 16. Changes in culinary preparation and table wares from the 'Belgic' to the Roman periods are clearly demonstrated by a comparison between the frequency of bowls in Fabrics 20 and 1 with 4.9% and 25.7% respectively. Similarly, there is a marked increase in the use of flagons and jugs, from 0.18% to 7.2%. Numerically there is a similar ratio of shallow bowls/platters between the 'Belgic' and Verulamium fabrics although the percentages 5.3% and 3.0% suggest that the coarser Verulamium products were less favoured. This is perhaps supported by the 8.7% ratio for the finer wares of Fabric 16. The use of Fabric 16 for finer table wares is clearly demonstrated in the beakers with 3.4% compared to 0.18% and 0.4% for Fabrics 20 and 1.

The medieval pottery (Figs 158 and 159)

by David S Neal

Medieval pottery was concentrated in two areas, area 19–2114–17 and in the filling of quarry pits, area 12–1322 to the west of the site (Fig 1). Three principal fabrics can be identified: 15, 28 and 118; the earliest, 118 (p 190), being a shelly ware of St Neots type with smooth, 'soapy' surfaces. It was found in area 2016 in horizons (549) associated with a bowl-shaped pit (607) containing charred grain and believed to have been a simple corn-drying oven. Two cooking pots were represented (Nos 119 and 120, Fig 158) and were also associated with vessels in Fabric 15 (p 188) and 28 (p 189), the ubiquitous 'Hertfordshire grey' or 'reduced wares' which come in a variety of shades depending on the reduction process.

Unfortunately, no single medieval deposit produced a wide assemblage of pottery in Fabrics 15 and 28 and therefore the forms represented (Nos 119–178, Fig 158) are taken from a variety of contexts including the following:

Nos 119–130	549	Possible corn-drying oven, area 2016
Nos 131–143	590, 1334, 1337	Gully post-dating 549 above, area 2116
Nos 144–157	1322	Lime kiln, Structure 57 (Fig 109), area 2116–17
Nos 158–174	519, 1217	Hollow in area 2015–16 interpreted as a pond (Fig 107)
Nos 175–176	4	Lower ploughsoil
No 177	546	Cesspit, area 2018
No 178	501	Upper fill of ditch; south side of Enclosure B, area 20–2316

The quantity of medieval pottery recovered from the excavation was perhaps too small for reliable statistical work to be carried out but cooking pots appear to have been the most common class of vessel followed by bowls and jugs. More specialised forms included skillets (No 141), cressets (No 157), curfews (No 158), storage jars (No 178) and 'bottles' (No 179, Fig 159).

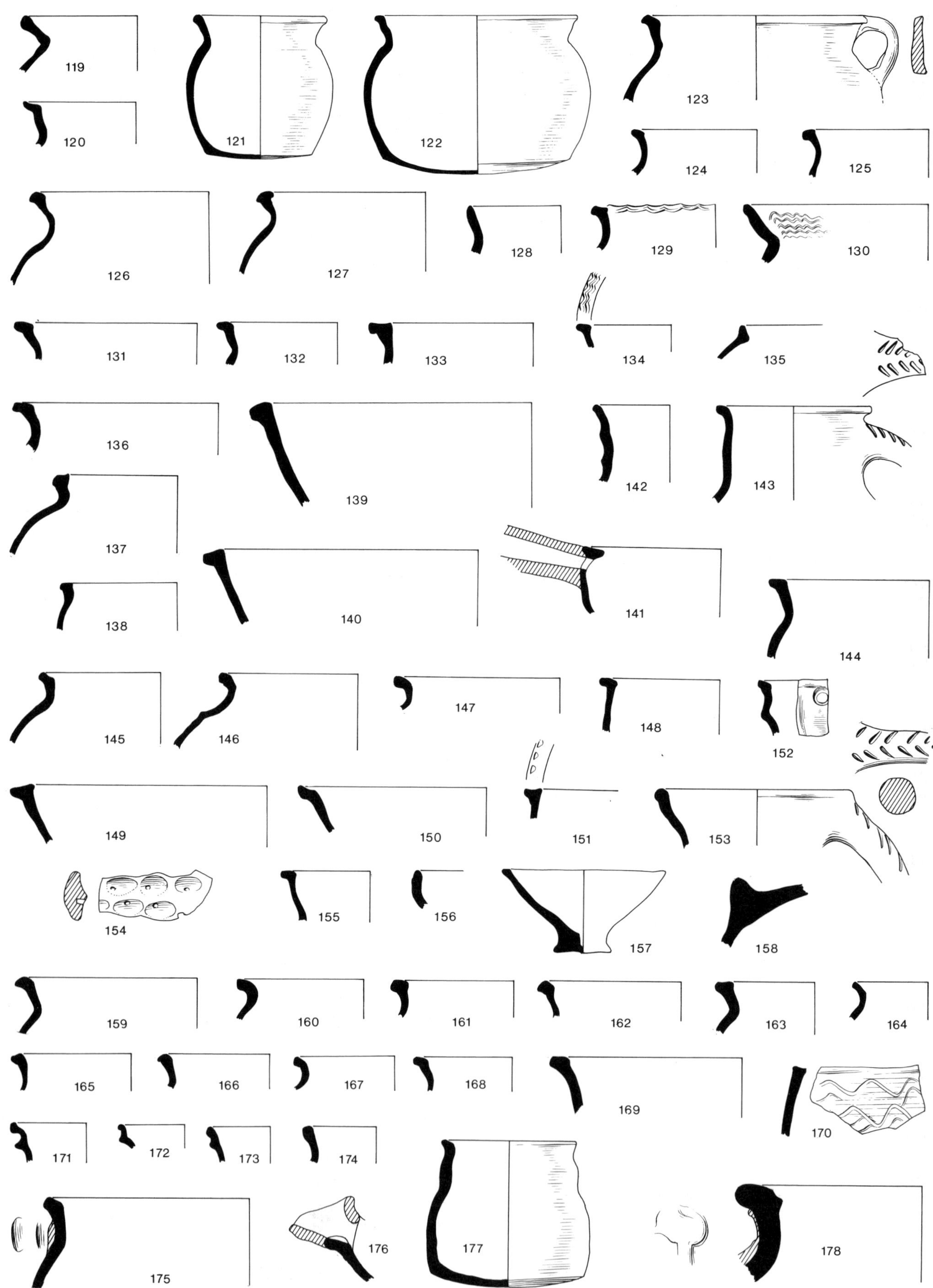

Fig 158 Medieval pottery, Nos 119–175 (Scale 1:4)

Cooking pots

Two sizes of vessel can be identified: medium and large, with rim diameters ranging from approximately 200–300mm and 300–400mm respectively. The larger vessels, which could also have been used as storage jars, were reinforced with horizontal applied strips with finger-impressed decoration (as No 175). Several examples, as No 129, had finger-impressed decoration on the rim, while another, larger form (No 130) had combing on the inside rim. The rim profiles were unusually 'squared', although it is possible that early examples were generally more rounded since several examples of this type were found with the St Neots ware type in a demonstrably earlier context. No 123 had a small strap-handle, possibly one of a pair.

Bowls

This type of vessel is exemplified by Nos 139, 149 and 150. Some rims are either rounded or slightly 'squared' while others, such as No 150, are kicked up and slightly concave on the inside surface, perhaps as a lid seating. No 151, which might be a straight-walled bowl, had finger-nail decoration on its upper rim.

Another possible bowl (No 170) had a fairly vertical wall with only a slight 'rim' which, from its 'kicked-up' outer edge, may have had an applied spout or a handle. Unusually, it was decorated with shallow horizontal grooves superimposed by wavy lines, a technique noted on a possible jug (No 134).

Jugs

No complete profile was recovered. The rims and necks appear to be of two types: simple straight-necked vessels with rounded, slightly splayed rims, such as No 143, and cordoned-necked vessels as No 142. No distinction in date is possible. The jugs were unglazed, except No 152 which had an impressed circle, possibly the eye from a face-jug. A very small sherd had indications of an applied horse. The handles were all unglazed; some were plain rod handles while others such as No 153 had slashed decoration. Handle No 154 had deep finger impressions, each impression stabbed.

Skillets

A bowl-shaped form (No 141) had a tubular ?handle opening through the wall of the vessel just below the rim. Whether it doubled as a pouring vessel is uncertain. Another skillet or bowl (No 176), possibly somewhat shallower, had a spout.

Cressets

Two cressets (as 157), almost identical in type, were found; one was fire-blackened (possibly a lid has been used as a cresset).

Curfew

No 158, a fragment from the upper part of a fire cover, has a diameter of approximately 500mm. No 'rim' sherds which could be attributed to this vessel type were noted although their forms can easily be mistaken for large bowls.

Bottle (Fig 159)

This 'bottle' or narrow-necked flask was also in Hertfordshire grey ware (Fabric 15) with fairly smooth, buff surfaces. Its wall was slightly dented by contact with other vessels in the kiln and it had a scar on the base, which was slightly kicked and had 'cheese-wire' marks. It is complete. It was found in 1956 and came from the filling of a ditch, believed to be the upper filling of the late Iron Age, Period 4, enclosure ditch, area 2316. No other examples of the form have been identified in the assemblage found between 1972 and 1982, nor was the type represented among the products from the Chandlers Cross kiln (see discussion). Dr D Renn, who notified the writer of the existence of this vessel in Verulamium Museum, comments that it is of the same form as 'bottles' produced in London-type ware found at Trigg Lane, London and dated *c* AD 1240 (Pearce *et al* 1985, fig 64.302), although these vessels are smaller.

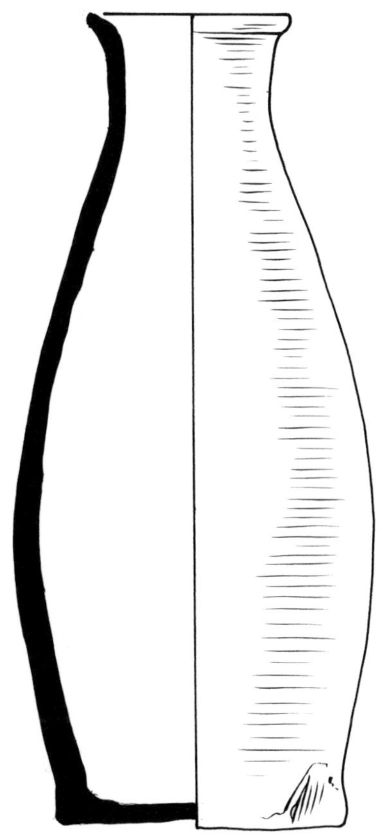

Fig 159 Medieval pottery: 'bottle' No 179 (Scale 1:2)

Discussion

The bulk of the assemblage can be attributed to the eleventh to thirteenth centuries, with the St Neots type vessels possibly being of tenth- to eleventh-century date. The lack of other classes of fabrics, such as Surrey wares, a lack also noted at Kings Langley (Hurst 1977, 155) in late thirteenth-century contexts, would suggest that occupation of the medieval site ceased at about this time. Much of the pottery can be paralleled in form to the pottery produced at the Chandlers Cross kiln (Neal forthcoming) with the exception of the combed vessels. A dearth of glazed products was also noted at Chandlers Cross where glaze was restricted to decorated jugs which, from the evidence of many hundredweight of sherds, represented only a fraction of the overall output. It appears that they may have been special products, perhaps to order, fired with the more mundane forms. Reference to the Chandlers Cross kiln is not intended to suggest that the kiln in question supplied the St Albans area, but that the vessels produced by contemporary potters in Hertfordshire and Buckinghamshire were of very similar type. The unusual 'bottle' suggests that London-type ware products were also being copied.

Fabric descriptions

All fabrics are Roman except where stated otherwise; some fabrics are unprovenanced. For mortaria fabrics see Nos 1, 1A, 2, 14, 35, 44, 47, 65, 68, 77, 79, 168, 197, 205, 220 and 221.

Fabric no

1 Verulamium region kiln products. This covers the range of local wares in cream fabric; however those firing with a distinct difference in colour have been given separate fabric numbers. Inclusions are generally abundant quartz particles of similar size evenly distributed throughout the fabric. For mortaria fabric description see p 193
Decoration: sparse on most forms but frilling, faces etc on jugs
Munsell range: 7.5YR 8/3 – 5YR 7/6 core

1A Verulamium region fabric used for mortaria. As No 1 but finer. For K Hartley's description see p 193

2 Oxford oxidised wares. Smooth micaceous fine sandy fabric generally dull reddish-brown with a grey core; used for mortaria also (for K Hartley's description see p 194)
Decoration: red slip, white barbotine, impressed rosettes etc (Young 1977)
Munsell range: 5YR 6/4 – 5/6 & 5YR 4/4

3 Fine oxidised ware. Pale reddish-buff sandy fabric, very micaceous throughout and often with mica-dusted surfaces. Forms comparable to early fine wares from London (Marsh 1978)
Decoration: mica dusting, incised lines, rouletting and embossing
Munsell range: 10YR 8/3 surfaces – 8/1 core

4 Amphora fabric: Dressel 20. Rough thick, pale brown on surfaces and in section. Large rounded inclusions and visible mica flakes on surfaces and core. The necks and handles of several vessels show serrated surfaces left by the saw
Munsell range: 7.5YR 8/4 – 6/2/; 8/2 and 5/2

5 Black-burnished wares. Well-burnished surfaces with large abundant inclusions throughout the fabric, and noticeable colour variation
Decoration: lattice, arcading
Munsell range: 5YR N3/ – 5/2; 2.5YR N3/

6 Shell-tempered ware. Forms and fabrics similar to those from the Harrold area. Variations in surface colour from pale buff to grey-black and with considerable shell within the clay
Munsell range: 2.5YR N3/0; N4/0 – 4/2

7 Reduced ware. Harsh grey fabric with large quartz in section, visible without magnification, some measuring up to 1mm. The fabric has much in common with sherds from a kiln at Fulmer, Buckinghamshire
Decoration: white slip
Munsell range: 5YR5/4; 2.5YR N5/0; 2.5YR 4/2

9 Gallo-Belgic wares. Mostly fine butt beakers, Camulodunum form 113 and flagons. Fine hard white fabric which can have a pinkish core with very small coloured quartz inclusions and traces of mica
Decoration: rouletting
Munsell range: 10YR 8/3 surfaces – 8/1 core

11 Much Hadham oxidised wares. Bright orange or brownish-orange throughout, with sometimes a variation in the core colour. Sandy with smooth surfaces and very micaceous; the fabric is heavily gritted, with fine black inclusions and white quartz, with occasional larger pieces
Decoration: white slip, burnish
Munsell range: 5YR 6/8 surfaces; 7/6 core

12 Black-burnished wares, very similar to Fabric 5, but with finer inclusions
Decoration: lattice
Munsell range: 10YR 4/1 surfaces – 3/1 core

13 Nene Valley colour-coated wares. White fabric, on surfaces and in section, containing fine evenly-sized quartz with some larger shell pieces, which can be up to 1mm across. Scatter of pale or darker red iron
Decoration: barbotine, rouletting, scale
Munsell range: 5YR 8/4

14 Mortaria fabric. A Colchester product. For K Hartley's description see p 193
Munsell range: 7.5YR 8/4

15 Medieval. Thin, hard fabric, mid-grey throughout core with paler surfaces. In section large rounded quartz inclusions are evenly distributed, with frequent voids. See also fabric 28.
Munsell range: surfaces 2.5Y N6/ – core 2.5Y N5

16 Grey wares. Mid- to dark-grey dense fabric with fine gritty quartz particles throughout, sometimes a few blacker grits, surfaces generally paler than the core. Used for tablewares
Decoration: white slip, barbotine dots, vertical lines
Munsell range: 10YR 5/1 – 6/2; 10YR 5/3

17 Grey ware. Mid-grey coarse fabric with rounded grits on surfaces and in section
Decoration: rusticated, white slip, barbotine dots
Munsell range: 10YR 6/3

18 Much Hadham reduced wares. Fabric identical in content to Fabric 11, with the same black and white quartz grits. Generally mid-grey throughout but can have highly burnished black surfaces
Decoration: burnish lines, vertical etc
Munsell range: 5YR 4/1 – 4/3

20 Local 'Belgic' native wares. 'Belgic' grog-tempered fabric used for forms which are paralleled in Verulamium and Prae Wood. Generally reddish-brown soft surfaces with grey-black section. The clay contains much grog tempering, up to 4mm in size with a scatter of shell. The surfaces are reduced on some vessels with good burnishing; both types feel smooth and soapy
Decoration: burnish, scored lines
Munsell range: 10YR 4/2 – 5/1 & 5YR N3/0 – N4/

21 Oxidised fabric. Bright orange rather micaceous fabric, sometimes quite coarse in texture with rounded quartzite inclusions throughout. Surfaces can have a white slip or mica dusting and the vessels are quite diverse in form. See 596 AV5 Face bowl
Decoration: white slip, rouletting, mica dusting
Munsell range: 5YR 6/6; 2.5YR 6/8 – 5/6

22 Reduced ware. Pale grey fabric, darker on surfaces with large rounded quartz inclusions throughout, giving a rough gritty finish. Generally used for heavy jars; the constituents of the fabric are very similar to those in Verulamium cream wares
Decoration: rustication, white slip
Munsell range: 7.5YR N7/0

23 Probably different firing of Fabric 1. Verulamium region
Munsell range: 7.5YR 7/6 surface – N3/0 core

25 Oxidised fabric. Hard fine fabric usually with oxidised surfaces and grey core. In the section infrequent rounded quartzite and some shell, generally micaceous throughout
Munsell range: 7.5YR 6/4; 5YR 6/8; 10YR 7/4

27 Reduced ware. Fine sandy micaceous fabric, reddish corein section and surfaces brownish-black. The core is fine and sandy with some larger quartz inclusions
Decoration: 'London' ware types, impressed patterns, compass-inscribed patterns
Munsell range: 2.5YR 5/6 – 10YR 4/2

28 Medieval. Much as fabric 15 but coarser and uneven in fabric. The inclusions are similar but larger and still rounded. The fabric is more laminated in section. Surfaces and core are grey-black in colour
Munsell range: 5Y 2.5/2 throughout

35 Mortaria fabric. Surrey/West Sussex. For description by K Hartley see p 193
Decoration: mortaria grits
Munsell range: 7.5YR 7/4

36 Grey ware. Very pale grey fabric with slightly darker surfaces very similar to Fabric 22 but finer
Decoration: white slip
Munsell range: 2.5Y N8/0

37 'Native' fabric. Probably slightly later in date than Fabric 20. The grog content is finer and the whole fabric more sandy and harder. The core is generally paler grey with visible grog, surfaces are reddish-brown
Munsell range: 10YR 5/3 – 6/1

38 Micaceous oxidised fabric. Generally pale orange-brown, sometimes with greyer surfaces, the whole noticeably micaceous. In section the core is fine and sandy with an even distribution of quartz. See 703 AV6 bowl with colander base. The fabric has similarities to the Hadham wares
Munsell range: 7.5YR N6/; 10YR 6/4

44 Oxford white wares. Fine hard pinkish-white fabric with some larger quartz pieces in the core, up to 2mm in size, sparse scatter of red iron pieces. Fabric also used for mortaria
Munsell range: 7.5YR 8/4

46 Coarse grey fabric, paler grey in section with mid-grey surfaces, very rough to touch and with large quartz particles throughout and occasional flint
Munsell range: 10YR 5/1 – 5YR 5/4

47 Nene Valley mortaria. For description by K Hartley see p 194
Munsell range: 5YR 8/1

48 Reduced sandy fabric, fine in section with smooth surfaces. Generally brownish or bluish-grey with no large inclusions but elongated black rods or voids up to 2mm in length; also very micaceous
Munsell range: 7.5YR 5/2

49 'Belgic' fabric similar to 20 but with smaller grog inclusions and altogether finer
Munsell range: 10YR 3/2

50 Prehistoric. Coarse sandy fabric with mixed flint and quartz inclusions some measuring up to 3mm in size. Reddish/brown smoothed hard surfaces with grey core
Munsell colour: 2.5YR 6/6 surfaces – 7.5YR 5/2 core

65 Mortaria fabric. A Colchester product. For K Hartley's description see p 193
Decoration: pink trituration grits
Munsell range: 7.5YR 8/4 surfaces – 7/4 core

66 Prehistoric. Hard fabric, heavily gritted with crushed flint visible throughout core and in section. The fabric is thin with some variation in the flint sizes. Colour varies from black/grey throughout to mid/grey core with reddish surfaces
Munsell colour: 7.5YR 6/6 surface – 5/2 core to 7.5YR N2/ throughout

68 Mortaria fabric: Gallo-Belgic import. For K Hartley's description see p 193
Decoration: trituration grits
Munsell range: 7.5YR 6/4

71 'Belgic' native fabric. Quite sandy with fewer grog pieces, very dark grey-black throughout, occasional orange red patches
Munsell range: 5YR 4/1 core – 4/4 surface

72 Reduced fabric, similar to 7. Harsh blue-grey fabric with paler surfaces, and similar-sized quartz throughout the core
Decoration: white slip, rusticated
Munsell range: 10YR 4/1

73 Fine ware. Fine creamy-white fabric, thin, hard and well-made, with fine quartz inclusions in section, pinkish in colour. Used for beakers and fine bowls; possible import, but could be very finely made local ware.
Decoration: painted circles
Munsell range: 10YR 7/3 surfaces and core

76 'Belgic' native ware. Brownish-black fabric, paler surfaces and quite fine and hard in texture. In section there are sparse grog pieces and fine quartz
Munsell range: 7.5YR N3/0 – 4/2

77 Mortaria fabric; Oxford. For K Hartley's description see p 194
Munsell range: 7.5YR 8/2

78 Terra nigra. Very fine ware, greyish-white with blue-grey surfaces, sometimes mottled and fairly micaceous throughout. In section there is fine quartz and some grey particles, the latter are fairly sparse
Decoration: burnish
Munsell range: 5YR 8/4

79 Mortaria fabric. Very similar to 77 and same provenance
Munsell range: 7.5YR – N7/0

80 Fabric number given to bowl or lid 1667 AV24. A later 'Belgic' native type of fabric, coarser and sandier than normal but still with grog inclusions, although smaller in size. Core mid blue-grey, surfaces reddish-brown with smoothed finish
Munsell range: 5YR 5/1 – 5/6

81 Fabric number given to platter 612 AV4. Visibly granulated fabric with cream surfaces and pale grey interior. The quartz inclusions are so similar to those in fabrics from Brockley Hill, that it is possible that the vessel could be from that source
Decoration: The platter is painted with black concentric circles and panels of latticing around vessel interior, and circles with centre dots around vessel side
Munsell range: 2.5Y N8/0

88 Grey ware. Coarse, sandy, hard fabric, paler grey in section with visible smallish grog throughout fabric. Surfaces are brownish grey and sometimes bright orange. The structure and appearance of this fabric is closely allied to that from the second kiln at Caldecotte, Buckinghamshire, which produced pottery which was more Roman in form but still contained grog
Munsell range: 5YR 5/3 – 5/1

90 Micaceous grey wares. Very fine smooth fabric, micaceous throughout, with some black grits in section and one or two larger inclusions
Munsell range: 7.5YR 5/2

92 Fabric used for butt beakers, could be fine 'Belgic'. Very thin and hard fabric, pale reddish-brown on surfaces with fine black grog in the core and the whole very micaceous
Decoration: vertical lines; rouletting
Munsell range: 5YR 5/4 surfaces – 10YR 5/2 core

94 Oxidised fabric. Sandy fabric, pale orange in section with speckled orange inclusions, mid-grey surfaces, some mica and quite hard. No rims in this fabric, a few sherds only
Munsell range: 7.5YR 4/24/2

96 Fine black ware, speckled throughout with shell and some grog in section. A finer 'Belgic' ware
Munsell range: 7.5YR 4/2

97 Shell-tempered fabric with grog and flint inclusions. Rather coarse in section with equal proportions of shell, flint and grog evenly distributed. Core dark blue-grey, surfaces hard are well made and generally reddish buff. An early 'Belgic' fabric type
Munsell range: 2.5YR N5/0 – N4/0

106 Rhenish ware. Fine, hard ware, mid-grey in section with very fine speckled white inclusions throughout and glossy grey-brown glazed surfaces
Decoration: indented; barbotine
Munsell range: 10YR 4/1

111 'Belgic' fabric. Rough hard grey-black fabric, paler on surfaces and with very large shell pieces visible in section, sometimes up to 5mm in length; large pieces of grog and scattered quartz
Munsell range: 5YR 3/1

115 Grey core fine and sandy in section, sparse shell, some large quartz pieces in core. Surfaces buff, very smooth with possible cream slip and visible fine mica. Fabric from pedestal base 2248 AV6 and collared flagon 1669 AV 117, probably import
Munsell range: 2.5YR 6/6

118 Medieval. Shelly fabric, coarse and uneven in fracture, and containing random crushed shell, elongated pieces are up to 2mm in size. Other inclusions, quite large but sparser throughout fabric, are red iron particles and possible grog, buff-orange in colour. Surfaces are smoothly finished and 'soapy' to the touch
Munsell colour: surfaces 2.5YR 5/4 – core 2.5YR N3/

119 Grey ware – mostly copies of black burnished wares. Could be a local product from the Verulamium region: the fabric is similar in content and structure. Grey-brown in colour and can have a black finish, fabric surface hard and gritty
Decoration: arcading
Munsell range: 10YR 4/2; 7.5YR N4/ – 4/2

122 Fabric copying terra nigra forms. Mid-grey sandy fabric, well finished with fine quartz in section and visible mica throughout
Munsell range: 5YR 6/1 surfaces – 5/1 core

124 Prehistoric. Pale buff/brown thick fabric, coarse in section with smoothed buff/red surfaces. Abundant large shell is visible throughout
Munsell colour: 5YR 6/3 – 6/4

127 Pink grogged fabric. Buff-pink surfaces which are sometimes powdery, pale grey in section with visible large irregularly sized grog pieces. Common in third century contexts but vessels do appear earlier
Decoration: not common but on occasional pots there are traces of painted decoration and burnish
Munsell range: 5YR 6/6 core; surfaces 7.5 6/4

140 Prehistoric. Thin sandy fabric, finer than 50 with abundant small flint inclusions. Colour varies through pale grey to dark brown
Munsell colour: 7.5YR 6/4 – 5/6 surfaces – 10YR 4/1 core

143 Oxidised fabric similar to samian ware with abundant fine shell in section. No colour coat or other finish but decorated with raised vertical lines
Munsell range: 5YR 5/6

144 Lyons ware. Pale greeny-cream or cream fabric, can be very powdery on surfaces and often considerably abraded. In section the fabric is smooth and dense with a few larger quartz pieces and some linear voids. Surface glaze is pale brown, sometimes quite hard but at Gorhambury mostly very worn
Decoration: scale, roughcast
Munsell range: 10YR 8/3 core – 4/3 colour coat

145 One vessel only: 628 AV1. Fine white fabric with remains of glaze and barbotine decoration. Central Gaulish glazed ware beaker
Munsell range: 10YR 8/3

153 Very smooth fine fabric, quite soft on surfaces, close textured and waxy in section. Forms: carinated cups, probable minature copy of Drag 27 cup and lid. Remains of colour on the surface suggest colour coat, possibly marbled. In 260 AV6 the fabric is almost as fine as eggshell. Fabric colour cream throughout
Decoration: marbling, colour coating, rouletting
Munsell range: 10YR 8/1 approximately

154 Prehistoric. One vessel only: 915 AV1. A finer fabric than 124, harder and sandier and containing small shell pieces. Buff/brown throughout with smoothed surfaces
Munsell colour: 7.5YR 7/4

157 Prehistoric. Visible flint on surfaces and in core. The fabric is hard and sandy with some large quartz. Dark grey/brown core with red/brown surface
Munsell colour: 5YR 4/2 surfaces – 5YR 2.5/1 core

158 Nene Valley oxidised fabric. Fine pale orange fabric, similar to No 13 in texture, with rounded shell and red iron inclusions. Surfaces are hard, smooth and paler than the core
Decoration: colour coating
Munsell range: 2.5YR 6/6

161 Coarse mid-brown fabric, slightly paler in section, very heavily gritted. Probably from local Verulamium region, as the structure and physical appearance are the same. Used for heavy vessels and found with first century material
Munsell range: 10YR 6/3

162 Fine ware import: Gallo-Belgic. Pale buff to pale brown hard, fine fabric and fine mica throughout. In section the core is of fine sandy particles with very few inclusioons. Forms include beakers
Decoration: clay barbotine dots, applied barbotine circles, and triangular decoration, raised bosses, mica dusting, rouletting
Munsell range: 5YR 7/8 – 5/2 and 7.5YR 7/4

164 Much Hadham reduced. Fabric similar in content to 18 but surfaces very highly burnished: third century
Munsell range: 7.5YR N4/0

167 Fine ware. Fine dense fabric with pinkish red core and black surfaces, possibly burnished. In section the inclusions are mostly small rounded quartz
Munsell range: 5YR 3/1 – 6/6

168 Mortaria fabric: Gallo-Belgic. For K Hartley's description see p 193
Munsell range: 2.5Y 8/2

169 Amphora fabric. Rather coarse sandy fabric with deep buff surfaces, more orange through the core with a scatter of larger quartz, red iron and shell. Very similar to 14
Munsell range: 7.5YR 6/4 – 6/6

170 Fine ware. Almost 'eggshell' fabric with thin, hard, smooth black surfaces, 2mm thick. The core is quite coarse with abundant quartz of varying sizes
Decoration: burnish
Munsell range: 2.5Y N3/

171 Shell- and flint-gritted ware. Fabric given to one vessel 191 AV2. Lid-seated jar, pinky-brown core with grey surfaces. The fabric is speckled with large gold mica flakes, flint pieces, fine and coarse shell and some larger quartz
Munsell range: 2.5YR 5/4 – N4/0

173 Fine ware. Reduced 'eggshell' fabric with fine sandy core and smooth glossy surfaces. The core is mid-grey and the exterior surfaces, black. Terra nigra 'eggshell', source North Gaul, or perhaps the Rhineland. Vessels are mostly carinated cups
Munsell range: 10YR 3/1

174 Similar fabric to 173 but pale reddish-brown in colour. More obviously micaceous than 173 and beaker 369 AV29 has good mica dusting. Provenance as 173
Munsell range: 5YR 6/6

175 Fabric for 'London' ware vessels. Fine, very micaceous brown-grey fabric, softer and less sandy than 27. In section the core is red-brown
Decoration: geometric incised circles, fine stabbed dots, inscribed 'swags', diagonal lines
Munsell range: 5YR 4/1 – 5/3

177 Glazed wares. Grey sandy fabric, sometimes with oxidised margins. Mostly small quartz in section, with some larger pieces, and a scatter of red iron and flecks of mica. Both surfaces are glazed, white slip decoration below exterior green glaze. Forms and fabric are similar to those from the Staines area
Decoration: barbotine slip circles, zig-zag
Munsell range: 2.5Y N4/0

179 Pompeian red ware. Generally rather thick fabric, buff throughout with a very fine sandy core and visible mica, shell and some red iron; on plain surfaces the fabric is very micaceous. The dishes have a good interior red colour coat, lids are without. The bases of the dishes are densely gritted and usually blackened. The same fabric was used in a much finer vessel lid, with both surfaces finely colour-coated. 624 AV 1288. Vessels imported from Central France
Munsell range: 5YR 7/4 surface; 5YR 6/4 core. Colour coat – 2.5YR 4/8

185 Miscellaneous gritty reduced fabric, core full of coarse quartz. Surfaces black and section reddish-brown
Decoration: lines of impressed dots
Munsell range: 5YR 4/4 core; 3/1 surfaces

187 Prehistoric. Sandy fabric, very rough to the touch, with large flint inclusions which can be up to 6mm across, and a scatter of fine shell
Munsell colour: 10YR 4/3 surface – 7.5YR 5/4 core

188 Prehistoric. Hard thin sandy fabric with dark brown surfaces and core with some flint throughout. Flint varies in size, with some pieces up to 4mm. The fabric is thinner and denser than 187
Munsell colour: 10YR 3/1 throughout

189 Nene Valley grey wares. The fabric is basically the same as fabric 13 but the surfaces are mottled mid-grey
Munsell range: 10YR 8/2 core; 5/1 surface

192 Prehistoric. Very coarse fabric heavily gritted with flint of varying sizes, which stand proud above the surface. The surfaces are bright reddish/brown with a dark brown core
Munsell colour: 5YR 6/6 surface – 7.5YR N2/ core

193 Rough and hard fabric with red-brown surfaces and brown-grey core which is coarse in section with numbers of elongated voids, quartz and fine shell; also abundant rounded shell throughout
Munsell range: 5YR 7/6 – 5/2 core

195 Sandy fabric, soft on surface with few visible inclusions in the core other than abundant fine rounded shell and a scatter of larger quartz pieces. Gallo-Belgic platter form 465 AV45. Reddish-brown surface and dark grey core
Munsell range: 5YR 6/3

197 Mortaria fabric. For K Hartley's description see p 193
Munsell range: 7/5YR 7/4

198 Fabric number given to one nearly complete vessel: 2397 AV1. Surfaces and core are black, fairly micaceous throughout and very dense in section with an occasional visible quartz grain. The fabric is both thin and hard
Munsell range: 2.5Y 2/0

200 Amphora fabric. Fine dense pale-buff range fabric with gold mica flakes visible throughout and fine shell scatter in section
Munsell range: 7.5YR 8/4

201 Terra rubra. Very fine waxy fabric with good burnish on exterior surface and bright red-orange throughout; noticeably micaceous and with red inclusions which are visible on the surface. Some vessels have a red slip. Vessel forms are small cups, bowls, and beakers
Decoration: red slip, burnishing, rouletting
Munsell range: 2.5YR 6/6

202 Amphora fabric. Coarse fabric with large white grits; surfaces are buff-orange and the core pale brown
Munsell range: 10YR 6/8 surfaces – 2.5YR 6/4 core

205 Mortaria fabric. See K Hartley's description p 193
Munsell range: 2.5Y 8/2

206 Grey ware. Dark grey fabric with smooth finish and in section some grog inclusions and large rounded white quartz; some mica visible on surfaces
Decoration: rusticated wares, white slip, barbotine dots
Munsell range: 7.5YR 4/0

207 Similar to fabric 153. Grey-white surface, pinkish white in the core, which is fine and waxy and without any real inclusions
Munsell range: 7.5YR 7/2

211 Fine ware. Thin hard white fabric with very few inclusions, uneven in fracture, with thin glossy colour coat generally dark brown but often with orange patches. Colour coat can split off in flakes. Vessels are small cups and beakers
Decoration: clay rough-cast, barbotine ridged
Munsell range: 10YR 8/1

212 Part of one vessel only without rim: remains of rough-cast beaker in fine sandy fabric. Dull orange-brown throughout and with an even dark brown matt colour-coat. The roughcast is made from clay particles. The core has a few larger pieces of quartz, some voids and very fine shell
Munsell range: 2.5YR N4/ – 6/6

213 Prehistoric. One vessel only: 1882 AV1. Hard, fine buff/grey fabric, coarse in section with visible fine shell inclusions
Munsell colour: 5YR 5/4 – 6/4 surface – 3/2 core

214 Miscellaneous grey ware. Hard fabric, fine in section with sparse shell and quartz, all of which are very rounded; some sparse iron particles. Fabric from carinated cup 91 AV19. Lattice decoration between girth grooves, below rim and on carination

215 Fabric may be the same as 144, Lyons ware, but subjected to more favourable soil conditions. The fabric is thin and hard, slightly darker cream in section than 144 and the colour coat more lustrous. The roughcast is sand particles but seem more sparsely scattered
Munsell range: 10YR 8/3 core – 5/3 colour coat

216 Fabric for one vessel only: 1804 AV23. Micaceous terra nigra platter base, with either highly burnished or mica-dusted surface. Pale grey surfaces and grey-white core, with few inclusions. Visible mica flakes throughout fabric
Munsell range: 7.5 N8/ YR core – N6/ surfaces

218 One vessel only, 91 AV40. Globular beaker in hard smooth fabric with fine mica throughout. Brown-orange on surfaces, slightly brighter in section. Smooth core with occasional larger quartz and iron particles
Munsell range: 2.5YR 6/6 – 6/8

220 Mortaria fabric. A Colchester product. For K Hartley's description see p 193

221 Mortaria fabric from the Soller kilns: for description see p 193

The mortaria

by Kay Hartley

Fragments from a minimum of 127 mortaria were examined. These range in date from the Claudian period to the late third or early fourth century. The different sources of supply are shown on Fig 160 along with the numbers of vessels involved. The earliest supplies came in small quantities from various sources including the Rhineland, central France, Gallia Belgica and Colchester but, as at Verulamium, local potteries had probably taken the market over entirely by the late Neronian period. The absence of any mortaria from the very important potteries, probably in the Pas de Calais, which produced form Gillam 238 (Gillam 1968), is particularly interesting. It parallels the situation in Verulamium and points to the local potteries being already in control of the market before AD 70.

Potters were probably making mortaria in the Verulamium region before AD 50; by AD 70 they were selling mortaria and perhaps flagons at least throughout the midlands. During the next decade, if not earlier, these potteries had prospered to such a degree that they had the lion's share of the market in mortaria throughout the major part of the province. Only places like Colchester, which had extensive potteries of its own, or areas with easy access to the coast or a port of some importance, would have the majority of their mortaria from a different source – usually the potteries in the Pas de Calais.

We know there were kilns at Brockley Hill, Radlett, Bricket Wood and Verulamium, but the workshops may have stretched intermittently along the area adjacent to Watling Street between Verulamium and Brockley Hill. For reasons unknown these potteries declined in importance from about AD 130, having only a toehold in markets outside the Verulamium–London region after AD 150/160 and they ceased production altogether during the latter part of the second and the first half of the third century. They were, however, of prime importance for places like Gorhambury, situated in the heart of the Verulamium region, from about AD 50 until the early third century.

Nothing highlights their decline more clearly than the virtual takeover of the market by the Oxford potteries in the middle of the third century. In this sample there are approximately 18 mortaria of Young type M17 (Young 1977), 12 of Young type M18, one M19 and one M21, making a total of 32 mortaria dated AD 240–300. There are nine examples of Young type

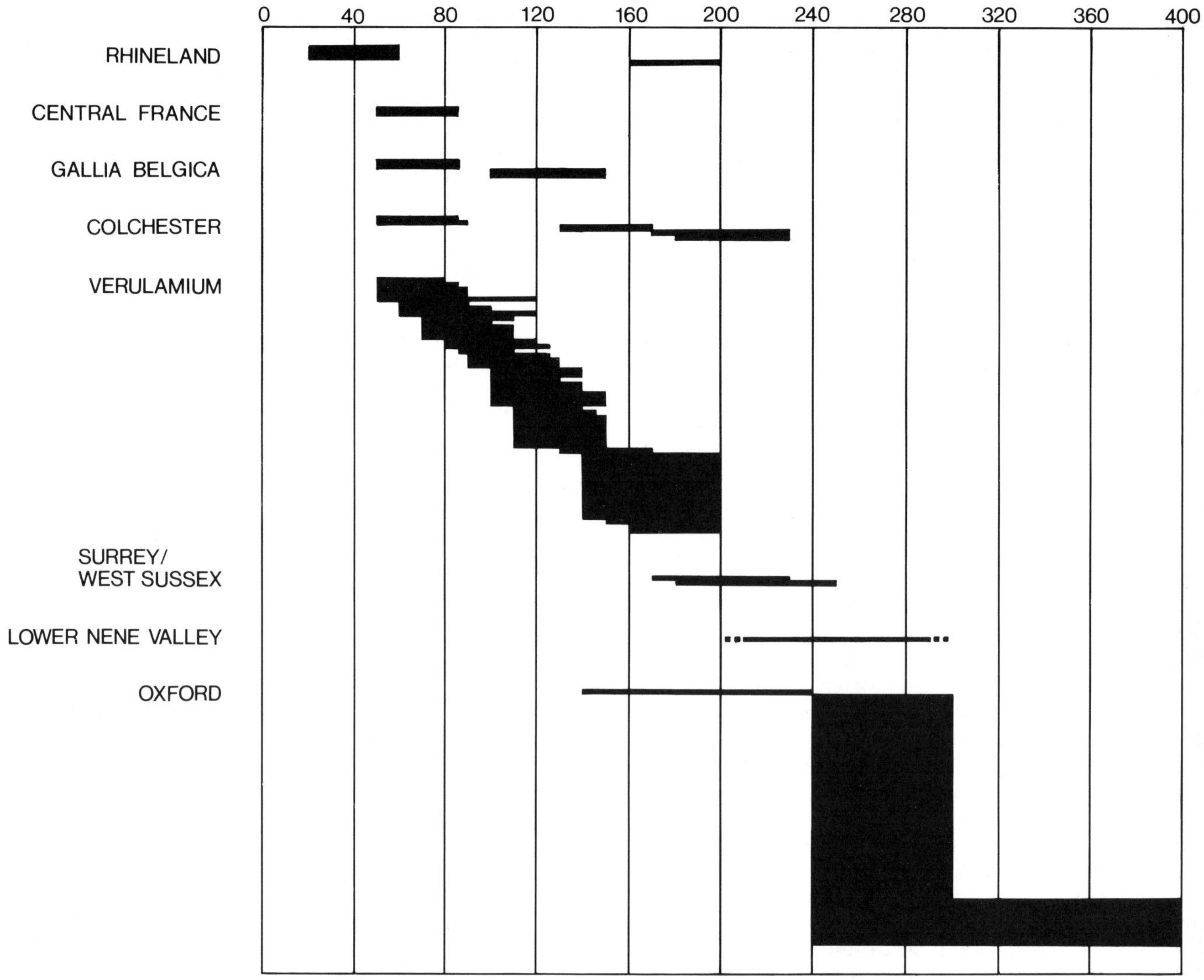

0 40 80 120 160 200 240 280 320 360 400

RHINELAND

CENTRAL FRANCE

GALLIA BELGICA

COLCHESTER

VERULAMIUM

SURREY/
WEST SUSSEX

LOWER NENE VALLEY

OXFORD

A

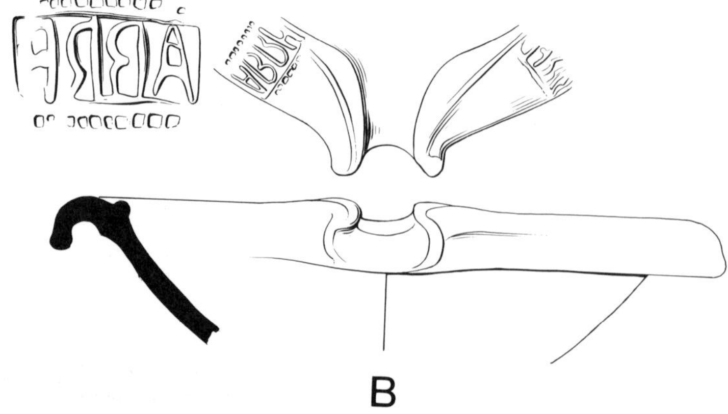

Fig 160 Graph showing mortaria by industry and date range (A) and mortaria of an uncertain potter (B) (see p 195, No 49) (Scales: vessel 1:4, stamp 1:2)

M22 and one of type C97, both types dated AD 240–400, but no examples of Young type C100 which is dated only to the fourth century. There are also no examples of any of the types made in these potteries before the mid third century.

These facts suggest either that few mortaria were being used in the first half of the third century or that there were still sufficient being made in the Verulamium region to cater for most of the needs of the area. Two locally made mortaria (nos 55 and 60) are so unlike the earlier products of these potteries and so similar to Young form M17 and M18 as to suggest that some slight production did continue in the first half of the third century. The total of purely third-century mortaria from the Oxfordshire potteries is strikingly high, while the relatively common type, C97, has only one example on a site which was by now dependent on these potteries for supplies. The implication must be that there is a virtual absence of fourth-century mortaria, but a considerable third-century presence.

A distribution plot of the assemblage was made and, as might be expected, most of the first and second century mortaria were located beneath or around Buildings 27 and 37, with a general scatter over much of the site especially in the upper filling of ditches. However a Sheepen Type 14 mortarium (No 1) dated AD 20–60 came from the primary filling of Ditch 74 and was probably associated with the occupation of Building 8 (Period 5 or 6). Mortaria of the period AD 140–200 were represented by only three vessels around Buildings 27 and 37, but of the nine mortaria from Building 39 four are of this period, including a massive Rhineland mortarium of Verecundus dated AD 160–200. These support the general conclusions drawn from the other coarse wares (p 65) that Building 39 was perhaps occupied longer and more intensively than the main villa. The massive mortarium also emphasises the communal occupation taking place in this structure: it is also of interest that a similar sized mortarium by Verecundus was found at Dicket Mead in Building 1, a building perhaps of similar function (Rook 1986, 81).

Of the 54 (100%) third–fourth-century Oxford mortaria found on the excavations only three (5.55%) were found over Building 39, probably post-dating its occupation and related to a later hut (Building 47). Eleven Oxfordshire mortaria (20.37%) were scattered to the west and south of Building 37, but 20 (37.04%) were found outside Building 30, which also reinforces the view that occupation of this structure continued later than some others.

Fabrics
(arranged in approximate date sequence)

The numbers are included in the general list of fabrics, pp 188ff

Rhineland

205 Fine-textured, brownish-cream fabric with pink core. Powdery to the touch. Trituration grit not used.
Four vessels are represented, all dating to the period AD 20–60

221 Fine-textured, brownish-cream matrix, fired to cream at the surface; packed with largish sub-angular quartz and only occasional black and red-brown inclusions. Trituration probably all quartz.
Only one vessel is represented and can be attributed to the Soller Kilns, Kr Duren, Lower Germany (Haupt 1984) and dated AD 160–200+. (On the graph this fabric has been combined with other material from the Rhineland and not shown separately)

Central France

197 Fine textured, pinkish brown fabric with occasional quartz inclusions with hackly fracture: trituration grit consists of quartz with occasional gold mica.
Two vessels are represented, both attributed to the period AD 50–85

Gallia Belgica

68 Hard, fine-textured, buff-cream, fabric with frequent, well sorted tiny inclusions which include quartz, flint and occasional black and red-brown material. Trituration grit mostly quartz and flint with occasional black and red-brown material.
Two examples from different workshops, dating AD 50–85 and AD 100–150 respectively

168 A fairly soft, almost greenish-cream fabric with fine black and occasional red-brown streaks. Trituration includes flint and quartz.
One example is recorded, AD 100–150

Colchester

220 Fine-textured, cream fabric sometimes with a pink core. Few tiny quartz and occasional opaque red-brown iclusions. Trituration grit consists of quartz, including pink quartz, and occasional flint.
Three examples are recorded, dated AD 50–85; these include a stamp of Sextus Valerius C[

14 Yellowish-cream fabric with very moderate, ill-sorted quartz and flint inclusions with occasional black and red-brown material. Trituration grit consists of flint, quartz and occasional black and red-brown material.
One example is recorded, AD 130–70

65 Smooth, very fine-textured, brownish-cream with few, mostly tiny, red-brown and black inclusions: smooth fracture. Trituration includes quartz and probably flint. Two examples are recorded, AD 170–230

Verulamium region

1 Kilns are known at Bricket Wood, Brockley Hill, Radlett and Verulamium but unless the specific kiln-site is known or suspected, the term 'Verulamium region' is used.
Granular, greyish-cream fabric, sometimes with pink core; occasionally brownish in colour. The fabric is packed with well-sorted quartz inclusions, with occasional flint and rare red-brown inclusions. The trituration grit consists of flint, quartz and red-brown material, the flint predominating

1A A similar fabric to No 1, with a finer texture; the inclusions are smaller and perhaps less abundent, giving the fabric a slightly smoother finish

Surrey/West Sussex

35 Fine-textured, buff-brown fabric; frequent, mostly ill-sorted quartz and some red-brown and black inclusions. Trituration grit consists of flint and quartz

Lower Nene Valley

47 From the Castor-Stibbington area of the lower Nene Valley. Hard, fine-textured, slightly off-white fabric with some quartz inclusions but too small to be visible at X10 magnification. Trituration all ironstone

Oxford

77 Cowley, Headington, Sandford etc, Oxford (Young 1977). Slightly sandy, off-white fabric, sometimes with pink core; tiny quartz and occasional red-brown inclusions. The frequency of inclusions can vary considerably so that the fabric may be quite fine-textured or have a surface like fine sandpaper. All of the mortaria have abundant trituration grit consisting of well-sorted transparent, pink and brownish quartz

2 Dorchester, Cowley, Sandford, Baldon etc, Oxford (Young 1977)
Fine-textured, slightly micaceous, orange-brown fabric with red-brown, samian-like slip. The trituration is identical with that of Fabric 77

Catalogue of the mortaria

Rhineland

1 **2223** (3373). Fabric 205. Probably an import, perhaps from the Rhineland. Sheepen Type 14 (Niblett 1985, fig 50). AD 20–60. A circular hole drilled through base is not central; its purpose is unknown but it could have been for a rivet

2 **2424** (3141) 3. Fabric 205. Probably an import, perhaps from the Rhineland. Sheepen Type 14 (Niblett 1985, fig 50). AD 20–60

3 **2021** (3021) 27. Not seen. Fabric type likely to be Fabric 205. Form probably as above. Drawing suggests date AD 20–60

4 **2123** (3393) 1. Fabric 205. Probably an import, perhaps from the Rhineland. Sheepen Type 14 (Niblett 1985, fig 60). AD 20–60

5 **3816** (2074) 1. Fabric 221. Form 7. Fragment from a huge mortarium, with stamp of Verecundus, whose workshop was at Soller, Kr Düren in Lower Germany (Haupt 1984; Frere 1984, 289, no 100). AD 160–200+

Central France

6 **2819** (1599) 5. Fabric 197. AD 50–85

7 **4019** (2392) 1. Fabric 197. Probably from central France. AD 50–85

Gallia Belgica

8 **2018** (545) 5. Fabric 168. AD 50–85

9 **2619** (1112) 9. Fabric 168. AD 50–85

10 **2019** (218) 2. Fabric 168. Probably from Gallia Belgica. AD 100–150

11 **2816** (1478) 1. Fabric 220. Probably from Gallia Belgica. AD 100–150

Colchester

12 **2118**, 21/2217 (641) 10. Fabric 220. Probably Colchester. AD 50–85

13 **2117** (660) 4. Fabric 220. Probably Colchester. AD 50–85. Slightly burnt. Circular rivet-hole surviving

14 **2319** (1028) 19. Fabric 220. Flange fragment with a broken stamp of Sextus Valerius C[. AD 50–90 (see Cunliffe 1971, 171, No 1 for details)

15 **2123** (410) 10. Fabric 14. Probably Colchester. Probably AD 130–70

16 **2019** (8). Fabric 14. (Hull 1963, Type 501B). AD 170–230

17 **2618** (1063) 17. Fabric 14. AD 180–230. Joins 2816, (1477) 1

Verulamium region (all fabrics are 1 unless stated otherwise)

18 **2621** (881). Two joining fragments with two stamps, reading LVGD, impressed close together along the flange, one above the other. These are counter-stamps of the potter Oastrius who worked at Bricket Wood (Little Munden), Herts. AD 50/55–75/80 (Saunders and Havercroft 1977)

19 **2822** (1657). AD 50–85

20 **2019** (91) 45. Flange fragment. Joins with another from 2821 (1578) 22. Slightly burnt. AD 50–90

21 **2821** (1616). AD 50–90

22 **2117** (624) 7. AD 50–120

23 **2823** (1540) 4. Broken counterstamp FLVGVDV, from the same die as Cunliffe 1968, pl LXXXVIII, no 4 (identical with Frere 1972, fig 145, no 6 except that the top of the F is joined to the L) AD 60–90. For further details see Frere 1972, 371–2, nos 2–11; 1984, 281–2, nos 55–61

24 U/S (1) 64. Two pieces join. Worn. AD 60–100

25 **2218** (615) 20 and 21. Two fragments from the same vessel which do not join. Burnt before fracture. AD 60–120

26 Gor 1961 H12 1 137. Three fragments probably from the same worn mortarium. The broken potter's stamps would read MARINVS//FECIT if they were complete. The two stamps were impressed close together. Marinus had a workshop at Brockley Hill, Middx in the period AD 70–110 (Frere 1972, 376, no 26; and 1984, 285, no 80–81). Probably part of 2122 (1) 432 4, and of GOR 61 (1), 108

27 **2121** (77B) 3. About half of a small mortarium. Probably AD 70–100

28 **2022** (369) 41. Worn. Both pieces burnt after fracture. AD 70–110. Joins with Gor 1975, 2018 (586) 10

29 **2017** (1414) 2592. Burnt. Flange fragment with incomplete stamp of Moricamulus (see Frere 1972, 376, no 29; 1984, 286 no 88). AD 70–110

30 **3917** (2247) 1. Slightly burnt. AD 70–110

31 **3817** (2187) 1. Slightly burnt. AD 80–120

32 **2817** (1287) 2586. Flange fragment with broken stamp of Matugenus,]ENV[, from the same die as Frere 1984, fig 118, no 83. Matugenus worked at Brockley Hill within the period AD 80–125

33 **2120** (45), 32. The broken stamp is from the latest die of Doinus, AD 85–110 (Frere 1972, 375, nos 19–20). There is adequate evidence to show that Doinus worked at Brockley Hill, Middx (Castle 1972)

34 **2018** (546) 3. Flange fragment. Joins GOR 75 63 3–7. There is a fragmentary, retrograde stamp of Lallaius, who had a workshop at Brockley Hill, Middx. probably within the period AD 90–125 (Frere 1972, 376, no 24; 1984, 280, no 24)

35 **2822** (1454) 1. AD 90–130. Joins GOR 79, 2822 (1651) 22

36 **2822** (1651) 144. AD 90–130

37 **2022** (275) 435, 62 and 46 joining. A large portion of a worn mortarium, smashed into fragments. The last three letters survive,]NVS, of the two-line stamp of Saturninus 1. He had a workshop at Brockley Hill. AD 100/110–130/140 (Frere 1972, 379, no 39 and 1984, 287, no 96 for other details)

38 **2123** (3392) 1. Four joining and one other fragments from a worn and slightly burnt mortarium with a stamp of Saturninus 1. Dates and details as 37 above

39 **3822** (2670) 4. AD 100–130

40 **2522** (722) 1884. Flange fragment with broken stamp TM[h. AD 100–140 (see Frere 1972, 379, no 39; 1984, 285 nos 78 and 79 for further details)

41 **3021** (3091) 2. Some wear. A border survives, perhaps of a stamp of Aebris. AD 100–150

42 **2218** (615) 18. AD 100–150

43 **2720** (1053) 1. AD 100–150

44 **2017** (1412) 1. Fragmentary stamp likely to be from the same die as Frere 1972, Fig 146, no 42. AD 100–150

45 **2117** (536) 2. Some wear. Fragmentary retrograde stamp of Aebris. AD 110–140. Joins with 2822 (1651) 18

46 **2823** (1540). A worn mortarium with stamp TM[h (see No 40 above for details). AD 100–140

47 **2121** (258) 7. Fabric 1A. Incompletely impressed stamp; not identified. AD 110–150

48 **2123** (410) 16. AD 110–150

49 **2617** (741) 2466. Fig 160B. Both of the potter's stamps survive, allowing the reading ABRF retrograde. No other stamps from the same die have been recorded. They have some characteristics in common with stamps of Aebris and a stamp which reads ABB[, but the profiles used with the three dies are quite different and they should be regarded as three separate potters unless evidence to the contrary appears. AD 110–150. Fragments of the same vessel were also recorded from 2617 (1271) and 2617 (1274)

50 **2822** (1454) 4. Burnt before fracture. AD 110–150

51 **27/2823** (1540) 85. AD 110–150

52 **2822** (1651) 25. Border of an illiterate stamp. AD 110–150

53 **2019** (11) 65. The poorly impressed two-line stamp is from a die which permits the reading MII/RTVC retrograde. Mertucus seems to be the name intended, two verticals being quite commonly used for E. His work can be attributed to Brockley Hill (2–3 vessels) and/or Radlett, Herts (4–5 vessels) (Castle 1976B, 216, fig 8, MS 92–93, with the best published drawings of his stamp, and 219; also Castle 1976A, 152, M13–16). His morrtaria have also been noted from Fenny Stratford, Bucks; London (5); Maryport; Melandra Castle; Milton Keynes; Otford, Kent; Staines (2); and Wilderspool. The rim-forms point to activity within the period AD 110–150 (120–140 is the optimum period)

54 **2816** (1286) 48. Burnt. AD 130–70

55 **3820** (2665) 1. Fabric 1. Form 7 (Frere 1972, nos 1053 and 1054). AD 140–200

56 **2620** (721) 33. Fabric 1A. Young form M18. Probably third century (Frere 1984, fig 112, no 2697). This mortarium is very unusual because it combines a fairly typical Verulamium region fabric with the equally typical Oxford form M18/17

57 **1922** (110) 19. Fabric 1A (Frere 1972, fig 131, nos 1053 and 1054). AD 140–200

58 **2117** (9) 1. Fabric 1A. Burnt. Unusual form. AD 140–220+

59 **2018** (544c) 16. Fabric 1A. Very heavily burnt. AD 140–200+

60 **2521** (704). Fabric 1A (Frere 1972, nos 1053 and 1054). AD 140–220

61 **2721** (773) 6. Fabric 1A. Young form M17. Probably third century. Closely similar to 2620 (721) (No 56), but may be a different vessel

62 **2621** (848) 7. Fabric 1A (Frere 1972, nos 1053 and 1054). AD 140–200+. Joins 2723 (1543) 1

63 **2620** (1013) 5. AD 140–220+ (Frere 1984, fig 112, no 2672)

64 U/S (1) 86. Fabric 1A (Frere 1972, nos 1053 and 1054). AD 140–200+

65 **2816** (1471). Fabric 1A (Frere 1972 *ibid*). AD 140–200+

66 **3817** (2001). Fabric 1A (Frere 1972 *ibid*). AD 140–200+

67 **3820** (2344) 1. Fabric 1A. Burnt (Frere 1972 *ibid*). AD 140–200+

68 **3020** (3059) 1. Fabric 1A. Worn and slightly burnt (Frere 1972 *ibid*). AD 140–200

69 **2918** (1448) 2. Burnt. AD 150–200+

70 **3917** (2016) 7. Fabric 1A. AD 160–230+

71 **3816** (2017) 4. Fabric 1A. AD 160–230+

72 **3820** (2560) 4. Fabric 1A (Frere 1972, nos 1053 and 1054). AD 140–200+

Surrey/West Sussex

73 **2218** (509) 2. Fabric 35. Probably made in a small pottery in the Surrey–West Sussex area. AD 170–230

74 **1921** (110) 12. Two joining fragments from a small, very neatly made, wall-sided mortarium in Fabric 35. Form 7.14. This is a fine-ware form, very expertly made despite the grit which has been added to the clay. It was probably made in a small pottery in the Surrey–West Sussex area, whose products are found primarily at such sites as Chichester, Rapsley, Binscombe, Chiddingfold and Fishbourne and occasionally as far away as London. The pottery was active in the period AD 135–250 and the only kiln known to date is at Wiggonholt, near Pulborough (Evans 1974). This mortarium is likely to have been made within the period AD 180–250. A mortarium from 2218 (494) 16 could well be from the same vessel

Lower Nene Valley

75 **2618** (1063) 16. Fabric 47. Made in the Castor–Stibbington area of the lower Nene Valley. Perhaps more likely to be third rather than fourth century. Slightly burnt

Oxford

76 **2018** (520) 14. Fabric 77. Form incomplete. Probably AD 140/180–240

77–95 Fabric 77. Young form M17. AD 240–300.
1921 and **2021** (110) 15 joining **2018** (547) 3; **2021** (162) 7; **2217** (491) 1; **2218** (494) 15; **2018** (544c) 18; **2520** (701) 29 and **2670** (721) 27 and **2823** (741) 1 and **2823** (1540) 79 = 1 vessel; **2720** (721) 201; **2721** (721) 9 and **2721** (786) 37 = 1 vessel; **2721** (786) 38; **2621** (796) 3; **2720** (721) 9 (not 201); **2723** (1540) 82; **3716** (1881) 1; **3716** (1883) 9; **3817** (1904) 1; **3817** (2016) 59; **3816** (2017) 14; **2721** (701) 13

96–109 Fabric 77. Young form M18. AD 240–300. **1921** and **2021** (110) 14; **2018** (586) 7; **2522** (701) 30; **2522** (701) 32; **2721** (701) 79; **2620** (1013) 1; **2517** (1258) 3; **3718** (1920) 1; **3918** (1956) 1; **3820** (2302) 1; **3820** (2302) 4; **3820** (2560) 4; **2021** (162) 8; **2223** (3361) 1

110 Fabric 77. Young form M19. AD 240–300. **3817** (2016) 60

111 Fabric 77. Young form M21. AD 240–300. **3917** (2016) 4

112–120 Fabric 77. Young form M22. AD 240–400. **2019** (40) 3; **1923** (278) 1; **2522** (701) 33; **2621** (823) 2; **2618** (996) 12; **2517** (1258) 2; **2816** (1475) 1; **4215** (1707); **3021** (3021) 10

121 Fabric 2. Young form C97. AD 240–400. **4019** (4) 117

Potters' stamps on imported vessels

by Valery Rigby

1 GOR 73 **2121** 77C 1
ANDOCAVLO Central stamp; three incised circles. Platter Camulodunum form 8. Terra nigra (Fabric 78), white fine-grained smooth matrix; pale blue surfaces, naked and laminated; no finish survives.
Andocaulo die IAI. From the same die as stamps on three terra nigra platters found at Camulodunum (2) and Bavay, Nord (1), and four terra rubra platters found at Trier (3) and Cologne (1). Both Trier and Cologne are possible sources. *c* AD 25–60

2 IVLO Central stamp. Cup with internal moulding and applied footring, probably Camulodunum form 56. Terra nigra (Fabric 78): grey smooth matrix; black surfaces.
Julo die IAI or Jul(l)ios die 9G10. Possibly a mis-spelling of Jul(l)ios, one of the most common names to occur on Gallo-Belgic products, particularly terra nigra (Rigby 1981). If it is a product of the potters Jul(l)ios, then it is die 9G10 and the vessel was probably made in the Marne-Vesle potteries of Gallia Belgica. The quality of the typological details is poor, indicating a comparatively late date of manufacture, after *c* AD 50. Should the name in fact be Julo or Lulo, then the die designation becomes Die IAI; the source is unknown, but would have been somewhere in Gallia Belgica or Lower Germany and it remains a late product: *c* AD 50–75

3 [NOVID]VS General stamp; single incised circle. Small platter with internal moulding, probably Camulodunum form 8.
Terra nigra (Fabric 78): white fine powdery matrix; abraded blue/grey surfaces; no finish survives.
Novidos die IAI. From the same stamps as four on terra nigra platters found at Skeleton Green (GB12), Camulodunum (no 180), Trier and Wederath (Burial 1057), and three on terra rubra platters Camulodunum form 8 from Bingen, Mainz and Fouches (Burial 10a).
Probably made near Trier, or in Lower Germany *c* AD 40–65

4 GOR 73 **2121** 77B 4
SILVANVS Underside of base. Carinated beaker Holwerda 26.
Fabric 173: black eggshell ware. Fine-grained smooth black ware; abraded grey surfaces; no finish survives.
Silvanus die IAI. No other stamps from this die have been identified. As yet no definite source of origin has been established for black eggshell beakers although they occur on sites in Lower Germany and Gallia Belgica. Larger and rather coarser versions, also stamped, were made at Bavay, Nord, and Metz, Moselle, in Gallia Belgica.
In Britain, very few stamped examples have been found; the joint list of finds from Londinium and its extra-mural settlement at Southwark is by far the longest with seven examples. Because the fabric is so distinct, sherds from both the carinated and necked beaker forms are easily identifiable, so the typological distribution is much wider than that of the stamps.
There is a certain Nero–Flavian military connection to the distribution with examples from Usk, Cirencester, Wroxeter, Richborough, the Lunt, Southampton and Ilkley. Here, when it occurs, the association is with late Gallo-Belgic imports, particularly the terra nigra platter Camulodunum form 16 (Greene 1979, 120). Locally, none was identified in the King Harry Lane cemetery, although there are sherds from Verulamium itself (Stead and Rigby 1989). The date of manufacture is likely to lie in the period *c* AD 60–85

5 GOR 74 **2122, 2022** 77 84
Illegible impression, of the same size and shape as no 1. Underside of base. Carinated beaker, Holwerda 26. Fabric 173: black eggshell ware; highly polished outer surface. Probably another product of Silvanus

6 GOR 73 **2121** 77 365
Illegible impression. Underside of base. Bobble pot, with undefined bosses, Camulodunum form 95B.
Mica-coated ware, Fabric 162: cream fine sandy-textured matrix with occasional red grog inclusions; mica-coating (muscovite) on the outer surface only. The impression is illegible, and the size and proportions of the die face cannot be matched exactly with any recorded stamp on a mica-coated vessel. This is however not surprising since only *14* such stamps are recorded, representing nine different dies. An identical beaker, although unstamped, was found in the Leaholm fort ditch at Cirencester, with a large group of pottery dating to the Neronian and early Flavian periods (Rigby 1982, fig 58, 289).
The source of origin is unknown; it was presumably imported from Gallia Belgica or Lower Germany. Stamps from the same die of the potter Inducius show that mica-coated and black eggshell beakers could be made by the same potter or firm; the former occur at Baldock (1) and London (1), and the latter at London (2). The date of manufacture should lie in the Neronian or Vespasianic periods. It may be chronologically significant that none was found in the King Harry Lane cemetery which was in use *c* AD 5–60 (Stead and Rigby 1989)

A potter's stamp on a local product

1 GOR 72 **2020** Q13 68
MARK Central; one incised circle. Platter copying the Gallo-Belgic import Camulodunum form 16. Fabric: blue-grey fine sand-tempered ware with burnished finish. The die-style is simple and combines four V- and two I-motifs. No other examples from this die have been identified, although very similar dies are represented at Verulamium (2), Baldock, Herts and Alchester, Oxon. The imported prototypes Camulodunum form 16, was the most widely distributed Gallo-Belgic vessel form, examples have been identified on Agricolan forts in Scotland, and Nero–Flavian military establishments in Wales and the South-West (Rigby 1977). Local potteries made more or less close copies in a variety of sand-tempered fabrics from *c* AD 70 until *c* AD 130. This is presumably a fairly local product

The decorated samian (Figs 161 and 162)

by G B Dannell

Catalogue

Note: The first number in the catalogue description gives the samian form number, the second the small find number, followed by the context number.

Abbreviations:

D = Déchelette 1904
O = Oswald
R–F = Ricken and Fischer 1963

1 29 SF 2039 **2220** (403). Ivy-leaves in the form used by the LICINVS/VOLVS workshop, cf Knorr 1952, taf 63E.
c AD 40–60 South Gaulish. Not illustrated

2 29 SF 114 **2019** (96). Lanceolate leaves, used by many Claudio–Neronian potters.
c AD 45–60 South Gaulish

3 29 SF 2566 **2517** (1403). This looks like a fragment of straight wreath, cf generally, Oswald, *J Roman Stud*, **28**
c AD 45–60? Le Joux

4 29 SF 1070, **2118** (626), SF 1276 **2218** (660). The details on this bowl are associated with interior stamps of FELIX, but almost certainly are from moulds made in the MODESTVD workshop. For the upper zone, cf Knorr 1952, taf 40F; the segmented leaf of the lower zone is on a MODESTVS bowl from London (Mus of Lond 1042), the small frond on a FELIX bowl from Colchester (Hull 1958, fig 101). The wreath is on a bowl stamped FELICIS from La Graufesenque, and the frond on a similar bowl from Rodez.
c AD 50–65 South Gaulish

5 29 SF 114 and 125 **2019** (96). The scroll in the upper zone terminates in a small ivy leaf, used by MATVGENVS, PRIMVS and NIGER. The lower zone has a goose, 0.2260 in a medallion, flanked by the smaller geese 0.2244 and 2286. These details appear in the work of the potter stamping S VIIRIV. Note the small group of circles.
c AD 65–80 South Gaulish

6 29 SF 2001 **2022** (403). SECVNDVS style, cf Knorr 1919, taf 74E. Not illustrated
c AD 70–85 South Gaulish

7 29 SF 2224 **2618** (741). It is difficult to place this piece, because the details of the upper zone first appeared in the later Neronian period, and continued into the Flavian. SEVERVS used the wreath (Wroxeter, layer 98, 84).
c AD 75–90? South Gaulish. Not illustrated

8 30 **2120** (77). Double-bordered ovolo with tongue to right ending in small rosette. The panel decoration has blocks of small segmental leaves, separated from cross motifs by upright V-shaped leaves.
I have not noted the ovolo previously, but the ivy leaf in the cross is diagnostic, and appears on a form 29 from La Nautique (*Archaeonautica*, 1978) fig 7.8, stamped by FELIX. The leaf also appears there with a nautilus motif in the lower zone (ibid 8.1).
The compound bifid leaf motif in the cross is similar to, but different from that used by the MVRRANVS group.
The leaf looks like the one from which the infilling on the form 29 from London and Camulodunum is made, cf Stanfield 1930, A, and Hawkes and Hull 1947, pl XXVI, 20. The birds there are similar to ones used by MODESTVS (Mus of Lond, S 431GH), and he is known to have moulds used by FELIX.
c AD 50–65 South Gaulish

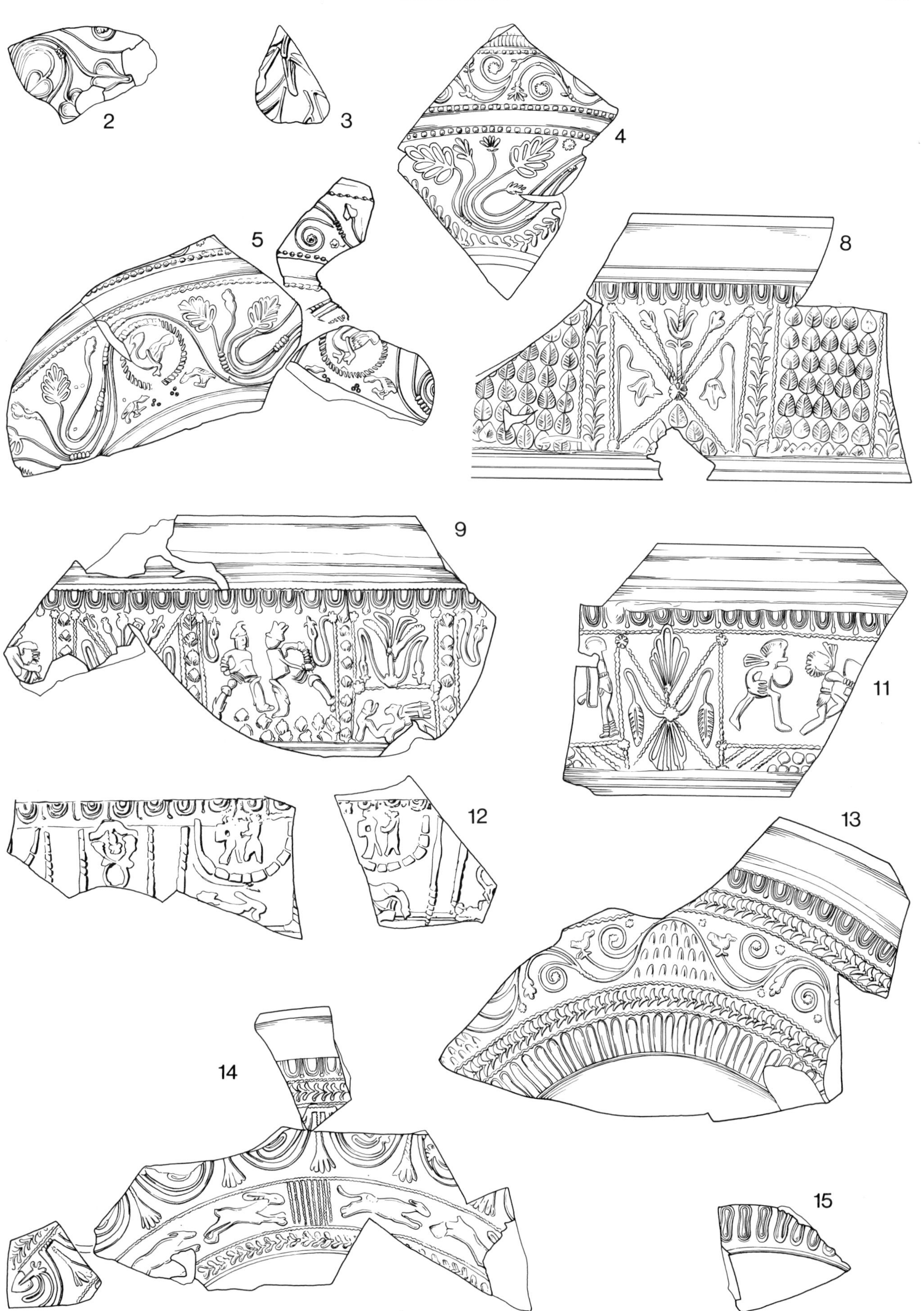

Fig 161 The decorated samian (Scale 1:2)

9 30 SF 2014 **2122** (320), SF 2016 **2022** (69), SF 2023 **2122** (349). The ovolo is used on bowls of IVSTVS, and possibly MOMMO. The gladiators are 0.1013A and B, the figure to the left is too fragmentary for identification. Thê gryphon is 0.882. These three types are associated with the ovolo on bowls from London (Mus of Lond 11812G and 4692G).
The upright frond also appears there (11815G) and the leaf-tip is on a form 78 from Wroxeter. The small putto, 0.411 is recorded on a form 30, cf Hermet 1934, pl 120.10, there with a Minerva associated with the present ovolo on a London bowl.
The frequent recurrence of the types in association suggest a single mould-maker.
c AD 65–80 South Gaulish

10 30 **2122**. SABINVS style; the ovolo is not obvious, being that shown by Stanfield 1937, detail 27, with an added rosette. This habit was affected by a number of workshops in the Neronian period and needs careful study. The rod is detail 61 and the leaf 90. Not illustrated

11 30 SF 185 **2120** (77). the ovolo is that attributed to M CRESTIO and C VALERIVS ALBANVS, the bowls of the former having a rather larger repertoire of poinçons. The gladiators are, from the left, 0.1013F, 1007 and 1021, the latter known from a stamped form 37 by M CRESTIO from Vindonissa. The palmate leaf and the segmental leaf are known with this ovolo (Mus of Lond 6545L and 11893G).
c AD 75–90 South Gaulish

12 30 SF 1362 **2721** (721), SF 1361, 1368, **2621** (721), SF 1703 **2621** (787). A small bowl in the style of PRIMITIVVS (probably IV); the ovolo is R-F E 11, the acanthus is probably P 113, the corded rod is probably 0 232, the deer is T 82b, the festoon is KB 101 and the trophy, 0 160a. The small dog is a variant of T 139b, but has a straight rather than curved tail. The warrior and captive, M 269, appear to be incomplete as the feet are missing.
T 139b was used by PRIMITIVVS I; M 269 was used by a number of potters including PRIMITIVVS I, all of the other motifs are known from the work of PRIMITIVVS IV.
First half third century, Rheinzabern

13 37 SF 350 **2121** (77), SF 656 **2022** (77). The ovolo has been attributed to IVSTVS, but there is nothing which I have recorded in his style to go with the detail on this bowl, and the sparrow is uncatalogued.
c AD 70–85 South Gaulish

14 37 SF 3321 **3916** (2071). This single-bordered ovolo with a straight tongue ending in a small circle is rare; it occurs with the same dog both at Fishbourne (Cunliffe 1971, fig 135.93) and at Richborough (Cunliffe 1968, pl LXXX, 15). The dog is 0.1929 and the hare 0.2072.
c AD 70–85 South Gaulish

15 37 SF 2805 **2819** (1569). A number of potters used these eccentric, small gadroons, cf Atkinson 1914, no 78.
c AD 70–85 South Gaulish

16 37 SF 1237 **2016** (91). Large double-bordered ovolo with trident tongue, the centre spike detached. Used by SEVERVS; a very similar cross-motif is on a form 30 with the ovolo from London (Mus of Lond 1932.162), the lanceolate leaf being replaced there by a bottle-shaped bud.
c AD 75–90 South Gaulish. Not illustrated

17 37 SF 78 **1920** (123). Entwined dolphins, 0.2407, and hound, 0.1994 type. Not from Banassac, so mid-Flavian.
c AD 75–90 South Gaulish

18 37 SF 1873 **2621** (847). The more commonly used ovolo of the M CRESTIO/CRVCVRO workshop. The hound is 0.2013.
c AD 75–90. South Gaulish. Not illustrated

19 37 SF 2552 **2017** (1416). Four-pronged ovolo in the style of M CRESTIO/CRVCVRO. The boar is on a form 37 in the style from London (Mus of Lond 4399G).
c AD 75–90 South Gaulish

20 37 SF 2858 **2821** (1552). Bent-tongued ovolo used by M CRESTIO, and the wreath is also known in combination with it, cf Richborough (Box 310).
c AD 75–90 South Gaulish. Not illustrated

21 37 SF 1036 **2016** (596). Large mastiff, 0.1994, above grass tuft; used by PASSIENVS, among others.
c AD 75–90? South Gaulish

22 37 SF 78 **1920** (123). DONNAVCVS style? Trajanic, Les Martres-de-Veyre. Not illustrated

23 37 SF 2468 **2417** (1263). Ovolo replacement, Rogers 1974 C 294.
c AD 100–120, Les Martres-de-Veyre

24 37 SF 2485 **2417** (1267), SF 3096 3717 US. Ovolo of potter X-3.
c AD 100–120, Les Martres-de-Veyre

25 37 SF 2712 **2822** (1454), SF 2857 **2822** (1630). DONNAVCVS style; all of the detail is shown in Stanfield and Simpson 1958, pls 44–49.
c AD 100–120, Les Martres-de-Veyre

26 37 SF 2904 **2822** (1651). Rogers' (1974) ovolo B44.
c AD 100–120, Les Martres-de-Veyre. Not illustrated

27 37 SF 2152 **2720** (741), SF 2306 **2619** (1016). Panel decoration on soft-fired sherd which has suffered from surface erosion. The small spiral is Rogers' M35, the winged figure, a variety of D 234, and the Bacchus is D.322. Rogers (1974) records the spiral for GEMINVS and another unidentified potter; the figures belong to the Hadrianic group too.
c AD 120–140? Lezoux

28 **37 SF 2904 2822 (1651). Rogers 1974 ovolo B 208.**
Hadrianic Central Gaulish. Not illustrated

29 **37 SF 2955 29188 (1643). Rogers 1974 ovolo b 61**
Hadrianic Central Gaulish. Not illustrated

30 3 SF 2142 **2419** (920). A Hadrianic piece, the figures are largely known from the repertoire of ACAVNISSA. The Minerva is D 78; the Venus, D 193 type; the two small warriors are D 139 and 382, while Rogers (1974) also attributes the leaf motif G 76 to him. The style is very different, and more like DOCILIS.
c AD 125–140 Central Gaulish

31 37 SF 109 **1920**)123), SF 2320 **2720** (1058), SF 2365 **2720** (1056). Rogers 1974 ovolo B19, attributed by him to potter P 16. The figures are: satyr, D 362; nude man, D 398; Pan, D 411; panthers, D 799 and 805, and stag, 0.1704A.
c AD 125–145 Central Gaulish

32 37 SF 2300 **2720** (1054), SF 2365 **2720** (1056). Rogers 1974 Q 65; danseuse, D 210; Hercules, D 469; female figure, cf Stanfield and Simpson 1958, pl 88.8; Pan, 0.715, type; panther or lioness, cf 0.1549. Probably by DRVSVS.
c AD 125–145 Central Gaulish

33 37 SF 3384 **3819** (1972). The ovolo is incomplete, the figure is 0.205 used by ACAVNISSA.
c AD 125–145 Central Gaulish

34 37 SF 3901 **3821** (2344). Rogers 1974 ovolo B 86
Hadrianic–Antoine Central Gaulish. Not illustrated

35 37 SF 488 **1923** (315). CINNAMVS style; for details cf Stanfield and Simpson 1958 pl 162.
c AD 145–165 Central Gaulish

36 37 SF 1703 **2621** (787). Rogers 1974 ovolo B 27, attributed to SERVVS II.
c AD 150–180 Central Gaulish. Not illustrated

37 37 SF 2685 **2723** (1492). PATERNVS style, the ovolo appears very similar to Rogers 1974 B 106, but caution is required, because the leaf is not shown for him by Rogers or Stanfield and Simpson 1958. The small toothed circle is Rogers' E 57.
c AD 160–190 Central Gaulish

38 67 SF 2552 **2017** (1416). The small bordered-palm leaf looks to be Neronian.
c AD 50–65? South Gaulish

The Arretine ware (Fig 162, 39)

Ritt 8. Stamped M 1 (MAHES). The die is recorded (Oxé, ed Comfort 1968, 74.86a, probably from a similar vessel. The description in Camulodunum (Hawkes and Hull 1947, S 16, 187) fits this cup exactly.
Kam (1965) attributes MAHES' work to the later Augustan and early Tiberian period. However, some caution is necessary. The fabric consists of a soft and very calcareous matrix with obvious red and black inclusions, the slip is red/orange, fine and smooth, with some evidence of differential firing; the form of the vessel is very close to those from Gaul, and although almost certainly Italian, sufficiently close to its Gaulish successors to suggest a Tiberian date

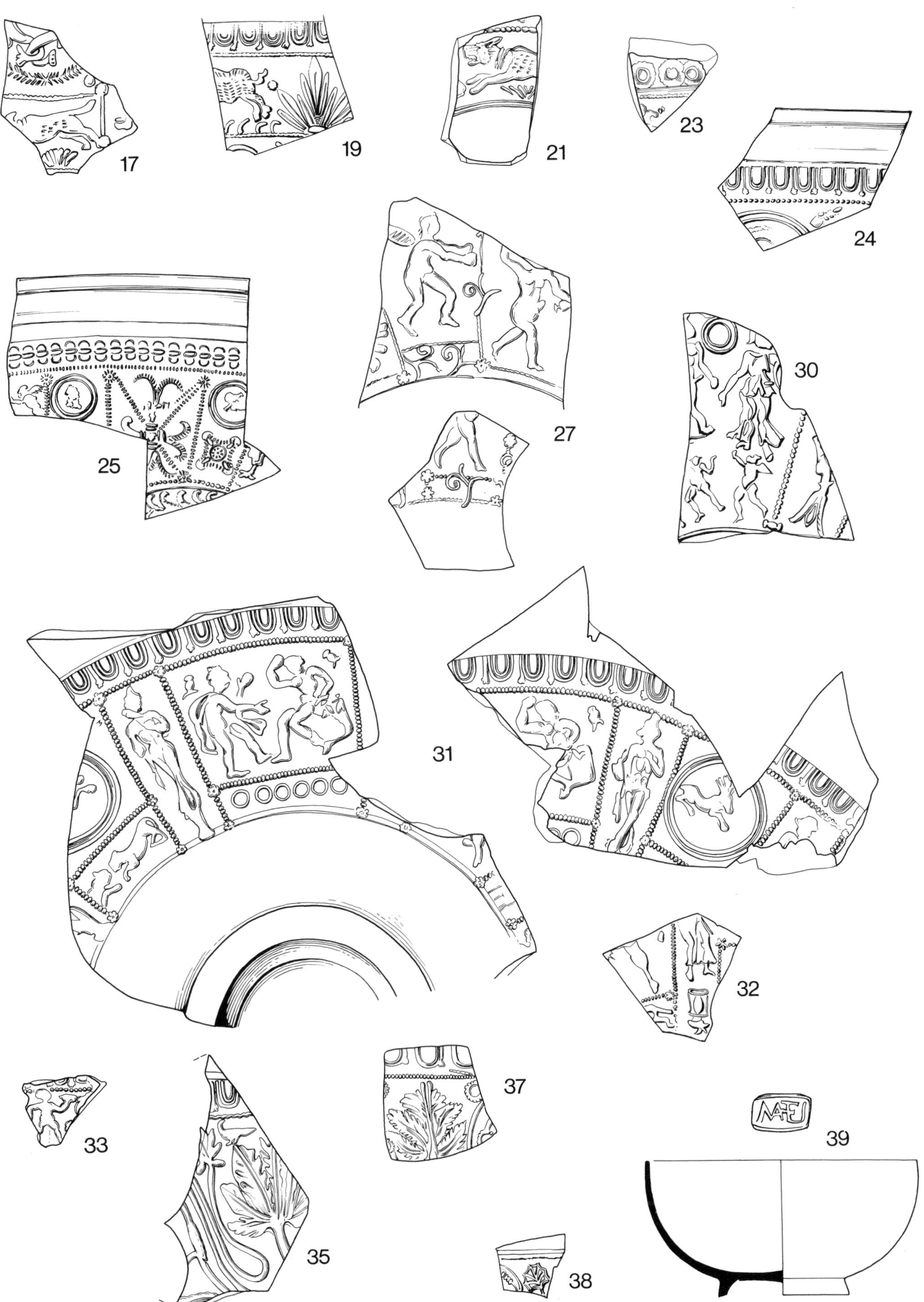

Fig 162 The decorated samian (Scale 1:2)

General remarks

The Gorhambury samian falls outside the normal collection from a private, as opposed to public, rural site with a late Iron Age origin. There is more pre-Flavian pottery, probably reflecting the status of the inhabitants, the proximity of Prae Wood as a trading centre, and the establishment of Verulamium as its commercial successor. The populations of stamps and decorated vessels are not so large as to invite elaborate statistical analysis, but the general correlation of proportions of both site and date is interesting.

In both cases some 40% is Flavian, and just under 60% comes from La Graufesenque; similarly, in the second century, Lezoux contributes some 30%, but this is spread out over a longer period, with for both categories some 10% attributable to the Hadrianic–Antonine, but a clear divergence elsewhere. While some 13% of the stamps are late Antonine, as opposed to 5% of the decorated, there is less representation in the Hadrianic, by about the same proportion. Les Martres-de-Veyre provides 12% of the decorated ware, and 8% of the stamps. While the former are conventionally dated to the Trajanic period (for mainstream pieces), the stamps are spread fairly evenly from the Trajanic to the Hadrianic/Antonine. East Gaul rates 2% of the decorated and 3% of the stamps.

Taken together the picture is not dissimilar to town collections, reflecting availability as well as economic and social activity.

Samian potters' stamps

by Brenda Dickinson

Note:
(a) A stamp attested at the pottery in question.
(b) Not attested at the pottery in question, though the potter is known to have worked there.
(c) Assigned to the pottery on the evidence of fabric, distribution, etc.

Each entry gives: excavation number, potter (i, ii, etc, where homonyms are involved), die number, form of vessel, reading, pottery of origin

1 75 *2108* (595) 1073 Advocisus 1b 18/31R–31R ADVOCISI.OF Lezoux. (b) In view of the form, this dish probably belongs to the 160s, rather than later. There is a grafitto, Caiu[, inscribed under the base, after firing

2 75 *2118* (644) 1267 Ardacus 9a 29 OF.(AR)DAC La Graufesenque. (b) *c* AD 40–60

3 76 *2521* (802) 1903 and 76 1956, almost certainly going together, Beliniccus i 11a 33 BELI/NICIM retrograde Lezoux. (a) *c* AD 135–160

4 77 *2419* (920) 2138 Biga 1a 18/31R [BIG[A.FEC Lezoux. (a) *c* AD 125–150

5 73 *2910* 1 89 Buccula 3a 27 BVCCVLΛ.Λ retrograde Les Martres-de-Veyre. (c) Hadrianic

6 79 *2918* (1642) 2860 Cauterra 3a 27 (slightly burnt) CΛV[TERRA] Lezoux. (a). *c* AD 145–175

7 56 *1995* Celsus ii 2a 33 CELSI[M[Lezoux. (a). *c* AD 169–190

8 79 *2819* (1569) 2807 Censor i 3b 18 [OFC.]EN La Graufesenque. (b). *c* AD 65–90

9 79 *2819* (1571) 2903 Censor 3d 27 OF.CIIN retrograde La Graufesenque. (a). *c* AD 65–90

10 79 *2821* (1594) 3007 Censor i 3h 15/17R or 18R OFCEN La Graufesenque (b). *c* AD 65–90

11 77 *2319* (1028) 2209 Cosius Rufinus 12a 27 CO[SRVF] La Graufesenque. (b). *c* AD 70–90

12 77 *2718* (741) 2161 Crestio 5b 29 ·OFCR[ESTIO] La Graufesenque. (a). *c* AD 45–65

13 79 *2822* (1669) Crestio 5c 18R [OFCRES]TIO La Graufesenque. (b). *c* AD 70–90

14 79 *2822* (1669) Crestus 1a 18 OFCREƧTI retrograde La Graufesenque. (b). *c* AD 70–90

15 75 U/S & 75 *2017* (4) 885 Epapra 1b 27 IIPΛPRΛ//Les Martres-de-Veyre. (a). *c* AD 100–120

16 58 Cellar 4 55 1996 Fabianus ii 2a 33 FΛBIΛNIMΛ retrograde Lezoux. Antonine

17 79 *2822* (1630) 2857 Firmo ii 3a 15/17 or 18 [O.FIR]MONIS La Graufesenque. (b). *c* AD 60–75

18 82 24/2524 (3144B) 4213 Fuscus ii 9b 27g FVSC, in a frame with swallow-tail ends, La Graufesenque. (b). *c* AD 80–110

19 72 *2019* (77) 144 Iullinus i 3a 27g [IVLLI]NI. La Graufesenque. (b). *c* AD 70–100

20 61 F6 (3) 1998 Licinus 23b 15/17 or 18 OFLICIN La Graufesenque. (b). *c* AD 45–65

21 82 *2321* (4) 4258 Licinus 49c 29 [L]ICNVS La Graufesenque. (b). *c* AD 45–65

22 73 *2120* R13/14 185 Logirnus 10a 18 LOGIRNM La Graufesenque. (a). *c* AD 65–85

23–4 73 *2120* (45) R15 176; 80 *3716* (2067) 3423 Maccalus 3a 38 or 44; 33 MACC[; MACCALIM Lezoux. (a). *c* AD 160–200

25 60 F4 1984 Maguanus 1a 18/31R[MA]GVΛVIM:Lezoux. (a). *c* AD 150–180

26 79 *2918* 1643 Mallus 2b 27 MΛLLIM Lezoux. (b). *c* AD 125–155

27 72 *2019* (77) Manduilus 18a 15/17 or 18 MΛN[DV.] La Graufesenque. (b). *c* AD 65–85

28 72 *2723* (1542) 2785 Marcellinus ii 2a 31 MARC[ELLIИI⊦] Lezoux. (a). *c* AD 160–200

29 1978 Survey TL1130–0825 Marcellus iii 2a 33 MARCELLI.M, in a frame with swallow-tail ends, Lezoux. (a). *c* AD 125–155

30 76 *2722* (701) 1399 Marcus vi 2a – [MAR]CV[SF] Rheinzabern. (a). Late second- or early third-century

31 75 *2117* (624) 1288 Modestus i 5a 15/17R OFW[ODEI] La Graufesenque. (b). *c* AD 45–65

32 74 *2022/2122* (77) 686 Murranus 10a 15/17 or 18 [O]F.MVRRA La Graufesenque. (b). *c* AD 55–70

33 72 *2019* (77) 144 Niger ii 2a 18 OFNIGRI La Graufesenque. (a). *c* AD 55–70

34 74 *2022*, 2122 (77) 687 Pass(i)enus 9a 15/17 or 18)FPASSE (from a reduced die originally giving OFPASSE) La Graufesenque. (b). *c* AD 65–80

35 *73 1920* (30) 86 Paterclus ii 12a or 12a' 18/31 [PATE]RCL[VSF] or PATE]RCL[I\] Les Martres-de-Veyre. (a). *c* AD 110–125

36 79 *2821* (1594) 3007 Patricius i 3h 15/17 or 18 OFPATRIC(I) La Graufesenque. (b). *c* AD 65–90

37 78 *2517* (1393) 2493 Patricius i (?) 13c(?) 15/17 or 18 [PΛTRIC]I La Graufesenque. (b). The attribution is very tentative, but the penultimate letter is almost certainly a C. *c* AD 70–95

38 79 *2822* (1552) 2880 Patricius i 13e 27g PΛTRIC[I] La Graufesenque. (b). *c* AD 70–95

39 77 *2721* (881) 1994 Peregrinus i 3a 18 [PERE]GRIИ La Graufesenque. (a). *c* AD 75–100

40 75 *2117* (624) 1137 Perrus i 6b Ritterling 9 PERRIMN La Graufesenque, (a), Banassac. (a). This example is in La Graufesenque fabric. *c* AD 55–70

41 *73 2121* (77) 351 Pontus 8h 27g OΛONT(I) LaGraufesenque. (b). *c* AD 70–100

42 79 *2821* (1594) 3007 & 76 *2721* 770 1905 Pudens 3a 27g)FPVDƎNT La Graufesenque. (a). *c* AD 70–85

43 80 *3917* (2016) Reginus ii 1a or 1a' REG[INI.M] Les Martres-de-Veyre. (b). *c* AD 130–150

44 *75 2118* (661) 1262 Regulus 3a 31 [.ꓘRƎGVLI.]MΛK· Lezoux. (b). CAD 140–160

45 79 *2819* (1569) 2807 Rufus iii 3g 27 OFRVFI retrograde La Graufesenque. (b). *c* AD 65–90

46 1956–61. Sq 2 Area B 36 1997 Scoplus 1a 31 (burnt) [SCOPL]I.M Lezoux. (a). *c* AD 160–190

47 *73 2118* (661) 1262 Scotnus 5a 15/17 or 18 ·SCOT[NS·] La Graufesenque. (b). *c* AD 45–60

48 79 *2822* (1669) Secundus i 8c′ OF.SECVΛ‹/D› La Graufesenque. (b). *c* AD 65–90

49 77 *2418* (741) Secundus ii 12d 33a OFSEC La Graufesenque. (b). *c* AD 65–90

50 80 *3716* (2073) 3218 Serullus 1a 31 SERV[LLLIM] (sic) Lezoux. (c). *c* AD 155–190

51 74 *2022* (414) 631 Severus i 7p OFSEVERI (F in the O) La Graufesenque. (a). *c* AD 70–90

52 *76 2121* (812) 1895 Silvius ii 1a 18/31 SILVI[.OF] Lezoux. (b). *c* AD 125–145

53 74 *2122* (5130) 2165 Tauricus i 1a 33 (T)AVRICIOF Lezoux. (a). *c* AD 150–180

54–5 74 *2022, 2122* (77) 685; 77 *2718* (1073) 2321 Tertius ii 4a 18R; 15/17R or 18R TERTI.MA;]RTI.MA La Graufesenque. (b). *c* AD 40–65.

56 79 U/S Tittius 2a 18/31 TITTIVSFE Lezoux. (a). *c* AD 130–160

57 77 *2720* (1053) 2298 Verecundus vi 6a 31 VƎRECVИDV. A stamp from a die used, successively, at La Madeleine, Ittenweiler, Heiligenberg and Haute-Yutz, and belonging to a potter whose other dies are attested at Rheinzabern. The Gorhambury piece is most likely to have been made at Heiligenberg. Mid- to late-Antonine

58 77 *2418* (714). Victor iv 6a 33 VIC.F Lezoux. (b). No other examples of this stamp have been noted. *c* AD 160–200

59 74 *2022* (369) 623 Virilis i 6c 18 ORVIIRIL[I] La Graufesenque. (b). The first vertical stroke comes from a scratch on the die, and is present on most examples of the stamp. *c* AD 75–100

60 *72 2019* (77) Vitalis ii 6c 18 OF.VITΛL La Graufesenque. (b). *c* AD 70–95

61 *75 2018* (91) 1024 Vitalis ii 24a or 24a′ 27g VITALIS[F] or VITALIS La Graufesenque. (a). *c* AD 65–90

Unidentified

62 79 *2821* (1578) 3008 An illegible stamp on form 29, South Gaulish. Probably Neronian

63 81 *3720* (2540) 3868 Λ...IN on form 15/17r or 18R, South Gaulish. Pre-Flavian

64 73 *2021* (29)^298 GAL..(?) on form Ritterling 8 (?), South Gaulish. Pre-Flavian

65 74 *2121* (449)^708A \[ ]COC(?) retrograde on form 27g, South Gaulish. Pre-Flavian

66 *73 2121* 77^356] И on form 18, South Gaulish. Neronian or early-Flavian

67 *73 2121* (77)^351 [IИ on form 27g, South Gaulish. Neronian or early-Flavian

68 79 *2821* (1574)^3015]. . . . X on form 27g, South Gaulish. First-century

69 79 *2819* (1572)^2903 FV[(?) on form 33a, South Gaulish. Flavian–Trajanic

70 56(?) J6 2^1989]CΛSV[retrograde on form 31, from Les Martres-de-Veyre. Hadrianic–Antonine

71 80 *3917* (2016)^3218 CR[retrograde on form 33, Central Gaulish. Hadrianic or early-Antonine

72 78 *2417* (1267)^2485 An illegible stamp on form 33, Central Gaulish. Antonine

Illiterate

73 82 *3023* (3107)^4100 IIIIII(?) on form 15/17R or 18R, South Gaulish. Pre-Flavian

74 79 *2821* (1594)^3007 INV on form 27g, South Gaulish. Flavian or Flavian–Trajanic

75 79 *2822* (1669)]IN·I on form 27, South Gaulish. Flavian or Flavian–Trajanic

76 73 *2120* (45)^260 FΛΛ III-I\I on form 27, Central Gaulish. Hadrianic or early-Antonine

77 80 *3716* (2018) AI...[on form 31, Central Gaulish. Early-Antonine

78 77 *2419* (920)^2141 IVN on form 33, Central Gaulish. Antonine

The glass (Figs 163–165)

Five hundred and thirty samples of vessel and window glass were recovered from the excavations. Some contain multiple fragments from the same vessel, or fragments from different vessels (hence the duplication of several small find numbers). The writer has examined all these items and made drawings of virtually every different vessel rim or fragment with decoration. These drawings form the basis of the catalogue. Only rarely was it possible reliably to relate base and body fragments, but nevertheless a wide range of bases is also illustrated. Unfortunately, owing to an oversight, insufficient time was allowed for specialist study of the glass but through the good offices of the Romano-British Glass Project, Leeds, it has been possible to identify the general form and type of glass of the illustrated assemblage. The non-drawn material has not yet been identified but the Project hopes to publish a full report including that material at a later date. No attempt is made here, therefore, to date the material or to provide the discussion which it deserves, though it may be observed that the assemblage includes a large proportion of high quality tablewares of the first and second centuries.

As with the other general finds, the majority of the samples were recovered from the filling of the ditches. A vessel of particular interest is a cast segmental bowl in green/blue glass with small millefiori insets (No 3, Fig 163).

Window glass was also found over much of the site and was mostly blue/green but of interest is the use of blue glass in both the bath-house (Building 41) and the bath-suite in Building 37. No pane size could be established. A tessera of opaque green glass was found over the mosaic pavement in Room 1, Building 37.

Cast vessels

1	(77/2323)	Blue/green pillar moulded bowl
2	(79/2892)	Cast millefiori wide-rimmed bowl; emerald green ground with opaque yellow spots and occasional opaque red ones
3	(79/2869)	Cast segmental bowl. Green/blue (peacock) ground with slices from a cane with a pattern of 6 opaque yellow petals and central dot in an opaque red ground, set at intervals on the interior
4	(75/1193)	Cast colourless shallow bowl with wide rim.
5	(75/994)	Cast (?) colourless bowl
6	(75/947)	Cast (?) colourless bowl
7	(77/2318)	Cast (?) colourless bowl
8	(75/1233)	Cast colourless bowl
9	(79/2748)	Cast colourless bowl

Blown vessels

Deep blue

10	(74/441)	Tubular-rimmed bowl
11	(77/2092)	Jar with fire-rounded rim
12	(75/1188)	Cylindrical-neck fragment of jug or flask

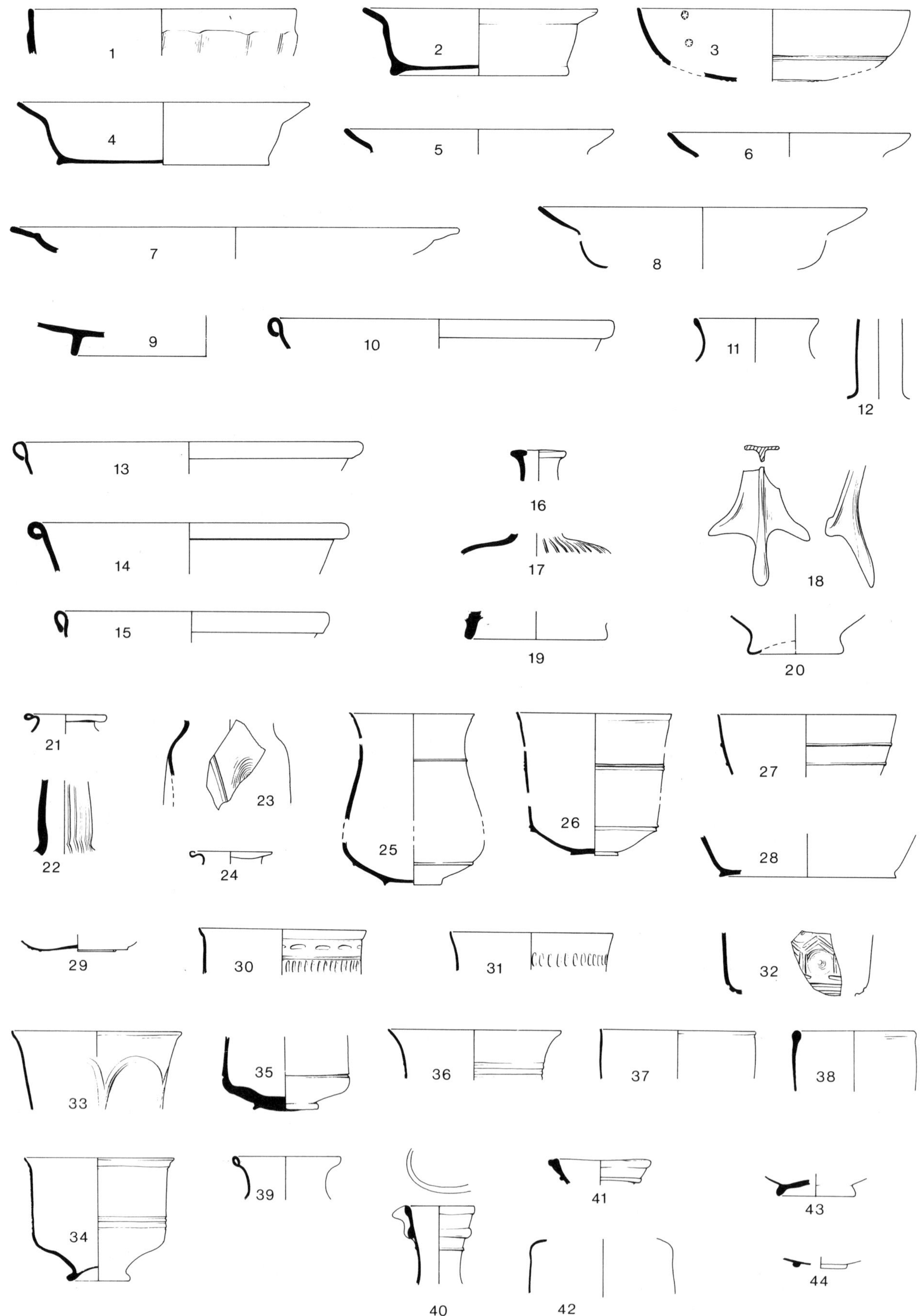

Fig 163 The glass (Scale 1:3)

Yellow-brown

13	(76/1849)	Tubular-rimmed bowl; dark yellow/brown
14	(79/2893)	Tubular-rimmed bowl; dark yellow/brown
15	(79/2878)	Tubular-rimmed bowl; yellow with greenish tinge
16	(74/636)	Folded rim of jug or flask; dark yellow/brown
17	(74/627)	Ribbed body fragment from (globular) jug: dark yellow/brown
18	(77/383)	Handle fragment of jug; light yellow
19	(81/3802)	Base with applied true base ring; side grozed; dark yellow/brown
20	(74/514)	Open pushed-in base ring of jar or jug; light yellow/brown

Yellow/green

21	(77/2505)	Jar with rim edge rolled in
22	(77/2069)	Ribbed neck fragment from jug

Light green

23	(74/640)	Arcaded beaker; light greenish colourless
24	(79/2954)	Jar with rim edge rolled in

Colourless

25	(75/897)	Beaker; exterior ground and polished to leave decoration in relief
26	(75/1187)	Beaker; exterior ground and polished to leave decoration in relief
27	(77/342)	Cup; exterior ground and polished to leave decoration in relief
28	(72/122)	Bowl; exterior ground and polished to leave decoration in relief
29	(77/2340)	Cup; exterior ground and polished to leave decoration in relief, interior polished
30	(74/795)	Facet-cut bowl
31	(74/467)	Facet-cut bowl
32	(74/459)	Facet-cut bowl
33	(75/1218)	Arcaded beaker
34	(74/556)	Wheel-cut cylindrical beaker with pushed-in base ring
35	(79/2716)	Wheel-cut carinated beaker; separately blown foot, grozed off and ground
36	(77/2204)	Wheel-cut cylindrical beaker; greenish colourless
37	(72/47)	Wheel-cut beaker
38	(80/3308)	Cylindrical cup
39	(73/392)	Jar with rolled rim
40	(76/1517)	Spouted jug decorated with trails, rim edge rolled in
41	(76/1338)	Funnel-mouthed jug decorated with trails; fire rounded rim
42	(76/1503)	Shoulder fragment of cylindrical bottle
43	(76/1534)	Base and lower body with tubular pushed-in base ring
44	(76/1578)	Base with tubular pushed-in base ring

Blue/green

45	(82/4170)	Beaker
46	(72/82)	Conical Beaker
47	(77/2204)	Tubular-rimmed bowl
48	(74/653)	Tubular-rimmed bowl
49	(82/4171)	Tubular-rimmed bowl
50	(75/1242)	Body fragment of tubular-rimmed bowl
51	(80/3313)	Bowl with cut-out fold
52	(74/582)	Body fragment from bowl with cut-out fold
53	(73/101)	Body fragment from bowl with cut-out fold
54	(77/2131)	Body fragment from bowl with cut-out fold
55	(75/819)	Collared jar
56	(77/2339)	Collared jar
57	(78/2559)	Collared jar, rim edge first rolled in
58	(79/2847)	Collared jar, rim edge first rolled in
59	(76/1330)	Jar
60	(74/567)	Jar
61	(72/45)	Jar
62	(72/123)	Jar
63	(74/493)	Jar
64	(74/629)	Jar
65	(75/1048)	Jar
66	(79/2893)	Jar
67	(82/4370)	Jar
68	(79/2984)	Ribbed conical jug with concave base
69	(77/339)	Ribbed handle fragment of jug
70	(74/514)	Open pushed-in base ring of jug or jar
71	(76/1582)	Funnel-mouthed jug
72	(75/896)	Rim of flask or jug
73	(76/1978)	Rim of flask or jug
74	(76/1577)	Rod-handle fragment of jug
75	(79–2820)	Rod-handle with pinched lower attachment from jug
76	(74/694)	Conical-bodied unguent bottle
77	(77/2270)	Base with tubular pushed-in base ring
78	(73/247)	Prismatic or cylindrical bottle
79	(75/1247)	Prismatic or cylindrical bottle
80	(75/1279)	Prismatic or cylindrical bottle
81	(75/1247)	Prismatic or cylindrical bottle
82	(74/603)	Prismatic bottle; base design 2 concentric circular mouldings with a central dot
83	(82/4279)	Square bottle; base design 1 circular moulding with petal pattern inside
84	(79/2894)	Ribbed barrel jug; base design 1 central circular moulding with other, possibly fortuitous, marks

Late Roman greenish colourless

85	(73/155)	Hemispherical cup
86	(76/1526)	Cylindrical beaker; blue-tinged
87	(73/223)	Cup or beaker with fire-rounded rim
88	(81/3511)	Jug with pushed-in base ring
89	(75/764)	Body fragment of ribbed barrel-jug
90	(76/1431)	Concave base with pontil scar
91	(76/1922)	Base with tubular pushed-in base ring

Early finds (1956–61) (Fig 165)

Colourless

92	(56/49)	Cylindrical facet-cut bowl
93	(58/59)	Cylindrical cup
94	(56/38)	Indented cup or beaker
95	(56/39)	Body fragment, facet-cut
96	(59/99)	Body fragment, colourless snake-thread decoration

Blue/green

97	(56/39)	Jar
98	U/S	Square bottle; base design 1 circle
99	(6/11)	Ribbed barrel-jug; base design 3 concentric circles with letters 'FRO' (Frontinus)

Late Roman greenish colourless

100	(61/hypocaust channel)	Hemispherical cup

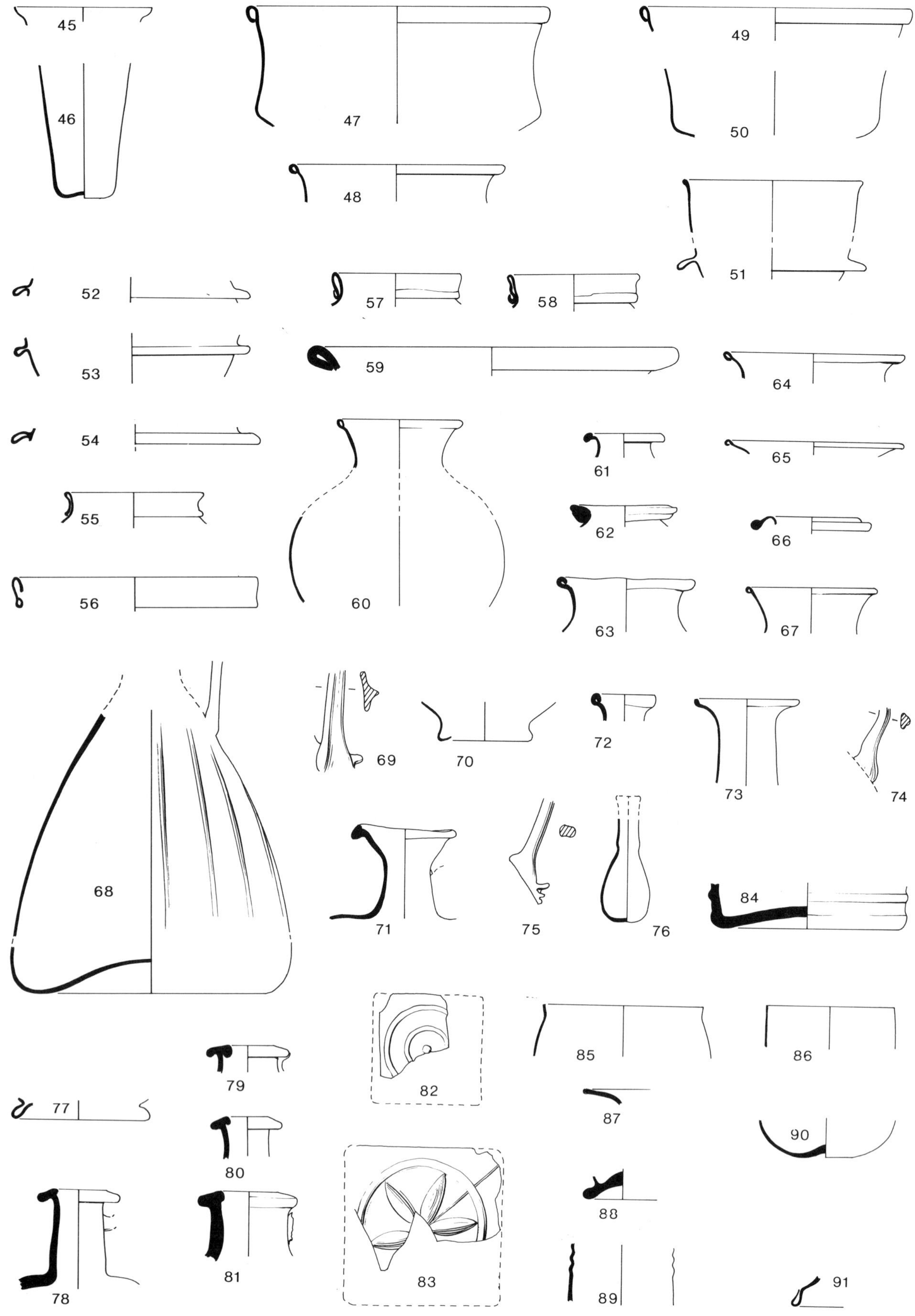

Fig 164 The glass (Scale 1:3)

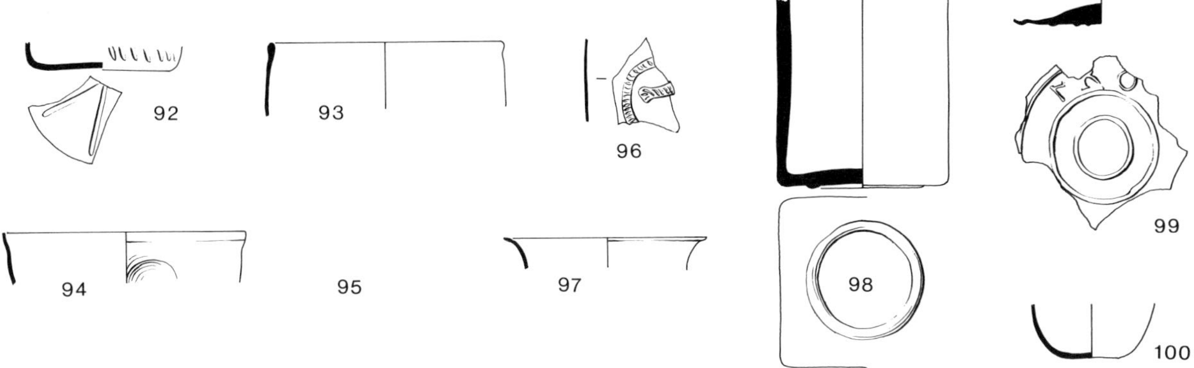

Fig 165 *The glass (Scale 1:3)*

The mammal, bird and fish bones

by Alison Locker

Introduction

A total of 15,815 larger mammal bones was recovered from securely dated deposits of Iron Age, Roman and medieval date. Bird, small mammal and fish remains were also found; these were examined and have been made the subject of separate reports (pp 210 and 212). The larger mammals, birds and small mammals were recorded using the method of Jones *et al* 1981; copies of the descriptive and metrical archives are held at the Ancient Monuments Laboratory. The bones are stored at Verulamium Museum. Sieving was carried out on most major deposits based on a 10kg sample size; this facilitated the recovery of many bird, small mammal and fish bones that might otherwise have been missed.

The larger mammals

Detailed tables held in archive form summarise the number of bones for each species in each layer; Table 18 summarises the number of bones in each general phase.

Table 18 Bones of larger mammals, by period

	Iron Age	*1st century AD*	*2nd century AD*	*3rd/4th centuries AD*	*Medieval*	*Total*
Ox *Bos* domestic	81	441	473	370	81	1446
Ovicaprid *Ovis* domestic/ *Capra* domestic	39	248	355	186	110	938
Pig *Sus* domestic	42	334	362	137	76	951
Horse *Equus* domestic	18	42	82	74	61	277
Large ungulate (ox-sized)	192	1474	1922	1205	281	5074
Small ungulate (ovic-sized)	73	737	1044	407	189	2450
Red deer *Cervus elaphus*	1	3	7	5	5	21
Roe deer *Capreolus capreolus*	–	4	4	1	–	9
Dog *Canis* domestic	22	60	44	38	4	168
Cat *Felis* domestic	–	–	–	1	–	1
Hare *Lepus* sp	–	8	12	5	1	26
Rabbit *Oryctolagus cuniculus*	–	2	–	–	–	2
Unidentifiable	139	1382	1622	1017	292	4452
Total	607	4735	5927	3446	1100	15815

Goats were positively identified from horn cores and a single femur, and sheep from a horn core. The Boessneck (1969, 354) index for separating sheep and goat based on the relative proportions of the distal ends of the metapodials did not suggest goats were present, so it is assumed that the large majority of ovicaprids are sheep. The large ungulate group could also include fragments of horse and red deer, although it is likely to be largely ox. The small ungulate group is mainly ovicaprid material, but could also include pig and roe deer. Loose teeth were included in the counts.

To assess the relative proportions of the three main domestic animals in each period two methods of counting were employed. The 'epiphyses only' method, devised by Grant (1971, 377) and used on both the Fishbourne and the Portchester material, was compared with the relative percentages of the total number of fragments. Both methods were calculated excluding the large and small ungulate categories (Table 19).

The total number of fragments should favour ox since the fragmentation of the carcase should be greater than for ovicaprid or pig. The importance of cattle in the Iron Age is reduced in the 'epiphyses only' method, with an increase in the percentage of ovicaprids. However both methods suggest that cattle were most important in the Iron Age and Roman deposits, particularly the late Roman. Here the 'epiphyses only' method highlights the importance of cattle and shows pig to be at its relatively lowest percentage. The same trend is shown in the total number of fragments but the differences are less diverse. In the medieval occupation, where the sample is very small (the total number of fragments for the three species is 267), the epiphyses method suggests cattle are still most numerous, but the total number of fragments shows ovicaprids to be the highest percentage for the first time. This difference could reflect a change in the fragmentation pattern of either species, but with such a small sample it cannot be evaluated.

Butchery

Evidence of butchery has been recorded on the basis of marks or breakage points caused by a specific instrument such as a chopper or knife. A few saw marks were observed but these are thought to be associated with bone-working. Fragmentation which does not show specific butchery marks may also be the result of tertiary butchery such as the smashing of bones for marrow extraction. Since the majority of the bone from this site is from Roman deposits most of the evidence of butchery is Roman. The Iron Age and medieval bone was insufficient to suggest any different techniques for dismembering carcases.

Ox: Only a few horn cores were present and there was no evidence of the method of their removal from the skull. They may have been taken from the site so that the horn could be removed elsewhere for working. Skull fragments tend to be very heavily fragmented, with a few examples of knifecuts, probably a result of skinning. On the mandible chopmarks were seen about the gonion, diastema and through the molar alveoli (the latter may be a tertiary activity for marrow extraction) in the first- and second-century material. On one third/fourth-century mandible knifecuts were seen across the diastema. In the separation of joints scapulae were mainly chopped across the neck and occasionally across the glenoid cavity (as at Exeter, Maltby 1979, 39). Humeri were chopped midshaft and across the distal articulation; the proximal ends of this bone do not survive well. Similarly radii were chopped midshaft and also across the proximal joint surface. Ulnae (all first-century) were chopped across the articulation, part of the same action as chopping through the proximal radius. Butchered metacarpals were only found in Roman deposits and were chopped through the midshaft as were the metatarsals. Since metapodials bear little meat this is unlikely to be for joint preparation and Maltby (1979, 39) has suggested the midshaft may be chopped for marrow

Table 19 The relative proportions of the three main domestic animals

Epiphyses only

	IA	*1st century AD*	*2nd century AD*	*3rd/4th centuries AD*	*Medieval*
Ox	43%	48%	49%	69%	40%
Ovic	30%	28%	27%	19%	36%
Pig	27%	24%	24%	12%	24%

Total numbers

	IA	*1st century AD*	*2nd century AD*	*3rd/4th centuries AD*	*Medieval*
Ox	50%	43%	40%	53%	30%
Ovic	24%	24%	30%	27%	41%
Pig	26%	33%	30%	20%	28%

extraction. Ossa coxae, largely from second-century deposits, were usually chopped through the acetabulum and also the ilium neck. The number of femora present is low, both in the ox and large ungulate categories. The few butchered examples were chopped through the midshaft and one second-century example through the proximal joint surface associated with the chopping of the acetabulum of the pelvis. Similarly tibiae were scarce with few examples of proximal and midshaft chopping. The tibiae from Exeter (Maltby 1979) were very fragmentary; perhaps the tibiae and femora from Gorhambury were also so fractured for marrow removal that their remains are classified within the large ungulate long bones fragments. The few examples of butchered calcanea and astragali represent the limits of the meat-bearing area of the hind limb. Many rib fragments were cut by knives, a result of cutting along the flanks of the animal. Phalanges were mainly whole with only two examples of knifecuts.

Knifecuts may be evidence of skinning (particularly when they occur on the limb extremities and on the skull) and also evidence of the 'boning out' of joints and other cuts of meat.

Ovicaprids: butchery tended to be less intense than for ox since the carcase is much smaller; however skulls were still fragmented – one had the horns chopped off. A second-century goat horncore was chopped above the junction with the skull and also had been cut, while one ovicaprid horncore fragment was chopped from the skull. Mandibles were fairly complete showing little indication of butchery and seem to have been regarded as waste material. The few examples of scapula and humerus butchery could be evidence that these two bones formed a single meat joint, although some instances of chopmarks across the midshaft of the humerus may suggest some preference for a smaller joint. Radii are chopped across the midshaft; one had knifecuts across the proximal joint surface. Saw marks across a second-century radius shaft are likely to be bone-working waste. No butchery was recorded on metacarpals except one small ungulate fragment chopped across the midshaft. On the hindlimb, ossa coxae are sometimes chopped through the acetabulum and occasionally through the ilium neck; the femur was chopped through the midshaft (including the only goat femur, identified from second-century deposits). Tibiae tend to be broken or chopped across the midshaft; the most commonly found parts of the tibia are the shaft and distal end. The distal end is more robust than the proximal end since it fuses earlier, and may also represent the waste end of the limb, leg joints commonly being cut off at the midshaft of the tibia as suggested at Exeter (Maltby 1979, 53). Metatarsals showed more evidence of ?butchery than metacarpals: three were chopped across the midshaft, one with knifecuts at the midshaft and another with cut marks at the proximal end. These marks may be more closely associated with bone-working than butchery since two first-century and one second-century metatarsals were perforated at the proximal ends; one midshaft section had been slightly shaved and polished. Phalanges were invariably complete. Ovicaprid rib fragments often had knifecuts indicating cutting along the flanks as with ox. Vertebrae were chopped both medio-laterally and also in the sagittal/axial direction, probably in the preparation of cutlets.

Pig: Butchery included skull fragments that had been chopped and cut; one first-century atlas had been chopped and cut with a knife but only one mandible had been chopped, at the diastema. Most butchery of scapulae was across the neck, repeatedly chopped and cut, with occasional instances across the glenoid cavity. Humeri were mostly chopped across the midshaft and, less frequently, at the distal joint surface. Similarly the radius was most often chopped across the midshaft and sometimes across the proximal joint surface. Three second-century ulnae were chopped across the articulation. On the hind limb examples of butchered ossa coxae and femora are few, although many of the bones are fragmentary; some chop marks and knifecuts were seen on the ischium of the pelvis, and femora showed a few chop-marks on the midshaft and proximal joint surface. All tibia butchery is on the shaft; one second-century tibia shaft was sawn through and is likely to be bone-working waste. Two second-century astragali were chopped, but the numerous metapodials did not show any evidence of butchery.

Horse bones were generally little fragmented; two tibiae had cut marks on the shaft and an Iron Age metatarsal shaft had been perforated; the former may be evidence of skinning and the latter bone-working. The low level of fragmentation suggests that horse was not eaten in any period.

A red deer scapula had been chopped across the neck (first-century), a medieval metacarpal chopped across the shaft, and Roman and medieval antlers had been chopped and sawn. A medieval roe deer humerus was chopped across the shaft and an antler chopped at the cranial end.

A second-century hare femur had a knifecut at the proximal end; this could have occurred at the table rather than preliminary butchery.

Knifecuts were observed on the midshaft of a dog tibia in second-century and medieval deposits. These may be skinning marks.

Ageing

Two methods can be used for ageing domestic animals: tooth eruption and wear or the epiphysial fusion of long bones; however the former method is more reliable. The method for scoring eruption and wear in ox, ovicaprid and pig devised by Grant (1975) was used, but since this requires a fair degree of completeness in the mandible this method tended to be inconclusive for this site. The stages devised by Maltby (1979) were also used which require a less complete jaw; the results are summarised in Tables 20–22. No ageing was attempted on loose teeth, only those teeth attached to fragments of mandible.

Ox: a total of 96 ox mandibles had some ageing information (Table 20); at the lowest level this was represented by a single tooth in a mandible fragment.

Table 20 Ox: aged by mandibles according to Maltby 1979

Stage	*1*	*2*	*3*	*4*	*5*	*6*	*no unaged*	*Total*
Iron Age	–	1	1	–	–	2	2	6
1st century AD	–	4	–	–	8	10	5	27
2nd century AD	–	5	–	4	9	14	1	33
3rd/4th centuries AD	–	1	–	1	3	8	5	18
Medieval	2	1	2	1	3	2	1	12

Key:
Stage 1 = The fourth deciduous premolar in wear
Stage 2 = Both columns of the first molar in wear
Stage 3 = Both columns of the second molar in wear
Stage 4 = The first column of the third molar in wear
Stage 5 = All columns of the third molar in wear
Stage 6 = The fourth premolar in wear

Although numbers are low, apart from the first- and second-century deposits it appears that the majority of cattle attained at least stage 5 and often 6 during the Roman period. The small quantity of ageable material from the late Roman period did not permit any speculation as to a change in the slaughtering pattern allied to the relative increase in cattle previously suggested. The most diverse ageing is seen in the medieval mandibles, but again the quantity is too small to be reliable.

A study of the epiphysial fusion, which is not discussed in detail here as it is a less reliable method, also supports the view that the majority of the cattle in the Iron Age and Roman period at Gorhambury were mature animals. The age attributed to them cannot be precise, but their primary functions were breeding, traction and milk, with the quality of meat as a secondary consideration. Three mandibles (two first-century and one third/fourth-) had the third pillar of the third mandible missing; this is a genetic anomaly.

Ovicaprid (it is likely that these are mainly sheep): the mandibles were generally less fragmented than ox, providing more detailed information about their age structure. Using the Maltby stages the results set out in Table 21 were found (the stage achieved should be regarded as a minimum since not all mandibles were complete).

Table 21 Ovicaprid: aged by mandibles according to Maltby 1979

Stage	*1*	*2*	*3*	*4*	*%1–3*	*no unaged*	*total*
Iron Age	4	–	2	2	75%	–	8
1st century AD	11	2	13	8	76%	12	46
2nd century AD	6	4	12	15	59%	7	44
3rd century AD	1	1	2	2	67%	4	10
Medieval	2	1	–	5	38%	5	13

Key:
Stage 1 = Both columns of the first molar in wear
Stage 2 = Both columns of the second molar in wear
Stage 3 = Fourth premolar in wear
Stage 4 = All columns of the third molar in wear

The percentages represent the proportion of ovicaprid mandibles that did not achieve stage 4 or later. Maltby has suggested (1979, 42) that stages 2 and 3 are animals of 15–26 months. Although the small samples must be treated with caution the percentages are particularly high for the Iron Age and the first century, and in the latter for stage 1. Maltby has suggested that the slaughter of non-breeding stock between stages 2 and 3 could have already provided at least one fleece (1979, 43).

It would seem that, as at Exeter and Portchester, flocks of mature breeding stock were maintained, with a few aged individuals, while a proportion of 'fat lambs' and older juveniles were culled. The evidence from epiphysial fusion does not contradict this interpretation.

Pig: the percentages in Table 22 represent the proportion that did not achieve stage 6. Because of the low figures only the first and second centuries may have any validity, the remainder being included for completeness. However well over half the pigs were slaughtered before all columns of the third molar were in wear. In the second century the four mandibles on stage 1 are from young animals, possibly under 6 months old (Silver 1969, 299). The high fecundity rate of pig, an animal whose main uses are breeding and meat, results in a more variable age structure than is usually found for cattle and ovicaprids. From the measurements of the third molar it would appear that the pigs in all periods at Gorhambury were within the domestic range.

All the horse remains were from adult animals; as mentioned earlier there is no evidence that horse was eaten. All these are likely to have been working animals, either for riding or traction. A horse's working life can begin at three to four years and with care can continue until its twenties.

Similarly the dog remains all suggested adult animals, except for a single mandible from the third to fourth centuries in which the third and fourth premolars had not erupted, which takes place at 5–6 months (Maltby 1979, 299). These may have been household dogs or working animals; their size is discussed in the next section.

Size determination

A number of measurements of complete bones permitted the estimation of the shoulder heights of some domestic species. The following ranges were calculated.

Ox (using Fock 1966 and Matolcsi 1970):

Iron Age	1.075m	n = 1
1st century AD	1.101–1.217m	n = 2
2nd century AD	1.073–1.230m	n = 4
3rd/4th centuries AD	1.043–1.144m	n = 3
Medieval	1.20m	n = 1

The numbers of withers heights are really too small to suggest any significance other than that they fit generally into the expected ranges for sites in south-eastern England.

Table 22 Pig: aged by mandibles, using Maltby 1979

Stage	*1*	*2*	*3*	*4*	*5*	*6*	*%1–5*	*no unaged*	*total*
Iron Age	–	1	–	1	2	2	67%	1	7
1st century AD	–	4	3	7	3	14	55%	2	33
2nd century AD	4	5	2	8	–	14	58%	4	37
3rd/4th centuries AD	1	–	–	1	3	4	56%	1	10
Medieval	–	–	–	7	–	6	54%	–	13

Key:
Stage 1 = Deciduous premolar 4 in wear
Stage 2 = Both columns of the first molar in wear
Stage 3 = Both columns of the second molaar in wear
Stage 4 = Fourth premolar in wear
Stage 5 = The first column of the third molar in wear
Stage 6 = All columns of the third molar in wear

More measurements were available for the distal width of the tibia. The Gorhambury tibiae compare well with both Magiovinium, a roadside settlement on Watling Street, Bucks (Locker 1988) and Portchester (Grant 1975, 399) although the Exeter cattle have a smaller range than those from the other three sites.

Gorhambury	range 50.5–68.7mm	n = 20
Portchester	range 50.0–69.0mm	n = 143
Magiovinium	range 50.8–71.5mm	n = 19
Exeter	range 49.7–65.1mm	n = 20

Ovicaprid (using Teichert 1975): the number of withers height that could be calculated were few and are shown below; again these fit generally into the expected ranges for sites in south-eastern England.

1st century AD	0.59 m	n = 1
2nd century AD	0.568–0.629 m	n = 4
3rd/4th centuries AD	0.613 m	n = 1
Medieval	0.561–0.638 m	n = 5

Horse (using Kiesewalter in von den Driesch and Boessneck 1974):

Iron Age	1.183–1.317m	n = 3	(approx 11 to 13 hh)
1st century AD	1.347m	n = 1	(approx 13 hh)
2nd century AD	1.276–1.456m	n = 4	(approx 12 to 14 hh)
3rd/4th centuries AD	1.295–1.554m	n = 2	(approx 13 to 15 hh)
Medieval	1.255–1.382m	n = 4	(approx 12 to 14 hh)

The approximate conversion to hands height shows that, apart from the upper range of the third and fourth centuries, most horses were of small to large pony size. A withers height of 15 hands is considered to be a small horse. These were adult, probably working animals and compare well in size with those from Magiovinium (Locker 1988), for which the metapodials suggested a size of 12 to just under 15 hh (n = 25). The few horse bones from Gadebridge (Harcourt 1974b, 259) were also from ponies of 13–14 hh.

Dog: estimated shoulder heights are given below calculated from Harcourt (1974a):

1st century AD	368mm	n = 1
2nd century AD	375mm	n = 1
3rd/4th centuries AD	547mm	n = 1

The dog was represented by a variety of forms during the Roman period, as shown by Harcourt (1974b), from veryy small lap dogs to large hunting or guard dog types. Columella describes the desirable attributes of both farm and sheep dogs, most of which would not be discernible from skeletal material, eg the 'ample bulk' required for a guard dog on the farm. Columella also makes brief references to 'sporting hounds' although he does not discuss them further. The size range of dogs from Gorhambury is not remarkable however, as can be seen from the measurements above.

Hunting

Neither red deer nor roe deer are present in large quantities, but would have provided both sport, possibly hunted on horseback using dogs, and a welcome variety in diet. Their antlers would also have provided a valuable raw material.

Hares could have been trapped or hunted with dogs. The two rabbit bones in a first-century deposit are likely to be intrusive.

Pathology

The incidence of pathology was low. Malocclusion in ox was observed on the fourth premolar and the first molar of a first-century mandible, and on the third molar of two second-century mandibles. Antemortem loss of the second premolar was seen on a first-century mandible. Exostoses occurred on two first-century metatarsals, one on the distal joint surface and one on the midshaft lateral surface. These conditions might be attributable to some sort of stress from traction. Exostoses were observed on two first phalanges, of first-century date, both over the shaft area.

Ovicaprids showed less incidence of pathology and are probably less prone to any post-cranial pathology since they were not used for any work. One first-century mandible showed swelling around the alveoli of the first molar, the result of infection. Ossified tendons were seen on a third/fourth-century tibia.

Pig pathology was restricted to the mandibles and feet. A second-century mandible had caries in the second molar and one third-century mandible showed antemortem loss of the first molar with associated pathology in the mandible. One second-century metapodial showed evidence of a fracture and a third/fourth-century metapodial had exostoses on the shaft.

A second-century horse metatarsal was fused at the proximal end with the tarsal bones, a relatively common condition in both cattle and horse called 'spavin' which could be related to stress in work. A third/fourth-century metatarsal had exostoses developing across the proximal joint surface.

In the third/fourth-century deposits a dog mandible showed antemortem loss of the fourth premolar, and on a humerus exostoses covered the distal joint surface.

Conclusions

Analysis of the animal bones from Gorhambury suggests that from the Iron Age farmstead through the Roman villa occupation cattle were the most important stock, particularly in the late Roman occupation, as at Gadebridge (Neal 1974). Conversely sheep numbers are low through the Roman period but increase in the medieval period, as do pig. One of the methods used to assess the relative percentages of the three species suggests that sheep were the most numerous species in the medieval occupation, but the sample is too small for any firm conclusions to be made.

In his survey of Roman sites in Britain, King (1978, 211) has shown that it is common for sheep to decline in relation to ox and pig at the end of the Roman period. But in his view the native sites tend to favour sheep more. However at Gorhambury in the limited material available for the Iron Age both methods used to assess the importance of cattle, sheep and pig favour cattle. The suitability of the landscape for cattle may have outweighed the traditional trends. During the Roman period the town of Verulamium may have provided an important outlet for surplus stock. Wooded areas around the villa would have been useful both for hunting and to provide pannage for pigs.

The small mammals

Small mammal bones were recovered from a number of sieved deposits; although two intrusive rabbit (*Oryctolagus cuniculus*) bones were found in first-century deposits it is assumed that the remainder are contemporary (see Table 23).

Of the many small mammal remains from the second century, 76 of the 107 fragments came from the granary robber trench, context 920. Bank vole, field vole, wood mouse and black rat were specifically identified from this feature.

The habitats preferred by these species suggest a mixed environment including some long grass and scrubby cover all of which could probably be found round the settlement.

The black rat has only been identified from Roman levels relatively recently. Previously thought to have been introduced to Britain in the medieval period and associated with the spread of bubonic plague in Europe, it has now been identified from Roman levels at York, London and Wroxeter. At the latter site the deposits may also be second-century (Armitage *et al* 1984, 381). At Gorhambury black rat was identified from context 920, a second-century granary robber trench, so there may be some element of doubt regarding its contemporaneity. Two rat femora were found in medieval deposits but these could not be identified specifically.

The bird remains

Some 301 bird bones were recovered from securely dated contexts, 78% being found in first and second century contexts (the measurements are available in the archive).

Table 24 shows the total number of each species found in each period. The many unidentifiable bird fragments are mainly from splintered long bones.

Domestic fowl was the most commonly identified species in the Roman and medieval periods. However, none were found in the Iron Age deposits; fowl are known to have been kept at this time, but Caesar has remarked they were not kept for meat. Domestic fowl were all identified from post-cranial fragments except for one broken skull from the third/fourth century. One spurred metatarsal represented a male, or possibly a capon, from the second century (West 1985). Knifecuts were observed close to the distal end of a first-century humerus and across the midshaft of a second-century humerus. A second-century ulna showed exostoses over the midshaft; this may be the result of an injury to the wing.

Geese were also identified from the Roman levels; whether these geese were domestic or the greylag (*Anser anser*) type from which the domesticate is thought to have originated is not clear. Similarly it was not possible to separate domestic duck from mallard, which were the second most commonly identified birds; these two groups may represent the slaughter of domestic birds kept at the villa or the catch of wild fowlers. Wild pigeons may have been encouraged to use 'columbaria' for nesting and breeding, as have been found at a few villa sites (Wilson 1973, 114).

Wild fowlers would also have caught teal, Britain's smallest duck, and woodcock, which can be found in forests and heathlands with scattered trees, feeding on swampy and marshy ground, conditions probably prevailing along the River Ver.

Today crane only occurs in Britain as an annual migrant, but used to be much more common. Two tibiotarsus shafts were tentatively identified from a first-century context (69). The adult birds tended to make tough eating and a Roman method for overcoming this recommended that the bird be cooked with the head outside the water; when the crane was cooked it was wrapped up in a warm cloth and the head pulled so that the it came off with the

Table 23 Bones of small mammals by period

	Iron Age	*1st century AD*	*2nd century AD*	*3rd/4th centuries AD*	*Medieval*	*Total*
Common shrew (*Sorex araneus*)	–	1	8	2	–	11
Bank vole (*Clethrionomys glareolus*)	–	–	2	1	–	3
Field vole (*Microtus agrestis*)	–	–	2	–	–	2
Wood mouse (*Apodemus* sp)	–	1	3	–	–	4
House mouse (*Mus musculus*)	–	–	1	1	–	2
Black rat (*Rattus rattus*)	–	–	1	–	–	1
Rat indet	–	–	–	–	2	2
Mouse indet	–	1	4	2	–	7
Weasel (*Mustela nivalis*)	–	–	–	1	–	1
Bat indet (*Chiroptera*)	–	1	–	–	–	1
Frog/Toad (*Rana* sp/*Bufo* sp)	–	1	5	2	–	8
Small mammal indet	1	14	81	16	9	121
Total	1	19	107	25	11	163

Table 24 Bones of birds by period

	Iron Age	*1st century AD*	*2nd century AD*	*3rd/4th centuries AD*	*Medieval*	*Total*
Domestic fowl (*Gallus* domestic)	–	24	32	11	3	70
Goose (*Anser* sp)	–	2	9	1	–	12
Duck/Mallard (*Anas* sp/*Anas platyrhynchos*)	–	9	11	1	–	21
Duck indet	–	1	–	1	–	2
Teal (*Anas crecca*)	–	2	–	–	–	2
?Crane (*Grus grus*)	–	2	–	–	–	2
Woodcock (*Scolopax rusticola*)	–	2	6	–	–	8
Pigeon (*Columba* sp)	–	–	–	2	1	3
Blackbird (*Turdus merula*)	–	5	1	–	–	6
?Song thrush (*Turdus philomelos*)	–	1	–	1	1	3
Finches (Fringillidae)	1	2	–	–	–	3
Rook (*Corvus frugilegus*)	–	–	1	–	–	1
Crow (*Corvus corone corone*)	–	–	1	2	–	3
Jackdaw (*Corvus monedula*)	2	1	–	–	1	4
Unident	–	63	62	16	20	161
Total	3	114	123	35	26	301

sinews attached leaving only the meat and bones (Wilson 1973, 115).

Small birds such as thrushes etc may have been netted, as in other Roman provinces, and were added to dishes containing many ingredients such as meat, brains, vegetables, pulses and herbs (Wilson 1973, 115). The corvids (rook, crow and jackdaw) have been eaten in the past and could also have been killed as pests scavenging round the villa. Butchery marks were seen only on domestic fowl and goose.

The fish bones

A total of 331 fish bones was recovered from sieved samples. It was not always possible to identify the remains precisely; for example the chub-dace pharyngeals were from such small specimens as to make the distinction between these closely related species very difficult. Table 25 indicates the total number of each species in each period.

Even when account is taken of the proportionately high number of vertebral centra per fish compared with the other species present, eel is still the most numerous species in the Roman period. Both skull remains and vertebral centra were found. Eels could have been caught in rivers using spears or in basket-like traps called 'eel-bucks' which are stretched across the water facing up stream to trap the eels migrating seawards (Wheeler 1979, 61). By the medieval period eels were also being stored live in ponds (Hickling 1972, 119). The salmonid (either salmon or trout), cyprinid (including dace/chub) and percoid remains are also evidence of local river catches. Neither dace nor chub are particularly good to eat and the presence of such small specimens may imply an incidental catch.

Any marine fish is likely to have reached the villa in a preserved state given its inland situation. The herring may have been pickled in amphorae, as was suggested for the herring and sprat remains from Peninsular House, London (Bateman and Locker 1982, 204–7). The mackerel remains, of which two vertebral centra (of first- and second-century date) were more akin to the Spanish mackerel (*Scomber japonicus*) than mackerel (*Scomber scombrus*), are oily fish and quickly decompose; they may have been preserved in the same manner as herring. Spanish mackerel has been identified from Roman Southwark in association with amphorae (Locker unpublished). Since the British distribution of this species only covers the south-west it would have to be marketed pickled in brine. In the medieval period herring fishing was a very important industry; smoking was the most popular technique for preserving them.

Apart from local fishing activities the markets of Verulamium may have sold a variety of preserved marine fish.

Acknowledgements

The writer would like to thank Roger Jones of the Ancient Monuments Laboratory for help in processing the computerised data and identifying some of the small mammal and bird remains. Acknowledgements are also extended to Angus Wainwright for taking the samples on site and to Alwyne Wheeler (British Museum Natural History) for help in identifying the fish bones and making accessible reference material.

Table 25 Bones of fish by period

	1st century AD	*2nd century AD*	*3rd/4th centuries AD*	*Medieval*	*Total*
Eel (*Anguilla anguilla*)	206v	26v 1d 1sk	2v	8v	244
Herring (*Clupea harengus*)	1v	5v	–	8v	14
Salmonid	–	2v	–	–	2
Dace/Chub (*Leuciscus leuciscus/ Leuciscus cephalus*)	3ph	–	–	–	3
Cyprinid (Cyprinidae)	–	1pre	–	–	1
Percoid	1sc	2sc	–	–	3
Scombroid	2v	1v 1sk	1v	–	5
Plaice/Flounder (*Pleuronectes platessa/ Platichthys flesus*)	1v	–	–	–	1
Flatfish	1v	–	–	–	1
Unident	13	25	3	16	57
Total	228	65	6	32	331

Key:
v = vertebral centra
pre = premaxilla
sc = scale
ph = pharyngeal
d = dentary
sk = skull fragment

The mollusc and seed remains

by Angus Wainwright

Method

As many deposits as possible were sampled with the aim of recovering seeds, mollusc remains and small bones. To obtain reasonable results it was found necessary to take large samples, normally 10kg. These were processed on site. A conventional flotation machine could not cope with the clay soils, so most samples were recovered by wet sieving and flotation, the sieve used having a mesh of 1mm. Although numbers of juveniles and smaller mollusc species were lost using this method, it was felt that this loss was worthwhile considering the number of deposits that could be sampled cheaply and quickly on site; comparative samples processed through graded sieves in laboratory conditions showed that the losses were small enough to have no significant effect on the conclusions drawn.

Samples from ditches cut through chalk were taken in columns through the section. Normally 2 kg loads were taken at 100mm intervals, but where closer sampling was required (eg from buried soils), they were taken at 20mm intervals. The high concentration of shells in these chalky soils and the ease with which they could be broken down (compared with those from clay soils) allowed wet sieving through graded sieves down to 0.5mm.

On the villa area the low pH of the soil would not normally allow the preservation of molluscs. However, where soil pH had been raised by the presence of alkaline materials such as mortar, cob and chalk, molluscs were preserved. For this reason most shells were recovered close to the site of buildings.

The results have been presented as bar graphs showing percentages of the whole for each species. Some of the more typical samples are presented here. The results of other samples mentioned in the text can be found in the site archive.

Molluscs

General interpretation

In the Roman period the most frequently occurring species were *Trichia hispida* (Linné), *Discus rotundatus* (Müller) and *Vallonia costata* (Müller). Of the *Zonitidae*, *Oxychilus cellarius* (Müller) and *Aegopinella nitidula* (Draparnaud) were the most frequent. The low numbers of *Carychium tridentatum* (Risso) were confirmed by processing comparative samples through finer sieves.

The snail shells were normally found in deposits along with pottery sherds, bones and rubble, often in the upper fills of such features as ditches, wells and robber trenches such as context 920 (Fig 166A).

The molluscan evidence suggests shaded habitats, perhaps overgrown with scrub and thick herbage. The low numbers of *Carychium tridentatum* suggest that these habitats suffered some disturbance, possibly due to the periodic dumping of domestic refuse and the everyday movement of livestock and people around the site. Given this interpretation, the high proportion of *Vallonia costata* (normally an open country species) is unusual, but as Evans (1972) points out, this species does occasionally behave syncanthropically: on the Gorhambury estate it has been found in large numbers amongst nettles and brambles around farm buildings.

The presence of such woodland species as *Acanthinula aculeata* (Müller), *Macrogastra rolphii* (Turton), *Cochlodina laminata* (Montagu), *Ena obscura* (Müller) and *Helicigona lapicida* (Linné), so close to human habitation, is of great interest. These species were originally restricted to woodland habitats, but may now be found in hedgerows. Their presence here indicates the proximity of such habitats; these species would have found it impossible to colonise a suitable, isolated, habitat across any extent of open ground. Two explanations for their presence are possible:

(i) The villa site was adjacent to an area of relic woodland removed, perhaps, during the occupation of the site leaving hedges only.
(ii) The villa site was surrounded by a hedge which joined another long established hedgerow, itself derived from or joined to relic woodland.

Species typical of open habitats such as *Vallonia excentrica* (Sterki), *Pupilla muscorum* (Linné), *Vertigo pygmaea* (Draparnaud) and *Helicella itala* (Linné) were present in most samples. These must have strayed from nearby grassy areas (eg cattle enclosures and yards) which ran up close to the features from which the samples were taken.

The samples from medieval layers (Fig 167B) produced small numbers of shells. These deposits did not contain the alkaline material found in the Roman period. Instead, the shells were found amongst ash and charcoal in ovens and grain driers. These indicate a different environment from that implied in the Roman period. Open country species predominate, particularly *Vallonia costata* and *Vallonia excentrica*. Amongst the species of shaded habitats only *Oxychilus cellarius* and *Aegopinella nitidula* occur in any numbers. Apart from three specimens of *Clausilia bidentata* (Ström), woodland species were absent. *Helix aspersa* (Müller) appears for the first time on this site. The environment indicated is one of long grass with disturbed areas, perhaps around the various ovens. The specimen of *Clausilia bidentata* may have lived under ivy on the buildings of the site or may have arrived with fire wood.

Samples from dyke sections

(for location of dyke sections see Fig 6)

The preservation of snails from the dyke sections, as opposed to elsewhere on the site, was very good. They are described in some detail here as they represent a

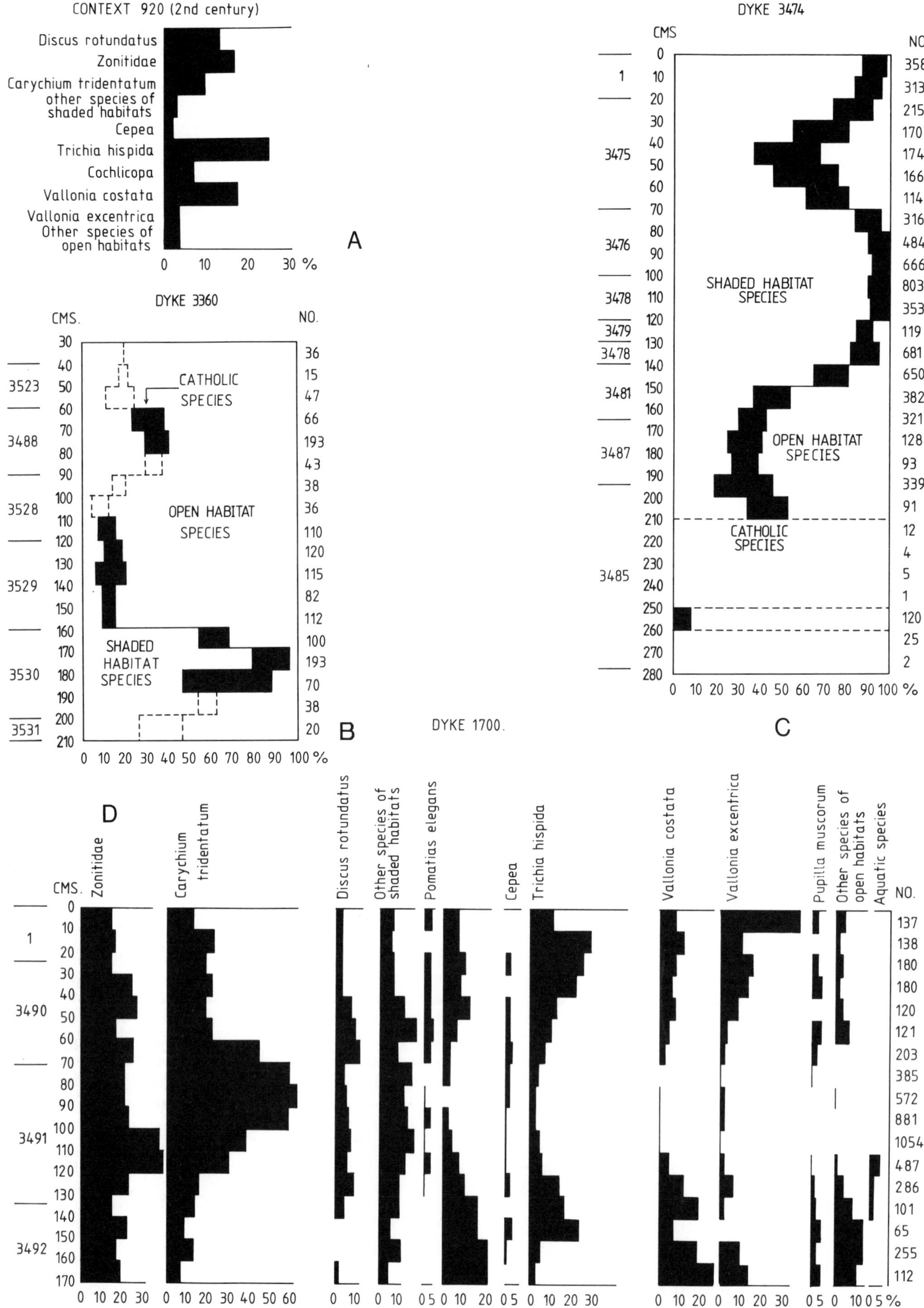

Fig 166 Graphs showing varieties and frequency of snails recovered from the filling of specific features

sequence from the late Iron Age to the present day. Although the snails may be reflecting merely local conditions they do seem to show evidence for environmental changes in a wider context.

Column samples through White Dyke (3360) (Fig 166 B; Section, Fig 24)

Buried soils

Layer 3489 The profile of the buried soil indicates some disturbance perhaps by ploughing, chalk lumps being spread evenly throughout. The molluscan evidence suggests an open dry environment, dominated by *Vallonia excentrica*. Only in the top 40mm does a significant change occur with a rise in the numbers of *Pupilla muscorum* to 38% of the sample. A more disturbed soil surface is indicated.

3531 Primary deposit of broken chalk, a few shells in similar proportions to the buried soil (these shells perhaps derive from fallen turf).

3530 The lower 200 mm of this deposit shows a change from an open environment dominated by *Vallonia excentrica*, to a more humid and overgrown one with the *Zonitidae*, *Carychium tridentatum* and *Trichia hispida*, dominating.

3529 The bottom 150 mm of this deposit continues the trend seen in the layer below with species of shaded habitats dominating. These include *Ena obscura*, *Marpessa laminata* and *Clausilia bidentata*. A damp, shaded woodland/hedgerow environment is indicated. The rest of this deposit contained snails in very similar proportions to those of the buried soils. A grassland habitat is indicated.

3528 A rapidly laid down deposit with few shells.

3588 Open country species predominate here particularly *Pupilla muscorum*. Dry broken turf is indicated. Woodland species constitute 25% of these samples. These include *Acicula fusca* (Montagu), *Ena obscura* and *Cochlodina laminata* and therefore part of this soil must derive from an established woodland or hedgerow habitat.

3523 Few shells in this plough soil. *Vallonia excentrica* is the largest constituent of this open country group.

Column sample through bank

Layer 3353 Similar fauna to that preserved in the buried soil.

3355 Few shells preserved here.

3356 Open country species dominate. Unlike the buried soil, *Pupilla muscorum* comprises only 2%. *Carychium tridentatum* occurs in values up to 10%. A grassland environment with more surface stability than the buried soil is indicated.

Ploughwash predating bank (3488)

Layer 3526 *Vallonia excentrica* predominates here with *Carychium tridentatum* reaching 24% of the sample. Moist grassland with a stable soil surface is indicated.

3525 Few shells of snails of open habitats.

3524 Similar sample to that taken from below, but here a few woodland species occurred (*Acicula fusca*, *Cochlodina laminata*).

3523 Shells concentrated in the bottom 200mm. These were predominantly species preferring open habitats.

Dyke 3474 (Fig 166 C; Section Fig 24)

3485 One sample towards the centre of this primary deposit contained shells presumably derived from a fallen turf. *Pupilla muscorum* reaches a value of 35%; a similar proportion to that reached in the top 40mm of the buried soil profile. An open, dry habitat with a disturbed soil surface is indicated.

Top 100mm of 3485, 3487 & 3481 The fauna here is dominated by species of open habitats, particularly *Vallonia costata*.

The *Nesovitrea hammonis* (Ström), *Euconolus fulvus* (Müller), *Punctum pygmaeum* (Draparnaud) and *Vitrina pellucida* (Müller) group described by Evans as typical of the secondary fill of ditches, is particularly well represented here. Although such woodland species as *Ena montana*, *Cochlodina laminata* and *Clausilia bidentata* are present in 3487, species of shaded habitats do not begin to dominate until the deposition of layer 3481.

These samples indicate a ditch with unstable sides, partially grass covered with, perhaps, isolated patches of undergrowth. The woodland species may well be intrusive, remembering that these deposits represent recuts of the original ditch.

It is worth noting that this fauna is quite different from those of any of the plough wash deposits found in Dyke 3360, where *Vallonia excentrica* always dominates. This suggests that these shells were derived from snails living in the immediate vicinity of the ditch rather than individuals arriving in plough wash from further afield.

The top 100mm of 3481 sees the fauna being dominated by species of shaded environments. The sides of the ditch must now be stabilised and covered by thick grass and patches of scrubby undergrowth

Recuts 3478 and 3476

Samples from these deposits show a progressive increase in the numbers of species of shaded habitats and an increase in the variety of these species. For instance *Helicigona lapidica*, *Colomella edentula* (Draparnaud) and *Acicula fusca* appear for the first time. A stable well established woodland habitat is indicated with a depth of leaf mould building up in the ditch.

Layer 3479, a thin band of material in the midst of 3478, shows a drop in the numbers of shells retrieved and a slight increase in the proportion of open country snails. A phase of disturbance is indicated probably due to an opening up of the tree canopy: tree felling may have taken place. *Pomatias elegans* (Müller) is present throughout, no doubt burrowing into the loose soil of the bank.

Towards the top of 3476 woodland species decrease in numbers, a trend which is carried on into the middle of layer 3475. Tree felling followed by ploughing up to the bank would explain this (the phase of ploughing represented by layer 3475).

From the middle of 3475 onwards to the most recent deposits, species preferring shaded habitats show a steady increase indicating the re-establishment of trees and undergrowth over the side of the ditch, a situation that continues today.

It is worth noting that from the bottom of recut 3487 onwards the graph follows the curve that might normally be expected had the ditch not been recut several times. This is because the digging of the various ditches did not disturb the evolving habitat of the steep bank that overshadowed all these ditches.

Column sample through Dyke 1700 (New Dyke) taken from south end of ditch near terminal close to White Dyke (3474, Figs 166D and 167A)

Layer 3493 Primary deposit with few shells.

3492 Samples from this deposit are dominated by snails of open habitats; *Vallonia costata* and the *Cochlicopa* species. The fauna here is very similar to that found in the secondary ditch deposits of dyke 3474. Grasses and other herbage must have established themselves on the unstable ditch sides.

At the interface 3492 and 3493 there is a sudden decrease in the proportion of *Vallonia costata* and an increase in that of *Trichia hispida* and also a decrease in the total number of shells retrieved. It is difficult to interpret this information, though it is worth noting that at the interface of these layers, water snails begin to appear.

3491 This layer sees the re-establishment of *Vallonia costata*. *Trichia hispida* remains fairly common but decreases (along with *V costata*) as species preferring shaded habitats increase in number and variety. This change in snail fauna reflects a change in environment; from thick grass to scrubby undergrowth.

By the middle of 3491, open country species are very scarce and the fauna has become a woodland one. This is probably because a tree canopy had become firmly established over the ditch and a rich damp layer of leaf mould had formed there. *Pomatias elegans* is present here and throughout the rest of the history of the ditch.

At the interface of 3491 and 3490 there is quite a dramatic reduction in the proportion of woodland snails, and an increase in the numbers of open country species and of *Trichia hispida*. This suggests an opening up of the tree canopy resulting in the dessication of the habitat. Presumably this is a result of post-medieval quarrying in this area. The sample from the top 100mm is dominated by *Vallonia excentrica* but with species of shaded habitats still constituting 34% of the sample. This reflects today's dry edge of field habitat with isolated trees and patchy undergrowth within a few metres.

Dyke 1700; section in Stoney Valley

(bar graph not illustrated)

Samples taken from the ditch section and from deposits behind the bank produced few snails perhaps due to the acid conditions prevailing during periods of waterlogging. The molluscs that were recovered here proved interesting. They included *Planorbis planorbis, Pisidium amnicum* and one of the *Bithynia* species. The presence of these species suggests that the area behind the bank and the ditch itself were filled with water for a considerable time, allowing the establishment of settled, open water fauna.

3497, the upper deposit behind the bank, contained a quite different group of species. Here, shells were well preserved. The fauna is dominated by *Carychium tridentatum* and the *Zonitidae*: a few woodland species also occur. Open country species comprise 20% of the whole. A habitat of scrub and occasional grassy clearings is suggested, although later ploughing may have mixed open country species with an earlier woodland fauna.

Summary of samples from dyke sections

The earliest ditch deposits in Dykes 3474 and 1700 are dominated by open country species particularly *Vallonia costata* and *Vallonia excentrica*. In both these dykes a gradual stabilisation of the ditch sides by grass and bushes can be detected. Later, the dyke was overhung by trees and filled with a damp layer of leaf mould. The woodland fauna from these samples included such species as *Acicula fusca* (Montagu) and *Columella edentula* (Draparnaud).

The later history of these dykes shows a resurgence of open country species as the ditches were filled in by the ploughing up of adjacent fields and the thinning out of trees.

In the case of Dyke 3474 the steady increase in the numbers of woodland species amongst the trees and shrubs around the ditch was unaffected by a series of recuts of this ditch.

The fauna preserved in the buried soil under the bank of Dyke 3474 is an open country one dominated by *Vallonia excentrica*. A large number of *Pupilla muscorum* shells occur in the top 40mm. This perhaps represents the remains of a turf line. The soil profile indicates light cultivation with the formation of a rather broken dry turf prior to the building of the bank. Very similar faunas were found in ploughwash deposit in the top two-thirds of the ditch 3360. Samples from the lower third produced a fauna which changed from one of open habitats to one of shaded environments with some woodland species present. These perhaps derived from a nearby hedge.

A series of samples were taken from a section through Dyke 1700 at the lowest point of Stony Valley. Shells were very badly preserved in these samples. Identifiable examples proved to be of water species such as *Planorbis planorbis, Pisidium amnicum* and one of the *Bithynia* species. These species indicate that the ditch and the area behind the bank were filled with water for long periods. Samples from the deposit above contained a fauna of shaded habitats with a significant open country constituent, suggesting a scrub habitat with occasional clearings, though it is possible that later ploughing has mixed two different faunas.

Macrogastra rolphii, a species that occurred in samples from shaded habitats on the villa, is entirely absent from the dyke sections, whereas *Aegopinella pura* (Alder), a very common species in these samples, was found relatively infrequently on the villa site, and it is assumed that these species are showing some habitat preference relating to the different soil types of these two areas. *Vallonia costata*, a species of open habitats which occurred in shaded habitats on the villa, was not able to survive in the true woodland environment which developed around the dykes. *Carychium tridentatum* occurred in low numbers on the villa, but in the undisturbed, shaded dykes it occurred in great numbers, up to 30% of some samples.

Seed remains (Fig 167C)

Carbonised seed remains were retrieved from floor surfaces, deposits of rubble or domestic rubbish. The total number of seeds recovered was small: 5,500, of which 34% were unidentifiable; the condition of the rest was not good. The badly abraded surfaces of the majority of the grain suggests that these may have been residual from earlier deposits. The seeds were often found with large amounts of charcoal suggesting that they may have derived from the inclusion of chaff or straw in domestic fires.

Rachis fragments were very rarely preserved so identification relied on the morphology of the grains; the accuracy of this, therefore, cannot be guaranteed. The small number, bad preservation and uncertain origin of the seeds mean that conclusions as to trends in arable agriculture at Gorhambury also have to be treated with caution.

Throughout the Roman period wheat is the most

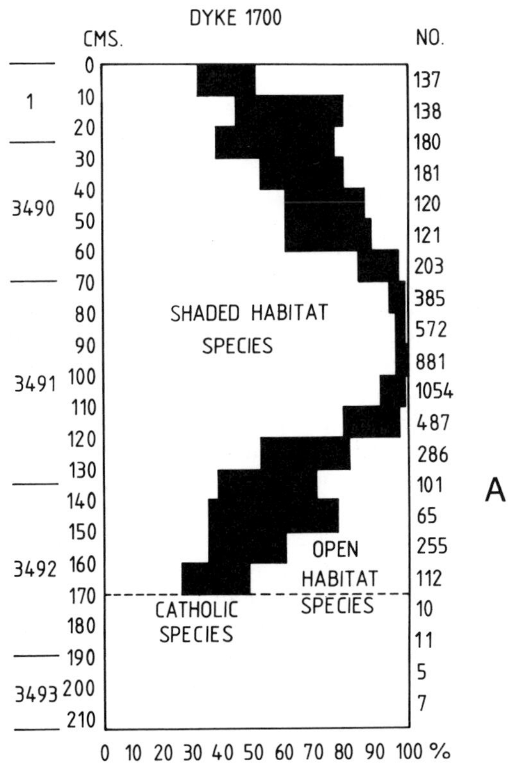

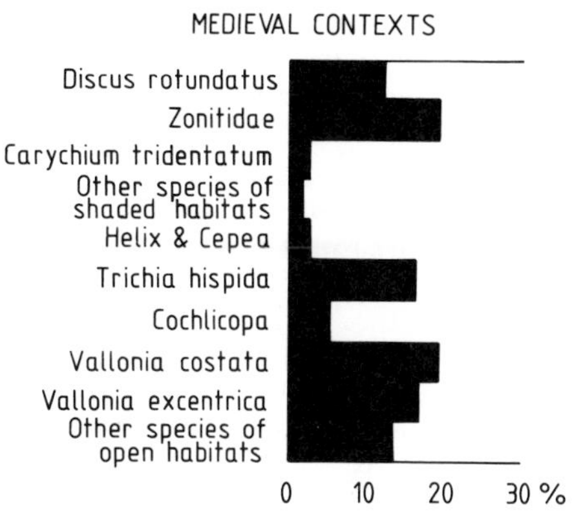

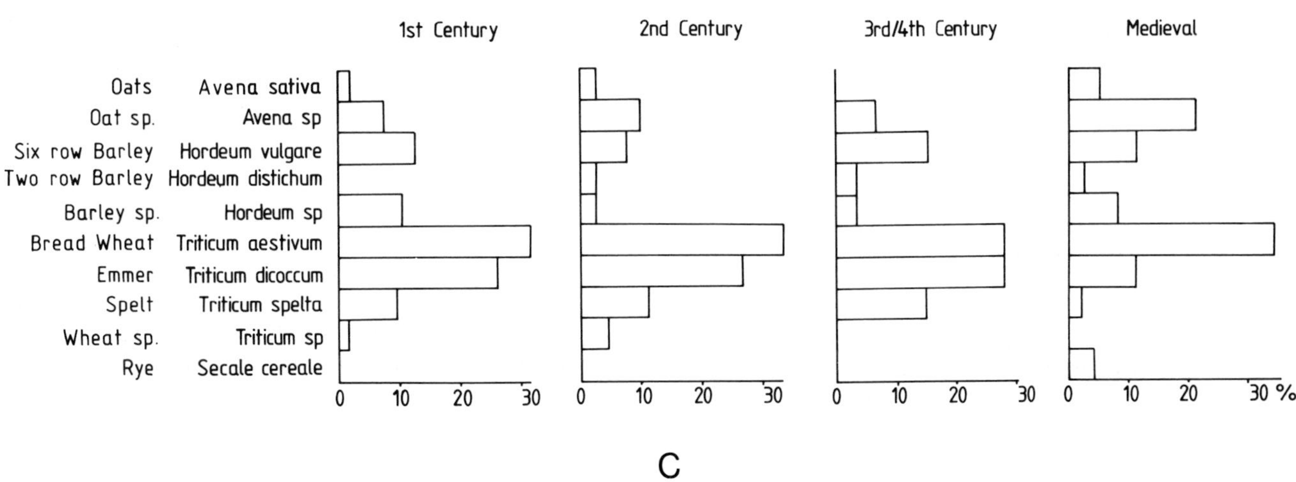

Fig 167 Graphs showing percentage of snail species (A and B) and percentage of cereal types (C)

common cereal found. *Triticum dicoccum* and *Triticum aestivum* occur most frequently in first- and second-century deposits. In the third and fourth centuries *Triticum spelta* occurs in larger numbers than before but *T aestivum* and *T dicoccum* remain the most commonly occurring species in samples.

Barley was noticeably absent: only one sample from a second-century context contained any; in this case *Hordeum distichum*.

Small grains of oat species occurred fairly frequently; these seeds may result from crop contamination rather than the cultivation of oats.

In medieval contexts *Triticum aestivum* was the most commonly occurring species however. One sample was composed almost entirely of *Hordeum distichum* grains, indicating that barley was grown at this time.

Oat grains were found in a higher proportion of samples from medieval contexts but perhaps not in large enough numbers to prove deliberate cultivation. Crop contamination may explain the presence of *Secale cereale* in one sample; it is unusual for this to be grown as a crop in the south of England.

Only one sample is worth mentioning in detail: this is from a third/fourth-century grain drier (context 1953). Of the grain in this sample, 35% was not identifiable but of the identifiable grain 13.7% was *Triticum aestivum*, 35.9% *Triticum dicoccum*, and 50.2% *Triticum spelta*. One grain of *Hordeum vulgare* was also found. As this sample comes from a grain drier it is possible that these proportions are close to the actual crop grown at this period.

Weed seeds were found in small numbers: they were all from plants typically found in field and field-edge habitats. *Papaver somnifera* occurred in one third/fourth-century sample and could have been a relic of cultivation or a crop contaminant; the same applies to *Brassica*. Leguminosae seeds occur frequently, particularly in medieval contexts. These may have derived from weeds in grain crops, though *Vicia sativa* and *Vicia faba* may have been grown as a crop in their own right.

The seeds of trees and shrubs such as the *Prunus* species and Hawthorn (*Crataegus*) may have been accidentally included with firewood. Shells of Hazelnuts (*Corylus avellana*) are likely to have been deliberately gathered. The Walnut (*Juglans*) shell is almost certain to have come from a cultivated tree.

Mineralised seeds

Some mineralised seeds were recovered from a first-century cesspit. These included seeds of a number of edible plants. Some such as *Prunus spinosa* (sloe) would have been gathered from wild or hedgerow plants. All could have grown locally though it seems likely that fig (*Ficus*) seeds arrived in imported dried fruit. The fruit species indicate a fairly varied diet including some more exotic species such as grape (*Vitis*) and fig. The surprisingly large number of sloe stones may be explained by the ease with which these small stones are swallowed compared with the larger ones from the other plum species. The absence of pear and apple pips could result from selective preservation or because cores were not eaten! The small numbers of pulses and the absence of grain from the sample suggest that these were thoroughly ground during food processing; this may also explain the low number of food flavouring seeds. Some weed seeds were also found but may have been washed or blown into the pit, or derived from contaminants of flour.

The flints (Figs 168 and 169)

by Andrew Pye

The lithic assemblage recovered from the excavations numbered some 327 pieces. The raw material consists entirely of flint, which varies considerably in colour, quality and patination. As it contains no obvious imported examples, it was presumably derived from local deposits of glacial drift and outwash material, and of weathered chalk bedrock. In this it appears typical of other similar local assemblages (Alison Turner-Rugg, pers comm).

Furthermore, most of the assemblage, except some 18 pieces from a slot belonging to Building 1 (a mere 5.5% of the total), came from residual contexts of Iron Age, Romano-British or later date, principally from medieval and later ploughsoils. Recovery of the flintwork from the latter was mostly in bulk, with moreover much of the ploughsoil being removed by machine. Also much of the assemblage has suffered edge damage, presumably as a consequence of ploughing. Thus neither distributional nor microwear analyses would seem to be worthwhile, and consequently have not been undertaken. However, the general diagnostic features of the assemblage and their dates can be summarised as follows (a complete breakdown of the elements is provided below).

Parent waste forms a minute part of the assemblage, and consists of one single platform conical blade core (no 1), together with three other heavily damaged possible cores of indefinite type. The use of the former for the production of blades would suggest either a Neolithic or Mesolithic date. Of the remainder of the flintwork, some 241 pieces (75%) represent product waste, and 82 (25%) have been retouched or utilised.

Blades, here defined as flakes having a length of at least double their breadth (nos 2–8, 10 and 11), form 25.6% of the total product waste, a proportion which differs little (ie 25.2%) on the inclusion of the retouched and utilised components. Of the total blade assemblage (79 pieces), 13 (some 16.6%) appear to have been utilised (eg nos 5–8), of which nos 5 and 7 clearly display visible edge gloss, and 4 (5%) have been retouched (nos 3 and 4). Also, excluding the 24 snapped blades, 35 (47.8%) have pointed distal ends, indicating perhaps that they were produced from single platform cores, and 20 (24.3%) have square distal ends, suggesting production from a double platform core, with in one case (no 4) flake scars struck from the distal end of the blade as well as from the bulbar.

Of the retouched component, the only clearly diagnostic pieces are two fine Earlier Bronze Age ('Beaker') scrapers (nos 15 and 16). The remainder consists of types which generally occur throughout much of the Neolithic and Bronze Age, though for example the small 'borers' or spurred implements (nos 23–27), which here seem relatively numerous, do seem to occur most commonly in the later Neolithic-Earlier Bronze Age period.

Thus, apart from an insignificant Mesolithic element represented by the three burin spalls (eg no 14), the assemblage seems to be largely Neolithic in date, on the basis of its generally ill-defined and nondescript nature and the substantial blade component. However, an Earlier Bronze Age element is also indicated especially by the 'Beaker' scrapers (nos 15 and 16). As such, although the assemblage is largely residual in context, its general Neolithic date certainly does not contradict the radiocarbon date of 3513–3389 cal BC from the earliest structure on site (Building 1). The latter date is further supported by the presence of four blades (typically Neolithic or earlier; including no 7) in one of the 'slots' belonging to the building. Thus the presence of the assemblage clearly indicates a Neolithic-Earlier Bronze Age phase of activity on or near the site of the later Iron Age and Romano-British occupation, and is wholly typical, in its range and relatively low quality, of other local lithic assemblages from St Albans and the surrounding area (Alison Turner-Rugg, pers comm).

Acknowledgements

My thanks especially to Alison Turner-Rugg, formerly of Verulamium Museum, for her comments on the assemblage as a whole and to Dr Roger Jacobi of Lancaster University.

Summary of the assemblage

The numbers in brackets refer to illustrated examples.

Cores: 1 definite (no 1), 3 possible.

Flakes: Plain – 177
Utilised – 10 (no 9)
Miscellaneous retouch – 23 (nos 12, 29, 30)

Blades: With pointed distal ends: Plain – 32
Utilised – 3 (no 6)

Blades: With square distal ends: Plain – 12 (no 2)
Utilised – 5 (nos 5, 7 and 18)
Miscellaneous retouch – 3 (nos 3 and 4)

Blades: Snapped/damaged ends: Plain – 17
Utilised – 6
Miscellaneous retouch – 1

Burin spalls: 3 (no 14)

Serrated blades: 2 (nos 10 and 11)

Denticulated flakes: 1 possible (no 13)

Choppers: 1 (no 28)

Scrapers: Side – 2 (nos 15 and 17)
End – 3 (nos 19 and 20)
End and side – 1 (no 18)
End and double side – 1 (no 16)

Awls: 2 (nos 21 and 22)

Small borers/spurred implements: 8 definite (nos 23–27)
8 possible

Catalogue of illustrated flints (Figs 168 and 169)

L = length; B = breadth; T = thickness (all measurements in millimetres); the numbers in brackets are context numbers

1 Core. Single platform. Small blades removed from one side only. Slightly conical in shape, with a 70 degree angle of strike. SF 1231 (666A). L33; B20; T11

2 Blade. Square distal end. Flat striking platform, soft hammer blow. SF 59 (4). L45; B15; T6

3 Blade. Some possible retouch on one side towards bulbar end, though as the context had been ploughed some may be edge damage. Square distal end with cortex. Flat striking platform, soft hammer blow. SF 79 (29). L59; B27; T7

4 Blade. Some possible abrupt retouch at bulbar end. Distal end snapped off. Direction of flake scars at distal end indicate this blade has been struck from a double platform core. SF 2511a (1269). L58; B28; T8

5 Utilised blade. Several very tiny squills and possible edge gloss on its 'left' edge (as illustrated). Square distal end with cortex. Irregular platform, soft hammer blow. SF 3071 (4). L43; B9; T2

6 Utilised blade. Squills along one edge. Pointed distal end. Flat platform, soft hammer blow. SF 3755 (2318). L43; B19; T6

7 Utilised blade. Squills and noticeable gloss on one edge. No patina or edge damage. Square distal end. Fractured platform, soft hammer blow. SF 3023 (1715). L48; B20; T6

8 Utilised blade. Squills at (square) distal end. Fractured platform, soft hammer blow. SF 3562 (US). L32; B15; T4

9 Utilised flake. Squills on both edges. Flat platform, hard hammer blow. SF 3013 (1). L48; B35; T11

10 Serrated blade. Distal end snapped. Flat platform, soft hammer blow. SF 124 (161). L57; B20; T6

11 Serrated blade, or possibly a worn saw. Serrations rough and worn, probably due in part to damage sustained whilst in context 4 – a post-Roman–medieval ploughsoil. Square distal end. Flat platform, soft hammer blow. SF 3595 (4). L45; B22; T8

12 Flake. Possible rough worn serrations on one edge. Pointed distal end. Flat platform, soft hammer blow. SF 414 (29). L66; B35; T15

13 Flake. Retouched, possibly denticulated. Fractured platform, soft hammer blow. SF 2082 (741). L52; B34; T11

14 Burin spall. SF 3860 (2302). L24; B5; T3

15 Side scraper, plano-convex in profile. Abrupt retouch produced by pressure flaking, with the angle of retouch varying from 70–90 degrees. Size, quality, and 'neatness' suggest an Earlier Bronze Age date. Flat striking platform, hard hammer blow. SF 3435 (2248). L39; B31; T9

16 Double-sided end scraper. Abrupt retouch produced by pressure flaking, with the angle of retouch varying from 45 degrees on the sides to 70 degrees on the distal end. Some wear on latter. Size, quality, and 'neatness' suggest an earlier BA date. Flat platform, hard hammer blow. SF 3436 (2247). L42; B30; T11

17 Side scraper. Angle of retouch about 80 degrees. Flat platform, hard hammer blow. SF 2119 (741). L69; B49; T13

18 Side and end scraper. Angle of retouch on side 50 degrees, on distal end 90. Distal end worn and chipped. Flat platform, hard hammer blow. SF 2653 (1487). L50; B62; T10

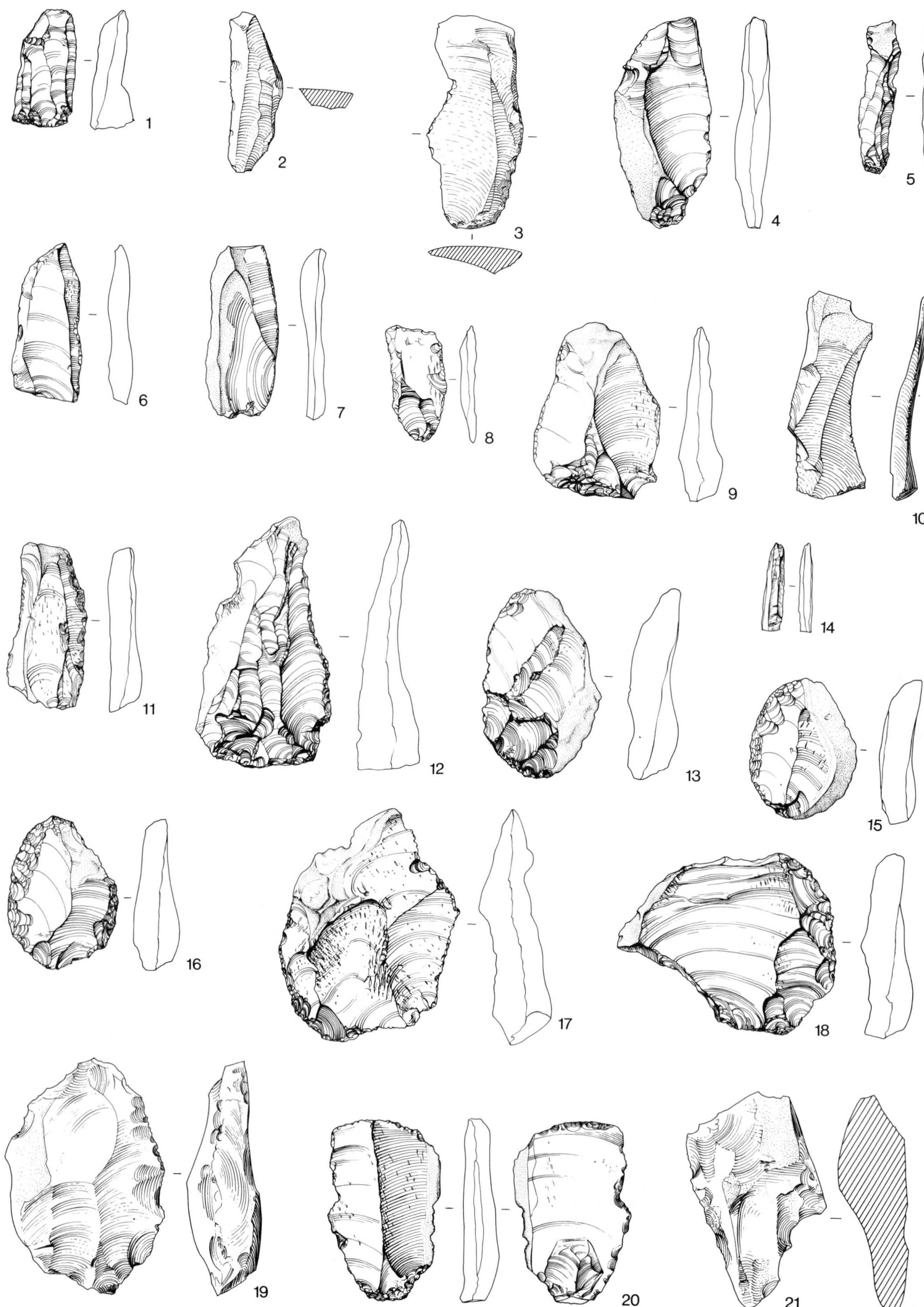

Fig 168 The worked flint (Scale 2:3)

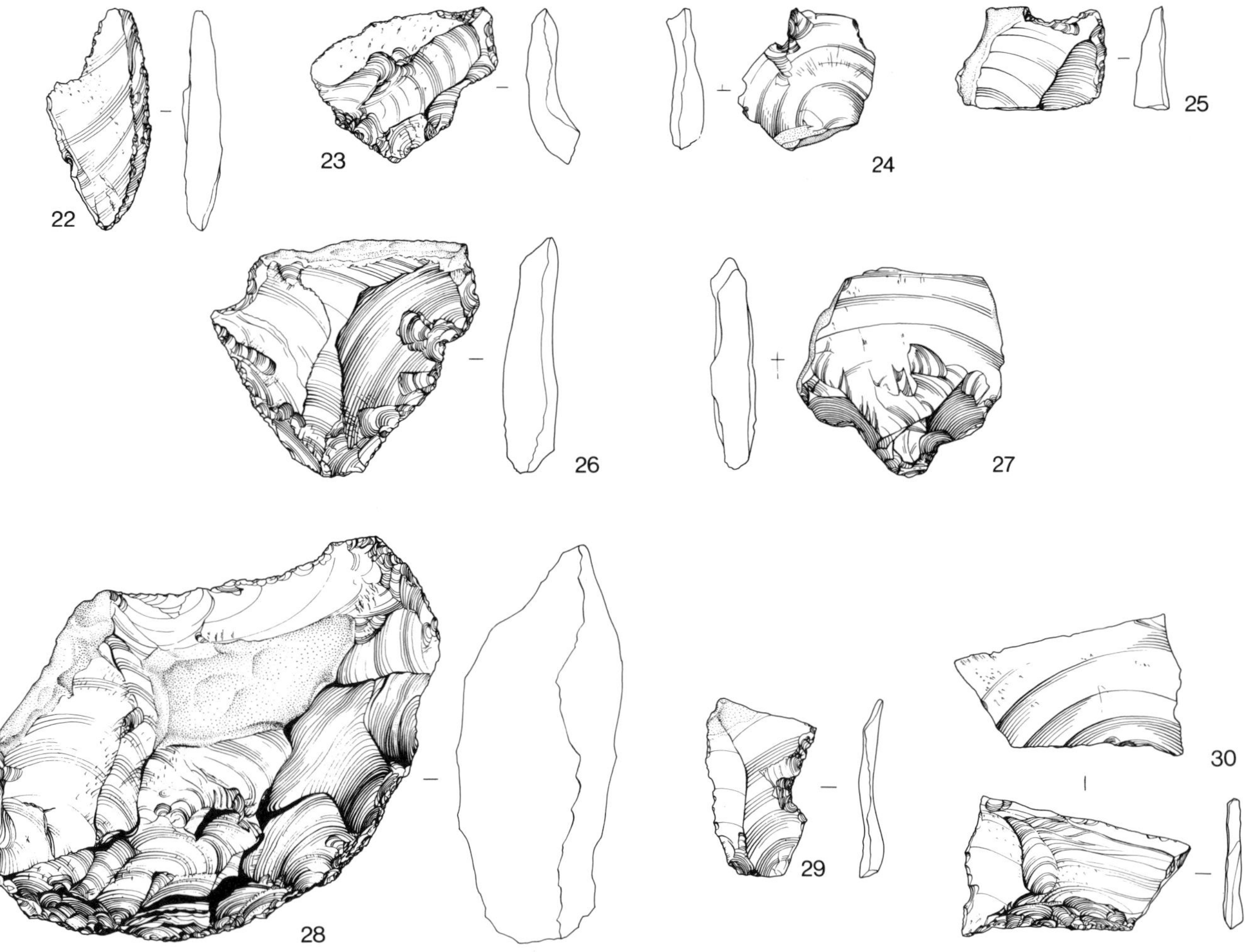

Fig 169 The worked flint (Scale 2:3)

19 A possible core converted into an end scraper. The unillustrated side consists of a 'pot boiler' scar and does not have a bulb of percussion or any related conchoidal fractures. Angle of retouch at scraper end (top of drawing) 80–90 degrees. SF 4410 (29). L65; B44; T20

20 End scraper. Retouched edge is in two portions set slightly askew to one another, in effect forming two separate working edges. Atypical in that retouch is on the bulbar side at the distal end (not illustrated) rather than on the more usual dorsal side. Angle of retouch 90 degrees. Flat platform, soft hammer blow. SF 4250 (3301). L52; B33; T9

21 Possible awl, with a small nodule being utilised for its manufacture. Abrupt retouch on sides and base of point. SF 429 (29). L59; B44; T22

22 Awl. Distal end of flake utilised as the point and subsequently snapped. SF 1162 (549). L45; B21; T7

23 Spur or borer. At distal end of flake. Flat platform, soft hammer blow. SF 4068 (3016). L38; B26; T67

24 Spur or borer. On bulbar side (not illustrated) at distal end of the flake. Flat cortical platform, soft hammer blow. SF 3213 (1880). L27; B30; T6

25 Spur or borer. At distal end of flake. Bulbar end snapped off. Abrupt retouch (45 degrees) on dorsal side. SF 3126 (4). L20; B30; T5

26 Borer, or spurred implement. Point on side of flake. Abrupt retouch on dorsal side. Flat platform, probable soft hammer blow. SF 3553 (US). L45; B54; T11

27 Borer. Point at bulbar end of flake. SF 3567 (US). L41; B41; T9

28 Chopper. Possibly originally a failed axe blank. Produced from a flint nodule. One edge heavily abraded and fractured. SF 2284 (1132). L103; B72; T31

29 Miscellaneous retouch. Flake (distal end snapped off) with shallow retouch produced by pressure flaking. Is not any recognisable form of knife. Flat striking platform, soft hammer blow. SF 4252 (3297). L32; B22; T4

30 Miscellaneous retouch. Abrupt retouch (70 degrees). Unidentified. Does not appear either to be a burin or a borer (R Jacobi, pers comm).SF 2844 (1641). L44; B28; T6

Appendix 1 10 metre grid squares

List of 10 metre grid squares with relevant archive plan and section(s) numbers. When an area number reads **19–2021**, for example, it refers to a building or context spanning both areas **1921** and **2021**. All site context records have the same cross reference system.

Area no	*Plan nos*
1320	256
1419	257, 299(S)
1420	256, 299(S)
1819	258
1820	259, 298(S)
1821	260
1822	46
1915	165, 197(S)
1916	166
1917	167
1919	16, 22
1920	25
1921	26, 27, 40
1922	47, 48, 65(S)
1923	49, 65(S)
2014	168, 196
2015	169, 170, 196, 197(S)
2016	69–75, 97(S), 98(S)
2017	76, 77, 171, 198(S)
2018	14, 78, 79, 98(S), 99(S)
2019	14, 17, 18, 23(S)
2020	19, 20, 24(S)
2021	29, 31, 41
2022	50–52, 66(S)
2023	53, 54, 67(S)
2114	172, 196
2115	173, 196
2116	174–178, 199(S)
2117	80, 81, 100(S), 101(S)
2118	14, 82–85, 101(S)
2119	14, 21, 23(S)
2120	32, 33, 43, 44
2121	34–36, 42(S)
2122	55–58, 66
2123	59, 60, 67(S)
2216	179, 180
2217	86–88, 102(S), 103(S)
2218	89–92, 103(S)
2219	1(S), 2, 3(S), 8(S), 9(S)
2220	28, 37, 43(S), 44(S)
2221	38, 39, 45(S)
2222	58, 61–63, 68(S)
2316	181, 200(S)
2317	93, 94, 104(S)
2318	95, 96, 104(S)
2319	135–137, 159(S)
2320	138
2321	105, 134(S)
2322	64
2417	182–185, 201(S), 202(S)
2418	139, 140, 157(S), 158(S)
2419	141–143, 157(S), 158(S)
2420	144, 158(S)
2421	105
2422	106, 131(S), 132(S), 134(S)
2424	203(S)
2517	186–189, 202(S)
2519	145, 146
2520	107, 108, 147
2521	109–114, 132(S)
2522	115–118, 132(S)
2616	190, 204(S)
2617	191–194, 204(S), 205(S)
2618	148–150, 160(S), 162(S)
2619	151–153, 164(S)
2620	119, 133(S)
2621	111–114, 120–122, 133(S)
2622	123, 124, 133(S)
2716	190, 205(S)
2717	194, 195, 205
2718	154, 163(S)
2719	154Z, 163(S)
2720	155, 156, 161–163(S)
2721	122, 125–127, 134(S)
2722	128, 129, 134(S)
2723	130, 132(S), 207, 249(S)
2724	208
2815	209, 250(S)
2816	206(S), 209, 250(S)
2817	195, 205(S), 210
2818	211, 213
2819	214–218, 251(S)
2820	218–221, 252(S), 253((
2821	220–224
2822	225, 226, 253(S)
2823	227, 228, 249(S)
2824	208
2916	206(S)
2917	210, 211
2918	229, 230
2919	231, 232
2920	233, 261
2921	261
2922	234–237, 252(S)
2923	228
3017	238–241
3018	242
3020	243
3116	206(S)
3117	244
3118	245
3120	246
3219	262, 263
3220	263, 264
3316	265, 299(S)
3317	266, 299(S)
3318	311
3319	263, 312
3320	263, 267
3416	268, 299(S)
3417	269, 299(S)
3418	313
3419	270, 314
3420	270, 315
3421	316
3422	317
3516	271
3517	272
3519	270, 318
3520	270, 319
3521	320
3522	321
3616	273
3617	274, 275
3618	322
3619	322
3620	319, 323
3621	324
3622	325
3716	276–278, 300(S), 301(S)
3717	277–279, 301(S), 302(S)
3718	280, 303(S)
3719	281
3720	326–329
3721	330
3722	331
3723	299
3816	282–284, 300(S)
3817	285–287, 302(S)
3818	332–335, 359(S)
3819	288, 335
3820	289, 336–339, 364
3821	337, 340–342, 364
3822	343, 344
3916	284, 290
3917	291–293
3918	294, 332–335
3919	295, 296, 335, 345–348, 360(S)
3920	297, 348–350, 360(S), 364
3921	351, 352, 364
3922	353
4013	354, 355
4014	354, 355, 361(S)
4016	247–254(S)
4017	362(S)
4018	304, 307, 356, 362(S)
4019	304, 345, 346, 348, 357, 363(S)
4020	348, 350, 363(S)
4022	248, 255(S)
4024	358
4116	247, 254(S)
4117	308
4118	304, 307
4119	304, 307
4120	304, 305, 307
4124	358
4215	247, 254(S)
4219	305
4220	305
4315	247, 254(S)
4319	309

Appendix 2 Conjectural storage capacity of the Gorhambury granary

by Michelle Ramsay

Granary

Cubic capacity of ground floor (3.2 × 4 × 4.6) = 58.88 cu m
or 3,593,111.9 cu ins
Cubic capacity of first floor (2.6 × 4 × 4.6) = 47.84 cu m
or 2,919,408.4 cu ins

Capacity of ground floor	1,619.6 bushels (1620)
Capacity of first floor	1,315.94 bushels (1316)

Data used:

1 sextarius = 1 pint = approx 34½ cu ins
1 modius = 1 peck (corn) = approx 554½ cu ins
1 iugerum = 240 feet × 120 feet = 28,800 Roman square feet
= 64% of an acre
(27,849.6 English square feet)
1 iugerum = 26% of an hectare (1 hectare = 10,000 sq metres)
1 hectare = 2.471 acres
16 pints = 1 peck
4 pecks = 1 bushel
1 bushel = 60 lb wheat
47 lb barley
40 lb oats
2218½ cu ins

Seed corn (figures based on Columella, *De Re Rustica,* II, ix

Barley (6 rowed)	5 modii/pecks per iugerum	7.8 pecks per acre	19.3 pecks per hectare
(2 rowed)	6 modii/pecks per iugerum	9.4 pecks per acre	23.2 pecks per hectare
Panic & Millet	4 sextarii/pints per iugerum	(6.2 pints per acre) (0.39 pecks per acre)	(15.3 pints per hectare) (0.96 pecks per hectare)
Wheat (Rich land)	4 modii/pecks per iugerum	6.2 pecks per acre	15.3 pecks per hectare
(Medium land)	5 modii/pecks per iugerum	7.8 pecks per acre	19.3 pecks per hectare
Spelt (fertile land)	9 modii/pecks per iugerum	14.1 pecks per acre	34.8 pecks per hectare
(ordinary land)	10 modii/pecks per iugerum	15.6 pecks per acre	48.5 pecks per hectare

Granary: total storage capacity

Crop	Ground floor 1620 bushels lbs	First floor 1316 bushels lbs	Total 2936 bushels lbs
Barley			
1) 2 rowed)	76,140	61,852	137,993
2) 6 rowed)			
Panic & Millet			
Wheat			
1) Rich land			
2) Medium land			
Spelt	97,200	78,960	176,160
1) Fertile land			
2) Ordinary land			

Seed: Land area catered for in the granary

Crop	Ground floor Acres	First floor Acres	Total Acres
Barley			
1) 2 rowed	830	674	1,504
2(6 rowed	691	562	1,253
Panic & Millet	16,591	13,481	30,072
Wheat			
1(Rich land	1,037	842	1,879
2) Medium land	829	674	1,503
Spelt			
1) Fertile land	461	374	835
2) Ordinary land	415	337	752

Crop	Ground floor Iugera	First floor Iugera	Total Iugera
Barley			
1) 2 rowed	1,296	1,053	2,349
2) 6 rowed	1,080	877.5	1,957.5
Panic & Millet	25,924	21,064	46,988
Wheat			
1) Rich land	1,620	1,316	2,936
2) Medium land	1,296	1,053	2,349
Spelt			
1) Fertile land	720	585	1,305
2) Ordinary land	648	526	1,174

	50% storage of the granary capacity. Figures are for either 100% food storage or 100% grain storage				Taking 50% storage as the norm: 1) 50%50% storage				2) 25% (food)/75% (seed) storage				3) 25% (seed)/75% (food) storage			
Crop	Food lbs	Seed Iugera	Seed Acres	Seed Hectares	Food lbs	Seed Iugera	Seed Acres	Seed Hectares	Food lbs	Seed Iugera	Seed Acres	Seed Hectares	Food lbs	Seed Iugera	Seed Acres	Seed Hectares
Barley																
1) 2 rowed	68,996	1,174.5	752	304	34,498	587	376	152	17,249	880.5	564	228	51,747	293.5	188	76
2) 6 rowed	68,996	976.8	627	254	34,498	498.4	313	127	17,249	734	470	190	51,747	244.7	167	63
Panic & Millet	–	23,494	15,036	6,085	–	11,747	7,518	3,042	–	17,620	11,277	4,564	–	5,874	3,759	1,517
Wheat																
1) Rich land		1,468	989	380		734	470	190		1,101	705	285		367	235	95
2) Medium land		1,175	752	304		588	376	152		882	564	228				
Spelt	88,080				44,040				22,020				66,060			
1) Fertile land		653	418	169		326	209	85		489	314	127		166	104	43
2) Ordinary land		587	375	152		293	187	76		441	281	114		147	93	38

	$33^1/3$% storage of granary				Taking $33^1/3$% storage as the norm: 1) 50%50% Storage				2) 25% (Food)/75% (seed) storage				3) 25% (seed)/75% (food) storage			
Crop	Food lbs	Seed Iugera	Seed Acres	Seed Hectares	Food lbs	Seed Iugera	Seed Acres	Seed Hectares	Food lbs	Seed Iugera	Seed Acres	Seed Hectares	Food lbs	Seed Iugera	Seed Acres	Seed Hectares
Barley																
1) 2 rowed	45,997	783	501	203	999	392	250	107	11,500	588	375	152	34,499	196	125	50.5
2) 6 rowed	45,999	652.5	418	169	22,999	326	209	85	11,500	489	314	127.5	34,499	163	105	42
Panic & Millet	–	15,663	10,024	4,057	–	7,832	5,012	2,028	–	11,748	7,518	3,042	–	3,916	2,506	1,014
Wheat																
1) Rich land		979	626	253		490	313	126		735	470	189		245	156	63
2) Medium land		783	501	203		392	250	101		588	375	152		196	125	50.5
Spelt	58,720				29360				14,680				44,046			
1) Fertile land		435	278	113		218	139	57		327	209	85		109	69	28
2) Ordinary land		391	250	107		196	125	50.5		294	188	76		98	63	25.5

Appendix 3: List of coins with site context

British coins

Pub no	*Small find no*	*AML no*	*Trench*	*Coordinate*	*Context*
1	2998	813838	2821	2.75 3.00	(1804)
2	310	756076	2220	1.00 8.00	(241)
3	4202	826255	3221	7.00 9.40	(3185)
4	992	756055	2017	1.00 1.00	(596)
5	3870	813979	4019	4.80 4.70	(2391)
6	80	813725	2221	7.00 7.00	(140)
7	37	956075	1921	2.00 1.00	(4)
8	2106	813794	2520	4.95 9.00	(703)
9	1350	813764	2421	3.70 5.00	(741)
10	1206	756064	2117	3.50 9.00	(650)
11	3884	813980	4019	5.00 3.65	(2391)
12	499	756058	2222	5.00 5.00	(319)
13	449	756056	2122	1.40 3.89	(287)
14	4625	826258	2220	9.25 9.60	US

Roman coins

Pub no	*Small find no*	*AML no*	*Trench*	*Coordinate*	*Context*
1	692	813736	2121	7.00 7.00	(449)
2	982	756062	2218	4.50 0.80	(615)
3	1178	756063	2117	4.50 8.00	(658)
4	140	725300	2019	8.00 8.00	(77)
5	1202	756054	2318	4.25 0.75	(616)=(29)
6	85	813716	2019	6.00 8.00	(63)
7	1212	756061	2217	8.20 8.50	(664)
8	1198	756052	2218	3.50 5.00	(691)
9	1716	813783	2520	9.90 8.90	(756)
10	4203	826256	2321	1.50 4.60	(4)
11	4270	826261	2321	2.40 1.00	(3301)
12	4028	826250	3021	4.00 7.60	(3021)
13	69	756059	2220	–	US
14	2933	813837	2821	4.00 1.00	(1594)
15	2256	813804	2620	9.20 0.05	(1105)
16	2366	813808	2619	4.80 2.55	(1140)
17	2107	813795	2620	2.10 1.25	(741)
18	2259	813805	2620	8.05 3.10	(1118)
19	86	813717	2019	5.00 5.00	(63)
20	248	756077	2221	8.00 8.00	(217)
21	4081	526252	3320	8.80 6.80	(3158)
22	1	813718	2220	–	(1)
23	3368	813892	3816	7.20 3.50	(2033)
24	1451	813773	2620	9.50 5.95	(721)
25	2183	813800	2720	–	US
26	438	756060	1922	3.70 1.87	(29)
27	1089	756051	2218	4.50 1.00	(615)
28	1300	813759	2721	0.20 3.30	(701)
29	3226	813874	3816	3.40 7.10	(2002)
30	2714	813832	2723	4.50 4.50	(1538)
31	2222	813802	2620	1.30 0.45	(1019)
32	–	826263	2122	8.00 2.00	–
33	536	813732	2322	–	(1)
34	–	813758	2721	5.50 4.60	(769)
35	3294	813885	3716	1.20 9.80	(2073)
36	714	756071	2318	4.70 3.00	(488)
37	10	813707	2219	–	–
38	1512	813775	2521	5.40 8.00	(703)
39	691	756057	2121	7.00 7.00	(449)
40	2627	813826	–	8.00 5.00	(US)

Pub no	*Small find no*	*AML no*	*Trench*	*Coordinate*	*Context*
41	1615	813778	2721	2.10 4.30	(773)
42	3532	813954	3820	8.50 3.40	(4)
43	3138	813861	3817	7.50 7.00	(1904)
44	854	756072	2018	9.40 1.40	(513)
45	58	813710	2218	–	–
46	3075	813845	3717	7.10 1.00	(1890)
47	3230	813876	3717	3.00 4.50	(2018)
48	1616	813779	2721	1.60 2.70	(773)
49	2638	813828	2922	2.80 3.50	US
50	3251	813883	3617	7.60 0.80	(1880)
51	443	813728	2222	7.30 0.25	(1)
52	2068	813792	2420	3.20 2.60	(741)
53	2066	813791	2418	7.40 5.00	(741)
54	2756	813834	2823	2.00 1.50	(1550)
55	3223	813872	3717	2.50 4.00	(2018)
56	472	756067	2023	9.00 1.00	(1)
57	3483	813924	3819	7.80 0.50	US
58	2637	813827	2822	9.60 4.50	US
59	3349	813890	3716	2.00 8.00	(2032)
60	53	813724	1921	8.00 8.00	(110)
61	614	813734	2322	6.05 6.05	(2)
62	2223	813803	2620	6.80 0.70	(1019)
63	51	813709	2118	–	–
64	3462	813907	3820	2.00 1.90	(2301)
65	413	813727	2122	7.35 7.20	(1)
66	5	813720	1920	5.00 8.00	(4)
67	3495	813930	3820	4.00 3.40	(4)
68	3110	813857	3718	1.40 5.25	(1921)
69	3135	813860	3716	9.00 9.00	(1881)
70	3510	813943	3818	7.40 9.90	US
71	3087	813854	3716	6.15 7.50	(1881)
72	3478	813921	3920	3.78 3.16	(2350)
73	3328	813886	3819	1.75 2.43	(1972)
74	1514	813776	2621	7.00 2.50	(787)
75	4	813719	1920	2.00 8.00	(4)
76	2048	813788	2420	–	US
77	1948	813786	2723	2.40 1.00	(916)
78	3450	813901	3820	4.80 6.20	(2301)
79	966	813753	2217	6.30 6.25	(494)
80	3455	813903	3921	0.45 3.50	(2301)
81	3536	813955	3820	8.25 7.20	(2302)
82	3361	813891	3918	–	(4)
83	3505	813939	3819	8.25 0.05	US
84	3541	813960	3721	8.00 1.00	(4)
85	3474	813918	3919	3.70 2.35	(4)
86	3453	813902	3819	5.60 2.95	US
87	3236	813880	3719	8.25 8.05	(1920)
88	709	813737	2016	–	US
89	3491	813928	3821	5.00 0.50	(2301)
90	3147	813862	3816	–	US
91	1301	813760	2521	8.25 2.80	(701)
92	133	813726	2121	8.00 8.00	(167)
93	3077	813847	3718	4.30 3.50	(1911)
94	3898	813981	3819	5.50 4.50	(2465)
95	3529	813951	3820	6.80 9.90	(2302)
96	33	813723	1920	5.00 8.00	(4)
97	857	813750	2018	0.90 3.30	(520)
98	3198	813870	3816	2.50 4.00	(2017)
99	3217	813871	3918	2.95 9.60	(1956)
100	3665	813964	3720	9.50 8.80	(4)
101	3482	813923	3820	9.80 5.47	(US)
102	3078	813848	3719	5.55 4.65	(1911)
103	4027	826249	3020	1.90 8.00	(4)

Pub no	*Small find no*	*AML no*	*Trench*	*Coordinate*	*Context*
104	3518	813948	3819	7.40 0.40	US
105	3513	813945	3819	8.70 0.55	US
106	3691a	813975a	3818	9.50 9.50	(1956)
107	3082	813852	3619	9.35 0.60	(1917)
108	593	813733	2322	6.50 1.60	(2)
109	3481	813922	3921	0.80 0.30	(US)
110	841	756053	2017	2.95 9.75	(547)
111	3688	813972	3820	6.50 1.50	(2302)
112	743	813741	2018	6.50 0.50	(1)
113	2471	813817	2116	5.60 6.20	(501)
114	48	813708		–	
115	518	813731	2222	6.00 4.00	(290c)
116	772	813746	2118	9.50 2.00	(494)
117	2442	813815	2216	1.80 3.50	(501)
118	3515	813946	3819	3.20 1.80	(US)
119	767	813744	2217	4.90 0.50	(488)
120	3476	813919	3919	3.40 8.95	(2351)
121	27	813722	1921	7.00 2.00	(4)
122	3690	813974	3821	5.90 0.55	(2302)
123	5	813711	2020	8.50 6.70	(23)
124	3081	813851	3718	3.95 2.35	(1914)
125	3057	813840	3716	3.10 8.60	(1881)
126	3187	813867	3716	8.00 6.00	(1883)
127	3093	813856	3719	9.25 8.30	(1920)
128	851	813749	2018	1.50 2.00	(547)
129	3519	813949	3818	4.20 9.90	US
130	876	756070	2018	3.00 2.00	(544a)
131	2489	813819	2617	4.50 5.00	(1276)
132	2487	813818	–	–	US
133	3079	813849	3718	2.96 2.46	(1914)
134	3059	813841	3716	1.10 5.50	(1881)
135	228	756078	1921	3.00 1.00	(159)
136	735	813740	2317	3.00 2.35	(488)
137	953	813735	2117	8.00 8.00	(562)
138	1126	813757	2018	2.50 0.50	(544 c)
139	834	756069	2018	4.50 1.55	(543)
140	3504	813938	3818	3.50 6.10	(US)
141	3666	813965	3720	4.00 9.70	(2409)
142	3485	813926	3820	3.00 7.90	(2301)
143	3522	813950	3920	0.50 8.00	(2301)
144	710	813738	2218	6.50 3.50	(US)
145	3060	813842	3716	1.00 5.50	(1881)
146	309	813855	3917	–	(US)
147	3065	813844	3716	6.95 6.10	(1881)
148	3484	813925	3820	7.80 8.20	(US)
149	3445	813896	3820	6.60 4.90	(2301)
150	984	824624	2117	8.20 7.00	(562)
151	2618	813825	2819	9.00 4.65	(US)
152	3083	813853	3716	6.50 6.00	(1883)
153	3975	813982	4124	4.35 5.00	(2658)
154	3540	813959	3720	5.00 5.00	(4)
155	3448	813899	3820	3.80 6.20	(2301)
156	3468	813912	3820	5.00 0.10	(2301)
157	3500	813935	3821	2.80 6.65	(2301)
158	3689	813973	3820	1.90 9.00	(2302)
159	883	813751	2018	0.45 2.00	(543)
160	962	756074	2018	3.00 3.00	(544 b)
161	2342	813806	2718	1.35 8.20	(1042)
162	3443	813894	3820	4.00 5.70	(2301)
163	3473	813917	3919	0.03 4.80	(4)
164	3496	813931	3821	2.80 3.60	(2301)
165	3539	813958	3920	0.20 8.70	(2302)
166	3509	813942	3818	4.10 2.10	(US)

Pub no	*Small find no*	*AML no*	*Trench*	*Coordinate*	*Context*
167	3670	813969	4019	2.80 6.20	(2356)
168	3668	813967	4019	5.00 1.35	(2350)
169	3530	813952	3820	5.50 4.60	(2301)
170	3461	813906	3821	6.00 0.10	(2301)
171	3531	813953	3820	8.00 4.10	(4)
172	3693	813977	3818	0.50 7.50	(2473)
173	3669	813968	3820	0.10 9.00	(2318)
174	3664	813963	4019	4.85 4.70	(2350)
175	3537	813956	3820	7.50 6.30	(2301)
176	3508	813941	3818	2.90 2.10	(US)
177	3663	813962	3819	5.50 4.50	(2451)
178	3460	813905	3820	1.00 9.20	(2301)
179	3465	813910	3821	6.20 2.30	(2301)
180	18	813715	1919	5.00 5.00	(US)
181	1027	813755	2117	7.00 7.00	(562)
182	833	813748	2117	5.00 8.00	(494)
183	954	813752	2117	2.50 8.50	(562)
184	1617	813780	2721	3.00 1.00	(773)
185	1404	813769	2620	4.00 6.05	(1)
186	1407	813771	2620	0.60 5.50	(1)
187	2441	813814	2116	8.50 1.50	(501)
188	2403	813809	1917	8.20 0.05	(4)
189	2405	813811	1915	2.30 0.30	(4)
190	3227	813875	3816	5.00 6.00	(2027)
191	3056	813839	3716	2.85 6.30	(1881)
192	3691 b	813975 b	3818	9.50 9.50	(1956)
193	3507 a	813940 a	3818	3.80 5.80	(US)
194	3667	813966	3919	5.00 3.95	(2350)
195	3503	813937	3821	4.50 7.20	(4)
196	3488	813927	3822	2.50 1.40	(4)
197	3472	813916	3821	5.95 0.50	(2301)
198	3471	813915	3820	0.50 9.90	(2301)
199	1340	813763	2621	9.30 3.00	(701)
200	1575	813777	2621	8.00 3.50	(787)
201	3507 b	813940 b	3818	3.80 5.80	(US)
202	3692	813976	3818	3.00 8.00	(2468)
203	3687	813971	3821	3.80 7.00	(4)
204	3538	813957	3820	2.50 6.50	(2301)
205	11	813721	2120	2.00 5.00	(US)
206	2047	813787	2319	8.50 2.70	(741)
207	–	813823	2723	5.00 5.00	(1490)
208	2757	813835	2723	4.50 4.50	(1490)
209	3501	813936	3821	2.00 7.40	(4)
210	1120	813756	2017	5.00 6.00	(545)
211	3469	813913	3820	6.40 9.55	(2301)
212	3470	813914	3821	6.40 0.30	(2301)
213	985	813754	2118	5.80 2.10	(621)
214	3148	813863	3817	8.00 9.00	(1904)
215	3076	813846	3719	8.90 4.65	(4)
216	2	813706	–	–	–
217	3234	813878	3719	8.40 2.35	(4)
218	3263	813884	3816	2.00 5.50	(1898)
219	4267	826259	2321	7.80 9.60	(140)
220	1635	813782	2721	3.20 0.70	(773)
221	3233	813877	3719	8.75 3.40	(4)
222	3442	813893	3820	7.60 8.90	(2301)
223	1623	813781	2621	7.00 1.25	(787)
224	2219	813801	2618	0.25 6.00	(1063)
225	1351	813765	2421	2.20 8.50	(741)
226	4083	826254	2424	5.55 2.53	(3139a)
227	12	813713	1919	9.80 5.00	(2)
228	2084	813793	2519	1.00 5.00	(741)
229	4082	826253	2424	5.55 2.53	(3139a)

Pub no	Small find no	AML no	Trench	Coordinate	Context
230	2050	813789	2319	–	US
231	1352	813766	2421	3.65 7.78	(741)
232	734	813739	2317	3.85 1.05	(488)
233	–	813703	–	–	–
234	–	826262	2118	–	–
235	–	813704	2018	–	–
236	3237	813881	3719	8.05 8.15	(1920)
237	3463	813908	3821	4.10 0.10	(2301)
238	2438	813813	2617	4.50 4.00	(1275)
239	4033	826251	3021	5.00 4.30	(3021)
240	3114	813859	3816	7.80 5.50	(1901)
241	1303	813762	2621	1.00 9.50	(701)
242	–	813705	2219	–	–
243	2057	813790	2418	2.50 8.50	(741)
244	3497	813932	3820	2.75 9.40	(2301)
245	3542	813961	3720	9.50 9.00	(4)
246	412	756065	1822	9.00 9.30	(29)
247	3797	813978	3821	3.00 3.00	(2346)
248	13	813714	2020	2.00 8.00	(3)
249	3459	813904	3821	5.40 0.30	(2301)
250	3449	813900	3820	8.20 5.90	(2301)
251	3447	813898	3820	2.50 7.00	(2301)
252	1406	813770	2620	1.00 9.00	(1)
253	3330	813887	3819	2.60 4.00	(1972)
254	3235	813879	3719	7.10 2.30	(4)
255	1408	813772	2620	6.00 8.00	(701)
256	1353	813767	2421	0.80 6.00	(741)
257	2680	813830	2822	1.35 5.60	(1456)
258	765	813743	2117	2.00 1.80	(488)
259	1363	813768	2622	8.00 5.00	(721)
260	3499	813934	3820	1.40 0.90	(2301)
261	3250	813882	3617	6.70 0.70	(1880)
262	3080	813850	3718	3.80 2.10	(1914)
263	3446	813897	3820	4.20 7.40	(2301)
264	3111	813858	3718	5.55 1.05	(1914)
265	1500	813774	2520	6.70 7.15	(721)
266	2374	820272	2617	4.50 9.50	(1145)
267	516	813730	2023	5.00 4.00	(319)
268	830	813747	2317	3.60 4.15	(488)
269	2668	813829	2822	4.70 6.00	(741)
270	3193	813869	3816	6.90 8.10	(2024)
271	3151	813865	3817	8.10 5.20	(2001)
272	3150	813864	3817	7.50 6.10	(2001)
273	3061	813843	3417	1.10 9.90	(4)
274	2705	813831	2819	9.65 2.55	(1448)
275	1927	813784	2723	4.00 2.80	(916)
276	3341	813888	3816	1.10 8.00	(2064)
277	1928	813785	2723	4.25 2.50	(916)
278	3189	813868	3817	7.00 2.50	(4)
279	2749	813833	2917	8.00 9.95	(1448)
280	2135	813797	2518	2.00 0.50	(996)
281	2582	813821	2817	3.00 3.00	(1287)
282	2121	813796	2618	0.25 1.00	(741)
283	2788	813836	2818	2.70 3.00	(1521)
284	2136	813798	2618	4.00 5.00	(997)
285	2589	813822	2116	1.70 7.25	(549)
286	2163	813799	2618	7.42 0.40	(741)
287	3464	813909	3821	6.10 1.15	(2301)
288	2617	813824	2820	3.40 7.40	(US)
289	3444	813895	3820	5.20 4.80	(2301)
290	2345	813807	2718	4.65 7.80	(1073)
291	3976	813983	4124	0.45 4.50	(2658)
292	447	813729	1923	6.00 2.00	(US)

Pub no	Small find no	AML no	Trench	Coordinate	Context
293	760	813742	2418	0.35 2.05	(488)
294	3477	813920	3920	5.00 1.10	(2350)
295	3686	813970	3820	4.00 9.00	(2302)
296	2437	813812	2216	1.40 5.20	(501)
297	431	756068	2122	–	(1)
298	771	813745	2016	3.00 3.70	(4)
299	2461	813816	2316	3.90 1.80	(501)
300	2539	813820	2116	6.80 8.20	(1322)
301	3224	813873	3816	5.00 6.25	(2027)
302	3153	813866	3817	2.00 5.20	(2001)
303	3492	813929	3821	8.00 3.40	(2301)
304	3498	813933	3820	2.70 9.60	(2301)
305	3516	813947	3819	6.20 1.70	US
306	3466	813911	3820	4.60 9.75	(2301)
307	3512	813944	3818	0.32 9.60	US
308	4204	826257	2816	3.20 6.40	(1282)
309	3344	813889	3816	1.20 6.00	(2017)
310	4269	826260	2125	9.00 8.00	(3381)

Appendix 4

Copper alloy objects: analytical results

Cat no	*Object*	*Zn*	*Pb*	*Sn*	*Alloy*
1	brooch	+		++	bronze
2	brooch	+		++	bronze
3	brooch	.2	1.4	16.2	bronze
4	brooch	+	+	++	bronze
5	brooch	+		++	bronze
6	brooch	.0	.0	12.5	bronze
7	brooch			++	bronze
8	brooch	+		++	bronze
9	brooch			+	bronze
10	brooch	+		++	bronze
11	brooch	17.3	.5	2.8	brass/gunmetal
12	brooch	17.5	.6	2.7	brass/gunmetal
13	brooch	19.0	1.1	2.7	brass/gunmetal
14	brooch	+		+	bronze/gunmetal ?
15	brooch	++			brass
16	brooch	1.0	13.2	13.7	leaded bronze
17	brooch	++		+	brass
18	brooch	++			brass
19	brooch	++			brass
20	brooch	++		+	brass
21	brooch	++		+	brass
22	brooch	+		+	brass/gunmetal ?
23	brooch	22.8	.3	.6	brass
24	brooch	16.6	.3	1.5	brass
25	brooch	1.8	.4	13.0	bronze
26	brooch	++		+	brass/gunmetal
27	brooch	++			brass
28	brooch	20.3	.0	.0	brass
29	brooch	++			brass

Key: Major and minor amounts of alloying elements are indicated by ++ and + respectively while blanks indicate only negligible amounts. Where figures are given, they are percentages. * = not in catalogue.

30	brooch			++	bronze
31	brooch	.0	18.3	7.6	leaded bronze
32	brooch	+	++	++	leaded bronze
33	brooch	2.4	6.6	12.9	(leaded) bronze
34	brooch	1.8	6.5	12.4	(leaded) bronze
35	brooch	.5	9.9	13.1	leaded bronze
36	brooch	.0	16.3	8.7	leaded bronze
37	brooch	+	++	++	leaded bronze
38	brooch		++	++	leaded bronze
39	brooch	1.2	5.3	9.6	(leaded) bronze
40	brooch	.0	17.0	12.6	leaded bronze
41	brooch	+	++	++	leaded bronze
42	brooch	.4	20.3	12.0	leaded bronze
43	brooch	+		++	bronze
44	brooch		++	++	leaded bronze
45	brooch	15.1	4.0	2.8	brass/gunmetal
46	brooch	++		+	brass/gunmetal
47	brooch fragment	++	++	+	leaded gunmetal
48	brooch fragment		++	++	leaded bronze
51	brooch fragment	.2	1.3	12.1	bronze
52	brooch fragment	+		++	bronze ?
54	brooch fragment	++			brass
55	brooch fragment	+			brass
57	brooch pin	++			brass
58	brooch fragment?	++			brass
61	ring	+	++	++	(leaded) bronze
69	ring			+	bronze ?
72	ring		+	++	bronze
75	bracelet	++		+	brass
77	bracelet	+	++	++	(leaded) gunmetal/bronze
78	bracelet		++	++	(leaded) bronze
79	bracelet		++	++	(leaded) bronze
80	bracelet	++	+	++	gunmetal
81	bracelet		+	++	bronze
83	bracelet	++		+	brass
86	pin	+	+	+	bronze/gunmetal ??
87	pin	+	+	++	bronze
88	pin	+	+	++	bronze
89	pin		++	++	(leaded) bronze
90	pin	+	++	++	(leaded) bronze/gunmetal
91	pin		+	++	bronze
92	pin	+	++	++	(leaded) bronze
93	pin	+	+	++	bronze
94	pin	++	++	++	(leaded) gunmetal
95	pin	+	+	++	bronze
96	pin	++	+	++	gunmetal
97	pin	++		+	brass/gunmetal
98	pin	+	+	++	bronze
99	pin		+	++	bronze
100	pin		+	+	bronze
101	pin		+	++	bronze
102	pin	++	++	++	(leaded) gunmetal
103	pin	+	++	++	(leaded) bronze/gunmetal
104	pin		++	++	(leaded) bronze
105	pin	++			brass
108	pin	+	+	++	bronze/gunmetal
110	ear scoop	+	++	+	(leaded) gunmetal
111	nail cleaner		+	++	bronze/gunmetal
112	tweezers			++	bronze
117	tweezers	+	+	++	gunmetal
119	tweezers	++	+	++	gunmetal
120	tweezers		++	+.001	(leaded) bronze
121	tweezers	+	+	++	bronze/gunmetal
122	tweezers		+	++	bronze
123	tweezers	+	++	++	(leaded) bronze

129	tweezers	++		+	brass
133	nail cleaner	+	++	++	(leaded) bronze
138	nail cleaner		+	++	bronze
139	ear scoop	+	++	+	leaded bronze
140	ear scoop		+	++	bronze
145	ligula	+	+	++	bronze
147	ligula	+		++	bronze
151	folding knife	++			brass
152	razor handle	++			brass
153	file	+	+	++	bronze
154	spatula	++	+	++	gunmetal
157	needle	++		+	brass/gunmetal
160	needle	+	+	++	bronze/gunmetal
161	needle			+	bronze
162	needle	+	+	++	bronze/gunmetal
163	needle	+	+	++	gunmetal
165	needle	++			brass
168	mount	++	+	+	brass
169	mount	+		+	brass/gunmetal
170	mount	+	+	+	brass/gunmetal
171	mount		++	+	leaded bronze/gunmetal
172	mount	++	++	+	(leaded) gunmetal
175	mount	++	++	++	leaded gunmetal
176	mount/boss	++	++	++	(leaded) gunmetal
178	mount	++	+	+	brass/gunmetal
179	scabbard runner	+	++	++	(leaded) gunmetal
181	stud	+	++		(leaded) brass
190	fragment of disc		++	++	(leaded) bronze
191	disc mount			++	bronze
194	wing		++	+	(leaded) bronze
195	hand and grapes	+	++	++	(leaded) bronze/gunmetal
197	lion-headed stud	++	++	+	(leaded) brass/gunmetal
198	foot	++	+	+	gunmetal
199	escutcheon		++	++	leaded bronze
200	cockerel	+	++	++	(leaded) bronze
201	decorated strip		+	++	bronze
202	seal box lid		++	+	(leaded) bronze
203	seal box	+	++	++	(leaded) bronze/gunmetal
204	seal box base	++	++	++	(leaded) gunmetal/bronze
205	seal box lid		++	++	leaded bronze
206	stylus/pin shaft		++	++	leaded bronze
207	fastener	+	+	++	bronze
209	stud	++	++	++	(leaded) gunmetal
210	stud		++	++	(leaded) bronze
211	stud		+	++	bronze
212	stud		+	+	bronze ?
213	lock pin	+	+	++	bronze/gunmetal
217	stud	++		+	brass
220	weight (disc)	+	++	++	leaded bronze
221	weight (disc)		++	++	(leaded) bronze
222	weight (disc)	+	++	++	leaded bronze
223	weight (disc)		++	++	(leaded) bronze
224	weight (disc)		++	++	leaded bronze
225	weight (disc)	+	++	++	leaded bronze
236	buckle fragment	++	+	++	gunmetal
239	spoon bowl		+		base silver
240	spoon bowl		++	++	bronze
241	spoon	+	++	++	leaded bronze/gunmetal
242	spoon	+	++	++	(leaded) bronze
243	spoon	++		+	brass
244	spoon		++	+	leaded gunmetal
245	key	++		+	brass
247	lock bolt	+	++	+	leaded gunmetal
248	lock bolt	+	++	+	leaded gunmetal
252	ring key	++	++	++	leaded gunmetal

254	drop handle			++	bronze ?
255	drop handle	++			brass
261	binding			++	bronze
263	plate			++	bronze
270	binding			++	bronze
307	ring	+	++	++	leaded bronze
316	ring	++	++	++	leaded bronze/gunmetal
317	ring	+	++	++	leaded bronze
321	chain	++			brass
325	chain	++			brass
330	strip			++	bronze
340	fragment of casting		+	++	bronze
341	padlock		++	++	(leaded) bronze
*	rivet/pinhead	+	+	++	bronze
*	rivet/pinhead	++		++	gunmetal
*	link	+		+	brass/gunmetal
*	pin	++		++	gunmetal
*	ring	++	++	++	leaded bronze/gunmetal

Appendix 5: Finds listed by context

Context	*Publication nos (Bracketed numbers are illustrated in the archive)*
1956 exc	(50); 91; 106; (150); 174; 194; 196; 266; 308; (319); 333; 342; 369; 378; 395; 409; 439; 441; (468); 520; 523; 554; 558; 574; (621); 678; 741; (752); (753); (883); (884); 919; 946; 969; 976; 1004; 1019; 1044; 1059
1	(58); 75; 82; 87; 88; 93; (125); (126); 136; (149); 189; 240; 262; 264; (291); 334; 341; 344; 345; 349; 350; 351; (397); 416; (508); (518); (590); (637); 641; (656); (658); (659); 682; (762); (775); (845); (884); 981; (985); (986); 1015; (1047); 1048; 1063
2	(56); 943
3	212
4	8; 183; 274; (290); 298; 323; 346; 353; 354; 358; 359; 371; (399); 408; (451); (457); 480; 482; (499); (512); (513); (515); (517); 538; (657); (669); (691); (692); (705); (713); 733; 738; (751); (843); (885); (886); 948; 991; 999
5	2; 35
6	188
8	177
9	987
20	757; 953
24	235; 347; 521; 984
26	(166); 949
29	259; 622; 807
35	185
36	105
37	1041
42	338; (599)
43	361
45	132; 242; 374; 442; (811)
63	(121); 340; 628; 982
64	(464)
67	224
71	339
77	15; 34; 191; 236; 237; 270; 273; 437; (460); 471; (670); 725; 732; 758; (759); (786); (846); 907; (909); 968; 1008; 1034
86	404
91	20; 33; (51); (122); 133; 140; 325; 990
109	47; 954
110	62; 443; 573; 575; 662; (812); 936; 938; 941; (963); 1017
120	728
130	(582); 731
131	(55); (302)
135	(304); 995; 1033
139	1020
151	940
158	1029
162	631
163	730
171	251
179	411; 638
194	977
199	89; 218
201	557
208	332
233	896
234	204; 506
254	(813)
258	102
263	248
266	22
275	68; 99; 104; 114; 211; 213; 214; 256; 327; 610; 923; 924; 925; (957); (958); (959); (960); (961); (962); 979; (983); 989; 1036; 1039
276	219
278	(379)
287	31; 997
314	(561)
317	324
318	43; 1038
319	(54); (289); 624
320	276
337	623
339	666
348	13
367	1030
369	16; 66; 130; 135; 238; 272; 278; 281; 560; 611; 612; (700); (814); 908; 926; (927); 931; (956); 965
374	(760)
384	96
389	614
394	(715)
396	155; (158)
409	14
410	98; 142; 144; 285; 286; 532; (761); 790; 975
488	156; (292); 336; 438; (514); 740; (887)
491	192
493	357; (567)
494	234; 239; (428); 435; 988; 1024; 1037
499	519
501	231; 233; 331; (445); 502; (509); (510); (815); (816); (817); (818)
502	1006

Context	*Publication nos (Bracketed numbers are illustrated in the archive)*
506	173; (446); (694); (754); 922; 945
509	939
519	193; 504; (511); (649); (819)
520	206; (680)
530	29
535	(847)
538	545
539	277
544	9; 703
544b	40; (604)
545	103
546	1043
547	172; (398)
549	478; 505; (772); (779)
550	609; 640; 947
556	(507); 765
562	95; (288); 293; 312; 375; 418; 526; (579); 596; (650); (848); (951); 1013
563	193; 980
566	90
574	(820)
584	937
586	(585)
590	326; (821)
591	660; (1045)
592	(124)
595	942
596	294; (305); (822)
615	21; 92; (313); 430; (462); (651); (823); (824); 952; 970
628	116
641	297; (620)
648	973
652	115; (141); (615); 1028
653	134
659	745
660	24; (57); (699); 964
661	(586)
666	(547)
667	208
694	198
701	216; (318); (320); 352; 360; (380); 417; 424; (465); (516); 572; 735; 767; (888); (889); (890); (891); 905; (1005)
702	(287); (493); (494); 593; 739; (749); (849); (850)
703	(314); 627; (636); (677); (851); (910)
711	(716); (852); 966
713	18
714	253
721	10; 25; 28; 107; 171; 205; 215; 226; 227; 228; 271; (381); (382); (383); (426); 440; 476; (491); (492); 527; (528); 533; (589); (597); (598); (653); (671); (695); (721); (722); (771); (782); (783); (788); 797; 799; 801; 802; 803; 804; (825); (826); (827); (828); (829); (830); (853); (854); (855); (856); (857); (858); (859); (860); (861); 904; 978; 1023
735	(455); 530
736	415
741	11; 12; 39; 42; 70; 113; (167); 229; 249; 279; 283; 296; 337; 343; 348; 355; 356; 362; (387); 402; (466); 503; 562; 569; 571; (616); (676); 683; 768; 805; (844); (892); (893); (894); (895); 899; 902; (994); 1022
745	199
748	413
751	1012
756	(720); 1035
768	221; 295; 996
769	23; 306; 710
770	(862)
773	(52); (127); 220; (552); (577); (773); (619); (674); (707); (781)
779	(551)
786	5; 65; 269; (448); 555; (654); 736; (773); (863); (864); (865); 935; 1049
787	275; 535; (617); 664; (714); (719); (723); (866); (867); (868); (869); 906; (911); 972; 974; 1042
790	(950)
796	219; (578); 743; 934
797	186; 469
798	(384); (453); (548); (756); (870); (871); (872); (873)
802	(603)
805	(49)
809	1032
812	570
815	220
817	30
848	179; 742; (831); 1027
849	32; (315)
859	232
916	(458)
917	967
920	(159); 257; 522; 524; (588); 625; 626; (652); (673); (750); 920; 930; 1054
996	(164); 328; (425); (755); 800; (832)
1013	(463); (833)
1028	282; (993)
1033	(874)
1040	131
1052	225
1056	(955)
	169
1062	1067
1063	543; (834)
1075	(912)
1082	200
1118	(875)
1140	1; (1046)
1142	94
1149	607; 1068
1195	1052
1218	(48)
1258	482
1263	64; 372
1264	501
1267	(568)
1269	4
1271	241; 250
1282	(1060)
1283	81; 202; (601)
1286	389; 1066
1298	180
1322	(452)
1333	(618)
1334	390
1398	322
1399	672
1413	178
1414	(137)
1416	(85)
1445	(876)
1446	246
1448	734
1450	76; 79
1451	793
1454	27; 170
1456	897
1474	(461)
1490	60; 118; 1016
1492	260
1495	(84); 421; 550
1499	(128)
1516	(655)
1520	(450)
1521	37; 74; (146)
1535	(148); 311
1540	45; (138); 307; (675); (835)
1551	19; (109); 268; 992
1552	67; 280; 284; 300; (780)
1569	63; 157; 223; 595; (698); 1007; 1018; 1051
1572	(147); 261; (836); (877)
1575	217
1578	(165)
1581	247
1586	41; (123); (1010)
1587	3; 303
1588	(53); 243; 244
1594	6; 7; 154; (161); 254; 255
1596	151; (498)
1597	207; 303

Context	Publication nos (Bracketed numbers are illustrated in the archive)
1599	59; (163); 245; (634); (690)
1622	605
1630	299; (837)
1641	789; 806
1642	153; 420; (600)
1643	263
1651	139; (913); 1021
1657	(108); 120; (145); (162); 929; 1064
1662	69; 321
1663	542
1665	36; 222
1668	928
1669	86; 110; 111; 112; 330; 679
1678	898
1679	1025; (1031)
1723	681
1724	903
1799	(693)
1804	971
1810	363
1857	301
1880	544
1881	97; 190; (316); 632; 932; 1040
1883	(777); 1003
1888	(129); (489); 766
1890	(486)
1895	(160)
1898	77; (78); 422; 474; 1898
1902	176
1903	203
1904	365
1906	(385); 729; 1000
1909	201; (645)
1910	(444); 566; 592; 900
1919	727
1920	(467); 933
2001	(317); 364; 367; (386); (388); 414; 432; 539; 549; (559); 630; (704); 737; 746; (747); 764; 998
2002	152; 377; (686); (687); 701; (787); 796; (877)
2003	794
2004	1011
2010	117
2015	(709)
2016	368; 472; (490); 531; 536; (688); (689); (879); (914)
2017	534; 546; 565; 629; (648); (776); 795; (838); (839)
2018	401; 431; (485); (580); (584); (633); 667; (748); 1050; 1055
2019	419; (915)
2020	252; 366; 370; 410; 537; (576); 606; 642; (643); (644); (916)
2032	391; (646); 1053
2033	529
2061	763
2065	396; 400; (488); 553; (581); (583); 639; (647); 661; (840); 1058
2066	423; 470; 556; 920; 921
2067	44; (487)
2086	(1056)
2090	119
2187	(778)
2192	258
2247	181; 479
2301	72; 80; 376; (403); 406; 433; (447); 483; (495); 525; 594; 711; (841); (880)
2302	175; 197; (427); (429); 434; 473; 484; (496); (587); (635); (696); (697); 701; (706); 724; (785); 791; 792; 808; (842); (881); (917); 1062
2303	168
2330	394; (784)
2344	230; 309; (449); 475; 613; 684; 809; 810
2345	(541); (882)
2346	663; (708)
2350	(770)
2355	(918)
2357	(718)
2361	(497)
2372	(602)
2387	17
2457	726

Context	Publication nos (Bracketed numbers are illustrated in the archive)
2462	798
2574	685
2606	1057
2619	38
2665	61; 540; (712)
2670	901
2680	(774)
2691	392
2731	(717)
2844	564; 668
3021	26; 143; 184; 407; (456); 1002
3091	71; 73; 101; 477
3107	608
3122	1061
3142	1026
3246	329
3258	182; 373
3270	335
3285	412
3312	665
3364	(459)
3367	(454)
3400	436

Summary

The aim of the excavations at Gorhambury, situated close to Verulamium, Herts, was to excavate a Roman villa complex fully and to establish whether the pattern of development noted at the Gadebridge villa, Hemel Hempstead, excavated between 1962 and 1968, was typical of the villas in the Verulamium area. The site at Gorhambury was chosen because incomplete excavations in 1956–62 suggested that the site had a long history and that evidence for the early development of the villa might be found.

The report describes the results of this work and demonstrates that, as at the villa at Park Street to the south of Verulamium, the settlement began in the late Iron Age (although a Neolithic building and Bronze Age pottery attest that the site had a longer history). A rectangular ditched enclosure with an entrance on its eastern side was enlarged at various times and contained an aisled barn which continued as the site for an aisled house until the third century. Further Iron Age buildings within a secondary enclosure included a circular house constructed over a massive nine-post granary. A sequence of buildings was constructed on the same spot including an early first-century timber house, the embryonic villa, which may well have been destroyed by Boudicca. Further timber buildings were followed in *c* AD 100 by a small but luxurious masonry villa which underwent various modifications, including the insertion of a cellar containing in its filling fragments of moulded wall plaster, mosaics and stucco. Associated buildings included a tower granary and a bath-house.

In the late second century this villa was rebuilt; other structures of this date included a bath-house for the farm workers and general ancillary structures. The area of the original enclosures was now divided into a series of paddocks.

In the third century the villa was abandoned temporarily and, even though it was repaired, the villa and farm structures gradually declined; unlike Gadebridge, there was no Constantinian revival although both villas ceased *c* AD 350. In the medieval period the site was occupied by a croft.

The report gives detailed descriptions and plans of all the buildings period by period and is accompanied by a discussion of the villas in the Verulamium area and reasons for their demise at such an early date. An attempt is made to investigate the coincidence between the late Iron Age earthworks on the Gorhambury estate with the medieval boundaries of Westwick manor, to establish a hypothetical area for the Roman villa estate. Earthworks related to those excavated by Wheeler in Prae Wood are published for the first time.

The finds catalogue illustrates over 1000 objects making possible comparison with the finds from Gadebridge; many of the copper alloy objects have been subjected to qualitative analysis, providing an interesting insight into the various alloys used for specific classes of object. Among the iron objects are tools and implements which are informative about the economic life of the villa estate. The report on the pottery concentrates on the large assemblage of late Iron Age vessels.

Résumé

Le but des fouilles entreprises à Gorhambury, site qui se trouve à proximité de Verulamium, comté de Hertfordshire, était d'explorer complètement une villa romaine et ses dépendances et d'essayer d'établir si les phases du dévelopement de ce type de site, telles qu'on les avaient observées lors de l'excavation de la villa Gadebridge, à Hemel Hempstead, entre 1962 et 1968, étaient caractéristiques des villas de la région de Verulamium. On a choisi le site de Gorhambury parce qu'un début de fouilles, entrepris là entre 1956 et 1962, laissait supposer que l'histoire du site couvrait une longue période et que l'on était susceptible de trouver des témoignages de l'occupation de la villa à une époque reculée.

Le compte-rendu décrit les résultats de ce travail et démontre que, comme pour la villa de Park Street, au sud de Verulamium, l'occupation du site avait commencé à l'âge de fer tardif (toutefois, une construction néolithique et de la poterie de l'âge de bronze indiquent que l'histoire du site s'étend au delà de cette période). Une enceinte rectangulaire, entourée d'un fossé et comportant une ouverture du côté est, avait été agrandie à plusieurs reprises et comprenait une grange avec bas-côtés dont l'emplacement fut utilisé plus tard pour une maison à bas-côtés qui survécut jusqu'au troisième siècle. Parmi d'autres édifices, datant également de l'âge de fer mais situés à l'intérieur d'une deuxième enceinte, on a découvert une maison circulaire construite au-dessus d'un imposant grenier à neuf poteaux. Par la suite, des bâtiments divers se succédèrent à ce même endroit, entre autres une maison en bois primitive du premier siècle – la villa à l'état embryonnaire – qui fut probablement détruite par Boudicca. A d'autres édifices en bois succéda, aux environs de l'an 100 après J-C, une petite mais luxueuse villa en pierres qui subit diverses modifications, dont l'adjonction d'un cellier recélant dans son remplissage des fragments de revêtement mural en plâtre moulé, de mosaïque et de stuc. Les dépendances comprenaient un grenier en forme de tour et un établissement de bains.

Vers la fin du second siècle cette villa fut reconstruite; on a également identifiés comme appartenant à cette même période d'autres vestiges: un établissement de bains pour les travailleurs de la ferme et des dépendances d'utilité générale. Les aires délimitées par les enceintes d'origine étaient maintenant divisées en une série d'enclos.

Au troisième siècle la villa fut momentanément abandonnée, et bien qu'elle fût réparée par la suite, la villa et ses dépendances perdirent peu à peu de leur importance mais, contrairement à ce qui se passa à Gadebridge, elle ne connut pas de renaissance à l'époque de Constantin et en fin de compte, les deux villas cessèrent d'exister vers 350 après J-C. Au moyen-âge le site fut occupé par une petite ferme.

Le compte-rendu offre des descriptions détaillées, ainsi que des plans, de tous les bâtiments époque par époque, on y examine les villas de la région de Verulamium et on y traite des raisons pour lesquelles elles ont connu un déclin si précoce. On a essayé d'analyser la correspondance entre les travaux de terrassement de l'âge de fer tardif de l'exploitation de Gorhambury et les limites médiévales du manoir de Westwick afin de délimiter un emplacement hypothétique pour le domaine de la villa romaine. Des travaux de terrassement, en rapport avec ceux mis au jour par Wheeler à Prae Wood, sont publiés pour la premiére fois.

Dans le catalogue des fouilles sont illustrés plus de 1000 objets qu'on peut ainsi comparer avec les trouvailles faites à Gadebridge; un grand nombre des objets en alliage de cuivre ont été soumis à une analyse qualitative qui a fourni d'intéressants renseignements sur les divers alliages utilisés pour des types particuliers d'objets. Parmi les objets en fer on trouve des outils et des instruments qui nous instruisent sur la vie économique de l'exploitation rurale. Le rapport sur la poterie se concentre sur l'importante collection de récipients de la fin de l'âge de fer.

Zusammenfassung

Ziel der Ausgrabungen in Gorhambury, das in der Nähe von Verulamium in Hertfordshire liegt, war es einen römischen Villenkomplex vollständig auszugraben und festzustellen, ob das Entwicklungsschema, das bei der zwischen 1962–68 in Gadebridge in Hemel Hempstead ausgegrabenen Villa sichergestellt wurde, auf alle Villen im Gebiet um Verulamium zutrifft. Die Wahl war auf die Fundstätte in Gorhambury gefallen, weil teilweise Ausgrabungen in den Jahren zwischen 1956–62 angedeutet haben, daß diese Fundstelle eine weitzurückreichende Geschichte besitzt und so möglicherweise Hinweise auf die frühen Entwicklungsphasen der Villa gefunden werden könnten.

Der Bericht beschreibt die Ergebnisse dieser Arbeiten und zeigt auf, dass, wie bei der Villa in Park Street südlich von Verulamium, die Besiedlung im ausgehenden Eisenzeitalter begann (obwhol ein Gebäude aus der Jungsteinzeit und bronzezeitliche Keramik bezeugen, daß die Fundstelle eine noch weiterzurückgehende Geschichte besitzt). Ein rechteckiges durch Gräben eingefriedetes Areal, dessen Zugang auf seiner Ostseite lag, war mehrfach vergrößert worden. Es enthielt eine mehrschiffige Scheune, deren Position dann für ein mehrschiffiges Haus bis in das 3 Jahrhundert hin weiterbenutzt worden war. Unter einer Anzahl weiterer eisenzeitlicher Bauten in einer Nebeneinfriedung befand sich ein Rundhaus, das über einem massiven Kornspeicher mit neun Pfosten errichtet worden war. Eine Folge von Gebäuden war dann auf der selben Stelle errichtet worden, eines davon ein Holzbau aus dem 1 Jahrhundert, die Keimzelle der Villa. Er wurde möglicherweise von Boudicca zerstört. Weitere Holzbauten wurden um ungefähr 100 n Chr von einer kleinen aber luxuriösen, in Mauerwerk erbauten Villa abgelöst. In dem mehrfachgeänderten Bau wurde unter anderem ein Keller eingebaut, der in seiner Auffüllung Fragmente von geformten Putz, von Mosaiken und Stuck enthielt. Zu den Nebengebäuden gehörten ein Turmspeicher und ein Badehaus.

In ausgehenden 2 Jahrhundert wurde die Villa neugebaut; zu den weiteren Bauten aus dieser Zeit zählen ein Badehaus für die Landarbeiter und Wirtschaftsgebäude. Die Areale der ursprünglichen Einfriedungen waren jetzt in eine Reihe von Koppeln aufgeteilt.

Im 3 Jahrhundert wurde die Villa zeitweilig aufgegeben und obwohl dann repariert, verfielen sie und die Wirtschaftsbebäude allmählich; es gab hier im Gegansatz zu der Villa in Gadebridge keine Neusiedlung zur Zeit Konstantins, obwohl beide Villen um 350 n Chr verlassen wurden. Während des Mittelalters lag auf der Lokalität ein Kleinbauernhof.

Der Bericht enthält detailierte Beschreibungen und Pläne aller Bauten, Bauphase für Bauphase. In einer begleitenden Diskussion werden die Villen im Gebiet von Verulamium und die Gründe für ihre frühzeitige Aufgabe besprochen. Es wird versucht zu ermitteln, welche Übereinstimmungen zwischen den späteisenzeitlichen Anlagen auf dem Gebiet des Gutes Gorhambury und der Ausdehnung der mittelalterlichen Gutsherrschaft Westwick bestehen, um so ein hypothetisches Areal für den Gutsbereich der römischen Villa festzulegen. Neuentdeckte Bodendenkmäler, die mit jenen von Wheeler in Prae Wood ausgegrabenen in Verbindung stehen, werden hier zum ersten Mal veröffentlicht.

Der Fundkatalog registriert bildlich über 1000 Gegenstände und macht so den Vergleich mit den Funden aus Gadebridge möglich. Viele der aus Kupferligierungen hergestellten Gegenstände wurden einer qualitativen Analyse unterzogen. Dies erlaubt einen interessanten Einblick in den Gebrauch der einzelnen Ligierungen für spezifische Gruppen von Gegenständen. Unter den Eisengegenständen befanden sich Werkzeuge und Gerätschaften, die über das Wirtschaftsleben auf dem zu einer römischen Villa gehörenden Gutes Auskunft geben. Der Bericht über die Keramik befaßt sich hauptsächlich mit dem großen Fundaufkommen an Gefäßen aus der späten Eisenzeit.

Bibliography

Allason-Jones, L, and Miket, R, 1984 *The catalogue of small finds from South Shields*, Newcastle upon Tyne

Anthony, I E, 1960 Rural Hertfordshire in the Iron Age and Roman period, *Hertfordshire past and present*, **1**

———, 1961 A Roman building at Gorhambury, St Albans, *Trans St Albans Hertfordshire Archit Archaeol*, 21–30

Applebaum, S, 1972 The boundaries of the Ditchley villa estate, Oxfordshire, in *The Agrarian history of England and Wales* (Finberg H P R), **I**, II, 266–7, Cambridge

———, 1975 Some observations on the economy of the Roman villa at Bignor, Sussex, *Britannia*, **6**, 118–132

Armitage, P, West, B, and Steedman, K, 1984 New Evidence of Black Rat in Roman London, *London Archaeol*, **4**, 14, 375–83

Atkinson, D A, 1914 A hoard of samian ware from Pompeii, *J Roman Stud*, 4, 27–64

Aubert, X, 1929 Evolution des hipposandales: essai de classification rationelle, *Revue des Musées*, Dijon, **19**, 5, 53, 75

Baker, A R H, and Butlin, R A, 1973 *Studies of field systems in the British Isles*, Cambridge

Barker, G, and Webley, D, 1977 An integrated economy for Gatcombe, in Branigan 1977, 198–200

Bateman, N, and Locker, A, 1982 The Sauce of the Thames, *London Archaeol*, **4**, 8, 204–7

Bayley, J, 1984 *Qualitative analysis of Roman spoons from Richborough, Kent*, AM Lab Report 4304

———, 1985a Brass and brooches in Roman Britain, *Masca J*, **3** (6), 189–91

———, 1985b The analysis of copper alloy objects and The technological finds, in Niblett 1985, 115, London

———, 1986a *The evidence for metalworking from Gorhambury Villa, Herts*, AM Lab Report No 28/86

———, 1986b A crucible from St Sepulchre Gate (Site DEH), Doncaster, in *The archaeology of Doncaster I. The Roman civil settlement*, BAR, **148**, Oxford

Bayley, J, and Wilthew, S, 1986 *Qualitative analysis of copper alloy objects from Gorhambury Villa, Herts*, AM Lab Report No 37/86

Bersu, G, 1940 Excavations at Little Woodbury, Wiltshire, *Proc Prehist Soc*, **6**, 30–111

Bishop, M C, 1988 Cavalry equipment of the Roman army in the first century AD, in *Military equipment and the identity of Roman soldiers* (ed J C Coulston), BAR, **S394**, 67–194, Oxford

Black, E W, 1981 An additional classification of granaries in Roman Britain, *Britannia*, **12**, 163–5

———, 1987 *The Roman villas of south-east England*, BAR, **171**, Oxford

Boessneck, J, 1969 Osteological differences between sheep (*Ovis aries* Linne) and Goat (*Capra hircus* Linne), in *Science in archaeology* (eds D Brothwell and E Higgs), 311–58, London

Böhme, A, 1972 Die Fibeln der Kastelle Saalburg und Zugmantel, *Saalburg Jahrbuch*, **29**, 5–112

Boon, G C, 1957 *Roman Silchester: the archaeology of a Romano-British town*, London

Brailsford, J, 1962 *Hod Hill*, **I**, *Antiquities from Hod Hill in the Durden collection*, London

Branigan, K, 1967 'Romano-British rural settlement in the western Chilterns', *Archaeol J*, **124**, 129–59

———, 1971 *Latimer: Belgic, Roman, Dark Age and early modern farms*, Chess Valley Archaeol Hist Soc, Chesham

———, 1977 *Gatcombe. The excavation and study of a Romano-British Villa estate 1967–1976*, BAR, **44**, Oxford

Brodribb, A C C, Hands, A R, and Walker, D R, 1968–73 *Excavations at Shakenoak Farm near Wilcote, Oxfordshire*, **1–4**, Oxford

Bushe-Fox, J P, 1916 *Third report on the excavations on the site of the Roman town at Wroxeter, Shropshire 1914*, Rep Res Comm Soc Antiq London, **4**, Oxford

Cameron, R A D, and Kerney, L, 1979 *A field guide to the land snails of Britain and north-west Europe*, London

Castle, S A, 1972 A kiln of the potter Doinus, *Archaeol J*, **129**, 69–88

———, 1976a Roman pottery from Radlett, 1959, *Hertfordshire Archaeol*, 4, 149–52

———, 1976b Roman pottery from Brockley Hill, Middlesex, 1966 and 1972–4, *Trans London Middlesex Archaeol Soc*, **27**, 206–27

Clarke, G, 1979 *Winchester Studies*, **3**, *Pre-Roman and Roman Winchester*, **2**, *The Roman cemetery at Lankhills*, Oxford

Clifford, E M, 1961 *Bagendon: a Belgic oppidum, a record of excavations of 1954–1956*, Cambridge

Cocks, A H, 1921 A Romano-British homestead in the Hambleden valley, Bucks, *Archaeologia*, **71**, 141–98

Columella trans Forster, E S, and Heffer, E, 1954 *De Re Rustica*, V–IX, Loeb Classical Library

Cool, H E M, and Price, J, 1987 The glass, in Meates 1987, 110–42

Cunliffe, B W (ed), 1968 *Fifth report on the excavations of the Roman fort at Richborough, Kent*, Rep Res Comm Soc Antiq London, **23**, Oxford

———, 1971 *Excavations at Fishbourne 1961–1969*, **2**: *The finds*, Rep Res Comm Soc Antiq London, **27**, Leeds

Crummy, N, 1979 A chronology of bone pins, *Britannia*, **10**, 157–64

———, 1983 *The Roman small finds from excavations in Colchester, 1971–79*, Colchester Archaeol Rep, **2**, Colchester

Curle, J, 1911 *A Roman frontier post and its people: the fort of Newstead in the Parish of Melrose*, Glasgow

Curnow, P, 1974 Coin lists: some problems of the smaller site in *Coins and the archaeologist* (ed J Casey and R Reece), BAR, **4**, 52–63

———, 1985 The Roman coins in *West Stow: the Anglo-Saxon village* (S West) **1**, 76–81, *East Anglian Archaeol*, **24**, Ipswich

Davey, N, and Ling, R, 1982 *Wall painting in Roman Britain*, Britannia Monog, **2**

Davies, W, 1979 Roman settlements and post-Roman estates in south-west Wales, in *The end of Roman Britain* (ed P J Casey), BAR, **71**, 153–73

Déchelette, J, 1904 *Les vases ornées de la Gaule romaine*, Paris

de Laet, S J, 1952 De romeinse nederzetting te Hofstade bij Aalst, *Cultureel Jaarboek der Provincie Oostvlaanderen*, **2**, 281–302

Dix, B, 1981 The Romano-British farmstead at Odell and its setting: some reflections on the Roman landscape of the SE Midlands, *Landscape Hist*, **3**, 17–26

Down, A, 1981 *Chichester excavations*, **5**, Chichester

Down, A, and Rule, M, 1971 *Chichester excavations*, **1**, Chichester

Von den Driesch, A, and Boessneck, J, 1974 Kritische Anmerkungen zur Widerristhoherberechnung aus Langenmassen vor- und fruhgeschichtlicher Tierknochen, *Saugetierkundliche Mitteilungen*, **22**, 325–48

Dudley, D, 1968 Excavations on Nor'nour in the Isles of Scilly, 1962–6, *Archaeol J*, **124**, 1–64

Ekwall, E, 1960 *The Concise Oxford dictionary of English place-names*, 4 edn, Oxford

Ettlinger, E, 1973 *Die römischen Fibeln in der Schweiz*, Bern

Evans, J, 1853 *Account of excavations on the sites of two Roman villas at Box Moor, Hertfordshire*, London

Evans, J G, 1972 *Land snails in archaeology*, London

Evans, K J, 1974 Excavations on a Romano-British site, Wiggonholt, 1964, *Sussex Archaeol Collect*, **112**, 1–56

Finberg, H P R, 1955 *Roman and Saxon Withington: a study in continuity*, Dept English Local History, Occas Pap, **8**, Univ Leicester

Fock, J, 1966 *Metrische Untersuchungen an Metapodien einiger europäischer Rinderassen*, Fakultat der Universitat München

Fossing, P, 1929 *The Thorvaldsen Museum, Catalogue of the antique engraved gems and cameos*, Copenhagen

Freeman, M, unpublished records, Verulamium Museum

Frere, S S, 1967 *Britannia, a history of Roman Britain*, London

———, 1972 *Verulamium excavations*, **I**, Rep Res Comm Soc Antiq London, **28**, London

———, 1983 *Verulamium excavations*, **2**, Rep Res Comm Soc Antiq London, **41**, London

———, 1984 *Verulamium excavations*, **3**, Oxford University Committee for Archaeology

Furtwängler, A, 1896 *Königliche Museen zu Berlin, Beschreibung der Geschnittenen Steine*, Berlin

Gaffney, V, and Tingle, M, 1985 The Maddle Farm (Berks) project and micro-regional analysis, in Macready and Thompson 1985, 67–73

Gaitzsch, W, 1980 *Giserne römische Werkzeuge, Studien zur römischen Werkzeugkunde in Italien und nördlichen Provinzen des Imperium Romanum*, BAR **S78**, i and ii

Gelling, M, 1978 *Signposts to the past*, London

Gesta Abbatum Monasterii Sancti Albani, ed H T Riley, London, 1869

Gillam, J P, 1968 *Types of Roman coarse pottery in northern Britain*, Newcastle

Goodburn, R, 1984 The non-ferrous metal objects, in Frere 1984, 19–67

Grant, A, 1971 The animal bones, in Cunliffe 1971, 377–88

———, 1975 The animal bones, and Appendix B: the use of tooth wear as a guide to the age of domestic animals, in *Excavations at Portchester Castle*, **1**, *Roman*, B W Cunliffe Rep Res Comm Soc Antiq London, **32**, 378–408, 438–450, London

Green, M J, 1976 *The religions of civilian Roman Britain*, BAR, **24**, Oxford

Greene, K T, 1979 The pre-Flavian fine wares, in *Report on the Excavations at Usk 1965–1976*

Grimston, C, 1821 MS, Gorhambury House Library

Hadman, J, 1978 Aisled buildings in Roman Britain, in *Studies in the Romano-British villa* (ed M Todd), 187–95, Leicester

Harcourt, R, 1974a The dog in prehistoric and early historic Britain, *J Archaeol Sci*, **1** (2), 151–76

———, 1974b Animal bones, in Neal 1974, 256–61

Hartley, B R, 1959 A Romano-British villa at High Wycombe, *Rec Buckinghamshire*, **16** (4), 227–57

Hassall, M W C, and Tomlin, R S O, 1982 Roman Britain in 1981: **2**, Inscriptions, *Britannia*, **13**, 396–422

Haupt, D, 1984 Römischer Töpfereibezirk bei Soller, Kreis Düren, *Rheinische Ausgrabungen, Band 23*, 1984: Beiträge zur Archäologie des Römischen Rheinlands, **4**, 391–476, Bonn

Hawkes, C F C, and Hull, M R, 1947 *Camulodunum: First Report on the Excavations at Colchester 1930–1939*, Rep Res Comm Soc Antiq London, **14**, Oxford

Hayfield, C, 1987 *An archaeological survey of the parish of Wharram Percy, E Yorks, the evolution of the Roman landscape*, BAR, **172**, Oxford

Henig, M, 1972 The origin of some ancient British coin types, *Britannia*, **3**, 209–23

———, 1977 Death and the maiden: funerary symbolism in daily life, in *Roman life and art in Britain* (eds J Munby and M Henig), BAR, **41**, 347–66

———, 1978 *A corpus of Roman engraved gemstones from British sites*, BAR, **8**, 2 edn, Oxford

———, 1979 Objects from a Romano-British temple on West Hill, Uley, Gloucestershire, **2**, The bronze figurines and stone altar, *Antiq J*, **58**, 369

———, 1986 *Classical gems, ancient and modern intaglios and cameos in the Fitzwilliam Museum, Cambridge*, Cambridge

Hermet, F, 1934 *La Graufesenque*, Paris

Hickling, C F, 1972 Prior More's Fishponds, *Medieval Archaeol*, **15–16**, 118–123

Hull, M R, 1958 *Roman Colchester*, Rep Res Comm Soc Antiq London, **20**, Oxford

———, 1963 *The Roman potters' kilns of Colchester*, Rep Res Comm Soc Antiq London, **21**, Oxford

Hunn, J R, 1980 The earthworks of Prae Wood: an interim account, *Britannia*, **11**, 21–30

———, forthcoming *A reconstruction and measurement of landscape change: a study of six parishes in the St Albans area*, PhD thesis, Univ Southampton, 1989

Hunn, J R, and Blagg, T F C, 1984 Architectural fragments from the vicinity of Verulamium, *Antiq J*, **64**, 362–5

Hurst, J G, 1977 Discussion of Pottery, in Neal, D S, 'Excavations at the Palace of Kings Langley, Hertfordshire 1974–1976', *Medieval Archaeol*, **21**, 1977, 124–165

JRS passim *Journal of Roman Studies*

Jackson, D A, and Ambrose, T M, 1978 Excavations at Wakerley Northants 1972–75, *Britannia*, **9**, 115–242

Jarret, M G, and Wrathmell, S, 1981 *Whitton, an Iron Age and Roman farmstead in South Glamorgan*, Cardiff

Johnston, D, 1969 Sparsholt, *Current Archaeol*, **12**, **2** (1), 14–18

Jones, M J, 1975 *Roman fort-defences to AD 117 with special reference to Britain*, BAR, **21**, Oxford

Jones, M, 1986 Towards a model of the villa estate, in Miles 1986, 38–42

Jones, R, Langley, P, and Wall, S, 1985 The animal bones from the 1977 excavations, in *Excavations at Brancaster 1974 and 1977* (J Hinchliffe and C S Gree), *East Anglian Archaeol*, **23**, 132–75

Jones, R T, Wall, S M, Locker, A M, Coy, J, and Maltby, M, 1981 *Ancient Monuments Laboratory DOE computer based osteometry, Data capture user manual (1)*, Ancient Monuments Lab Rep 3342

King, A, 1978 A comparative survey of bone assemblages from Roman sites in Britain, *Institute Archaeol Bull*, **15**, 207–32

Knorr, R, 1919 *Töpfer und Fabriken verzierter Terra-sigillata des ersten Jahrhunderts*, Stuttgart

———, 1952 *Terra-sigillata-Gefasse des ersten Jahrhunderts mit Töpfernamen*, Stuttgart

Krug, A, 1980 Antike Gemmen in Römisch-Germanischen Museum Köln, *BRGK*, **61**, 151–260

Leech, R, 1982 *Excavations at Catsgore 1970–1973; a Romano-British village*, Western Archaeol Trust, Excavation Monog, **2**, Gloucester

Levett, A E, 1938 *Studies in manorial history*, Oxford

Locker, A, 1988 The animal bones, in Neal 1988

Lowther, A W G, 1948 *A study of the patterns on Roman flue-tiles and their distribution.* Res Pap Surrey Archaeol Soc, **1**, Guildford

Lyneborg, L, 1977 *Mammals in colour*, Blandford

Maaskant-Kleibrink, M, 1978 *Catalogue of the engraved gems in the Royal Coin Cabinet, The Hague, The Greek, Etruscan and Roman collections*, The Hague

MacGregor, A, 1985 *Bone, antler, ivory and horn, the technology of skeletal material since the Roman period*, London

Mack, R P, 1964 *The coinage of ancient Britain*, London

Macready, S, and Thompson, F H, 1985 *Archaeology and field survey in Britain and beyond*, Soc Antiq Occas Pap, **6**, London

Maltby, M, 1979 *Faunal studies on urban sites, the animal bones from Exeter 1971–1975*, Exeter Archaeol Rep, **2**, Sheffield

Manning, W H, 1972 The iron objects, in Frere 1972, 163–95

———, 1974 Objects of iron, in Neal 1974, 157–87

———, 1976 *Catalogue of Romano-British ironwork in the Museum of Antiquities, Newcastle upon Tyne*, Newcastle upon Tyne

———, 1984a The iron objects, in Frere 1984, 83–106

———, 1984b Objects of iron, in Excavations at Dorchester-on-Thames, 1963 (S S Frere), *Archaeol J*, **141**, 91–174

———, 1985 *Catalogue of the Romano-British iron tools, fittings and weapons in the British Museum*, London

Manning, W H, and Scott, I R, 1986 Iron objects, in Stead and Rigby 1986, 145–62

Marsh, G, 1978 Early second-century fine wares in the London area, in *Early fine wares in Roman Britain* (eds P Arthur and G Marsh), BAR, **57**, 119–224, Oxford

Matolsci, J, 1970 Historische erforschung der Korpergross der Rindes aus Grund von ungarischen Knockenmaterial, *Zeitschrift fur Tierzuchtg und Zuchtungsbiol, Hamburg*, **87**, 89–137

Maxfield, V, forthcoming *Excavations at Camelon*

Meates, G W, 1987 *The Roman villa at Lullingstone Kent*, **2**, Kent Archaeol Soc Monog, **3**

Miles, D, 1986 *Archaeology at Barton Court Farm, Abingdon, Oxon*, CBA Res Rep, **50**, London

Neal, D S, 1974 *The excavation of the Roman villa in Gadebridge Park, Hemel Hempstead, 1963–68*, Rep Res Comm Soc Antiq London, **21**, London

———, 1976 Northchurch, Boxmoor and Hemel Hempstead Station: the excavation of three Roman buildings in the Bulbourne Valley, *Hertfordshire Archaeol*, **4**, 1–135

———, 1978 in *Studies in the Romano-British villa* (ed M Todd), 33–58, Leicester

———, 1981a *Roman mosaics in Britain: an introduction to their schemes and a catalogue of paintings*, Britannia Monog, **1**, London

———, 1981b The Gorhambury mosaic, in *Mosaic*, **5**, 12–13, Association Study, Preserving Roman Mosaics (ASPROM)

———, 1982 A green stone from the Roman villa at Gorhambury, St Albans, Herts, *Antiq J*, **62**, 365

———, 1983 Unusual buildings at Wood Lane End, Hemel Hempstead, Herts, *Britannia*, **14**, 73–86

———, 1984 A sanctuary at Wood Lane End, Hemel Hempstead, *Britannia*, **15**, 193–215

———, 1989 Excavations at Magiovinium, *Rec Buckinghamshire*, **29**, 1–24

Neal, D S, and Butcher, S A, 1974 Miscellaneous objects of bronze, in Neal 1974, 128–35

Niblett, R, 1985 *Sheepen: an early Roman industrial site at Camulodunum*, CBA Res Rep, **57**, London

Oldenstein, J, 1976 Zur Ausrustung römischer Auxiliareinheiten, *Bericht der Römisch-Germanischen Kommission*, **57**, 49–316

Olivier, A, forthcoming The brooches, in Excavations at Braughing (T Potter), *Hertfordshire Archaeol*

O'Neil, H E, 1945 The Roman villa at Park Street, near St Albans, Hertfordshire: report on the excavations of 1943–45, *Archaeol J*, **102**, 21–110

Oswald, F, 1936–7 *Figure-types on terra sigillata*, Liverpool

Oxé, A, ed Comfort, H, 1968 *Corpus Vasorum Arretinorum*, Bonn

Partridge, C, 1981 *Skeleton Green, a late Iron Age and Romano-British site*. Britannia Monog, **2**, London

Pearce, J E, Vince, A G, and Jenner, M A, 1985 *A dated type-series of London medieval pottery, Part 2, London-type ware*, London and Middlesex Archaeological Society, Spec Pap, **6**

Pearson, G W, Pilcher, J R, Baille, M G, Corbett, D M, and Qua, F, 1986 *Radiocarbon*, **28**, 911–34

Rahtz, P, and Greenfield, E, 1977 *Excavations at Chew Valley Lake, Somerset*, DoE Archaeol Rep, **8**, London

RCHM (England), 1962 *An inventory of the historical monuments in the City of York*, **1**, *Eburacum, Roman York*, London

Reece, R, 1972 A short survey of the Roman coins found in fourteen sites in Britain, *Britannia*, **3**, 269–76

———, 1982 The coins from the Cow Roast, Herts – a commentary, *Hertfordshire Archaeol*, **8**, 60–6

———, 1986 The coins, in Rook 1986, 144–5

Rees, S E, 1979 *Agricultural implements in prehistoric and Roman Britain*, BAR, **69**, Oxford

Ricken, H, and Fischer, C, 1963 *Die Bilderschüsseln de Romischer Töpfer von Rheinzabern*, Bonn

Richter, G M A, 1971 *Engraved gems of the Romans*, London

Rigby, V, 1977 The Gallo Belgic pottery from Cirencester in *Roman pottery studies in Britain and beyond* (eds J Dore and K T Green), BAR **S30**, Oxford

———, 1981 The potter Julios – a suitable case for study, in *Roman pottery research in Britain and north-west Europe* (eds A C and AS Anderson), BAR, **S123**, Oxford

———, 1982 The coarse pottery, in *Early Roman occupation at Cirencester* (J S Walker and A D McWhirr), Cirencester Excavations, **1**

Riha, E, 1979 *Die römischen Fibeln aus Augst und Kaiseraugst*, Basel

Rivet, A L F, 1969 Social and economic aspects, in *The Roman villa in Britain* (ed A L F Rivet), 173–216, London

Roden, D, 1973 Field systems of the Chiltern Hills and their environs, in Baker and Butlin 1973, 325–76

Rodwell, W J, and Rodwell, K A, 1986 *Rivenhall: investigation of a villa, church and village 1950–1977*, CBA Res Rep, **55**, London

Rogers, G, 1974 *Poteries sigillées de la Gaule Centrale*, Paris

Rogers, J C, 1933 The manor and houses of Gorhambury, *Trans St Albans Hertfordshire Archit Archaeol Soc*, n ser, **4**, 35–113

Rook, T, 1986 The Roman site at Dicket Mead, Lockleys, Welwyn, *Hertfordshire Archaeol*, **9**, 79–175

Saunders, A, 1961 Excavations at Park Street 1954–57, *Archaeol J*, **118**, 100–35

Saunders, C, and Havercroft, A B, 1977 A kiln of the potter Oastrius and related excavations at Little Munden Farm, Bricket Wood, *Hertfordshire Archaeol*, **5**, 109–56

Scott, P, forthcoming *Excavations at Piercebridge*

Selkirk, A, 1971 Dicket Mead, Lockleys, *Current Archaeol*, **27**, **3**, (4), 106–9

Sena Chiesa, G, 1966 *Gemme del Museo Nazionale di Aquileia*, Aquileia

Silver, I A, 1969 The ageing of domestic animals, in *Science in archaeology* (eds D Brothwell and E Higgs), 283–302, London

Smith, J T, 1963 Romano-British aisled houses, *Archaeol J*, **120**, 1–30

Spitaels, P, forthcoming The provincial-Roman enamelled fibula

Stanfield, J A, 1930 Further examples of Claudian 'terra sigillata' from London, *Antiq J*, **10**, 114–25

———, 1937 Romano-Gaulish decorated jugs and the work of the potter Sabinus, *J Roman Stud*, **28**, 168–79

Stanfield J A, and Simpson, G, 1958 *Central Gaulish potters*, London

Stead, I M, 1969 Verulamium 1966–68, *Antiquity*, **43**, 45–52

———, 1976 *Excavations at Winterton Roman Villa and other Roman sites in North Lincolnshire 1958–67*, DoE Archaeol Rep, **9**, London

———, 1980 *Rudston Roman Villa*, Yorkshire Archaeol Soc, Leeds

Stead, I M, and Rigby, V, 1986 *Baldock, the Excavation of a Roman and pre-Roman Settlement, 1968–72*, Britannia Monograph Series, **7**, 1986

———, and ———, 1989 *Verulamium: the King Harry Lane site*, HBMC Archaeol Rep, **12**, London

Teichert, M, 1975 Osteometrische Untersuchungen zur Berechnung der Widerristhohe bei Schafen, in *Archaeozoological studies* ed A Clason, 51–69, Amsterdam

Thompson, I, 1982 *Grog-tempered 'Belgic' pottery of south-eastern England*, BAR, **108**, Oxford

Toynbee, J M C, 1964 *Art in Britain under the Romans*, Oxford

Wacher, J, 1974 *The towns of Roman Britain*, London

Wainwright, G J, 1968 The Excavation of a Durotrigan Farmstead near Tollard Royal in Cranborne Chase, Southern England, *Proc Prehist Soc*, **34**, 102–47

Walthew, C V, 1975 The town house and the villa house in Roman Britain, *Britannia*, **6**, 189–205

Wardle, A, 1982 Kings Langley Roman Villa, *Hertfordshire's Past*, **13**, 20–2

Ward-Perkins, J B, 1938 The Roman villa at Lockleys, Welwyn, *Antiq J*, **18**, 339–76

Waugh, H, and Goodburn, R, 1972 The non-ferrous objects, in Frere 1972, 115–62

Webster, G, 1958 The advance under Ostorius Scapula, *Archaeol J*, **115**, 49–98

Wedlake, W J, 1958 *Excavations at Camerton, Somerset 1926–56*, Camerton Excavation Club

West, B, 1985 Chicken legs revisited, *Circaea, J Assoc Environmental Archaeol*, **3** (1), 11–14

Wheeler, A, 1979 *The tidal Thames*, London

Wheeler, R E M, 1932 *Excavations of the prehistoric, Roman and post-Roman site in Lydney Park, Gloucestershire, 1932*, Rep Res Comm Soc Antiq London, **9**, Oxford

Wheeler, R E M, 1943 *Maiden Castle, Dorset*, Rep Res Comm Soc Antiq London, **12**, Oxford

Wheeler, R E M, and Wheeler, T V, 1936 *Verulamium, a Belgic and two Roman cities*, Rep Res Comm Soc Antiq London, **11**, Oxford

Wild, J P, 1970a *Textile manufacture in the northern Roman Provinces*, Cambridge

———, 1970b Button-and-loop fasteners in the Roman provinces, *Britannia*, **1**, 137–55

Wilson, C A, 1973 *Food and drink in Britain*, London

Wilson, D R, 1975 Roman Britain in 1974, *Britannia*, **6**, 258

Young, C J, 1977 *The Roman pottery industry of the Oxford Region*, BAR, **43**, Oxford

Zazoff, P, 1975 *Antike Gemmen in Deutschen Sammlungen*, **4**, *Hannover Kestner-Museum*, Wiesbaden

Zwierlein-Diehl, E, 1979 *Die Antiken Gemmen des Kunsthistorischen Museums in Wien*, **2**, Munich

Index

compiled by Sarnia Butcher

Figures in bold refer to pages on which illustrations occur.